DATABASE SYSTEMS: Management and Design

Programming books from boyd & fraser

Structuring Programs in Microsoft BASIC
BASIC Fundamentals and Style
Applesoft BASIC Fundamentals and Style
Complete BASIC: For the Short Course
Fundamentals of Structured COBOL
Advanced Structured COBOL: Batch and Interactive
Comprehensive Structured COBOL
Pascal
WATFIV-S Fundamentals and Style
VAX Fortran
Fortran 77 Fundamentals and Style
Learning Computer Programming: Structured Logic, Algorithms, and Flowcharting

Also available from boyd & fraser

Database Systems: Management and Design
Using Pascal: An Introduction to Computer Science I
Using Modula-2: An Introduction to Computer Science I
Data Abstraction and Structures: An Introduction to Computer Science II
Fundamentals of Systems Analysis with Application Design
Data Communications for Business
Data Communications Software Design
Microcomputer Applications: Using Small Systems Software
The Art of Using Computers
Using Microcomputers: A Hands-On Introduction

Shelly, Cashman and Forsythe books from boyd & fraser

Computer Fundamentals with Application Software
Workbook and Study Guide to accompany Computer Fundamentals with Application Software
Learning to Use SUPERCALC®3, dBASE III®, and WORDSTAR® 3.3: An Introduction
Learning to Use SUPERCALC®3: An Introduction
Learning to Use dBASE III®: An Introduction
Learning to Use WORDSTAR® 3.3: An Introduction
BASIC Programming for the IBM Personal Computer
Structured COBOL — Flowchart Edition
Structured COBOL — Pseudocode Edition
Turbo Pascal Programming

DATABASE SYSTEMS: Management and Design

PHILIP J. PRATT

JOSEPH J. ADAMSKI

Grand Valley State College

BOYD & FRASER PUBLISHING COMPANY
BOSTON

CREDITS:

Editor: Tom Walker
Director of Production: Becky Herrington
Ancillaries Editor: Donna Villanucci
Manufacturing Director: Erek Smith

COVER PHOTOGRAPHY AND DESIGN:
Tom Norton – TOM NORTON DESIGNS

© 1987 by Boyd & Fraser Publishing Company

Manufactured in the United States of America

Library of Congress Cataloging-in-Publication Data

Pratt, Philip J., 1945-
   Database systems.

   Includes index.
   1. Data base management. 2. System design.
I. Adamski, Joseph J., 1945-   . II. Title.
III. Title: Data base systems.
QA76.9.D3P72929 1987   005.74   86-28409
ISBN 0-87835-227-9

4 5 6 7 8 D 3 2 1 0 9

Dedication

To Judy, Randy, and Tammy — Phil
To Judy — Joe

Without their love, understanding, support, and encouragement, this project would not have been possible.

To the memory of
Dr. Daniel Kemp, a friend and an inspiration.

CONTENTS

Chapter 6: DATABASE DESIGN I — INTRODUCTION TO DATABASE DESIGN

Chapter 7: DATABASE DESIGN II — INFORMATION LEVEL DESIGN

Chapter 8: CODASYL MODEL I — INTRODUCTION TO THE CODASYL MODEL

Chapter 13: THE FOURTH-GENERATION ENVIRONMENT

Chapter 14: DATABASE ADMINISTRATION

Chapter 15: ALTERNATIVES: DISTRIBUTED SYSTEMS, DATABASE COMPUTERS, MICROCOMPUTER SYSTEMS

PREFACE

The past few years have produced a number of dramatic developments that make the process of managing a database accessible to a wide variety of users. These developments include commercial relational model systems, microcomputer database systems, the fourth-generation environment, and the integration of database software with other types of software such as spreadsheets and graphics. Since its inception, database management has always been an important area. It is even more important now, with an ever-increasing audience needing to be familiar with database concepts.

ABOUT THIS BOOK

This book is intended to be used as the textbook for a course in Database Management. The vast majority of people who will take a serious course in database management in the coming years will eventually be users of database management systems. That is, they will *use* a database management system to create application software, either for themselves or for others. This book is intended for these people and not for the minority who will be "builders" of database management systems. Thus the book is an appropriate text for a database course in an information systems curriculum, a business curriculum, or a computer science curriculum in which applications are important.

Students using this text should have experience with some programming language and with the basics of file processing. They should be familiar with the terms *files*, *records*, and *fields*. They should be at least minimally familiar with the general characteristics of modern computing equipment (e.g., the fact that files are stored on disk, the role of CRTs, and the role of microcomputers). Students with this background should certainly be able to successfully use this text.

To receive maximum benefit from the text, it would be helpful for students to have a good background in the file organization and data structures concepts covered in Appendix A of this textbook. This background ideally will have been obtained from a prior course. If that is not possible, then the material in Appendix A can be presented near the beginning of the database course. (Many textbooks in database management cover such material in two or three chapters early in the book. If desired, this book can be used in a similar fashion; i.e., the material in Appendix A could be taught near the beginning of the database course, immediately following the introduction.) The time spent covering this material will, of course, mean that less of the book can be covered in the remainder of the course. If the course is part of a two-term sequence, this will not be a problem. In a single course, however, some of the later material will need to be omitted.

DISTINGUISHING FEATURES

THE RELATIONAL MODEL EMPHASIZED

The relational model is given a special place of prominence befitting its importance, both today and in the future. It is the first model covered, with three complete chapters devoted to exploring its basic structure, methods of manipulating relational databases and the relational model's impact on database design. In addition, two major commercial implementations of the model are presented and discussed.

THE HIERARCHICAL, CODASYL AND INVERTED FILE MODELS

The hierarchical, CODASYL, and inverted file models also receive detailed coverage. In each case, the coverage includes the basic and advanced features of the model as well as details of a significant commercial implementation of the model.

Study of these additional models is motivated by the fact that many commercial implementations of them still exist. Additionally, a comparative analysis of the various models can be quite instructive.

The book is designed in a modular fashion to allow the instructor the maximum flexibility regarding the order in which the models are to be presented. Chapters concerning the hierarchical, CODASYL and inverted file models (chapters 8, 9, 10 and 11) can be taught in any sequence or completely omitted. These chapters can also be covered early in the course where students are working with systems that follow one of these models in their projects.

DATABASE DESIGN COVERED IN DETAIL

The very important process of database design is covered in great detail, both the information level of database design and the physical level. In the two chapters (6 and 7) devoted to the information level, a methodology is presented that has the relational model as its foundation. This methodology, a non-graphical approach, is compared and contrasted with one of the popular graphical methodologies, the entity-relationship model, in chapter 7. In chapter 12, after all of the models have been examined, the physical level of design is examined in detail.

In attempting to master the topic of database design, examples are crucial. In addition to the examples given in the chapters on database design, there are two detailed database design examples in Appendix B which emphasize all facets of the process.

THE FOURTH-GENERATION ENVIRONMENT

There is a detailed discussion of the fourth-generation environment. The data dictionary, the central component of this environment, other components such as report writers, query languages, screen generators, program generators, teleprocessing monitors, and fourth-generation languages are also covered. The role of the fourth-generation environment in the prototyping process is examined. Large numbers of fourth-generation products are available today, and more are being developed. These easier-to-use, integrated products will be tomorrow's technology and are a required part of the database student's background.

IN-DEPTH COVERAGE OF THE DATABASE ADMINISTRATION FUNCTION

There is a detailed discussion of the role of database administration in computing today. Central and distributed databases require central management, coordination and control, and database administration is assigned this responsibility. In addition to a review of the organizational placement and structure of database administration, there is detailed coverage of the characteristics of successful database administration groups and of their administrative, application and technical functions.

EARLY TREATMENT OF DBMS FUNCTIONS

The functions that should be provided by a full-scale DBMS are presented early in the book. These functions are presented in chapter 2, immediately following the general introduction to database management. There are three important benefits to the early treatment of DBMS functions. First, to satisfy the natural curiosity of students about the overall capabilities of DBMS. Second, an understanding of this material provides students with an excellent foundation for the remaining material in the text. Finally, when the various commercial systems are discussed later in the text, students gain an appreciation for the manner in which these systems furnish the required functions.

DETAILED COVERAGE OF IMPORTANT COMMERCIAL SYSTEMS

Some of the most significant of today's commercial systems, DB2, INGRES, IDMS/R, IMS and ADABAS, are examined in the text along with the manner in which these systems provide the features expected from a full-scale commercial DBMS.

NUMEROUS REALISTIC EXAMPLES

The book contains numerous examples illustrating each of the concepts. The examples presented throughout the text are based on two hypothetical organizations, Marvel College and Premiere Products. The examples are realistic and representative of the kinds of problems that professionals encounter in designing, manipulating, and administering databases.

QUESTIONS AND EXERCISES

Q&As — At key points within the chapters, there are Q&As. These are questions that the students are to answer to ensure that they understand the material before they proceed. The answers to these questions are given immediately following the questions themselves.

REVIEW QUESTIONS — At the end of each chapter, there are Review Questions, which test the student's recall of the important points in the chapter. The answers to all of the odd-numbered review questions are given at the end of the text. The answers to the even-numbered review questions are given in the Instructor's Manual.

EXERCISES — There are also Exercises in which the students must apply what they have learned. The answers to all of the exercises are given in the accompanying Instructor's Manual.

PROJECTS

Projects in which the students actually use a DBMS are essential in a database course. We suggest assigning a single project with several parts that runs throughout the semester. Eight such projects are presented in the instructor's manual together with tips for administering the projects. These projects vary in size and can be implemented by students working in either microcomputer or mainframe environments. These projects can also be used as the basis for database design exercises by students.

ANCILLARY MATERIALS

A comprehensive instructors' support package accompanies *Database Systems: Management and Design*. These ancillaries are available to instructors upon request from our publisher, Boyd & Fraser.

INSTRUCTOR'S MANUAL

Material in the Instructor's Manual follows the organization of the text. Chapters of the Instructor's Manual include:

- Purpose
- Vocabulary Words
- Chapter Objectives
- Lecture Outlines [keyed to Transparency Masters]
- Teaching Suggestions [keyed to Lecture Outline]
- Answers to Exercises [found in the text]
- Test Questions
- Answers to Test Questions
- Solutions to Database Design Exercises [found in Appendix B]
- Database Design (and/or Implementation) Projects

TRANSPARENCY MASTERS

An extensive set of over 250 transparency masters is also available. These masters include figures, program segments and tables from the text.

ProTest

Boyd & Fraser's fourth-generation test-generating program, ProTest, has been designed specifically to accompany this text.

ORGANIZATION OF THIS BOOK

The textbook contains 15 chapters and two appendices which are organized as follows:

INTRODUCTION

Chapter 1 provides a general introduction to the field of database management.

THE FUNCTIONS OF A DBMS

Chapter 2 discusses the features that should be provided by a full-functioned database management system. In later chapters, the manner in which the commercial systems examined in the text furnish these functions is explored.

THE RELATIONAL MODEL

Chapters 3, 4, and 5 concern the relational model. In chapter 3, the general model is presented along with methods for manipulating relational databases. Chapter 4 deals with normalization, the contribution of the relational model to the field of database design. Finally, chapter 5 covers advanced features of the model together with a discussion of two of the major implementations of the relational model: DB2 and INGRES.

DATABASE DESIGN (INFORMATION LEVEL)

Chapters 6 and 7 deal with database design. Chapter 6 introduces the information level of database design together with a specific methodology for performing database design. Chapter 7 expands on this material with some specific tips. It also presents another design methodology, the entity-relationship model, which is compared and contrasted with the methodology of the text. A method for converting between the two methodologies is also presented.

THE CODASYL MODEL

Chapters 8 and 9 cover the CODASYL model. The basic model is presented and discussed in chapter 8. Advanced features of the model are covered in chapter 9 which also includes a discussion of a prime example of the CODASYL model: IDMS. Along with the discussion of IDMS is a discussion of IDMS/R, an enhancement of IDMS that includes relational-like features.

THE HIERARCHICAL AND INVERTED FILE MODELS

Chapter 10 covers the hierarchical model and the major hierarchical system: IMS. Chapter 11 covers the inverted file model and one of the major inverted file systems: ADABAS.

DATABASE DESIGN (PHYSICAL LEVEL)

Chapter 12 completes the discussion of database design by covering the physical part of the design process; i.e., the implementation of the information level design on a specific database management system. A methodology is given for this process.

THE FOURTH-GENERATION ENVIRONMENT

Chapter 13 examines the fourth-generation environment. The data dictionary and other major components of this environment are covered along with the information center, prototyping and emerging fifth-generation software.

DATABASE ADMINISTRATION

Chapter 14 covers the role of database administration. Major emphasis is devoted to an examination of the administrative, application and technical functions of database administration.

DISTRIBUTED SYSTEMS, DATABASE COMPUTERS, MICROCOMPUTER SYSTEMS

Chapter 15 presents a discussion of some alternatives to the conventional centralized processing of databases on a single mainframe computer: distributed systems, database computers and micro-computer database management systems.

FILE ORGANIZATION AND DATA STRUCTURES

Appendix A presents material on file organization and data structures that relate to database management.

DATABASE DESIGN EXAMPLES

Appendix B includes two major database design examples illustrating the design methodology, both the information level and the physical level.

ANSWERS TO ODD-NUMBERED REVIEW QUESTIONS

Answers to the odd-numbered review questions are given at this point in the text.

GLOSSARY

There is a glossary containing definitions to over 300 of the most important terms in the text. Important terms, which are printed in **boldface** within the text are either defined on the same page on which they appear or are defined in the glossary.

FLEXIBILITY OF THIS BOOK

The textbook can be used successfully in a variety of database courses. The following suggests sections of the text which might be covered in introductory or advanced courses both at the undergraduate and graduate levels. Sections followed by an * can be completely omitted if so desired. We have also outlined ways in which the text can be used in a two-semester sequence, as well as in a course devoted solely to the relational model.

INTRODUCTORY COURSE — UNDERGRADUATE

CHAPTER 1: all
CHAPTER 2: all
CHAPTER 3: 3.1, 3.2, 3.3, 3.4 (up to the examples on querying multiple tables).
CHAPTER 4: 4.1, 4.2, 4.3, 4.4.
CHAPTER 6: 6.1, 6.2, 6.3, 6.4, 6.5, 6.6*.
CHAPTER 8: 8.1, 8.2.
CHAPTER 10: 10.1*, 10.2*.
CHAPTER 12: 12.1, 12.2.
CHAPTER 13: 13.1, 13.2.
CHAPTER 14: 14.1, 14.2, 14.3, 14.4*, 14.5*.

ADVANCED COURSE — UNDERGRADUATE

CHAPTER 1: all
CHAPTER 2: all
CHAPTER 3: all
CHAPTER 4: all
CHAPTER 5: 5.1, 5.2, 5.3*, either 5.4* or 5.5*.
CHAPTER 6: all
CHAPTER 7: all
CHAPTER 8: 8.1, 8.2, 8.3, 8.4, 8.5*.
CHAPTER 9: 9.1, 9.2, 9.8*.
CHAPTER 10: 10.1*, 10.2*, 10.5*.

CHAPTER 11: 11.1*, 11.2*.
CHAPTER 12: 12.1, 12.2, 12.3, 12.4*, 12.5, 12.6*, 12.7*.
CHAPTER 13: all
CHAPTER 14: all
CHAPTER 15: all

> *Note:* Either the material on IDMS (9.3 – 9.7) or DL/I (10.3 - 10.5) should be included. If DL/I happens to be a dominant system in the industry in your area, you may want to choose it as the system to be studied. Otherwise, choose IDMS.

Comment: Some of the advanced material in this course requires a knowledge of the data and file structures topics contained in appendix A. If students have not had such material in prior courses, appendix A should be a part of this course, immediately following chapter 1. Some of the optional sections will probably need to be omitted to make room for this material.

INTRODUCTORY COURSE — GRADUATE

CHAPTER 1: all
CHAPTER 2: all
CHAPTER 3: 3.1, 3.2, 3.3, 3.4 (up to and including the examples on querying multiple tables), 3.6*.
CHAPTER 4: 4.1, 4.2, 4.3, 4.4.
CHAPTER 5: 5.1, 5.2.
CHAPTER 6: 6.1, 6.2, 6.3, 6.4, 6.5, 6.6*.
CHAPTER 8: 8.1, 8.2.
CHAPTER 10: 10.1*, 10.2*.
CHAPTER 11: 11.1*, 11.2*.
CHAPTER 12: 12.1, 12.2.
CHAPTER 13: 13.1, 13.2, 13.3*.
CHAPTER 14: 14.1, 14.2, 14.3, 14.4*, 14.5*.
CHAPTER 15: all

ADVANCED COURSE — GRADUATE

CHAPTER 1: all
CHAPTER 2: all
CHAPTER 3: all
CHAPTER 4: all
CHAPTER 5: 5.1, 5.2, 5.3, 5.4, 5.5*.
CHAPTER 6: all
CHAPTER 7: all
CHAPTER 8: 8.1, 8.2, 8.3, 8.4, 8.5*.
CHAPTER 9: 9.1, 9.2, 9.3*, 9.4*, 9.5*, 9.6*, 9.7*, 9.8.
CHAPTER 10: 10.1*, 10.2*, 10.3*, 10.4*, 10.5*.
CHAPTER 11: 11.1*, 11.2*, 11.3*, 11.4*.
CHAPTER 12: 12.1, 12.2, 12.3, 12.4*, 12.5, 12.6, 12.7*.
CHAPTER 13: all

CHAPTER 14: 14.1, 14.2, 14.3, 14.4, 14.5.
CHAPTER 15: all

Comment: Some of the advanced material in this course requires a knowledge of the data and file structures topics contained in appendix A. If students have not had such material in prior courses, appendix A should be a part of this course. If so, it should immediately follow chapter 1. Some of the optional sections will probably need to be omitted to make room for this material.

TWO-SEMESTER SEQUENCE

Two-semester sequences in database management are becoming increasingly common. While there are a variety of possible arrangements of topics in such sequences, the following represents the two most popular.

SECOND COURSE AS PROJECT COURSE — In this arrangement, the first database course is taught in exactly the same manner as the one-semester courses described earlier. The second course is a course in which the students, often working in teams, develop and implement a major application system utilizing a DBMS. The last four of the eight projects described in the instructor's manual are ideal as projects for such a course.

SECOND COURSE AS DATABASE DESIGN COURSE — In this arrangement, the focus of the second course is database design. To use the text for such an arrangement, remove the database design material (chapters 6, 7, and 12) from the first course and place the material in the second course. (You might want to cover chapter 6 in the first course to introduce the topic of database design there.) In addition, go through the detailed design example worked out in appendix B and have the students work through the other design example on their own. Any of the project assignments in the instructor's manual can be used as additional database design assignments, in case more design projects are desired.

RELATIONAL MODEL COURSE

If a course focusing strictly on the relational model is desired, this can be easily achieved by omitting chapters 8, 9, 10, and 11 and sections 12.3 and 12.4 from the course.

TO THE STUDENT

BOLDFACED TERMS

Terms that are printed in **boldface** are either defined where they appear or are defined in the glossary. If you encounter a term in boldface whose definition does not accompany the term, it has been defined earlier in the text and you should be familiar with it. If you are not, you could look it up in the glossary.

EMBEDDED QUESTIONS

There are a number of places in the text where special questions have been embedded. Sometimes the purpose of these questions is to ensure that you understand some crucial material before you proceed. In other cases, the questions are designed to give you the chance to consider some special concept in advance of its actual presentation. In all cases, the answer to the question is given immediately after the question. You could simply read the question and its answer. To receive maximum benefit, however, you should take the time to work out your own answer and then check it against the one given in the text.

END-OF-CHAPTER MATERIAL

The end-of-chapter material consists of three elements: a summary, review questions, and exercises. The summary briefly describes the material covered in the chapter. The review questions require you to recall the important material in the chapter. The answers to the odd-numbered review questions are given in the text. The exercises require you to apply what you have learned.

We suggest that, upon completion of a chapter, you read the summary to make sure that you are generally familiar with the main concepts of the chapter. Next, answer the review questions and compare your answers to the odd-numbered questions with those given in the text. Finally, work whatever exercises your instructor has assigned.

A NOTE ON NOTATION

There are many inconsistencies in notation in computing in general and in the database area in particular. Most of these will not cause any problem in our study of database management, but one of them can be troublesome. It concerns the use of the hyphen as opposed to the underscore. In some situations, the underscore is a legal symbol and the hyphen is not. For example, CUSTOMER_ NUMBER is legal, but CUSTOMER–NUMBER is not. In others, the roles are reversed: the hyphen, rather than the underscore is a legal symbol. In these situations, CUSTOMER–NUMBER is legal but CUSTOMER_NUMBER is not.

Do not be concerned with these differences. In this text, the symbols are used in whichever way is correct based on the particular topic being studied. If you simply use the symbols in the same way that they are used in the text, your usage will be correct. Further, if you are working with a new system, simply consulting the manual will indicate which symbol is appropriate. Even if you happen to use the wrong symbol, the system will let you know (and rapidly) that what you are doing is wrong. Fortunately, it is an easy correction to make.

A FINAL NOTE

We wish you the best in your study of the exciting, important, and rapidly-changing area of database management. We hope that you find it as interesting, challenging, and rewarding as we do.

ACKNOWLEDGEMENTS

We would like to acknowledge several individuals for their contributions in the preparation of this book.

We are grateful to our students in the database course at Grand Valley State College who used preliminary versions of this text. We appreciate not only their many helpful suggestions but also their support and encouragement.

We also greatly appreciate the efforts of the following individuals who class-tested or reviewed the text and made many helpful suggestions: John M. Atkins, West Virginia University; Madeline Baugher, Southwestern Oklahoma State University; C. Andrew Belew, Ferris State College; Alfred

Boals, Western Michigan University; Donald Dawley, Miami University; John Demel, Ohio State University; Gary Heisler, Lansing Community College; Carl Penziul, Corning Community College; Darleen V. Pigford, Western Illinois University; Phil Prins, Calvin College; David D. Riley, University of Wisconsin-LaCrosse; Constantine Ruossos, Lynchburg College; Marguerite Summers, University of North Carolina.

The efforts of the following members of the staff of Boyd & Fraser have been invaluable: Tom Walker, president; Sharon Cogdill, development editor; Donna Villanucci, ancillaries editor; Becky Herrington, director of production; Jeanne Black, typesetting manager; and the entire production department for all their hard work. We would also like to express our thanks and appreciation to our copy editor, Toni Rosenberg, for her many helpful suggestions.

Allendale, Michigan   Philip J. Pratt
January, 1987   Joseph J. Adamski

INTRODUCTION TO DATABASE MANAGEMENT

1.1 INTRODUCTION

Marvel College's programmers recently talked about traditional file processing and database processing:

Mary: This might be a good time to compare notes on how we are each progressing in our work on the new computer. Mike, how are you coming along?

Mike: I'm working on a payroll system for the college. I have part of it done and it's already being used. What I've finished is the departmental earnings report. The users seem to be quite happy with it. Here's a sample of the report [see figure 1.1]. I have two main files that I work with, a department file that contains a

```
   9/05/87                   MARVEL COLLEGE                      PAGE   1
                           DEPARTMENTAL LISTING

      DEPT: 1    DESC: COMPUTER SCI. LOCATION: 408 KELLY HALL

      FACULTY                                          EARNINGS
      NUMBER       NAME            ADDRESS       SALARY   YTD
         119    BARB MARTIN    94 RIDGE,GRANT,MI   22500  15425.00
         421    AL JONES      121 COLTON,HART,MI   20000  11402.50
         462    TOM JOHNSON   604 46TH,LOWELL,MI   25000  16952.12
```

```
DEPARTMENT
   DEPT_NUMBER
   DESCRIPTION
   LOCATION

FACULTY
   FACULTY_NUMBER
   NAME
   ADDRESS
   SALARY
   EARNINGS_YTD
   DEPT_NUMBER
```

record for each department and a faculty master file that contains a record for each faculty member. Included in the faculty record, among other things, is the number for the department in which the faculty member works.

Bill: How can you include the number of the department in which a faculty member works in the faculty record? What if a faculty member is assigned to more than one department? What would you use for the number in that case?

Mike: That's a good question. The same thought occurred to me early in the design of the system. I asked the users if a faculty member could be assigned to two or more departments and they said no. I was just as glad. I'm not sure exactly how I would have handled it if the answer had been yes. [Note to the reader: Mike has not taken a course in database design. If he had, he would have known what to do.] What are you working on, Bill?

FIGURE 1.1a
Mike's report

FIGURE 1.1b
Mike's files

Bill: I'm working on a system for the personnel department. It will be used by the person who oversees the medical insurance for the college. I've still got a long way to go, but here's one of the main reports that's being used now. It should give you an idea of the kinds of things I'm working on [see Figure 1.2]. Like you,

```
9/05/87                      MARVEL COLLEGE                    PAGE   1
                          INSURANCE PLAN LISTING

        PLAN: 1    DESC: REGULAR

           FACULTY                            DEPENDENTS
           NUMBER        NAME        ADDRESS    COVERED

              209    JANE NEWTON   210 LEONARD,ADA,MI    YES
              507    ROB CANTON    5 STATE,CUTLER,MI     YES
              564    TIM FERRIS    16 W. 9TH,TROY,MI      NO
               .         .             .                 .
               .         .             .                 .
               .         .             .                 .
```

```
PLAN
    PLAN_NUMBER
    DESCRIPTION

FACULTY
    FACULTY_NUMBER
    NAME
    ADDRESS
    DEPS_CVD
     (DEPENDENTS
      COVERED –
       YES or NO)
    PLAN_NUMBER
```

Mike, I have two main files. In my case, they are an insurance policy file that gives information on the possible insurance plans available to the faculty at Marvel, and a faculty master file. I see that my faculty master file is similar to yours, but there are some differences. You have department number, salary and earnings year-to-date, which I don't have. I have the insurance plan number and a code called DEPENDENTS_COVERED. If the value in this field is "YES", dependents are covered by the faculty member's policy. If it is "NO", they are not. Your record layout does not include either of these fields.

Mary: I also have a faculty master file, but I can see that it's different from either of yours. I'm working for a development group on campus that is in the process of setting up a speakers' bureau. They want to keep information on topics on which various faculty members are prepared to speak. Here's a sample of the main report [see Figure 1.3]. Notice the difference in my faculty master file. I

FIGURE 1.2a
Bill's report

FIGURE 1.2b
Bill's files

FIGURE 1.3a
Mary's report

FIGURE 1.3b
Mary's files

```
9/05/87                      MARVEL COLLEGE                    PAGE   1
                             SPEAKING TOPICS

FACULTY                                                    TIMES    LAST
NUMBER     NAME        ADDRESS      DEGREE   FIELD      TITLE          GIVEN   GIVEN

  119  BARB MARTIN  94 RIDGE,GRANT,MI  MA   COMM.    DISTRIBUTED DATABASE  5   3/21/87
                                                     WHY NETWORK MICROS?   2   5/15/87
                                                     COMMUNICATIONS        1   9/02/87

  462  TOM JOHNSON  462 MACK,HARPER,MI MS   OP. SYS. THE FUTURE OF UNIX    3   5/13/87

  485  PAM SPARKS   201 OLIVE,HOLT,MI  PhD  ANALYSIS THE REGULAR POLYHEDRA 2  11/15/86

  507  ROB CANTON   5 STATE,CUTLER,MI  MS   VOLCANOES MOUNT ST. HELENS     1   2/11/87

  683  FRANK NILSON 46 CRESTON,ADA,MI  PhD  LASER TECH LASER TECHNOLOGY    3   5/22/87
                                                       NUCLEUR POWER PRO&CON 1 6/15/87
```

```
FACULTY
    FACULTY_NUMBER
    NAME
    ADDRESS
    DEGREE
    FIELD

SPEAKING_TOPICS
    FACULTY_NUMBER
    TITLE
    TIMES_GIVEN
    LAST_GIVEN
```

don't need some of the fields that you people do, but I need a field for the highest degree earned by the faculty member and one for the field in which the degree was earned.

Joan: You're not going to believe this, but I have a faculty master file also, and mine is different from any of yours. I'm also working on a project for the personnel department, but mine involves keeping track of when each faculty member was promoted and to what rank. Here's what my main report looks like [see Figure 1.4]. Notice the differences in my faculty master file. I need the highest

```
 9/05/87                          MARVEL COLLEGE                    PAGE  1
                              JOB HISTORY INFORMATION

 FACULTY                                   CURRENT                    DATE
 NUMBER      NAME            ADDRESS       DEGREE   RANK       RANK   ATTAINED

    119   BARB MARTIN   94 RIDGE,GRANT,MI    MA   ASST PROF  ASST PROF  9/15/81

    209   JANE NEWTON   210 LEONARD,ADA,MI   MS   ASSO PROF  ASST PROF  9/01/76
                                                             ASSO PROF  9/13/83

    421   AL JONES      121 COLTON,HART,MI  PhD   ASST PROF  ASST PROF  8/15/83

    462   TOM JOHNSON   604 46TH,LOWELL,MI   MS   ASSO PROF  ASST PROF  4/12/71
                                                             ASSO PROF  9/14/81

    485   PAM SPARKS    201 OLIVE,HOLT,MI   PhD   PROF       ASST PROF  4/02/65
                                                             ASSO PROF  9/12/74
                                                             PROF       9/13/83

    507   ROB CANTON    5 STATE,CUTLER,MI    MS   ASST PROF  ASST PROF  9/12/81

    564   TIM FERRIS    16 W. 9TH,TROY,MI   PhD   ASSO PROF  ASST PROF  5/21/76
                                                             ASSO PROF  9/01/87

    683   FRANK NILSON  46 CRESTON,ADA,MI   PhD   PROF       ASST PROF  6/11/66
                                                             ASSO PROF  8/02/74
                                                             PROF       8/12/83
```

```
FACULTY
    FACULTY_NUMBER
    NAME
    ADDRESS
    DEGREE
    CURRENT_RANK

JOB_HISTORY_
    INFORMATION
    FACULTY_NUMBER
    RANK
    DATE_ATTAINED
```

FIGURE 1.4a
Joan's report

FIGURE 1.4b
Joan's files

degree attained, just as Mary does, but I don't need the field in which the degree was attained. I also need the current rank of the faculty member, and none of you need that.

Mary: I can't believe all the duplication that we have. Each one of us stores a faculty member's number, name, and address. It looks to me like this data is getting stored four times for each faculty member!

Bill: Better make that at least four times. There may be others we don't even know about yet. By the way, the common term for such duplication is **redundancy**. We say that we have redundancy or that the data is stored redundantly.

Joan: Whatever it's called, it sure wastes a lot of space.

Bill: Wasted space is only the beginning. Think about what happens when a faculty member moves. We have to make sure the address is changed in each of our systems. What a headache!

Mary: I hate to tell you this, but we already have a problem. Look at the address for Tom Johnson on Mike's report, and then look at it on mine. I hope nobody looks at these reports side by side. Have you recently changed any addresses in your system, Mike?

Mike: I believe the users entered a number of changes yesterday.

Mary: Evidently my users are either not as conscientious as yours or they have not yet been notified of the changes.

Joan: While this is a big headache, it seems to me we also have another problem. The personnel department asked me for a report grouping the full professors, the associate professors, and the assistant professors in each department. I'm supposed to show when they were promoted to each rank. They would also like to include the topics on which these professors are prepared to speak. This was a problem for me, since my system does not contain any information concerning either departments or speaking topics. I see that some of your systems do. It's going to be a monstrous headache, but I wonder if I could get the data I need from your systems?

Mike: I see a couple of problems. My data includes salary information, and I don't know if your users should be able to access the salary. Also, as I understand it, you wrote your application in COBOL using indexed sequential files. Mary's was written in Pascal using what Pascal calls "files of records", and mine is written in FORTRAN using a special type of direct access file. Even if the salary problem can be overcome, what language are you going to use for your program that can access all of these different types of files?

Joan: Wow! I hadn't thought about all of those problems. I don't suppose that each of you would be willing to write a little program to convert your files into a format that I could work with, would you?

Mike: We like you, Joan, but there is a limit!

Joan: Isn't there some way we could pool our data so that we could all use it but we wouldn't have all of these problems?

Mike: Say, that's a good idea. Instead of a bunch of separate files, we could build a single pool of data. I've read something about this idea. It's called a **database**.

Joan: Exactly what is a database?

Mike: I don't know the fancy definition, but basically it seems pretty simple. Instead of holding information about a single entity, like employees or customers or parts or whatever, the way a normal file does, a database holds information about many different types of entities. In a single database we could have information about sales reps, customers, orders, parts, and so on.

Joan: Or faculty members, departments, insurance plans, job history info, and speaking topics.

Mike: Exactly. You're getting the idea. But there's another difference between a database and a regular file.

Mary: What's that?

Mike: A database also contains information about *relationships*. A database containing information about sales reps and customers could also contain information that indicates which sales rep represents which customer. You could then start with a customer and find the sales rep that represents this customer, or you could start with a sales rep and find all of the customers that he or she represents.

Mary: Let me see if I get the idea. In a database for the college, we would have information not only about departments and faculty members but also about which faculty member works in which department.

Mike: That's right. We would also have information relating insurance plans and faculty members as well as information relating faculty members to their job history records and to their speaking topics.

Joan: So, in this database, each faculty member would be stored only once, right?

Mike: Right. I would use faculty members and departments and the relationship between them for my report.

Bill would use faculty members and insurance plans together with the relationship between them.

Mary: I would use faculty members and speaking topics. Joan would use faculty members and job history records. Since we all use the same set of faculty members, each faculty member really would be stored only once. We don't have all that waste of space, and changing an address is easy. There's only one place to change it.

Joan: This is a great improvement, but there's another issue. The various users must agree on who has the right to change an address. Otherwise, they all might be changing addresses every which way, and we'd have a real mess.

Mike: That's a good point, Joan. Policies will have to be developed to address that. Do you agree, though, that the approach we are talking about will definitely improve things as far as the systems being developed for these users are concerned?

Joan: Sure. I see that. I also see that the special report that I was asked to develop, which included departments, faculty members, job history information, and speaking topics, would be much easier using this approach. All the information that I need is right within the database.

Bill: I hate to bring up a potential problem just when everything seems so rosy. As you have been talking, I started remembering a class in which we had to write programs to maintain one of these databases. We had to use a scheme called **hashing** to decide where to place records in the database.

Then we used things called **linked lists** to maintain the relationships. Another group in the class had to do the same thing except that they maintained their relationships using **inverted files**.

Joan: Hashing, linked lists, inverted files. I haven't heard of these topics before. Are they difficult?

Bill: They aren't difficult once you get the hang of it. The biggest problem is that they make every program in the system a little bit more complicated than it would be if it were accessing simple files. Also, if even a single program has a problem, it can destroy the whole structure of the database for everyone.

Mary: It sounds to me like we could be losing more than we would gain if Bill's assessment is correct. Besides, don't we still have some of the problems mentioned earlier? What language do we use to access this database? What could its structure be so that it could be accessed from all of the different languages we are using? Also, what about the issue that Mike raised earlier concerning salary? Wouldn't that be a real problem here, where everyone could access the salary field? Wouldn't the payroll office have a fit?

Mike: All of your objections are valid, Mary. I think, though, that things are not as glum as they may seem. There's a software product I've heard about that does most of the work Bill was talking about. It's technically called a **database management system**. Most of the time, though, they just call it a **DBMS**.

Joan: What all does it do?

Mike: I'm not really sure. Do you want me to look into it?

Bill, Joan, Mary: Please do.

Mike: Okay. I'll report back to you soon with the information.

— Some time later —

Mary: Did you find out anything about these database management systems, or DBMS's, as you called them?

Mike: I sure did. They're fantastic. I don't know exactly where to begin. I'll try to list all of the really neat things they can do, but I'm sure I'll forget something.

One of the things they do relates to what Bill was talking about the last time we got together. Remember, he was mentioning the special structures that might be used to maintain the information and the relationships. He mentioned things like hashing, linked lists, and inverted files, and he pointed out the added complexity that these would bring to each program.

Mary: I seem to remember making a comment that we would lose more than we would gain if we had to worry about all of that in every program.

Mike: With a DBMS, we don't. The DBMS handles all of that kind of activity. We only have to say things like STORE a faculty member. The system does its own thing with whichever of those structures it uses. If we want to find a department, we only need say FIND. We can then find all of the faculty members within the department by simply asking the system to repeatedly FIND the NEXT faculty member within the department. In fact, in some systems, we can find all of the faculty members in a department in a single command. We don't even need a loop. We just say things like SELECT FACULTY_NAME, FACULTY_NUMBER FROM FACULTY WHERE DEPT_NUMBER = 3, for example.

Mary: That sounds great, but I'm a little confused. Exactly where do you say these things: the FIND or the STORE or the SELECT? What does this have to do with COBOL or FORTRAN programs?

Mike: Good question. Sometimes you can use these things in sort of a stand-alone mode. You could just sit at a terminal and type the SELECT command I mentioned, for example. As another possibility, you can embed these commands in a regular programming language, like COBOL or FORTRAN. If you do that, you have all of the power of those languages at your disposal in addition to the easy way the DBMS gives you for manipulating the database.

Joan: It sounds almost too good to be true. What about some of the other objections we mentioned before? You said that you could put these commands in languages like COBOL and FORTRAN. Surely you couldn't use both of those languages to process the same database.

Mike: With a good DBMS, you could use either of these two or several others to process the same database. The system allows users to have their own views of the database. Sometimes this is called a view, sometimes it's called a subschema. Anyhow, this is what is used when the database is accessed.

Bill: Where did they get the term subschema?

Mike: In the systems that use the term subschema, the overall picture of the database is called a schema, kind of like a schematic diagram. I suppose they picked subschema because this is the individual user's *sub* set of the *schema.* Anyhow, when a user gets a subschema, he or she can get it in a form that is tailored for some specific language. The DBMS will take it from there. I might have a COBOL subschema and write COBOL programs to access this database, and you might have a FORTRAN subschema and write FORTRAN programs to access the same database.

Joan: What about the other objection, the one you brought up, Mike, when I asked to use some of your data? You said that my users should not be able to access the salary of a faculty member. That salary would be in this one database that all users are accessing. Won't my users be able to access the salary field?

Mike: There are a couple of solutions to that problem. One involves the same subschema idea that I was just talking about. Since each user must access the database via a subschema or view, we just don't include the salary field in your users' subschema. By doing that, as far as they are concerned, there is no salary field in the whole database.

There's another nice aspect to the idea of subschemas, incidentally. Occasionally, it's necessary to change the overall structure of the database, either because of a change in requirements or perhaps to make the system run more efficiently. Provided that we didn't do something that would invalidate a given user's subschema, like remove one of the fields the user needs to access, we don't need to change the user's programs at all. *The programs don't even need to be recompiled.*

Mary: That would be tremendous. I've already been through an experience where we needed to change the structure of a number of files that were used in a system and then go back and make appropriate changes to all of the programs in the system. It was a colossal hassle.

I do see a problem, though. You said that if a given user was not to access the salary field, you simply did not include it in that user's subschema. What about users who are allowed to *see* faculty members' salaries but not change them? If you don't include salary in their subschema, it seems to me that they couldn't even see a salary. Yet, if you do include it, won't they be able to start making salary changes?

Mike: That brings me to the second solution to the problem. Most of the good DBMS's allow an additional level of protection. Even though the salary field is included in a given subschema, a user accessing the database via this subschema can be forced to furnish a certain password or have a certain user ID in order to even see the salary, and perhaps a different password or different ID in order to be able to both see the salary and change it. You could say that the password "ABRACADABRA" would allow a user to be able to see and change a salary, whereas the password "FLINTSTONE" would allow a user to see the salary but not change it. The password "BASEBALL" could allow a user to see other fields but *not* salary. We could then have three different users all running the *same* program and using the *same* subschema but with different privileges. In fact, some systems go so far as to allow us to restrict users to where they can only see and/or change salaries for faculty members within their own department. That's getting pretty fancy.

Bill: It certainly does sound like there are a number of sophisticated security features available. I can't help but wonder, though, about someone who bypasses the DBMS and tries to somehow read information in the database directly. None of the DBMS security features would apply to this person.

Mike: Even in this case, the DBMS does help. Of course, the database itself can be protected with the normal operating system passwords and so on, but, if a person could somehow get through these layers of protection, it is true that that person could read the information in the database. The help the DBMS provides here is what is called encyphering, or encryption. When anything is stored or modified in the database, the DBMS will actually encode it. When a legitimate user retrieves data through the DBMS, the DBMS will decypher it and the user will see it in a normal fashion. An actual user of the DBMS will not even be aware that this encyphering is happening. Someone bypassing the DBMS would have to crack the code and decypher all of the data in order to make any sense out of it.

Bill: The security features really are impressive. What else do these DBMS's do?

Mike: You can specify what are termed integrity constraints. You can say that a given field must contain only numeric data, or that another field must be in the range one hundred to five hundred. You can specify that the department for a given faculty member must exist in order for the faculty member to be stored in the database. You could prevent deletions of departments which contain any faculty members. The DBMS will then enforce these things.

The DBMS will handle all of the tricky problems associated with shared update. It will also take care of backup and recovery.

Mary: I always thought backup and recovery were pretty simple. You make a backup copy of the file each night before it is updated with the transactions from the day. Then, if there is ever a problem, you recover the file by copying the backup version over the live version and redoing the update.

Mike: But what if the file, or in this case the database, is being updated on-line? When users make changes, they are really changing the data in the database and not just adding transactions to some transaction file for update the following night. And what if there is not just a single user, but a hundred users, all updating the database? We still need a backup copy, of course; but suppose that copy was made at 10:00 p.m. last night and users have been updating the database since 8:00 a.m. this morning. What do we do if a problem in the database is discovered at 2:00 p.m. this afternoon? We can't merely copy this backup copy over the live copy. What about all of the user updates that have taken place in the meantime? I would hate to have to call all of these users and tell them that they need to repeat the previous six hours' work.

Mary: I see what you mean. What does the DBMS do about that problem?

Mike: It keeps track of the updates that have taken place in a special file called a **log** or **journal**. Then, if a recovery is necessary, it uses the information in the log to reconstruct the activity that has taken place. The users don't have to do it.

Joan: That sounds great. Are there many of these DBMS's available?

Mike: From what I read, it seems like there must be hundreds. You find them on everything from the largest mainframe to the smallest micro. Some have all of the features we have been talking about and more; others are much more limited.

Bill: How do you decide which one to get?

Mike: That's not an easy question. There are many factors. Certainly one is price, but there are many others. For example, if you already have hardware in place, the DBMS you buy must run on this hardware under whatever operating system is currently in operation. The best thing is to build a chart on which you list all of the different possible features a DBMS might possess. Then you rate each of these according to how important the feature is to you. If you are going to be doing a lot of shared updating, then you might assign the category "SUPPORT FOR SHARED UPDATE" a high value. If this were not so important, you might assign it a low value.

After this is done, you could evaluate each of the DBMS's that you are considering to see how they stack up in these different categories. There are a number of different reports available to help you do this. You could also talk to current users of these systems to get their impressions of the quality of the product in the different categories.

Bill: It sounds like a lot of work.

Mike: It is, but it's such an important decision that it's well worth it. In fact, we are about to begin this process right here at Marvel.

Joan: It sounds like there are some exciting times ahead.

Mike: You bet there are. There are a number of extraordinary features we haven't even talked about. One example is **query languages**.

Mary: I know a query is a request for information from a file or database, but what is a query language?

Mike: It's a language that's intended to be used to query the database in a quick and easy way. Without these languages, if a user wanted to get information in a manner that was not already built into the system, he would have to request that the data processing staff write a program in a language like COBOL. Given how overworked most data processing departments are, it could take quite a while for the request to be honored. In addition, it takes a while to write a COBOL program, even a fairly simple one. With a query language, the user can do it by himself or herself in a matter of moments.

Bill: What do they look like?

Mike: They take many different forms. To give you a general idea, suppose the user wanted a list of all faculty members earning less than $25,000. He would type something like:

```
DISPLAY FACULTY_NUMBER, NAME
     WHEN SALARY < 25000
```

Bill: That's all?!

Mike: That's all. Naturally, the syntax varies somewhat from one query language to another, but this is about all you have to do. In fact, there's a type of query language they call a **natural language**, in which the user types commands and requests in plain everyday English. A user could type something like:

```
Give me the numbers and names of all faculty earning less
than 25000.
```

If a user then wanted to know which of those faculty members listed in the answer were in the math department, she could type something like:

```
Which ones are in the math department?
```

These systems are smart enough to realize that the user wanted a list of all the people who were a part of the answer to the previous question and, in addition, were in the math department.

Bill: That's really impressive. I'll bet it takes a pretty large computer to run some of those languages, especially the natural languages.

Mike: That's what I thought, but I was wrong. They have some very impressive natural language systems running on microcomputers. A friend of mine saw one of them demonstrated and said that it was really impressive. In fact, when the person sitting at the keyboard typed "hird" instead of the word "hired", the system asked him if he meant to type the word "hired". The kinds of things these systems can do are really incredible.

Mary: It all looks great, but I must confess that as a programmer it makes me uneasy. If it's so easy for users to get results themselves, is there going to be a need for me? Is this whole area going to put me out of a job?

Mike: Initially, that concerned me, too. The more I looked into it, however, the more I realized that there is still plenty to do. Designing databases, administering databases, developing systems, and so on are all going to be critical areas that need professional expertise. In addition, as nice as some of these new languages are, they cannot do it all. There are still a number of tasks that can't be done unless you have a language like COBOL. If you're concerned about job security, the best thing you can do is to make yourself as flexible as possible. It seems to be especially critical to have a good working knowledge of database concepts. [Note to the reader: Mike is really putting in a plug for you to read the rest of the book.]

Joan: I repeat: it sounds like there are some exciting times ahead.

— End of conversation —

The preceding conversation is fictitious, and the reports and file layouts have been greatly simplified from what they would be in an actual setting. However, the four programmers did discover and discuss the major problems with the file-oriented approach, and the points Mike made concerning database management systems were valid.

This textbook deals with the topic of database management. In it we will examine a variety of database management systems. We will look at the various categories, or models, into which these systems are grouped. We will study the process of database design, i.e., how a database is structured to meet the needs of a given organization. We will look at the people involved in database management. We will also look at what is happening in the world of computing today, and what is likely to happen tomorrow, in relation to database management. In this chapter, we begin our study of this very important topic.

Section 1.2 presents some background material and terminology concerning database management. In section 1.3, we will study the history of the topic. Finally, in sections 1.4 and 1.5, we will examine some of the advantages and disadvantages of using database management systems.

1.2 BACKGROUND

This section introduces some crucial background terminology and ideas. You are probably familiar with some of the terms from previous work you have done with files.

ENTITIES, ATTRIBUTES, AND RELATIONSHIPS

Among the most fundamental terms are entity, attribute, and relationship. An entity is really just like a noun; it is a person, place, or thing. The entities of interest to the group from Marvel College that we encountered in section 1.1 are faculty members, departments, insurance plans, job history records, and speaking topics. We will soon meet another organization, called Premiere Products, that is interested in entities like sales reps, customers, orders, and products.

An attribute is a property of an entity. The term is used here exactly as it is used in everyday English. You certainly might speak of the attributes of a person, such as eye color and height. At Marvel College, on the other hand, for the entity called faculty member, the attributes of interest are faculty number, name, address, and so on. While these properties may not be as physical as eye color or height, they are indeed properties of faculty members.

Figure 1.5 on the following page, shows two entities, department and faculty. It also shows a number of attributes. The department entity has three attributes: department number, description, and location. The faculty entity has five attributes: faculty number, name, address, salary, and earnings year-to-date.

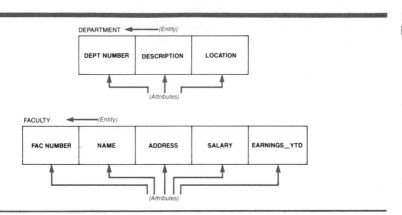

FIGURE 1.5
Entities and attributes

When we speak of **relationship**, we really mean an association between entities. There is a relationship between departments and faculty members, for example. A department is related to all of the faculty members who work in the department, and a faculty member is related to the department in which he or she works.

Figure 1.6 shows the relationship between the department and faculty entities. The arrow represents the relationship. In this case, it is a **one-to-many** relationship; i.e., one department is associated with many faculty members, but each faculty member is associated with only one department. (In this type of relationship, "many" is used in a slightly different manner than in everyday English. It would actually be better to state that a department is associated with *any number* of faculty members. This number can even be zero! Certainly this is not the normal use of the word "many.")

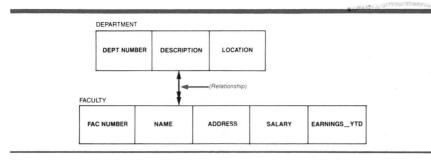

FIGURE 1.6
One-to-many
relationship with single
arrowhead indicating
the "one" part of the
relationship and
double arrowhead
indicating the "many"
part of the relationship

In the type of drawing shown in the figure, a single arrowhead is used to indicate the "one" part of the relationship and a double arrowhead is used to indicate the "many" part. In another common type of drawing used in the database environment, the same type of relationship is indicated by having only a single arrowhead indicating the "many" part and no arrowhead for the "one" part. This type of diagram is shown in Figure 1.7 and represents the style that will be encountered most often in this text. Fortunately, when examining either type of diagram, it is usually clear which style has been used.

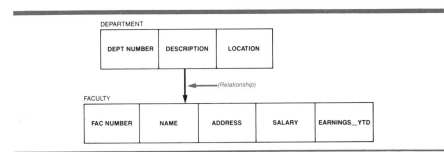

FIGURE 1.7
One-to-many
relationship with single
arrowhead indicating
the "many" part of
the relationship.

FILES, RECORDS, AND FIELDS

In a file processing environment, the critical terms are field, record, and file. The smallest amount of data that can be stored is the bit. Bits are grouped into bytes (or characters). Collections of characters form a field. Collections of fields form a record. Collections of occurrences of a specific type of record form a file.

For an example, consider the data needed by Mike for faculty members as shown in Figure 1.1. The fields shown are FACULTY_NUMBER, NAME, ADDRESS, SALARY, EARNINGS_YTD, and DEPT_NUMBER. Collectively, all of these fields form a record (technically, a record type). The collection of all of the occurrences of this record type (one for each faculty member) forms a file. Both the file and the record type would be given names, of course. We might choose to call the file EMPLOYEE_FILE and the record type EMPLOYEE_FILE_REC, for example.

How are entities, attributes, and relationships handled in a file processing environment? As you might expect, for each entity, we will have a separate file. For each attribute of that entity in which we are interested, we will have a field. Relationships will be implemented by having fields within one file identify records in another.

Consider, for example, Mike's requirements from section 1.1. There were two entities: departments and faculty members. The attributes of interest for departments were department number, description, and location, and the attributes of interest for faculty members were employee number, name, address, salary, and earnings year-to-date. We thus have two files, a department file and a faculty file. The attributes become the fields in these records. In addition, there was a relationship between departments and faculty members in which each department was related to all faculty members who worked in the department and each faculty member was related to the unique department in which he or she worked (the same relationship shown pictorially in Figures 1.6 and 1.7). This relationship is accomplished by placing the department number, which is the key to the department file, as one of the fields in the faculty file record. Given a specific faculty member, the value in this field indicates the number of the department in which the faculty member works. If we want any further information about the department, using this value as the key to the department file enables us to find any information about the department that we desire. On the other hand, if we wish to find all of the faculty members who work in a given department, say department 3, we search through the faculty member file looking for any faculty records that have the number 3 in the department number field.

DATABASES

In a typical file processing environment, each user area, such as payroll, personnel, and the speakers' bureau, has its own collection of files and programs that access these files [see Figure 1.8]. This type of environment leads to the

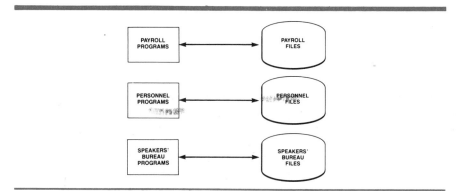

FIGURE 1.8
Classical file approach

problems mentioned in the discussion at Marvel College. Since there is usually overlap of data between user areas, there is **redundancy** in the system. The address of a faculty member can occur in many places, for example. While this is certainly wasteful of space, the problems it causes for update are potentially much more serious. In addition, trying to produce reports or respond to queries that span user areas can be extremely difficult. These problems lead to the idea of a pool of data, or database, rather than separate collections of individual files.

Is a database the next step in the progression? (Fields → records → files → database?) Is a database merely a collection of files? Although there is some justification for viewing a database in this way, it is insufficient. Some mention must be made of relationships among the records in these files.

> *Def:* A **database** is a structure that can house information about multiple types of entities as well as relationships among the entities.

Note that the definition doesn't indicate that all the entities must be housed within the same actual physical file on disk. While a database may be contained in a single file, it can also be stored within a number of different files, one for each entity, for example. The crucial point is that there must be some way of implementing relationships among the records.

Different definitions of a database exist. Some definitions include the word **self-describing**. This means that a database contains within it a *description of itself*. This would be analogous to a file containing its record description as part of the contents of the file. It makes the database a logically complete structure; i.e., it does not rely on a separate structure for information about itself. Every DBMS discussed in this text has this property. Another word often used is **integrated**. This simply means that the database contains the relationships mentioned in our definition. The final word that is sometimes included is **shared**, which simply means that more than one user has access to the data. After all, if a database is not shared, its full potential value will not be available to the organization.

We could eliminate the problems associated with a straight file processing environment by moving to a database environment. One way to do this would be to have a single database that users from each area would access, as shown in Figure 1.9. In this database, an individual faculty member would be found only once.

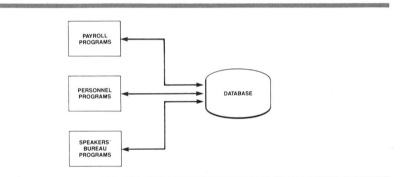

FIGURE 1.9
Database
(user-maintained)

This faculty member would somehow be related to the department in which he or she worked, the insurance plan that covered that faculty member, all of that faculty member's job history information, and all the lectures that faculty member would be willing to give. With this structure, all of the programmers at Marvel would be able to complete their tasks.

As Bill correctly pointed out, however, managing a database is a complicated task. The underlying structure is inherently more involved than a simple file. Whether we use linked lists, inverted files, or anything else to accomplish the task, we have added complexity to the structure. If we are to manage this structure ourselves, each program in the system will be more complex than a comparable program in a corresponding file processing environment. In addition, a failure on the part of any of these programs could actually destroy the structure of the database.

DATABASE MANAGEMENT SYSTEMS

Fortunately, software packages called database management systems can do the job of manipulating actual databases for us. A database management system (or **DBMS**), at its simplest, is a software product through which users interact with a database. The actual manipulation of the underlying database structures is handled by the DBMS [see Figure 1.10]. Using a DBMS, we can request the system to find

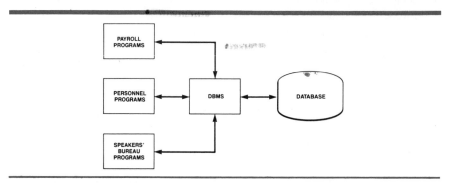

FIGURE 1.10
Database (using a Database Management System)

department 3, for example, and the system will either locate the desired department or tell us that no such department exists. All the work in accomplishing this task is done by the system. We do not have to worry about hashing, indexing, or any other mechanisms used to accomplish the task. We could then ask for the faculty members in the department and again the system would perform all the work of locating these faculty members. Likewise, when we store a new faculty member in the database, the DBMS performs all the tasks necessary to ensure that the faculty member is, in fact, connected to the appropriate department and insurance plan.

DATA MODELS

Database management systems are characterized by the model of data that they follow. A data model has two components — structure and operations. The structure refers to the way the system structures data or, at least, the way the users of the DBMS feel that the data is structured. The operations are the facilities given to the users of the DBMS to manipulate data within the database. What is crucial is the way things *feel* to the user. It does not matter how the designers of the DBMS choose to implement these facilities behind the scenes.

There are three models, or categories, for the vast majority of DBMS's: the relational model, the network model, and the hierarchical model. These models will be investigated in detail in later chapters of the text. At this point, we just wish to give a brief introduction to them and to the sample databases that we will use throughout the text. Although we need to touch on some of the terminology at this point in order to present the ideas of the models, don't be overly concerned with it. It will all be covered in detail later.

RELATIONAL MODEL

A relational model database is perceived by the user as being just a collection of tables. Formally, these tables are called relations, and this is where the relational model gets its name. Relationships are implemented through common columns in two or more tables. Consider the relational database in Figure 1.11.

FACULTY

FACULTY_NUMBER	NAME	ADDRESS	SALARY	EARNINGS_YTD	DEPT_NUMBER	DEGREE	FIELD	RANK	PLAN_NUMBER	DEPS_CVD

DEPARTMENT

DEPT_NUMBER	NAME	LOCATION

INSURANCE_PLAN

PLAN_NUMBER	DESCRIPTION

SPEAKING_TOPICS

FACULTY_NUMBER	TITLE	TIMES_GIVEN	LAST_GIVEN

JOB_HISTORY_INFORMATION

FACULTY_NUMBER	RANK	DATE_ATTAINED

In this database, we have a table for each entity: faculty members, departments, insurance plans, speaking topics, and job history records. If you examine the department and faculty tables, you will see that they both contain a column, DEPT_NUMBER. Do you see how this column will allow us to accomplish the relationship between departments and faculty members?

FIGURE 1.11
Marvel College relational database structure

Consider the sample occurrence of this database in Figure 1.12. Using the common column of department number, we can see that faculty member 507 is in department 3. On the other hand, we can find all of the faculty members in the math department by examining the department table to find that math is department 2, and then looking for all of the faculty members in the faculty table who have a 2 in the department number column.

There are many ways of manipulating a relational database. These will be discussed in detail in chapter 3. One of the most prevalent of these is a

FIGURE 1.12
Marvel College sample data

FACULTY

FACULTY_ NUMBER	NAME	ADDRESS	SALARY	EARNINGS_ YTD	DEPT_ NUMBER	DEGREE	FIELD	RANK	PLAN_ NUMBER	DEPS_ CVD
119	BARB MARTIN	94 RIDGE,GRANT,MI	22500	15425.00	1	MA	COMM.	ASST PROF	2	NO
209	JANE NEWTON	210 LEONARD,ADA,MI	29000	18945.50	2	MS	TOPOLOGY	ASSO PROF	1	YES
421	AL JONES	121 COLTON,HART,MI	20000	11402.50	1	PhD	DATABASE	ASST PROF	2	NO
462	TOM JOHNSON	604 46TH,LOWELL,MI	25000	16952.12	1	MS	OP. SYS.	ASSO PROF	2	YES
485	PAM SPARKS	201 OLIVE,HOLT,MI	33500	20115.35	2	PhD	ANALYSIS	PROF	3	YES
507	ROB CANTON	5 STATE,CUTLER,MI	19500	11010.00	3	MS	VOLCANOES	ASST PROF	1	YES
564	TIM FERRIS	16 W. 9TH,TROY,MI	28500	18540.40	3	PhD	MINERALS	ASSO PROF	1	NO
683	FRANK NILSON	46 CRESTON,ADA,MI	36500	22050.55	5	PhD	LASER TECH	PROF	2	YES

DEPARTMENT

DEPT_ NUMBER	NAME	LOCATION
1	COMPUTER SCI.	408 KELLY HALL
2	MATHEMATICS	253 WATSON HALL
3	GEOLOGY	707 CASE TOWER
5	PHYSICS	118 FONT TOWER

INSURANCE_PLAN

PLAN_ NUMBER	DESCRIPTION
1	REGULAR
2	DELUXE
3	SPECIAL

SPEAKING_TOPICS

FACULTY_ NUMBER	TITLE	TIMES_ GIVEN	LAST_ GIVEN
119	DISTRIBUTED DATABASE	5	32187
119	WHY NETWORK MICROS?	2	51587
119	COMMUNICATIONS	1	90287
462	THE FUTURE OF UNIX	3	51387
485	THE REGULAR POLYHEDRA	2	11586
507	MOUNT ST. HELENS	1	21287
683	LASER TECHNOLOGY	3	52287
683	NUCLEAR POWER PRO&CON	1	61587

JOB_HISTORY_INFORMATION

FACULTY_ NUMBER	RANK	DATE_ ATTAINED
119	ASST PROF	91581
209	ASST PROF	90176
209	ASSO PROF	91383
421	ASST PROF	81583
462	ASST PROF	41271
462	ASSO PROF	91481
485	ASST PROF	40265
485	ASSO PROF	91274
485	PROF	91383
507	ASST PROF	91281
564	ASST PROF	52176
564	ASSO PROF	90187
683	ASST PROF	61166
683	ASSO PROF	80274
683	PROF	81283

language called SQL (Structured Query Language) that was developed by IBM. The basic form of an SQL command is simply SELECT . . . FROM . . . WHERE . . . . We list the columns that we wish to see printed after the word SELECT. After the word FROM, we list all tables that contain these columns. Finally, we list any restrictions to be applied after the word WHERE. For example, if we wish to print the number, name, and address of all faculty members whose salary is over $25,000, we would type

```
SELECT FACULTY_NUMBER, NAME, ADDRESS
      FROM FACULTY
      WHERE SALARY > 25000
```

and the computer would respond with:

FACULTY NUMBER	NAME	ADDRESS
209	JANE NEWTON	210 LEONARD, ADA, MI
485	PAM SPARKS	201 OLIVE, HOLT, MI
564	TIM FERRIS	16 W. 9TH, TROY, MI
683	FRANK NILSON	46 CRESTON, ADA, MI

If we wished to see the number and name of each department together with the number and name of each faculty member within the department, we would type:

```
SELECT DEPT.DEPT_NUMBER, DEPT.NAME,
      FACULTY.FACULTY_NUMBER, FACULTY.NAME
      FROM DEPT, FACULTY
      WHERE DEPT.DEPT_NUMBER = FACULTY.DEPT_NUMBER
```

and the computer would respond with:

DEPT NUMBER	DEPT NAME	FACULTY NUMBER	FACULTY NAME
1	COMPUTER SCI.	119	BARB MARTIN
2	MATHEMATICS	209	JANE NEWTON
1	COMPUTER SCI.	421	AL JONES
1	COMPUTER SCI.	462	TOM JOHNSON
2	MATHEMATICS	485	PAM SPARKS
3	GEOLOGY	507	ROB CANTON
3	GEOLOGY	564	TIM FERRIS
5	PHYSICS	683	FRANK NILSON

Why did we write DEPT.NAME instead of just NAME? By writing DEPT.NAME, we are indicating that we are referring to the NAME column *within the* DEPT *table*. Since the other table involved in this problem also includes a column called NAME, it is essential that we indicate which NAME we are interested in. This is called **qualification.** We say that we have **qualified NAME.** Note that we have also qualified FACULTY_NUMBER, even though there is only one such column. It is not wrong to do so, although it is not necessary.

NETWORK MODEL

A **network model** database is perceived by the user as a collection of record types and relationships between these record types. Such a structure is called a **network,** and it is from this that the model takes its name. In contrast to the relational model, in which relationships were *implicit* (being derived from matching columns in the tables), in the network model the relationships are *explicit* (presented as part of the structure itself). Consider the database in Figure 1.13,

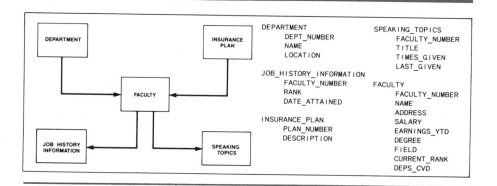

for example. The rectangles represent the record types in the database. There is one for each of the entities: departments, faculty members, insurance plans, job history information, and speaking topics. The arrows represent the relationships. In particular, they represent the one-to-many relationship that was discussed earlier. The arrow goes from the "one" part of the relationship to the "many" part. Since one department is related to many faculty members but each faculty member is related to exactly one department, we have a one-to-many relationship, and thus an arrow, from department to faculty, for example.

We manipulate a network model database by essentially *following the arrows.* This procedure is often referred to as **database navigation.** Arrows may be followed in either direction. Suppose that we need to print a list of all of the faculty members in department 3. We first ask the DBMS to FIND department 3. Assuming there is such a department, we then repeatedly ask to FIND the NEXT faculty member within this department until reaching the end of the list of faculty mem-

FIGURE 1.13
Marvel College
network database
structure

bers in this department. While we are on a given faculty member, we can ask to find the insurance plan related to that faculty member. Here we would be following the arrow from insurance plan to faculty member in the reverse direction. If we also wanted to print all the faculty member's job history information, we could repeatedly ask the DBMS to FIND the NEXT job history record for this faculty member until there were no more.

Note that we find the department to which a faculty member is related by following the arrow, not by looking at a department number field in a faculty record. There is thus no need for such a field. In general there is no need to have fields in network model records to implement the relationships.

HIERARCHIAL MODEL

A hierarchical model database is perceived by a user as a collection of hierarchies (or trees). A hierarchy is really a network with an added restriction: no box can have more than one arrow entering the box. (It doesn't matter how many arrows leave a box.) A hierarchy is thus a more restrictive structure than a network. Since two arrows enter the faculty box in the Marvel College database shown in Figure 1.13, it is not a hierarchy and cannot be implemented directly in a hierarchical model DBMS.

PREMIERE PRODUCTS

It is time to meet Premiere Products, the other organization that we will use as an example throughout the text. A distributor of appliances and sporting goods, Premiere Products needs to maintain the following information:

1. For sales reps, they need to store the sales rep's number, name, address, total commission, and commission rate.
2. For customers, they need to store the customer's number, name, address, current balance, credit limit, and the number of the sales rep who represents the customer.
3. For parts, they need to store the part's number, description, units on hand, item class, the number of the warehouse in which the item is stored, and the unit price.

Premiere Products also must store information on orders. A sample order is shown in Figure 1.14 on the following page. Note that there are three parts to the order. The heading (top) of the order contains the order number, date, customer number, name, address, sales rep number, and sales rep name. The body of the order contains a number of order lines, sometimes called line items. Each order line contains a part number, part description, the number of the part that was ordered, and the quoted price for the part. It also contains a total (usually called an extension) which is the product of the number ordered and the quoted price.

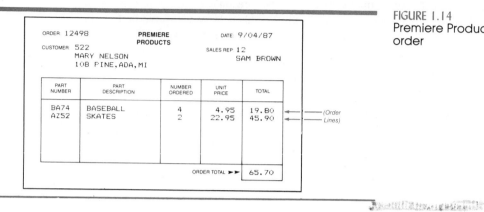

FIGURE 1.14
Premiere Products
order

Finally the footing (bottom) of the order contains the order total. The following are the additional items that Premiere Products must store concerning orders:

4. For orders, they need to store the order number, date the order was placed, and the number of the customer who placed the order. Note that the customer's name, address, and the number of the sales rep who represents the customer are stored with customer information. In addition, the name of the sales rep is stored with sales rep information.
5. For each order line, they need to store the order number, part number, number ordered, and the quoted price. Note that the part description is stored with part information. The product of number ordered and quoted price is not stored, since it can easily be computed when needed.
6. The overall order total is not stored but will be computed when the order is produced.

Figure 1.15 represents a relational model database for Premiere Products.

FIGURE 1.15
Premiere Products
relational database
structure

SLSREP	SLSREP_NUMBER	SLSREP_NAME	SLSREP_ADDRESS	TOTAL_COMMISSION	COMMISSION_RATE

CUSTOMER	CUSTOMER_NUMBER	NAME	ADDRESS	CURRENT_BALANCE	CREDIT_LIMIT	SLSREP_NUMBER

ORDER	ORDER_NUMBER	DATE	CUSTOMER_NUMBER

ORDER_LINE	ORDER_NUMBER	PART_NUMBER	NUMBER_ORDERED	QUOTED_PRICE

PART	PART_NUMBER	PART_DESCRIPTION	UNITS_ON_HAND	ITEM_CLASS	WAREHOUSE_NUMBER	UNIT_PRICE

Figure 1.16 shows the same database, but filled in with sample data that will be used throughout the book.

FIGURE 1.16
Premiere Products
sample data

SLSREP

SLSREP_ NUMBER	SLSREP_NAME	SLSREP_ADDRESS	TOTAL_ COMMISSION	COMMISSION_ RATE
3	MARY JONES	123 MAIN,GRANT,MI	2150.00	.05
6	WILLIAM SMITH	102 RAYMOND,ADA,MI	4912.50	.07
12	SAM BROWN	419 HARPER,LANSING,MI	2150.00	.05

CUSTOMER

CUSTOMER_ NUMBER	NAME	ADDRESS	CURRENT_ BALANCE	CREDIT_ LIMIT	SLSREP_ NUMBER
124	SALLY ADAMS	481 OAK,LANSING,MI	418.75	500	3
256	ANN SAMUELS	215 PETE,GRANT,MI	10.75	800	6
311	DON CHARLES	48 COLLEGE,IRA,MI	200.10	300	12
315	TOM DANIELS	914 CHERRY,KENT,MI	320.75	300	6
405	AL WILLIAMS	519 WATSON,GRANT,MI	201.75	800	12
412	SALLY ADAMS	16 ELM,LANSING,MI	908.75	1000	3
522	MARY NELSON	108 PINE,ADA,MI	49.50	800	12
567	JOE BAKER	808 RIDGE,HARPER,MI	201.20	300	6
587	JUDY ROBERTS	512 PINE,ADA,MI	57.75	500	6
622	DAN MARTIN	419 CHIP,GRANT,MI	575.50	500	3

ORDER

ORDER_ NUMBER	DATE	CUSTOMER_ NUMBER
12489	90287	124
12491	90287	311
12494	90487	315
12495	90487	256
12498	90587	522
12500	90587	124
12504	90587	522

ORDER_LINE

ORDER_ NUMBER	PART_ NUMBER	NUMBER_ ORDERED	QUOTED_ PRICE
12489	AX12	11	14.95
12491	BT04	1	402.99
12491	BZ66	1	311.95
12494	CB03	4	175.00
12495	CX11	2	57.95
12498	AZ52	2	22.95
12498	BA74	4	4.95
12500	BT04	1	402.99
12504	CZ81	2	108.99

PART

PART_ NUMBER	PART_ DESCRIPTION	UNITS_ ON_HAND	ITEM_ CLASS	WAREHOUSE_ NUMBER	UNIT_ PRICE
AX12	IRON	104	HW	3	17.95
AZ52	SKATES	20	SG	2	24.95
BA74	BASEBALL	40	SG	1	4.95
BH22	TOASTER	95	HW	3	34.95
BT04	STOVE	11	AP	2	402.99
BZ66	WASHER	52	AP	3	311.95
CA14	SKILLET	2	HW	3	19.95
CB03	BIKE	44	SG	1	187.50
CX11	MIXER	112	HW	3	57.95
CZ81	WEIGHTS	208	SG	2	108.99

For sales reps, we have columns for the number, name, address, total commissioned earned, and commission rate. For customers, we have the number, name, address, balance, and credit limit. In addition, we have a column for the number of the sales rep who represents the customer. Using it, we can find the one sales rep who represents a particular customer. Thus, we see that customer 256 (ANN SAMUELS) is represented by sales rep 6 (WILLIAM SMITH). On the other hand, by looking for all of the customers who have some specific number in this column, we can find all the customers whom a given sales rep serves. Thus, we see that sales rep 12 (SAM BROWN) represents customers 311 (DON CHARLES), 405 (AL WILLIAMS), and 522 (MARY NELSON).

For orders, we have the number and the date of the order. In addition, we have a column for the customer who placed an order. This column relates orders to customers in the same way that the sales rep column in the customer table related customers to sales reps. For parts, we have columns for the part number, description, number of units on hand, the item class the part belongs in (housewares, sporting goods, or appliances), the number of the warehouse in which the part is stored, and the price.

In the ORDER_LINE table, we have columns for the order number that a given order line corresponds to, the number of the part that is present on that order line, the number of units of that part that were ordered, and the price that was quoted for that part on that order. The seventh row of the ORDER_LINE table tells us, for example, that there is a line on order 12498 on which four units of part BA74 (BASEBALL) were ordered at a price of 4.95 each.

To test your understanding of the relational model database for Premiere Products, answer the following questions using the data in Figure 1.16.

1. Give the numbers of all the customers represented by MARY JONES.
2. Give the name of the customer who placed order 12491. Give the name of the sales rep who represents this customer.
3. List all of the parts that appear on order 12491. For each part, give the description, number ordered, and quoted price.
4. Why is the column QUOTED_PRICE a part of the ORDER_LINE table? Can't we just take the PART_NUMBER and look up the price in the PART table?

Answers:

1. 124, 412, and 622. (Look up the number of MARY JONES in the SLSREP table and obtain the number 3. Then find all customers in the CUSTOMER table that have the number 3 in the SLSREP_NUMBER column.)
2. DON CHARLES. SAM BROWN. (Look up the customer number in the ORDER table and obtain the number 311. Then find the customer in the CUSTOMER table that has customer number 311. Using this customer's sales rep number of 12, find the name of the sales rep in the SLSREP table.)
3. PART_NUMBER – "BZ66", PART_DESCRIPTION – "WASHER", NUMBER_ORDERED – 1, QUOTED_PRICE – 311.95. Also PART_NUMBER – "BT04", PART_DESCRIPTION – "STOVE", NUMBER_ORDERED – 1, QUOTED_PRICE – 402.99. (Look up each ORDER_LINE table row in which the order number is 12491. Each of these rows contains a part number, the number ordered, and the quoted price. The only thing missing is the description of the part. Use the part number to look up the corresponding description in the PART relation.)

continued

Q&A continued

4. If we do not have the QUOTED_PRICE column in the ORDER_LINE table, the PRICE for a part on an order line must be obtained by looking up the PRICE in the PART table. While this may not be bad, it does prevent Premiere Products from charging different prices to different customers for the same part. Since Premiere Products wants the flexibility to quote different prices to different customers, we include the QUOTED_PRICE column in the ORDER_LINE table. If you examine the ORDER_LINE table, you will see cases in which the QUOTED_PRICE value matches the actual price in the PART table and cases in which it differs.

Figure 1.17 shows a network model database for Premiere Products that will be used in the discussion of the network model in chapter 8.

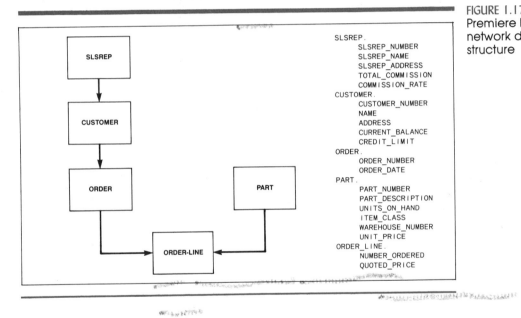

FIGURE 1.17
Premiere Product network database structure

1.3 HISTORY OF DATABASE MANAGEMENT

Although it is difficult to pinpoint exactly when the area of database management began, there is good reason to place its beginnings with the Apollo project of the 1960s, which was launched in response to President John F. Kennedy's stated goal of landing a man on the moon by the end of the decade. This project was certainly a vast and complex undertaking. Since, at the time, no available systems were capable of handling the coordination of the vast amounts of data required, North American Rockwell, the prime contractor for the project, asked IBM to develop one. In response, IBM developed the Generalized Update Access Method (GUAM), which went into production in 1964.

It soon became clear to IBM that this product was useful in other environments and, in 1966, the company made the product available to the general public under the name Data Language/I (DL/I). This product is really the data management component of the Information Management System (IMS), which was certainly one of the most important of the early database management systems. IMS has been enhanced over the years and is still offered by IBM.

Another development was taking place in the mid-1960s. A system called Integrated Data Store (I-D-S) was developed at General Electric by a team headed by Charles Bachman. This system led to a whole class of database management systems, the CODASYL systems, which are still popular and influential today.

In the late 1960s, the COnference on DAta SYstems Languages (CODASYL), the group responsible for COBOL, tackled the problem of providing a standard for database management systems. CODASYL charged a task group, the DataBase Task Group (DBTG) with the job of developing specifications for database management systems. The DBTG did this and in 1971, CODASYL presented these specifications to the American National Standards Institute (ANSI) for adoption as a national standard. Although these specifications were not accepted as a standard by ANSI, a number of systems were developed following the CODASYL guidelines. These systems are usually called CODASYL systems or DBTG systems.

In 1970, Dr. E. F. Codd presented a paper that was to have a profound impact on the database community. In it, he proposed a new and, at the time, radically different approach to the management of data: the relational model. Throughout the decade of the 1970s, the relational model was the subject of intense research activity. In addition to purely theoretical research, prototype systems were developed, the most important being a system called System R, which was developed by IBM. It was not until the 1980s, however, that commercial relational DBMS's began to appear. Systems that are at least partly relational now exist in abundance on computers ranging from the smallest micro to the largest mainframe. While System R never became a commercial system, it led to IBM's commercial relational offering, DB2.

The 1970s and 1980s have seen the development of a number of support products to go along with DBMS's. Data dictionaries, report generators, query facilities, and nonprocedural languages have all been developed and, along with the DBMS, they are now a part of an entire environment, the so-called fourth generation environment. We speak of systems that contain all of these facilities as fourth generation languages (4GL) or as application generators. They represent a tremendous increase in productivity. (This environment will be discussed in chapter 13.) In addition, the 1980s have seen the development of microcomputer DBMS's. As the decade has progressed, these systems have increased greatly in functionality, to the point where they rival their mainframe counterparts in a number of areas.

For an excellent account of the early history of database management, see the March 1976 issue of the *ACM Computing Surveys*; in this issue, [6] gives the history of database management and an overview of the various models; [4] discusses the relational model; [11] discusses the CODASYL approach; [12] examines the hierarchical model; and [10] presents a comparison between the relational and CODASYL approaches.

1.4 ADVANTAGES OF DATABASE PROCESSING

There are a number of advantages to the database approach to processing, particularly when a powerful, full-functioned DBMS is used. These advantages are listed in Figure 1.18.

1. Economy of scale
2. Getting more information from the same amount of data
3. Sharing of data
4. Balancing conflicting requirements
5. Enforcement of standards
6. Controlled redundancy
7. Consistency
8. Integrity
9. Security
10. Flexibility and responsiveness
11. Increased programmer productivity
12. Improved program maintenance
13. Data independence

1. ECONOMY OF SCALE

The concentration of applications in one location allows for the possibility of smaller numbers of larger and more powerful computers, which usually results in an *economy of scale* (not unlike buying the "large economy size"). The same economy of scale may be realized by the concentration of technical expertise. Furthermore, since many users are sharing the database, any improvement in the database will potentially benefit many different users. In general, economy of scale refers to the fact that the collective cost of several combined operations may be less than the sum of the cost of the individual operations. Database processing makes this type of combination possible.

2. GETTING MORE INFORMATION FROM THE SAME AMOUNT OF DATA

The primary goal of a computer system is to turn data (recorded facts) into information (knowledge gained by processing these facts). Even though all the data that Joan needed for a requested report was in computer files, she could not easily access it and thus could not obtain the desired information. If, however, that data were in a common database, she would be able to access it (provided, of course, that she were authorized to do so). Thus, this added *information* would now be available even though the database might not contain additional *data* not already present in the files.

3. SHARING OF DATA

The data can be shared among authorized users, allowing users access to more of the data. Several users might have access to the same piece of data, e.g., a faculty member's address, but use it in a variety of ways. When a faculty member's address is changed, the change is immediately relayed to all users. In addition, new applications can be developed using the existing data in the database without the added burden of creating separate collections of files.

4. BALANCING CONFLICTING REQUIREMENTS

In order for the database approach to function adequately, there must be a person or group within the organization in charge of the database itself. This body is often called Database Administration (DBA). By keeping the overall needs of the organization in mind, DBA can structure the database to the benefit of the entire organization, not just a single user group. While this may potentially mean that an individual user group is served less well than it might have been if it had its own isolated system, the overall organization will benefit. If the organization benefits, then, ultimately, so do the individual user groups.

5. ENFORCEMENT OF STANDARDS

With the central control mentioned in the previous paragraph, DBA can ensure that standards for such things as data names, usages, and formats are followed uniformly throughout the organization.

6. CONTROLLED REDUNDANCY

Since data that was kept separate in a file oriented system is now integrated into a single database, we no longer have multiple copies of the same data. Each of the four programmers at Marvel had his or her own FACULTY file containing, among other things, a faculty member's address. Thus the address of each faculty member appeared in at least four different places. In the database approach, since there will be only one occurrence of each faculty member, this redundancy will be eliminated. In practice, there are places where we might actually introduce some limited amount of redundancy into a database for performance reasons. But, even in these cases, we are able to keep it under tight control. This is why it is better to say that we *control* redundancy rather than *eliminate* it.

7. CONSISTENCY

Consistency follows from the control or elimination of redundancy. If a faculty member's address appears in only one place, there is no possibility that faculty member 111 will have the address 123 MAIN ST at one spot within our data and 466 WILLOW RD in another, for example.

8. INTEGRITY

An **integrity constraint** is a rule that data in the database must follow. Here is an example of an integrity constraint: the department number given for a faculty member must be that of a department that *actually exists*. A database has **integrity** if data in the database satisfies all integrity constraints that have been established. In the database approach, DBA can define validation procedures that will ensure the integrity of the database.

9. SECURITY

Security is the prevention of access to the database by unauthorized users. Since DBA has control over the operational data, it can define authorization procedures to ensure that only legitimate users access the data. DBA can further allow different users to have different types of access to the same data. The payroll department at Marvel College may be able to view and change the salary of a faculty member. The insurance department may be able to view the salary of a faculty member but not change it. The speakers' bureau may not even be able to view a salary. One way DBA achieves this security is through user views. Any data items not included in the user view for a given user will not be accessible to that user. Another means of achieving security is through the use of sophisticated password schemes.

10. FLEXIBILITY AND RESPONSIVENESS

Since the data that was previously kept in several different files by several different user areas is now in the same database, it is possible to respond to requests for data from multiple areas in a much easier and more flexible way. Even within a single user area, the flexibility furnished by the DBMS to locate and access data in a number of different ways aids programmers in developing new programs to satisfy user requests. The use of high-level languages allows users to do some of their own programming in a very easy way. A user who employs one such language, for example, to find all the faculty members who are assigned to department 3, who are covered by insurance plan 2, and who have a salary under $20,000, need only type

```
SELECT FACULTY_NUMBER, NAME
     FROM FACULTY
     WHERE DEPT_NUMBER = 3 AND
          PLAN_NUMBER = 2 AND
          SALARY < 20000
```

Employing yet another language, called **a natural language**, a user may actually be able to type

Give me the names and numbers of all faculty members who
are in department 3, covered by plan 2 and make less than
20000.

In both cases, the user can get a response to a question concerning data in the
database rapidly and easily, without having to submit a request for the creation of a
special program to an already overworked data processing department.

II. INCREASED PROGRAMMER PRODUCTIVITY

Since programmers accessing a database do not have to worry about the mun-
dane data manipulation activities, as they would when accessing files, they will be
more productive. Studies have shown that on the average they will be two to four
times more productive; i.e., a new application can be developed in one-quarter to
one-half of the time it would take if it were a straight file-oriented application. In
addition, with the advent of fourth-generation languages built around database
management systems, the productivity increases can be much more dramatic. Ten-
to twentyfold increases (and more) in productivity are not uncommon.

I2. IMPROVED PROGRAM MAINTENANCE

When interacting with a DBMS, programs are relatively independent of the
actual data in the database. This means that many changes to the structure of the
data itself may not require maintenance to existing application programs. In a
straight file environment this is not true. Even simple changes to file layouts can
require substantial changes in every program that accesses the file. In addition,
since the low-level data manipulation is handled by the DBMS, details concerning
this manipulation do not appear in programs. Thus, the complexity of maintaining
such logic is not a concern in a DBMS environment.

I3. DATA INDEPENDENCE

While improving program maintenance is one important advantage of having
programs independent of the structure of the database, this independence has other
advantages as well. Without such independence, changes to the database structure
to improve performance and to meet changing corporate requirements become
very difficult. The fact that all of the programs in the system need maintenance
every time a change is made to the database structure would be a strong incentive
not to make any of these changes. Data independence removes this obstacle to
changing the structure.

Data independence occurs when the structure of the database can change without requiring the programs that access the database to change. Data independence
is achieved in the database environment through the use of external views or
subschemas. Each program accesses data through an external view. The underlying structure of the database can change without requiring a change in the external
view. Thus, programs would not have to change. (There is an obvious stipulation.
If the change to the database structure invalidated a user view, then the user view

and consequently any programs using the view would have to change. An example of such a change would be the removal of a required field from the database structure.)

To address the independence issue in a general way, a committee within the American National Standards Institute called the American National Standards Institute/Committee X3/Standards Planning And Requirements sub-Committee (ANSI/X3/SPARC or ANSI/SPARC), proposed the model illustrated in Figure 1.19. The external schemas are views of data furnished to application programs.

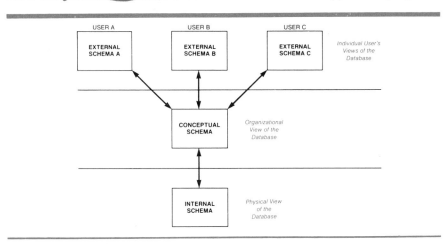

FIGURE 1.19
ANSI/SPARC model

The conceptual schema is the overall global organizational view of data. Finally, the internal schema is the view of the database as seen by the computer. It is the responsibility of the DBMS to map one view to another.

The only requirement imposed on the external schemas is that they can be derived from what is in the conceptual schema. Certainly, if there is no SALARY field within the conceptual schema, there can be no SALARY field within an external schema. If there is no relationship between customers and employees in a conceptual schema, for example, there can be no relationship between them in any external schema. The important point is that the conceptual schema could change (fields added, relationships added, formats changed) without affecting the external schemas. Obviously, an external schema would need to be changed if some field that it required were deleted from the conceptual schema.

Similarly, an internal schema can be changed without affecting the conceptual schema. Storage details or access strategies could change, for example. Where a given field was stored as zoned decimal, we may now wish to store it as packed decimal or, perhaps, in a binary format. Where direct access to a faculty member had previously been accomplished through one scheme, say hashing, we may now wish to use another scheme, perhaps some kind of index, for this purpose. (Don't worry about the technical terminology at this point.)

DBA could thus make changes to the internal schema to improve the performance of the database. DBA could also make changes to the conceptual schema to respond to new requirements within the organization. In both cases, the external schemas could remain the same (subject, of course, to the stipulation that the data they require is still present in the new structure). In this way the independence described earlier is achieved.

Any decent DBMS supports the external schemas of the ANSI/SPARC model. CODASYL systems call them subschemas. Many relational model systems call them views. In any case, the idea is the same: users can have their own views of what the database looks like.

Likewise, any decent DBMS supports, in general, the conceptual and internal schemas. In this case, however, the support is often not as complete as we would like. In the ANSI/SPARC model, logical details about the structure of the database belong in the conceptual schema, and physical details about such things as the actual storage and access methods for the database belong in the internal schema. Many DBMS products do not have this clear breakdown. Their designers may not have attempted to separate the logical from the physical at all or, if they have, the separation may not be nearly as complete as the ANSI/SPARC model requires. This is the direction in which systems are moving, however, and we have already discussed why it is a worthy goal.

1.5 DISADVANTAGES OF DATABASE PROCESSING

As you would expect, if there are advantages to doing something a certain way, there are also disadvantages. The database area is no exception. There are several disadvantages regarding database processing, and they are listed in Figure 1.20.

1. Size
2. Complexity
3. Cost
4. Additional hardware requirements
5. Higher impact of a failure
6. Recovery more difficult

FIGURE 1.20
Disadvantages of database processing

1. SIZE

To support all the complex functions that it must provide to users, a database management system must, by its very nature, be a large program occupying megabytes of disk space as well as a substantial amount of internal memory.

2. COMPLEXITY

Again, the complexity and breadth of the functions furnished by a DBMS make it a complex product. Programmers and analysts must understand the features of the system in order to take full advantage of it. There is a great deal for them to learn. In addition, with many choices to make when designing and implementing a new system using a DBMS, it is possible to make these choices incorrectly, especially if the understanding of the system is not thorough enough. Unfortunately, a few incorrect choices can spell disaster for the whole project.

3. COST

A good DBMS is an expensive product. By the time all the appropriate components related to the DBMS are purchased for a major mainframe system, the total price can easily run into the $100,000 to $400,000 range.

4. ADDITIONAL HARDWARE REQUIREMENTS

Because of the size and complexity of a DBMS, greater hardware resources are required than would be necessary without the DBMS. This means that if the hardware resources are not increased when a DBMS is purchased, users of the system may very well notice a severe degradation in performance. Purchasing (or leasing) additional hardware resources represents yet another added cost.

5. HIGHER IMPACT OF A FAILURE

Since many of the data processing resources are now concentrated in the database, a failure of any component has a much more far-reaching effect than in a nondatabase environment.

6. RECOVERY MORE DIFFICULT

Because of the added complexity, the process of recovering the database in the event of a catastrophe is a more complicated one, particularly if the database is being updated by a large number of users concurrently (i.e., at the same time).

1.6 SUMMARY

While a conventional file is capable of housing information concerning only a single type of entity (such as customers), a database is capable of housing information concerning several different types of entities (such as customers, sales reps, orders, and parts). In addition, a database also contains information concerning relationships among the various entities (such as the relationship between a sales rep and all of the customers whom he or she represents). In contrast to the file approach to processing, the database approach offers the possibility of controlling or eliminating redundancy; it also offers greater flexibility in drawing relationships among diverse entities.

A database management system (DBMS) is a software product that manages a database. Any interaction between users and the database is through the DBMS. The DBMS takes all responsibility for the actual storage and retrieval of data.

Database management systems began to appear in the mid-1960s. They are classified by the model of data they support. There are three basic models of data: the relational model, the network model (which includes systems following the specifications proposed by CODASYL), and the hierarchical model.

Taking the database approach to processing involves pooling data into a common database and managing this database with a DBMS. Some advantages of this approach include the ability to control redundancy, share data among users, get more information from the same data, and increase programmer productivity. Some disadvantages of this approach include the cost of the DBMS and related additional hardware, the complexity of a DBMS, and the higher potential impact of any type of failure.

For other information concerning the background of database processing, along with the advantages and disadvantages, see numbers [1], [2], [3], [5], [7], [8], [9], and [13] in the references section at the end of this chapter.

REVIEW QUESTIONS

1. Define redundancy. What redundancy currently exists in systems at Marvel College? What are the problems associated with redundancy?
2. Why is satisfying the request made to Joan by the personnel department difficult with the present system? Would it be easier to satisfy this request if Marvel were currently using a database approach? Why or why not?
3. What was Bill's initial concern about using a database? Do you think his concern was justified?
4. Define entity, attribute, and relationship.
5. Explain how entities, attributes, and relationships are implemented in a straight file environment.
6. Define database.
7. What does it mean to say a database is self-describing? Why is this a desirable feature?
8. What does it mean to say a database is integrated? Why is this a desirable feature?
9. What does it mean to say a database is shared? Why is this a desirable feature?
10. What is a DBMS? What is the fundamental function of a DBMS?
11. What is a data model? What are the three main data models?
12. If the beginning of database technology could be traced to a single event, which event would that be?
13. What contribution did CODASYL make to the database area?
14. What contribution did Dr. E. F. Codd make to the database area?
15. Describe what is meant by "economy of scale." How does database processing achieve an economy of scale?
16. How is it possible to get more information from the same amount of data when a database approach is used as opposed to a file approach?
17. What is DBA? What kinds of things does DBA do in a database environment?
18. How does consistency result from controlling or eliminating redundancy?
19. What is meant by integrity as it is used in this chapter?
20. What is meant by security? How is it achieved in the database environment?
21. How does the database approach furnish additional flexibility and responsiveness?
22. Why are programmers more productive in the database environment?
23. What is meant by data independence? How is it achieved in the database environment?
24. How does the ANSI/X3/SPARC model relate to data independence?
25. How can the size of a DBMS be a disadvantage to using one?
26. How can the complexity of a DBMS be a disadvantage?
27. Why could the impact of a failure in the database environment be more serious than in a file environment?
28. Why could recovery be more difficult in the database environment?

EXERCISES

1. Using the data for Marvel College as shown in Figure 1.12, answer each of the following questions .
   a. How many faculty members in the computer science department have a salary that is at least $25,000?
   b. How many faculty members covered by the regular insurance plan have coverage for dependents?
   c. What are the names of the faculty members who have at least two different speaking topics?
   d. What are the names of the faculty members who are still at the rank at which they were hired?
   e. How many talks have been given by members of the Computer Science Department?
   f. Give all of the information currently in the database concerning Barb Martin.

2. Using the data for Premiere Products as shown in Figure 1.16, answer each of the following questions.
   a. Give the names of all customers represented by William Smith.
   b. How many customers have a balance that is over their credit limit?
   c. Which sales reps represent customers whose balance is over their credit limit?
   d. Which customers placed orders on 9/05/87?
   e. Which sales reps represent any customers who placed orders on 9/05/87?
   f. Which customers currently have a STOVE on order?
   g. List the number and description of all parts that are currently on order by any customer represented by William Smith.

3. Indicate the changes that should be made to the Marvel College relational database structure shown in Figures 1.11 and 1.12 to satisfy the following additional requirements:
   a. Store the birthdate of each faculty member.
   b. Store the name of the secretary of each department.
   c. Store the number, name, and address of each student of Marvel College. In addition, there is a relationship between faculty and students in which each faculty member advises many students but each student is advised by exactly one faculty member.
   d. Store the number and description of each course offered at Marvel College as well as the number of credits each course is worth. Each course is offered by exactly one department. Each department offers many courses.
   e. Store the grade each student received in each course taken by the student. (This one is a little tricky.)

4. Indicate the changes that should be made to the Premiere Products relational database structure shown in Figures 1.15 and 1.16 to satisfy the following additional requirements:
   a. Store the phone number for each customer.
   b. Premiere Products is divided into territories. For each territory, store the number and description. Each sales rep is located in a single territory. Many sales reps can be located in the same territory.
   c. Each customer is located in a single territory.
   d. What change should be made if the territory in which a customer is located must be the same as the territory in which his or her sales rep is located?

REFERENCES

1] Atre, S. *Data Base: Structured Techniques for Design, Performance and Management*. Wiley-Interscience, 1980.

2] Bradley, James. *Introduction to Data Base Management in Business*. Holt, Rinehart & Winston, 1983.

3] Cardenas, Alfonso F. *Data Base Management Systems*, 2d ed. Allyn & Bacon, 1984.

4] Chamberlin, Donald D. "Relational Data-Base Management Systems." *ACM Computing Surveys* 8, no. 1 (March 1976).

5] Date, C. J. *Introduction to Database Systems, Volume I*, 4th ed. Addison-Wesley, 1986.

6] Fry, James P., and Sibley, Edgar H. "Evolution of Data-Base Management Systems." *ACM Computing Surveys* 8, no. 1 (March 1976).

7] Goldstein, Robert C. *Database Technology and Management*. John Wiley & Sons, 1985.

8] Kroenke, David. *Database Processing*, 2d ed. SRA, 1983.

9] McFadden, Fred R., and Hoffer, Jeffrey A. *Data Base Management*. Benjamin Cummings, 1985.

10] Michaels, Ann S.; Mittman, Benjamin; and Carlson, J. Robert. "A Comparison of the Relational and CODASYL Approaches to Data-Base Management." *ACM Computing Surveys* 8, no. 1 (March 1976).

11] Taylor, Robert W., and Frank, Randall L. "CODASYL Data-Base Management Systems." *ACM Computing Surveys* 8, no. 1 (March 1976).

12] Tsichritzis, D. C., and Lochovsky, F. H. "Hierarchical Data-Base Management: A Survey." *ACM Computing Surveys* 8, no. 1 (March 1976).

13] Vasta, Joseph A. *Understanding Data Base Management Systems*. Wadsworth, 1985.

FUNCTIONS OF A DATABASE MANAGEMENT SYSTEM

2.1 INTRODUCTION

In chapter 1, we discussed the concepts of a database and a database management system (DBMS). Throughout the remainder of the text, we will be investigating various aspects of database management in detail. We will look at the various models followed by DBMS's as well as some specific DBMS implementations. We will study the process of database design. We will discuss the people involved in the management of databases, especially those who handle database administration (DBA) functions. Before beginning any of this study, however, we really need to know more about what this object called a DBMS is supposed to do.

The main function of a DBMS, as we learned in chapter 1, is to store, update, and retrieve data in a database. Several other functions were mentioned briefly. In this chapter, we will examine these and other functions in some detail to set the stage for the remainder of the text. As we study various DBMS implementations, we will see to what degree these functions are actually present and how they are implemented.

In [4], Dr. E. F. Codd lists eight capabilities, or services, that should be provided by any full-scale DBMS. This list has found general acceptance and forms the basis of our study of the functions of a database management system. In addition, there are two important services not covered in Dr. Codd's list that we will also investigate. In the complete list that follows, the first eight services are those presented by Codd.

1. **data storage, retrieval** and **update**

   A DBMS must furnish users with the ability to store, retrieve, and update data in the database.

2. a user-accessible **catalog**

   A DBMS must furnish a catalog in which descriptions of data items are stored and which is accessible to users.

3. **transaction** support

   A DBMS must furnish a mechanism which will ensure that either all of the updates corresponding to a given transaction are made or that none of them are made.

4. **concurrency** control services

A DBMS must furnish a mechanism to ensure that the database is updated correctly when multiple users are updating the database concurrently.

5. **recovery** services

A DBMS must furnish a mechanism for recovering the database in the event that the database is damaged in any way.

6. **authorization** services

A DBMS must furnish a mechanism to ensure that only authorized users can access the database.

7. support for **data communication**

A DBMS must be capable of integrating with communication software.

8. **integrity** services

A DBMS must furnish a mechanism to ensure that both the data in the database and changes to the data follow certain rules.

9. services to promote **data independence**

A DBMS must include facilities to support the independence of programs from the actual structure of the database.

10. utility services

A DBMS should provide a set of utility services.

The preceding list is summarized in Figure 2.1.

1. Data storage, retrieval, and update
2. A user-accessible catalog
3. Transaction support
4. Concurrency control services
5. Recovery services
6. Authorization services
7. Support for data communication
8. Integrity services
9. Services to promote data independence
10. Utility services

FIGURE 2.1
Functions of a DBMS

2.2 STORAGE, RETRIEVAL, AND UPDATE (Function 1)

A DBMS must furnish users with the ability to store, retrieve, and update data in the database.

It almost goes without saying that a DBMS must allow its users to store, update, and retrieve data in a database. This is the fundamental capability. Without it, there is no point in talking about anything else. In storing, updating, and retrieving data, the user should *not* have any need to be aware of the system's

internal structures (such as **linked lists, inverted files,** and **indexes**) or the procedures used to manipulate these structures. The manipulation of these structures is
totally the responsibility of the system.

.3   CATALOG (Function 2)

> *A DBMS must furnish a* catalog *in which descriptions*
> *of data items are stored and which is accessible to users.*

It is very important for those who are responsible for a given database to have
a catalog they can access to determine what the database "looks like" and how
various programs access the database. In particular, they need to be able to easily
get answers to questions like:

- What records and fields are included in the current structure? What are the
  characteristics of these fields? Is the NAME field within the CUSTOMER record
  twenty characters long or thirty?
- What are the possible values for the various fields? Are there any restrictions on
  the possibilities for CREDIT_LIMIT, for example?
- What is the meaning of the various fields? What, exactly, is ITEM_CLASS, for
  example, and what does an item class of "HW" mean?
- What relationships are present? What is the meaning of each of the relationships? Must the relationship always exist? Does a customer, for example, have
  to have a sales rep?
- Which programs within the system access which data within the database? How
  do they access it? Do they merely retrieve it or do they actually update it? What
  kinds of updates do they do? Can a certain program add a new customer, for
  example, or can it merely make changes to existing customers? When it makes a
  change to a customer, can it change all of the fields or only the address?

Providing answers to these questions is crucial if a complex database is to be
managed effectively. Since the DBMS uses the layout of the database in order to
function, some of this information is available from the DBMS itself. In general,
however, the information available from the DBMS may be limited to such things
as record names, field names, and field characteristics (such as the fact that the
sales rep number is a two-digit number).

What the DBMS "knows" does not necessarily include meanings of records,
fields, and relationships, or the relationship between the data in the database and
the programs that access the database. This additional information is often furnished by a software tool called a **data dictionary system**. This product, which
complements the DBMS to furnish a highly useful catalog, can be a module of the
DBMS itself or a separate software product.

For additional discussion of the catalog, see [10] and [11].

2.4 LOGICAL TRANSACTIONS (Function 3)

A DBMS must furnish a mechanism which will ensure that either all of the updates corresponding to a given transaction are made or that none of them are made.

A **logical transaction** (often simply called a *transaction*) is a sequence of steps that will accomplish a single task (or, at least, what feels to the user like a single task). Following are some examples of logical transactions: add a customer, enter an order, enroll a student in a course, deactivate an employee, increase the units on hand of a particular part by 50. To a user, all of these seem to be single tasks. As we shall see shortly, accomplishing one "single task" may require that many changes are made to the database. Provided all of these changes are indeed made, everything is fine. We would have *severe* problems if some were made and others were not. A DBMS should furnish services that will ensure this does not happen. If it does happen, the database will not be consistent with reality.

Suppose that, in the Premiere Products database, there are some additional columns, as shown in Figure 2.2. In the SLSREP table, there is a column labeled ON_ORDER. This column contains the total dollar value of all of the orders currently on file for each customer of the given sales rep. There is also a similar column in the CUSTOMER table that represents the total dollar value of all of the orders for each customer. Finally, there is a column labeled ALLOCATED in the PART table that represents the number of units of a given part that are currently on order.

FIGURE 2.2
Premiere Products
sample data

SLSREP	SLSREP_NUMBER	SLSREP_NAME	SLSREP_ADDRESS	TOTAL_COMMISSION	COMMISSION_RATE	ON_ORDER
	3	MARY JONES	123 MAIN,GRANT,MI	2150.00	.05	567.44
	6	WILLIAM SMITH	102 RAYMOND,ADA,MI	4912.50	.07	815.90
	12	SAM BROWN	419 HARPER,LANSING,MI	2150.00	.05	998.62

CUSTOMER	CUSTOMER_NUMBER	NAME	ADDRESS	CURRENT_BALANCE	CREDIT_LIMIT	SLSREP_NUMBER	ON_ORDER
	124	SALLY ADAMS	481 OAK,LANSING,MI	418.75	500	3	567.44
	256	ANN SAMUELS	215 PETE,GRANT,MI	10.75	800	6	115.90
	311	DON CHARLES	48 COLLEGE,IRA,MI	200.10	300	12	714.94
	315	TOM DANIELS	914 CHERRY,KENT,MI	320.75	300	6	700.00
	405	AL WILLIAMS	519 WATSON,GRANT,MI	201.75	800	12	.00
	412	SALLY ADAMS	16 ELM,LANSING,MI	908.75	1000	3	.00
	522	MARY NELSON	108 PINE,ADA,MI	49.50	800	12	283.68
	567	JOE BAKER	808 RIDGE,HARPER,MI	201.20	300	6	.00
	587	JUDY ROBERTS	512 PINE,ADA,MI	57.75	500	6	.00
	622	DAN MARTIN	419 CHIP,GRANT,MI	575.50	500	3	.00

ORDER	ORDER_NUMBER	DATE	CUSTOMER_NUMBER
	12489	90287	124
	12491	90287	311
	12494	90487	315
	12495	90487	256
	12498	90587	522
	12500	90587	124
	12504	90587	522

ORDER_LINE	ORDER_NUMBER	PART_NUMBER	NUMBER_ORDERED	QUOTED_PRICE
	12489	AX12	11	14.95
	12491	BT04	1	402.99
	12491	BZ66	1	311.95
	12494	CB03	4	175.00
	12495	CX11	2	57.95
	12498	AZ52	2	22.95
	12498	BA74	4	4.95
	12500	BT04	1	402.99
	12504	CZ81	2	108.99

PART	PART_NUMBER	PART_DESCRIPTION	UNITS_ON_HAND	ITEM_CLASS	WAREHOUSE_NUMBER	UNIT_PRICE	ALLOCATED
	AX12	IRON	104	HW	3	17.95	11
	AZ52	SKATES	20	SG	2	24.95	2
	BA74	BASEBALL	40	SG	1	4.95	4
	BH22	TOASTER	95	HW	3	34.95	0
	BT04	STOVE	11	AP	2	402.99	2
	BZ66	WASHER	52	AP	3	311.95	1
	CA14	SKILLET	2	HW	3	19.95	0
	CB03	BIKE	44	SG	1	187.50	4
	CX11	MIXER	112	HW	3	57.95	2
	CZ81	WEIGHTS	208	SG	2	108.99	2

FIGURE 2.2
Premiere Products
sample data
(continued)

With these changes, let us consider what would happen when a user enters an order, a single logical transaction. Suppose the user enters order 12506, with a date of 9/06/87, for customer 405. This order is for 2 AX12's at 17.95 each and 3 CZ81's at 100.00 each (which represents a discount of 8.99). Behind the scenes, the steps described in Figure 2.3 must take place.

FIGURE 2.3
Sample logical
transaction

1. The customer's balance and credit limit are checked to ensure that the new order will not raise the balance over the credit limit.
   — assuming that we can proceed —

2. The total value of the order
   $(335.90 = 2 \cdot 17.95 + 3 \cdot 100.00)$
   must be added to the value in the ON_ORDER column for customer 405. In addition, depending on how soon the order is to be shipped, it may also be added to the customer's balance.

3. This same total must be added to the value in the ON_ORDER column for sales rep 12 (the sales rep who represents customer 405).

4. Order 12506 must be added to the ORDER table with a date of 9/06/87 and a customer number of 405.

5. Two order lines must be added to the ORDER_LINE table. They both will have an order number of 12506. One will have part number AX12, number ordered 2, quoted price 17.95 and the other will have part number CZ81, number ordered 3, quoted price 100.00.

6. The allocated column for part AX12 must be increased by 2 and the allocated column for part CZ81 must be increased by 3.

All of these steps must be performed when a user submits the single logical transaction, enter an order. While they do not necessarily have to happen in the order stated, they had better all happen or we have problems. Consider a hypothetical situation, for example, in which the ON_ORDER figures in the CUSTOMER and SALESREP tables are updated but, for some reason, perhaps a hardware or software failure, the order itself is never added to the database!

TRANSACTION SUPPORT

What must a DBMS do about this problem? First of all, you should realize that a program accomplishing these updates can be processing more than just a single logical transaction. This may have been the forty-third of the transactions it must process, for example, with 151 transactions yet to go. Each of these transactions may very well require several updates to the database. The DBMS has no inherent way of knowing which updates are grouped together in response to a single transaction. Thus, it must furnish the programmer with a mechanism to communicate this information to the DBMS.

It could, for example, allow a programmer to issue a command, BEGIN TRANSACTION, when the program is ready to begin a series of updates in response to a single logical transaction, and END TRANSACTION when the last of the updates has been completed. When the DBMS receives END TRANSACTION it knows that these updates can be made permanent and available to other users (the technical term is that the transaction is **committed**). If a problem occurs before the END TRANSACTION is received, we say that the transaction is to be **aborted**. The DBMS should then undo all of the changes made since the last BEGIN TRANSACTION was received. (The technical term is that the database has been **rolled back**.) In addition to accomplishing this task, the DBMS should also notify the user that this has happened. Once a transaction has been committed, the updates caused by the transaction should be available to all programs accessing the database; i.e., they should see the new data. If, on the other hand, a transaction is aborted, no program should see the results of *any* of the updates that were accomplished along the way.

For additional discussion of logical transactions, see [6], [10], and [11].

2.5 SHARED UPDATE (Function 4)

> *A DBMS must furnish a mechanism to ensure that the database is updated correctly when multiple users are updating the database concurrently.*

By **shared update** we mean two or more users involved in making updates to the database at the same time. We say that these users are updating the database **concurrently** or that *concurrent update* is taking place. On the surface, it might seem as though shared update is no problem. Why can't two or three (or fifty, for that matter) different users update the database at the same time? What's the problem?

THE PROBLEM

To illustrate the problems involved in shared update, let's assume that we have two users: user A and user B. User A is currently accessing the database to process orders and, among other things, to increase customers' balances by the amount of the orders. In particular, let's assume that customer 124's balance is to be increased by $100.00. User B is accessing the database to post payments and, among other things, to decrease customers' balances by the amount of the payments. As it happens, customer 124 (SALLY ADAMS) has just made a $100.00 payment and so her balance is to be decreased by $100.00. The balance of customer 124 was $418.75 prior to the start of this activity and, since the amount of the increase exactly matches the amount of the decrease, it should still be $418.75 after the activity has been completed. Will it? That depends.

How exactly does user A make the required update? First, the data concerning customer 124 is read from the database into user A's work area. Second, any changes are made to the data in the work area; in this case, $100.00 is added to the current balance, $418.75, bringing it up to $518.75. This change has *not* yet taken place in the database, *only* in user A's work area. Finally, the information is written to the database and the change is now made in the database itself, (see Figure 2.4).

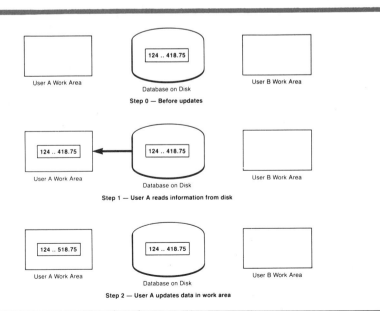

FIGURE 2.4a
User A updates database (continued on the following page)

FIGURE 2.4b

Step 3 — User A updates database with data in work area

Suppose, at this point, user B begins his or her update. The data for customer 124 would be read from the database, including the new balance of $518.75. The amount of the payment, $100.00, would then be subtracted from the balance, thus giving a balance of $418.75 *in user B's work area*. Finally, this new information is written to the database, and customer 124's balance is what it should be (see Figure 2.5).

FIGURE 2.5
User B updates
database

Step 0 — Database after User A's update, before user B's update

Step 1 — User B reads information from disk

Step 2 — User B updates data in work area

Step 3 — User B updates database with data from work area

Do you see another way for things to happen whereby the result would not be correct? What if the following scenario had occurred instead? User A reads the data from the database into user A's work area. User B reads the data from the database into user B's work area. At this point, both user A and user B have the data for customer 124, including a balance of $418.75. User A adds $100.00 to the balance in user A's work area, and user B subtracts $100.00 from the balance in user B's work area. At this point, in user A's work area the balance reads $518.75, while in user B's work area it reads $318.75. User A now writes to the database. At this moment, customer 124 has a balance of $518.75 in the database. Finally, user B writes to the database. Now, customer 124's balance in the database is *$318.75*! (A very good deal for SALLY ADAMS. Unfortunately, not such a good deal for Premiere Products, the company that is paying our salary; see Figure 2.6.)

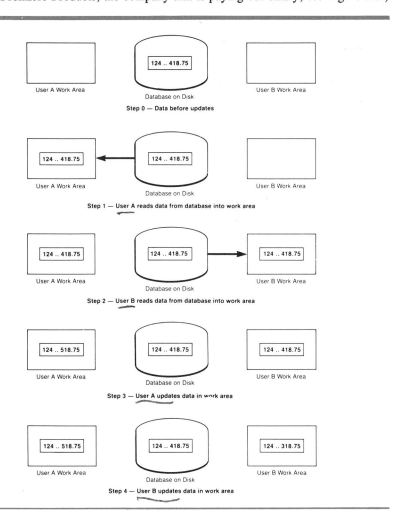

FIGURE 2.6a
User A and User B update database in manner that leads to inconsistent data (continued on the following page)

FIGURE 2.6b

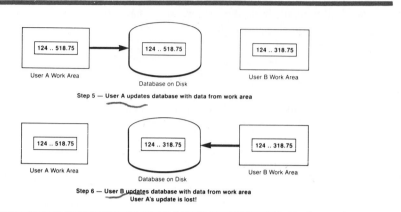

Had the updates taken place in the reverse order, the final balance would have been $518.75. In either case, we now have incorrect data in our database (one of the updates has been *lost*). This cannot be permitted to happen.

AVOIDING THE PROBLEM

One way to prevent this situation from occurring is to prohibit the opportunity for shared update. While this may seem a little drastic, it is not quite as farfetched as it may appear. We could permit several users to access the database, but for *retrieval* only; i.e., they would be able to read information from the database but they would not be able to write anything to the database. When these users entered some kind of transaction to update the database (like posting a payment), the database would not really be updated at all. Instead, a record would be placed in a separate file of transactions. A record in this file might indicate, for example, that $100.00 had been received from customer 124 on a certain date. Periodically, a single update program would read the records in these transaction files and actually perform the appropriate updates to the database. Since this program would be the only program actually updating the database, we would not have the problems associated with shared update.

Using this approach avoids one set of problems, those associated with shared update, but creates another. From the time users start updating, i.e., placing records in the update files, until the time the update program actually runs, the data that is actually in the database is out of date. Where a customer's balance in the database is $49.50, it may, in fact, be $649.50, if a transaction has been entered that would increase the balance by $600.00. Assuming that the customer has an $800 credit limit, we should prohibit him or her from charging, say, a $200 item. However, as far as the data currently in the database is concerned, this should be no problem. After all, the customer has $750.50 of available credit ($800 - $49.50). If we are in such a situation, where the data in the database must be current, then this scheme for avoiding the problems of shared update will not work.

LOCKING

Assuming that we cannot solve the shared update problem by avoidance, we need a mechanism for dealing with the problem. We need to be able to keep user B from even beginning the update on customer 124 until user A has completed his or her update (or vice versa). This could be accomplished by some kind of **locking** scheme. Suppose that once user A had read customer 124's record, the record became locked (no other user could access it) and remained locked until user A had completed the update. During the duration of the lock, any attempt by user B to read the record would be rejected. User B would be notified that the record was locked. User B could, if desired, keep attempting to read the record until it was no longer locked, at which time his or her update could be completed. Thus, we have a scenario as shown in Figure 2.7. In at least this simple case, the problem of a "lost update" seems to have been solved.

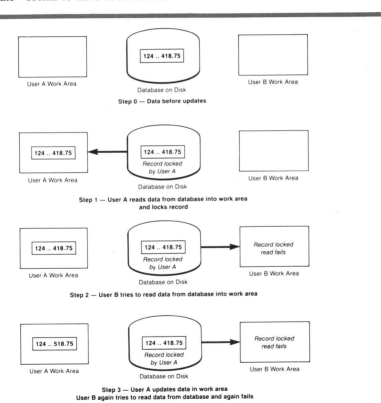

FIGURE 2.7a
User A and User B update database. Locking prevents inconsistent data (continued on the following page)

FIGURE 2.7b

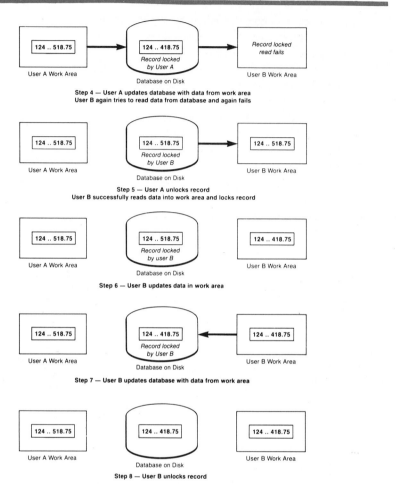

Step 4 — User A updates database with data from work area
User B again tries to read data from database and again fails

Step 5 — User A unlocks record
User B successfully reads data into work area and locks record

Step 6 — User B updates data in work area

Step 7 — User B updates database with data from work area

Step 8 — User B unlocks record

TWO-PHASE LOCKING

Suppose that user A is in the process of updating the database as shown in Figure 2.3 on page 43; user A has updated customer 405's record, but has not completed the entire transaction. Because the record has been updated, it is locked. When should the record be unlocked? Suppose it was unlocked at this time and user B proceeded to change customer 405's balance to $300.00. Now suppose that, for whatever reason, user A's transaction is aborted. As indicated in the discussion of logical transactions, all of the activity thus far completed must be undone. The database must be rolled back to the state it was in before the transaction was performed. In particular, the data for customer 405 reverts to its original state, *with its original balance*. User B's update is *lost* even though we are using a locking mechanism.

Obviously, user A gave up the lock on customer 405 too early. Until user A's transaction has actually been committed (completed successfully), the possibility of this problem exists. Thus, user A should retain all of his or her locks until the last update for the given transaction has actually been made. At this point, *all* locks should be released. This approach is called **two-phase locking**. There is a **growing phase** in which more and more records are being locked but none are being released, and a **shrinking phase** in which all locks are released and no new ones added. This two-phase approach solves the lost update problem.

DEADLOCK

There is another problem to deal with, however. Suppose that user A has completed steps 1 through 5 of the updates and is about to complete step 6. One part of step 6 involves updating part AX12. Suppose that this record is locked by another user, user B. User A must wait for this record until user B is done with it. As it turns out, user B needs to update customer 405 in order to finish his or her update. Since user A currently has this record locked, user B must wait until user A is done. Thus, user A cannot proceed until user B is done and user B cannot proceed until user A is done. This situation is called **deadlock** or the **deadly embrace** (see Figure 2.8 a).

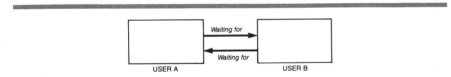

USER A   Waiting for   Waiting for   USER B

FIGURE 2.8a
Two users each
waiting for resources
held by the other —
DEADLOCK!

The final problem then is: What do we do about deadlock? One possible scheme is to make each user lock all the records that he needs to update at the beginning, before any updates have actually taken place. If he encounters a record that another user currently has locked, he must release *all* of his locks and try again. While this scheme technically works, it is difficult to implement in the database environment, since the collection of records that need to be updated is often not known until the update is already under way. This approach is designed to *prevent* deadlock.

Another approach that is, in general, more workable is to let users lock records as they need them, thus allowing deadlock to occur, but then to detect and break any deadlocks that actually take place. To detect deadlock, the system must keep track of the collection of records that each user has locked as well as the records each user is waiting for. If a situation is encountered in which two users are each waiting for records held by the other, a deadlock has occurred. Actually, more than two users could be involved. User A might be waiting for a record held by user B while user B is waiting for a record held by user C, who is in turn waiting for user A (see Figure 2.8b on the following page). This situation, however, is extremely rare.

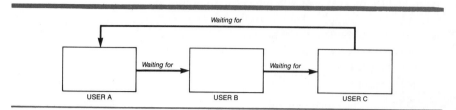

FIGURE 2.8b
Three users each
waiting for resources
held by the other —
DEADLOCK

Once a deadlock has been detected, it must be broken. To break the deadlock, one of the deadlocked users is chosen to be the **victim**. This user's transaction is aborted; i.e., all of the updates already accomplished are undone. In addition, all locks are released and the program is notified that all of this has taken place. Each program in the system should be prepared to take appropriate action in the event that a transaction has been aborted in this way. The action taken may be as simple as retrying all of the updates. In this case, the only divergence from normal processing that the user would notice would be a delay in the time the update takes to complete. In other situations, the program may need to notify the user that there has been a problem, and if this happens, the user must indicate what action he or she wishes to take.

SHARED AND EXCLUSIVE LOCKS

A locking scheme in which users obtain an **exclusive lock** on a record when they read it is unduly harsh: as long as they hold this type of lock, no other user can gain any kind of lock. The act of reading in itself does not cause any problems. It is only an eventual update that brings about difficulties. One hundred different users all reading the same record would not cause any problems. In general, granting exclusive locks every time any record is read can create performance problems, with far too much of the database locked at any time. (Picture those hundred users all standing in line waiting for their turn to read and exclusively lock the one record they all are interested in. Each must wait until the previous user gives up his lock before being able to access it. While the likelihood of one hundred users all wanting precisely the same record at the same time is obviously very slim, we think you get the point about how the use of only exclusive locks can really tie up the database.)

In actual practice, there are usually two different types of locks: *shared* and exclusive. A user *reading* a record holds a **shared lock** on the record, thus allowing other users to also read the record. In order to update a record, the lock must be *promoted* to exclusive. Once the user holds an exclusive lock, no other users may obtain even a shared lock on the record until this user has released the lock. If, when the user attempts to gain an exclusive lock, other users currently hold shared locks on the same record, the user must wait until the other users release their shared locks. This brings up another deadlock possibility, of course. Suppose both user A and user B hold shared locks on customer 405 and part BT04. If user A attempts to gain an exclusive lock on customer 405, he or she must wait until user B releases his or her shared lock. If instead of doing this, user B attempts to gain an exclusive lock on part BT04, we again have two users waiting on each other: DEADLOCK!

LOCK GRANULARITY

So far, it has been assumed that any locking that took place occurred at the *record level*; i.e., it was individual records that were locked. This need not be the case. Locking can occur at the field level, in which individual fields can be locked, or at the block (or page) level. (A database, like any file, is organized in blocks or pages, the amount that is physically accessed when data is read from or written to the disk.) If customer 405 is found on page 13 of the database, then the lock would actually be placed on all of page 13, not just on customer 405. While this effectively locks many records that are not being accessed (the page might contain 4K bytes' worth of various kinds of data, for example), it is often easier to administer than field-level locks or record-level locks. Finally, the lock might take place at the file or database level, allowing only one user to update anything at all in the database.

The level of the lock is called the **lock granularity**. As we have seen, the lock level could be:

1. the whole file or database
2. a block or page
3. a record
4. an individual field

The larger the amount of data locked, the easier the locks are for the DBMS to administer. The smaller the amount, the less contention ("bumping heads") there will be among users. If the locking occurs at the page level, for example, two users attempting to access records on the same page will be in contention, even though they might be attempting to update *totally different records*. If locking occurs at the record level, the same two users would not be in contention. In actual practice, locking at the page level is usually the most common.

For additional discussion of the shared update, see [3], [6] [9], [10], [11], [13], and [15].

2.6 RECOVERY (Function 5)

> *A DBMS must furnish a mechanism for recovering the database in the event that the database is damaged in any way.*

There are, of course, many different types of things that could happen to damage a database. Programs could abort or behave incorrectly. There could be problems with the disk or disks on which the database resides. The computer could suffer some kind of hardware failure as the database is being processed. The

DBMS must be able to restore the database to some correct state following any kind of catastrophe. This process is called **recovery**.

In a straight batch environment, where master files are updated by running update programs that access files of transactions, the whole process is fairly simple. A copy called a **backup** or **save** of the master file is made before the update takes place. If the updated master is destroyed or damaged in any way, it can be recreated by copying the backup over the actual master file and then rerunning the update program against the same transaction file. In the database environment, however, we have many different users updating the database, typically interactively. If the database is destroyed at 2:00 p.m. and the backup copy was made at 10:00 p.m. the previous evening, what do we do about all of the transactions the users have entered since they came on-line at 8:00 a.m. this morning? Do we phone each of these users and ask them to repeat the entire day's worth of activity? Clearly, this is not acceptable. The DBMS must furnish a mechanism to recover the database in a much simpler fashion.

To facilitate this recovery, the DBMS should provide facilities to:

1. back up the database
2. maintain a journal (or log)
3. recover the database

BACKUP

The DBMS should provide the facility to make a *backup* or *save* copy of the database. This copy will be used to recover the database if the active copy of the database is destroyed. This operation should take place on a regular basis.

JOURNALING

The process of **journaling** involves keeping a **log** or **journal** of all of the activity that updates the database. Several types of information are typically kept in the log for each transaction. This includes the transaction ID and the time (and date) of each individual update, together with a record of what the data in the database looked like before the change (called a **before image**) and a record of what the data looked like after the change (called an **after image**). In addition, a record will be kept in the log indicating the beginning of a transaction as well as a record indicating the end (**COMMIT**) of a transaction.

To illustrate the use of such a log, consider the sample transactions shown in Figure 2.9 on the opposite page. There are four transactions. Three of them, CST1, PRT1, and PRT2, represent single-update transactions, i.e., transactions requiring that only a single update be made to the database. One of them, ORD1, involves several updates. (This transaction is, in fact, the logical transaction described in Figure 2.3.) Assume that these four transactions are the first transactions in a given day and that they all complete successfully. In this case the log might look like the sample log shown in Figure 2.10 (opposite).

FIGURE 2.9
Sample transactions

TRANS ID	TRANSACTION DESCRIPTION
CST1	1. Change the balance of customer 256
ORD1	1. Change the ON_ORDER value for customer 405
	2. Change the ON_ORDER value for sales rep 12
	3. Add order (order number _ 12506, date _ 90687, customer _ 405)
	4. Add order line (order _ 12506, part _ AX12, number ordered _ 2, quoted price _ 17.95)
	5. Add order line (order _ 12506, part _ CZ81, number ordered _ 3, quoted price _ 100.00)
	6. Change ALLOCATED value for part AX12
	7. Change ALLOCATED value for part CZ81
PRT1	1. Add part BV57
PRT2	1. Delete part BH22

FIGURE 2.10
Sample log (All
transactions
committed normally)

TRANS ID	TIME	ACTION	OBJECT OF ACTION	BEFORE IMAGE	AFTER IMAGE
CST1	8:00	START			
PRT1	8:02	START			
CST1	8:03	MODIFY	CUSTOMER (256)	(Old Values)	(New Values)
ORD1	8:05	START			
CST1	8:06	COMMIT			
ORD1	8:08	MODIFY	CUSTOMER (405)	(Old Values)	(New Values)
PRT2	8:09	START			
PRT1	8:12	INSERT	PART (BV57)		(New Values)
ORD1	8:13	MODIFY	SLSREP (12)	(Old Values)	(New Values)
PRT1	8:14	COMMIT			
ORD1	8:16	INSERT	ORDER (12506)		(New Values)
ORD1	8:18	INSERT	ORDER_LINE (12506, AX12)		(New Values)
PRT2	8:19	ERASE	PART (BH22)	(Old Values)	
ORD1	8:20	INSERT	ORDER_LINE (12506, CZ81)		(New Values)
ORD1	8:22	MODIFY	PART (AX12)	(Old Values)	(New Values)
PRT2	8:23	COMMIT			
ORD1	8:24	MODIFY	PART (CZ81)	(Old Values)	(New Values)
ORD1	8:26	COMMIT			

Before investigating the manner in which the log is used in the recovery process, let us examine the log itself. Each record in the log includes the ID of the transaction as well as the time the particular event occurred. (The actual time recorded in a log would be much more precise than in this example and would also include the date on which the event occurred. For the sake of simplicity in the example, the time is only given to the nearest minute.) The event can be START, indicating that a transaction has begun, or COMMIT, indicating that a transaction has successfully completed. In addition, the event can be an actual update to the database: an INSERT (add data), a MODIFY (change data), or an ERASE (delete data). For the updates, the log record also contains the before image and the after image. For an INSERT, there is effectively no before image, since the data did not exist in the database prior to the operation. Similarly, for an ERASE, there is effectively no after image.

This particular log indicates, for example, that transaction ORD1 began at 8:05. The updates necessary to accomplish the complete transaction occurred at 8:08 (customer 405 is modified); 8:13 (slsrep 12 is modified); 8:16 (order 12506 is inserted); 8:18 (the first order line is inserted); 8:20 (the second order line is inserted); 8:22 (the first part is modified); and 8:24 (the other part is modified).

Finally, at 8:26, the transaction is committed. During this same period of time, other transactions were also processed.

To illustrate the use of before images, suppose that the MODIFY for transaction ORD1 at 8:24 is unsuccessful. Instead, the transaction aborts at this time and all previous updates must be undone. This is accomplished by changing the database to match the before images of all of the updates for transaction ORD1 in reverse order (technically, before images are **applied** to the database.) Thus, the first update undone will be the MODIFY of part AX12 that occurred at 8:22. This is followed by undoing the insert of the order line for order 12506, part CZ81 that occurred at 8:20. Note that since the before image for an insert is nonexistent, this action will delete the order line. Each of the updates is undone in this fashion. The process is complete when the system has worked back to the START for ORD1, which occurred at 8:05. (Incidentally, this is one reason that the START must be recorded. Without it, the system would have to look all the way back to the beginning of the log for updates for transaction ORD1. In this small example, this may not seem so bad. With an actual log in a heavily used system, this would be prohibitive.)

To illustrate the use of after images, suppose that a system crash occurs at 8:21, as shown in Figure 2.11. Suppose further that the actual database is

TRANS ID	TIME	ACTION	OBJECT OF ACTION	BEFORE IMAGE	AFTER IMAGE
CST1	8:00	START			
PRT1	8:02	START			
CST1	8:03	MODIFY	CUSTOMER (256)	(Old Values)	(New Values)
ORD1	8:05	START			
CST1	8:06	COMMIT			
ORD1	8:08	MODIFY	CUSTOMER (405)	(Old Values)	(New Values)
PRT2	8:09	START			
PRT1	8:12	INSERT	PART (BV57)		(New Values)
ORD1	8:13	MODIFY	SLSREP (12)	(Old Values)	(New Values)
PRT1	8:14	COMMIT			
ORD1	8:16	INSERT	ORDER (12506)		(New Values)
ORD1	8:18	INSERT	ORDER_LINE (12506,AX12)		(New Values)
PRT2	8:19	ERASE	PART (BH22)	(Old Values)	
ORD1	8:20	INSERT	ORDER_LINE (12506,CZ81)		(New Values)

/\
/\ ◄—CRASH!!
/\

FIGURE 2.11
Sample log
(Malfunction occurs at 8:21)

destroyed in some way. In this case, we copy the most recent backup version of the database over the live database. We now can recreate the updates that have taken place, since this backup was made by applying the after images stored in the log in chronological order. Thus the after image of the MODIFY that occurred at 8:03 for transaction CST1 would be the first to be applied. This would effectively recreate the effect of the MODIFY command. Next the after image for the MODIFY for transaction ORD1 that occurred at 8:08 would be applied. The process proceeds in this fashion.

There is, however, a very serious question that needs to be resolved concerning the application of after images. Exactly when does the process stop? If we apply all of the after images, we are left with two transactions, PRT2 and ORD1, that are technically still in progress, but there is no practical way to continue them. (The programs that were processing these transactions aborted when the system crashed.) The answer to the question is that we only apply the after images of transactions that had successfully completed prior to the crash, i.e., transactions for which there is a COMMIT in the log. This can be accomplished by applying *all* after images and then undoing the transactions for which there is no COMMIT, using the before images in the manner described earlier. It can also be accomplished by prescanning the log to determine which transactions have actually been committed and then selectively applying only the after images of these transactions.

WRITE-AHEAD LOG

For each change made to the database, we now have extra activity to perform: the log must be updated. Which should be done first: the update to the database or the update to the log? If everything completes successfully, it doesn't make any difference. What if, however, there is a failure partway through an update? If the database is updated first and then, before the log can be updated, the system fails, we have changes in the database *that have never been recorded in the log*. Thus, there is no way for the system to undo these changes since, as far as the log is concerned, *they don't even exist!* If, on the other hand, the log is updated first and then, before the database is updated, the system fails, there will be enough information in the log to allow the database to be returned to a correct state. Thus, it is crucial that the log be updated first.

RECOVERY

Recovery means returning the database to a state that is known to be correct from a state known to be incorrect. With the facilities listed above, all of the pieces necessary for recovery are in place. The way they will be used depends on the kind of recovery that must be accomplished, which in turn depends on the kind of problem that occurred. Let us examine the different types of problems that might be encountered to see what process would be necessary to recover the database.

FORWARD RECOVERY

If all or part of the database has actually been destroyed, then the recovery must begin with the most recent backup copy of the database. Since this copy is no longer current, it must be brought up to date. This can be accomplished by applying the after images of updates from committed (completed) transactions to this copy of the database. In its simplest form this consists of copying the after image of a given record or page over the actual record or page in the database in chronological order. This process can be improved by realizing that if a given page were updated ten times, this page would be changed ten times in the process just described. In reality, the first nine of those would be unnecessary. The tenth after image actually includes all of the changes accomplished in the first nine. Thus, we can improve things considerably by scanning the log before the recovery and only applying the most recent after image.

BACKWARD RECOVERY

If the database has not actually been destroyed, then the problem must involve transactions that were either incorrect or, more likely, transactions that were stopped in midstream. The database is currently not in a valid state, but we can return it to a valid state by undoing the transactions that are currently in progress. This can be accomplished by processing the log backwards, using the before images to undo changes that have been made.

The actual problem may be systemwide: perhaps a hardware or software problem caused the whole system to go down and there were many transactions halted in progress. In this case, the before images of all transactions could be used to roll the database back to the most recent correct state. At that point, the database would be brought forward by applying the after images of those transactions that had completed before the problem occurred.

The problem could involve only a single transaction. In this case, the individual transaction would be undone by using its before images.

CHECKPOINT

In the rollback of the full database, the procedure was to use the before images to roll the database back to its most recent correct state. What was the time of this most recent correct state? With large numbers of transactions from large numbers of users in various stages of progress, it is not clear exactly when everything is known to be correct. We would want a point where we were sure that the database and the log matched and, ideally, where no transactions were currently in progress. Do we have to go all the way back to the most recent backup to achieve this state? Fortunately not. Most systems incorporate a feature known as **checkpoint**. When this feature is used, the system will periodically refuse to accept any new requests and will complete any updates of the database and the log that are currently in progress. Once this has been completed, the system will again accept new requests. These checkpoints do not involve much overhead and are usually employed frequently, perhaps every fifteen minutes or so. They then help identify the correct states.

RECOVERY THROUGH OFFSETTING TRANSACTIONS

Suppose that a transaction is erroneous; i.e., it puts faulty data in the database. The transaction runs to completion and, on the surface, everything seems fine. Because of a program or user error, however, the database is now actually in an incorrect state. Suppose, for example, that a user inadvertently enters a $100 payment for customer 315 when the payment was really made by customer 311. If the problem is not discovered in time, rolling back the transaction will not be effective. The only alternative is to enter another transaction (or other transactions) to correct the data in the database. In our example, we could enter a payment of $100 for customer 311 and a negative $100 payment (or adjustment) for customer 315 to offset the payment entered earlier.

DIFFERENTIAL FILES

The problem of recovery is not difficult if the database is not being updated on-line, i.e., if the update is done in a batch type of environment. If the data in the database must be up-to-date, however, batch update is probably not appropriate. There is a way, however, of obtaining the ease of recovery that is present in a batch update environment while making the data in the database seem up-to-date. This approach uses a separate file that contains the changes to the database. This file is called a **differential file** (see [12]).

Under this scheme, an update entered by a user does not actually update the database at all. Instead, an entry is made in the differential file to indicate the change. When a user retrieves data from the database, the differential file must first be scanned, in reverse order, to determine whether any changes have been made to the appropriate record. Once this has been done, the appropriate data can be presented to the user, whether it be data directly from the database or from the differential file. The user will not know the difference.

Periodically, a program will actually update the database with data from the differential file in a fashion similar to ordinary batch update programs. Thus, recovery can be accomplished with the same relative ease found in a batch update environment. Yet, since the differential file is scanned whenever data is retrieved from the database, the data feels up-to-date to the user. It would seem that this approach allows the best of both worlds. Unfortunately, if the volume of updates is at all large, the overhead of continually having to access the differential file is often more than can be tolerated.

For additional discussion of recovery, see [1], [3], [6], [9], [10], [11], [12], [13], and [14].

2.7   SECURITY (Function 6)

A DBMS must furnish a mechanism to ensure that
only authorized users can access the database.

The term **security** refers to the protection of the database against unauthorized (or even illegal) access, either intentional or accidental. The features of a DBMS that provide for security are:

1. Encryption
2. Subschemas or views
3. Authorizations
4. User-defined procedures

ENCRYPTION

Encryption refers to the storing of the data in the database in an encrypted format. Any time a user stores or modifies data in the database, the DBMS will encrypt the data before actually updating the database. When any legitimate user retrieves the data via the DBMS, it will be decrypted before the user sees it. The whole encryption process is transparent to a legitimate user; i.e., he or she is not even aware that it is happening. However, if an unauthorized user attempts to bypass all of the controls of the DBMS and get to the database directly, he or she will only be able to see the encrypted version of the data.

SUBSCHEMAS OR VIEWS

A DBMS should furnish a **subschema** or **view** facility (external schemas in the terminology of ANSI/SPARC). While this facility encompasses more than strictly security, it plays an important role in this area.

If, for example, a given user is not to be able to see or change the balance of any of the customers, we simply do not include the balance field in his or her view. As far as this user is concerned, there is no balance field in the database. Thus, he or she cannot access it in any way. A different user may be able to access all information about a customer, but only for customers of sales rep 3. This user can be furnished a view that contains all of the fields within the customer record, but, as far as this user is concerned, the only customers in the database are those represented by sales rep 3. Thus, it would not be possible for this customer to even see any information about customer 405, for example, much less change it, since this customer is represented by sales rep 12.

AUTHORIZATIONS

In [8], Fernandez, Summers, and Wood proposed a model for database security using a table of **Authorization Rules**. An authorization rule has four parts: a subject, an object, an action, and a constraint. An example of an authorization rule would be that Jane (subject) is allowed to delete (action) customers (object) whose balance is 0 (constraint).

The subject of an authorization rule can be any entity that can access the database. It could be a person, a department, a program, or some specific kind of transaction. Subjects are identified in a variety of ways. Usually they are identified by a password, or a password in conjunction with an account number. Occasionally, where more stringent controls are required, they may be identified through such things as fingerprints or voiceprints.

The object of an authorization rule is the set of database entities that can be updated by the subject. These usually are records, although they could be individual fields or, at the other extreme, the whole database.

The action referred to in the authorization rule is really the action that the subject can take on the object. The actions typically permitted are read, insert, modify, and delete. An action of read allows the subject to retrieve information about the object. Insert allows the subject to add new occurrences of the object.

Modify allows the subject to change data for existing occurrences. Delete allows the subject to delete existing occurrences of the object. It is permissible, of course, to assign multiple actions to a given subject. Jane may be able, for example, to read, modify, and delete customers. In this case, Jane could retrieve information about existing customers. She could also change or delete customers. She would not, however, be able to add new customers.

The constraint specifies limitations on when the subject can take the action on the object. In the authorization rule listed earlier, Jane can only delete a customer *if the balance is 0*. The fact that the balance must be 0 is a constraint on Jane's taking the indicated action. It is possible to have a constraint of "none", indicating that the subject can take the action without any restriction. It is also possible to have complicated constraints; for example, Tom may add an order provided *the total obtained by adding the number ordered multiplied by the quoted price on each order line is no more than $500 and, additionally, that there is enough of each part that was requested in the order available to satisfy the order*.

Most systems currently offer a limited form of support for authorization rules. Usually a given user can take a given action on a given object. It is often not possible to specify much in the way of further constraints. Most often, the actions available are retrieve and update. Retrieve corresponds to read. Update corresponds to the combination of read, insert, modify, and delete. Authorizations are usually accomplished through the combination of subschemas and passwords, although some of the relational systems offer more powerful authorization support through additional features.

USER-DEFINED PROCEDURES

A **user-defined procedure** is just what it says. It is a procedure written by the users of the DBMS in some programming language. The DBMS provides a *user exit* to these procedures. When the database is accessed in a particular way, the DBMS will invoke the procedure. The procedure will, in turn, perform whatever action it was designed to take. Information about when these procedures are to be invoked will be described in the schema.

For example, suppose that the only way a customer can place an order that would bring the customer's balance over his or her credit limit is if a special authorization exists for this customer. Information about these special authorizations is kept outside of the database in a separate file. A user-defined procedure could be created which would check to see whether an order would raise the customer's balance over the credit limit and, if so, would check the information in this file to see whether the order should be accepted. This procedure would be invoked whenever an attempt was made to store an order.

User-defined procedures allow users to build a wide variety of authorization tests. They can be used to supplement the capabilities of a DBMS. Deficiencies in the security facilities of the DBMS can potentially be overcome by using these procedures. However, this means that the burden for developing and testing these procedures falls on the enterprise using the DBMS rather than on the DBMS itself.

It is desirable for the DBMS to possess sophisticated enough security facilities that user-defined procedures become unnecessary.

PRIVACY

While **privacy** has become a complex societal issue whose scope goes far beyond what is appropriate for a text such as this one, no discussion of security would be complete without at least a brief mention of privacy. Although often the two terms are used synonymously, in reality they are different, but related, concepts. Technically, privacy refers to the right of an individual to have certain information concerning him or her kept confidential. Privacy and security are related, since it is only through appropriate *security* measures that *privacy* can be ensured.

The need for privacy (or the lack thereof) can be dictated by law or, alternatively, can be a matter of organizational policy. If Marvel College is a state-supported institution, for example, it may be that employees' salaries are considered to be public information, available to anyone who wishes to examine it. Even if Marvel is not state-supported, it may still be college policy that salaries are public. On the other hand, they may be considered private, with strict rules concerning who can see another individual's salary.

Suppose that salaries at Marvel were considered private. The policy could be, for example, that an appropriate person within the payroll department could see the salary of any employee, whereas a department chairperson could only see the salaries of the faculty members within the department; an individual faculty member could not see the salaries of any other employee. Finally, suppose there were a certain employee who could not view the salary of any employee but who was allowed to see statistics, e.g., average salary within departments.

STATISTICAL DATABASES

This brings us to the interesting but tricky topic of statistical databases. A **statistical database** is a database that is intended to supply only statistical information to its users. A census database would be an example of a statistical database. Since the database at Marvel College is not only supplying statistical information but information on individuals as well, it is technically not a statistical database. It does function in this way for the last user mentioned, however, and we will use it to illustrate a tricky little problem associated with this kind of database.

In a statistical database, the user should *not* be able to infer information about any individual, and this brings up a problem. We will not discuss a solution here, but merely illustrate the problem. (For a more detailed discussion see [6] and [7].)

Suppose there were only one employee, Gus Flavian, in the Latin department. Obviously, in this case, the average salary for the Latin department would be Gus Flavian's salary. Thus, by obtaining a statistic — the average salary for faculty within the Latin department — the user could infer information about an individual, namely, Gus's salary. Similarly, if there were only one female, Diane Smith, within the history department, the average salary for females within the history department would be Diane's salary. It might seem as if we could avoid this problem by reporting a statistic only when there were some minimum number of values upon which the statistic was calculated. The system could potentially report an average salary, for example, only if there were at least five employees within the sample. Even this is not good enough, however. Suppose there were ten faculty members in the history department, with Diane Smith being the only female. If a user requested the average salary within the history department, the system would give an answer, since ten faculty members would be involved. It would not give an answer if the average salary of all females in the history department were requested, but it would answer if the average salary *of all males were requested* since nine faculty members would be involved. From these two figures, however, Diane's salary could be computed, thus circumventing the controls built into the system!

For additional discussion of security, see [1], [3], [5], [6], [7], [8], [9], [10], [11], [12], and [13].

.8   COMMUNICATIONS (Function 7)

A DBMS must be capable of integrating with communication software.

In the typical database environment today, most users access the database through terminals, both to retrieve data from the database and to update the data. While batch users usually interface directly with the DBMS, terminal users often do not, instead interacting with a **teleprocessing (TP) monitor**. This TP monitor routes transactions from the terminal users to the appropriate application programs, which in turn interface with the DBMS (see Figure 2.12).

There is an overlap in services between the DBMS and a TP monitor. Both provide support for concurrent update. Both provide recovery services. For everything to function smoothly, then, these two must be carefully integrated.

For additional discussion of communications, see [3], [5], [6], [7], [8], [9], [10], [11], [12], and [13].

FIGURE 2.12
Use of a TP monitor

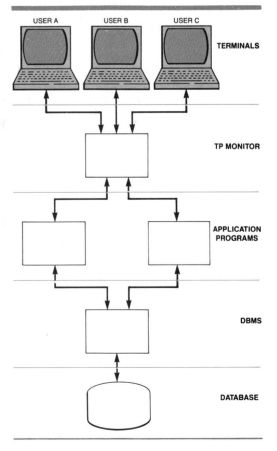

2.9 INTEGRITY (Function 8)

> *A DBMS must furnish a mechanism to ensure that*
> *both the data in the database and changes to the data*
> *follow certain rules.*

In any database, there will be *constraints* i.e., conditions that the data within the database must satisfy or conditions that apply to the processing that may take place. These are usually called **integrity constraints**. The database has **integrity** if these constraints are currently met. If any of these constraints are violated, it does not have integrity.

Some examples of possible integrity constraints within the Premiere Products database are:

1. Customer numbers must be numeric.
2. Commission rates must be between .01 and .25.
3. Credit limits must be $300, $500, $800 or $1000.
4. The sales rep for a given customer must exist; i.e., the sales rep number for a customer must correspond to the sales rep number of a sales rep actually on file.

While the preceding constraints really apply to data within the database, they are effectively constraints on storing and updating. We should not be allowed to store or update anything within the database in such a way that any of these constraints is violated. If, for example, there is no sales rep 4 within the database, we should not be able to store a customer who is represented by sales rep 4.

There are other constraints that just affect the updating of the database and not necessarily the data within it. Consider the following, for example:

5A. No customer may be deleted who currently has any orders on file.
    This constraint says that a certain kind of update, namely the deletion of a customer, cannot take place if certain conditions are met, namely that the customer has orders. An alternate version might be:
5B. A customer may be deleted at any time. If the customer currently has orders, then all of these orders must also be deleted.
    In version 5B, when a deletion of a customer occurs and a certain condition is met, namely that the customer has orders, then further action is required, namely deleting those orders.

We have seen two different types of constraints. One type is a constraint that effectively states that the database is not to be updated in such a way that the resulting data within it violates some condition or conditions. Examples 1 through 4 are in this category. A second type is one that states that a certain type of processing must (or must not) occur if the database is in a certain state prior to the update. Examples 5A and 5B are in this category. Example 5A states that a deletion *must not* take place if there are any orders for the customer, whereas example 5B says that in the event of the deletion of a customer who has orders, those orders *must* also be deleted.

A DBMS should enforce integrity constraints. If the DBMS does not enforce these constraints and if our database is to have integrity, then the programs that access the database must enforce them. This is undesirable for two reasons. First, it adds unnecessary complications to the programs. Second, if any program does not enforce the constraints correctly, we can easily find ourselves in a state in which our database does not have integrity *and we are not even aware that there is a problem!*

For additional discussion of integrity, see [3], [5], [6], [9], [10], [11], and [13].

.10   DATA INDEPENDENCE (Function 9)

> **A DBMS must include facilities to support the independence of programs from the actual structure of the database.**

Data independence basically means that users are unaffected by changes to the logical and/or physical structure of the database. If a DBMS truly furnishes data independence, then the structure of the database should be able to be changed one night and the programs that ran the preceding day will still run the next day *without any changes*. In fact, we should not even have to recompile these programs. There is, of course, an obvious stipulation that should be added: if any data used by a given program is *removed* from the database structure, then changes will certainly have to be made. If a particular program uses the credit limit field and we no longer store credit limits in the database, clearly something will have to be done to the program.

There are really two types of data independence: logical and physical.

Logical data independence occurs when changes to the logical structure of the database do not affect the programs that access the database. Changes to the logical structure include adding, deleting, or changing fields, records, or relationships. The addition of the field CUSTOMER_TYPE to the customer record would be an example of such a change. This change should not affect any existing programs. Logical data independence allows us to change the structure of the database to keep pace with changes in the organization without having to continually change application programs.

Physical data independence occurs when changes to the underlying physical structure of the database do not affect the programs that access the database. Changes to the physical structure include changing the storage characteristics of fields, changing the placement strategies for records in the database, changing encryption schemes, changing underlying structures used to directly access records, etc.; i.e., changes to the way the database is physically stored and manipulated. Changing the BALANCE field from zoned decimal to packed decimal is an example of a physical change. Another example would be changing the underlying structure used to find all of the customers of a given sales rep. Physical data independence allows us to *tune* the database for performance, i.e., to make changes that will improve the overall performance of our applications without having to change the application programs themselves.

Usually, in a DBMS, data independence is achieved through a **subschema** or **view** type mechanism. The level of data independence obtained by a given DBMS is determined by the kinds of changes (logical and/or physical) that can be made to the database structure without a subschema or view having to change. Most systems are quite respectable in terms of physical data independence; i.e., there are a number of kinds of changes that can be made to the physical characteristics of the database without affecting the subschemas. Virtually all nonrelational systems fall short of true logical independence. The addition of new fields and records can usually be handled, but *not* changes to relationships. While current relational systems are better about handling changes to relationships, there is still room for improvement. There is every reason to believe that improvement in this area will occur in the near future.

2.11 UTILITIES (Function 10)

A DBMS should provide a set of utility services.

There are a number of services that a DBMS can provide which would be of assistance in the general maintenance of the database. Services to facilitate the accomplishment of the physical and logical changes just described, services to gather and report on statistics involving patterns of database usage, and services to examine the data in the database in order to look for any irregularities (bad pointers, for example) are just a few of the utility-type services that a DBMS can and should provide. To do an effective job administering and monitoring a database, services like these are required. If the DBMS does not provide them, then the enterprise using the DBMS must provide its own.

2.12 SUMMARY

In this chapter, we have examined the capabilities that should be provided by any full-scale DBMS. Ten such capabilities were examined:

1. The DBMS must support data storage, retrieval, and update.
2. The DBMS must include a catalog that is accessible to the user and that gives descriptions of the various fields, records, and relationships in the database. In addition, the catalog contains information concerning the programs that access the database, including the set of data items accessed by each program and how that data is accessed.

3. The DBMS should provide support for logical transactions. A logical transaction is a sequence of steps that will accomplish what feels to the user like a single task. An example was given of the logical transaction of entering an order. To a user, that was a single task. For the system, however, there were many steps that had to be accomplished. Many different updates had to occur. To say a DBMS supports logical transactions means that the DBMS will ensure that either all of these updates will take place or none of them will take place; i.e., we will not be left in that unacceptable middle ground where some of the updates occurred and others did not. If all of the updates occur, we say the transaction has been committed. If something prevents all of the updates from occurring, we say the transaction has been aborted. In this case, a rollback will be performed in which all of the updates that have been made will be undone, thus returning the system to the state it was in before the transaction was started.

4. The DBMS should provide support for shared update. When two or more users update the database at the same time, there is a potential for incorrect results and lost updates. In order to prevent these problems, the DBMS must allow some form of locking. The amount of material to be locked (called the lock granularity) could be a field, record, page, or the whole database. A lock can be either shared, which permits other programs to read the same data, or exclusive, which prohibits other programs from accessing the data in any way. To ensure that correct results are obtained, programs should use two-phase locking. In this approach, locks are first gained but never released until a transaction is complete, following which all locks are released. Locking brings up the potential problem of deadlock, which must be resolved in some way. The most common approach is to pick one of the transactions that is in deadlock and abort it (i.e., roll it back).

5. The DBMS should provide recovery services. If the database is damaged in any way, the system should be able to recover the database to a correct state. The DBMS must be capable of backing up the database; maintaining a journal, or log, of all activities that update the database as well as before and after images of portions of the database; and, finally, using the data in the journal to recover the database. If the database is destroyed, a forward recovery is done, which starts with the backup copy and then applies after images from the journal to roll the database forward. If the database has not been destroyed, then a backward recovery may be done, in which before images from the journal are applied in reverse order to roll the database back to the most recent state when the database was known to be correct. After the database has been rolled back, it may be brought forward by applying after images of only committed transactions (transactions that have completed successfully).

6. The DBMS should provide services that protect the database from unauthorized access. There are four basic features of a DBMS that provide for security. Encryption refers to storing the data in the database in an encrypted format. Users that access the database through the DBMS will see the correct information; users that bypass the DBMS will need to break the

code in order to make sense out of the data. Subschemas or views provide for security by furnishing a mechanism whereby a given user can be kept from even knowing about the existence of a particular field or record. If a given user does not have the salary field in his or her subschema, he or she cannot retrieve or update any salaries. In fact, as far as that user is concerned, there is no salary field in the database. Authorization rules allow us to specify that a given subject (person, department, etc.) can take a given action (read, insert, modify, delete) on a given object (record, field, etc.), subject to a given constraint. Finally, user-defined procedures allow the users of a DBMS to add security checks of their own in some programming language. This facility allows users of the DBMS to supplement the security features of the DBMS itself.

The related topic, privacy, refers to the right of an individual to have certain information conerning him or her kept confidential. It is through appropriate security measures that privacy is ensured.

Finally, the statistical database concept was briefly examined. A statistical database is one from which statistics (average, sum, max, etc.) are to be drawn but no information about individual entities is to be available.

7. The DBMS should provide support for related communications software. In particular, since a good TP monitor provides some services that overlap the services of the DBMS, the two should be carefully integrated.

8. The DBMS should provide services to ensure that the database has integrity. An integrity constraint is a condition that the data in the database must satisfy or, alternatively, a condition that describes the kinds of processing that may or may not take place. The DBMS should ensure that none of these constraints are violated.

9. The DBMS should provide facilities to promote data independence. Data independence means that the overall physical and/or logical structure of the database can be changed without affecting the users or the programs that are accessing the database. Data independence is often divided into physical data independence and logical data independence. Logical data independence occurs when changes to the logical structure do not affect the programs that access the database, and physical data independence occurs when changes to the underlying physical structures do not affect these programs. While many systems do a creditable job of achieving physical data independence, most systems currently fall short of true logical data independence. Good relational model systems come the closest to true logical data independence.

10. The DBMS should provide utility services. There are a number of valuable services that a DBMS can and should provide that do not fall in any of the preceding categories and that are more properly termed utilities. These would include services to facilitate the changes to the logical and/or physical structure of the database mentioned in the section on data independence, services to report on statistics concerning different types of database usage, and services to examine the database structure in order to look for any irregularities.

REVIEW QUESTIONS

1. What do we mean when we say that a DBMS should provide facilities for storage, retrieval, and update?
2. What is the purpose of the catalog?
3. Discuss why the DBMS (or related software product) should maintain the catalog.
4. When and how is the catalog used? Give examples.
5. Define logical transaction. Give an example of a logical transaction that can be accomplished by updating a single record. Give an example of a logical transaction for which several records must be updated.
6. Why must a system support logical transactions? Why do we even need to worry about them?
7. Describe what is meant by a transaction being committed. Describe what is meant by a transaction being aborted.
8. What is a rollback?
9. Give two different reasons that a transaction might be aborted.
10. What is meant by shared update? What is another name for it?
11. What is meant by locking?
12. Describe a situation, other than the example used in the text, in which uncontrolled shared update produces incorrect results.
13. What is meant by two-phase locking? Give an example illustrating how lack of adherence to two-phase locking would cause a problem.
14. What is deadlock? Why must one transaction be rolled back instead of merely held up and allowed to continue when the other user is done?
15. What is the difference between a shared lock and an exclusive lock? Why is it better to use these two types of locks than just exclusive locks?
16. What is meant by lock granularity? What are the possibilities?
17. What is meant by recovery?
18. What kinds of events might precipitate the need for a recovery?
19. If the database is updated by a single batch program running once a day, how could recovery be accomplished?
    In questions 20 through 26, assume that the database is being updated interactively.
20. What activities must the DBMS perform in order to be able to do a recovery?
21. What is the journal? What kinds of information are kept in the journal?
22. Which should be updated first, the database or the journal? Why?
23. Describe forward recovery. How is it accomplished? When is it appropriate?
24. Describe backward recovery. How is it accomplished? When is it appropriate?
25. If an erroneous transaction has produced invalid data in the database, how may the situation be corrected?
26. What is a differential file? What purpose does it serve?
27. What is meant by security?
28. What is encryption? How does it promote security?
29. How does the subschema facility relate to security?
30. What is an authorization rule? What are the four components of an authorization rule? Give three examples of authorization rules.

31. What types of authorization rules are most commonly supported by current DBMS's? How are they most often supported?
32. What is a user-defined procedure? How does it relate to security?
33. What is privacy? How does it relate to security?
34. What is a statistical database?
35. What is meant by integrity? What is an integrity constraint?
36. What is meant by physical data independence? What benefit is achieved by having a high level of physical data independence?
37. What is meant by logical data independence? What benefit is achieved by having a high level of logical data independence?
38. How does the subschema facility relate to data independence?
39. Give two examples of utility services that a DBMS should provide.

EXERCISES

For questions 1 through 6, assume that the log shown in Figure 2.10 has been expanded to include the time when records are read and that the result is shown in Figure 2.13.

TRANS ID	TIME	ACTION	OBJECT OF ACTION	BEFORE IMAGE	AFTER IMAGE
CST1	8:00	START			
CST1	8:01	READ	CUSTOMER (256)		
PRT1	8:02	START			
CST1	8:03	MODIFY	CUSTOMER (256)	(Old Values)	(New Values)
ORD1	8:05	START			
CST1	8:06	COMMIT			
ORD1	8:07	READ	CUSTOMER (405)		
ORD1	8:08	MODIFY	CUSTOMER (405)	(Old Values)	(New Values)
PRT2	8:09	START			
ORD1	8:10	READ	SLSREP (12)		
PRT1	8:12	INSERT	PART (BV57)		(New Values)
ORD1	8:13	MODIFY	SLSREP (12)	(Old Values)	(New Values)
PRT1	8:14	COMMIT			
PRT2	8:15	READ	PART (BH22)		
ORD1	8:16	INSERT	ORDER (12506)		(New Values)
ORD1	8:17	READ	PART (AX12)		
ORD1	8:18	INSERT	ORDER_LINE (12506,AX12)		(New Values)
PRT2	8:19	ERASE	PART (BH22)	(Old Values)	
ORD1	8:20	READ	PART (CZ81)		
ORD1	8:21	INSERT	ORDER_LINE (12506,CZ81)		(New Values)
ORD1	8:22	MODIFY	PART (AX12)	(Old Values)	(New Values)
PRT2	8:23	COMMIT			
ORD1	8:24	MODIFY	PART (CZ81)	(Old Values)	(New Values)
ORD1	8:26	COMMIT			

FIGURE 2.13

Sample Log (Including READ operations)

1. Assume that the DBMS being used issues locks whenever a READ, MODIFY, INSERT, or ERASE command is given and releases all locks held by a transaction when a COMMIT command is executed.

   Assume also that locking occurs at the record level. Indicate the locks held by each transaction at each point in time throughout the session shown in Figure 2.13.

Time	Trans.	Locks Held
8:00		
8:01	CST1	CUSTOMER 256
8:02	CST1	CUSTOMER 256
8:03	CST1	CUSTOMER 256
8:05	CST1	CUSTOMER 256
8:06		
8:07	ORD1	CUSTOMER 405
.	.	.
.	.	.
.	.	.

2. Some systems, in particular many microcomputer systems, will issue a lock to a transaction when a READ command is executed and will release the lock as soon as a MODIFY or ERASE command is executed for the same record. In addition, the lock will be released if another record of the same type is read. (Two separate PART records could not be locked by the same transaction at the same time, for example.) No record is locked for an INSERT command. Indicate the locks that would be held if the DBMS being used operates in such a fashion.

Time	Trans.	Locks Held
8:00		
8:01	CST1	CUSTOMER 256
8:02	CST1	CUSTOMER 256
8:03		
8:05	⏤	
8:06		
8:07	ORD1	CUSTOMER 405
.	.	.
.	.	.
.	.	.

3. Assume that the DBMS being used issues shared locks whenever a READ command is issued and promotes the locks to exclusive when a subsequent MODIFY, INSERT, or ERASE command is issued. All other assumptions are the same as in question 1. Indicate the locks held by each transaction at each point in time throughout the session shown in Figure 2.13. For each lock, indicate whether it is shared or exclusive. Use (S) for shared and (E) for exclusive.

Time	Trans.	Locks Held
8:00		
8:01	CST1	CUSTOMER 256 (S)
8:02	CST1	CUSTOMER 256 (S)
8:03	CST1	CUSTOMER 256 (E)
8:05	CST1	CUSTOMER 256 (E)
8:06		
8:07	ORD1	CUSTOMER 405 (S)
.	.	.
.	.	.
.	.	.

4. Suppose another transaction, CST2, started at 8:04, read CUSTOMER 405 at 8:06:30, modified CUSTOMER 405 at 8:08:30, and committed at 8:11. What effect, if any, would this have on the sequence of operations shown in the log?

5. Suppose transaction PRT2 erased PART "CZ81" rather than PART "BH22". What effect, if any, would this have on the sequence of operations shown in the log?

6. Suppose that transaction CST1 read and modified CUSTOMER 405 rather than 256. Suppose further that transaction CST1 did not commit at 8:06 but, instead, read SLSREP 12 and later, at 8:15:30, attempted to modify SLSREP 12. What effect, if any, would this have on the sequence of operations shown in the log?

7. What problems would the absence of the COMMIT records in the log cause for backward and forward recovery?

8. Indicate the subject, object, action, and constraint associated with each of the following:
   a. Sales reps may retrieve customer data for their own customers but may not update this data.
   b. The order entry staff may add orders and order lines.
   c. Tom may delete customers who do not have any orders on file and whose balance is zero.
   d. Mary may perform any type of update on any item in the database.

9. Give three examples of integrity constraints that pertain to data in the database.

10. Give an example of an integrity constraint that gives conditions under which a given type of processing *may not* take place. Give an example of an integrity constraint that gives conditions under which a given type of processing *must* take place.

REFERENCES

1] Atre, S. *Data Base: Structured Techniques for Design, Performance and Management.* Wiley-Interscience, 1980.

2] Bradley, James. *Introduction to Data Base Management in Business.* Holt, Rinehart & Winston, 1983.

3] Cardenas, Alfonso F. *Data Base Management Systems* 2d ed. Allyn & Bacon, 1984.

4] Codd, E. F. "Relational Database: A Practical Foundation for Productivity." *Communications of the ACM* 25, no. 2 (February 1982).

5] Date, C. J. *Introduction to Database Systems, Volume I* 4th ed. Addison-Wesley, 1986.

6] Date, C. J. *Introduction to Database Systems, Volume II.* Addison-Wesley, 1983.

7] Denning, D. E., and Denning, P. J. "Data Security." *ACM Computing Surveys* 11, no. 3 (September 1979).

8] Fernandez, Eduardo B.; Summers, Rita C.; and Wood, Christopher. *Database Security and Integrity.* Addison-Wesley, 1980.

9] Goldstein, Robert C. *Database Technology and Management.* John Wiley & Sons, 1985

10] Kroenke, David. *Database Processing* 2d ed. SRA, 1983.

11] McFadden, Fred R., and Hoffer, Jeffrey A. *Data Base Management.* Benjamin Cummings, 1985.

12] Teorey, Toby J., and Fry, James P. *Design of Database Structures.* Prentice-Hall, 1982.

13] Vasta, Joseph A. *Understanding Data Base Management Systems.* Wadsworth, 1985.

14] Wood, J. Chris. "Restart and Recovery in DBMS's." In *A Practical Guide to Data Base Management* ed. John Hannan. Auerbach, 1982.

15] Young, John W., Jr. "Concurrency in DBMS's." In *A Practical Guide to Data Base Management* ed. John Hannan. Auerbach, 1982.

RELATIONAL MODEL I INTRODUCTION TO THE RELATIONAL MODEL

.I   INTRODUCTION

In a landmark paper in 1970, Dr. E. F. Codd proposed "A relational model of data for large shared databanks" (see [3]). Throughout the 1970s, this **relational model** was the subject of a great deal of theoretical research activity. Prototype relational systems were being developed, most notably a system called System R from IBM. With the advent of the 1980s, commercial relational systems began appearing, first in the mainframe environment and then in the microcomputer environment. These have now proliferated to the extent that there are large numbers of systems which are, at least in some sense, relational.

When compared to the other DBMS models, the **hierarchical model** and the **network model**, the relational model offers the following advantages:

1. The logical and physical characteristics of the database are separated.
2. The model is much more easily understood. Data is viewed in a much more natural way, with no complex paths to be followed.
3. There are powerful operators available which enable even very complex operations to be accomplished with very brief commands.
4. The model provides a sound framework for the design of databases. Until the introduction of the relational model, database design was very definitely a "seat of the pants" process in which designs were used simply because they felt right. On occasion, reasonably correct designs were produced in this manner. Usually, however, designs were incorrect, problem ridden, and the direct cause of some major computing disasters.
The relational model provides important tools that allow us to determine whether there are potential problems in a design, and, if such problems do exist, it provides a mechanism for correcting the design.

Like the other models, the relational model has its proponents and its critics. Even its critics will admit that relational model systems are much easier to use and are more flexible than nonrelational systems. The critics claim, however, that relational model systems are not nearly as efficient as some of the good hierarchical and network systems and that this makes them inappropriate for large applications. Its proponents respond that there is no reason a relational model system cannot be as efficient as any other. The view of the authors of this text is that while at the present time the relational model systems are in general less efficient than some of the best of the nonrelational model systems, the gap is narrowing. When the time comes, and it will, that the relational systems are comparable in efficiency, new application development will, with rare exceptions, take place using only relational or relational-like systems. The other systems will continue to exist for a number of years, owing to the sheer volume of current applications that have been developed with them, but they will not be the subject of many new applications.

In this chapter we study the basic relational model. In section 3.2, we look at the model itself and some of the important terminology. In section 3.3, we examine how various types of relationships are implemented within the relational model. Sections 3.4 through 3.8 deal with various approaches to the problem of manipulating data within the relational model, including both updating what is currently in the database (**data manipulation**) and producing reports using the data in the database (**data retrieval**).

3.2 TERMINOLOGY

In its simplest terms, a relation is just a two-dimensional table. Figure 3.1 on the opposite page, shows the five tables, or relations, for Premiere Products that were discussed in chapter 1.

In examining these tables, we can see that there are certain restrictions that we would probably want to place on relations. Each column should have a unique name, and entries within each column should all "match" this column name; i.e., if the column name is CREDIT_LIMIT, all entries in that column should actually be credit limits. Also, each row should be unique. After all, if two rows are absolutely identical, the second row does not give us any information that we didn't already have. In addition, for maximum flexibility, the ordering of the columns and the rows should be immaterial. Finally, the table will be simplest if each position is restricted to a single entry, i.e., if we do not allow repeating groups or arrays in an individual location in the table. These ideas lead to the following definitions:

Def: **A RELATION** is a two-dimensional table in which

1. The entries in the table are single-valued.
2. Each column has a distinct name (called the attribute name).
3. All of the values in a column are values of the same attribute (namely, the attribute identified by the column name).
4. The order of columns is immaterial.
5. Each row is distinct.
6. The order of rows is immaterial.

Def: **A RELATIONAL DATABASE** is a collection of relations.

SLSREP

SLSREP_NUMBER	SLSREP_NAME	SLSREP_ADDRESS	TOTAL_COMMISSION	COMMISSION_RATE
3	MARY JONES	123 MAIN,GRANT,MI	2150.00	.05
6	WILLIAM SMITH	102 RAYMOND,ADA,MI	4912.50	.07
12	SAM BROWN	419 HARPER,LANSING,MI	2150.00	.05

CUSTOMER

CUSTOMER_NUMBER	NAME	ADDRESS	CURRENT_BALANCE	CREDIT_LIMIT	SLSREP_NUMBER
124	SALLY ADAMS	481 OAK,LANSING,MI	418.75	500	3
256	ANN SAMUELS	215 PETE,GRANT,MI	10.75	800	6
311	DON CHARLES	48 COLLEGE,IRA,MI	200.10	300	12
315	TOM DANIELS	914 CHERRY,KENT,MI	320.75	300	6
405	AL WILLIAMS	519 WATSON,GRANT,MI	201.75	800	12
412	SALLY ADAMS	16 ELM,LANSING,MI	908.75	1000	3
522	MARY NELSON	108 PINE,ADA,MI	49.50	800	12
567	JOE BAKER	808 RIDGE,HARPER,MI	201.20	300	6
587	JUDY ROBERTS	512 PINE,ADA,MI	57.75	500	6
622	DAN MARTIN	419 CHIP,GRANT,MI	575.50	500	3

ORDER

ORDER_NUMBER	DATE	CUSTOMER_NUMBER
12489	90287	124
12491	90287	311
12494	90487	315
12495	90487	256
12498	90587	522
12500	90587	124
12504	90587	522

ORDER_LINE

ORDER_NUMBER	PART_NUMBER	NUMBER_ORDERED	QUOTED_PRICE
12489	AX12	11	14.95
12491	BT04	1	402.99
12491	BZ66	1	311.95
12494	CB03	4	175.00
12495	CX11	2	57.95
12498	AZ52	2	22.95
12498	BA74	4	4.95
12500	BT04	1	402.99
12504	CZ81	2	108.99

PART

PART_NUMBER	PART_DESCRIPTION	UNITS_ON_HAND	ITEM_CLASS	WAREHOUSE_NUMBER	UNIT_PRICE
AX12	IRON	104	HW	3	17.95
AZ52	SKATES	20	SG	2	24.95
BA74	BASEBALL	40	SG	1	4.95
BH22	TOASTER	95	HW	3	34.95
BT04	STOVE	11	AP	2	402.99
BZ66	WASHER	52	AP	3	311.95
CA14	SKILLET	2	HW	3	19.95
CB03	BIKE	44	SG	1	187.50
CX11	MIXER	112	HW	3	57.95
CZ81	WEIGHTS	208	SG	2	108.99

Each row of the relation is technically called a **tuple** and each column is technically called an **attribute**. Thus, we have two different sets of terms: relation, tuple, attribute and table, row, column. There is actually a third set. The table could be viewed as a file (in fact, this is how relational databases are often, but not always, stored, with each relation, or table, in a separate file). In this case, we

FIGURE 3.1
Premiere Products
sample data

would call the rows records and the columns fields. We now have *three* different sets of terms! Their correspondence is shown below.

FORMAL TERMS	ALTERNATIVE ONE	ALTERNATIVE TWO
relation	table	file
tuple	row	record
attribute	column	field

Of these three sets of choices, the one that is becoming the most popular is alternative one: tables, rows, and columns. One reason for its popularity is that it seems the most natural to the nontechnical user. A second reason is that many of the commercial relational DBMS's, including IBM's offering in the relational database market, use these terms. In this text, as well as many other references, the formal terms and the corresponding terms from the first alternative will be used interchangeably.

As a sort of shorthand representation of the structure of these tables, we write the name of the table and then within parentheses list all of the columns in the table. Thus, this sample database consists of:

SLSREP (SLSREP_NUMBER, SLSREP_NAME, SLSREP_ADDRESS,
            TOTAL_COMMISSION, COMMISSION_RATE)

CUSTOMER (CUSTOMER_NUMBER, NAME, ADDRESS, CURRENT_
            BALANCE, CREDIT_LIMIT, SLSREP_NUMBER)

ORDER (ORDER_NUMBER, DATE, CUSTOMER_NUMBER)

ORDER_LINE (ORDER_NUMBER, PART_NUMBER, NUMBER_ORDERED,
            QUOTED_PRICE)

PART (PART_NUMBER, PART_DESCRIPTION, UNITS_ON_HAND,
            ITEM_CLASS, WAREHOUSE_NUMBER, PRICE)

Notice that there is some duplication of names. The attribute SLSREP_NUMBER appears in *both* the SLSREP relation *and* the CUSTOMER relation. If a situation exists wherein the two might be confused, we **qualify** the names by placing the relation name in front of the attribute name, separated by a period. Thus, we would write CUSTOMER.SLSREP_NUMBER or SLSREP.SLSREP_NUMBER. It is *always* acceptable to qualify data names, even if there is no possible confusion. There will be times, however, when it is absolutely essential to do so.

Two important terms will be discussed briefly here. The **primary key** of a relation is the attribute (column) or collection of attributes that uniquely identifies a given tuple (row). In the SLSREP relation, for example, the sales rep's number uniquely identifies a given row. (Sales rep 6 occurs in only one row of the table, for example.) Thus SLSREP_NUMBER is the primary key. As indicated in the shorthand representation, the common practice is to underline the primary keys.

Why does the primary key to the ORDER_LINE relation consist of two attributes, not just one?
Answer:
No single attribute uniquely identifies a given row. It requires two: ORDER_NUMBER and PART_NUMBER.

There is another kind of key that is extremely important. An attribute in one relation that is required to match the primary key of another relation is called a **foreign key**. As an example, the SLSREP_NUMBER in the customer relation should match a real sales rep, i.e., the SLSREP_NUMBER of an actual sales rep in the SLSREP table. We say the sales rep number in the CUSTOMER table (CUSTOMER.SLSREP_NUMBER) is a foreign key that identifies SLSREP. This provides a mechanism for explicitly specifying relationships between two different relations as well as a mechanism for ensuring integrity. It tells us that there is a relationship between customers and their sales reps. It also prohibits us from entering a customer whose sales rep does not exist.

When we consider the data represented by a set of tuples in a relation at a given instant, as we did for the five relations in Figure 3.1, we have what is called an **extension** of the relations. On the other hand, the permanent part of the relation, the listing of the attributes or columns of the relation, is called an **intension** of the relation. Thus, a shorthand representation of a relation can be called an intension of the relation.

It is frequently very useful to consider collections of legitimate values that attributes within a relation may assume. Both customer and sales rep's names should be chosen from the pool of "names". A customer's credit limit must be chosen from the pool of "credit limits". This collection of legitimate values is called a **domain.**

> *Def:* A domain is a pool of values from which the values for a given column must be chosen.

We might have, for example, a domain called CREDIT_LIMIT which consisted of all possible legitimate credit limits. In that case, we might be able to give a precise definition of this collection. A credit limit might be 300, 500, 800, or 1000, for example, in which case the pool would be precisely these four numbers. Commissions might be decimal numbers with two decimal places and range from .00 to .25, in which case this would be the pool of values for the domain COMMISSION. The domain NAME on the other hand, might consist of all valid names (not a particularly precise definition). It would still be of value to specify this domain, however. Anyone looking at that domain definition would then know that it was a name rather than an address or part description or anything else that could belong in that column.

It is perfectly legitimate to have the name of a domain be the same as the name of a column whose values are to be drawn from this domain. Having values for the column BALANCE drawn from the domain BALANCE certainly will not cause confusion. In general, in fact, this approach is advisable, unless it causes a problem in a particular situation. If, in the CUSTOMER relation, for example, we record the name of the customer *and* the name of his or her spouse, both columns will be drawn from a domain of names. Since we cannot give the same name to two different columns within the table, we cannot give the domain name to each of these columns. In this case, we might choose, for example, to call the domain "NAME", the customer's name "CUSTOMER_NAME", and the spouse's name "SPOUSE_NAME". Both columns would be drawn from the domain NAME.

A word about repeating groups is in order. A structure that satisfies all of the properties listed earlier is often called a **normalized** relation. A structure that satisfies all but property 1 (i.e., repeating groups are allowed) is sometimes called an **unnormalized** relation. Thus, according to the definition, an unnormalized relation is technically not a relation at all!

It is always possible to replace an unnormalized relation with a normalized relation that is equivalent, i.e., that represents the same information. The following unnormalized relation contains a repeating group.

ORDER(ORDER_NUMBER, DATE, PART_NUMBER, NUMBER_ORDERED)

This notation indicates an unnormalized relation called ORDER consisting of a primary key, ORDER_NUMBER, an attribute, DATE, and a repeating group containing two attributes, PART_NUMBER and NUMBER_ORDERED. Figure 3.2 gives

ORDER	ORDER_NUMBER	DATE	PART_NUMBER	NUMBER_ORDERED
	12489	90287	AX12	11
	12491	90287	BT04	1
			BZ66	1
	12494	90487	CB03	4
	12495	90487	CX11	2
	12498	90587	AZ52	2
			BA74	4
	12500	90587	BT04	1
	12504	90587	CZ81	2

FIGURE 3.2
Unnormalized
ORDER relation

a sample extension of this relation. To **normalize** this relation, the repeating group is removed, giving the following:

ORDER(<u>ORDER_NUMBER</u>, DATE, <u>PART_NUMBER</u>, NUMBER_ORDERED)

The corresponding extension of the new relation is shown in Figure 3.3. Note that the second row of the unnormalized relation indicated that part BT04 and part BZ66 were both present for order 12491. In the normalized relation, this information is represented by *two* rows, the second and third. Notice also that the primary key of the new relation is no longer just the order number but the combination of the order number and the part number. (Technically, it is called the **concatenation** of the order number and part number.)

ORDER	ORDER_NUMBER	DATE	PART_NUMBER	NUMBER_ORDERED
	12489	90287	AX12	11
	12491	90287	BT04	1
	12491	90287	BZ66	1
	12494	90487	CB03	4
	12495	90487	CX11	2
	12498	90587	AZ52	2
	12498	90587	BA74	4
	12500	90587	BT04	1
	12504	90587	CZ81	2

FIGURE 3.3
Normalized
ORDER relation

.3 EXPRESSING RELATIONSHIPS

A database contains not only information about several different types of entities, e.g., sales reps, customers, orders, but also information about relationships between these entities. A sales rep is related to the customers whom he or she represents. A customer is related to the orders that he or she has placed. In the relational model, these relationships are achieved by having common attributes in two separate tables. The relationship between sales reps and the customers whom they represent, for example, is achieved by having the sales rep number in both the SLSREP table and the CUSTOMER table.

The three different types of relationships with which we must contend are one-to-one, one-to-many, and many-to-many. If the relationship between entity A and entity B is *one-to-one* every occurrence of A is related to one occurrence of B, and every occurrence of B is related to one occurrence of A. If the relationship between entity A and entity B is *one-to-many* every occurrence of A is related to many occurrences of B, but every occurrence of B is related to one occurrence of A. If the relationship between entity A and entity B is *many-to-many* every occurrence of A is related to many occurrences of B, and every occurrence of B is related to many occurrences of A. We will now examine the manner in which each of these types of relationships may be implemented in the relational model.

1. ONE-TO-ONE

Suppose that at Premiere Products not only is each customer represented by only one sales rep but each sales rep represents *only one customer* (It is a very exclusive establishment that lavishes a lot of personal attention!). In this case, we could actually put both customers and sales reps in a single table, as shown in Figure 3.4.

SLSREP	SLSREP_NUMBER	SLSREP_NAME	CUSTOMER_NUMBER	NAME
	3	MARY JONES	124	SALLY ADAMS
	6	WILLIAM SMITH	256	ANN SAMUELS
	12	SAM BROWN	311	DON CHARLES

FIGURE 3.4
One-to-one relationship implemented in a single table

In addition, we would also have other columns containing further information about sales reps (address, commission, etc.) and columns containing further information about customers (address, balance, credit limit, etc.). Each sales rep would appear on a single row along with the one customer that the sales rep represented. Likewise, each customer would appear on a single row along with the one sales rep who represented that customer. Thus, we would indeed have a one-to-one relationship. There is a slight problem in choosing the primary key. We have two possibilities: sales rep number and customer number. Both are unique! If two possibilities for the primary key are encountered in actual practice (quite rare), we choose one of the two as the primary key and designate the other as a **candidate key** (some people will use the term **alternate key** in this circumstance).

While this is one way of implementing the one-to-one relationship, it does not seem to be very natural. We have a single table in which we are storing *both* information about sales reps *and* customers, two different types of entities. A more common approach would be to have one table for sales reps and a separate table for customers. We would include the primary key of each table as one of the attributes (actually a foreign key) as shown in Figure 3.5.

SLSREP	SLSREP_NUMBER	SLSREP_NAME	CUSTOMER_NUMBER
	3	MARY JONES	124
	6	WILLIAM SMITH	256
	12	SAM BROWN	311

CUSTOMER	CUSTOMER_NUMBER	NAME	SLSREP_NUMBER
	124	SALLY ADAMS	3
	256	ANN SAMUELS	6
	311	DON CHARLES	12

FIGURE 3.5
One-to-one relationship implemented by including the primary key of each relation as an attribute in the other

Since each row in the SLSREP table contains the number of a single customer and each row in the customer table contains the number of a single sales rep, we have indeed accomplished what we wanted, a one-to-one relationship between the two entities. In addition, any other information concerning sales reps (address, commission, etc.) will be in additional columns in the sales rep table and any other information concerning customers (address, balance, etc.) will be in additional columns in the customer table.

While this is perhaps the simplest way of implementing a one-to-one relationship, it does incur problems that are beyond the scope of the current discussion. These problems will be discussed in chapter 7; by that time, you will have enough background to understand them as well as the alternatives that will be presented. For now, we will assume that this approach is an acceptable method for treating one-to-one relationships.

2. ONE-TO-MANY

Suppose that at Premiere Products each customer is represented by only one sales rep but each sales rep represents many customers. In this case, we will have one table for sales reps and a separate table for customers. We will include the primary key of the "one" part of the relationship, in this case sales reps, as one of the attributes in the "many" part of the relationship, but not vice versa, as shown in Figure 3.6.

CUSTOMER	CUSTOMER_NUMBER	NAME	SLSREP_NUMBER
	124	SALLY ADAMS	3
	256	ANN SAMUELS	6
	311	DON CHARLES	12
	315	TOM DANIELS	6
	405	AL WILLIAMS	12
	412	SALLY ADAMS	3
	522	MARY NELSON	12
	567	JOE BAKER	6
	587	JUDY ROBERTS	6
	622	DAN MARTIN	3

SLSREP	SLSREP_NUMBER	SLSREP_NAME
	3	MARY JONES
	6	WILLIAM SMITH
	12	SAM BROWN

FIGURE 3.6
One-to-many relationship implemented by including the key of the "one" part of the relationship as an attribute in the "many" part of the relationship

Since each customer appears in only one row in the CUSTOMER relation and this row contains a single sales rep number, each customer is associated with exactly one sales rep. On the other hand, since the SLSREP relation itself contains no customer number column, the only way to find the customer or customers whom a given sales rep represents is to find those rows within the CUSTOMER relation that contain the desired sales rep number. Since an individual sales rep number can occur in many rows within the CUSTOMER relation, a given sales rep is associated with many customers.

3. MANY-TO-MANY

Suppose that at Premiere Products each order contains lines for many different parts and each part is found on lines in many different orders. We will need an ORDER table and a PART table. To implement the many-to-many relationship between orders and parts, we introduce a third table containing as its key the concatenation of the keys of the original tables. In this case, the key is the concatenation of ORDER_NUMBER and PART_NUMBER. In addition, there may be other columns in this new table if there are any attributes that depend on both ORDER_ NUMBER and PART_NUMBER. Here, the number of units of a given part that were ordered and the quoted price could be the third and fourth columns in the relation. In this case, the third table effectively represents lines within the orders and we call it ORDER_LINE. The relations are shown in Figure 3.7.

ORDER

ORDER_ NUMBER	DATE
12489	90287
12491	90287
12494	90487
12495	90487
12498	90587
12500	90587
12504	90587

PART

PART_ NUMBER	PART_ DESCRIPTION
AX12	IRON
AZ52	SKATES
BA74	BASEBALL
BH22	TOASTER
BT04	STOVE
BZ66	WASHER
CA14	SKILLET
CB03	BIKE
CX11	MIXER
CZ81	WEIGHTS

ORDER_LINE

ORDER_ NUMBER	PART_ NUMBER	NUMBER_ ORDERED	QUOTED_ PRICE
12489	AX12	11	14.95
12491	BT04	1	402.99
12491	BZ66	1	311.95
12494	CB03	4	175.00
12495	CX11	2	57.95
12498	AZ52	2	22.95
12498	BA74	4	4.95
12500	BT04	1	402.99
12504	CZ81	2	108.99

To find the parts that are related to a given order, we find the part numbers that appear in any row in the ORDER_LINE relation which contains the appropriate order number. Since any number of such rows is possible, an order is related to many parts. Likewise, to find the orders that are related to a given part, we find the order numbers that appear in any row in the ORDER_LINE relation that contains the appropriate part number. Again, any number of such rows is possible and a part is related to many orders.

FIGURE 3.7
Implementation of a many-to-many relationship

3.4 SQL

The remaining sections of this chapter are devoted to studying a variety of approaches to data manipulation within the relational model, i.e., relational **data manipulation language (DML)**. The examples throughout these sections will use the database described in Figure 3.1. Most of the examples will involve retrieval, i.e., getting information out of the database for either a printed report or for display on a screen. Obtaining this information from the data in the database is also called **querying the database** and we refer to the commands that request this information as "queries."

From a theoretical standpoint, perhaps the most important approach to manipulating relational databases is the **relational calculus**. It is based on the *predicate calculus* a term whose origin is the discipline known as mathematical logic. The idea of a relational calculus was first proposed by Codd (see [4]). He also presented a language called ALPHA which was based on this calculus (see [5]). Although this language was never implemented, a language with a similar flavor, called QUEL, is used as the manipulation language in the relational DBMS,

INGRES, which will be examined in chapter 5. Basically, the importance of the relational calculus is in the theoretical arena, and we will not discuss it here. The only other point that we wish to make regarding the relational calculus concerns the concept of *relational completeness*, a concept defined by Codd (see [4]). A language is said to be **relationally complete** if any relation that can be retrieved by using the relational calculus can also be retrieved using that other language, i.e., if the other language is as "powerful" as the relational calculus. Thus, the relational calculus forms a yardstick by which other languages for relational data manipulation can be measured. For further information on the relational calculus, see [2], [6], and [11].

Other relational DML approaches to be studied here include the relational algebra in section 3.5, Query-by-Example in 3.6, and natural languages in 3.7. In this section we will examine a language called **SQL** (Structured Query Language), which is perhaps the most important relational DML of all. Many, if not most, relational DMBS's use a version of SQL, or something similar to it, as their data manipulation language. In addition, there is every reason to believe that this trend will continue as new systems are developed.

SQL is an example of a *transform-oriented* language; i.e., it is a language designed to use relations to transform inputs into desired outputs. It does bear some similarity to the relational calculus mentioned earlier. It was developed under the name SEQUEL at the IBM San Jose research facilities as the DML for IBM's prototype relational model DBMS, System R, in the mid-1970s. In 1980, it was renamed SQL to avoid confusion with an unrelated hardware product called SEQUEL. It is used as the DML for IBM's current production offerings in the relational DBMS arena, SQL/DS and DB2.

Before beginning our study of SQL, we should note that even though we have referred to it as a relational DML, it is really more than that. It also contains facilities to *define* data, i.e., to describe the structure of the database. This facility is usually called a **data definition language (DDL)**. Thus SQL is both a DML and a DDL.

Some points concerning these examples should be made before we begin. As you might expect, SQL, like most modern languages, is basically free format. The purpose of the indenting scheme shown in this chapter is strictly readability. Commas, where used, are essential. The SQL reserved words we will encounter must not be used in any way other than that for which they were intended. This does pose one problem for us: ORDER is a reserved word and we cannot use it as a name for a table. For this reason, throughout these examples, we will change the name of the ORDER table to ORDERS.

In the examples that follow, we will investigate the manner in which tables may be described, data may be retrieved, new data may be added, data may be changed, and data may be deleted.

DATA DEFINITION

Example 1: Database creation.

STATEMENT: Describe the layout of the sales rep relation to the DBMS.

```
CREATE TABLE SLSREP
     (SLSREP_NUMBER    DECIMAL(2),
      SLSREP_NAME      CHAR(15),
      SLSREP_ADDRESS   CHAR(25),
      TOTAL_COMMISSION DECIMAL(7,2),
      COMMISSION_RATE  DECIMAL(2,2))
```

In this SQL statement, which uses the data definition features of SQL, we are describing a table that will be called SLSREP. It contains five columns: SLSREP_NUMBER, SLSREP_NAME, SLSREP_ADDRESS, TOTAL_ COMMISSION, and COMMISSION_RATE. SLSREP_ NUMBER is a two-digit number. SLSREP_NAME is fifteen-character alphanumeric field and SLSREP_ ADDRESS is a twenty-five-character alphanumeric field. TOTAL_ COMMISSION is numeric and is seven digits long, including two decimal places. Similarly, COMMISSION_RATE is two digits long, and both of those are decimal places. We can visualize this statement as setting up for us a blank table with appropriate column headings (see Figure 3.8).

SLSREP	SLSREP_ NUMBER	SLSREP_NAME	SLSREP_ADDRESS	TOTAL_ COMMISSION	COMMISSION_ RATE

FIGURE 3.8
Newly created SLSREP table

We now consider the data manipulation features of the language, beginning with those aspects of the language devoted to retrieval of information from the database. It should be noted that when the statements below are executed, a nicely formatted report, including column headings, will be produced. The output of the process is actually another relation, however. This is the way we can and should think of the process, as one whose input is a collection of relations, together with the formulation of the query, and whose output is a relation.

SIMPLE RETRIEVAL

The basic form of an SQL expression is quite simple. It is merely SELECT . . . FROM . . . WHERE. After the SELECT, we list those columns that we wish to have displayed. After the FROM, we list the table or tables that are involved in the query. Finally, after the WHERE, we list any conditions that apply to the data we wish to retrieve.

Example 2: Retrieve certain columns and all rows.

STATEMENT: List the number, name, and balance of all customers.

Since we want all customers listed there is no need for the WHERE clause (we have no restrictions). The query is thus:

```
SELECT CUSTOMER_NUMBER, NAME, CURRENT_BALANCE
      FROM CUSTOMER
```

The computer will respond with:

CUSTOMER_NUMBER	NAME	CURRENT_BALANCE
124	SALLY ADAMS	418.75
256	ANN SAMUELS	10.75
311	DON CHARLES	200.10
315	TOM DANIELS	320.75
405	AL WILLIAMS	201.75
412	SALLY ADAMS	908.75
522	MARY NELSON	49.50
567	JOE BAKER	201.20
587	JUDY ROBERTS	57.75
622	DAN MARTIN	575.50

Example 3: Retrieve all columns and all rows.

STATEMENT: List the complete part table.

We could certainly use the same structure shown in example 2. However, there is a shortcut. Instead of listing all of the column names after the SELECT we can use the symbol "*". This indicates that we want all columns listed (in the order in which they have been described to the system during data definition). If we want all columns but in a different order, we would have to type the names of the columns in the order in which we want them to appear. In this case, assuming that the normal order is appropriate, the query would be

```
SELECT *
    FROM PART
```

PART_NUMBER	PART_DESCRIPTION	UNITS_ON_HAND	ITEM_CLASS	WAREHOUSE_NUMBER	UNIT_PRICE
AX12	IRON	104	HW	3	17.95
AZ52	SKATES	20	SG	2	24.95
BA74	BASEBALL	40	SG	1	4.95
BH22	TOASTER	95	HW	3	34.95
BT04	STOVE	11	AP	2	402.99
BZ66	WASHER	52	AP	3	311.95
CA14	SKILLET	2	HW	3	19.95
CB03	BIKE	44	SG	1	187.50
CX11	MIXER	112	HW	3	57.95
CZ81	WEIGHTS	208	SG	2	108.99

Example 4: Use of the WHERE clause.

STATEMENT: What is the name of customer 124?

We use the WHERE clause to restrict the output of the query to customer 124 as follows:

```
SELECT NAME
     FROM CUSTOMER
     WHERE CUSTOMER_NUMBER = 124
```

NAME
_____
SALLY ADAMS

The condition in the WHERE clause need not involve equality. Any of the normal comparison operators $=$, $>$, $>=$, $<$, $<=$ may be used as well as $\sim =$ (NOT EQUAL).

Example 5: Use of a compound condition within the WHERE clause.

STATEMENT: List the descriptions of all parts that are in warehouse 3 and have more than 100 units on hand.

Compound conditions are possible within the WHERE clause using AND, OR, and NOT. In this case, we have

```
SELECT PART_DESCRIPTION
     FROM PART
     WHERE WAREHOUSE_NUMBER = 3
     AND UNITS_ON_HAND > 100
```

PART_DESCRIPTION
_____
IRON
MIXER

Example 6: Use of computed fields.

STATEMENT: Find the available credit for all customers who have at least an $800 credit limit.

There is no column AVAILABLE_CREDIT in our database. It is, however, computable from two columns which are present, CREDIT_LIMIT and BALANCE (AVAILABLE_CREDIT = CREDIT_LIMIT – BALANCE). There are two possible ways around this problem. If the DBMS that we are using supports VIRTUAL columns (columns that are not physically stored but rather are computed from existing columns when needed), then AVAILABLE_ CREDIT could have been described to the system as a VIRTUAL column during the definition of the CUSTOMER table, and we could use it in this query. Assuming that, for whatever reason, this has not been done, we have a second

solution to the problem. SQL permits us to specify computations within the
SQL expression. In this case, we would have:

```
SELECT CUSTOMER_NUMBER, NAME, CREDIT_LIMIT –
       CURRENT_BALANCE
    FROM CUSTOMER
    WHERE CREDIT_LIMIT >= 800
```

CUSTOMER_NUMBER	NAME	3
256	ANN SAMUELS	789.25
405	AL WILLIAMS	598.25
412	SALLY ADAMS	91.25
522	MARY NELSON	750.50

Note that the heading for the available credit column is simply the number
3. Since this column does not exist in the CUSTOMER table, the computer does
not know how to label the column and instead uses the number 3 (for the *third*
column). There is a facility within SQL to change any of the column headings
to whatever we desire. For now, though, we will just accept the headings that
SQL will produce automatically. (There is some variation among different versions of SQL concerning column headings for computed columns. Your version
may very well treat them differently.)

Example 7: Use of "LIKE".

STATEMENT: List the number, name, and address of all customers who live in
Grant.

Normally, we would have a column labeled CITY and this would be a very
simple query. In this case, however, the city is just a portion of the column
labeled ADDRESS, and thus anyone living in Grant has "GRANT" somewhere
within his or her address, but *we don't know where.* Fortunately, there is a
facility within SQL that we can use in this situation. It is illustrated in the
following:

```
SELECT CUSTOMER_NUMBER, NAME, ADDRESS
    FROM CUSTOMER
    WHERE ADDRESS LIKE '%GRANT%'
```

CUSTOMER_NUMBER	NAME	ADDRESS
256	ANN SAMUELS	215 PETE, GRANT, MI
405	AL WILLIAMS	519 WATSON, GRANT, MI
622	DAN MARTIN	419 CHIP, GRANT, MI

The symbol "%" is used as a "wild card." Thus, we are asking for all customers whose address is "LIKE" some collection of characters, followed by
GRANT, followed by some other characters. Note that this query would also
pick up a customer whose address was "123 GRANTVIEW, ADA, MI". We
would probably be safer to have asked for addresses like '%,GRANT,%'

although this would have missed an address entered as "215 PETE, GRANT , MI" since this address does not contain the string of characters ",GRANT," but rather ",GRANT ,".

SORTING

Example 8: Use of ORDER BY and IN.

STATEMENT:

    A. List all customers ordered by name.
    B. List all customers having a credit limit of $300, $500 or $1000.
    C. List all customers whose name begins with "S".

You will recall that the order of rows in a relation is considered to be immaterial. From a practical standpoint, this means that in querying a relational database, there are no guarantees concerning the order in which the results will be displayed. It may be in the order in which the data was originally entered, but even this is not certain. Thus, if the order in which the data is displayed is important to us, we should *specifically* request that the results be displayed in the desired order. In SQL, this is done with the ORDER BY clause. In all three queries for this example, we will assume that the data is to be ordered by name and we will use the appropriate clause. In addition, in the second query we will use a new approach to the problem of determining whether a credit limit is $300, $500, or $1000 using the SQL word "IN". (We could have obtained the same answer by saying CREDIT_LIMIT = 300 OR CREDIT_LIMIT = 500 OR CREDIT_LIMIT = 1000. This new approach is just a little simpler.) Finally, in the third query, we will observe a use of the SQL word LIKE that is slightly different from the one in the previous example. It should be noted that since the names are stored as FIRST LAST, the ordering by name produces an order that is alphabetic by *first* name.

8A:

```
SELECT CUSTOMER_NUMBER, NAME, ADDRESS
      FROM CUSTOMER
      ORDER BY NAME
```

CUSTOMER_NUMBER	NAME	ADDRESS
405	AL WILLIAMS	519 WATSON,GRANT,MI
256	ANN SAMUELS	215 PETE,GRANT,MI
622	DAN MARTIN	419 CHIP,GRANT,MI
311	DON CHARLES	48 COLLEGE,IRA,MI
567	JOE BAKER	808 RIDGE,HARPER,MI
587	JUDY ROBERTS	512 PINE,ADA,MI
522	MARY NELSON	108 PINE,ADA,MI
412	SALLY ADAMS	16 ELM,LANSING,MI
124	SALLY ADAMS	481 OAK,LANSING,MI
315	TOM DANIELS	914 CHERRY,KENT,MI

8B:
```
SELECT CUSTOMER_NUMBER, NAME, ADDRESS
    FROM CUSTOMER
    WHERE CREDIT_LIMIT IN (300, 500, 1000)
    ORDER BY NAME
```

CUSTOMER_NUMBER	NAME	ADDRESS
622	DAN MARTIN	419 CHIP,GRANT,MI
311	DON CHARLES	48 COLLEGE,IRA,MI
567	JOE BAKER	808 RIDGE,HARPER,MI
587	JUDY ROBERTS	512 PINE,ADA,MI
412	SALLY ADAMS	16 ELM,LANSING,MI
124	SALLY ADAMS	481 OAK,LANSING,MI
315	TOM DANIELS	914 CHERRY,KENT,MI

8C:
```
SELECT CUSTOMER_NUMBER, NAME, ADDRESS
    FROM CUSTOMER
    WHERE NAME LIKE 'S%'
    ORDER BY NAME
```

CUSTOMER_NUMBER	NAME	ADDRESS
124	SALLY ADAMS	481 OAK,LANSING,MI
412	SALLY ADAMS	16 ELM,LANSING,MI

Why did we use NAME LIKE 'S%' and not NAME LIKE '%S%' as in the previous example?
Answer:
Using NAME LIKE '%S%' would have yielded all customers whose name contained the letter S anywhere within the name.

Example 9: Sorting with multiple keys, descending order.

STATEMENT: List the customer number, name, and credit limit of all customers, ordered by decreasing credit limit and by customer number within credit limit.

This example calls for sorting on multiple keys (customer number within credit limit) as well as the use of descending order for one of the keys. This (shown on the next page), is accomplished as follows:

```
SELECT CUSTOMER_NUMBER, NAME, CREDIT_LIMIT
    FROM CUSTOMER
    ORDER BY CREDIT_LIMIT DESC, CUSTOMER_NUMBER
```

CUSTOMER_NUMBER	NAME	CREDIT_LIMIT
412	SALLY ADAMS	1000
256	ANN SAMUELS	800
405	AL WILLIAMS	800
522	MARY NELSON	800
124	SALLY ADAMS	500
587	JUDY ROBERTS	500
622	DAN MARTIN	500
311	DON CHARLES	300
315	TOM DANIELS	300
567	JOE BAKER	300

BUILT-IN FUNCTIONS

Example 10: Use of the built-in function COUNT.

STATEMENT: How many parts are in item class "HW"?

SQL has the usual collection of built-in functions:

COUNT — count of the number of values in a column
SUM — sum of the values in a column
AVG — average of the values in a column
MAX — largest of the values in a column
MIN — smallest of the values in a column

In this query, we are interested in the number of rows in the relation produced by selecting only those parts that are in item class "HW". We could count the number of part numbers in this relation or the number of descriptions or the number of entries in any other column. It doesn't make any difference. (Rather than requiring us to arbitrarily pick one of these, some versions of SQL allow us to use the symbol "*".) The query could thus be formulated as follows:

```
SELECT COUNT(PART_NUMBER)
    FROM PART
    WHERE ITEM_CLASS = 'HW'
```

$$\frac{1}{4}$$

Example 11: Use of COUNT and SUM.

STATEMENT: Find the number of customers and the total of their balances.

The only real difference between COUNT and SUM (other than the obvious fact that they are computing different statistics) is that in the case of SUM, we *must* specify the column for which we want a total. (It doesn't make sense to use the "*", even if this is permitted for COUNT.) This query is thus:

```
SELECT COUNT(CUSTOMER_NUMBER), SUM(CURRENT_BALANCE)
      FROM CUSTOMER
```

1	2
10	2944.8

SUBQUERIES

Example 12: Nesting queries.

STATEMENT:

A. What is the largest credit limit awarded to any customer of sales rep 3?
B. Which customers have this limit?
C. Find the answer to part B in a single step.

Parts A and B do not require anything new, other than using the built-in function MAX.

12A:

```
SELECT MAX(CREDIT_LIMIT)
      FROM CUSTOMER
        WHERE SLSREP_NUMBER = 3
```

1
1000

12B: After viewing the answer to part A (1000)

```
SELECT CUSTOMER_NUMBER, NAME
      FROM CUSTOMER
        WHERE CREDIT_LIMIT = 1000
```

CUSTOMER_NUMBER	NAME
412	SALLY ADAMS

12C:

In part C, we are to accomplish the same thing as A and B but in a single step. We can do this using a feature permitted in SQL called nesting of queries. The form for query nesting is illustrated in the solution:

```
SELECT CUSTOMER_NUMBER, NAME
      FROM CUSTOMER
        WHERE CREDIT_LIMIT IN
              (SELECT MAX(CREDIT_LIMIT)
                    FROM CUSTOMER
                      WHERE SLSREP_NUMBER = 3)
```

CUSTOMER_NUMBER	NAME
412	SALLY ADAMS

The portion in parentheses is called a subquery. The subquery is evaluated first and produces a new relation. The outer query can now be evaluated. In this case, we will only obtain the names of customers whose credit limit is in the relation produced by the subquery. Since that relation contains only the maximum credit limit for the customers of sales rep 3, we will obtain the desired list of customers. Incidentally, since the subquery in this case will produce a relation containing only a single value (the maximum credit limit, this query could have been formulated in another way, and that is:

```
SELECT CUSTOMER_NUMBER, NAME
     FROM CUSTOMER
     WHERE CREDIT_LIMIT =
          (SELECT MAX(CREDIT_LIMIT)
              FROM CUSTOMER
              WHERE SLSREP_NUMBER = 3)
```

CUSTOMER_NUMBER	NAME
412	SALLY ADAMS

In this formulation we are asking for those customers whose credit limit *is equal to* the one unique credit limit obtained by the subquery. In general, unless you know that the subquery *must* produce a unique value, the prior formulation using IN would be the one to use.

Example 13: Use of DISTINCT.

STATEMENT:

A. Find the numbers of all customers who currently have orders.
B. Find the numbers of all customers who currently have orders, making sure to list each customer exactly once.
C. Count the number of customers who currently have orders.

13A:

The formulation seems fairly simple. If a customer currently has an order, there must be at least one row in the ORDER table on which that customer's number appears. Thus we could say:

```
SELECT CUSTOMER_NUMBER
     FROM ORDERS
```

CUSTOMER_NUMBER
124
311
315
256
522
124
522

13B:

If you look at the solution to 13A, you will see that some customer numbers are repeated. Those customers with more than one order appear in the result more than once. If we want to ensure uniqueness, we formulate the query in the following manner:

```
SELECT DISTINCT CUSTOMER_NUMBER
      FROM ORDERS
```

CUSTOMER_NUMBER
124
256
311
315
522

13C:

The final part of this example involves counting, as we discussed before. The reason it is mentioned here is that if we are not careful, we might end up counting the duplicate customer numbers, as in the following:

```
SELECT COUNT(CUSTOMER_NUMBER)
      FROM ORDERS
```

$\frac{1}{7}$

To overcome this difficulty, we again use the word DISTINCT as:

```
SELECT COUNT(DISTINCT CUSTOMER_NUMBER)
      FROM ORDERS
```

$\frac{1}{5}$

Unfortunately, not all implementations of SQL support this construction (the use of DISTINCT within COUNT). In such implementations, the same effect can be achieved by:

```
SELECT COUNT(CUSTOMER_NUMBER)
      FROM CUSTOMER
      WHERE CUSTOMER_NUMBER IN
            (SELECT DISTINCT CUSTOMER_NUMBER
            FROM ORDERS)
```

$\frac{1}{5}$

Example 14: Use of a built-in function in a subquery.

STATEMENT: List all customers whose balance is over the average balance.

In this case, we use a subquery to obtain the average balance. Since this produces a single number, we can compare each customer's balance with this number, as:

```
SELECT CUSTOMER_NUMBER, NAME, ADDRESS, CURRENT_BALANCE
    FROM CUSTOMER
    WHERE CURRENT_BALANCE >
        (SELECT AVG(CURRENT_BALANCE)
            FROM CUSTOMER)
```

CUSTOMER_ NUMBER	NAME	ADDRESS	CURRENT_ BALANCE
124	SALLY ADAMS	481 OAK,LANSING,MI	418.75
315	TOM DANIELS	914 CHERRY,KENT,MI	320.75
412	SALLY ADAMS	16 ELM,LANSING,MI	908.75
622	DAN MARTIN	419 CHIP,GRANT,MI	575.50

GROUPING

Example 15: Using GROUP BY and HAVING.

STATEMENT:

A. List the order total for each order.
B. List the order total for those orders amounting to more than $200.

15A:

The order total is equal to the total of the products of number ordered and quoted price for all of the order lines within the order. These queries thus involve the sum of computed fields. However, there is a little more to it than just including SUM(NUMBER_ORDERED * QUOTED_PRICE) in the query. This would only give us the grand total over all order lines; the grand total would not be broken down by order. To get individual totals we use the GROUP BY clause. In this case, saying GROUP BY ORDER_NUMBER will cause the order lines for each order to be "grouped together"; i.e., all order lines with the same order number will form a group. Any statistics, such as totals, requested in the SELECT clause will be calculated for each of these groups. It is important to note that the GROUP BY clause does not imply that the information will be sorted. To produce the report in a particular order, the ORDER BY clause must be used. Assuming that the report is to be ordered by order number, we would have the following formulation for part A:

```
SELECT ORDER_NUMBER, SUM(NUMBER_ORDERED * QUOTED_PRICE)
    FROM ORDER_LINE
    GROUP BY ORDER_NUMBER
    ORDER BY ORDER_NUMBER
```

ORDER_NUMBER	2
12489	164.45
12491	714.94
12494	700.00
12495	115.90
12498	65.70
12500	402.99
12504	217.98

When rows are grouped, one line of output is produced for each group. The only things that may be displayed are statistics calculated for the group or columns whose values are the same for all rows in a group. In this example, it is appropriate to display the order number, since the output is grouped by order number and thus the order number on one row in a group must be the same as the order number on any other row in the group. It would *not* be appropriate, however, to display a part number, since this will vary from one row in a group to another. (The computer would not know which part number to display for the group.)

15B:

In part B there is a restriction, namely, we only want to display totals for those orders that amount to more than $200. This restriction does not apply to individual rows but rather to *groups*. Since the WHERE clause applies only to rows, it is not the appropriate clause to accomplish the kind of selection that we have here. Fortunately, there is a facility that is to groups what WHERE is to rows. It is the HAVING clause, and it is illustrated in the following solution to part B:

```
SELECT ORDER_NUMBER, SUM(NUMBER_ORDERED * QUOTED_PRICE)
    FROM ORDER_LINE
    GROUP BY ORDER_NUMBER
    HAVING SUM(NUMBER_ORDERED * QUOTED_PRICE) > 200
    ORDER BY ORDER_NUMBER
```

ORDER_NUMBER	2
12491	714.94
12494	700.00
12500	402.99
12504	217.98

In this case, the row created for a group will be displayed only if the sum calculated for the group is larger than 200.

Example 16: HAVING vs. WHERE.

STATEMENT:

A. List each credit limit together with the number of customers who have this limit.
B. Same as query A, but only list those credit limits held by more than one customer.
C. List each credit limit together with the number of customers of sales rep 3 who have this limit.
D. Same as query C, but only list those credit limits held by more than one customer.

16A:

In order to count the number of customers who have a given credit limit, the data must by GROUPed BY this credit limit. Thus the formulation would be:

```
SELECT CREDIT_LIMIT, COUNT(CUSTOMER_NUMBER)
    FROM CUSTOMER
    GROUP BY CREDIT_LIMIT
```

CREDIT_LIMIT	2
300	3
500	3
800	3
1000	1

16B:

Since this condition involves a group total, a HAVING clause is used. The formulation would be:

```
SELECT CREDIT_LIMIT, COUNT(CUSTOMER_NUMBER)
    FROM CUSTOMER
    GROUP BY CREDIT_LIMIT
    HAVING COUNT(CUSTOMER_NUMBER) > 1
```

CREDIT_LIMIT	2
300	3
500	3
800	3

16C:

The condition only involves rows, so the WHERE clause is appropriate and the formulation would be:

```
SELECT  CREDIT_LIMIT,  COUNT(CUST
     FROM  CUSTOMER
     WHERE  SLSREP_NUMBER  =  3
     GROUP  BY  CREDIT_LIMIT
```

CREDIT_LIMIT	2
500	2
1000	1

16D:

Since the conditions involve both rows and
and a HAVING clause are required and the form

```
SELECT  CREDIT_LIMIT,  COUNT(CUSTOM
     FROM  CUSTOMER
     WHERE  SLSREP_NUMBER  =  3
     GROUP  BY  CREDIT_LIMIT
     HAVING  COUNT(CUSTOMER_NUMBER)
```

CREDIT_LIMIT	2
500	2

In this final example, rows from the original table will be considered only if the sales rep number is 3. These rows are then grouped by credit limit and the count is calculated. Only groups for which the calculated count is greater than 1 will be displayed.

QUERYING MULTIPLE TABLES

Example 17: Joining two tables together.

STATEMENT: For each part that is on order, find the number ordered, the price quoted, the actual price, and the description of the part.

A part is considered to be on order if there is a row in the ORDER_LINE table in which the part appears. To find the order number, the number ordered, and the price quoted we need only examine the ORDER_LINE table. To find the description and the actual price, however, we need to look in the PART table. Thus, to satisfy this query we need to **join** two tables together. (The term join is actually a term used in the relational algebra. The process of joining, however, is common to all approaches to manipulating relational databases and often the term is applied to this process with regard to other approaches besides the relational algebra.) We need to find rows in the ORDER_LINE relation and rows in the PART relation that match, i.e., rows on which there is the same part number. This is accomplished in SQL as follows:

```
                    _LINE.PART_NUMBER,
                NUMBER_ORDERED, QUOTED_PRICE,

             ,  PART
            NE.PART_NUMBER  =  PART.PART_NUMBER
```

	PART_ DESCRIPTION	NUMBER_ ORDERED	QUOTED_ PRICE	UNIT_ PRICE
.12	IRON	11	14.95	17.95
BT04	STOVE	1	402.99	402.99
BZ66	WASHER	1	311.95	311.95
494 CB03	BIKE	4	175.00	187.50
12495 CX11	MIXER	2	57.95	57.95
12498 AZ52	SKATES	2	22.95	24.95
12498 BA74	BASEBALL	4	4.95	4.95
12500 BT04	STOVE	1	402.99	402.99
12504 CZ81	WEIGHTS	2	108.99	108.99

Here we indicate all fields we wish displayed in the SELECT clause. In the FROM clause, we list all the tables involved in the query. Finally, in the WHERE clause, we give the condition that will restrict the data to be retrieved to only those rows from the two relations that match. Note that since there is a column in ORDER_LINE called PART_NUMBER and a column in PART called PART_ NUMBER, it is necessary to qualify them, i.e., to specify ORDER_ LINE.PART_NUMBER and PART.PART_NUMBER. We could, of course, have qualified other attributes as well (ORDER_LINE.NUMBER_ORDERED, for example), but since there is only one NUMBER_ORDERED, qualification of this name is not necessary.

Example 18: Comparison of JOIN and the use of IN.

STATEMENT: Find the descriptions of all parts included in order 12491.

Since this query also involves the ORDER_LINE and PART tables, as did the previous example, we could approach it in a similar fashion. There are two basic differences: this query does not require as many fields, and we are only interested in order 12491. The fact that there are not as many columns only means there are going to be fewer attributes listed in the SELECT clause. Restriction of the query to a single order is accomplished by adding the condition ORDER_NUMBER = 12491 to the WHERE clause. Thus one formulation of this query would be:

```
SELECT  PART_DESCRIPTION
    FROM  ORDER_LINE, PART
    WHERE  ORDER_LINE.PART_NUMBER  =  PART.PART_NUMBER
    AND  ORDER_NUMBER  =  12491
```

PART_DESCRIPTION
STOVE
WASHER

Notice that ORDER_LINE was listed in the FROM clause even though there were no fields from the ORDER_LINE relation that were to be displayed. There were fields from this relation mentioned in the WHERE clause, however, and thus it was involved in the query.

There is another approach that could be taken, and it involves the IN clause and a subquery. We could first find all of the part numbers in the ORDER_LINE relation that appear on any row in which the order number is 12491 as a subquery. Next we find the descriptions of any parts whose part number is in this list. The formulation to do this would be:

```
SELECT PART_DESCRIPTION
FROM PART
WHERE PART.PART_NUMBER IN
        (SELECT ORDER_LINE.PART_NUMBER
              FROM ORDER_LINE
              WHERE ORDER_NUMBER = 12491)
```

PART_DESCRIPTION
_____
STOVE
WASHER

Example 19: Comparison of IN and EXISTS.

STATEMENT:

A. Find the number and date of those orders that contain part "BT04".
B. Find the number and date of those orders that do not contain part "BT04".

19A:

The query is similar to that of the previous example but involves the ORDERS table instead of the PART table. It could thus be handled in either of the ways discussed in the previous example. Using the formulation involving IN would give:

```
SELECT ORDERS.ORDER_NUMBER, DATE
    FROM ORDERS
    WHERE ORDERS.ORDER_NUMBER IN
          (SELECT ORDER_LINE.ORDER_NUMBER
                FROM ORDER_LINE
                WHERE PART_NUMBER = 'BT04')
```

ORDER_NUMBER	DATE
12491	90287
12500	90587

19B:

This query could be handled in essentially the same fashion, except that "IN" would be replaced by "NOT IN". An alternative formulation can be given using the SQL word "EXISTS". (In this case, we actually use "NOT EXISTS".) This formulation would be:

```
SELECT ORDER_NUMBER, DATE
     FROM ORDERS
     WHERE NOT EXISTS
          (SELECT *
               FROM ORDER_LINE
               WHERE ORDERS.ORDER_NUMBER =
                    ORDER_LINE.ORDER_NUMBER
               AND PART_NUMBER = 'BT04')
```

Here, for each order number in the ORDERS table, the subquery is selecting those rows of the ORDER_LINE table on which the order number matches the order number from the ORDERS table and the part number is "BT04". If the order number from the order table does not appear on any row in ORDER_LINE on which the part is "BT04", the result of the subquery will be an empty relation. In this case the "NOT EXISTS" condition will be true (no rows exist in the relation created by the subquery) and this order number and corresponding date will be printed. If, on the other hand, the order does contain part "BT04", there will be at least one row in the relation created by the subquery, and the "NOT EXISTS" condition will be false, so that this order number would not be displayed.

Note that this formulation could also be used in part A, but with "EXISTS" instead of "NOT EXISTS".

Example 20: Subquery within a subquery.

STATEMENT: Find all of the numbers and dates of those orders that include a part located in warehouse 3.

One way to approach this problem is to first of all determine the list of part numbers in the PART relation for those parts that are located in warehouse 3. Once this has been done, we can obtain a list of order numbers in the ORDER_LINE relation where the corresponding part number is in our part number list. Finally, we can retrieve those order numbers and dates in the ORDERS relation for which the order number is in the list of order numbers obtained during the second step. This approach would be formulated in SQL as follows:

```
SELECT ORDER_NUMBER, DATE
     FROM ORDERS
     WHERE ORDER_NUMBER IN
           (SELECT ORDER_NUMBER
                FROM ORDER_LINE
                WHERE PART_NUMBER IN
                      (SELECT PART_NUMBER
                           FROM PART
                           WHERE WAREHOUSE_NUMBER = 3))
```

ORDER_NUMBER	DATE
12489	90287
12491	90287
12495	90487

As you would expect, the queries are evaluated from the innermost query to the outermost query and thus this formulation matches exactly the procedure we specified. There is, of course, an alternative formulation involving the joining of three tables, ORDERS, ORDER_LINE, and PART. The formulation to do this would be:

```
SELECT ORDERS.ORDER_NUMBER, DATE
     FROM ORDER_LINE, ORDERS, PART
     WHERE ORDER_LINE.ORDER_NUMBER =
        ORDERS.ORDER_NUMBER
     AND ORDER_LINE.PART_NUMBER = PART.PART_NUMBER
     AND WAREHOUSE_NUMBER = 3
```

ORDER_NUMBER	DATE
12489	90287
12491	90287
12495	90487

In this case, the condition ORDER_LINE.ORDER_NUMBER = ORDERS.ORDER_NUMBER and the condition ORDER_LINE.PART_NUMBER = PART.PART_NUMBER will accomplish the appropriate joining of the tables. The condition WAREHOUSE_NUMBER = 3 is what restricts the output to only those parts located in warehouse 3.

The response produced will be correct regardless of which of these two formulations is used. Thus, the user can employ whichever approach is more comfortable.

You may be wondering whether one approach will be more efficient than another. Good mainframe systems have built-in optimizers that analyze queries to determine the best way to satisfy them. Given a good optimizer, it should not make any difference how the query is formulated. If we are using a system without such an optimizer, like one of the many microcomputer database management systems, then the formulation of a query can make a difference.

Example 21: A comprehensive example.

STATEMENT: List the customer number, the order number, the order date, and the order total for all of those orders whose total is over $100.

This query involves several of the features already discussed. The formulation is:

```
SELECT CUSTOMER_NUMBER, ORDERS.ORDER_NUMBER, DATE,
       SUM(NUMBER_ORDERED * QUOTED_PRICE)
    FROM ORDERS, ORDER_LINE
    WHERE ORDERS.ORDER_NUMBER =
       ORDER_LINE.ORDER_NUMBER
    GROUP BY ORDERS.ORDER_NUMBER, CUSTOMER_NUMBER, DATE
    HAVING SUM(NUMBER_ORDERED * QUOTED_PRICE) > 100
    ORDER BY ORDERS.ORDER_NUMBER
```

CUSTOMER_NUMBER	ORDER_NUMBER	DATE	4
124	12489	90287	164.45
311	12491	90287	714.94
315	12494	90487	700.00
256	12495	90487	115.90
124	12500	90587	402.99
522	12504	90587	217.98

This example illustrates the use of all the major clauses that can be used within the SELECT command. It also illustrates the order in which these clauses must appear.

In this example, the ORDERS and ORDER_LINE tables are joined by listing both tables in the FROM clause and relating them in the WHERE clause. Data selected is sorted by ORDER_NUMBER, using the ORDER BY clause. The GROUP BY clause indicates that the data is to be grouped by order number, customer number, and date. For each group, the SELECT indicates that the customer number, order number, order date, and order total, (SUM(NUMBER_ ORDERED * QUOTED_PRICE), are to be displayed. Not all groups will be displayed, however. The HAVING clause indicates that only groups for which the SUM(NUMBER_ORDERED * QUOTED_PRICE) is greater than 100 are to be printed.

Note that for each order, the order number, customer number, and date are the same. Thus, it would seem that merely grouping by order number should be sufficient. Most implementations of SQL, however, still require that both customer number and date also be listed in the GROUP BY clause. (Recall that the SELECT can only include statistics calculated for groups or columns whose values are known to be the same for each row in a group. By stating that the data is to be grouped by the order number, customer number, and date, the system knows that the values of these columns must be the same for each row in a group. A more sophisticated implementation would realize that by the structure of this database, grouping by order number alone is sufficient to ensure the uniqueness of both customer number and date.)

USING AN ALIAS

Example 22: Use of an alias.

STATEMENT: List the number and name of all sales reps together with the number and name of all of the customers they represent.

When tables are listed in the FROM clause, it is possible to give each table an **alias** or alternate name that can be used throughout the rest of the statement. This is done by immediately following the name of the table with the alias. There are no commas separating the two. If there were, SQL would assume that the alias was, in fact, the name of another table. There are two basic uses for aliases. One is simplicity. In the following example, we will assign the SLSREP table the alias "S" and the CUSTOMER table the alias "C". By doing this, we can type "S" instead of "SLSREP" and "C" instead of "CUSTOMER" in the remainder of the query. The following query is relatively simple, so the full benefit of this feature is not really felt. If the query is very involved, however, requiring much qualification of names, this feature can simplify the process greatly.

The formulation for this query using aliases is:

```
SELECT S.SLSREP_NUMBER, S.SLSREP_NAME,
       C.CUSTOMER_NUMBER, C.NAME
    FROM SLSREP S, CUSTOMER C
    WHERE S.SLSREP_NUMBER = C.SLSREP_NUMBER
```

SLSREP_ NUMBER	SLSREP_NAME	CUSTOMER_ NUMBER	NAME
3	MARY JONES	124	SALLY ADAMS
3	MARY JONES	412	SALLY ADAMS
3	MARY JONES	622	DAN MARTIN
6	WILLIAM SMITH	256	ANN SAMUELS
6	WILLIAM SMITH	315	TOM DANIELS
6	WILLIAM SMITH	567	JOE BAKER
6	WILLIAM SMITH	587	JUDY ROBERTS
12	SAM BROWN	311	DON CHARLES
12	SAM BROWN	405	AL WILLIAMS
12	SAM BROWN	522	MARY NELSON

In addition to their role in simplifying queries, there are certain situations, like the one in the next example, in which the use of aliases is essential.

MORE INVOLVED JOINS

Example 23: Joining a table to itself.

STATEMENT: Find the list of any pairs of customers who have the same name.

If we had two different tables of customers and the query requested us to find customers in the first table who have the same name as customers in the second table, this would be a regular join operation. Here, however, there is only the one table, CUSTOMER. We can actually treat it as two tables in the query by using the alias feature of SQL presented in the previous example. In this query we use this feature in the following way. In the FROM clause, we state:

```
FROM CUSTOMER FIRST, CUSTOMER SECOND
```

As far as SQL is concerned, we are requesting the querying of two tables, one that has the alias FIRST and another that has the alias SECOND. The fact that both tables are really the single table CUSTOMER is not a problem. Thus the query could be formulated:

```
SELECT FIRST.CUSTOMER_NUMBER, FIRST.NAME,
       SECOND.CUSTOMER_NUMBER, SECOND.NAME
    FROM CUSTOMER FIRST, CUSTOMER SECOND
    WHERE FIRST.NAME = SECOND.NAME
    AND FIRST.CUSTOMER_NUMBER < SECOND.CUSTOMER_NUMBER
```

CUSTOMER_ NUMBER	NAME	CUSTOMER_ NUMBER	NAME
124	SALLY ADAMS	412	SALLY ADAMS

We are requesting a customer number and name from the FIRST table, followed by a customer number and name from the SECOND table, subject to two conditions. The names must match, and the customer number from the first table must be less than the customer number from the second table. If we did not include the second condition, we would get a result like the following:

```
SELECT FIRST.CUSTOMER_NUMBER, FIRST.NAME,
       SECOND.CUSTOMER_NUMBER, SECOND.NAME
    FROM CUSTOMER FIRST, CUSTOMER SECOND
    WHERE FIRST.NAME = SECOND.NAME
```

CUSTOMER_ NUMBER	NAME	CUSTOMER_ NUMBER	NAME
124	SALLY ADAMS	124	SALLY ADAMS
124	SALLY ADAMS	412	SALLY ADAMS
256	ANN SAMUELS	256	ANN SAMUELS
311	DON CHARLES	311	DON CHARLES
315	TOM DANIELS	315	TOM DANIELS
405	AL WILLIAMS	405	AL WILLIAMS
412	SALLY ADAMS	124	SALLY ADAMS
412	SALLY ADAMS	412	SALLY ADAMS
522	MARY NELSON	522	MARY NELSON
567	JOE BAKER	567	JOE BAKER
587	JUDY ROBERTS	587	JUDY ROBERTS
622	DAN MARTIN	622	DAN MARTIN

Example 24: An example involving joining all five tables.

STATEMENT: List the number and name of all sales reps who represent any customers who currently have any orders on file for parts in item class "HW".

Conceptually, we need to examine each customer of each sales rep. For each of these customers, we need to examine all orders placed. For each of these orders we need to look at each order line. For each order line, we need to examine the appropriate part to see if that part is in item class "HW". If we find that one of these parts is in item class "HW", the corresponding sales rep should appear on the report. If no such part exists among all the lines of all the orders of all the customers for a given sales rep, that rep should not appear on the report. This query thus involves effectively joining all five tables together. This is accomplished in exactly the same manner as joining two or three tables together. We need conditions that specify how the tables are to be related in addition to a condition that restricts the result of the query only to parts that are in item class "HW". The formulation is:

```
SELECT  SLSREP.SLSREP_NUMBER,  SLSREP.SLSREP_NAME
     FROM SLSREP, CUSTOMER, ORDERS, ORDER_LINE, PART
     WHERE  SLSREP.SLSREP_NUMBER =
        CUSTOMER.SLSREP_NUMBER
     AND  CUSTOMER.CUSTOMER_NUMBER =
        ORDERS.CUSTOMER_NUMBER
     AND  ORDERS.ORDER_NUMBER = ORDER_LINE.ORDER_NUMBER
     AND  ORDER_LINE.PART_NUMBER = PART.PART_NUMBER
     AND  ITEM_CLASS = 'HW'
```

SLSREP_NUMBER	SLSREP_NAME
3	MARY JONES
6	WILLIAM SMITH

UNION, INTERSECTION, AND DIFFERENCE

SQL supports the normal set operations: union, intersection, and difference. The union of two relations is a relation containing all rows that are in either the first relation or the second or both. The intersection of two relations is a relation containing all rows that are in both relations. The difference of two relations, A and B (referred to as A minus B), is the set of all rows that are in relation A but are not in relation B. There is an obvious restriction for any of these operations. It does not make sense to talk about the union of the CUSTOMER table and the ORDER table, for example. What would rows in this union look like?! The two relations must have the same structure. The technical term is **union-compatible.**

> _Def:_ Two relations are union-compatible if they have the same number of attributes (columns) and if their corresponding attributes have the same domain.

Note that the definition does not state that the column headings of the two relations have to be identical but rather that the columns must come from the same domain, i.e., must be of the same type.

Example 25: Use of UNION.

STATEMENT: List the number and name of all customers who are either represented by sales rep 12 or who currently have orders on file, or both.

We can create a relation containing the number and name of all customers who are represented by sales rep 12 by selecting customer numbers and names from the CUSTOMER table in which the sales rep number is 12. We can create another relation containing the number and name of all customers who currently have orders on file by creating a join of the customer table and the order table. The two relations created by this process have the same structure: two columns, a customer number, and a name. Since they are thus union-compatible, it is legitimate to take the union of these two relations. This is accomplished in SQL by:

```
SELECT CUSTOMER_NUMBER, NAME
     FROM CUSTOMER
     WHERE SLSREP_NUMBER = 12
UNION
SELECT CUSTOMER.CUSTOMER_NUMBER, NAME
     FROM CUSTOMER, ORDERS
     WHERE CUSTOMER.CUSTOMER_NUMBER =
        ORDERS.CUSTOMER_NUMBER
```

CUSTOMER_NUMBER	NAME
124	SALLY ADAMS
256	ANN SAMUELS
311	DON CHARLES
315	TOM DANIELS
405	AL WILLIAMS
522	MARY NELSON

If an implementation truly supports the union operation, it will remove any duplicate rows; i.e., any customers who are represented by sales rep 12 *and* who currently have orders on file will not appear twice. Some implementations of SQL have a "union" operation but will not remove such duplicates.

Example 26: Use of INTERSECT (INTERSECTION).

STATEMENT: List the number and name of all customers who are represented by sales rep 12 and who currently have orders on file.

The only difference between this query and the previous one is that the appropriate operation is INTERSECT. The query is thus:

```
SELECT CUSTOMER_NUMBER, NAME
     FROM CUSTOMER
     WHERE SLSREP_NUMBER = 12
INTERSECT
SELECT CUSTOMER.CUSTOMER_NUMBER, NAME
     FROM CUSTOMER, ORDERS
     WHERE CUSTOMER.CUSTOMER_NUMBER =
        ORDERS.CUSTOMER_NUMBER
```

CUSTOMER_NUMBER	NAME
311	DON CHARLES
522	MARY NELSON

Example 27: Use of MINUS (DIFFERENCE).

STATEMENT: List the number and name of all customers who are represented by sales rep 12 but who do not currently have orders on file.

The only difference between this query and the previous two is that the appropriate operation is MINUS. The query is thus:

```
SELECT CUSTOMER_NUMBER, NAME
      FROM CUSTOMER
      WHERE SLSREP_NUMBER = 12
MINUS
SELECT CUSTOMER.CUSTOMER_NUMBER, NAME
      FROM CUSTOMER, ORDERS
      WHERE CUSTOMER.CUSTOMER_NUMBER =
            ORDERS.CUSTOMER_NUMBER
```

CUSTOMER_NUMBER	NAME
405	AL WILLIAMS

ALL AND ANY

Example 28: Use of ALL.

STATEMENT: Find the number, name, current balance, and sales rep number of those customers whose balance is larger than the balances of all customers of sales rep 12.

While this query can be satisfied by finding the maximum balance of the customers represented by sales rep 12 in a subquery and then finding all customers whose balance is greater than this number, there is an alternative. The word ALL can be used, as in the following query:

```
SELECT CUSTOMER_NUMBER, NAME, CURRENT_BALANCE,
        SLSREP_NUMBER
    FROM CUSTOMER
    WHERE CURRENT_BALANCE > ALL
            (SELECT CURRENT_BALANCE
                FROM CUSTOMER
                WHERE SLSREP_NUMBER = 12)
```

CUSTOMER_ NUMBER	NAME	CURRENT_ BALANCE	SLSREP_ NUMBER
124	SALLY ADAMS	418.75	3
315	TOM DANIELS	320.75	6
412	SALLY ADAMS	908.75	3
622	DAN MARTIN	575.50	3

To some users, this formulation might seem more natural than finding the maximum balance in the subquery. For other users, just the opposite might be true. Users can employ whichever approach they find more comfortable.

Example 29: Use of ANY.

STATEMENT: Find the number, name, current balance, and sales rep number of those customers whose balance is larger than the balance of any customer of sales rep 12.

This query can be satisfied by finding the minimum balance of the customers represented by sales rep 12 in a subquery and then finding all customers whose balance is greater than this number. Again there is an alternative. The word ANY can be used, as in the following query:

```
SELECT CUSTOMER_NUMBER, NAME, CURRENT_BALANCE,
        SLSREP_NUMBER
    FROM CUSTOMER
    WHERE CURRENT_BALANCE > ANY
            (SELECT CURRENT_BALANCE
                FROM CUSTOMER
                WHERE SLSREP_NUMBER = 12)
```

CUSTOMER_ NUMBER	NAME	CURRENT_ BALANCE	SLSREP_ NUMBER
124	SALLY ADAMS	418.75	3
311	DON CHARLES	200.10	12
315	TOM DANIELS	320.75	6
405	AL WILLIAMS	201.75	12
412	SALLY ADAMS	908.75	3
567	JOE BAKER	201.20	6
587	JUDY ROBERTS	57.75	6
622	DAN MARTIN	575.50	3

UPDATE

The remainder of the SQL examples involve the update features of SQL.

Example 30: Change existing data in the database.

STATEMENT: Change the name of customer 256 to "ANN JONES".

The SQL command to make changes to existing data is the UPDATE command. For this example, the formulation would be:

```
UPDATE CUSTOMER
    SET NAME = 'ANN JONES'
    WHERE CUSTOMER_NUMBER = 256
```

Example 31: Add new data to the database.

STATEMENT: Add sales rep (14, "ANN CRANE", "123 RIVER, ADA, MI", 0, 0.05) to the database.

Addition of new data is accomplished through the INSERT command. If we have specific data, as in this example, we can use the insert command as follows:

```
INSERT INTO SLSREP
     VALUES
     (14,'ANN CRANE','123 RIVER,ADA,MI',0.00,0.05)
```

Example 32: Delete data from the database.

STATEMENT: Delete from the database the customer whose name is "AL WILLIAMS".

To delete data from the database, the DELETE command is used, as in the following:

```
DELETE CUSTOMER
     WHERE NAME = 'AL WILLIAMS'
```

Note that this type of deletion can be very dangerous. If there happened to be another customer whose name is also 'AL WILLIAMS', this customer would also be deleted in the process. The safest type of deletion occurs when the condition involves the primary key. In such a case, since the primary key is unique, we are certain that we will not cause accidental deletion of other rows in the table.

Example 33: Change data in the database based on a compound condition.

STATEMENT: For each customer with a $500 credit limit whose balance does not exceed his/her credit limit, increase the credit limit to $800.

The only difference between this and the previous update example is that the condition is compound. Here, the formulation would be:

```
UPDATE CUSTOMER
     SET CREDIT_LIMIT = 800
     WHERE CREDIT_LIMIT = 500
     AND CURRENT_BALANCE < CREDIT_LIMIT
```

Example 34: Create a new relation with data from an existing relation.

STATEMENT: Create a new relation called "SMALLCUST" containing the same columns as "CUSTOMER" but only the rows for which the credit limit is $500 or less.

The first thing we need to do is to describe this new table using the data definition facilities of SQL, as follows:

```
CREATE TABLE SMALLCUST
     (CUSTOMER_NUMBER   DECIMAL(4),
     NAME               CHAR(15),
     ADDRESS            CHAR(25),
     CURRENT_BALANCE    DECIMAL(7,2),
     CREDIT_LIMIT       DECIMAL(4),
     SLSREP_NUMBER      DECIMAL(2))
```

Once this is done, we can use the same INSERT command that we encountered in example 32. Here, however, we use a SELECT command to indicate what is to be inserted into this new table. The exact formulation is:

```
INSERT INTO SMALLCUST
    SELECT *
    FROM CUSTOMER
    WHERE CREDIT_LIMIT <= 500
```

This section contained examples illustrating many features of the SQL language. It is not intended to represent an exhaustive list of all of the SQL features (exhausting, maybe, but not exhaustive). If you are at an installation in which you will be working with a version of SQL, you should, of course, consult the manual both for a complete list of features and for ways in which your version of SQL may differ from what has been presented here.

It should be clear from these examples that SQL is a very powerful language that allows comprehensive queries to be satisfied with brief formulations. The use of SQL is also very widespread. It is used with many relational DBMS's, on everything from the largest mainframe to the smallest microcomputer, and thus it is a good idea to gain familiarity with this language.

For other examples of SQL queries, see [1], [2], [6], [8], [10], and [11].

3.5   THE RELATIONAL ALGEBRA

Like the **relational calculus**, the **relational algebra** is a theoretical way of manipulating a relational database. In the relational algebra, there are operations that act on relations to produce new relations, just as the operations of + , –, etc., act on numbers to produce new numbers in the algebra with which you are familiar. Retrieving data from a relational database through the use of the relational algebra involves issuing relational algebra commands to operate on existing relations in order to form a new relation that contains the desired information. It may be that successive commands will be required to form intermediate relations before the final result is obtained, as some of the following examples demonstrate. As you will notice in these examples, each command ends with a clause that reads GIVING followed by a relation name. This clause is requesting that the result of the execution of the command is to be placed in a relation with the name we have specified.

The relational algebra is **relationally complete**; i.e., anything that can be accomplished using the relational calculus can also be accomplished using the relational algebra. In fact, many people use the relational algebra as an alternate standard for relational completeness. In this section, we will briefly consider the operations of the relational algebra and will give a few examples of their use.

I. SELECT

The SELECT command within the relational algebra takes a horizontal subset of a relation, i.e., it causes only certain rows to be included in the new relation. (It should not be confused with the SQL SELECT command, which actually includes the power to accomplish all of the relational algebra commands.) This SELECT causes a new table to be created, including rows of a single table that meet some specified criteria.

STATEMENT: List all information from the CUSTOMER relation concerning customer 256.

Relational algebra:

```
SELECT CUSTOMER WHERE CUSTOMER_NUMBER = 256
GIVING ANSWER
```

SQL:

```
SELECT * FROM CUSTOMER WHERE CUSTOMER_NUMBER = 256
```

STATEMENT: List all information from the CUSTOMER relation concerning those customers who have an $800 credit limit.

Relational algebra:

```
SELECT CUSTOMER WHERE CREDIT_LIMIT = 800 GIVING ANSWER
```

SQL:

```
SELECT * FROM CUSTOMER WHERE CREDIT_LIMIT = 800
```

2. PROJECT

The PROJECT command within the relational algebra takes a vertical subset of a relation, i.e., it causes only certain columns to be included in the new relation.

STATEMENT: List the number and name of all customers.

Relational algebra:

```
PROJECT CUSTOMER OVER (CUSTOMER_NUMBER, NAME)
GIVING ANSWER
```

SQL:

```
SELECT CUSTOMER_NUMBER, NAME FROM CUSTOMER
```

STATEMENT: List the number and name of all customers who have an $800 credit limit.

This is accomplished in a two-step process. We first use a SELECT command to create a new relation that contains only those customers with the appropriate credit limit. Then we project that relation to restrict the result to only the indicated columns.

Relational algebra:

```
SELECT CUSTOMER WHERE CREDIT_LIMIT = 800
GIVING TEMP
PROJECT TEMP OVER (CUSTOMER_NUMBER, NAME)
GIVING ANSWER
```

SQL:

```
SELECT CUSTOMER_NUMBER, NAME FROM CUSTOMER
     WHERE CREDIT_LIMIT = 800
```

3. JOIN

The JOIN operation is at the heart of the relational algebra. It is the command that allows us to pull together data from more than one relation. In the most usual form of the JOIN, we **join** two tables together, based on a common attribute. A new table is formed containing the columns of both the tables that have been joined. Rows in this new table will be the concatenation of a row from the first table and a row from the second that match on the common attribute (often called the JOIN column). For example, suppose we wish to JOIN the following tables on SLSREP_NUMBER (the join column), creating a new relation called TEMP:

	CUSTOMER_NUMBER	NAME	ADDRESS	SLSREP_NUMBER
CUSTOMER	124	SALLY ADAMS	481 OAK, LANSING, MI	3
	256	ANN SAMUELS	215 PETE, GRANT, MI	6
	311	DON CHARLES	48 COLLEGE, IRA, MI	12
	315	TOM DANIELS	914 CHERRY, KENT, MI	6
	405	AL WILLIAMS	519 WATSON, GRANT, MI	12
	412	SALLY ADAMS	16 ELM, LANSING, MI	3
	522	MARY NELSON	108 PINE, ADA, MI	12
	567	JOE BAKER	808 RIDGE, HARPER, MI	6
	587	JUDY ROBERTS	512 PINE, ADA, MI	6
	622	DAN MARTIN	419 CHIP, GRANT, MI	3
	701	ART PETERS	111 20TH, KENT, MI	5

and

	SLSREP_NUMBER	SLSREP_NAME
SLSREP	3	MARY JONES
	6	WILLIAM SMITH
	12	SAM BROWN
	15	JOAN LEWIS

The result of the join would be:

TEMP	CUSTOMER_NUMBER	NAME	ADDRESS	SLSREP_NUMBER	SLSREP_NAME
	124	SALLY ADAMS	481 OAK, LANSING, MI	3	MARY JONES
	256	ANN SAMUELS	215 PETE, GRANT, MI	6	WILLIAM SMITH
	311	DON CHARLES	48 COLLEGE, IRA, MI	12	SAM BROWN
	315	TOM DANIELS	914 CHERRY, KENT, MI	6	WILLIAM SMITH
	405	AL WILLIAMS	519 WATSON, GRANT, MI	12	SAM BROWN
	412	SALLY ADAMS	16 ELM, LANSING, MI	3	MARY JONES
	522	MARY NELSON	108 PINE, ADA, MI	12	SAM BROWN
	567	JOE BAKER	808 RIDGE, HARPER, MI	6	WILLIAM SMITH
	587	JUDY ROBERTS	512 PINE, ADA, MI	6	WILLIAM SMITH
	622	DAN MARTIN	419 CHIP, GRANT, MI	3	MARY JONES

Note that the column on which the tables are joined appears only once. Other than that, all columns from both tables are present in the result. Certain points need to be emphasized concerning this join operation:

a. If there is a row in one table that does not match any row in the other table, it will not appear in the result of the join. Thus, sales rep 15, JOAN LEWIS, and customer 701, ART PETERS, do not appear, since they do not match anything.

b. In this case, since sales rep number is the primary key, there cannot be two rows in the SLSREP relation on which there is the same sales rep number. Consequently, each customer will appear on one row at most in the new relation created by the join. If, however, for some reason the sales rep table were allowed to have multiple rows with the same sales rep number, each customer could appear several times. If the SLSREP relation also contained a row in which the sales rep number were 3 and the name were BOB JOHN-SON, the relation created would be:

TEMP	CUSTOMER_NUMBER	NAME	ADDRESS	SLSREP_NUMBER	SLSREP_NAME
	124	SALLY ADAMS	481 OAK, LANSING, MI	3	MARY JONES
	124	SALLY ADAMS	481 OAK, LANSING, MI	3	BOB JOHNSON
	256	ANN SAMUELS	215 PETE, GRANT, MI	6	WILLIAM SMITH
	311	DON CHARLES	48 COLLEGE, IRA, MI	12	SAM BROWN
	315	TOM DANIELS	914 CHERRY, KENT, MI	6	WILLIAM SMITH
	405	AL WILLIAMS	519 WATSON, GRANT, MI	12	SAM BROWN
	412	SALLY ADAMS	16 ELM, LANSING, MI	3	MARY JONES
	412	SALLY ADAMS	16 ELM, LANSING, MI	3	BOB JOHNSON
	522	MARY NELSON	108 PINE, ADA, MI	12	SAM BROWN
	567	JOE BAKER	808 RIDGE, HARPER, MI	6	WILLIAM SMITH
	587	JUDY ROBERTS	512 PINE, ADA, MI	6	WILLIAM SMITH
	622	DAN MARTIN	419 CHIP, GRANT, MI	3	MARY JONES
	622	DAN MARTIN	419 CHIP, GRANT, MI	3	BOB JOHNSON

The output from the join relation can be restricted to include only desired columns by using the project command, as the following example illustrates:

STATEMENT: List the number and name of all customers together with the number and name of the sales rep who represents each customer.

Relational algebra:

```
JOIN CUSTOMER SLSREP
    WHERE CUSTOMER.SLSREP_NUMBER =
        SLSREP.SLSREP_ NUMBER GIVING TEMP
PROJECT TEMP OVER (CUSTOMER_NUMBER, NAME,
        SLSREP_NUMBER,SLSREP_NAME) GIVING ANSWER
```

SQL:

```
SELECT CUSTOMER_NUMBER, NAME, SLSREP_NUMBER, SLSREP_NAME
    FROM CUSTOMER, SLSREP
    WHERE CUSTOMER.SLSREP_NUMBER =
        SLSREP.SLSREP_NUMBER
```

Although this is by far the most common kind of join, there are other possibilities worth mentioning. If we are distinguishing between different types of joins, the one described above is called the **natural join**. In this form of the join, the column on which the table was joined appeared only once. If we follow the same process but leave both copies of the join column in the table that is created, we have the **equijoin**. In the preceding example, an equijoin would have contained two SLSREP_NUMBER columns, one for the SLSREP_NUMBER from the CUS-TOMER relation and the other for the SLSREP_NUMBER from the SLSREP relation. If we join on a condition other than equality, we have the **theta-join**. For example, we could join each customer to any sales rep whose commission was more than 10 percent of the customer's balance. The final type of join, the **outer join** differs from the natural join only for rows in the original relations that do not match any row in the other relation. Recall that in the natural join these rows are eliminated. In the outer join they are maintained, and values of the columns from the other table are left vacant or **null**. In the case of the original example from this section, the outer join operation would give:

TEMP	CUSTOMER_ NUMBER	NAME	ADDRESS	SLSREP_ NUMBER	SLSREP_NAME
	124	SALLY ADAMS	481 OAK,LANSING,MI	3	MARY JONES
	256	ANN SAMUELS	215 PETE,GRANT,MI	6	WILLIAM SMITH
	311	DON CHARLES	48 COLLEGE,IRA,MI	12	SAM BROWN
	315	TOM DANIELS	914 CHERRY,KENT,MI	6	WILLIAM SMITH
	405	AL WILLIAMS	519 WATSON,GRANT,MI	12	SAM BROWN
	412	SALLY ADAMS	16 ELM,LANSING,MI	3	MARY JONES
	522	MARY NELSON	108 PINE,ADA,MI	12	SAM BROWN
	567	JOE BAKER	808 RIDGE,HARPER,MI	6	WILLIAM SMITH
	587	JUDY ROBERTS	512 PINE,ADA,MI	6	WILLIAM SMITH
	622	DAN MARTIN	419 CHIP,GRANT,MI	3	MARY JONES
	701	ART PETERS	111 20TH,KENT,MI	5	.
				15	JOAN LEWIS

4. UNION

The UNION operation is conceptually identical to the SQL union encountered earlier. As you might expect, the same requirement for **union compatibility** exists here.

STATEMENT: List all customers who either have orders or are represented by sales rep 12, or both.

We can form the list of all customers who have orders by projecting the ORDER relation over customer number. We can form the list of all customers represented by sales rep 12 by first selecting those rows in the CUSTOMER relation where the sales rep number is 12 and then projecting that result over the customer number. Finally, taking the union of these two intermediate results will satisfy the query. Since both of these relations consist only of a customer number, they are union-compatible; thus, forming the union is a legitimate operation.

Relational algebra:

```
PROJECT ORDER OVER (CUSTOMER_NUMBER) GIVING TEMP1
SELECT CUSTOMER WHERE SLSREP_NUMBER = 12 GIVING TEMP2
PROJECT TEMP2 OVER (CUSTOMER_NUMBER) GIVING TEMP3
UNION TEMP1 WITH TEMP3 GIVING ANSWER
```

SQL:

```
SELECT CUSTOMER_NUMBER
     FROM ORDER
UNION
SELECT CUSTOMER_NUMBER
     FROM CUSTOMER
     WHERE SLSREP_NUMBER = 12
```

5. INTERSECTION

STATEMENT: List all customers who have orders and are represented by sales rep 12.

This process is virtually identical to the one encountered in the UNION example. Here, however, at the end, we should INTERSECT the two tables, not take their union. The structure is thus:

Relational algebra:

```
PROJECT ORDER OVER (CUSTOMER_NUMBER) GIVING TEMP1
SELECT CUSTOMER WHERE SLSREP_NUMBER = 12 GIVING TEMP2
PROJECT TEMP2 OVER (CUSTOMER_NUMBER) GIVING TEMP3
INTERSECT TEMP1 WITH TEMP3 GIVING ANSWER
```

SQL:

```
SELECT CUSTOMER_NUMBER
     FROM ORDER
INTERSECT
SELECT CUSTOMER_NUMBER
     FROM CUSTOMER
     WHERE SLSREP_NUMBER = 12
```

6. DIFFERENCE

The difference operation, which is accomplished by the SQL MINUS, is performed by the SUBTRACT statement in the relational algebra.

STATEMENT: List all customers who have orders but are not represented by sales rep 12.

Relational algebra:

```
PROJECT ORDER OVER (CUSTOMER_NUMBER) GIVING TEMP1
SELECT CUSTOMER WHERE SLSREP_NUMBER = 12 GIVING TEMP2
PROJECT TEMP2 OVER (CUSTOMER_NUMBER) GIVING TEMP3
SUBTRACT TEMP3 FROM TEMP1 GIVING ANSWER
```

SQL:

```
SELECT CUSTOMER_NUMBER
     FROM ORDER
MINUS
SELECT CUSTOMER_NUMBER
     FROM CUSTOMER
     WHERE SLSREP_NUMBER = 12
```

The last two operations, PRODUCT and DIVISION, are not nearly as common as the others. They are mentioned here for the sake of completeness.

7. PRODUCT

The product of two relations (mathematically called the Cartesian product) is the relation obtained by concatenating every row in the first relation with every row in the second relation. Thus, the product of

ORDER	ORDER_NUMBER	DATE
	12489	90287
	12491	90287
	12494	90487

and

PART	PART_NUMBER	PART_DESCRIPTION
	BT04	STOVE
	BZ66	WASHER

would be

ANSWER	ORDER_NUMBER	DATE	PART_NUMBER	PART_DESCRIPTION
	12489	90287	BT04	STOVE
	12491	90287	BT04	STOVE
	12494	90487	BT04	STOVE
	12489	90287	BZ66	WASHER
	12491	90287	BZ66	WASHER
	12494	90487	BZ66	WASHER

Every row of ORDER is matched with every row of PART. If ORDER has m rows and PART has n rows, there would be $m \times n$ rows in the product. If, as is typically the case, the tables have a large number of rows, the number of rows in the product can be so great that it is not practical to form the product. Usually, we would only want combinations that satisfy certain restrictions and so we would virtually always use the join operation instead of product.

8. DIVISION

The division process is best illustrated by considering the division of a relation with two columns by a relation with a single column. As an example let us divide the relation

ORDER_LINE	ORDER_NUMBER	PART_NUMBER
	12489	AX12
	12491	BT04
	12491	BZ66
	12494	CB03
	12495	CX11
	12498	AZ52
	12498	BA74
	12500	BT04
	12504	CZ81

by the relation

PART	PART_NUMBER
	BZ66
	BT04

The quotient will be a new relation with a single column ORDER_NUMBER. The rows in this new relation will consist of those ORDER_NUMBERS from ORDER_LINE which are "matched" to *all* of the parts appearing in the PART relation. In this case that means that an order number will appear if there is a row in ORDER_LINE with this order number in the ORDER_NUMBER column and "BZ66" in the PART_NUMBER column and another row in ORDER_LINE with this same order number in the ORDER_NUMBER column and "BT04" in the PART_NUMBER column. It does not matter if there are other rows in ORDER_LINE containing the same order number as long as the rows with "BZ66" and "BT04" are present. With our sample data, only order 12491 qualifies, and thus the result would be

ANSWER

ORDER_NUMBER
12491

Before leaving the relational algebra, it is worth noting that of the eight operations listed, not all are necessary. The five operations SELECT, PROJECT, PRODUCT, UNION, and DIFFERENCE are the "primitive" operations; i.e., the other operations can be specified in terms of these five. To do a JOIN, for example, we could first take a PRODUCT, followed by a SELECT, followed by a PROJECT. The other three operations, especially the JOIN operation, are so useful in practice that they are usually included in any list of operations within the relational algebra.

For further discussion of the relational algebra, see [1], [2], [6], [8], and [10].

3.6 QBE

In this section, we will investigate an approach to manipulating relational databases that is very different from the approaches discussed earlier in this chapter. It is called **Query-By-Example** (or **QBE** for short) and was developed by M. M. Zloof at the IBM Yorktown Heights Research Laboratory (see [12] and [13]). It is intended for use on a visual display terminal. Not only are results displayed on the screen in tabular form, but users actually enter their requests by filling in portions of the displayed tables. Studies have shown (see [7]) that in regard to the time it takes to learn QBE, the time it takes to formulate a query using QBE, and the accuracy with which these queries are formulated, the figures for the use of QBE are as good as, if not better than, those obtained for other approaches.

In using QBE, we are first presented with a blank form on the screen:

We indicate which table we wish to manipulate by typing the name of the table in the first box:

ORDER				

At this point, we could fill in the column headings for those columns we wish to have included in our queries. If we wish to include all columns from the table, there is a shortcut. We merely type:

ORDER P.				

The **P.** stands for print. The system will respond with

ORDER	ORD #	ORD DATE	CUST #

It should be pointed out that we are abbreviating the column headings here in order to adjust the width of the examples so that they will easily fit on a book page. In actual implementations of QBE, if the requested data will not fit on the screen it is possible to scroll from right to left to view any piece of information.

In the following queries, we will give the QBE formulation but leave it to the reader to determine the results that the computer would produce. For the first few examples, assume that we have requested the part table with the following columns:

PART	PRT #	PRT DESC	UNONHND	I TM CLS	WRE HSE

Example 1: Retrieve certain columns and all rows.

STATEMENT: List the part number and description of all parts.

Using the same **P.** that we encountered earlier, we request all part numbers to be printed by putting a **P.** in the PRT # and PRT DESC columns:

PART	PRT #	PRT DESC	UNONHND	I TM CLS	WRE HSE
	P.	P.			

The system would then respond by filling in the part number and description columns for all parts currently on file. If there are more rows than will fit on the screen, which will probably be the case, they will be displayed one screen at a time. If desired, the **P.** can be followed with either **AO** (ascending order) or **DO** (descending order) so that the output will be sorted appropriately.

Example 2: Retrieve all columns and all rows.

STATEMENT: List the complete part table.

We could certainly put a **P.** in each column in the table to obtain the desired result. There is a simpler method, however, and that is to put a single **P.** in the first column:

PART	PRT #	PRT DESC	UNONHND	I TM CLS	WRE HSE
P.					

This indicates that we want the full table printed.

Example 3: Retrieval with a simple condition.

STATEMENT: List the part numbers of all parts in item class "HW".

We use the **P.** as before, to indicate the columns that are to be printed. We can also place a specific value in a column:

PART	PRT #	PRT DESC	UNONHND	I TM CLS	WRE HSE
	P.			HW	

This indicates that the part numbers to be printed should only be those for which the item class is "HW".

Example 4: Retrieval with a compound condition involving "AND".

STATEMENT: List the part numbers for all parts that are in item class "HW" and are located in warehouse 3.

As you might expect, we can put specific values in more than one column. Further, QBE also supports the normal comparison operators =, >, >=, <, <=, as well as ~ = (NOT EQUAL). It is common in QBE to omit the " = " symbol in "equal" and "not equal" comparisons, although it may be used if desired.

PART	PRT #	PRT DESC	UNONHND	I TM CLS	WRE HSE
	P.			HW	3

In this case, we are requesting those parts for which the item class is "HW" *and* the warehouse is 3.

Example 5: Retrieval with a compound condition involving "OR".

STATEMENT: List the part numbers for those parts that are in item class "HW" or warehouse 3.

What we essentially have in this query is two queries. We want all parts that are in class "HW". We also want all parts that are in warehouse 3. This is effectively how we enter our request, as two queries:

PART	PRT #	PRT DESC	UNONHND	I TM CLS	WRE HSE
	P.			HW	
	P.				3

The first row indicates that we want all parts that are in class "HW". The second row indicates that we also want all parts that are in warehouse 3.

Example 6: Retrieval using "NOT".

STATEMENT: List the part numbers of all parts that are not in item class "HW".

We use the symbol ~ for not and enter:

PART	PRT #	PRT DESC	UNONHND	I TM CLS	WRE HSE
	P.			~HW	

In each of the above examples, we could have used a feature of the QBE language from which it draws its name: an example. The queries above were simple enough, so there was no real need to use an example, but it would certainly have been legitimate to do so. To use an example, we pick a sample response that the computer could give to the query and actually enter it in the table. To indicate that it is merely an example, we underline it. Thus, in the previous query, we could have entered:

PART	PRT #	PRT DESC	UNONHND	I TM CLS	WRE HSE
	P.XYZ			~HW	

We are indicating that XYZ is an example of the response we are expecting. It does *not* have to be an actual response that would be generated in response to this query. In this case, in fact, there is not even a part XYZ in the database. Notice the difference between the part number XYZ and the item class HW. The part number is underlined, indicating that it is strictly an example. The item class is not, indicating that it is an actual value we are interested in.

The following queries will use tables:

ORDER	ORD #	ORD DATE	CUST #

and

CUSTOMER	CST #	NAME	BALANCE	CR L I M	SLSR #

Example 7: Retrieval using more than one table

STATEMENT: List the name and number of those customers who placed an order on 9/02/87.

This query cannot be satisfied using a single table. The customer name is in the customer table, whereas the order date is in the order table. We need the equivalent of a **join** operation. This is accomplished by having two tables on the screen and filling them in as follows:

CUSTOMER	CST #	NAME	BALANCE	CR L I M	SLSR #
	P.123	P.			

ORDER	ORD #	ORD DATE	CUST #
		90287	123

In this example, there is a **P.** in both the CUSTOMER_NUMBER and NAME columns of the CUSTOMER table, indicating that there are the columns in which results are to be printed. Further, there is an example, 123, in the CUSTOMER number column of the customer table as well as *the same* example in the CUSTOMER_NUMBER column of the ORDER table. These examples are necessary, and the fact that they are the same is crucial. This is what tells the system how the tables are to be joined. Finally, since the 90287 is not underlined, it is *not* an example but rather a specific restriction. In words, we are telling the system to:

PRINT the number and name of any customers in the CUSTOMER table for whom there is a row in the ORDER table where the customer number matches the customer number in the CUSTOMER table and the order date is 90287.

Example 8: Retrieval using more than one table with "NOT".

STATEMENT: List the name and number of those customers who did not place an order on 9/02/87.

This query, which is similar to the last one except for the negation, can be solved in virtually the same way. The only difference is that we include the not symbol (~) in the ORDER relation. The formulation would thus be:

CUSTOMER	CST #	NAME	BALANCE	CR L I M	SLSR #
	P.123	P.			

ORDER	ORD #	ORD DATE	CUST #
~		90287	123

In this example, we are telling the system to:

PRINT the number and name of any customers in the CUSTOMER table for whom there is *no* row in the ORDER table where the customer number matches the customer number in the CUSTOMER table and the order date is 90287.

Example 9: Joining a table to itself.

STATEMENT: Find the number and name of all the customers represented by the same sales rep who represents customer 256.

We could certainly satisfy this query in two stages using techniques that we have already encountered. We could first find the sales rep of customer 256 and then, when we have seen the answer, find all customers of that particular sales rep. The query could be satisfied, however, in a single operation, using the idea of joining tables together demonstrated in the previous example. The difference here is that we are only dealing with a single table. Applying those same ideas to the one table, CUSTOMER would yield:

CUSTOMER	CST #	NAME	BALANCE	CR LIM	SLSR #
	P.	P.			88
	256				88

In this example, we are asking the system to:

PRINT the number and name of any customers in the CUSTOMER table for whom there is a row in the customer table where the sales rep number matches the original sales rep number and the customer number is 256.

Example 10: Use of a condition box.

STATEMENT: Find the number and name of those customers who are represented by either sales rep 6 or sales rep 12 and who have a credit limit of either $500 or $800.

In this example, we introduce the condition box. Rather than enter conditions in the table itself, we can place them in a condition box. As might be expected, we then reference these conditions by example, as follows:

CUSTOMER	CST #	NAME	BALANCE	CR LIM	SLSR #
	P.	P.		C1	C2

```
CONDITIONS
C1 = (500 / 800)
C2 = (6 / 12)
```

By these conditions, we are requiring the credit limit to be either $500 or $800 *and* the sales rep number to be either 6 or 12.

How would you fill in the tables if the two individual conditions were to be connected with the word "OR"?

Answer:

CUSTOMER	CST #	NAME	BALANCE	CR LIM	SLSR #
	P.	P.		C1	
	P.	P.			C2

Example 11: Use of built-in functions.

STATEMENT: Find the number of customers who are represented by sales rep 6.

There is the usual collection of built-in functions in QBE. These are CNT.ALL. (count), SUM.ALL. (sum), AVG.ALL. (average), MAX.ALL. (maximum), and MIN.ALL. (minimum). Further, if duplicates are to be eliminated before the statistic is calculated, UNQ is specified as CNT.UNQ.ALL., SUM.UNQ.ALL., or AVG.UNQ.ALL.. If this is not specified, duplicates *will* be used in the calculation of the indicated statistic. In this example, uniqueness is guaranteed, since no customer appears more than once in the CUSTOMER table. We would thus enter:

CUSTOMER	CST #	NAME	BALANCE	CR LIM	SLSR #
	P.CNT.ALL.				6

Example 12: Additions.

STATEMENT: Add order 12520 (date – 90687, customer – 256) to the database.

Just as there is a command **P.** to print, there is a command **I.** to insert a new row. It is used as follows:

ORDER	ORD #	ORD DATE	CUST #
I.	12520	90687	256

Example 13: Single-record update.

STATEMENT: Change the credit limit of customer 256 to $1000.

There is a command, **U.**, for update. It is used as follows:

CUSTOMER	CST #	NAME	BALANCE	CR LIM	SLSR #
U.	256			1000	

Since CUSTOMER_NUMBER is the primary key, which cannot be updated in this kind of operation, it is used to identify the row to be changed. Thus, the credit limit of customer 256 will be changed to $1000 in the database.

Example 14: Multiple-record update.

STATEMENT: Change the credit limit of all customers who currently have a $300 limit to $350.

Using the **U.** command, we can request that several records be updated at once. This is done as follows:

CUSTOMER	CST #	NAME	BALANCE	CR LIM	SLSR #
	123			300	
U.	123			350	

We use 123 as an example of a customer number and include the restriction that the credit limit is $300. The second row says to update any customer who matches the restriction by changing his or her credit limit to $350.

Example 15: Multiple-record update.

STATEMENT: Add $50 to the credit limit of all customers of sales rep 12.

There are two differences between this example and example 13. The restriction involves a column other than the column to be changed; in addition, the change is not to a specific entry, but rather to a value that is computed from the old value. Neither of these differences poses any problem for QBE. The formulation would be:

CUSTOMER	CST #	NAME	BALANCE	CR LIM	SLSR #
	123			100	12
U.	123			100 + 50	

Note that the 100 is underlined, which emphasizes that it is an example, not a specific value. On the second row the *100* + 50 indicates that the old value, whatever it was, is to be increased by 50. The fact that the 12 is not underlined indicates that it is a restriction, i.e., the process of increasing the credit limit will be applied only to customers of sales rep 12.

Example 16: Single-record delete.

STATEMENT: Delete customer 256.

The command for delete in QBE is **D.** To delete a single customer we fill in the table as follows:

CUSTOMER	CST #	NAME	BALANCE	CR LIM	SLSR #
D.	256				

Example 17: Multiple-record delete.

STATEMENT: Delete all customers of sales rep 6.

The formulation here would be:

CUSTOMER	CST #	NAME	BALANCE	CR L IM	SLSR #
D.					6

All customers represented by sales rep 6 will be deleted. It goes without saying that multiple-record deletes (as well as multiple-record updates) are very risky and should either be avoided or used with extreme caution. In this query, for example, the slip of a finger when entering the sales rep number could cause a totally incorrect set of customers to be deleted.

As with SQL, the above examples are certainly not intended to be a complete treatment of QBE but rather are presented to give you the flavor of this very different and very important approach to manipulating relational databases. For further examples of QBE, see [1], [2], [6], [9], [10], and [11].

3.7   NATURAL LANGUAGES

Another approach to manipulating databases for the purpose of retrieval (querying databases) involves the use of so-called **natural languages**. Employing these languages, users type their queries as normal English questions or requests. These languages possess a built-in dictionary of words that they can interpret. Users can add words to this dictionary to tailor it to their particular application. In addition, these languages recognize names of relations and attributes in the database. Finally, they can recognize alternate names, or aliases, for relation and attribute names, e.g., account number may be another name for customer number.

These languages are discussed here since they represent an important way of retrieving data from a relational database. (Actually, they can be used with databases that follow other models, but, to reach their full potential, the flexibility of the relational model is crucial.) We will look at a few examples of querying a database using a fictitious (but representative) natural language called NL and, in each case, an SQL formulation for the same query will be presented.

STATEMENT: Find the name of customer 256.

NL:

USER: What is the nme of customer 256?

COMPUTER: I don't recognize "nme". Did you mean "name"?

USER: Yes.

COMPUTER: NAME
               ANN SAMUELS

SQL:

```
SELECT NAME
      FROM CUSTOMER
      WHERE CUSTOMER_NUMBER = 256
```

STATEMENT: Find the names of all of the customers of sales rep 6.

NL:

USER: Give me the names of the customers of sales rep 6.

COMPUTER: NAME
                 ANN SAMUELS
                 TOM DANIELS
                 JOE BAKER
                 JUDY ROBERTS

SQL:

```
SELECT NAME
      FROM CUSTOMER
      WHERE SLSREP_NUMBER = 6
```

STATEMENT: Of the names found in the previous query, which ones had a credit limit of $300?

NL:

USER: Which ones had a credit limit of 300?

COMPUTER: NAME
                 TOM DANIELS
                 JOE BAKER

SQL:

```
SELECT NAME
      FROM CUSTOMER
      WHERE SLSREP_NUMBER = 6
      AND CREDIT_LIMIT = 300
```

As a final note, if the user had defined in the dictionary a term "small customer" as a customer whose credit limit is $300, then that last query could have been formulated as "Which ones are small customers?"

For further information on natural languages, see [9] as well as chapter 13 of this text.

3.8 SUMMARY

In this chapter, we began the study of the relational model of data. A relational model database consists of a collection of relations. Relations are simply two-dimensional tables that are subject to some restrictions:

1. The entries in the table are single-valued.
2. Each column has a distinct name (called the attribute name).
3. Each column contains values about the same attribute (namely, the attribute identified by the column name).
4. The order of columns is immaterial.
5. Each row is distinct.
6. The order of rows is immaterial.

Each row is technically called a tuple and each column is called an attribute (although the terms table, row, and column are finding widespread use themselves). The permanent part of the relation, the actual structure of the relation, is called an intension of the relation.

Some critical relational model terms were discussed. The primary key of a relation is the attribute or collection of attributes that uniquely identifies a given tuple. A foreign key is an attribute in one relation that is required to match an attribute in another relation. A structure that satisfies all of the properties listed above for a relation except property one is called an unnormalized relation. One that satisfies all of the properties is sometimes called a normalized relation.

Next, the relational model implementation of the various types of relationships (one-to-one, one-to-many, and many-to-many) was discussed. In the most common approach to the one-to-one relationship, the key of each table is an attribute in the other table. In implementing a one-to-many relationship, the key of the "one" table is an attribute (specifically a foreign key) in the "many" table, but not vice versa. In implementing a many-to-many relationship, a third table is constructed whose key is the concatenation of the keys of the original tables.

Finally, a variety of approaches to the manipulation of relational databases were discussed. The relational calculus, a form of manipulation based on the predicate calculus of mathematical logic, was discussed only briefly. It is of theoretical importance as a standard by which other approaches are judged. That is, a language is relationally complete if it is as "powerful" as the relational calculus. The language SQL, Structured Query Language, is perhaps the most important approach of all because of its widespread use. It is an example of a transform-oriented language, one which uses relations to transform inputs into desired outputs. Many features of this very important language were illustrated through examples. The relational algebra, an approach in which operations act on relations to produce new relations, and QBE (Query-by-Example), a language in which users visually fill in forms on the screen to manipulate the data in the database, were also discussed.

Finally, some brief examples of querying databases with English-like languages were presented.

REVIEW QUESTIONS

1. Define relation.
2. Define domain.
3. Define primary key and foreign key. What is the difference between the two?
4. What is the difference between a normalized and an unnormalized relation? How can an unnormalized relation be converted to an equivalent normalized relation?
5. Give two ways in which a one-to-one relationship may be implemented using relations.
6. How can a one-to-many relationship be implemented using relations?
7. How can a many-to-many relationship be implemented using relations?
8. Define union-compatible. Which of the relational algebra commands require union-compatibility? Why?
9. Describe four different types of joins. What are the differences between them? Where might each be used?

EXERCISES

Questions 1 through 23 are based on the sample database of Figure 3.1 and deal with the language SQL. For each question, give both the appropriate SQL formulation and the result that would be produced.

1. Find the part number and description of all parts.
2. List the complete sales rep table.
3. Find the names of all the customers who have a credit limit of at least $800.
4. Give the order numbers of those orders placed by customer 124 on 9/05/87.
5. Give the part number, description, and on-hand value (units on hand * price) for each part in item class "AP". (On-hand value is really units on hand * cost but we do not have a cost column in the PART table.)
6. Find the number and name of all customers whose last name is "NELSON".
7. List all details about parts. The output should be sorted by part number within item class.
8. Find out how many customers have a balance that exceeds their credit limit.
9. Find the total of the balances for all the customers represented by sales rep 12.
10. Find the number and name of all sales reps who represent at least one customer with a credit limit of $1000. Do this in two different ways: in one solution use a subquery; in the other, do not use a subquery.
11. List the totals of the balances for the customers of each sales rep. In a second query, list only the totals of the balances for sales reps with at least three customers.
12. List the number, name, and balance of each customer together with the number, name, and commission rate of each customer's sales rep.

13. List the number and name of all sales reps who represent at least one customer who lives in "LANSING". List the number and name of all sales reps who do *not* represent any customers who live in "LANSING".

14. Find the customer number and name of those customers who currently have an order on file for an "IRON".

15. List the number and name of those sales reps together with the number and name of any of their customers who have at least two orders on file.

16. List the number and description of those parts that are currently on order. (Make sure each part is listed only once.) In a second query, count the number of parts that are currently on order.

17. List the number, description, and item class of any pairs of parts that are in the same item class.

18. List the number and description of all parts that are currently on order by any customer who is represented by the sales rep whose name is "WILLIAM SMITH".

19. Change the description of part "BT04" to "OVEN".

20. Add $100 to the credit limit of all customers represented by sales rep 6.

21. Add order 12600 (date — 90687, customer — 311) to the database.

22. Delete all customers whose balance is 0 and who are represented by sales rep 12.

23. Describe a new relation to the database called "SPGOOD". It contains only part number, description, and price. Once this has been done, insert the part number description and price of all parts whose item class is "SG" into this new relation.

24. ***** COMPUTER PROJECT *******

    If you have access to a relational database management system, do each of the following:

    a. Create each of the five tables shown in Figure 3.1.

    b. Enter the sample data from Figure 3.1 into your database. For SLSREP, ORDER, ORDER_LINE, and PART use whatever default type of features are included in your system for entering the data. If your system allows you to design your own forms, use this feature to enter the data for the CUSTOMER table. Finally, determine whether it is possible in your system to ensure, first, that a customer will not be added if the corresponding sales rep does not exist and, second, that a customer will not be deleted if he or she has any orders currently on file. Use whatever features of your system that you need in order to accomplish this. (It may very well mean writing a program in some appropriate language.)

    c. Actually do each of the queries in problems 1 through 23. Point out how the formulation in your system differs from the answers you gave earlier. If any of these queries cannot be satisfied in your system, explain why.

Questions 25 through 31 are also based on the sample database of Figure 3.1 but deal with the relational algebra. For each question, give both the appropriate relational algebra formulation and an equivalent SQL formulation.

25. List all information from the part relation concerning part "BT04".

26. List the number and name of all sales reps.

27. List the order number, order date, customer number, and customer name for each order.

28. List the order number, order date, customer number, and customer name for each order placed by any customer represented by MARY JONES.

29. List all orders that were either placed on 90287 or placed by a customer with a $1000 credit limit.
30. List all orders that were placed on 90287 by a customer with a $1000 credit limit.
31. List all orders that were placed on 90287 but not by a customer with a $1000 credit limit.

Questions 32 through 45 are also based on the sample database of Figure 3.1 but deal with QBE. For each question, give the appropriate QBE formulation.

32. List the number and name of all sales reps.
33. List the complete CUSTOMER table.
34. List the number and name of all customers represented by sales rep 3 whose balance is at least $500.
35. List the number and name of all customers who are either represented by sales rep 3 or whose balance is at least $500.
36. List the number and name of all customers who do not have a credit limit of $1000.
37. List the number and name of all customers who are represented by MARY JONES.
38. List the number and name of all customers who are not represented by MARY JONES.
39. Find the number and name of all customers who have the same credit limit as ANN SAMUELS.
40. Find the number and description of all parts that are in either item class "HW" or "SG" and also are located in either warehouse 2 or 3. (Use a condition box.)
41. Find the total number of units on hand in warehouse 3.
42. Add sales rep 11 (name — JOAN THOMAS, address — 10 MAPLE, GRANT, MI, commission — 0, commission rate — 7 percent) to the database.
43. Change the description of part "BT04" to "OVEN".
44. Add 10 percent to the price of all parts that are in item class "HW".
45. Delete all parts that are in item class "SG".

REFERENCES

1] Bradley, James. *Introduction to Data Base Management in Business*. Holt, Rinehart & Winston, 1983.

2] Cardenas, Alfonso F. *Data Base Management Systems*, 2d ed. Allyn & Bacon, 1984.

3] Codd, E. F. "A Relational Model of Data for Large Shared Databanks." *Communications of the ACM* 13, no. 6 (June 1970).

4] Codd, E. F. "Relational Completeness of Data Base Sublanguages." In *Data Base Systems*, Courant Computer Science Symposia Series, vol. 6. Prentice-Hall, 1972.

5] Codd, E. F. "A Data Base Sublanguage Founded on the Relational Calculus." Proceedings of the ACM SIGFIDET Workshop on Data Description, Access and Control, 1971.

6] Date, C. J. *Introduction to Database Systems, Volume I*, 4th ed. Addison-Wesley, 1986.

7] Greenblatt, D., and Waxman, J. "A study of Three Database Query Languages" in *Databases: Improving Usability and Responsiveness*, ed. B. Schneideman. Academic Press, 1978.

8] Kroenke, David. *Database Processing*, 2d ed. SRA, 1983.

9] Martin, James. *Managing the Database Environment*. Prentice-Hall, 1983.

10] McFadden, Fred R., and Hoffer, Jeffrey A. *Data Base Management*. Benjamin Cummings, 1985.

11] Ullman, Jeffrey D. *Principles of Database Systems*, 2d ed. Computer Science Press. Prentice-Hall, 1982.

12] Zloof, M. M. "Query By Example." Proceedings of the NCC 44, May 1975.

13] Zloof, M. M. "Design Aspects of the Query-by-Example Data Base Management Language." in *Databases: Improving Usability and Responsiveness*, ed. B. Schneideman. Academic Press, 1978.

RELATIONAL MODEL II FUNCTIONAL DEPENDENCE, KEYS, AND NORMALIZATION

INTRODUCTION

In chapter 3, we discussed the basic relational model, its structure, and the various ways of manipulating data within a relational database. In this chapter, we discuss the **normalization** process and its underlying concepts and features. Normalization enables us to analyze the design of a relational database to see whether it is bad; that is, normalization gives us a method for identifying the existence of potential problems, called **update anomalies**, in the design. The normalization process also supplies methods for correcting these problems.

The process involves various types of **normal forms**. **First normal form** (1NF), **second normal form** (2NF), and **third normal form** (3NF) are three of these types. It is these three that will be of the greatest use to us during database design. They form a progression in which a relation that is in 1NF is better than a relation that is not in 1NF; a relation that is in 2NF is better yet; and so on. The goal of this process is to allow us to start with a relation or collection of relations and produce a new collection of relations that is equivalent to the original collection (i.e., that represents the same information) but is free of problems. For practical purposes, this means that relations in the new collection will be at least in 3NF.

There are two crucial concepts that are fundamental to the understanding of the normalization process: functional dependence, which is discussed in section 4.2, and keys, which are discussed in section 4.3. The discussion of first, second, and third normal form takes place in section 4.4. Fourth normal form is covered in section 4.5. In section 4.6, higher normal forms are examined briefly. Finally, the application of normalization to database design is discussed in section 4.7.

Most of the examples in this chapter use data from the Premiere Products example (see Figure 4.1 on the following page).

SLSREP

SLSREP_NUMBER	SLSREP_NAME	SLSREP_ADDRESS	TOTAL_COMMISSION	COMMISSION_RATE
3.	MARY JONES	123 MAIN,GRANT,MI	2150.00	.05
6	WILLIAM SMITH	102 RAYMOND,ADA,MI	4912.50	.07
12	SAM BROWN	419 HARPER.LANSING,MI	2150.00	.05

CUSTOMER

CUSTOMER_NUMBER	NAME	ADDRESS	CURRENT_BALANCE	CREDIT_LIMIT	SLSREP_NUMBER
124	SALLY ADAMS	481 OAK,LANSING,MI	418.75	500	3
256	ANN SAMUELS	215 PETE,GRANT,MI	10.75	800	6
311	DON CHARLES	48 COLLEGE,IRA,MI	200.10	300	12
315	TOM DANIELS	914 CHERRY,KENT,MI	320.75	300	6
405	AL WILLIAMS	519 WATSON,GRANT,MI	201.75	800	12
412	SALLY ADAMS	16 ELM,LANSING,MI	908.75	1000	3
522	MARY NELSON	108 PINE,ADA,MI	49.50	800	12
567	JOE BAKER	808 RIDGE,HARPER,MI	201.20	300	6
587	JUDY ROBERTS	512 PINE,ADA,MI	57.75	500	6
622	DAN MARTIN	419 CHIP,GRANT,MI	575.50	500	3

ORDER

ORDER_NUMBER	DATE	CUSTOMER_NUMBER
12489	90287	124
12491	90287	311
12494	90487	315
12495	90487	256
12498	90587	522
12500	90587	124
12504	90587	522

ORDER_LINE

ORDER_NUMBER	PART_NUMBER	NUMBER_ORDERED	QUOTED_PRICE
12489	AX12	11	14.95
12491	BT04	1	402.99
12491	BZ66	1	311.95
12494	CB03	4	175.00
12495	CX11	2	57.95
12498	AZ52	2	22.95
12498	BA74	4	4.95
12500	BT04	1	402.99
12504	CZ81	2	108.99

PART

PART_NUMBER	PART_DESCRIPTION	UNITS_ON_HAND	ITEM_CLASS	WAREHOUSE_NUMBER	UNIT_PRICE
AX12	IRON	104	HW	3	17.95
AZ52	SKATES	20	SG	2	24.95
BA74	BASEBALL	40	SG	1	4.95
BH22	TOASTER	95	HW	3	34.95
BT04	STOVE	11	AP	2	402.99
BZ66	WASHER	52	AP	3	311.95
CA14	SKILLET	2	HW	3	19.95
CB03	BIKE	44	SG	1	187.50
CX11	MIXER	112	HW	3	57.95
CZ81	WEIGHTS	208	SG	2	108.99

FIGURE 4.1
Premiere Products
sample data

4.2 FUNCTIONAL DEPENDENCE

Since most of the update anomalies possessed by relations are caused by inappropriate functional dependencies, we must discuss this concept before examining the normalization process.

Def: An attribute, B, is **functionally dependent** on another attribute, A (or possibly a collection of attributes), if a value for A determines a single value for B at any one time.

We can think of this as follows. If we are given a value for A, do we know that we will be able to find a single value for B? If so, B is functionally dependent on A (often written as A → B). If B is functionally dependent on A, we also say that A **functionally determines** B.

For example, in the CUSTOMER relation, is the NAME functionally dependent on CUSTOMER_NUMBER? The answer is yes. If we are given customer number 124, we would find the *single* name SALLY ADAMS associated with it.

In the same CUSTOMER relation, is ADDRESS functionally dependent on NAME? Here the answer is no since, given the name SALLY ADAMS, we would not be able to find a single address. (However, if the organization had a policy that would not allow two or more customers with the same name, then the answer would be yes.)

In the FACULTY relation at Marvel College, is DEPARTMENT_NUMBER (the number of the department in which a faculty member works) functionally dependent on FACULTY_NUMBER? Given a faculty number, say 123, do we know that we can find a single department number? The answer is yes, since college policy requires that each faculty member must be assigned to a single department. If joint appointments were allowed, the answer would be no.

In the relation ORDER_LINE, is the NUMBER_ORDERED functionally dependent on ORDER_NUMBER? No. ORDER_NUMBER does not give enough information. Is it functionally dependent on PART_NUMBER? No. Again, not enough information is given. In reality, NUMBERED_ORDERED is functionally dependent on the **concatenation** (combination) of ORDER_NUMBER and PART_NUMBER.

At this point, a question naturally arises: How do we determine functional dependencies? Can we determine them by looking at sample data, for example? The answer is no.

Consider Figure 4.2, in which customer names happen to be unique. It is very tempting to say that NAME functionally determines ADDRESS (or equivalently that ADDRESS is functionally dependent on NAME). After all, given the name of a customer, we can find the single address. But what happens when customer 412,

FIGURE 4.2
CUSTOMER relation

CUSTOMER

CUSTOMER_ NUMBER	NAME	ADDRESS	CURRENT_ BALANCE	CREDIT_ LIMIT	SLSREP_ NUMBER
124	SALLY ADAMS	481 OAK,LANSING,MI	418.75	500	3
256	ANN SAMUELS	215 PETE,GRANT,MI	10.75	800	6
311	DON CHARLES	48 COLLEGE,IRA,MI	200.10	300	12
315	TOM DANIELS	914 CHERRY,KENT,MI	320.75	300	6
405	AL WILLIAMS	519 WATSON,GRANT,MI	201.75	800	12
522	MARY NELSON	108 PINE,ADA,MI	49.50	800	12
567	JOE BAKER	808 RIDGE,HARPER,MI	201.20	300	6
587	JUDY ROBERTS	512 PINE,ADA,MI	57.75	500	6
622	DAN MARTIN	419 CHIP,GRANT,MI	575.50	500	3

whose name also happens to be SALLY ADAMS, is added to the database? We then
have the situation exhibited in Figure 4.3.

CUSTOMER

CUSTOMER_ NUMBER	NAME	ADDRESS	CURRENT_ BALANCE	CREDIT_ LIMIT	SLSREP_ NUMBER
124	SALLY ADAMS	481 OAK,LANSING,MI	418.75	500	3
256	ANN SAMUELS	215 PETE,GRANT,MI	10.75	800	6
311	DON CHARLES	48 COLLEGE,IRA,MI	200.10	300	12
315	TOM DANIELS	914 CHERRY,KENT,MI	320.75	300	6
405	AL WILLIAMS	519 WATSON,GRANT,MI	201.75	800	12
412	SALLY ADAMS	16 ELM,LANSING,MI	908.75	1000	3
522	MARY NELSON	108 PINE,ADA,MI	49.50	800	12
567	JOE BAKER	808 RIDGE,HARPER,MI	201.20	300	6
587	JUDY ROBERTS	512 PINE,ADA,MI	57.75	500	6
622	DAN MARTIN	419 CHIP,GRANT,MI	575.50	500	3

FIGURE 4.3
CUSTOMER relation
with second
SALLY ADAMS

If the name we are given is SALLY ADAMS, we can no longer find a single
address. Thus we were misled by our original sample data. The only way to really
determine the functional dependencies that exist is to examine the user's policies.

4.3. KEYS

A second underlying concept of the normalization process is that of the primary key. It builds on functional dependence, and it completes the background
required for an understanding of the normal forms.

> *Def:* Attribute A (or a collection of attributes) is the **primary key** for a
> relation, R, if
> 1. *All* attributes in R are functionally dependent on A.
> 2. No subcollection of the attributes in A (assuming A is a collection of
>   attributes and not just a single attribute) also has property 1.

For example, is NAME the primary key for the CUSTOMER relation? No, since
the other attributes are not functionally dependent on name. (Note that the answer
would be different in an organization that had a policy enforcing uniqueness of
customer names.)

Is CUSTOMER_NUMBER the primary key for the CUSTOMER relation? Yes,
since all attributes in the CUSTOMER relation are functionally dependent on
CUSTOMER_NUMBER.

Is ORDER_NUMBER the primary key for the ORDER_LINE relation? No,
since it does not uniquely determine NUMBER_ORDERED or QUOTED_PRICE.

Is the combination of the ORDER_NUMBER and the PART_NUMBER the primary key for the ORDER_LINE relation? Yes, since all attributes can be determined by this combination, and nothing less will do.

Is the combination of the PART_NUMBER and the PART_DESCRIPTION the
primary key for the PART relation? No. Though it is true that all attributes of the
PART relation can be determined by this combination, something less, namely, the

PART_NUMBER alone, also has this property.

Occasionally (but not often) there might be more than one possibility for the primary key. For example, in an EMPLOYEE relation either the EMPLOYEE_NUMBER or the SOCIAL_SECURITY_NUMBER could serve as the key. In this case one of these is designated as the primary key. The other is referred to as a **candidate key**. A candidate key is a collection of attributes that has the same properties presented in the definition of the primary key but which has not been chosen to function in that way. (Technically, the definition given for primary key really defines candidate key. From all of the candidate keys one is chosen to be the primary key.)

The primary key is frequently called simply the *key* in other studies on database management and the relational model. We will continue to use the term primary key in order to clearly distinguish among the several different concepts of a key that we will encounter.

.4 FIRST, SECOND, AND THIRD NORMAL FORMS

The first three of the normal forms were defined by Codd in 1972 (see [3]). Subsequently, it was discovered that in some situations the definition of third normal form was inadequate. A revised, and stronger, definition was given by Boyce and Codd in 1974 (see [4]). It is this new definition of third normal form (sometimes called **Boyce-Codd normal form**) that we shall examine later in this section.

FIRST NORMAL FORM

A relation that contains a repeating group is called an **unnormalized relation** (Technically, it is not a relation at all.) Removal of repeating groups is the starting point in our quest for relations that are as free of problems as possible. Relations without repeating groups are said to be in first normal form.

> *Def:* A relation is in **first normal form** (1NF) if it does not contain repeating groups.

As an example, consider the following ORDER relation, in which there is a repeating group consisting of PART_NUMBER and NUMBER_ORDERED. As the example shows, there is one row per order with PART_NUMBER, NUMBER_ORDERED repeated as many times as is necessary.

ORDER (ORDER_NUMBER, DATE, PART_NUMBER, NUMBER_ORDERED)

This notation indicates a relation called ORDER, consisting of a primary key, ORDER_NUMBER, an attribute, DATE, and a repeating group containing two attributes, PART_NUMBER and NUMBER_ORDERED.) Figure 4.4 shows a sample extension of this relation.

ORDER

ORDER_NUMBER	DATE	PART_NUMBER	NUMBER_ORDERED
12489	90287	AX12	11
12491	90287	BT04 BZ66	1 1
12494	90487	CB03	4
12495	90487	CX11	2
12498	90587	AZ52 BA74	2 4
12500	90587	BT04	1
12504	90587	CZ81	2

FIGURE 4.4
Sample unnormalized relation

To convert this relation to 1NF, the repeating group is removed, giving the following:

ORDER(<u>ORDER_NUMBER</u>, DATE, <u>PART_NUMBER</u>, NUMBER_ORDERED)

The corresponding extension of the new relation is shown in Figure 4.5.

ORDER

ORDER_NUMBER	DATE	PART_NUMBER	NUMBER_ORDERED
12489	90287	AX12	11
12491	90287	BT04	1
12491	90287	BZ66	1
12494	90487	CB03	4
12495	90487	CX11	2
12498	90587	AZ52	2
12498	90587	BA74	4
12500	90587	BT04	1
12504	90587	CZ81	2

FIGURE 4.5
Result of normalization (conversion to 1NF)

Note that the second row of the unnormalized relation indicates that part BZ66 and part BT04 are both present for order 12491. In the normalized relation, this information is represented by *two* rows, the second and third. The primary key to the unnormalized ORDER relation was the ORDER_NUMBER alone. The primary key to the normalized relation is now the combination of ORDER_NUMBER and PART_NUMBER. In general it will be true that the primary key will expand in converting a non-1NF relation to 1NF. It will typically include the original primary key concatenated with the key to the repeating group; i.e., the attribute that distinguishes one occurrence of the repeating group from another within a given row in the relation. In this case, PART_NUMBER is the key to the repeating group and thus becomes part of the primary key of the 1NF relation.

SECOND NORMAL FORM

Even though a relation is in 1NF, problems may exist within the relation that will cause us to want to restructure it. Consider the relation:

```
ORDER(ORDER_NUMBER, DATE, PART_NUMBER, PART_DESCRIPTION,
      NUMBER_ORDERED, QUOTED_PRICE)
```

with the functional dependencies

```
ORDER_NUMBER → DATE
PART_NUMBER → PART_DESCRIPTION
ORDER_NUMBER, PART_NUMBER → NUMBER_ORDERED, QUOTED_
      PRICE
```

Thus ORDER_NUMBER determines DATE, PART_NUMBER determines PART_DESCRIPTION, and the concatenation of ORDER_NUMBER and PART_NUMBER determines NUMBER_ORDERED and QUOTED_PRICE. Consider the extension of this relation, as shown in Figure 4.6.

FIGURE 4.6
Sample ORDER relation

ORDER	ORDER_NUMBER	DATE	PART_NUMBER	PART_DESCRIPTION	NUMBER_ORDERED	QUOTED_PRICE
	12489	90287	AX12	IRON	11	14.95
	12491	90287	BT04	STOVE	1	402.99
	12491	90287	BZ66	WASHER	1	311.95
	12494	90487	CB03	BIKE	4	175.00
	12495	90487	CX11	MIXER	2	57.95
	12498	90587	AZ52	SKATES	2	22.95
	12498	90587	BA74	BASEBALL	4	4.95
	12500	90587	BT04	STOVE	1	402.99
	12504	90587	CZ81	WEIGHTS	2	108.99

As you can see in the example, the description of a specific part, BT04 for example, occurs several times in the table. This redundancy causes several problems. It is certainly wasteful of space, but that in itself is not nearly as serious as some of the other problems. These other problems are called **update anomalies** and they fall into four categories:

1. UPDATE

   A change to the description of part BT04 requires not one change but several — we have to change each row in which BT04 appears. This certainly makes the update process much more cumbersome; it is more complicated logically and takes more time to update.

2. INCONSISTENT DATA

There is nothing about the design that would prohibit part BT04 from having two different descriptions in the database. In fact, if it occurs in twenty rows, it could conceivably have twenty *different* descriptions in the database!!!

3. ADDITIONS

We have a real problem when we try to add a new part and its description to the database. Since the primary key for the table consists of *both* ORDER_NUMBER *and* PART_NUMBER, we need values for both of these in order to add a new row. If we have a part to add but there are as yet no orders for it, what do we use for an ORDER_NUMBER? Our only solution would be to make up a dummy order number and then replace it with a real ORDER_NUMBER once an order for this part had actually been received. Certainly this is not an acceptable solution.

4. DELETIONS

In the example above, if we delete order 12489 from the database, we also *lose* the fact that part AX12 is called IRON.

The above problems occur because we have an attribute, PART_DESCRIPTION, that is dependent on only a portion of the primary key, PART_NUMBER, and *not* on the complete primary key. This leads to the definition of second normal form. Second normal form represents an improvement over first normal form since it eliminates these update anomalies in these situations. First, we need to define nonkey attribute.

Def: An attribute is a **nonkey attribute** if it is not a part of the primary key.

We can now provide a definition for second normal form.

Def: A relation is in **second normal form** (2NF) if it is in first normal form and no nonkey attribute is dependent on only a portion of the primary key.

For another perspective on 2NF, consider Figure 4.7. This type of diagram, sometimes called a **dependency diagram** indicates all of the functional dependen-

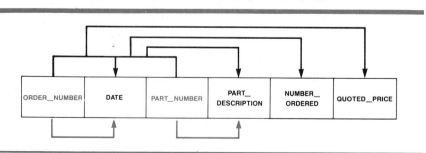

FIGURE 4.7
Dependencies in
ORDER relation

cies present in the ORDER relation through arrows. The arrows above the boxes indicate the normal dependencies that should be present; i.e., the primary key functionally determines all other attributes. (In this case, the concatenation of ORDER_NUMBER and PART_NUMBER determines all other attributes.) It is the arrows below the boxes that prevent the relation from being in 2NF. These arrows represent what is often termed **partial dependencies** which are dependencies on something less than the key. In fact, an alternative definition for 2NF is that a relation is in 2NF if it is in 1NF but contains no partial dependencies.

Either way we view 2NF, we can now name the fundamental problem with the ORDER relation: it is *not* in 2NF. While it may be pleasing to have a name for the problem, what we really need, of course, is a method to *correct* it. Such a method follows.

First, for each subset of the set of attributes that make up the primary key, begin a relation with this subset as its primary key. For the ORDER relation, this would give:

```
(ORDER_NUMBER,
(PART_NUMBER,
(ORDER_NUMBER, PART_NUMBER,
```

Next, place each of the other attributes with the appropriate primary key; that is, place each one with the minimal collection on which it depends. For the ORDER relation this would yield:

```
(ORDER_NUMBER, DATE)
(PART_NUMBER, PART_DESCRIPTION)
(ORDER_NUMBER, PART_NUMBER, NUMBER_ORDERED,
     QUOTED_PRICE)
```

Each of these relations can now be given a name that is descriptive of the meaning of the relation, such as ORDER, PART, or ORDER_LINE, for example. Figure 4.8 on the following page shows the extensions of the relations involved.

Note that the update anomalies have been eliminated. A description appears only once, so we do not have the redundancy that we did in the earlier design. Changing the description of part BT04 to OVEN is now a simple process involving a single change. Since the description for a part occurs in one single place, it is not possible to have multiple descriptions for a single part in the database at the same time. To add a new part and its description, we create a new row in the PART relation and thus there is no need to have an order exist for that part. Also, deleting order 12489 does not cause part number AX12 to be deleted from the PART relation, and thus we still have its description (IRON) in the database. Finally, we have not lost any information in the process. The data in the original design can be reconstructed from the data in the new design.

ORDER

ORDER_NUMBER	DATE	PART_NUMBER	PART_DESCRIPTION	NUMBER_ORDERED	QUOTED_PRICE
12489	90287	AX12	IRON	11	14.95
12491	90287	BT04	STOVE	1	402.99
12491	90287	BZ66	WASHER	1	311.95
12494	90487	CB03	BIKE	4	175.00
12495	90487	CX11	MIXER	2	57.95
12498	90587	AZ52	SKATES	2	22.95
12498	90587	BA74	BASEBALL	4	4.95
12500	90587	BT04	STOVE	1	402.99
12504	90587	CZ81	WEIGHTS	2	108.99

is replaced by

ORDER

ORDER_NUMBER	DATE
12489	90287
12491	90287
12494	90487
12495	90487
12498	90587
12500	90587
12504	90587

PART

PART_NUMBER	PART_DESCRIPTION
AX12	IRON
AZ52	SKATES
BA74	BASEBALL
BH22	TOASTER
BT04	STOVE
BZ66	WASHER
CA14	SKILLET
CB03	BIKE
CX11	MIXER
CZ81	WEIGHTS

ORDER_LINE

ORDER_NUMBER	PART_NUMBER	NUMBER_ORDERED	QUOTED_PRICE
12489	AX12	11	14.95
12491	BT04	1	402.99
12491	BZ66	1	311.95
12494	CB03	4	175.00
12495	CX11	2	57.95
12498	AZ52	2	22.95
12498	BA74	4	4.95
12500	BT04	1	402.99
12504	CZ81	2	108.99

THIRD NORMAL FORM

FIGURE 4.8
Conversion to 2NF

Problems can still exist with relations that are in 2NF. Consider the following CUSTOMER relation:

CUSTOMER (CUSTOMER_NUMBER, NAME, ADDRESS, SLSREP_
        NUMBER, SLSREP_NAME)

with the functional dependencies:

CUSTOMER_NUMBER → NAME, ADDRESS, SLSREP_
        NUMBER, SLSREP_NAME
SLSREP_NUMBER → SLSREP_NAME

(CUSTOMER_NUMBER determines all of the other attributes. In addition SLSREP_NUMBER determines SLSREP_NAME.)

As the extension of this relation, shown in Figure 4.9 on the opposite page, demonstrates, this relation possesses problems similar to those encountered earlier, even though it is in second normal form. (Any 1NF relation whose key consists of a single attribute is by default in 2NF. There can be no field dependent only on a portion of the key in this circumstance.) In this case it is the name of a sales rep

FIGURE 4.9
Sample CUSTOMER
relation

CUSTOMER	CUSTOMER_ NUMBER	NAME	ADDRESS	SLSREP_ NUMBER	SLSREP_NAME
	124	SALLY ADAMS	481 OAK, LANSING, MI	3	MARY JONES
	256	ANN SAMUELS	215 PETE, GRANT, MI	6	WILLIAM SMITH
	311	DON CHARLES	48 COLLEGE, IRA, MI	12	SAM BROWN
	315	TOM DANIELS	914 CHERRY, KENT, MI	6	WILLIAM SMITH
	405	AL WILLIAMS	519 WATSON, GRANT, MI	12	SAM BROWN
	412	SALLY ADAMS	16 ELM, LANSING, MI	3	MARY JONES
	522	MARY NELSON	108 PINE, ADA, MI	12	SAM BROWN
	567	JOE BAKER	808 RIDGE, HARPER, MI	6	WILLIAM SMITH
	587	JUDY ROBERTS	512 PINE, ADA, MI	6	WILLIAM SMITH
	622	DAN MARTIN	419 CHIP, GRANT, MI	3	MARY JONES

that can occur many times in the table; see sales rep 12 (SAM BROWN), for example. This redundancy results in the same exact set of problems that was described in the previous ORDER relation. In addition to the problem of wasted space, we have similar update anomalies, as follows:

1. UPDATE

   A change to the name of a sales rep requires not one change but several. Again the update process becomes very cumbersome.

2. INCONSISTENT DATA

   There is nothing about the design that would prohibit a sales rep from having two different names in the database. In fact, if the same sales rep represents twenty different customers (and thus would be found on twenty different rows), he or she could have twenty different names in the database!!!

3. ADDITIONS

   In order to add sales rep 47, whose name is MARY DANIELS, to the database, we must have at least one customer whom she represents. If she has not yet been assigned any customers, then either we cannot record the fact that her name is MARY DANIELS or we have to create a fictitious customer for her to represent. Again, this is not a very desirable solution to the problem.

4. DELETIONS

   If we were to delete all of the customers of sales rep 6 from the database, then we would also lose the name of sales rep 6 and there would be no record containing this information.

These update anomalies are due to the fact that SLSREP_NUMBER determines SLSREP_NAME but SLSREP_NUMBER is not the primary key. As a result, the same SLSREP_NUMBER and consequently the same SLSREP_NAME can appear on many different rows.

Though 2NF is an improvement over 1NF, we need an even better strategy for creating relations in our database to eliminate 2NF problems. Third normal form gives us the strategy. First, we need to define a determinant.

Def: Any attribute (or collection of attributes) that determines another attribute is called a **determinant.**

Certainly the **primary key** in a relation will be a determinant. By definition, any **candidate key** will also be a determinant. (You will recall that a candidate key is an attribute which could also have functioned as the primary key.) In this case, SLSREP_NUMBER is a determinant but it is certainly not a candidate key, and that is the problem.

Def: A relation is in **third normal form** (3NF) if it is in second normal form and if the only determinants it contains are candidate keys.

Again, for an additional perspective, we will consider a dependency diagram, as shown in Figure 4.10. As before, the arrows above the boxes represent the

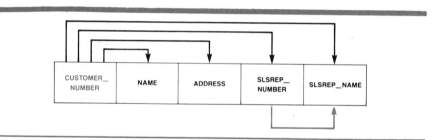

FIGURE 4.10
Dependencies in
CUSTOMER relation

normal dependencies of all attributes on the primary key. It is the arrow below the boxes that causes the problem. The presence of this arrow makes SLSREP_NUMBER a determinant. If there were arrows from SLSREP_NUMBER to all of the attributes, SLSREP_NUMBER would be a candidate key and we would not have a problem. The absence of these arrows indicates that this relation possesses a determinant that is not a candidate key. Thus, the relation is not in 3NF. *Note:* The definition given above is not the original definition of third normal form. This more recent definition, which is preferable to the original, is often referred to as **Boyce-Codd normal form** (BCNF) when it is important to make a distinction between this definition and the original. We will not make such a distinction but will take this to be *the* definition of 3NF.

We have now named the problem with the CUSTOMER relation: it is not in 3NF. What we need is a scheme to correct the deficiency in the CUSTOMER relation and in all relations having similar deficiencies. Such a method can now be given.

First, for each determinant that is not a candidate key, remove from the relation the attributes that depend on this determinant. Next, create a new relation containing all the attributes from the original relation that depend on this determinant. Finally, make the determinant the primary key of this new relation.

In the CUSTOMER relation, for example, SLSREP_NAME is removed since it depends on the determinant SLSREP_NUMBER, which is not a candidate key. A new relation is formed, consisting of SLSREP_NUMBER as the primary key and SLSREP_NAME. Specifically

CUSTOMER(CUSTOMER_NUMBER, NAME, ADDRESS, SLSREP_
          NUMBER, SLSREP_NAME)

is replaced by

CUSTOMER(CUSTOMER_NUMBER, NAME, ADDRESS,
          SLSREP_NUMBER)

and

SLSREP(SLSREP_NUMBER, SLSREP_NAME)

    Figure 4.11 shows extensions of the relations involved.

CUSTOMER

CUSTOMER_NUMBER	NAME	ADDRESS	SLSREP_NUMBER	SLSREP_NAME
124	SALLY ADAMS	481 OAK, LANSING, MI	3	MARY JONES
256	ANN SAMUELS	215 PETE, GRANT, MI	6	WILLIAM SMITH
311	DON CHARLES	48 COLLEGE, IRA, MI	12	SAM BROWN
315	TOM DANIELS	914 CHERRY, KENT, MI	6	WILLIAM SMITH
405	AL WILLIAMS	519 WATSON, GRANT, MI	12	SAM BROWN
412	SALLY ADAMS	16 ELM, LANSING, MI	3	MARY JONES
522	MARY NELSON	108 PINE, ADA, MI	12	SAM BROWN
567	JOE BAKER	808 RIDGE, HARPER, MI	6	WILLIAM SMITH
587	JUDY ROBERTS	512 PINE, ADA, MI	6	WILLIAM SMITH
622	DAN MARTIN	419 CHIP, GRANT, MI	3	MARY JONES

is replaced by

CUSTOMER

CUSTOMER_NUMBER	NAME	ADDRESS	SLSREP_NUMBER
124	SALLY ADAMS	481 OAK, LANSING, MI	3
256	ANN SAMUELS	215 PETE, GRANT, MI	6
311	DON CHARLES	48 COLLEGE, IRA, MI	12
315	TOM DANIELS	914 CHERRY, KENT, MI	6
405	AL WILLIAMS	519 WATSON, GRANT, MI	12
412	SALLY ADAMS	16 ELM, LANSING, MI	3
522	MARY NELSON	108 PINE, ADA, MI	12
567	JOE BAKER	808 RIDGE, HARPER, MI	6
587	JUDY ROBERTS	512 PINE, ADA, MI	6
622	DAN MARTIN	419 CHIP, GRANT, MI	3

SLSREP

SLSREP_NUMBER	SLSREP_NAME
3	MARY JONES
6	WILLIAM SMITH
12	SAM BROWN

FIGURE 4.11
Conversion to 3NF

    Have we now corrected all previously identified problems? A sales rep's name appears only once, thus avoiding redundancy and making the process of changing a sales rep's name a very simple one. It is not possible with this design for the same sales rep to have two different names in the database. To add a new sales rep to the database, we add a row in the SLSREP relation so that it is not necessary to have a customer whom the sales rep represents. Finally, deleting all of the customers of a given sales rep will not remove the sales rep's record from the SLSREP relation, so we do retain the sales rep's name; all of the data in the original relation can be reconstructed from the data in the new collection of relations. All previously mentioned problems have indeed been solved.

INCORRECT DECOMPOSITIONS

It is important to note that the decomposition of a relation into two or more 3NF relations *must* be accomplished by the method indicated even though there are other possibilities that might seem at first glance to be legitimate. Let us examine two other decompositions of the CUSTOMER relation into 3NF relations in order to understand the difficulties they pose.

What if, in the decomposition process,

CUSTOMER(<u>CUSTOMER_NUMBER</u>, NAME, ADDRESS, SLSREP_
            NUMBER, SLSREP_NAME)

is replaced by

CUSTOMER(<u>CUSTOMER_NUMBER</u>, NAME, ADDRESS, SLSREP_NUMBER)

and

SLSREP(<u>CUSTOMER_NUMBER</u>, SLSREP_NAME)

The extensions of these relations are shown in Figure 4.12 on the opposite page.

Both of the new relations are in 3NF. In addition, by joining these two relations together on CUSTOMER_NUMBER we can reconstruct the original CUSTOMER relation. The result, however, still suffers from some of the same kinds of problems that the original CUSTOMER relation did. Consider, for example, the redundancy in the storage of sales reps' names, the problem encountered in changing the name of sales rep 12, and the difficulty of adding a new sales rep for whom there are as yet no customers. In addition, since the sales rep number is in one relation and the sales rep name is in another, we have actually *split a functional dependence across two different relations*. Thus, this decomposition, while it may appear to be valid, is definitely not a desirable way to create 3NF relations.

CUSTOMER	CUSTOMER_NUMBER	NAME	ADDRESS	SLSREP_NUMBER	SLSREP_NAME
	124	SALLY ADAMS	481 OAK, LANSING, MI	3	MARY JONES
	256	ANN SAMUELS	215 PETE, GRANT, MI	6	WILLIAM SMITH
	311	DON CHARLES	48 COLLEGE, IRA, MI	12	SAM BROWN
	315	TOM DANIELS	914 CHERRY, KENT, MI	6	WILLIAM SMITH
	405	AL WILLIAMS	519 WATSON, GRANT, MI	12	SAM BROWN
	412	SALLY ADAMS	16 ELM, LANSING, MI	3	MARY JONES
	522	MARY NELSON	108 PINE, ADA, MI	12	SAM BROWN
	567	JOE BAKER	808 RIDGE, HARPER, MI	6	WILLIAM SMITH
	587	JUDY ROBERTS	512 PINE, ADA, MI	6	WILLIAM SMITH
	622	DAN MARTIN	419 CHIP, GRANT, MI	3	MARY JONES

is replaced by

CUSTOMER	CUSTOMER_NUMBER	NAME	ADDRESS	SLSREP_NUMBER
	124	SALLY ADAMS	481 OAK, LANSING, MI	3
	256	ANN SAMUELS	215 PETE, GRANT, MI	6
	311	DON CHARLES	48 COLLEGE, IRA, MI	12
	315	TOM DANIELS	914 CHERRY, KENT, MI	6
	405	AL WILLIAMS	519 WATSON, GRANT, MI	12
	412	SALLY ADAMS	16 ELM, LANSING, MI	3
	522	MARY NELSON	108 PINE, ADA, MI	12
	567	JOE BAKER	808 RIDGE, HARPER, MI	6
	587	JUDY ROBERTS	512 PINE, ADA, MI	6
	622	DAN MARTIN	419 CHIP, GRANT, MI	3

SLSREP	CUSTOMER_NUMBER	SLSREP_NAME
	124	MARY JONES
	256	WILLIAM SMITH
	311	SAM BROWN
	315	WILLIAM SMITH
	405	SAM BROWN
	412	MARY JONES
	522	SAM BROWN
	567	WILLIAM SMITH
	587	WILLIAM SMITH
	622	MARY JONES

There is another decomposition that we might choose, and that is to replace

FIGURE 4.12
Incorrect
decomposition

CUSTOMER(CUSTOMER_NUMBER, NAME, ADDRESS, SLSREP_
         NUMBER, SLSREP_NAME)

by

CUSTOMER(CUSTOMER_NUMBER, NAME, ADDRESS,
         SLSREP_NAME)

and

SLSREP(SLSREP_NUMBER, SLSREP_NAME)

The extensions of these relations are shown in Figure 4.13.

CUSTOMER

CUSTOMER_NUMBER	NAME	ADDRESS	SLSREP_NUMBER	SLSREP_NAME
124	SALLY ADAMS	481 OAK, LANSING, MI	3	MARY JONES
256	ANN SAMUELS	215 PETE, GRANT, MI	6	WILLIAM SMITH
311	DON CHARLES	48 COLLEGE, IRA, MI	12	SAM BROWN
315	TOM DANIELS	914 CHERRY, KENT, MI	6	WILLIAM SMITH
405	AL WILLIAMS	519 WATSON, GRANT, MI	12	SAM BROWN
412	SALLY ADAMS	16 ELM, LANSING, MI	3	MARY JONES
522	MARY NELSON	108 PINE, ADA, MI	12	SAM BROWN
567	JOE BAKER	808 RIDGE, HARPER, MI	6	WILLIAM SMITH
587	JUDY ROBERTS	512 PINE, ADA, MI	6	WILLIAM SMITH
622	DAN MARTIN	419 CHIP, GRANT, MI	3	MARY JONES

is replaced by

CUSTOMER

CUSTOMER_NUMBER	NAME	ADDRESS	SLSREP_NAME
124	SALLY ADAMS	481 OAK, LANSING, MI	MARY JONES
256	ANN SAMUELS	215 PETE, GRANT, MI	WILLIAM SMITH
311	DON CHARLES	48 COLLEGE, IRA, MI	SAM BROWN
315	TOM DANIELS	914 CHERRY, KENT, MI	WILLIAM SMITH
405	AL WILLIAMS	519 WATSON, GRANT, MI	SAM BROWN
412	SALLY ADAMS	16 ELM, LANSING, MI	MARY JONES
522	MARY NELSON	108 PINE, ADA, MI	SAM BROWN
567	JOE BAKER	808 RIDGE, HARPER, MI	WILLIAM SMITH
587	JUDY ROBERTS	512 PINE, ADA, MI	WILLIAM SMITH
622	DAN MARTIN	419 CHIP, GRANT, MI	MARY JONES

SLSREP

SLSREP_NUMBER	SLSREP_NAME
3	MARY JONES
6	WILLIAM SMITH
12	SAM BROWN

This seems to be a possibility. Not only are both relations in 3NF, but joining them together based on SLSREP_NAME seems to reconstruct the data in the original relation. Or does it? Suppose that the name of sales rep 6 is also MARY JONES. In that case, when we join the two new relations together, we will get a row in which customer 124 (SALLY ADAMS) is associated with sales rep 3 (MARY JONES) and *another* row in which customer 124 is associated with sales rep 6 (MARY JONES). Since we obviously want decompositions that preserve the original information (called **nonloss decompositions**), this scheme is not appropriate.

FIGURE 4.13
Second incorrect decomposition

NORMALIZATION PROCESS EXAMPLES

As a pictorial summary of the normalization process, we can visualize the following:

1. Convert to 1NF

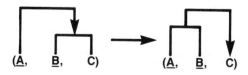

where A is the key to the relation and B is the key to the repeating group (B, C). B now becomes a part of the primary key of the new relation.

2. Convert to 2NF

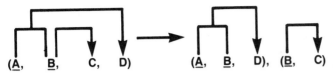

(A,   B,   C,   D)   →   (A,   B,   D), (B,   C)

Here the combination of A and B forms the primary key for the original relation but C depends only on B. This dependency is removed and placed in its own relation.

3. Convert to 3NF.

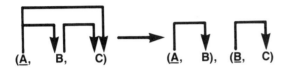

(A,   B,   C)   →   (A,   B), (B,   C)

Here A, which is the key in the original relation determines both B and C, but B also determines C. This dependency is removed and placed in its own relation.

Q&A

Using the types of entities found in a college environment (faculty, students, departments, courses, etc.), create an example of a relation that is in 1NF but not in 2NF and an example of a relation that is in 2NF but not 3NF. In each case justify the answers and show how to convert to the higher forms.

Answer:

There are many possible solutions. If your solution differs from the one we will look at, this does not mean that it is an unsatisfactory solution.

To create a 1NF relation that is not in 2NF, we need a relation that (a) has no repeating groups and (b) has at least one attribute that is dependent on only a portion of the primary key. For an attribute to be dependent on a portion of the primary key, the key must contain at least two attributes. Following is a picture of what we need:

(__1__ , __2__ ,   3 ,   4)

This relation contains four attributes, numbered 1, 2, 3, and 4, in which attributes 1 and 2 functionally determine both attributes 3 and 4. In addition, neither attribute 1 nor attribute 2 can

continued

Q&A continued

determine *all* other attributes, otherwise the key would contain only this one attribute. Finally, we want part of the key, say, attribute 2, to determine another attribute, say, attribute 4. Now that we have the pattern we need, we would like to find attributes from within the college environment to fit it. One example would be:

(STUDENT_NUMBER, COURSE_NUMBER, GRADE, COURSE_DESC)

In this example, the concatenation of STUDENT_NUMBER and COURSE_NUMBER determines both GRADE and COURSE_DESCRIPTION. Both of these are required to determine GRADE, and thus the primary key consists of their concatenation (nothing less will do). The COURSE_DESCRIPTION, however, is only dependent on the COURSE_NUMBER. This violates second normal form. To convert this relation to 2NF we would replace it by the two relations

(STUDENT_NUMBER, COURSE_NUMBER, GRADE)

and

(COURSE_NUMBER, COURSE_DESCRIPTION)

We would of course now give these relations appropriate names.

To create a relation that is in 2NF but not in 3NF, we need a 2NF relation in which there is a determinant that is *not* a candidate key. If we choose a relation that has a single attribute as the primary key, it is automatically in 2NF, so the real problem is the determinant. We need a relation like the following:

(__1__,   2 ,   3   )

This relation contains three attributes, numbered 1, 2, and 3, in which attribute 1 determines each of the others and is thus the primary key. If, in addition, attribute 2 determines attribute 3, it is a determinant. If it does not also determine attribute 1, then it is not a candidate key. One example that fits this pattern would be:

(STUDENT_NUMBER, ADVISOR_NUMBER, ADVISOR_NAME)

Here the STUDENT_NUMBER determines both the student's ADVISOR_NUMBER and the ADVISOR_NAME. The ADVISOR_NUMBER determines the ADVISOR_NAME but the ADVISOR_NUMBER does not determine the STUDENT_NUMBER, since one advisor can have many advisees. This relation is in 2NF but not 3NF. To convert it to 3NF, we replace it by

continued

Q&A continued

(STUDENT_NUMBER, ADVISOR_NUMBER)

and

(ADVISOR_NUMBER, ADVISOR_NAME)

Convert the following relation to 3NF:

STUDENT (STUDENT_NUMBER, NAME, NUMBER_CREDITS, ADVISOR_NUMBER, ADVISOR_
    NAME, COURSE_NUMBER, COURSE_DESCRIPTION, GRADE)

In this relation, STUDENT_NUMBER determines NAME, NUMBER_CREDITS, ADVISOR_
NUMBER, and ADVISOR_NAME. ADVISOR_NUMBER determines ADVISOR_NAME. COURSE_
NUMBER determines COURSE_DESCRIPTION. The combination of a STUDENT_NUMBER and a
COURSE_NUMBER determines a GRADE.

Answer:

Step 1. Remove the repeating group to convert to 1NF. This yields:

STUDENT (STUDENT_NUMBER, NAME, NUMBER_CREDITS, ADVISOR_NUMBER, ADVISOR_
    NAME, COURSE_NUMBER, COURSE_DESCRIPTION, GRADE)

This relation is now in 1NF, since it has no repeating groups. It is not, however, in 2NF, since
NAME is dependent only on STUDENT_NUMBER, which is only a portion of the primary key.

Step 2. Convert the 1NF relation to 2NF. First, for each subset of the primary key, start a relation
with that subset as its key yielding:

(STUDENT_NUMBER,
(COURSE_NUMBER,
(STUDENT_NUMBER, COURSE_NUMBER,

Next, place the rest of the attributes with the minimal collection on which they depend, giving:

(STUDENT_NUMBER, NAME, NUMBER_CREDITS, ADVISOR_NUMBER,
    ADVISOR_NAME)
(COURSE_NUMBER, COURSE_DESCRIPTION)
(STUDENT_NUMBER, COURSE_NUMBER, GRADE)

continued

Q&A continued

Finally, we assign names to each of the newly created relations:

```
STUDENT (STUDENT_NUMBER, NAME, NUMBER_CREDITS, ADVISOR_NUMBER,
    ADVISOR_NAME)
COURSE (COURSE_NUMBER, COURSE_DESCRIPTION)
GRADE (STUDENT_NUMBER, COURSE_NUMBER, GRADE)
```

While these relations are all in 2NF, both COURSE and GRADE are also in 3NF. The STUDENT relation is not, however, since it contains a determinant, ADVISOR_NUMBER, that is not a candidate key.

Step 3: Convert the 2NF STUDENT relation to 3NF by removing the attribute that depends on the determinant ADVISOR_NUMBER and placing it in a separate relation:

```
(STUDENT_NUMBER, NAME, NUMBER_CREDITS, ADVISOR_NUMBER)
(ADVISOR_NUMBER, ADVISOR_NAME)
```

Step 4: Name these relations and put the entire collection together, giving:

```
STUDENT (STUDENT_NUMBER, NAME, NUMBER_CREDITS, ADVISOR_NUMBER)
ADVISOR (ADVISOR_NUMBER, ADVISOR_NAME)
COURSE (COURSE_NUMBER, COURSE_DESCRIPTION)
GRADE (STUDENT_NUMBER, COURSE_NUMBER, GRADE)
```

For further discussion of the normalization process, see [1], [2], [5], [6], and [8].

STOP

4.5 MULTIVALUED DEPENDENCIES AND FOURTH NORMAL FORM

By converting a given collection of relations to an equivalent 3NF collection, we remove any problems arising from functional dependencies. Usually this means that the types of anomalies discussed in the previous section have been eliminated. This is not always the case, however. There is a different kind of dependency that can also lead to the same types of difficulties.

To illustrate the problem, suppose we are interested in sales reps, the customers they represent, and the children of these sales reps. Assume for the purposes of this example that a sales rep can represent many customers and a customer can be represented by many sales reps. Suppose that as an initial relational design for this situation we chose the following unnormalized relation:

SLSREP (SLSREP_NUMBER, CUSTOMER_NUMBER,
    SLSREP_CHILD_NAME)

The single relation SLSREP has a primary key of SLSREP_NUMBER and two separate repeating groups, CUSTOMER_NUMBER and SLSREP_CHILD_NAME. To convert this relation to 1NF, we might be tempted to merely remove the two repeating groups and expand the primary key to include both CUSTOMER_NUMBER and SLSREP_CHILD_NAME. This solution would give the relation:

SLSREP(SLSREP_NUMBER, CUSTOMER_NUMBER,
    SLSREP_CHILD_NAME)

Extensions of these relations are shown in Figure 4.14.

SLSREP	SLSREP_ NUMBER	CUSTOMER_ NUMBER	SLSREP_ CHILD_NAME
	123	12805	BILLY
		24139	JOAN
			TOM
	456	37573	MARY
		24139	
		36273	
	444	57384	TOM

is replaced by

SLSREP	SLSREP_ NUMBER	CUSTOMER_ NUMBER	SLSREP_ CHILD_NAME
	123	12805	BILLY
	123	24139	BILLY
	123	12805	JOAN
	123	24139	JOAN
	123	12805	TOM
	123	24139	TOM
	456	37573	MARY
	456	24139	MARY
	456	36273	MARY
	444	57384	TOM

FIGURE 4.14
Incorrect way to remove repeating groups

You may already have spotted some problems with this approach, and if so, you are correct. It is a strange way to normalize the original relation. Yet, it is precisely this approach to the removal of repeating groups that leads to the problems alluded to in the beginning of this section concerning multivalued dependencies. We will examine how this relation should have been normalized in order to avoid the problems altogether. Let us for the moment, however, push ahead with the relation we have created and discuss what kinds of problems are present.

The first thing we should observe about this relation is that it is in 3NF since there are no repeating groups, no attribute is dependent on only a portion of the primary key, and there are no determinants that are not candidate keys. There are several problems, however, with this 3NF relation:

1. UPDATE
    Altering the name of a child of sales rep 123 requires more than one change. If we change the name BILLY to WILLIAM, the change should be made in both of the first two rows in the table.
    After all, it doesn't make sense to say that the child's name is BILLY when associated with customer 12805 and WILLIAM when associated with customer 24139. It is the same child of the same sales rep. The sales rep does not refer to his or her son as Billy when calling on one customer and William when calling on another.

2. ADDITIONS

Suppose that sales rep 666 joins the sales force. Also suppose that this sales rep does not have a child. When this sales rep now begins to represent customer 44332, we have a problem, since SLSREP_CHILD_NAME is part of the primary key. We would need to enter a fictitious child name in this situation.

3. DELETIONS

If sales rep 444 no longer represents customer 57384 and we delete the appropriate row from the table, we lose the information that sales rep 444 has a child named SAM.

These problems are certainly reminiscent of those encountered in the discussions of both 2NF and 3NF, but there are *no* functional dependencies among the attributes in this relation. A given sales rep is not associated with *one* child name, as he or she would be if there were a functional dependency; however, the sales rep is associated with a *specific* collection of child names. More importantly, this association is *independent* of any association with customers. It is this independence that causes the problem.

We can now define multivalued dependency and fourth normal form.

Def: In a relation with attributes A, B, and C, there is a **multivalued dependency** of attribute B on attribute A (also read as "B is **multidependent** on A" or "A **multidetermines** B") if a value for A is associated with a specific collection of values for B, independent of any values for C. (This is usually written A $\rightarrow\rightarrow$ B.)

Def: A relation is in **fourth normal form** (4NF) if it is in 3NF (really BCNF) and there are no multivalued dependencies.

As might be expected, converting a relation to 4NF is similar to the normalization process encountered in the treatments of 2NF and 3NF. We split the relation into separate relations, each containing the attribute that multi-determines the others, in this case the sales rep number. This means we replace

SLSREP(<u>SLSREP_NUMBER</u>, <u>CUSTOMER_NUMBER</u>, <u>SLSREP_CHILD_NAME</u>)

with

SLSCUST(<u>SLSREP_NUMBER</u>, <u>CUSTOMER_NUMBER</u>)

and

SLSCHILD(<u>SLSREP_NUMBER</u>, <u>SLSREP_CHILD_NAME</u>).

Figure 4.15 shows extensions of these relations.

SLSREP	SLSREP_NUMBER	CUSTOMER_NUMBER	SLSREP_CHILD_NAME
	123	12805	BILLY
	123	24139	BILLY
	123	12805	JOAN
	123	24139	JOAN
	123	12805	TOM
	123	24139	TOM
	456	37573	MARY
	456	24139	MARY
	456	36273	MARY
	444	57384	TOM

is replaced by

SLSCUST	SLSREP_NUMBER	CUSTOMER_NUMBER
	123	12805
	123	24139
	456	37573
	456	24139
	456	36273
	444	57384

SLSCHILD	SLSREP_NUMBER	SLSREP_CHILD_NAME
	123	BILLY
	123	JOAN
	123	TOM
	456	MARY
	444	TOM

As before, the problems have disappeared. There is no problem with changing the name BILLY to WILLIAM since it occurs only in one place. To add the information that sales rep 666 represents customer 44332, we need only add a row to the SLSCUST relation. It does not matter whether or not this sales rep has a child. Finally, to delete the information that sales rep 444 represents customer 57384, we need only remove a row from the SLSCUST table. In this case, we do not lose the information that this sales rep has a child named SAM.

FIGURE 4.15
Conversion to 4NF

AVOIDING THE PROBLEM

While it is certainly true that a relation which is not in 4NF suffers some serious problems, there is a way to avoid dealing with the issue. What we need is a methodology for normalizing relations that will prevent this situation from occurring in the first place. We already have most of such a methodology in place from the discussion of the 1NF, 2NF, and 3NF normalization process. All we need is to expand the method for converting an unnormalized relation to 1NF.

The conversion of an unnormalized relation to 1NF requires the removal of repeating groups. When this was first demonstrated, we merely removed the repeating group symbol and expanded the key. You will recall, for example, that

ORDER(ORDER_NUMBER, PART_NUMBER, NUMBER_ORDERED)

became

ORDER(ORDER_NUMBER, PART_NUMBER, NUMBER_ORDERED)

The primary key was expanded to include the primary key of the original relation together with the key to the repeating group.

What if there are two or more repeating groups, however? The method we have just alluded to is inadequate for such situations. Instead we must remove each separate repeating group and place each in a separate relation. Each relation will contain all of the attributes that make up a given repeating group as well as the primary key to the original unnormalized relation. The primary key to each new relation will usually be the concatenation of the primary key of the original relation and the key to the repeating group.

For example, consider the following unnormalized relation containing two separate repeating groups:

```
SLSREP(SLSREP_NUMBER, NAME,
      CUSTOMER_NUMBER, CUSTOMER_NAME,
      SLSREP_CHILD_NAME, SLSREP_CHILD_AGE)
```

where NAME is the name of the sales rep and CUSTOMER_NAME is the name of the customer. The attributes SLSREP_CHILD_NAME and SLSREP_CHILD_AGE refer to the children of the sales rep. Among all of the children of a given sales rep, the names are unique. Applying this new method to create 1NF relations would produce

```
SLSREP(SLSREP_NUMBER, NAME)
SLSCUST(SLSREP_NUMBER, CUSTOMER_NUMBER,
      CUSTOMER_NAME)
SLSCHILD(SLSREP_NUMBER, SLSREP_CHILD_NAME,
      SLSREP_CHILD_AGE)
```

As you can see, the problems with multivalued dependencies have been avoided. At this point we have a collection of 1NF relations and we still need to convert them to 3NF. By using the above process, however, we are guaranteed that the result will also be in *4NF*.

4NF AND PRIMARY KEYS

Some people mistakenly believe that a relation is not in 4NF if its primary key consists of three or more attributes. That is *not* the problem. The problem is the independence mentioned earlier. For example, suppose we wish to keep track of the number of items each customer has purchased from each sales rep. We again assume that a customer can be represented by more than one sales rep. An appropriate relation for this example is:

```
SALES(SLSREP_NUMBER, CUSTOMER_NUMBER,
      PART_NUMBER, NUMBER_SOLD)
```

Consider the sample extension of this relation shown in Figure 4.16.

SALES	SLSREP NUMBER	CUSTOMER_ NUMBER	PART_ NUMBER	NUMBER_ SOLD
	3	124	AX12	15
	3	256	CB03	3
	3	412	AX12	21
	3	412	BZ66	2
	3	412	CZ81	5
	6	124	CZ81	7
	6	412	BT04	1
	6	412	AX12	4

FIGURE 4.16
4NF relation with concatenation of three attributes as the key

In this relation, we do not have the independence discussed earlier. It is certainly not true that a given sales rep is associated with the same set of customers *independent of parts* for example. Specifically, sales rep 3 sold part AX12 to customers 124 and 412 but sold part CB03 to customer 256. Similarly, the association between a sales rep and a collection of parts depends on customers. Specifically, to customer 412, sales rep 3 sold AX12, BZ66, and CZ81, but to customer 256, sales rep 3 sold only CB03. Likewise, the relationship between a customer and a given collection of parts depends on the sales rep. Specifically, customer 412 purchased parts AX12, BZ66, and CZ81 from sales rep 3 but purchased parts AX12 and BT04 from sales rep 6. Since there is no independence among the three attributes that make up the key, we are in 4NF and thus there is no problem. The *independence* is the root of the problem, not the fact that the key consists of the concatenation of more than two attributes.

6 HIGHER NORMAL FORMS

There are two higher normal forms that have been defined. These are currently the subject of a great deal of research and thus deserve mention. But at least at the present time, they do not appear to hold much value for the design process.

The first of these is fifth normal form (5NF). Fifth normal form involves yet another kind of dependency, a join dependency, which is an assertion that a relation can be constructed by the join of its projections. A relation is in **fifth normal form** (sometimes called project-join normal form) if every join dependency is "implied" by the candidate keys. For information concerning fifth normal form, see [5] and [9].

The other higher normal form was defined by Fagin [7] and is called domain-key normal form (DK/NF). A relation is in **domain-key normal form** if every constraint on the relation is a logical consequence of the definitions of keys and domains. In the same paper in which he defined DK/NF, Fagin also showed that a relation that is in DK/NF will suffer from no insertion or deletion anomalies. This fact then creates a boundary for the definition of normal forms; no higher normal forms will be needed. Unfortunately, no obvious general means is known for converting a relation to DK/NF. For further information on DK/NF, see [8].

4.7 APPLICATION TO DATABASE DESIGN

The normalization process used to convert an unnormalized relation or collection of relations to an equivalent collection that is in 3NF is a crucial part of the database design process and will be covered later in the text. By following a careful and appropriate normalization methodology, normal forms higher than 3NF will not need to be considered. There are two aspects of this methodology that warrant further discussion.

1. Conversion to 3NF should be done sensibly and not blindly. Consider the CUSTOMER relation

    CUSTOMER(CUSTOMER_NUMBER, NAME,
        ADDRESS, CITY, STATE, ZIP, ...)

    In addition to the functional dependencies that all the attributes have on the CUSTOMER_NUMBER, there are two other functional dependencies. ZIP determines STATE and, at least in most regions of the country, ZIP also determines CITY. Does this mean that we should replace this relation with

    CUSTOMER(CUSTOMER_NUMBER, NAME,
        ADDRESS, ZIP, ...)

    and

    ZIP_CODES(ZIP, CITY, STATE)

    If we are determined to ensure that every relation is in 3NF, then we should do this, but it is probably overkill. If you review the list of problems normally associated with relations that are not in 3NF, you will see that they really don't apply here. Are we likely to need to change the STATE in which ZIP 49428 is located? Do we need to add the fact that ZIP 49401 corresponds to ALLENDALE, MICHIGAN, if we have no customers with that ZIP? In addition, if we leave the relation in its original non-3NF format, it is much more natural.

2. By splitting relations to achieve 3NF, we create the need to express inter-relation constraints. In the example given earlier for converting to 3NF, we created the two relations

    CUSTOMER(CUSTOMER_NUMBER, NAME,
        ADDRESS, SLSREP_NUMBER)

    and

    SLSREP(SLSREP_NUMBER, SLSREP_NAME)

There is nothing about these two relations by themselves that would force the SLSREP_NUMBER in a row of the CUSTOMER relation to actually match a SLSREP_NUMBER in the SLSREP relation. Requiring this to take place is an example of an **interrelation constraint**, i.e., a condition that involves two or more relations. We cannot determine whether this condition has been satisfied merely by looking at the CUSTOMER relation. This type of interrelation constraint (there are others) is handled by FOREIGN KEY rules, which are discussed in chapter 6, the first chapter on database design. It is mentioned here only because the problem surfaces when relations are split in the normalization process.

.8 SUMMARY

In this chapter we have examined the relational model's normalization process. We began by discussing functional dependence. Attribute B is functionally dependent on attribute (or collection of attributes) A if a value for A determines a specific value for B. We next defined the primary key of a relation. An attribute (or collection of attributes), A, is the primary key for a relation if all attributes of the relation are dependent on A and if no subcollection of the attributes in A also has this property.

Next the various normal forms were discussed. A first normal form relation contains no repeating groups. A second normal form relation is a relation that is in first normal form and has no attribute dependent on only a portion of the primary key. A third normal form relation is a relation that is in second normal form and has no determinants that are not also candidate keys. (Technically this is called Boyce-Codd normal form, or BC/NF.) A fourth normal form relation is a relation that is in third normal form and has no multivalued dependencies. A fifth normal form relation is one in which every join dependency is "implied" by its candidate keys. Finally, a domain/key normal form relation is one in which every constraint on the relation is a consequence of the definitions of keys and domains.

A methodology was presented for converting unnormalized relations (those not in first normal form) to third normal form in such a way that the end result will also be in fourth normal form. Since the higher forms (fifth and domain/key) are of theoretical interest but not particularly applicable to the design process, reaching fourth normal form is the goal.

REVIEW QUESTIONS

1. Define functional dependence.
2. Give an example of an attribute, A, and an attribute, B, such that B is functionally dependent on A. Give an example of an attribute, C, and an attribute, D, such that D is not functionally dependent on C.
3. Define candidate key.
4. Define primary key.
5. Define first normal form. What is the relationship between first normal form and "normalized" relations as defined in chapter 3?
6. Define second normal form. What types of problems are encountered in relations that are not in second normal form?
7. Define third normal form. What types of problems are encountered in relations that are not in third normal form?
8. Define multivalued dependency. How does this concept differ from functional dependency?
9. Define fourth normal form.

EXERCISES

1. Consider a student relation containing student number, student name, student's major department, student's advisor number, student's advisor's name, student's advisor's office, student's advisor's phone, student's number of credits, and student's class standing (freshman, sophomore, etc.). List the functional dependencies that exist together with the assumptions that would support these dependencies. Change one or two of your assumptions and indicate the change this produces in the list of functional dependencies.
2. In the CUSTOMER relation of the example presented at the beginning of the chapter, the primary key is CUSTOMER_NUMBER. Give an assumption under which the primary key would be the concatenation of CUSTOMER_NUMBER and SLSREP_NUMBER.
3. In the ORDER relation of the example presented at the beginning of the chapter, the primary key is ORDER_NUMBER. Give an assumption under which the primary key would be the concatenation of ORDER_NUMBER and CUSTOMER_NUMBER.
4. In the ORDER_LINE relation of the example presented at the beginning of the chapter, the primary key is the concatenation of ORDER_NUMBER and PART_NUMBER. Give an assumption under which the primary key would be the ORDER_NUMBER alone.
5. In the PART relation of the example presented at the beginning of the chapter, the primary key is PART_NUMBER. Give an assumption under which the primary key would be the concatenation of PART_NUMBER and WAREHOUSE_NUMBER.
6. Using the types of entities found in a distribution environment (sales reps, customers, orders, parts, etc.), create an example of a relation that is in 1NF but not in 2NF and an example of a relation that is in 2NF but not 3NF. In each case justify the answers and show how to convert to the higher forms.

7. Convert the following relation to an equivalent collection of relations that is in 3NF.

PATIENT(<u>HH_NUMBER</u>, HH_NAME, HH_ADDRESS, BALANCE,
    <u>PATIENT_NUMBER</u>, PATIENT_NAME,
    <u>SERVICE_CODE</u>, SERVICE_DESCRIPTION, FEE, DATE)

This is a relation concerning information about patients of a dentist. Each patient belongs to a household. The head of the household is designated as HH in the relation. The following dependencies exist in PATIENT:

PATIENT_NUMBER → HH_NUMBER, HH_NAME, HH_ADDRESS,
    BALANCE, PATIENT_NAME
HH_NUMBER → HH NAME, HH ADDRESS, BALANCE
SERVICE_CODE → SERVICE_DESCRIPTION, FEE
PATIENT_NUMBER, SERVICE_CODE → DATE

8. List the functional dependencies in the following relation, subject to the specified conditions. Convert this relation to an equivalent collection of relations that are in 3NF.

INVOICE(<u>INVOICE_NUMBER</u>, CUSTOMER_
    NUMBER, CUSTOMER_NAME, CUSTOMER_ADDRESS, INVOICE_DATE,
    <u>PART_NUMBER</u>, PART_DESC, PRICE, NUMBER_SHIPPED)

This relation concerns invoice information. For a given invoice (identified by the invoice number) there will be a single customer. The customer's number, name, and address appear on the invoice as well as the invoice date. Also, there may be several different parts appearing on the invoice. For each part that appears, the part number, description, price, and number shipped will be displayed. The price is from the current master price list.

9. Using your knowledge of a college environment, determine the functional dependencies that exist in the following relation. After these have been determined, convert this relation to an equivalent collection of relations that are in 3NF.

STUDENT(<u>STUDENT_NUMBER</u>, NAME, NUMBER OF CREDITS,
    ADVISOR_NUMBER, ADVISOR_NAME, DEPT_NUMBER, DEPT_NAME,
    <u>COURSE_NUMBER</u>, COURSE_DESCRIPTION, TERM_TAKEN, GRADE)

10. Determine the multivalued dependencies in the following relation. Convert this relation to an equivalent collection of relations that are in 4NF.

COURSE(<u>COURSE_NUMBER</u>, <u>TEXTBOOK</u>, <u>INSTRUCTOR_NUMBER</u>)

Each course is associated with a specific set of textbooks independently of the instructors who are teaching the course; i.e., even though many instructors may be teaching the course, they will all use the same set of textbooks.

11. The following unnormalized relation is similar in content to the relation in the previous problem. Convert it to 4NF. Did you encounter the relation from the previous problem along the way?

COURSE(COURSE_NUMBER, COURSE_DESCRIPTION,
        NUMBER_OF_CREDITS, TEXTBOOK,
        INSTRUCTOR_NUMBER, INSTRUCTOR_NAME)

Note that this relation has two separate repeating groups, one listing the textbooks used for the course and the other listing the instructors who are teaching the course.

12. In the customer-sales rep example, we discussed the interrelation constraint that a customer cannot be added to the database unless the corresponding sales rep already exists. List two other related constraints that we might wish to impose. (*Hint:* Suppose customers represented by sales rep 6 are currently in the database. Consider the deletion of sales rep 6. Consider the process of changing sales rep 6's number to 5.)

REFERENCES

1] Cardenas, Alfonso F. *DataBase Management Systems* 2d ed. Allyn & Bacon, 1984.

2] Chamberlin, D. D. "Relational Data-Base Management Systems." *ACM Computing Surveys* 8, no. 1 (March 1976).

3] Codd, E. F. "Further Normalization of the Data Base Relational Model." In *Data Base Systems*, Courant Computer Science Symposia Series, vol. 6. Prentice-Hall, 1972.

4] Codd, E. F. "Recent Investigations into Relational Data Base Systems." Proceedings of the IFIP Congress, 1974.

5] Date, C. J. *Introduction to Database Systems, Volume I*, 4th ed. Addison-Wesley, 1986.

6] Date, C. J. *A Guide to DB2*, Addison-Wesley, 1984.

7] Fagin, Ronald. "A Normal Form for Relational Databases That is Based on Domains and Keys." *Transactions on Database Systems* 6, no. 3, (September 1981).

8] Kroenke, David. *Database Processing*, 2d ed. SRA, 1983.

9] Ullman, Jeffrey D. *Principles of Database Systems*, 2d ed. Computer Science Press, 1982; Prentice Hall, 1981.

RELATIONAL MODEL III

CHAPTER

1 INTRODUCTION

In this chapter, we continue our study of the relational model. We begin in section 5.2 by investigating some advanced concepts within the general model. We will look at

- the issues involved in supporting nulls
- the relational integrity rules
- the use of views and their relationship to subschemas
- the use of authorizations for security
- the way in which a special relationship, the bill-of-materials relationship, is implemented within the relational model
- the use of indexes to improve performance

We will also consider the question, What does it take to be relational? In section 5.3, we will continue our study of SQL by how nulls are supported in SQL. We will examine the way in which a table's basic structure can be changed, as well as the use of the catalog within SQL systems and the report formatting features within SQL. We will also see how SQL can be embedded in programs in languages like COBOL.

The remainder of the chapter will be spent discussing two major relational model implementations. The first of these, DB2, a product of IBM, will be examined in some detail. We will see that much of what we have been discussing applies directly to DB2. We will also investigate the way in which DB2 supports the functions of a DBMS that were described in chapter 2. Finally, we will discuss INGRES, which is a major alternative to the systems that support SQL and is marketed by Relational Technology, Inc.

5.2 ADVANCED TOPICS

NULLS

Occasionally, when a new row is entered into a database or an existing row is modified, the values for one or more columns are unknown. They may be merely unavailable for the moment; a customer may not yet have been assigned a sales rep or a credit limit. In other cases, these values may never be known; a customer may exist without ever having a sales rep. This concept of unknown (or nonapplicable) values is supported by many systems. Such values are called **null data values**, or simply **nulls**.

In any system that supports null values, the choice whether or not to allow them must be made for each column. This choice should be made carefully, since null values can present problems.

It does not make sense to allow null values for the primary key. The wisdom of storing a customer whose customer number is unknown is questionable at best. Further, if we have stored two such customers, there is no way to tell them apart.

Null values in numeric fields can cause strange results when statistics are computed. Suppose that CURRENT_BALANCE may accept null values. Suppose, further, that there are currently four customers on file, with respective balances of $100, $200, and $300, and one whose balance is null (unknown). When the average balance is calculated, most implementations will ignore the null value and obtain $200 (($100 + $200 + $300)/ 3). Similarly, if the total of the balances is calculated, the null value will be ignored and a total of $600 will be obtained. If a count of the number of rows in the table is made, however, the row containing the null will be included, yielding a result of 4. Thus the total balance ($600) divided by the number of customers (4) is not equal to the average balance ($200)!

Another problem occurs when tables are joined on columns that are allowed to be null. Suppose that in the Marvel College database the column indicating the field of specialization of a faculty member is allowed to be null. Suppose further that we are attempting to find pairs of faculty members who are in the same area of specialization by joining the FACULTY table to itself, based on matching fields of specialization. What happens when the areas of specialization of two faculty members are both null? Are these two faculty members to be joined or not? Both specializations seem to be the same, null; but, on the other hand, null means we don't know what their specializations really are. To claim that they are the same would certainly seem strange.

In addition, what happens if we request a list of all faculty members whose area of specialization is "TOPOLOGY" or whose salary is greater than $25,000? In SQL, this would be formulated as

```
SELECT * FROM FACULTY
     WHERE SALARY > 25000
     OR FIELD = 'TOPOLOGY'
```

Is the condition considered true for a faculty member whose salary is $30,000 and for whom the value of FIELD is null? In particular, if the value of FIELD is null, what about the single condition FIELD = 'TOPOLOGY'? Is it to be considered true or false? It certainly cannot be considered true; yet we can't really say it is false either. We really need a third possibility, perhaps called "maybe". Once we allow this third possibility for simple conditions, we need a way to assign values for compound conditions. If SALARY > 25000 is true, for example, and FIELD = 'TOPOLOGY' is maybe, what value should be assigned to the compound condition SALARY > 25000 OR FIELD = 'TOPOLOGY'? In this case, since the first condition in an "OR" is true, the overall condition should be true independently of the truth or falsity of the second condition, and thus it makes sense to assign it the value true.

We can, in fact, construct a new set of truth tables, as shown in Figure 5.1.

AND	T	M	F		OR	T	M	F		NOT			
T	T	M	F		T	T	T	T		T	F	**T** - *True*	
M	M	M	F		M	T	M	M		M	M	**F** - *False*	
F	F	F	F		F	T	M	F		F	T	**M** - *Maybe*	

These truth tables represent the net result of combining two simple conditions with AND or OR or taking the negation (NOT) of an individual simple condition. They give the resulting values based on the values of the simple conditions themselves. Thus, for example, if condition A is maybe and condition B is false, condition A AND B will be false, condition A OR B will be maybe, condition NOT A will be maybe, and condition NOT B will be true.

FIGURE 5.1
Three-way logic

This is not to imply that relational model systems (or any others, for that matter) actually implement this **three-way logic**, nor that implementing such logic is even necessarily desirable. It is, however, at least a theoretical way around some of the problems caused by nulls.

A final comment is in order before leaving the subject of nulls. As indicated earlier, nulls can be used when values are either unknown or nonapplicable. It is the "unknown" use of nulls that causes many of the above problems. If nulls are used only to support nonapplicable values, at least some of the problems disappear. These same problems do not arise, for example, if a null sales rep number in the CUSTOMER relation means specifically that a customer has no sales rep, not that we don't know who represents the customer; they also do not arise if a null value in FIELD indicates that the faculty member has no area of specialization. It is clear that when customers are related to sales reps, a customer number whose sales rep number is null should not be related to any sales reps. It is equally clear that for a faculty member for whom the value of FIELD is null, the value of the condition FIELD = 'TOPOLOGY' is false.

For other perspectives on nulls, see [4], [5], and [8].

RELATIONAL INTEGRITY RULES

In [2], Codd presents some extensions to the basic relational model in an attempt to capture more of the semantics, or meaning, of the actual data that is being modeled. His paper contains a summary of the main features of the model together with a statement of two integrity rules. While the ideas behind these integrity rules appeared in his original paper on the subjects as discussed in chapter 3, they were not listed explicitly.

ENTITY INTEGRITY

Since the function of the primary key is to uniquely identify a particular row in the relation, it does not make sense for the primary key to be null. The usefulness of storing a customer without a customer number, a part without a part number, or an employee without an employee number would certainly be questionable. Refusing to allow null values for any portion of the primary key is the property that Codd termed entity integrity.

> *Def:* **Entity integrity** is the rule that no attribute which participates in the primary key may accept null values.

This property guarantees that entities do indeed have an identity. There will be a way to distinguish one from another, namely, through the primary key. Entity integrity guarantees that the primary key can, indeed, serve this function.

REFERENTIAL INTEGRITY

A **foreign key** is an attribute (or collection of attributes) in one relation whose values are required to match the primary key of another relation. The example given was that the SLSREP_NUMBER in the CUSTOMER relation is a foreign key that must match the primary key of the SLSREP table. In practice this simply means that the sales rep number for any customer must be that of a *real* sales rep.

There is one possible exception to this. In some organizations a customer might exist *without* a sales rep. This could be indicated in the CUSTOMER table by setting such a customer's sales rep number to null. A null sales rep number would, however, violate the restrictions that we have indicated for a foreign key. Thus, we modify the definition of foreign keys to include the possibility of nulls. In doing so, we are describing the property that Codd called referential integrity.

> *Def:* **Referential integrity** is the rule that if a relation, A, contains a foreign key matching the primary key of a relation, B, then values of this foreign key must either match the value of the primary key for some row in relation B or be null.

Without foreign keys, the relational model suffers from two serious deficiencies. The first is that relationships are hidden. We have to notice the existence of a SLSREP_NUMBER column in the SLSREP table and a SLSREP_NUMBER column in the CUSTOMER table in order to be aware that there is a relationship between sales reps and customers. Even then we are not sure. The identical names could be a coincidence. Further, if the names happened to be different, say, SLSREP_NUMBER in the SLSREP table and SR_NUMB in the CUSTOMER table, we might not even be aware that the relationship existed. Foreign keys make such relationships explicit. Even if the names are different, indicating that the SR_NUMB within the CUSTOMER table is a foreign key which must match SLSREP_NUMBER within the SLSREP table leaves no doubt about the relationship.

The second deficiency concerns integrity. There is nothing about the basic relational model that would prevent us from storing a row in the CUSTOMER table in which the SLSREP_NUMBER were 11 even though there were no sales rep 11 in the database. Foreign keys solve this problem through the restrictions stated previously.

For other perspectives on integrity in the relational model, see [4], [5], [6], [8], and [9].

VIEWS

Many relational model systems support the concept of a view. The existing, permanent tables in a relational database are often called **base tables**. A **view**, on the other hand, is a derived, virtual table; i.e., it is a table that does not really exist although it appears to the user that it does. Rather, its contents are derived from data in existing base tables. The manner in which this data is to be derived is stored as part of the view definition.

In the discussion that follows, we will use SQL as a mechanism for defining and processing views. It should be emphasized, however, that many systems which do not support the SQL language provide support for views. Although the manner in which this is accomplished will vary slightly from one system to another, the basic concepts are the same.

In SQL, a view is defined through a **defining query**. Suppose, for example, that we wish to define a view, HOUSEWARES, that consists of the part number, description, units on hand, and unit price of all parts that are in item class "HW". This would be accomplished as follows:

```
CREATE VIEW HOUSEWARES AS
      SELECT PART_NUMBER, PART_DESCRIPTION,
            UNITS_ON_HAND, UNIT_PRICE
      FROM PART
      WHERE ITEM_CLASS = 'HW'
```

Conceptually, given the current data in the Premiere Products database, this view will contain the data shown in Figure 5.2. The data does not actually exist in

HOUSEWARES	PART_NUMBER	PART_DESCRIPTION	UNITS_ON_HAND	UNIT_PRICE
	AX12	IRON	104	17.95
	BH22	TOASTER	95	34.95
	CA14	SKILLET	2	19.95
	CX11	MIXER	112	57.95

FIGURE 5.2
HOUSEWARES view

this form, however, nor will it *ever* exist in this form. It is tempting to think that when this view is used, the query will be executed and will produce some sort of temporary table, called HOUSEWARES, which the user will then access. This is *not* what happens. Instead, this query is "merged" with the query issued by the user, thus forming the actual query that is executed. To illustrate the manner in which this is accomplished, suppose the user enters the following:

```
SELECT *
    FROM HOUSEWARES
    WHERE UNITS_ON_HAND > 100
```

Rather than execute this query, the computer merges this with the query that defines the view, thus producing:

```
SELECT PART_NUMBER, PART_DESCRIPTION,
    UNITS_ON_HAND, UNIT_PRICE
    FROM PART
    WHERE ITEM_CLASS = 'HW'
        AND UNITS_ON_HAND > 100
```

Notice that the selection is from the PART table rather than the HOUSEWARES view, the "*" is replaced by just those columns in the HOUSEWARES view, and the condition involves the condition in the query entered by the user together with the condition stated in the view definition. This new query is the one that is actually executed.

The user, however, is totally unaware that this kind of activity is taking place. It feels as though there actually is a table called HOUSEWARES that is being accessed. One advantage of this approach is that since HOUSEWARES never exists in its own right, any update to the PART table is *immediately* felt by someone accessing the database through the HOUSEWARES view. If HOUSEWARES were an actual stored table, this would not be the case.

The actual form of a view definition is illustrated in the HOUSEWARES view. It is CREATE VIEW view-name AS query. The query can be any legitimate SQL query. (This is not technically true for all relational model implementations. Some forbid the use of UNION in the query, for example.) Optionally the view-name can be followed by the names of the columns in the view, as:

```
CREATE VIEW HOUSEWARES (PART_NUMBER, PART_
        DESCRIPTION, UNITS_ON_HAND, UNIT_PRICE) AS
    SELECT PART_NUMBER, PART_DESCRIPTION,
            UNITS_ON_HAND,
        UNIT_PRICE
        FROM PART
        WHERE ITEM_CLASS = 'HW'
```

This feature can also be used to rename columns. For example, we could have:

```
CREATE VIEW HOUSEWARES (PNUM, DESC, ON_HAND, PRICE) AS
     SELECT PART_NUMBER, PART_DESCRIPTION,
          UNITS_ON_HAND,UNIT_PRICE
     FROM PART
     WHERE ITEM_CLASS = 'HW'
```

In this case, anyone accessing the HOUSEWARES view will refer to PART_ NUMBER as PNUM, PART_DESCRIPTION as DESC, UNITS_ON_HAND as ON_ HAND, and UNIT_PRICE as PRICE.

The HOUSEWARES view is an example of a row-and-column subset view; i.e., it consists of a subset of the rows and columns in some base table, in this case the PART table. Since the query can be any SQL query, a view could involve the join of two or more tables. It could also involve statistics. Here is an example of a view involving a join:

```
CREATE VIEW SALES_CUST (SNUMB, SNAME, CNUMB, CNAME) AS
     SELECT SLSREP.SLSREP_NUMBER,
          SLSREP.SLSREP_NAME,
        CUSTOMER.CUSTOMER_NUMBER, CUSTOMER.NAME
     FROM SLSREP, CUSTOMER
     WHERE SLSREP.SLSREP_NUMBER =
          CUSTOMER.SLSREP_NUMBER
```

Given the current data in the Premiere Products database, this view is conceptually the table shown in Figure 5.3.

SALES_CUST	SNUMB	SNAME	CNUMB	CNAME
	3	MARY JONES	124	SALLY ADAMS
	3	MARY JONES	412	SALLY ADAMS
	3	MARY JONES	622	DAN MARTIN
	6	WILLIAM SMITH	256	ANN SAMUELS
	6	WILLIAM SMITH	315	TOM DANIELS
	6	WILLIAM SMITH	567	JOE BAKER
	6	WILLIAM SMITH	587	JUDY ROBERTS
	12	SAM BROWN	311	DON CHARLES
	12	SAM BROWN	405	AL WILLIAMS
	12	SAM BROWN	522	MARY NELSON

FIGURE 5.3
SALES_CUST view

Following is an example of a view that involves statistics:

```
CREATE VIEW CREDLIM (CREDIT_LIMIT,
          NUMBER_OF_CUSTOMERS) AS
     SELECT CREDIT_LIMIT, COUNT(CUSTOMER_NUMBER)
          FROM CUSTOMER
          GROUP BY CREDIT_LIMIT
```

Given the current data in the Premiere Products database, this view is conceptually the table shown in Figure 5.4.

CREDLIM	CREDIT_ LIMIT	NUMBER_OF_ CUSTOMERS
	300	3
	500	3
	800	3
	1000	1

FIGURE 5.4
CREDLIM view

The use of views furnishes several advantages:

1. Views provide logical data independence. If the database structure is changed (columns added, relationships changed, etc.) in such a way that the view can still be derived from existing data, the user can still access the same view. If adding extra columns to tables in the database is the only change and these columns are not required by this user, the defining query may not even need to be changed. If relationships are changed, it may be that the defining query will be different, but since users need not even be aware of the defining query, this difference is unknown to them. They continue to access the database through the same view, as though nothing has changed. For an example of the type of change that requires modification of the defining query, consider the following:
   a. Customers are assigned to territories.
   b. Each territory is assigned to a single sales rep.
   c. A sales rep can have more than one territory.
   d. A customer is represented by the sales rep who covers the territory to which the customer is assigned.

To implement these changes, we might choose to restructure the database as follows:

SLSREP(SLSREP_NUMBER, SLSREP_NAME, SLSREP_ADDRESS,
           TOTAL_COMMISSION, COMMISSION_RATE)

TERRITORY(TERRITORY_NUMBER, TERRITORY_DESCRIPTION,
           SLSREP_NUMBER)

CUSTOMER(CUSTOMER_NUMBER, NAME, ADDRESS, CURRENT_
           BALANCE, CREDIT_LIMIT, TERRITORY_NUMBER)

Assuming that the SALES_CUST view shown earlier is still required, the defining query could be reformulated as follows:

```
CREATE VIEW SALES_CUST (SNUMB, SNAME, CNUMB,
        CNAME) AS
    SELECT SLSREP.SLSREP_NUMBER,
            SLSREP.SLSREP_NAME,
        CUSTOMER.CUSTOMER_NUMBER, CUSTOMER.NAME
    FROM SLSREP, TERRITORY, CUSTOMER
    WHERE SLSREP.SLSREP_NUMBER =
        TERRITORY.SLSREP_NUMBER
        AND TERRITORY.TERRITORY_NUMBER =
        CUSTOMER.TERRITORY_NUMBER
```

The user of this view will still be presented with the number and name of a sales rep together with the number and name of customers whom the sales rep represents. Such a user will be totally unaware of the new structure in the database.

2. Since each user has his or her own view, the same data can be viewed by different users in different ways.

3. A view should contain only those columns required by a given user. This practice accomplishes two things. First, since the view will, in all probability, contain far fewer columns than the overall database and since the view is effectively a single relation rather than a collection of relations, it greatly simplifies the user's perception of the database. Second, it furnishes a measure of security. Columns that are not included in the view are not accessible to this user. Omitting the CURRENT_BALANCE column from the view will ensure that a user of this view cannot access the balance of any customer. Likewise, rows that are not included in the view are not accessible. A user of the HOUSEWARES view, for example, cannot obtain any information about sporting goods, even though both housewares and sporting goods are stored in the same base table, PART.

All of the above advantages hold when views are used for retrieval purposes only; the story is a little different when it comes to update.

ROW AND COLUMN SUBSETS

Consider the row and column subset view HOUSEWARES. The main problem with this view is that there are columns in the underlying base table, PART, which are not present. Thus, if we attempt to add a row ('BB99', 'PAN', 50, 14.95), somehow the system must determine how to fill in the remaining columns from PART: ITEM_CLASS, and WAREHOUSE_NUMBER. In this case, it is clear how to fill in ITEM_CLASS. According to the definition of the view, it should be "HW". On the other hand, it is not at all clear how to fill in WAREHOUSE_NUMBER. The only possibility would be for it to be NULL. Thus, provided that any columns not included in a view may accept nulls, we can potentially add new rows in the fashion previously indicated. There is another problem, however. Suppose the user attempts to add the row ('AZ52', 'POT', 25, 9.95). This attempt *must* be rejected, since there is already a part numbered "AZ52" in the PART table. This rejection will certainly seem strange to the user, since there is no such part in this user's view! (It has a different item class.)

Updates or deletions cause no particular problem in this view. If the description of part "CA14' is changed from "SKILLET' to "PAN', this change will be made in the PART table. If part "CX11' is deleted, this deletion will occur in the PART table. One peculiar change could potentially take place, however. Suppose that ITEM_CLASS were included as a column in the HOUSEWARES view and suppose that a user changed the item class of part "CX11' from "HW' to "AP'. Since this item would no longer satisfy the criterion for being included in the HOUSEWARES view, it would effectively disappear as far as this user were concerned!

While some problems do have to be overcome, it seems possible to update the database through the HOUSEWARES view. This does not imply that *any* row and column subset view is updatable, however. Consider the following view:

```
CREATE VIEW SLS_CRED AS
        SELECT DISTINCT CREDIT_LIMIT, SLSREP_NUMBER
        FROM CUSTOMER
```

(The word distinct is used to omit duplicate rows in the resulting relation.) Conceptually, this view currently contains the data shown in Figure 5.5.

SLS_CRED	CREDIT_LIMIT	SLSREP_NUMBER
	500	3
	800	6
	300	12
	300	6
	800	12
	1000	3
	500	6

FIGURE 5.5
SLS—CRED view

It shows the relationship between sales reps and the credit limits of customers they represent.

How would we add the row (1000, 6) to this view? In the underlying base table, CUSTOMER, at least one customer must be added whose credit limit is $1000 and whose sales rep is 6, but who? We can't very well leave the other columns null in this case, especially since one of them is the CUSTOMER_NUMBER, which is the primary key. What would changing the row (800, 12) to (1000, 12) mean? Would it mean changing the credit limit of all of the customers who are represented by sales rep 12 and who currently have a credit limit of $800 to $1000? Would it mean changing the credit limit of one of these customers and deleting the rest? What would it mean to delete the row (500, 3)? Would it mean deleting all customers whose credit limit is $500 and whose sales rep is 3, or would it mean assigning these customers a different sales rep or a different credit limit? Potentially, we could also set their credit limit and/or their sales rep numbers to null.

Why does the view SLS_CRED involve a number of serious problems that are not present in HOUSEWARES? The basic reason is that HOUSEWARES includes, as one of its columns, the primary key of the underlying base table and SLS_CRED does not. This is true in general. A row and column subset view that contains the primary key of the underlying base table is updatable (subject, of course, to some of the concerns we have discussed).

JOINS

In general, views that involve joins of base tables can cause real problems for update. Consider the relatively simple view SALES_CUST, for example, described earlier (see Figure 5.3). The fact that some columns in the underlying base tables are not present in this view certainly presents some of the same problems discussed earlier. Even assuming that these problems can be overcome through the use of nulls, there are still other, more serious problems inherent in the attempt to update the database through this view. On the surface, changing the row (6, 'WILLIAM SMITH', 256, 'ANN SAMUELS') to (6, 'NANCY BAKER', 256, 'ANN SAMUELS') might not appear to pose any problems other than some inconsistency in the data. (In the new version of the row, the name of sales rep 6 is Nancy Baker; on the next row in the table, the name of sales rep 6 is William Smith.) The problem is actually more serious than that. It is not possible to make only this change! Since the name of the sales rep is stored just once in the underlying sales rep table, changing the name from WILLIAM SMITH to NANCY BAKER on this one row of the view will cause the same change to be made on all the other rows. Although in this case that would probably be a good thing, in general the occurrence of unexpected changes as a result of an update is definitely not desirable.

Additions and deletions can also cause problems. Consider the following questions, which will be restated in the exercises at the end of the chapter. What problems are caused by adding the row (3, 'SAM BROWN', 400, 'MARK WILSON')? Give an example of another row that we might try to add and would cause problems in the underlying base tables. What problems are caused by deleting the row (12, 'SAM BROWN', 311, 'DON CHARLES')?

Before leaving the topic of views that involve joins, it should be noted that not all joins create the preceding problem. If two base tables happen to have the same primary key and this primary key is used as the join field, updating the database will not be problematic. Consider the following, for example:

The actual database contains not a single SLSREP table but two:

SLSREP_DEMO(SLSREP_NUMBER, SLSREP_NAME, SLSREP_ADDRESS)

and

SLSREP_FIN(SLSREP_NUMBER, TOTAL_COMMISSION, COMMISSION_
RATE)

(see Figure 5.6). In this case, what was a single table in the Premiere Products

SLSREP_DEMO	SLSREP_NUMBER	SLSREP_NAME	SLSREP_ADDRESS
	3	MARY JONES	123 MAIN,GRANT,MI
	6	WILLIAM SMITH	102 RAYMOND,ADA,MI
	12	SAM BROWN	419 HARPER,LANSING,MI

SLSREP_FIN	SLSREP_NUMBER	TOTAL_COMMISSION	COMMISSION_RATE
	3	2150.00	.05
	6	4912.50	.07
	12	2150.00	.05

FIGURE 5.6
Salesrep data split
across two relations

design has been separated into two. Any user who expected to see a single table
could have been accommodated through a view that joined these two tables
together on SLSREP_NUMBER. We could, in fact, call the view SLSREP. The
view definition would be:

```
CREATE VIEW SLSREP AS
    SELECT SLSREP_DEMO, SLSREP_NUMBER, SLSREP_NAME,
            SLSREP_ADDRESS, TOTAL_COMMISSION,
            COMMISSION_RATE
        FROM SLSREP_DEMO, SLSREP_FIN
        WHERE SLSREP_DEMO.SLSREP_NUMBER =
            SLSREP_FIN.SLSREP_NUMBER
```

Conceptually, this view would contain the data shown in Figure 5.7.

SLSREP	SLSREP_NUMBER	SLSREP_NAME	SLSREP_ADDRESS	TOTAL_COMMISSION	COMMISSION_RATE
	3	MARY JONES	123 MAIN,GRANT,MI	2150.00	.05
	6	WILLIAM SMITH	102 RAYMOND,ADA,MI	4912.50	.07
	12	SAM BROWN	419 HARPER,LANSING,MI	2150.00	.05

FIGURE 5.7
SLSREP as a view that
is a join of
SLSREP_DEMO and
SLSREP_FIN

No difficulty is encountered in updating this view. To add the row (10, 'JEAN
PETERS', '14 BRINK,HART,MI', 107.50, .05) to the database merely means
adding the row (10, 'JEAN PETERS', '14 BRINK,HART,MI') to SLSREP_
DEMO and the row (10, 107.50, .05) to SLSREP_FIN. A change to any row in
the view requires only a change to the appropriate base table. If sales rep 3's name
is change to Mary Lewis, the name will be changed in SLSREP_DEMO. If her

commission rate is changed to .06, the change will be made in SLSREP_FIN. To delete any row from the view, we delete the corresponding rows from both underlying base tables. To delete sales rep 6 from SLSREP, we delete sales rep 6 from *both* SLSREP_DEMO *and* SLSREP_FIN.

The previously discussed view SLSREP is updatable. None of the types of updates (add, change, or delete) cause any problems. The main reason that this view is updatable and other views involving joins are not is that this view is derived from the joining of two base tables *on the primary key of each.* In contrast, the view SALES_CUST is derived from the joining of two tables by matching a *foreign* key of one with the primary key of the other. Even more severe problems are encountered if neither of the join columns is a primary key.

STATISTICS

A view that involves statistics calculated from one or more base tables is the most troublesome of all. Consider CREDLIM, for example (see Figure 5.4). How would we add the row (600, 3)? We would somehow have to add to the database three customers each of whose credit limit is $600. Likewise, changing the row (500, 3) to (500, 6) means adding three customers each of whose credit limit is $500. Clearly these are impossible tasks.

CURRENT SYSTEMS

The preceding discussion concerned what is *theoretically possible*, not what is actually implemented on current commercial systems. Many current systems support update of views that are row and column subsets. (In performing this kind of update, users must be mindful of some of the pitfalls we have discussed.) Views involving statistics are not even theoretically updatable. Views involving joins form the middle ground. Some such views are not theoretically updatable, others are. *Most current implementations will not support update of the database through any view that involves a join, even views that are updatable in theory.* The day will come when systems do support this type of update, however; progress is under way.

VIEWS AND SUBSCHEMAS

In chapters 1 and 2, we discussed the concept of a subschema, or individual user's view of the database. While it may seem that the relational model "view" is really what we termed a subschema, this is not quite accurate. The basic problem is that a view, even though it may be derived by joining more than one base table, is still essentially a single table. For some users, this will not be enough. If a given user required access to all the columns in all the tables of the Premiere Products database, it would not be practical to attempt to present this user with a single table that was the result of joining all existing tables together. The database is generally far more involved than the sample we have been using for Premiere Products, so an attempt to join all of the tables together in one view would be even less practical, if not impossible. Further, since some views involving joins are not updatable using today's systems, and others are not even theoretically updatable, such an approach would not be feasible for any user updating the database.

In reality, a subschema in a relational model system will consist of some combination of base tables and views. For some users, a single view may suffice. Others may require a combination. In general, views rather than base tables should be used wherever possible in order to obtain the advantages described earlier.

For other information on views, see [4], [5], [6], [8], and [9].

SECURITY

While views furnish a certain amount of security, the main security mechanism in relational model systems is achieved through some form of "GRANT" mechanism. The sample GRANT mechanism described here is that of DB2, one of the two relational model systems we will examine later in this chapter. It is representative, however, of the type of security mechanism found in many other systems.

The basic idea is that different types of privileges can be granted to users and, if necessary, later revoked. This is accomplished through GRANT and REVOKE statements. The following are examples of the GRANT statement:

GRANT SELECT ON SLSREP TO JONES
(User Jones will be able to retrieve data from the SLSREP table.)

GRANT INSERT ON PART TO SMITH, BROWN
(Users Smith and Brown will be able to add new parts.)

GRANT UPDATE ON CUSTOMER (NAME, ADDRESS) TO ANDERSON
(User Anderson will be able to change the name or address of customers.)

GRANT DELETE ON ORDER_LINE TO MARTIN
(User Martin will be able to delete order lines.)

GRANT SELECT ON PART (PART_NUMBER, PART_DESCRIPTION,
            ITEM_CLASS) TO PUBLIC
(Any user will be able to retrieve part numbers, descriptions and item classes.)

GRANT INDEX ON SLSREP TO ROBERTS
(User Roberts can create an index on the SLSREP table.)

GRANT ALTER ON CUSTOMER TO THOMAS
(User Thomas can change the structure of the CUSTOMER table.)

GRANT ALL ON SLSREP, CUSTOMER, ORDER TO WILSON
(User Wilson has all of the privileges on the SLSREP, CUSTOMER, and ORDER tables.)

The privileges that can be granted are SELECT (retrieve data), UPDATE (change data), DELETE (delete data), INSERT (add new data), ALTER (change the structure of a table), and INDEX (create an index). Any GRANT statement can be followed with the clause "WITH GRANT OPTION", which will allow the user mentioned in the GRANT statement not only the appropriate privileges but also the ability to GRANT these same privileges (or a subset of them) to still other users.

Any privileges granted in this fashion can later be revoked by using the REVOKE statement. The format of the REVOKE statement is essentially the same as that of the GRANT statement, but there are two differences. Instead of GRANT privileges TO users, the format is REVOKE privileges FROM users. In addition, the clause WITH GRANT OPTION is obviously not meaningful as part of a REVOKE statement. Incidentally, the revoke will cascade; i.e., if Jones was granted privileges WITH GRANT OPTION and then granted these same privileges to Smith, revoking the privileges from Jones will cause Smith's privileges to be revoked at the same time.

GRANT and REVOKE can also be applied to views. This provides the capability of restricting access to only certain rows within tables. If, for example, we wanted to permit sales rep 3 (Mary Jones) to access any data concerning the customers she represents but not permit her to access data concerning any other customers, this could be accomplished as follows:

```
CREATE VIEW SLSREP_3_CUSTOMERS AS
     SELECT *
          FROM CUSTOMER
          WHERE SLSREP_NUMBER = 3
GRANT SELECT ON SLSREP_3_CUSTOMER TO MARY_JONES
```

For other information on security, see [1], [4], [5], [6], [8], and [9].

BILL-OF-MATERIALS

Occasionally, we encounter a relationship between an entity and itself. The classic example of such a relationship is the **bill-of-materials relationship** in manufacturing organizations. In this relationship each part is related to its components, i.e., the parts that are assembled to create it. Each part is also related to its parents, i.e., those parts for which it is a component. In addition to knowing which parts are components of which other parts, we also need to know how many are required.

As an example, suppose that our final product is part A. Assembling part A requires three units of part B and two units of part C. Assembling a single part B requires one unit of part D and one unit of part E. Assembling a single part C requires two units of part D and one unit of part E. This information can be represented pictorially, as shown in Figure 5.8. In this type of drawing, we can

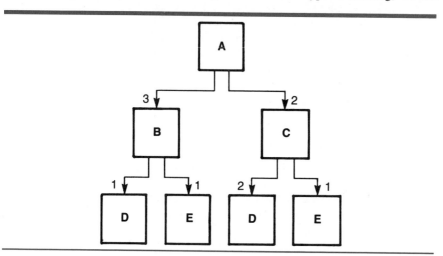

FIGURE 5.8
Sample bill-of-
materials relationship

determine the components of any part by following the arrows from the bottom of the part box to the collection of the parts at the next level in the drawing. The quantities that are required of each of these parts are written next to the arrows. Thus, we see that this figure represents exactly the set of requirements just described.

How would such a relationship be implemented in a relational database? Clearly, there is an entity "part", and there will be a corresponding relation, say, PART. Let's assume that the key to this relation is a column called PART_ NUMBER. We now have to implement a many-to-many relationship between this PART relation and itself. If we apply the ideas previously discussed for implementing many-to-many relationships, we will create a new relation whose key is the concatenation of PART_NUMBER and PART_NUMBER! Obviously, we need to do something a little different in this case.

Actually, we do use a concatenation of part numbers as the key, but we distinguish the part numbers. We could call the first part number the PARENT_PART_ NUMBER, for example, and the second part number the COMPONENT_PART_NUMBER. In addition to these two columns that constitute the key, we also include a column called QUANTITY_REQUIRED that indicates the number of units of the component used in assembling the parent. Since the information in this relation indicates the structure of the various products, we will call the relation PRODUCT_STRUCTURE. Thus, in addition to the PART relation, we will have the one additional relation

PRODUCT_STRUCTURE (PARENT_PART_NUMBER,
    COMPONENT_PART_NUMBER, QUANTITY_REQUIRED)

A sample extension of this relation is shown in Figure 5.9. The first row in

PRODUCT_STRUCTURE	PARENT_PART_NUMBER	COMPONENT_PART_NUMBER	QUANTITY_REQUIRED
	A	B	3
	A	C	2
	B	D	1
	B	E	1
	C	D	2
	C	E	1

FIGURE 5.9
Relational model implementation of the bill-of-materials relationship

this table indicates that three units of part B are used in assembling part A. The last row indicates that one unit of part E is used in assembling part C.

To find all of the immediate components (components at the next level in the structure shown in Figure 5.8) for part A, we determine all of the rows in which the parent part number is A. The component part numbers in each of these rows are the part numbers of the immediate components of A. In this case, the immediate components are B and C. If we so desire, we can determine the quantities required in the same fashion. We could then apply the same reasoning to each of these components to find their components. We would view both B and C as parents to find their components in turn. This process could continue until we obtained parts that had no components, such as D and E.

We could reverse the roles of parents and components to produce "WHERE-USED" information. If we wished to determine all of the immediate parents of part D, for example, we would locate the rows in which part D occurred as a component part number. The set of all the parent part numbers in these rows would be the immediate parents of D, in this case parts B and C. We could then determine where B and C were used in the same fashion, and so on.

While the bill-of-materials relationship is the most widely known example of a relationship with this type of structure, there are certainly others. As one example, in the next chapter we will encounter a relationship between courses at a college and their prerequisites that has essentially the same structure.

For other information on the bill-of-materials relationship, see [1].

INDEXES

Within relational model systems, the main mechanism for increasing the efficiency with which data is retrieved from the database is the use of **indexes**. Typically, an index can be created and maintained for any column or combination of columns in any table. Once an index has been created, it can be used to facilitate retrieval. In powerful mainframe relational systems, the decision concerning which index or indexes to use (if any) during a particular type of retrieval is one of the functions of the **optimizer** within the DBMS, i.e., no reference is made to any index by the user; rather, the system makes the decision behind the scenes. (In less powerful systems and, in particular, in many of the microcomputer systems, the user may have to specifically indicate in some fashion that a given index should be used.)

As you would expect, the use of any index is not purely advantageous or disadvantageous. The advantage was already mentioned: an index makes certain types of retrieval more efficient. There are two disadvantages: An index occupies space that is technically not required. (Any retrieval that can be made using an index can also be made without the index. The process may be less efficient, but it is still possible. Thus, an index is technically not necessary.) The other disadvantage is that the index must be updated whenever corresponding data in the database is updated. Since the index is really unnecessary, the update of the index is additional overhead that is also unnecessary. The main question when considering whether or not to create a given index is, Do the benefits derived during retrieval outweigh the additional storage required and the extra overhead incurred during update operations?

Indexes can be added and dropped at will. The final decision concerning the columns or combination of columns on which indexes should be built does not have to be made at the time the database is first implemented. If, after viewing the pattern of access to the database, the user determines that the overall performance would benefit through the creation of a new index on some combination of columns, the index can easily be added. Likewise, if it appears that an existing index is unnecessary, it can easily be dropped.

The command used to create an index varies from one system to another. The following are examples of commands for creating indexes for the Premiere Products database, using a DBMS, such as DB2, which supports SQL.

```
CREATE UNIQUE INDEX CUSTOMER_INDEX ON CUSTOMER
      (CUSTOMER_NUMBER)
```

(Creates an index on the CUSTOMER_NUMBER column within the CUSTOMER table. The index is called CUSTOMER_INDEX. The word UNIQUE indicates that the system is to maintain uniqueness of customer numbers; i.e., the system will not permit two customers with the same number to exist in the database. This index will be used to support direct retrieval based on the primary key, CUSTOMER_NUMBER.)

```
CREATE INDEX CUSTOMER_SLSREP_INDEX ON CUSTOMER
      (SLSREP_NUMBER)
```

(Creates an index, called CUSTOMER_SLSREP_INDEX, on the SLSREP_NUMBER column within the CUSTOMER table. This index will not be unique, since the same sales rep can appear on many rows in the CUSTOMER table. This index can be used to rapidly find all the customers of a given sales rep.)

```
CREATE UNIQUE INDEX ORDER_LINE_INDEX
      ON ORDER_LINE (ORDER_NUMBER, PART_NUMBER)
```

(Creates a unique index on the ORDER_NUMBER, PART_NUMBER combination, which is the primary key of the ORDER_LINE table.)

```
CREATE INDEX CREDIT_INDEX ON CUSTOMER (CREDIT_LIMIT
      DESC, NAME)
```

(Creates an index for the CUSTOMER table, called CREDIT_INDEX. If customers are listed using this index, they will appear in order of descending credit limit. Within any credit limit, the customers will be ordered by name.)

Likewise, the command used to drop an index varies from one system to another. The following is an example of a command for dropping an index for the Premiere Products database, also using a DBMS, such as DB2, that supports SQL.

```
DROP INDEX CUSTOMER_INDEX
```

These indexes are typically B-tree indexes (see Appendix A for a discussion of B-tree indexes). They are very efficient and, if a given type of retrieval is going to be performed with any frequency, an index to facilitate the process is usually worthwhile. The added efficiency will, in such situations, usually offset the additional storage required and the extra overhead in processing incurred when updating the database. The ability to create and drop indexes easily, together with an efficient optimizer, provides a great deal of flexibility. If an index were created on a given night which would increase the efficiency of a given type of retrieval, the optimizer should immediately begin making use of the index. No program need change. The only difference that a user might notice is that certain types of retrieval would be more rapid and certain types of updates might be less rapid. Likewise, if an index were dropped on a particular night, the optimizer would find new ways of satisfying any request that utilized that index. Again, no program need change. In this case, the only difference that might be noticed is that certain types of retrieval would be less rapid and certain types of update might be more rapid. The flexibility to make this type of change "on the fly" is one of the real benefits of the relational model which is not shared by systems following other models.

For other information on the use of indexes, see [1], [4], [6], [8], and [9].

WHAT DOES IT TAKE TO BE RELATIONAL?

In chapter 2, we discussed the functions that should be provided by database management systems in general. We will now examine the functions that should be provided by relational model systems in particular. This has become especially important with the popularity of the relational model and the fact that many systems unworthy of the title still call themselves "relational." We need a mechanism for distinguishing between true relational systems and the others.

Codd, in [3], defines a relational system as one in which:

1. Users perceive databases as collections of tables. There are no additional structures present of which the users are aware.
2. At least the operations of SELECT, PROJECT, and JOIN (see the material on the relational algebra in chapter 3) are supported. This support is independent of any predefined access paths.

The first characteristic is essentially a definition of the relational structure; it contains tables (relations) and nothing else. Note that the restriction concerns how the user *perceives* the data. It does not address how the data is actually stored. The way in which the system is to implement this structure is left totally to the system. The second characteristic indicates that not only must the three crucial operations of SELECT, PROJECT, and JOIN be supported, but the support must not be dependent on any predefined access path (such as an index). This means, for example, that we must be able to select information concerning customer 124 whether or not an index has been created on the customer number column. We must be able to join customers and their sales reps whether or not indexes are found on the sales rep columns in the SLSREP and CUSTOMER tables. Any system that supports these operations only when appropriate indexes exist does not meet the definition.

The definition states that the system must support the SELECT, PROJECT, and JOIN operations. It does not indicate that the system must use this terminology. SQL supports these three operations through the SELECT statement which is considerably more powerful than the relational algebra SELECT, which is the SELECT indicated in the definition. The following are examples of the manner in which SQL supports the operations:

SELECT (Choose certain rows from a table):

```
SELECT *
     FROM CUSTOMER
     WHERE CREDIT_LIMIT = 500
```

PROJECT (Choose certain columns from a table):

```
SELECT CUSTOMER_NUMBER, NAME, ADDRESS
     FROM CUSTOMER
```

JOIN (Combine tables based on matching columns):

```
SELECT SLSREP_NUMBER, SLSREP_NAME, SLSREP_ADDRESS,
       TOTAL_COMMISSION, COMMISSION_RATE,
       CUSTOMER_NUMBER, NAME, ADDRESS,
       CURRENT_BALANCE, CREDIT_LIMIT
    FROM SLSREP, CUSTOMER
    WHERE SLSREP.SLSREP_NUMBER =
          CUSTOMER.SLSREP_NUMBER
```

Date, in [4], discusses a classification scheme for systems that support at least the relational structure; i.e., systems in which the only structure that the user perceives is the table. There are four categories into which such systems may fall:

1. TABULAR

   In a **tabular** system, the only structure perceived by the user is the table, but the system does not support the SELECT, PROJECT, and JOIN operators in the unrestricted fashion indicated in Codd's definition. Inverted file systems typically fall in this category.

2. MINIMALLY RELATIONAL

   You will recall that the operations SELECT, PROJECT, and JOIN are not the only operations in the relational algebra. There are eight operations altogether. A **minimally relational** system is one that supports the tabular structure together with the SELECT, PROJECT, and JOIN operations but does not support the complete set of operations from the relational algebra. Many of the relational microcomputer systems fall into this category.

3. RELATIONALLY COMPLETE

   Any system that supports the tabular structure and all the operations of the relational algebra (without requiring appropriate indexes) is said to be **relationally complete**. There are many systems in this category, including the two we will examine in this chapter, DB2 and INGRES.

4. FULLY RELATIONAL

   A system that supports the tabular structure, all the operations of the relational algebra, and the two integrity rules (entity and referential integrity) described earlier in this section is said to be **fully relational**. This is the goal for which systems are (or should be) striving. At present, we are not aware of any systems that are fully relational according to this definition. The principal failing on the part of many systems is lack of support for referential integrity. Much progress is occurring in this area and soon we shall see a number of fully relational systems.

While the preceding guidelines form a valuable categorization for systems, there have been other requirements proposed for relational model systems. Kim, in particular (see [7]), proposed a number of other valuable properties for such systems to possess. Some of the properties Kim suggested have already been addressed in chapter 2, since they really relate to systems in general, not just to relational systems. Others properties, however, are specific to the relational model and are worth examining:

1. An interface for a high-level, nonprocedural language that has capabilities for data definition, data retrieval, and data manipulation. Such a language should be available to both programmers and nontechnical users.
2. Efficient structures in which to store the data and efficient mechanisms to support access to the data. This point does not address the question of what these structures must be, just that they must be present. Storing each table in a separate file and using B-tree indexes to enhance retrieval is one possibility.
3. An efficient optimizer. The DBMS must be able to respond to a user request for update or retrieval in an efficient manner. In nonrelational systems, optimization is done by programmers. The flexibility that is one of the main strengths of the relational model requires that optimization be removed from the shoulders of programmers and turned over to the DBMS itself.
4. User views and snapshots of the database. User views were discussed earlier. A snapshot is a view of the database at a particular point in time. SQL could be used, for example, to create an actual table (not a virtual table like a view) that contained data extracted from the main database. This data could then be used by users in whatever way was appropriate. The data in this new database, or snapshot, would reflect the data in the overall database at the time the SQL query was executed. Unlike views, any subsequent change made to the main database would *not* affect this snapshot.
5. A report generator in which attractive and useful reports against data in the database can be easily and quickly described and produced by users.

For more information concerning what it takes to make a system relational, see [3], [4], [6], [7], [8], and [9]. Also, watch the pages of any of the major computing periodicals, such as *ComputerWorld*, in which this topic is the subject of relatively frequent articles.

5.3   ADVANCED SQL

SQL, the language that was originally covered in chapter 3, is in many ways the dominant language for data definition and manipulation of relational databases. In the previous section, SQL was used as a vehicle to illustrate some further concepts within the relational model. In this section, we will expand further on SQL itself.

DATA DEFINITION

We have already encountered many of the data definition facilities of SQL. We examined the basic way in which tables are defined. We have seen how to create and drop views and how to create and drop indexes. We will now examine data types that may be used in table definition, and methods for allowing or disallowing nulls, for altering a table definition, and for dropping a table.

DATA TYPES

Besides the data types DECIMAL and CHAR, there are others available. While the actual data types that are supported will vary somewhat from one implementation of SQL to another, the following list is indicative of the types that are often encountered:

INTEGER
: fullword integer

SMALLINT
: halfword integer

DECIMAL (p,q)
: packed decimal number p digits in length with q of these being decimal places. For example, DECIMAL (5,2) represents a number with three places to the left of the decimal and two to the right. It is the equivalent of a picture of 9(3)v9(2) in COBOL.

CHAR (n)
: character string n characters in length

VARCHAR(n)
: variable length character string that has a maximum length of n characters

For any given implementation of SQL, the syntax may vary slightly from that listed above. It may be, for example, that to specify a variable length character string the word VARYING is used as an option within the CHAR data type, as in CHAR(20) VARYING. There may be options as to whether numbers are to be signed or unsigned and within the DECIMAL data type as to whether or not numbers are to be packed. Floating-point decimal numbers will also usually be supported in some fashion.

NULLS

In any implementation of SQL that supports **nulls**, there must be a mechanism to indicate which columns can accept null values and which cannot. This is usually accomplished through the clause NOT NULL. Those columns whose description includes NOT NULL are not allowed to accept null values. Other columns may accept such values.

For example, suppose that the sales rep number and name cannot accept null values but all other columns in the SLSREP table can. The corresponding CREATE TABLE command is shown in Figure 5.10. Any attempt to store a null value in either the sales rep number or name columns will be rejected by the system.

```
CREATE TABLE SLSREP
      (SLSREP_NUMBER      INTEGER      NOT NULL,
       SLSREP_NAME        CHAR(15)     NOT NULL,
       SLSREP_ADDRESS     CHAR (25),
       TOTAL_COMMISSION   DECIMAL (7,2),
       COMMISSION_RATE    DECIMAL (3,2))
```

FIGURE 5.10
SQL create statement
that involves nulls

ALTER

It is possible in SQL to easily alter the structure of an existing table. In contrast, such a change to the structure of existing databases in nonrelational systems is a much more complex process, involving not only a change to the description of the structure but utility programs to unload the data from the current structure and then reload it with the new structure.

Changing a table is accomplished through the ALTER table command. At a minimum, new columns may be added to the end of an existing table. Suppose that we now wish to maintain a customer type for each customer in the Premiere Products database. This type can be "R" for regular customers, "D" for distributors, and "S" for special customers. We need a new column in the customer table. This can be added as follows:

```
ALTER TABLE CUSTOMER
     ADD CUSTOMER_TYPE        CHAR(1)
```

At this point, the CUSTOMER table contains an extra column, CUSTOMER_TYPE. Any rows added from this point on will have this extra column. Effectively, existing records contain this extra column immediately. (The data in any existing row will only be changed to reflect the new column the next time the row is updated. However, any time a row is selected for any reason, the system will treat the row as though the column is actually present. Thus, to the user, it will feel as though the structure was changed immediately.)

For rows added from this point on, the value of CUSTOMER_TYPE will be assigned as the row is added. For existing rows, some value of CUSTOMER_TYPE must be assigned. The simplest approach (from the point of view of the DBMS, *not* the user) is to assign the value NULL as a CUSTOMER_TYPE on all existing rows. (This requires that CUSTOMER_TYPE accept null values, and some systems actually require this. That is, any column added to a table definition *will* accept nulls; the user has no choice in the matter.) A more flexible approach and one that is supported by some systems is to allow the user to specify an initial value. In our example, if most customers are of type "R", we might set all of the customer types for existing customers to "R" and later change those customers of type "D" or type "S" to the appropriate value. To change the structure and set the value of CUSTOMER_TYPE to "R" for all existing records, we would type:

```
ALTER TABLE CUSTOMER
     ADD CUSTOMER_TYPE        CHAR(1)    INIT = 'R'
```

Note that if a system will only set new columns to null, the above initialization can still be accomplished by following the alter with an update command:

```
UPDATE CUSTOMER
     SET CUSTOMER_TYPE = 'R'
```

While this is not particularly difficult, it still is an extra step. Further, it is desirable for a user to determine whether or not nulls are to be allowed rather than have the system require that they be allowed. Thus, it is preferable for the system to support initial values for added columns.

While some systems automatically position newly added columns at the end, others allow users to determine where such columns are to be positioned. If CUSTOMER_TYPE is to be positioned before CURRENT_BALANCE in such systems, the ALTER statement would read something like:

```
ALTER TABLE CUSTOMER
        ADD CUSTOMER_TYPE        BEFORE CURRENT_BALANCE
                                 CHAR(1)    INIT = 'R'
```

or, assuming CURRENT_BALANCE is the fourth column:

```
ALTER TABLE CUSTOMER
        ADD CUSTOMER_TYPE        BEFORE 4
                                 CHAR(1)    INIT = 'R'
```

Note that this column ordering becomes important only when a feature such as SELECT * FROM table name is used, i.e., where the system lists all columns in the order in which they are stored.

Some systems allow existing columns to be deleted. The syntax for deleting the WAREHOUSE column from the PART table would typically be something like:

```
ALTER TABLE PART
        DELETE WAREHOUSE
```

Finally, some systems allow changes in the data types of given columns. A typical use of such a change would be to increase the length of a character field that was found to be inadequate. Assuming that the NAME column in the CUS-TOMER table needed to be increased to thirty characters, the ALTER statement would be something like:

```
ALTER TABLE CUSTOMER
        CHANGE COLUMN NAME TO CHAR(30)
```

Interestingly enough, most mainframe systems currently do not support this useful type of change but many microcomputer systems do.

DROP

A table that is no longer needed can be deleted with the DROP command. If the SLSREP table were no longer needed in the Premiere Products database, the command would be:

```
DROP TABLE SLSREP
```

The table would be erased, as would all indexes and views defined on the table. References to the table would be removed from the system catalog.

DATA MANIPULATION

The only new aspect of data manipulation that will be discussed here is the impact of nulls. Two aspects must be covered: setting a given column to null and testing a given column to determine whether it is or is not null.

To set a given column to null, we merely use the word null in the appropriate assignment. To set the address of customer 124 to null, for example, we would enter:

```
UPDATE CUSTOMER
    SET ADDRESS = NULL
    WHERE CUSTOMER_NUMBER = 124
```

We can also test to see whether or not a given column is null. The syntax for the test is not ADDRESS = NULL, as you might expect, but rather ADDRESS IS NULL. To obtain a list of the customer numbers and names of all the customers whose address is null, we would type

```
SELECT CUSTOMER_NUMBER, NAME
    FROM CUSTOMER
    WHERE ADDRESS IS NULL
```

THE CATALOG

Information concerning the tables known to the system is kept in the system **catalog**. The following description of the catalog applies to DB2, but other systems are similar. The exact structure has been somewhat oversimplified, but it is certainly representative of the basic ideas.

The catalog contains three tables, SYSTABLES (information about the tables known to SQL), SYSCOLUMNS (information about the columns within these tables), and SYSINDEXES (information about indexes defined on these tables). While these tables have many columns, only a few are of concern to us here.

SYSTABLES contains columns NAME, CREATOR, and COLCOUNT. The NAME column identifies the name of a table. The CREATOR column contains an identification of the person or group who created the table. The COLCOUNT column contains the number of columns within the table that is being described. If, for example, the user whose ID is "SALESX01" created the sales rep table, and the sales rep table had five columns, there would be a row in the SYSTABLES table in which NAME was "SLSREP", CREATOR was "SALESX01", and COL-COUNT was five. Similar rows would exist for all tables known to the system.

SYSCOLUMNS contains columns NAME, TBNAME, and COLTYPE. The NAME column identifies the name of a column in one of the tables. The table in which the column is found is stored in TBNAME, and the data type for the column is found in COLTYPE. There will be a row in SYSCOLUMNS for each column in the SLSREP table, for example. On each of these rows, TBNAME will be "SLSREP". On one of these rows, NAME will be "SLSREP_NUMBER" and COLTYPE will be DECI-MAL(2). On another row, NAME will be "SLSREP_NAME" and COLTYPE will be CHAR(15).

SYSINDEXES contains columns NAME, TBNAME, and CREATOR. The name of the index is found in the NAME column. The name of the table on which the index was built is found in the TBNAME column. The ID of the person or group that created the index is found in the CREATOR column.

The system catalog is a relational database of its own. Consequently, in general, the same types of queries that are used to retrieve information from relational databases can be used to retrieve information from the system catalog. The following queries illustrate this process.

1. List the name and creator of all tables known to the system.

```
SELECT NAME, CREATOR
    FROM SYSTABLES
```

2. List all of the columns in the CUSTOMER table as well as their associated data types.

```
SELECT NAME, COLTYPE
    FROM SYSCOLUMNS
    WHERE TBNAME = 'CUSTOMER'
```

3. List all tables that contain a column called SLSREP_NUMBER.

```
SELECT TBNAME
    FROM SYSCOLUMNS
    WHERE NAME = 'SLSREP_NUMBER'
```

Thus, information concerning the tables that are in place in our relational database, the columns they contain, and the indexes built on them can be obtained from the catalog by using the same SQL syntax that is used to query any other relational database.

Updating the tables that constitute the catalog occurs automatically when users CREATE, ALTER, or DROP tables or when they CREATE or DROP indexes. Users should not update the catalog directly using the update features of SQL. The main concern with users updating the catalog directly is that inconsistent results may be produced. If a user were to delete the row in the SYSCOLUMNS table for the CUSTOMER_NUMBER column, the system would no longer have any knowledge of this column, which is the primary key, yet all of the rows in the database would still contain a customer number. The system might well now treat those customer numbers as names, since, as far as it is concerned, NAME is the first column in the CUSTOMER table.

REPORT FORMATTING

In addition to the sorting and totaling features available in the SELECT command, many implementations of SQL include some elementary report formatting capabilities, which we will now examine. Often these features are not used, since typically SQL will be found as just one component of a larger environment that includes much more sophisticated report formatting capabilities.

A SELECT statement produces a report following a rigid format. Once this report has been produced, the report may be reformatted and reprinted as often as desired. Reprinting the report with a new format does *not* cause the SELECT to be reexecuted. Rather, the process is applied to the temporary, saved relation produced by the execution of the SELECT statement.

Format details are supplied through appropriate FORMAT statements. The various options will be illustrated through an example. To begin, let's assume that we wish to list the number and name of all sales reps. For each sales rep, we will list the number and name of all customers represented by the sales rep. For each customer, we will list the number and date of all orders placed. Finally, for each order line within each of these orders, we will list the part number, the part description, the number ordered, the quoted price, and the extension (number ordered * quoted price). The report is to be sorted by sales rep number. Within sales rep number it is to be sorted by customer number, and within customer number it is to be sorted by order number.

Write an SQL query to produce the above report.
Answer:

```
SELECT SLSREP.SLSREP_NUMBER, SLSREP.SLSREP_NAME,
     CUSTOMER.CUSTOMER_NUMBER, CUSTOMER.NAME,
     ORDERS.ORDER_NUMBER, ORDERS.DATE,
     PART.PART_NUMBER, PART.PART_DESCRIPTION,
     ORDER_LINE.NUMBER_ORDERED, ORDER_LINE.QUOTED_PRICE,
     (ORDER_LINE.NUMBER_ORDERED * ORDER_LINE.QUOTED_PRICE)
     FROM SLSREP, CUSTOMER, ORDERS, ORDER_LINE, PART
     WHERE SLSREP.SLSREP_NUMBER = CUSTOMER.SLSREP_NUMBER
         AND CUSTOMER.CUSTOMER_NUMBER = ORDERS.CUSTOMER_NUMBER
         AND ORDERS.ORDER_NUMBER = ORDER_LINE.ORDER_NUMBER
         AND ORDER_LINE.PART_NUMBER = PART.PART_NUMBER
     ORDER BY SLSREP.SLSREP_NUMBER, CUSTOMER.CUSTOMER_NUMBER,
         ORDERS.ORDER_NUMBER
```

The output of this query (except for the last two columns, which do not fit) is shown in Figure 5.11. One concern about the report as it stands is that it is very

SLSREP_ NUMBER	SLSREP_NAME	CUSTOMER_ NUMBER	NAME	ORDER_ NUMBER	DATE	PART_ NUMBER	PART_ DESCRIPTION	NUMBER_ ORDERED	QUOTED_ PRI..
3	MARY JONES	124	SALLY ADAMS	12489	90287	AX12	IRON	11	14.9..
3	MARY JONES	124	SALLY ADAMS	12500	90587	BT04	STOVE	1	402.9..
6	WILLIAM SMITH	256	ANN SAMUELS	12495	90487	CX11	MIXER	2	57.9..
6	WILLIAM SMITH	315	TOM DANIELS	12494	90487	CB03	BIKE	4	17..
12	SAM BROWN	311	DON CHARLES	12491	90287	BZ66	WASHER	1	311.9..
12	SAM BROWN	311	DON CHARLES	12491	90287	BT04	STOVE	1	402.9..
12	SAM BROWN	522	MARY NELSON	12498	90587	AZ52	SKATES	2	22.9..
12	SAM BROWN	522	MARY NELSON	12498	90587	BA74	BASEBALL	4	4.9..
12	SAM BROWN	522	MARY NELSON	12504	90587	CZ81	WEIGHTS	2	108.9..

FIGURE 5.11
Sample SQL report

wide. The width is due, in large part, to some of the column headings. Sales rep number, for example, is only a two-digit number, yet because of the column heading, SLSREP_NUMBER, it occupies several extra columns on the report. Thus, we might wish to shorten some of the headings. In general, we may also wish to change headings to improve readability or because SQL has not given us an appropriate heading.

To change a column heading we refer to the column by number in a FORMAT statement. The following examples change the headings of all the columns to the new headings indicated in the statements.

```
FORMAT COLUMN 1 NAME = 'SNUM'
FORMAT COLUMN 2 NAME = 'NAME'
FORMAT COLUMN 3 NAME = 'CNUM'
FORMAT COLUMN 4 NAME = 'NAME'
FORMAT COLUMN 5 NAME = 'ONUM'
FORMAT COLUMN 6 NAME = 'DATE'
FORMAT COLUMN 7 NAME = 'PNUM'
FORMAT COLUMN 8 NAME = 'DESC'
FORMAT COLUMN 9 NAME = 'NUM'
FORMAT COLUMN 10 NAME = 'PRICE'
FORMAT COLUMN 11 NAME = 'EXT'
```

At this point, we type PRINT to see the results. The results of such a PRINT statement are shown in Figure 5.12 on the following page.

SNUM	NAME	CNUM	NAME	ONUM	DATE	PNUM	DESC	NUM	PRICE	EXT
3	MARY JONES	124	SALLY ADAMS	12489	90287	AX12	IRON	11	14.95	164.45
3	MARY JONES	124	SALLY ADAMS	12500	90587	BT04	STOVE	1	402.99	402.99
6	WILLIAM SMITH	256	ANN SAMUELS	12495	90487	CX11	MIXER	2	57.95	115.9
6	WILLIAM SMITH	315	TOM DANIELS	12494	90487	CB03	BIKE	4	175	700
12	SAM BROWN	311	DON CHARLES	12491	90287	BZ66	WASHER	1	311.95	311.95
12	SAM BROWN	311	DON CHARLES	12491	90287	BT04	STOVE	1	402.99	402.99
12	SAM BROWN	522	MARY NELSON	12498	90587	AZ52	SKATES	2	22.95	45.9
12	SAM BROWN	522	MARY NELSON	12498	90587	BA74	BASEBALL	4	4.95	19.8
12	SAM BROWN	522	MARY NELSON	12504	90587	CZ81	WEIGHTS	2	108.99	217.98

FIGURE 5.12
Sample SQL report with new column headings

Another difficulty occurs in the PRICE and EXT columns. The format of the numbers is not particularly desirable. We would prefer all of the numbers to have exactly two decimal places. This can be accomplished by the width option, which allows us to change the width of any of the columns. Within the width option, we can also specify the number of decimal places. In our example, the appropriate statements would be:

```
FORMAT COLUMN 10 WIDTH = 6,2
FORMAT COLUMN 11 WIDTH = 6,2
```

We are indicating that the tenth and eleventh columns should be six columns wide, including exactly two decimal places. Executing the PRINT command would produce the report shown in Figure 5.13.

SNUM	NAME	CNUM	NAME	ONUM	DATE	PNUM	DESC	NUM	PRICE	EXT
3	MARY JONES	124	SALLY ADAMS	12489	90287	AX12	IRON	11	14.95	164.45
3	MARY JONES	124	SALLY ADAMS	12500	90587	BT04	STOVE	1	402.99	402.99
6	WILLIAM SMITH	256	ANN SAMUELS	12495	90487	CX11	MIXER	2	57.95	115.90
6	WILLIAM SMITH	315	TOM DANIELS	12494	90487	CB03	BIKE	4	175.00	700.00
12	SAM BROWN	311	DON CHARLES	12491	90287	BZ66	WASHER	1	311.95	311.95
12	SAM BROWN	311	DON CHARLES	12491	90287	BT04	STOVE	1	402.99	402.99
12	SAM BROWN	522	MARY NELSON	12498	90587	AZ52	SKATES	2	22.95	45.90
12	SAM BROWN	522	MARY NELSON	12498	90587	BA74	BASEBALL	4	4.95	19.80
12	SAM BROWN	522	MARY NELSON	12504	90587	CZ81	WEIGHTS	2	108.99	217.98

We can obtain a total of the EXT column (the eleventh column) by typing:

```
FORMAT TOTAL 11
```

FIGURE 5.13
Sample SQL report with PRICE and EXT columns

Executing the PRINT command would produce the report shown in Figure 5.14 (Opposite).

SNUM	NAME	CNUM	NAME	ONUM	DATE	PNUM	DESC	NUM	PRICE	EXT
3	MARY JONES	124	SALLY ADAMS	12489	90287	AX12	IRON	11	14.95	164.45
3	MARY JONES	124	SALLY ADAMS	12500	90587	BT04	STOVE	1	402.99	402.99
6	WILLIAM SMITH	256	ANN SAMUELS	12495	90487	CX11	MIXER	2	57.95	115.90
6	WILLIAM SMITH	315	TOM DANIELS	12494	90487	CB03	BIKE	4	175.00	700.00
12	SAM BROWN	311	DON CHARLES	12491	90287	BZ66	WASHER	1	311.95	311.95
12	SAM BROWN	311	DON CHARLES	12491	90287	BT04	STOVE	1	402.99	402.99
12	SAM BROWN	522	MARY NELSON	12498	90587	AZ52	SKATES	2	22.95	45.90
12	SAM BROWN	522	MARY NELSON	12498	90587	BA74	BASEBALL	4	4.95	19.80
12	SAM BROWN	522	MARY NELSON	12504	90587	CZ81	WEIGHTS	2	108.99	217.98
										2381.96

FIGURE 5.14
Sample SQL report
with total reformatted

Rather than have the sales rep number, sales rep name, customer number, customer name, order number, and order date print on every line, we might choose to group them. Any column that has been grouped will display a value only when it changes. Blank lines will be inserted between groups. To group columns, the group option is used as follows:

```
FORMAT GROUP 1,2,3,4,5,6
```

The result of the PRINT command is shown in Figure 5.15. When fields are

SNUM	NAME	CNUM	NAME	ONUM	DATE	PNUM	DESC	NUM	PRICE	EXT
3	MARY JONES	124	SALLY ADAMS	12489	90287	AX12	IRON	11	14.95	164.45
				12500	90587	BT04	STOVE	1	402.99	402.99
6	WILLIAM SMITH	256	ANN SAMUELS	12495	90487	CX11	MIXER	2	57.95	115.90
		315	TOM DANIELS	12494	90487	CB03	BIKE	4	175.00	700.00
12	SAM BROWN	311	DON CHARLES	12491	90287	BZ66	WASHER	1	311.95	311.95
						BT04	STOVE	1	402.99	402.99
		522	MARY NELSON	12498	90587	AZ52	SKATES	2	22.95	45.90
						BA74	BASEBALL	4	4.95	19.80
				12504	90587	CZ81	WEIGHTS	2	108.99	217.98
										2381.96

FIGURE 5.15
Sample SQL report
with grouping

grouped, we can also create subtotals for each group by using the SUBTOTAL option. The results of this option are not shown here.

Finally, we may wish to print a title at the top of the report. This is accomplished with the TITLE option as follows:

```
FORMAT TITLE 'ORDER REPORT'
```

The result is shown in Figure 5.16. Note that the date and page number appear automatically when a title is requested.

SNUM	NAME	CNUM	NAME	ONUM	DATE	PNUM	DESC	NUM	PRICE	EXT
3	MARY JONES	124	SALLY ADAMS	12489	90287	AX12	IRON	11	14.95	164.45
				12500	90587	BT04	STOVE	1	402.99	402.99
6	WILLIAM SMITH	256	ANN SAMUELS	12495	90487	CX11	MIXER	2	57.95	115.90
		315	TOM DANIELS	12494	90487	CB03	BIKE	4	175.00	700.00
12	SAM BROWN	311	DON CHARLES	12491	90287	BZ66	WASHER	1	311.95	311.95
					90287	BT04	STOVE	1	402.99	402.99
		522	MARY NELSON	12498	90587	AZ52	SKATES	2	22.95	45.90
					90587	BA74	BASEBALL	4	4.95	19.80
				12504	90587	CZ81	WEIGHTS	2	108.99	217.98

9/06/87   **ORDER REPORT**   Page: 1

2381.96

All of the format details specified remain in force until another SELECT command is issued.

FIGURE 5.16
Sample SQL report with page heading

STOP

EMBEDDED SQL

Up to this point, we have only discussed the use of SQL in a stand-alone mode; i.e., an SQL query is entered and executed, results are produced, and the process terminates. It is possible to embed SQL commands in a language like COBOL, thus bringing to COBOL the benefits of SQL.

In the discussion that follows, we will examine the method of embedding SQL within COBOL, as accomplished in DB2. Other relational systems are similar.

A COBOL program in which SQL commands are embedded will have additional statements in both the DATA and PROCEDURE divisions beyond the standard COBOL statements. In both cases, these new statements are preceded by

        EXEC SQL

and followed by

        END—EXEC

giving the compiler an easy way to distinguish such statements from standard COBOL statements.

In the DATA DIVISION (in particular, in the WORKING-STORAGE SEC-TION), the new statements will serve to declare the tables that will be used in processing the database as well as a communications area for SQL that includes items which allow SQL to communicate various aspects of processing with the program. Of particular interest is the item SQLCODE. After the execution of any SQL statement, SQLCODE will contain a code indicating the fate of the statement that was executed. If the execution was normal, SQLCODE will be zero. If not, the value in SQLCODE will indicate the problem that occurred. Programs should check the value of SQLCODE after each SQL statement.

In the PROCEDURE DIVISION, the new statements will be essentially SQL statements, with some slight variations. The examples that follow will illustrate the use of SQL to retrieve a single row, insert new rows, update existing rows, and delete existing rows. Finally, we will examine the manner in which we can retrieve multiple rows. (Executing a SELECT statement that retrieves more than one row presents a problem for a language like COBOL, which is oriented toward processing a single record at a time. Thus, some special action must be taken in such situations.)

DATA DIVISION

Any tables to be processed must be declared in WORKING-STORAGE. This is accomplished by the DECLARE TABLE command, which is similar to the SQL CREATE TABLE command. If we were to process the SLSREP table, for example, we would code:

```
EXEC SQL
     DECLARE SLSREP TABLE
             (SLSREP_NUMBER        DECIMAL (2),
              SLSREP_NAME          CHAR (15),
              SLSREP_ADDRESS       CHAR (25),
              TOTAL_COMMISSION     DECIMAL (7,2),
              COMMISSION_RATE      DECIMAL (2,2))
END-EXEC.
```

Optionally, if the description of the SLSREP table were stored in a library under the name DECSLSREP, we could use:

```
EXEC SQL
     INCLUDE DECSLSREP
END-EXEC.
```

As we will see, in processing this table we will need to have regular COBOL variables corresponding to the columns in the table. For the SLSREP table, we might have, for example:

```
01 W-SLSREP.
       03   W-SLSREP-NUMBER     PIC S9(2)        COMP-3.
       03   W-SLSREP-NAME       PIC X(15).
       03   W-SLSREP-ADDRESS    PIC X(25).
       03   W-TOTAL-COMMISSION  PIC S9(5)V9(2)   COMP-3.
       03   W-COMMISSION-RATE   PIC SV9(2)       COMP-3.
```

Since this description is standard COBOL, it is not preceded by EXEC SQL. We have deliberately changed the names by prefacing each one with "W–" (for work variable). This procedure is not necessary; it is legitimate to use the same names that are in the table declaration. We feel, however, that the effect of the statements in the PROCEDURE DIVISION is more clear when different names are used.

Finally, the SQL communication area (SQLCA) is used by the system to provide feedback to the program. In particular, it is this area that contains SQLCODE. The SQLCA is included by coding:

```
EXEC SQL
      INCLUDE SQLCA
END-EXEC.
```

There is only one other new type of entry that appears in the DATA DIVISION. It is called a CURSOR and is used for the multiple-row SELECT mentioned earlier. We will defer discussion of CURSORs until we investigate the problems associated with multiple-row retrieval.

PROCEDURE DIVISION

Before looking at examples of the use of SQL statements in the PROCEDURE DIVISION, some general comments should be made. First, normal COBOL variables may be used in SQL statements. Such variables are called *host* variables; i.e., they are variables in the host language, in this case COBOL. When used, they must be preceded by colons. If W–SLSREP–NAME is used *within an SQL statement*, for example, it will appear as :W–SLSREP–NAME. For any other use, it will appear as the normal W–SLSREP–NAME. Second, the results of SQL queries must be placed in host variables through the use of the INTO clause, as in:

```
SELECT SLSREP_NAME
      INTO :W-SLSREP-NAME
      FROM SLSREP
      WHERE SLSREP_NUMBER = 3
```

Finally, provision must be made for exceptional conditions, for example when no data is found to satisfy a condition or when no space is available to add a new row. Of course, the specific condition will determine which action is to be taken. Mechanisms to check for and handle these conditions will be discussed after the examples have been presented.

In each of the following examples, only the PROCEDURE DIVISION code for accomplishing the task will be shown. Let's assume that all the tables in the Premiere Products database have been declared in the DATA DIVISION in the manner previously discussed. Let's assume further that work versions of all the columns in the tables have also been declared and that the SQLCA has been included.

Example 1: Retrieve a single row and column.

STATEMENT: Obtain the name of sales rep 3 and place it in W–SLSREP–NAME.

Since this retrieval is based on the primary key (SLSREP_NUMBER), it does not pose any problem for a record-at-a-time language like COBOL. If SQL were used in a stand-alone mode, the query would be:

```
SELECT SLSREP_NAME
       FROM SLSREP
       WHERE SLSREP_NUMBER = 3
```

In COBOL, the statement is only slightly different:

```
EXEC SQL
       SELECT SLSREP_NAME
              INTO :W-SLSREP-NAME
              FROM SLSREP
              WHERE SLSREP_NUMBER = 3
       END-EXEC.
```

The only difference other than the required EXEC SQL and END–EXEC is the INTO clause, which indicates that the result is to be placed in the host variable, W–SLSREP–NAME. This variable may now be used in any way it could be used in any other COBOL program. Its value could be printed on a report, displayed on a screen, compared with some other name, and so on.

Example 2: Retrieve a single row and all columns.

STATEMENT: Obtain all information about the sales rep whose number is stored in the host variable W–SLSREP–NUMBER.

After filling in W–SLSREP–NUMBER with an appropriate COBOL statement, such as a MOVE or an ACCEPT, this requirement could be satisfied by using a formulation similar to the one in example 1:

```
EXEC SQL
       SELECT SLSREP_NAME, SLSREP_ADDRESS,
              TOTAL_COMMISSION, COMMISSION_RATE
           INTO :W-SLSREP-NAME, :W-SLSREP-ADDRESS,
              :W-TOTAL-COMMISSION, :W-COMMISSION-RATE
           FROM SLSREP
           WHERE SLSREP_NUMBER = :W-SLSREP-NUMBER
END-EXEC.
```

In this formulation, several columns are listed after the SELECT, and the corresponding host variables that will receive the values are listed after INTO. In addition, the host variable W–SLSREP–NUMBER is used in the WHERE clause. Note that there was no need to select SLSREP_NUMBER and place it in W–SLSREP–NUMBER, since W–SLSREP–NUMBER already contained the desired number.

As you might expect, since we are selecting all of the columns in the SLSREP table, the above query could be formulated as:

```
EXEC SQL
      SELECT *
            INTO :W–SLSREP–NUMBER, :W–SLSREP–NAME,
             :W–SLSREP–ADDRESS, :W–TOTAL–COMMISSION,
                :W–COMMISSION–RATE
            FROM SLSREP
            WHERE SLSREP_NUMBER = :W–SLSREP–NUMBER
END–EXEC.
```

Note that in this example, W–SLSREP–NUMBER is listed as one of the fields to be filled in, even though it already contained the right number before the query was executed. This is because the SELECT * retrieves *all* columns, including SLSREP_NUMBER, and we must indicate to SQL where this value should be placed.

As a final change, since the fields W–SLSREP–NUMBER, W–SLSREP–NAME, W–SLSREP–ADDRESS, W–TOTAL–COMMISSION, and W–COMMISSION–RATE constitute the record W–SLSREP, the above query can actually be formulated as:

```
EXEC SQL
      SELECT *
            INTO :W–SLSREP
            FROM SLSREP
            WHERE SLSREP_NUMBER = :W–SLSREP–NUMBER
END–EXEC.
```

This formulation is appropriate only because we wish to select all of the columns from the SLSREP table *and* because the order of the fields within the W–SLSREP record match these columns exactly.

Example 3: Retrieve a single row from a join of two tables.

STATEMENT: Obtain the name and address of the customer whose customer number is stored in the host variable W–CUSTOMER–NUMBER as well as the number and name of the sales rep who represents this customer.

This query involves joining the customer and sales rep relations. Since the restriction involves the primary key of the CUSTOMER relation and since each customer is related to exactly one sales rep, the result of the query will be a single row. The method for handling this query is thus similar to that for the preceding queries. It would be formulated as:

```
EXEC SQL
     SELECT NAME, ADDRESS, SLSREP_NUMBER,
         SLSREP_NAME
             INTO :W-NAME, :W-ADDRESS,
                    :W-SLSREP-NUMBER, :W-SLSREP-NAME,
             FROM SLSREP, CUSTOMER
             WHERE SLSREP.SLSREP_NUMBER =
                    CUSTOMER.SLSREP_NUMBER
             AND CUSTOMER.CUSTOMER_NUMBER =
                    :W-SLSREP-NUMBER
END-EXEC.
```

Example 4: Insert a row into a table.

STATEMENT: Add a row to the sales rep table. The sales rep number, name, address, total commission, and credit limit have already been placed in the variables W-SLSREP-NUMBER, W-SLSREP-NAME, W-SLSREP-ADDRESS, W-TOTAL-COMMISSION, and W-CREDIT LIMIT, respectively.

To insert a row into a table, the INSERT command is appropriate. The values are contained in host variables, whose names must be preceded by colons, as follows:

```
EXEC SQL
     INSERT
             INTO SLSREP
         VALUES (:W-SLSREP-NUMBER, :W-SLSREP-NAME
                    :W-SLSREP-ADDRESS,
                    :W-TOTAL-COMMISSION,
                    :W-COMMISSION-RATE)
END-EXEC.
```

The values currently in the host variables included in the INSERT statement will be used to add a new row to the SLSREP table.

Example 5: Change a single row in a table.

STATEMENT: Change the name of the sales rep whose number is currently stored in W-SLSREP-NUMBER to the value currently stored in W-SLSREP-NAME.

Again, the only difference between this example and the update examples in chapter 3 is the use of host variables. The formulation is:

```
EXEC SQL
     UPDATE SLSREP
         SET SLSREP_NAME = :W-SLSREP-NAME
         WHERE SLSREP_NUMBER = :W-SLSREP-NUMBER
END-EXEC.
```

Example 6: Change multiple rows in a table.

STATEMENT: Add the amount stored in the host variable INCREASE—IN—RATE to the commission rate of all sales reps who currently represent any customers with a credit limit of $1000.

The necessity of updating multiple rows does not pose any problem for COBOL. The formulation is:

```
EXEC SQL
    UPDATE SLSREP
        SET COMMISSION_RATE = COMMISSION_RATE
            + :INCREASE-IN-RATE
        WHERE SLSREP_NUMBER IN
            (SELECT SLSREP_NUMBER
                FROM CUSTOMER
                WHERE CREDIT_LIMIT = 1000)
END-EXEC.
```

Example 7: Delete a single row from a table.

STATEMENT: Delete the sales rep whose number is currently stored in W—SLSREP—NUMBER from the SLSREP table.

The formulation is:

```
EXEC SQL
    DELETE
        FROM SLSREP
        WHERE SLSREP_NUMBER = :W-SLSREP-NUMBER
END-EXEC.
```

Example 8: Delete multiple rows from a table.

STATEMENT: Delete all parts in the item class currently stored in the host variable W—ITEM—CLASS.

The formulation is:

```
EXEC SQL
    DELETE
        FROM PART
        WHERE ITEM_CLASS = :W-ITEM-CLASS
END-EXEC.
```

MULTIPLE-ROW SELECT

All of the examples encountered thus far posed no problem for COBOL. The SELECT statements retrieved only individual rows. There was an UPDATE example in which multiple rows were updated and a DELETE example in which multiple rows were deleted, but these presented no difficulty. The SQL statements were executed and the updates or deletions took place. The program could now move on to the next task.

What if, however, a SELECT statement produced not one row but multiple rows? What if, for example, the select statement were to produce the number and name of all customers represented by the sales rep whose number was stored in W–SLSREP–NUMBER? Could we formulate this query as:

```
EXEC SQL
      SELECT CUSTOMER_NUMBER, NAME
            INTO :W–CUSTOMER–NUMBER, :W–NAME
            FROM CUSTOMER
            WHERE SLSREP_NUMBER = :W–SLSREP–NUMBER
      END–EXEC.
```

There is a problem. It stems from the fact that although COBOL is a language capable of processing an individual record at a time, this SQL command will produce a set of rows (or records). Whose number and name will be placed in W–CUSTOMER–NUMBER and W–NAME if 100 customers have been retrieved? Should we make both W–CUSTOMER–NUMBER and W–NAME arrays capable of holding 100 customers and, if so, what should the size of these arrays be?

Fortunately, there is a solution to this problem. It involves the use of a **cursor**. Through the use of a cursor, COBOL can process the set of rows retrieved just as though they were records in a sequential file. A cursor is essentially a pointer to a row in the collection of rows retrieved by an SQL statement. This pointer can be advanced a row at a time to provide sequential, record-at-a-time-type access to the retrieved rows.

Example 9: Retrieve multiple rows.

STATEMENT: Retrieve the number and name of all customers represented by the sales rep whose number is stored in the host variable W–SLSREP–NUMBER.

The first step in using a cursor is to declare the cursor and describe the associated query. This is accomplished in the WORKING–STORAGE SECTION of the DATA DIVISION, as follows:

```
EXEC SQL
      DECLARE CUSTGROUP CURSOR FOR
         SELECT CUSTOMER_NUMBER, NAME
            FROM CUSTOMER
            WHERE SLSREP_NUMBER = :W–SLSREP–NUMBER
      END–EXEC.
```

This formulation does *not* cause the query to be executed at this time. It merely indicates that we have a cursor called CUSTGROUP and that this cursor is associated with the indicated query.

Use of a cursor in the PROCEDURE DIVISION involves three facets: OPEN, FETCH, and CLOSE. Opening the cursor effectively causes the query to be executed and makes the results available to the program. Executing a fetch advances the pointer to the next row in the set of rows retrieved by the query and places the contents of this row in the indicated host variables. Finally, closing a cursor deactivates it. Data retrieved by the execution of the query is no longer available. (The cursor could later be opened again and processing could begin anew. If any host variables used in making the selection were changed, the set of rows retrieved might be totally different, however.)

The OPEN, FETCH, and CLOSE commands used in processing a cursor are analogous to the OPEN, READ, and CLOSE commands used in processing a sequential file. We will now examine the way in which each of these commands is coded in COBOL.

Open:

The formulation for the OPEN command is

```
EXEC SQL
      OPEN CUSTGROUP
END-EXEC.
```

Fetch:

The formulation for the FETCH command is

```
EXEC SQL
      FETCH CUSTGROUP
            INTO :W-CUSTOMER-NUMBER, :W-NAME
END-EXEC.
```

Note that the INTO clause is associated with the FETCH command itself, not the query used in the definition of the cursor. In all probability, the execution of that query will produce multiple rows. The execution of the FETCH command produces a single row and it is thus appropriate that the FETCH command causes data to be placed in the indicated host variables.

Close:

The formulation for the CLOSE command is

```
EXEC SQL
      CLOSE CUSTGROUP
END-EXEC.
```

The formulation of the query to define the cursor in the previous example was relatively simple. Any SQL query is legitimate in a cursor definition. In fact, the more complicated the requirements for retrieval, the more numerous the benefits derived by the programmer who uses embedded SQL. Consider the following query, for example:

STATEMENT: Retrieve the order number, order date, number and name of the customer who placed the order, and the number and name of the sales rep who represents the customer for each order that contains an order line for the part whose part number is stored in W-PART-NUMBER. The results should be sorted by customer number.

Opening and closing the cursor will be accomplished exactly as in the previous example. The only difference in the fetch command will be a different set of host variables in the INTO clause. Thus, the only real difference is in the definition of the cursor itself. In this case, the cursor definition would be:

```
EXEC SQL
    DECLARE ORDGROUP CURSOR FOR
      SELECT ORDER.ORDER_NUMBER, ORDER.DATE,
          CUSTOMER.CUSTOMER_NUMBER, CUSTOMER.NAME,
          SLSREP.SLSREP_NUMBER, SLSREP.SLSREP_NAME
          FROM ORDER_LINE, ORDER, CUSTOMER, SLSREP
          WHERE ORDER_LINE.PART_NUMBER = :W-PART-
              NUMBER AND ORDER_LINE.ORDER_NUMBER =
              ORDER.ORDER_NUMBER
          AND ORDER.CUSTOMER_NUMBER =
              CUSTOMER.CUSTOMER_NUMBER
          AND CUSTOMER.SLSREP_NUMBER =
              SLSREP.SLSREP_NUMBER
          ORDER BY CUSTOMER.CUSTOMER_NUMBER
END-EXEC.
```

The retrieval requirements for this program are fairly involved. Yet, beyond coding the preceding cursor declaration, the programmer doesn't have to worry at all about the mechanics of obtaining the necessary data or of placing it in the right order. This will all happen automatically when the cursor is opened. To the programmer, it is as though a sequential file already exists that has precisely the right data in it, sorted in the right order. This approach yields three major advantages.

First, the coding in the program is greatly simplified. Second, the system optimizer will determine the best way to execute the query. The programmer doesn't have to be concerned with the best way to pull the data together. In addition, if an underlying structure changes, e.g., if an additional index is created, the system optimizer will determine the best way to execute the query in view of the new structure. The program does not have to change at all. Third, if the database structure changes in such a way that the necessary information is still obtainable but through a differently formulated query, the only change required in the program is the cursor definition in WORKING-STORAGE. The PROCEDURE DIVISION code will not be affected.

UPDATING CURSORS

Rows encountered in processing cursors may be updated. In order to indicate that update is required, an additional clause, the FOR UPDATE OF clause, is included in the cursor definition. For example, consider the following update requirement:

STATEMENT: Add $100 to the credit limit of all customers who are represented by the sales rep whose number is currently stored in the host variable W—SLSREP—NUMBER, whose balance is not over their credit limit, and whose credit limit is $500 or less. Add $200 to the credit limit of all customers of the same sales rep whose balance is not over their credit limit and whose credit limit is more than $500. Write the number and name of all customers of this sales rep whose balance is greater than their credit limit.

In this example, the cursor declaration would be:

```
EXEC SQL
    DECLARE CREDGROUP CURSOR FOR
        SELECT CUSTOMER_NUMBER, NAME, CREDIT_LIMIT
            FROM CUSTOMER
            WHERE SLSREP_NUMBER = :W—SLSREP—NUMBER
            FOR UPDATE OF CREDIT_LIMIT
END—EXEC.
```

In order to update the credit limit, we include the clause FOR UPDATE OF CREDIT_LIMIT in the declaration. The PROCEDURE DIVISION code for the OPEN and CLOSE will be the same one discussed before. The code to fetch a row, determine whether it was actually fetched, and then take appropriate action would be:

```
EXEC SQL            •
    FETCH CREDGROUP
            INTO :W—CUSTOMER—NUMBER, :W—NAME,
                :W—CREDIT—LIMIT
END—EXEC.
IF SQLCODE = 100
        MOVE "NO" TO ARE—THERE—MORE—CUSTOMERS
    ELSE
        PERFORM CUSTOMER—UPDATE.

CUSTOMER—UPDATE.
    IF W—CREDIT—LIMIT > W—BALANCE
        print W—CUSTOMER—NAME
    ELSE IF W—CREDIT—LIMIT > 500
        EXEC SQL
            UPDATE CUSTOMER
                SET CREDIT_LIMIT = CREDIT_LIMIT + 200
```

```
                    WHERE CURRENT OF CREDGROUP
          END-EXEC
      ELSE
          EXEC SQL
              UPDATE CUSTOMER
                  SET CREDIT_LIMIT = CREDIT_LIMIT + 100
                  WHERE CURRENT OF CREDGROUP
          END-EXEC.
```

The preceding code will be in a loop that is performed until the flag "ARE-THERE-MORE-CUSTOMERS" is set to "NO". The FETCH command will either make the next row that was retrieved available to the program with the values placed in the variables W-CUSTOMER-NUMBER, W-NAME, and W-CREDIT-LIMIT, or it will set SQLCODE to 100, indicating that no more rows were retrieved. The code that comes after the FETCH command will set the flag to "NO" if SQLCODE is 100. If not, the update routine will be performed.

In the update routine, the credit limit is first compared with the balance. If it is larger, a message is printed. If not, the credit limit is compared with $500. If it is larger, the customer is updated by adding $200 to the credit limit. If not, the customer is updated by adding $100 to the credit limit.

Note the clause "WHERE CURRENT OF CREDGROUP". This clause indicates that the update is to apply only to the row just fetched. Without this clause and in the absence of any WHERE clause to restrict the scope of the update, *all* customers' credit limits would be updated at once.

ERROR HANDLING

Checking SQLCODE

Programs must be prepared to handle exceptional conditions that may arise when the database is being accessed. Since any problem encountered is communicated through a value in SQLCODE, one legitimate way to handle such conditions is to check the value in SQLCODE after each executable SQL statement and take appropriate action based on the problem indicated. With all the conditions that might conceivably be encountered, this method becomes very cumbersome. Fortunately, DB2 provides another way to handle such conditions.

Using WHENEVER

There are two distinct types of conditions that may arise. One type consists of the unusual but normal conditions, such as not retrieving any data to match a given condition, attempting to store a row that violates a duplicates clause, and so on. The value in SQLCODE for such conditions is a positive number. For many of these, the appropriate action may be printing an error message and going on. In fact, for one of these, END OF DATA (SQLCODE 100), the appropriate action is probably termination of some loop and continuation of the rest of the program. Not even an error message is required.

The other type of condition is far more serious. These are the abnormal and unexpected conditions or, in a very real sense, the fatal ones. Examples of this type include no more room in the database, a damaged database, and so on. The value in SQLCODE for such conditions is a negative number. The appropriate action for these will usually be printing some kind of final message that indicates which problem occurred and terminating the program.

The WHENEVER statement can be used to handle these errors in a global way. The following example of the WHENEVER statement illustrates a typical way of handling these conditions in a program.

```
EXEC SQL
    WHENEVER SQLERROR  GOTO ERROR-PROCESSING-ROUTINE
END-EXEC.
EXEC SQL
    WHENEVER SQLWARNING   CONTINUE
END-EXEC.
EXEC SQL
    WHENEVER NOT FOUND   CONTINUE
END-EXEC.
```

In the WHENEVER statement, SQLERROR represents the abnormal or fatal conditions (SQLCODE < 0), SQLWARNING represents the unusual but normal conditions (SQLCODE > 0), and NOT FOUND represents the special warning END OF DATA (SQLCODE = 100). The WHENEVER statement ends either with GOTO followed by a section or paragraph name or with the word CONTINUE. This statement indicates to DB2 how each of these conditions should be handled if and when it occurs.

In the preceding WHENEVER statements, we are indicating that if a fatal condition occurs, the program is to immediately proceed to a paragraph (or section) called ERROR-PROCESSING-ROUTINE. Such a paragraph has probably been constructed by the organization and will be the same in each program that accesses DB2. Typically, it would contain statements to display the SQLCODE together with any other information the organization deems useful in tracking down the problem, followed by a STOP RUN. With this paragraph in place, the remainder of the program does not have to continually check for all possible errors of this type.

If an unusual but normal condition arises, however, or the special NOT FOUND condition occurs, processing is to continue without any special action being taken. This means that appropriate tests of SQLCODE had better be included at appropriate places.

While these tests can also be accomplished through the WHENEVER clause, doing the testing ourselves provides a cleaner structure for the program. The built-in GOTO of the WHENEVER clause can play havoc with the attempt to create well-structured programs.

For other perspectives on SQL, see [1], [4], [6], [7], [8], and [9].

RESUME

.4 DB2

The prototype system called System R, which was developed in the 1970s by IBM, gave rise to IBM's commercial offering in the relational DBMS market, DB2. (DB2 is a DBMS for the MVS/370 and MVS/XA operating systems. There is actually another similar relational DBMS offered by IBM for the VM/CMS and DOS/VSE operating systems, called SQL/DS. The two systems are, for all practical purposes, identical. In this text, we shall discuss DB2.)

IBM has also offered for some time the premiere hierarchical model system, IMS, which is examined in chapter 10 of this text. While DB2 offers the flexibility and ease of use associated with the relational model, IMS offers the power to handle the major, high-volume applications. At the present time, IBM is suggesting that a typical installation should have both DB2 and IMS - DB2 for applications that do not necessarily need the power of IMS and which can benefit from the ease of use inherent in DB2, and IMS for applications for which DB2 is not currently efficient enough. Progress is under way in making DB2 more efficient. (The same progress is occurring in every relational system.) As this happens, the number of applications that require additional processing power beyond that furnished by DB2 will diminish.

It should be emphasized that, while IBM does furnish bridges between IMS and DB2, they are two separate products. This is in contrast to the route taken by the Cullinet Corporation, vendors of the premiere network model system, IDMS, another system capable of handling the high-volume applications. Cullinet added relational capabilities to IDMS and renamed it IDMS/R. IDMS/R is a single product with both relational-like capabilities and network capabilities.

Our study of DB2 is greatly simplified by the fact that we have really been studying it since chapter 3. Virtually all that we have studied about SQL applies to DB2. Much of the material in this chapter pertaining to advanced features of the relational model was illustrated with SQL and applies to DB2. Thus, we will give a brief explanation of the features of DB2 and indicate where it differs from what was discussed earlier.

As we have discussed, SQL can be used in both an interactive mode, and it can also be embedded in programs in languages like COBOL. The same is true for DB2. DB2I is the special name for the component of DB2 that supports the interactive mode (for DB2-Interactive). We will first examine the general characteristics of DB2, and then the four components that together support embedding SQL in programs. Finally, we will examine a related product, QMF, which furnishes alternative ways of manipulating DB2 databases.

DB2 — GENERAL

All of the previous discussion concerning data definition and manipulation in SQL applies to DB2. The syntax presented was entirely consistent DB2. The material presented earlier in this chapter on creating and using views applies to DB2, as does the material on granting and revoking privileges. Creating and dropping indexes in DB2 is also accomplished in the same manner, including the possibility of specifying an index as unique. Processing nulls in DB2 and restricting a column from containing null values is also consistent with what has been discussed. The description of the structure of the catalog together with the retrieval of information from the catalog is consistent with DB2.

In summary, virtually everything discussed earlier that concerned SQL was presented in a way that is entirely consistent with the way things are done in DB2. There is only one exception: altering a table. As of the time this book is being written, tables can indeed be altered, but not with the full flexibility discussed earlier. Existing columns may not be changed or deleted; the only alteration possible is the addition of new columns. Further, these columns will appear at the end of the list of columns for the relation (it is not possible to position them where we might want them). In addition, the new columns *must* accept null values. Finally, the values for these columns in all existing rows will be initialized to null. This falls far short of the flexibility in modifying a table structure that we discussed earlier. Increased flexibility will certainly be featured in future releases of the product.

Again, as of the time this book is being written, DB2 does not provide support for either primary or foreign keys. Primary key support can be implemented fairly easily by creating a unique index on the column or columns that constitute the primary key. (Such an index must *never* be dropped. Otherwise, the primary key support disappears.) Foreign key support is totally nonexistent. This is a major problem and certainly one that is the subject of research. In the near future, perhaps by the time you read this text, such support will exist.

EMBEDDED SQL

SQL is embedded in COBOL programs in DB2 in exactly the fashion discussed earlier. In this section, we will discuss the kind of work that DB2 does behind the scenes when this embedding takes place.

Before such a program is compiled, a component of DB2 called the *Precompiler* will examine the code and collect all requests to DB2 (SELECT, FETCH, UPDATE, etc.) into a *Database Request Module* (DBRM). These statements are replaced in the program by appropriate CALL statements. The resulting program can then be compiled and linked in the usual way.

The component called *Bind* will convert to machine code the database requests that have been placed in a DBRM in order to form what is termed an *application plan*. This component contains an optimizer, so the machine code produced is optimized; i.e., it represents not just one way to satisfy the given request but the best way to satisfy the request. The application plans are then stored in the system catalog.

At this point, the program can be run. When a given CALL inserted by the Precompiler is encountered for the first time during the running of the program, control will pass to another component, the *Runtime Supervisor*, which will fetch the appropriate application plan from the catalog into main memory. The program now proceeds to execute the application plan, in the process calling upon the *Stored Data Manager* component of DB2 to perform the actual database accesses.

Since the plan is now in main memory, if the same CALL statement is encountered a second time, the plan can simply be executed without the need to fetch it from the catalog. Thus, it is only on the first CALL of each type that the additional overhead to fetch an application plan will be felt.

There are other systems that do not perform the same type of separation. Rather, the statements that access the database are interpreted during the actual running of the program and any optimization that takes place occurs at that point. Clearly, from the standpoint of efficiency, optimization should take place prior to the running of the program.

On the other hand, an approach like the one implemented in DB2 does present a problem when some aspect of the structure of the database changes. Suppose, for example, that an index which was used in a given application plan is dropped. This would not present a problem for a system that interprets and optimizes requests during the execution of a program. Since the index is unavailable, the optimizer certainly will not choose to use it. In DB2, on the other hand, the application plan, *using this index*, has already been created and is stored in the catalog. What will happen when the application plan is fetched and the system attempts to execute it? Will it attempt to access a nonexistent index? What will happen if it does? This would seem to present a real problem for the approach implemented in DB2.

Actually, though, it is *not* a problem. In DB2, when an index is dropped, it is not only deleted and removed from the catalog, but, in addition, current application plans are examined and any application plan that utilizes this index is marked as invalid. (It is *not* redone at this point, however.) The next time a program encounters a CALL statement that corresponds to this application plan, the system notes that the plan is invalid and re-optimizes the corresponding DBRM (Database Request Module). The re-optimized code is then stored in the catalog and is also fetched into main memory to be executed. Someone carefully monitoring the execution of such a program would notice that the first occurrence of the given CALL statement did not execute as rapidly as usual. From that point on, however, execution would be the same.

By taking this approach, DB2 is able to secure additional efficiency by translating the database requests into optimized machine code before programs are executed. There is another problem with this approach, however, one which to date has not been solved. Suppose an index is created that should be used if a given request is going to be satisfied in the optimum way. In a system that interprets requests during program execution, no problem will arise. The next time a program is run that makes this type of request, the optimizer will notice the index and use it. This is not necessarily the case in DB2. Suppose the application plan for the request already existed before the index was created. Certainly, the application plan will not utilize the index. However, it will *not* be marked as invalid (it still represents a legitimate way, although not the best way, to satisfy the request). Consequently, when programs run which use this application plan, the plan that will be executed will not make use of the index and, consequently, will not really be optimal.

A method does exist for solving this problem. It requires human intervention, however. DB2 has a facility that invokes Bind to produce a new plan for a given request. If the database administrator has reason to believe that certain requests may benefit from a newly added index, he or she can request that these plans be redone. While this does guarantee that the plan will once again be optimal, the process is not automatic. Someone must make the determination that it is beneficial for a rebind to take place.

QUERY MANAGEMENT FACILITY (QMF)

The Query Management Facility (QMF) is a separate product that can be used with DB2. DB2 can exist without it, but when used it brings some added capabilities. (It can also be used with SQL/DS, by the way.) QMF is a front-end to DB2; i.e., a user interacts with QMF, which, in turn, interacts with DB2 on behalf of the user to satisfy the user's request.

SQL can be employed interactively by users of QMF. QMF furnishes to its users a very sophisticated mechanism for formatting reports created as the output of SQL queries. Its capabilities in this area go far beyond those discussed in the section on advanced SQL.

QMF also furnishes the ability to use QUERY-BY-EXAMPLE (QBE) to process DB2 databases. The output of QBE queries can be formatted using the report-formatting services of QMF previously discussed.

DB2 AND THE FUNCTIONS OF A DBMS

DB2 certainly supports the storage, retrieval, and update of data. We have already discussed the DB2 catalog. DB2 interfaces with the main IBM communications software and furnishes several utility services; it also provides facilities for recovery of the database as described in chapter two.

COMMIT AND ROLLBACK

The commands in DB2 that relate to support for logical transactions are COMMIT and ROLLBACK (or, optionally, COMMIT WORK and ROLLBACK WORK). The COMMIT command indicates a successful completion of a transaction. Updates are made permanent. Open cursors are closed. Locks are released. The ROLLBACK command signals an unsuccessful termination of a transaction. Updates accomplished since the end of the last successfully terminated transaction are undone. Open cursors are also closed, and locks are released.

LOGICAL TRANSACTIONS

DB2 provides support for **logical transactions** (although they are termed logical units of work). The start of the program marks the start of the first transaction. The COMMIT command is used to mark the end of a successful transaction and, consequently, the beginning of the next transaction. The end of the program marks the end of the last transaction (an implicit COMMIT). If a transaction cannot be successfully completed, any updates completed will be undone, either in response to a ROLLBACK command or as the result of a system-issued rollback.

SHARED UPDATE

DB2 supports shared and exclusive locks. When a program retrieves a record, the program is granted a **shared lock**. When the program attempts to update a record, the system attempts to **promote** the lock to **exclusive** status. Once successful, the update can be completed and no other program can acquire any type of lock on the record. Locks may be released by the application program itself, using the COMMIT and ROLLBACK commands previously described, and will also be released at the termination of the program. In addition, if a user is discovered to have caused a **deadlock**, the system will cause an automatic **rollback** to be performed, in which case locks will also be released.

SECURITY

DB2 has three features that provide security: **views**, GRANT, and **encryption**. If rows and/or columns are excluded from a given view, no user accessing the database through this view will be able to access them. (In nonrelational systems, it is easy to exclude columns from a given subschema. Excluding rows, though, is usually not possible. In relational systems that support the view mechanism, it is quite easy to define a given user's view as including only the rows that satisfy some condition in a particular table. A given view, for example, might include only the customers of sales rep 3.) The GRANT mechanism, which allows access privileges to be granted to and revoked from users, also provides security. Finally, DB2 supports encryption of data.

INTEGRITY

At present, **integrity** support in DB2 is somewhat lacking. Support is not provided for **foreign key** constraints or even for **primary keys**, although primary key support can be achieved by creating a unique index on the column or columns that constitute a primary key (provided, of course, that such an index is *never* dropped).

Support is also not provided for describing legal values to be accepted by a given column beyond the data type specification. A field can be specified as numeric and DB2 will ensure that only numbers are accepted. There is no way, however, to specify that a base table may only accept one of the numbers 300, 500, 800, or 1000, for example. Interestingly enough, there is a way to specify such restrictions on views, using the WITH CHECK OPTION clause. For example, consider a view defined as:

```
CREATE VIEW CUSTOMER_VIEW AS
     SELECT *
          FROM CUSTOMER
          WHERE CREDIT_LIMIT IN (300, 500, 800, 1000)
          WITH CHECK OPTION
```

The WITH CHECK OPTION clause guarantees that no updates that violate the conditionwill be permitted; i.e., no customer can be added or changed through this view in such a way that the credit limit will be other than $300, $500, $800 or $1000.

DB2 does allow fields to be specified as NOT NULL and will ensure that these fields do not accept null values. It allows indexes to be specified as UNIQUE and will ensure this uniqueness. Finally, user-defined procedures are allowed and these procedures are capable of accomplishing further integrity checking. They do have two important limitations, however: they are written in assembler language, and no database accesses may be performed within them.

DATA INDEPENDENCE

Like most relational systems, DB2 provides a fairly high degree of **data independence**. **Logical data independence** is furnished by views and cursors.**Physical data independence** is furnished through automatic **database navigation**.

Logical Data Independence

If a user is accessing the database through a view and the underlying structure of the database changes in such a way that the data needed by the user can still be found in the database, then all that needs to be changed is the defining query for the view. To the user, the view is still the same as it was before. Behind the scenes, however, the data for this user may be pulled together in a totally different way. This ability to change the logical structure without affecting users yields a high degree of logical data independence.

There is a little problem, however. While any user interested only in retrieval will be able to continue processing as before, a user interested in update may not be. You will recall that not all views are updatable. Some are not even theoretically updatable; others are not updatable in DB2. If the previous view was updatable but the new one is not, this will necessitate a change in the way the user manipulates the database.

In application programs, cursors furnish a degree of logical data independence. When the structure of a database changes, potentially all that needs to change is the cursor definition. The procedural code in the program need not be affected. Unfortunately, the cursor definition is found in the program, and thus the program does need to be modified, recompiled, and relinked, and a new application plan has to be created. It would be desirable for this to happen externally to the program itself. However, since no procedural code needs to change, we still have some of the benefits of logical data independence.

Good programming practice can also promote logical data independence. Formulating an SQL query as:

```
SELECT SLSREP_NUMBER, SLSREP_NAME, SLSREP_ADDRESS,
    TOTAL_COMMISSION, COMMISSION_RATE
    FROM SLSREP
```

may seem more tedious than formulating it as:

```
SELECT *
        FROM SLSREP
```

but yet it is better from standpoint of data independence. If a new column, TERRITORY_NUMBER, is added to the SLSREP table, the second formulation produces a new result: there is an extra column. The first formulation, in contrast, will continue to produce the same type of result for users even though the underlying database structure has been changed. For the most part, the second formulation should be used only when a user wants all columns from the SLSREP table, whatever they may be.

Physical Data Independence

The automatic database navigation — the fact that DB2 rather than the user determines how to access the database to satisfy a given request — furnishes a high degree of physical data independence. Physical changes, such as the addition or deletion of an index, will not affect the way a user processes the database, except possibly in terms of the efficiency with which processing takes place. It will not affect whether or not a user can continue to access the database with the same queries.

For further information on DB2, see [4], [6], or the manuals available from IBM.

STOP

.5 INGRES

During the 1970s a prototype relational system called System R was being developed by IBM. This work led, among other things, to the commercial product we have just studied, DB2. At the same time, work on another prototype relational system called INGRES (INteractive Graphics and REtrieval System) was taking place at the University of California at Berkeley. A commercial implementation of INGRES is now marketed by Relational Technology, Inc. Because this was one of the first relational efforts, it is an important system. In addition, a number of other systems have been developed using some of the ideas and, particularly, the data manipulation language of INGRES, just as other systems have been developed using the ideas in System R and its data manipulation language, SQL. For these reasons, we will briefly investigate this system and its data definition and manipulation capabilities, together with the manner in which programs in languages like COBOL can interface with INGRES.

INGRES is not considered an SQL system, although, as of late 1985, it does support SQL. Rather, it supports its own language, **QUEL** (QUEry Language). QUEL is usually classified as an implementation of the relational calculus. In what follows, we will give SQL equivalents of QUEL expressions wherever such equivalents exist.

DATA DEFINITION

CREATE

QUEL has a CREATE command that is similar to that of SQL. To define the Premiere Products SLSREP table, the command in QUEL would be

```
CREATE  SLSREP
       ( SLSREP_NUMBER      =  I1,
         SLSREP_NAME        =  C15,
         SLSREP_ADDRESS     =  C25,
         TOTAL_COMMISSION   =  MONEY,
         COMMISSION_RATE    =  F4 )
```

which is basically similar to the SQL

```
CREATE  TABLE  SLSREP
       ( SLSREP_NUMBER      DECIMAL(2),
         SLSREP_NAME        CHAR(15),
         SLSREP_ADDRESS     CHAR(25),
         TOTAL_COMMISSION   DECIMAL(7,2),
         COMMISSION_RATE    DECIMAL(2,2)  )
```

The syntax is slightly different and there is a different set of possible data types: I (integer), C (like CHAR), MONEY (up to sixteen digits with two decimal places), and F (floating point number). In addition, there is a data type DATE to store date and time, and TEXT, which is a variable-length character string. Possible integer formats are I1, I2, and I4 for one, two, or four-byte integers, respectively. Possible floating point formats are F4 and F8 for four-byte and eight-byte floating point numbers. For character data, the C is followed by the number of bytes as C25. Finally, for variable-length character data, the TEXT is followed by the maximum-length character string that needs to be stored as TEXT(25).

INDEX

Indexes can be created with the INDEX command. Creating an index on the customer number within the customer table is accomplished by

```
INDEX ON CUSTOMER IS CUSTOMER_INDEX (CUSTOMER_
     NUMBER)
```

as opposed to the SQL

```
CREATE INDEX CUSTOMER_INDEX ON CUSTOMER (CUSTOMER_
     NUMBER)
```

DESTROY

Indexes and/or base tables may be deleted using the DESTROY command. To delete the customer index just created, we would enter:

```
DESTROY CUSTOMER_INDEX
```

In SQL, the formulation would be:

```
DROP INDEX CUSTOMER_INDEX
```

MODIFY

The MODIFY command provides for changing of the underlying storage structure of a table or index. This effectively allows users to reorganize a table or an index or to convert a table or index to a different storage structure. It is *not* the equivalent of the SQL ALTER, which allows the addition of new columns to tables in the database. INGRES does not have a statement equivalent to ALTER.

Among the possible structures are BTREE (a **B-tree** structure) and HASH (a structure using **hashing**). In addition to specifying storage structures, tables or indexes may be requested to be compressed by preceding the storage structure code with the letter C (as in CBTREE).

For any structure that involves a key, such as BTREE and HASH (hashing must take place on some key field), a key is specified, as is the option of enforcing uniqueness for that key field.

To specify that SLSREP is to have a BTREE structure with SLSREP_NUMBER as a unique key, the formulation would be:

```
MODIFY SLSREP TO BTREE UNIQUE ON SLSREP_NUMBER
```

VIEWS

INGRES includes a view mechanism. View definition is similar to that in SQL, with a slightly different syntax. To define the HOUSEWARES view described in section 5.2 in INGRES, the command would be:

```
DEFINE VIEW HOUSEWARES
      (PNUM    = PART.PART_NUMBER
      DESC     = PART.PART_DESCRIPTION
      ON_HAND  = PART.UNITS_ON_HAND
      PRICE    = PART.UNIT_PRICE)
      WHERE PART.ITEM_CLASS = 'HW'
```

The corresponding SQL view definition is:

```
CREATE VIEW HOUSEWARES (PNUM, DESC, ON_HAND, PRICE) AS
     SELECT PART_NUMBER, PART_DESCRIPTION,
            UNITS_ON_HAND, UNIT_PRICE
        FROM PART
        WHERE ITEM_CLASS = 'HW'
```

In an SQL view definition, if the names of the columns in the view are the same as the names of the corresponding columns in the base tables, the names do not have to be listed. In INGRES, on the other hand, they *must* be listed, even if they are unchanged.

DATA MANIPULATION

The QUEL RETRIEVE command is analogous to the SQL SELECT. The basic form is RETRIEVE–WHERE. Note that there is no analog to the SQL FROM clause and, thus, every column must be qualified with its table name. The following examples from chapter 3 illustrate the basic use of the RETRIEVE command. For more detailed examples, see [5].

Example 3.2: List the number, name, and balance of all customers.

QUEL:

```
RETRIEVE CUSTOMER.CUSTOMER_NUMBER, CUSTOMER.NAME,
         CUSTOMER.CURRENT_BALANCE
```

SQL:

```
SELECT CUSTOMER_NUMBER, NAME, CURRENT_BALANCE
       FROM CUSTOMER
```

Example 3.3: List the complete part table.

In QUEL, the word ALL corresponds to the SQL *.

QUEL:

```
RETRIEVE PART.ALL
```

SQL:

```
SELECT *
     FROM PART
```

Example 3.4: What is the name of customer 124?

QUEL:

```
RETRIEVE CUSTOMER.NAME
       WHERE CUSTOMER.CUSTOMER_NUMBER = 124
```

```
SQL:
SELECT NAME
      FROM CUSTOMER
      WHERE CUSTOMER_NUMBER = 124
```

Example 3.6: Find the available credit for all customers who have at least an $800 credit limit.

In QUEL, computed fields must be assigned a name. This is done by giving the assigned name, followed by an equal sign, followed by the computation.

```
QUEL:
RETRIEVE CUSTOMER.CUSTOMER_NUMBER, CUSTOMER.NAME,
      AVAILABLE_CREDIT = CUSTOMER.CREDIT_LIMIT -
          CUSTOMER.CURRENT_BALANCE)
      WHERE CREDIT_LIMIT > = 800
```

```
SQL:
SELECT CUSTOMER_NUMBER, NAME, CREDIT_LIMIT -
      CURRENT_BALANCE
      FROM CUSTOMER WHERE CREDIT_LIMIT > = 800
```

Example 3.7: List the number, name, and address of all customers who live in Grant.

QUEL supports the same use of a "wild card" that SQL does. The symbol used is different: it is an asterisk.

```
QUEL:
RETRIEVE CUSTOMER.CUSTOMER_NUMBER, CUSTOMER.NAME,
      CUSTOMER.ADDRESS
      WHERE CUSTOMER.ADDRESS = "*GRANT*"
```

```
SQL:
SELECT CUSTOMER_NUMBER, NAME, ADDRESS
      FROM CUSTOMER
      WHERE ADDRESS LIKE '%GRANT%'
```

Example 3.8A: List all customers, ordered by name.

In QUEL, the SORT clause corresponds to the SQL ORDER BY.

```
QUEL:
RETRIEVE CUSTOMER.CUSTOMER_NUMBER, CUSTOMER.NAME,
      CUSTOMER.ADDRESS
      SORT BY CUSTOMER.NAME
```

SQL:
```
SELECT CUSTOMER_NUMBER, NAME, ADDRESS
     FROM CUSTOMER
     ORDER BY NAME
```

Example 3.10: How many parts are in item class "HW"?

QUEL supports all of the usual built-in functions. Unlike SQL, the result of a computation involving a built-in function must be assigned a name. In the following QUEL command, the value obtained is called HWCOUNT. Further, any restrictions are included as part of an argument for the function.

QUEL:
```
RETRIEVE ( HWCOUNT = COUNT (PART.PART_NUMBER WHERE
     PART.ITEM_CLASS = "HW" ) )
```

SQL:
```
SELECT COUNT(PART_NUMBER)
     FROM PART
     WHERE ITEM_CLASS = 'HW'
```

Example 3.14: List all customers whose balance is over the average balance.

In QUEL, functions can be used in the WHERE clause.

QUEL:
```
RETRIEVE CUSTOMER.CUSTOMER_NUMBER, CUSTOMER.NAME,
     CUSTOMER.ADDRESS, CUSTOMER.CURRENT_BALANCE
     WHERE CUSTOMER.CURRENT_BALANCE >
          (AVG (CUSTOMER.CURRENT_BALANCE) )
```

SQL:
```
SELECT CUSTOMER_NUMBER, NAME, ADDRESS,
     CURRENT_BALANCE
     FROM CUSTOMER WHERE CURRENT_BALANCE >
      (SELECT AVG(CURRENT_BALANCE)
          FROM CUSTOMER)
```

Although the examples thus far have not shown it, QUEL queries use *range variables*, i.e., variables whose values range over the rows of a given table. In SQL, they are termed aliases.

Example 3.22: List the number and name of all sales reps together with the number and name of all the customers they represent.

QUEL:

```
RANGE OF S IS SLSREP
RANGE OF C IS CUSTOMER

RETRIEVE S.SLSREP_NUMBER, S.SLSREP_NAME,
      C.CUSTOMER_NUMBER, C.NAME
    WHERE S.SLSREP_NUMBER = C.SLSREP_NUMBER
```

SQL:

```
SELECT S.SLSREP_NUMBER, S.SLSREP_NAME,
      C.CUSTOMER_NUMBER, C.NAME
    FROM SLSREP S, CUSTOMER C
    WHERE S.SLSREP_NUMBER = C.SLSREP_NUMBER
```

In QUEL, range variables are indicated with a separate RANGE clause. In the above query, S is a range variable for the SLSREP table and C is a range variable for the CUSTOMER table. These names will now be used in place of SLSREP and CUSTOMER in the retrieve command. If no RANGE clauses are present, QUEL assumes that the name of each table is also the range variable for the table. As far as QUEL is concerned, query 3.2 above, for example, contains the RANGE clause:

```
RANGE OF CUSTOMER IS CUSTOMER
```

As in SQL, there are instances in which the use of RANGE clauses is essential. The following example from chapter 3 illustrates this point.

Example 3.23: List any pairs of customers who have the same name.

QUEL:

```
RANGE OF FIRST IS CUSTOMER
RANGE OF SECOND IS CUSTOMER

RETRIEVE FIRST.CUSTOMER_NUMBER, FIRST.NAME,
     SECOND.CUSTOMER_NUMBER, SECOND.NAME
    WHERE FIRST.NAME = SECOND.NAME
    AND FIRST.CUSTOMER_NUMBER <
      SECOND.CUSTOMER_NUMBER
```

SQL:

```
SELECT FIRST.CUSTOMER_NUMBER, FIRST.NAME,
     SECOND.CUSTOMER_NUMBER, SECOND.NAME
    FROM CUSTOMER FIRST, CUSTOMER SECOND
    WHERE FIRST.NAME = SECOND.NAME
    AND FIRST.CUSTOMER_NUMBER <
      SECOND.CUSTOMER_NUMBER
```

For an explanation of this query, refer back to the discussion in chapter 3.

As you would expect, QUEL includes commands to update the database: REPLACE, DELETE, and APPEND, which are analogous to the SQL commands UPDATE, DELETE, and INSERT, respectively. The following examples illustrate the syntax and the use of these commands.

Example 3.30: Change the name of customer 256 TO "ANN JONES".

QUEL:

```
REPLACE CUSTOMER (NAME = "ANN JONES")
    WHERE CUSTOMER_NUMBER = 256
```

SQL:

```
UPDATE CUSTOMER
    SET NAME = 'ANN JONES'
    WHERE CUSTOMER_NUMBER = 256
```

Example 3.31: Add sales rep (14, "ANN CRANE", "123 RIVER, ADA, MI", 0, 0.05) to the database.

QUEL:

```
APPEND TO SLSREP (SLSREP_NUMBER = 14,
    SLSREP_NAME = "ANN CRANE",
    SLSREP_ADDRESS = "123 RIVER, ADA, MI",
    TOTAL_COMMISSION = 0.00,
    COMMISSION_RATE = 0.05)
```

SQL:

```
INSERT INTO SLSREP
    VALUES
    (14, 'ANN CRANE', '123 RIVER, ADA, MI', 0.00, 0.05)
```

Example 3.32: Delete the customer whose name is "AL WILLIAMS" from the database.

QUEL:

```
DELETE CUSTOMER WHERE CUSTOMER.NAME = "AL WILLIAMS"
```

SQL:

```
DELETE CUSTOMER
    WHERE NAME = 'AL WILLIAMS'
```

EMBEDDED QUEL

Like SQL in DB2, QUEL can be embedded in programs in a host language like COBOL. Embedded QUEL is referred to as EQUEL. While the process is similar to that described for SQL in DB2, there are three differences worth mentioning.

In DB2, SQL commands were identified to the precompiler by preceding them with EXEC SQL and following them with END—EXEC. In EQUEL, QUEL commands are identified by placing the characters "##" in the first two columns on any line containing a QUEL statement. The EQUEL preprocessor will then convert these statements to appropriate CALL statements.

There is no analog to a cursor. Rather, after a retrieve command, a block of code will be contained between two lines of code that are both:

[

This block of code will be executed for each row that has been retrieved. In this manner, INGRES circumvents the problem of returning multiple rows to a record-at-a-time-oriented language.

Finally, QUEL commands are interpreted and optimized at runtime, unlike DB2, in which the Bind processor prepares application plans for SQL queries in advance of program execution. The advantage of the INGRES approach is that the optimizer always uses the most current information. By contrast, an index created after an application plan has been prepared in DB2 will not be used, even if it provides a better way to satisfy the SQL command.

The INGRES approach has a corresponding disadvantage in terms of performance. Extra overhead is incurred during program execution. This overhead could be potentially serious for a QUEL statement occuring in a loop. (If, during each iteration of the loop, the command must be reinterpreted and re-optimized, the additional overhead must be multiplied by the number of iterations!) Fortunately, INGRES provides a solution to this problem. If a QUEL command is preceded by the word REPEAT, the code generated the first time this command is encountered is saved and used whenever the command is encountered during the remaining execution of the program. Thus, like SQL, it is only the first time a given command is encountered that the impact of additional overhead will be felt.

SECURITY AND INTEGRITY

INGRES supports sophisticated security features through the DEFINE PER-MIT command, which is analogous to the DB2 GRANT command. Any authorizations granted through a DEFINE PERMIT command can be revoked through the DESTROY PERMIT command, which is analogous to the DB2 REVOKE command.

The DEFINE PERMIT command has some interesting options, as the following example illustrates:

```
DEFINE PERMIT RETRIEVE, REPLACE
      ON   CUSTOMER (CUSTOMER_NUMBER, CUSTOMER_NAME)
      TO   MARY_JONES
      AT   VT100-3
      FROM 13:00 TO 16:00
      ON   THU  TO FRI
      WHERE CUSTOMER.SLSREP_NUMBER = 3
```

In this example, Mary Jones is allowed to retrieve or update the number and name of any customer represented by sales rep 3. This activity can take place, however, only at terminal VT100-3 between 1:00 and 4:00 in the afternoon on Thursday or Friday. Of course, any DEFINE PERMIT command does not have to use all of the features just illustrated.

When a user who has been issued a PERMIT accesses an INGRES database, the QUEL command is modified to include the conditions in the permit. If Mary Jones, for example, issued the query

```
RETRIEVE (CUSTOMER.CUSTOMER_NUMBER, CUSTOMER.NAME)
     WHERE CUSTOMER.CREDIT_LIMIT = 500
```

the query actually executed would be:

```
RETRIEVE (CUSTOMER.CUSTOMER_NUMBER, CUSTOMER.NAME)
     WHERE CUSTOMER.CREDIT_LIMIT = 500
     AND CUSTOMER.SLSREP_NUMBER = 3
```

Integrity is supported through the DEFINE INTEGRITY command. As commands are modified for security, so in a similar way are commands modified to include the integrity constraint. Suppose, for example, that the following integrity constraint has been defined:

```
DEFINE INTEGRITY
     ON CUSTOMER
     IS CREDIT_LIMIT = 300
     OR CREDIT_LIMIT = 500
     OR CREDIT_LIMIT = 800
     OR CREDIT_LIMIT = 1000
```

and a user attempts to add $200 to the credit limit for all customers of sales rep 3. According to the constraint, this should be permitted only if the customer's credit limit is $300 or $800. (Adding $200 to a credit limit of $500 or $1000 will produce an invalid credit limit.) INGRES enforces this constraint by converting the command the user would enter from:

```
REPLACE CUSTOMER (CREDIT_LIMIT =
     CUSTOMER.CREDIT_LIMIT + 200)
     WHERE CUSTOMER.SLSREP_NUMBER = 3
```

to

```
REPLACE CUSTOMER (CREDIT_LIMIT =
     CUSTOMER.CREDIT_LIMIT + 200)
     WHERE CUSTOMER.SLSREP_NUMBER = 3
     AND (   CUSTOMER.CREDIT_LIMIT = 300
        OR CUSTOMER.CREDIT_LIMIT = 500
        OR CUSTOMER.CREDIT_LIMIT = 800
        OR CUSTOMER.CREDIT_LIMIT = 1000 )
```

Certainly, many constraints cannot be handled in this simple way, and these constraints are not supported by INGRES. However, most other systems do not currently support such restrictions, either.

For other information on INGRES, see [4] or the manuals from Relational Technology, Inc.

.6 SUMMARY

In this chapter, we have examined some of the advanced topics within the relational model. We discussed the problems that pertain to the use of nulls. We looked at the integrity rules: entity integrity, which states that no attribute that is a part of the primary key may accept null values, and referential integrity, which states that if the value for a foreign key is not null, it must match the value of the primary key for some row in the relation identified by the foreign key. We discussed views, (derived, virtual tables), how they are defined, how they are manipulated, which types of views may be updated, and the role that views play in logical data independence and in security. We also discussed another typical security feature in relational model systems, the ability to grant various types of authorizations to different users. We discussed the special bill-of-materials relationship in which an entity, in this case the PART entity, is related to itself in a many-to-many fashion. We discussed the use of indexes to improve performance. Finally, we listed some criteria that systems must satisfy to be considered fully relational systems.

We then considered some advanced features of SQL. We examined the various data types supported by SQL. We looked at the features of SQL which relate to the support of nulls. We looked at the ALTER statement, which allow users to add columns to an existing table, change the characteristics of columns in a table, or delete columns from a table. We pointed out that some implementations of SQL, such as the one used in DB2, only support the addition of columns. We looked at the type of information stored in the catalog and how information can be retrieved from the catalog. We looked at some of the report formatting features of SQL. Finally, we looked at the issues involved in embedding SQL in a program in a language like COBOL. We discussed the problem created when an SQL command retrieves several rows that are then passed to a language designed to handle a single row (or record) at a time. We saw how this problem is solved through the use of cursors.

Next, we investigated the relational system DB2, a product of IBM that grew out of the prototype System R. Since much of the previous discussion in the text concerning SQL and advanced features of the relational model also pertained to DB2, we listed the ways in which DB2 differed. We saw the manner in which DB2 furnished the ten functions of a DBMS.

In the final section, we examined an alternative relational product, INGRES, that is not SQL based. (Although SQL is now supported in INGRES, it is not the principal language.) INGRES comes from a prototype system, also called INGRES, which was developed at the University of California at Berkeley at the same time that System R was being developed at IBM. INGRES supports a language called QUEL. We examined the data definition and manipulation features of QUEL, together with the manner in which QUEL can be embedded in application programs using the EQUEL (Embedded QUEL) processor. Finally, we examined the manner in which INGRES handles security and integrity restrictions.

REVIEW QUESTIONS

1. State the two integrity rules. Indicate why it is desirable to enforce each rule.
2. What is a view? What is the difference between a view and a base table? Does the data described in a view definition ever exist in that form? What happens when a user accesses a database through a view?
3. Name three advantages of using views.
4. Which types of views are theoretically updatable? Which types are not? Which types are updatable in most current systems? Which types are not?
5. What is the relationship between a view and a subschema?
6. Describe the GRANT mechanism and explain how it relates to security. What types of privileges may be granted? How are they revoked?
7. What are the advantages of using indexes? What are the disadvantages?
8. List the two properties specified by Codd that a system must satisfy to be considered relational.
9. List the four categories of systems proposed by Date. Describe the characteristics of systems in each category.
10. List and describe the data types supported by SQL.
11. How can the structure of a table be changed in SQL? What types of changes are possible in general?
12. Why should users not be able to update the catalog directly?
13. How are SQL commands that are embedded in a COBOL program identified to the precompiler? What are host variables? How are column names distinguished from host variables in an embedded SQL command?
14. What is the SQLCA? What function does it serve? How is it included in a COBOL program?
15. Why does a select that produces more than one row cause a problem for a language like COBOL? How do cursors solve this problem?
16. Describe two ways to handle exceptional conditions that involve processing the database in a COBOL program.
17. How do COMMIT and ROLLBACK relate to the support of logical transactions?
18. How do COMMIT and ROLLBACK relate to the support of shared update?
19. Describe how a user-defined procedure could be used for integrity support. What are the limitations involved in user-defined procedures in DB2?
20. Describe the major features through which DB2 furnishes logical and physical data independence.
21. What is EQUEL? How is the problem of retrieving multiple rows handled in EQUEL?

22. How is security handled in INGRES?   What happens when a user for whom some security restrictions have been defined enters a QUEL command?

23. How is integrity handled in INGRES? What happens when an update occurs that would affect a column for which an integrity constraint has been defined?

EXERCISES

1. A view, SMALLCUST, is to be defined. It consists of the customer number, name, address, balance, and credit limit for all customers whose credit limit is $500 or less.
   a. Write the view definition for SMALLCUST.
   b. Write an SQL query to retrieve the number and name of all customers in SMALLCUST whose balance is over their credit limit.
   c. Convert the query from part B to the query that will actually be executed.
   d. Are any problems created by updating the database through this view? If so, what are they? If not, why not?

2. A view, CUSTORD, is to be defined. It consists of the customer number, name, balance, order number, and order date for all orders currently on file.
   a. Write the view definition for CUSTORD.
   b. Write an SQL query to retrieve the customer number, name, order number, and order date for all orders in CUSTORD for customers whose balance is more than $100.
   c. Convert the query from part B to the query that will actually be executed.
   d. Are any problems created by updating the database through this view? If so, what are they? If not, why not?

3. A view, ORDTOT, is to be defined. It consists of the order number and order total for each order currently on file in which the total is more than $100. (The order total is the sum of the number ordered times the quoted price on each of the order lines for the order.)
   a. Write the view definition for ORDTOT.
   b. Write an SQL query to retrieve the order number and order total for all orders whose total is over $100.
   c. Convert the query from part B to the query that will actually be executed.
   d. Are any problems created by updating the database through this view? If so, what are they? If not, why not?

4. Let's assume that to manufacture part M requires three of part N, six of part P, and twelve of part R. Manufacturing part N requires two of part S and a single part T. Manufacturing part P requires three of part S, two of part T, and a single part V. Manufacturing part R requires a single part T and a single part V.
   a. Show an extension of the PRODUCT_STRUCTURE table representing the above data.
   b. Write an SQL query that will list all of the immediate components of part M, together with the quantity of each component that is required.
   c. Write the query that will list all of the immediate parents of part T.

5. How is support for nulls provided by SQL? Your answer should address both data definition and data manipulation capabilities.

6. Give the syntax required to add the column MTD_SALES to the CUSTOMER table. MTD_SALES is a dollar figure that will be less than $10,000. It should be placed before the CREDIT_LIMIT column. MTD—SALES for current customers should be set to zero.

7. Give the syntax required to delete the column ITEM_CLASS from the PART table.

8. Give the syntax required to expand PART_DESCRIPTION to thirty characters.

9. Describe the information stored in the catalog. Give an SQL query that will access the catalog to determine the creator of the SLSREP table. Give an SQL query that will access the catalog to determine all columns in all tables created by JONES.

10. Give an SQL query together with appropriate report-formatting commands which will produce the following report: List the number and name of each sales rep together with the number, name, and balance of each customer represented by the sales rep. Column headings for these columns should be 'SNUM', 'NAME', 'CNUM', 'NAME', and 'BAL', respectively. The report should be sorted by customer number within sales rep number. The balance column should be presented with two decimal places and should be totaled by sales rep. A sales rep number and name should appear only once. The heading for the report should be 'SALES REP REPORT'.

11. If you have access to an SQL system that supports the type of report formatting discussed in this chapter, produce the report indicated in exercise 10.

12. Assuming that the appropriate entries have been made in the DATA DIVISION of a COBOL program, give the procedure division code for each of the following:

   a. Obtain the description and unit price of the part whose part number is currently stored in W–PART–NUMBER. Place these values in the variables W–PART–DESCRIPTION and W–UNIT–PRICE, respectively.

   b. Obtain the order date, customer number, and name for the order whose number is currently stored in W–ORDER–NUMBER. Place these values in the variables W–ORDER–DATE, W–CUSTOMER–NUMBER, and W–NAME, respectively.

   c. Add a row to the PART table. The data is currently stored in the fields within the W–PART record.

   d. Change the description of the part whose number is stored in W–PART–NUMBER to the value currently found in W–PART–DESCRIPTION.

   e. Increase the price of all parts in item class 'HW' by 5 percent.

   f. Delete the part whose number is stored in W–PART–NUMBER.

13. Let's assume that we wish to retrieve all parts located in the warehouse whose number is stored in W–WAREHOUSE–NUM.

   a. Write an appropriate cursor description.

   b. Give all statements that will be included in the PROCEDURE DIVISION and that relate to processing the database through this cursor.

   c. Write the additional PROCEDURE DIVISION code that will update any of these parts that are in item class 'HW' by adding 5 percent to the unit price and any parts in item class 'SG' by adding 10 percent to the unit price. (The cursor must be used in the answer.)

14. Give an INGRES view definition for the SMALLCUST view described in exercise 1.

15. Give QUEL commands for the following:
    a. List the part number, description, and unit price for all parts.
    b. List the complete SLSREP table.
    c. List the description of part "BT04".
    d. Find the on-hand value (units on hand times the unit price) for all parts in warehouse 3.
    e. List the number, name, and balance of all customers named "SMITH". Sort the result by customer number.
    f. Count the number of customers of sales rep 3.
    g. List the number and name of all customers together with the number and date of all their orders. Use range variables in the query.
    h. Change the number of units on hand of part "BT04" to 15.
    i. Add order (12506, 90687, 124) to the database.
    j. Delete from the database all orders placed by customer 522.

REFERENCES

1] Bradley, James. *Introduction to Data Base Management in Business*. Holt, Rinehart & Winston, 1983.

2] Codd, E. F. "Extending the Relational Database Model to Capture More Meaning" *ACM TODS* 4, no. 4 (December 1979).

3] Codd, E. F. "Relational Database: A Practical Foundation for Productivity." *Communications of the ACM* 25, no. 2 (February 1982).

4] Date, C. J. *Introduction to Database Systems, Volume I*, 4th ed. Addison-Wesley, 1986.

5] Date, C. J. *Introduction to Database Systems, Volume II*. Addison-Wesley, 1983.

6] Date, C. J. *A Guide to DB2*. Addison-Wesley, 1984.

7] Kim, Won. "Relational Database Systems." *ACM Computing Surveys* 11 (September 1979).

8] Kroenke, David. *Database Processing*, 2d ed. SRA, 1983.

9] McFadden, Fred R., and Hoffer, Jeffrey A. *Data Base Management*. Benjamin Cummings, 1985.

DATABASE DESIGN I INTRODUCTION TO DATABASE DESIGN

CHAPTER

6

INTRODUCTION

In all the examples we have studied thus far, the design of the databases had already been completed. In the examples concerning the relational model, this meant that decisions had already been made regarding the collection of relations that made up the database as well as the collection of attributes contained in these relations.

In this chapter we begin the study of database design, which is the process of determining the content and arrangement of data in the database that is needed to support some activity on behalf of a user or group of users. **Database design** is really a two-step process. In the first step, user requirements are gathered together and a database is designed which will meet these requirements as cleanly as possible. This step is called **information-level design** and it is taken *independent* of any individual DBMS. In the second step, this information-level design is transformed into a design for the specific DBMS that will be used to implement the system in question. In this step, which is called **physical-level design**, we are concerned with the characteristics of the specific DBMS that will be used. We are also concerned with the adequate performance of the system. Though the concept of adequate performance is difficult to define precisely, it will involve taking some measure of the space occupied by the database and some measure of processing performance, such as response time and throughput.

Both of these database design steps are critical. A poor effort made with regard to the information-level design is extremely difficult to counteract when it comes to the physical-level design. On the other hand, even an excellent information-level design is not enough to avoid a poorly performing system if the physical-level design is not well done.

Various approaches, or methodologies, have been proposed for the information level of database design. Among them are the canonical schema of James Martin [7], the entity-relationship model of Dr. Peter Chen [1], and the semantic data model of Hammer and McLeod ([4] and [6]). In this text, another methodology is presented, one that depends heavily on the relational model. While it differs in a number of ways, the methodology in the text has been heavily influenced by the methodology described by C. J. Date in [2] and also uses some of the ideas that he suggests in [3]. Some of the terminology is the same as that proposed by Date.

The information-level database design process is such an important topic that two chapters of this text are devoted to it. In this chapter, we will study the basic information-level design methodology and will work through a number of examples. In chapter 7, we will go into greater detail regarding several issues within the information-level design process. We will also examine an alternative methodology, the entity-relationship model, in some detail. In chapter 12, we will discuss the physical level of database design. At that point, we will show that even though the information-level methodology is heavily grounded in the relational model, it can still be used quite successfully when a given DBMS follows another model.

6.2   DATABASE DESIGN GOALS

Database design is a process that takes a set of user requirements as input and produces database structures capable of supporting these requirements as output. As database designers, we have certain expectations of the user requirements and certain goals for the database structures.

First, we expect the user requirements to be as complete as possible. Specifically, this means that the user requirements for the system should address both the *functional requirements* and the *physical constraints* of the target system. The functional requirements must include:

- all reports that must be produced
- all inquiries that must be supported
- all other outputs that must be sent to other systems or to external destinations
- all update transactions that must be processed
- all calculations that must be performed
- all restrictions that the system must enforce; for example, not allowing a customer to be added for whom there is no matching sales rep and not allowing the deletion of a customer who currently has orders on file
- all synonyms that are used for each attribute. Synonyms are different names used by different users for the same attribute. For example, part number, product code, model number, and item number may all be used by different people in the same organization to refer to the same attribute.

When we turn our attention to the physical design process, we also need the user requirements to provide information about processing volumes and performance measurements. We call these volumes and measurements physical constraints. These would include, for example, the following estimates and constraints:

- the number of occurrences of each type of entity: sales reps, orders, customers, etc.
- the frequency with which each report will be printed
- the length in number of lines for each report
- the response-time requirements for each query
- the response-time requirements for each update transaction
- the special security constraints that define who can access which data and in what way

Taking these user requirements as input, the information-level and physical-level design processes should produce a database design for a specific DBMS which supports these requirements and performs in an acceptable manner. The information-level design process does not entail the physical constraints from the user requirements. Instead, the information-level design is based on all other user requirements. This process results in a logical design that cleanly supports the user requirements and is independent of the characteristics of any individual DBMS. The physical-level design process utilizes this design, the physical constraints from the user requirements, and information concerning the particular DBMS involved to produce the final database structure. The overall process is illustrated in Figure 6.1.

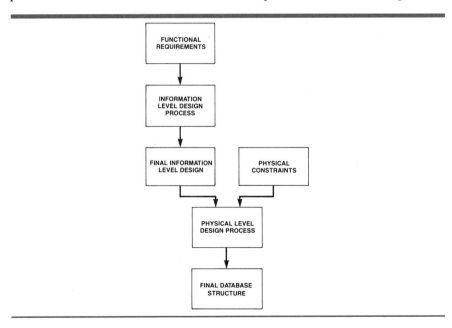

FIGURE 6.1
Database design process

We must keep certain goals in mind as we proceed through the information-level and the physical-level design processes. The information-level design process must result in a design that is complete. That is, *all* user functional requirements must be satisfied by this design. The design itself should enforce as many of the requirements as possible rather than force programs to do so. Among other things, this means that the design should be in 3NF or 4NF unless there is a good reason for it not to be so. Any requirements that the design cannot enforce should be noted in the form of a list of requirements that the programs in the system will have to enforce. Note that efficiency of processing is not a primary goal during this step; the ultimate goal is a clean, redundancy-free design that will enforce as many of the stated requirements as possible.

Using the output of step one along with the physical requirements, the physical-level design process must result in a DBMS-specific design that still meets the user requirements. Here, however, we are concerned about system efficiency in terms of storage space, processing time, and response time. The goals of this step can and often do conflict with the goals of the information-level design. We may not be able to achieve 3NF with the efficiency that is required. It may even be necessary to use a repeating group that was removed during the process of converting to 1NF. However, any changes that we make should be executed with the utmost care and in a very controlled way. In addition, the need for any deviation from the information-level design must be clearly documented. Since the physical-level design may not be able to enforce all the requirements and constraints that the information-level design did, a list of all additional burdens individual programs must now assume should be drawn up.

6.3 USER VIEWS

No matter which approach is adopted with regard to database design, design of a complete database that will satisfy the requirements can never be a one-step process. Unless the requirements are exceptionally simple, it is also usually necessary to subdivide the overall task of database design into smaller tasks. This is often done through the separate consideration of individual user views. A **user view** is the view of data necessary to support the operations of a particular user. For each user view, a database structure to support the view must be designed and then merged into a cumulative design. Each user view, in general, will be much simpler than the total collection of requirements, so working on individual tasks will be much more manageable than attempting to turn the design of the entire database into one task.

These user views are obtained through a variety of methods. In addition to interviewing users, we can examine reports, forms, and procedures, study existing file structures and observe the processing that is actually taking place. We will discuss the information-gathering process to some extent in chapter 7; a complete description of this process as a means of determining these user views can be found in a systems analysis and design text. It is worth noting that the smaller the unit we work with, the easier the design of the database structures to support this unit will be. Thus, if one user requires three different reports, we might well consider each report as a separate user view, unless, of course, the design of the structure for simultaneously supporting all three reports is obvious to us.

4   THE BASIC DATABASE DESIGN METHODOLOGY

The database design methodology we present involves representing individual user views, refining them to eliminate any problems, and then merging them into a cumulative design. A "user" could be an actual person or group who will use the system, a report the system must produce, or a type of transaction that the system must support. In the last two instances, you might think of the user as the person who will use the report or enter the transaction.

For this design methodology, we assume that the users have been interviewed, that report and transaction requirements have been gathered and analyzed, and that any ambiguities have been resolved. In other words, we are assuming that all requirements needed to begin the design process are in hand.

Another "must" is that appropriate documentation will be created and maintained during the design process. One type of documentation is addressed in the description of the methodology, but this is certainly not the only documentation that would be created during the design phase. Program specifications, test plans, training plans, conversion plans, screen layouts, and printer spacing charts, for example, are also crucial.

We now turn to the methodology itself. For each user view in turn, we need to complete the following five steps:

1. Represent the user view as a collection of relations. •
2. Normalize these relations. •
3. Represent all keys. •
4. Determine any other restrictions. •
5. Merge the result of the previous steps into the design. •

We will now examine each of these steps in detail.

1. REPRESENT THE USER VIEW AS A COLLECTION OF RELATIONS

When taking this step, we must make certain to identify the keys. In some situations this may not be much of a problem. A good and proper design may occur to you very naturally. Suppose, for example, that a given user view involves departments and employees. Suppose further that each department can employ many employees but that each employee is assigned to exactly one department (a typical restriction). The design

DEPARTMENT(<u>DEPARTMENT_NUMBER</u>, DEPARTMENT_NAME)

EMPLOYEE(<u>EMPLOYEE_NUMBER</u>, NAME, ADDRESS,
         WAGE_RATE, DEPARTMENT_NUMBER)

may have naturally occurred to you and is probably an appropriate design. The real question is, What procedure should be followed if a correct design is not so obvious? To find the answer, the following tips can be applied.

Tip 1. Create a separate relation for each type of entity.

If a user view involves departments and employees, begin by creating a DEPARTMENT relation and an EMPLOYEE relation. If a user view involves customers, sales reps, and orders, begin by creating a CUSTOMER relation, a SLSREP relation, and an ORDER relation. Note that this tip does not address the issue of which attributes should be included in each relation.

Tip 2. Determine the primary key for each of these relations.

Even though we have yet to determine the attributes in the relation, we can often determine the **primary key**. For example, the primary key to a EMPLOYEE relation will probably be the EMPLOYEE_NUMBER, and the primary key to a CUSTOMER relation will probably be the CUSTOMER_NUMBER.

Tip 3. Determine the properties for each of these entities.

Look at the user requirements and then determine the other properties of each entity that are required. For example, an employee entity may require NAME, ADDRESS, WAGE_RATE, HOURS_WORKED, and NUMBER_OF_DEPENDENTS. Or a customer entity may require NAME, ADDRESS, CUSTOMER_TYPE, BAL-ANCE, and CREDIT_LIMIT. These properties, along with the key identified in tip 2, will become the attributes in the relation.

Tip 4. Determine relationships among the entities.

The basic relationships that we will need to contend with are one-to-one, one-to-many, and many-to-many. We will consider each of these in turn and discuss a method to handle each relationship type.

a. One-to-one

Suppose that each student had exactly one advisor and each advisor had exactly one advisee. In this case we would include the primary key of the STUDENT relation as a **foreign key** (an attribute whose values are required to match the primary key of another relation) in the ADVISOR relation and the primary key of the ADVISOR relation as a foreign key in the STUDENT relation.

STUDENT(<u>STUDENT_NUMBER</u>, NAME, ..., ADVISOR_
           NUMBER, ...)

ADVISOR(<u>ADVISOR_NUMBER</u>, ADVISOR_NAME, ...,
           STUDENT_NUMBER, ...)

While this may be the simplest way of implementing a one-to-one relationship, it does present some difficulties that are beyond the scope of the current discussion. These problems will be discussed in chapter 7.

b. One-to-many

Suppose that each student had exactly one advisor but an advisor could have several advisees. In this case we would include the primary key of the ADVISOR relation as a foreign key in the STUDENT relation. We would *not* include the primary key of the STUDENT relation in the ADVISOR relation.

STUDENT(STUDENT_NUMBER, NAME, . . . , ADVISOR_
        NUMBER, . . .)

ADVISOR(ADVISOR_NUMBER, ADVISOR_NAME, . . .)

c. Many-to-many

Suppose that each student could have several advisors and each advisor could have several advisees. In this case we would create a new relation, ADVISES, whose primary key would be the combination of the STUDENT_NUMBER and the ADVISOR_NUMBER.

STUDENT(STUDENT_NUMBER, NAME, . . .)

ADVISOR(ADVISOR_NUMBER, ADVISOR_NAME, . . .)

ADVISES(STUDENT_NUMBER, ADVISOR_NUMBER, . . .)

The other attributes in the ADVISES relation would be those attributes which pertained to both the student and the advisor, if such attributes existed. One possibility, for example, would be the date when the advisor began advising the student. This would depend on both student and advisor.

2. NORMALIZE THESE RELATIONS

Normalize each relation, with the target being third normal form. The target is actually fourth normal form; but a little care in the early phases of the normalization process will usually alleviate the need to consider fourth normal form.

3. REPRESENT ALL KEYS

Identify all keys, primary, candidate, secondary, and foreign, and resolve specific issues for each one.

PRIMARY:

This is the **primary key** determined in the earlier steps.

CANDIDATE:

If there are any **candidate keys** (attributes that could have been chosen as primary key but were not), they should be represented at this point. It is not common to have candidate keys, other than the primary key; but if they do exist, and if the system is to enforce their uniqueness, they should be so noted.

SECONDARY:

If there are any **secondary keys** (attributes that are of interest strictly for the purpose of retrieval), they should be represented at this point.

FOREIGN:

This is in many ways the most important category, since it is through **foreign keys** that relationships are established and certain types of integrity constraints are enforced in the database. For each foreign key some decisions must be made at this point. To illustrate the issues involved, let's consider the following example:

```
DEPARTMENT(DEPARTMENT_NUMBER, DEPARTMENT_NAME)

EMPLOYEE(EMPLOYEE_NUMBER, EMPLOYEE_NAME, WAGE_RATE,
         DEPARTMENT_NUMBER)
```

As before, the DEPARTMENT_NUMBER in the EMPLOYEE relation indicates the department to which the employee is assigned. We say that the DEPARTMENT_NUMBER in the EMPLOYEE relation, written EMPLOYEE.DEPARTMENT_NUMBER, is a foreign key that *identifies* DEPART-MENT.

The issues to address are as follows:

1. Are nulls allowed? Can we store an employee without having a department number for that employee? The issue is not whether a department number must match. That is already settled by **referential integrity**, which guarantees that a department number that is actually entered must match the number of an actual department. The issue is whether or not a department number must actually be entered. Usually the answer to this question will be that nulls are not to be allowed.

2. What are the rules for changing a department's number in the DEPART-MENT relation? If no employees are currently assigned to that department, there is no problem. If there is a row in the EMPLOYEE relation indicating that JONES is in department 12, and we decide to change the DEPARTMENT_NUMBER of department 12 to 21 in the DEPARTMENT relation, what do we do about JONES? Do we even permit the operation? The answer, of course, depends on the circumstances. It depends on the policies of the organization for which we are designing the database. The possible answers to the question are summarized on the opposite page:

(a). One possibility is to forbid this change. In this case we would say that *update is restricted*.

(b). A second possibility is to allow the update but indicate that the DEPARTMENT_NUMBER for any employee in the old department had to be changed to the new department number. In this case we would say that *update cascades*.

(c). The third possibility is not nearly as common as the other two. The idea here would be to allow the update but change the department number to null for those employees who were in the old department (provided, of course, that nulls were even allowed). In this case we would say that *update nullifies*. x

In general, the most common choice is update cascades.

3. What are the rules for deleting a department? Again, if no employees are currently assigned to that department, there is no problem. If there is a row in the employee relation indicating that JONES is in department 12 and we decide to delete department 12, what do we do about JONES? Do we even permit the operation? The answer, as in the case of update, depends on the policies of the organization for which we are designing the database. The possible answers to the question are summarized below:

(a). One possibility is to forbid the operation. In this case we would say that *delete is restricted*.

(b). A second possibility is to allow the delete and also to delete any employee who was assigned to this department. In this case we would say that *delete cascades*.

(c). The third possibility is again not nearly as common as the other two. Here the deletion would be allowed but the department number for those employees who were in the old department would be changed to null (provided again, of course, that nulls were even allowed). In this case we would say that *delete nullifies*.

In general, the most common choice is delete is restricted.

DATABASE DESIGN LANGUAGE (DBDL)

We need a mechanism for representing the relations and keys together with the restrictions discussed above. The standard mechanism for representing relations is fine but it does not go far enough. There is no routine way to represent candidate, secondary, or foreign keys, nor is there a way of representing foreign key restrictions. There is no way of indicating that a given field or attribute can accept null values. Since the methodology is based on the relational model, however, it is desirable to represent relations with the standard method. We will add additional features capable of representing additional information. The end result is **Database Design Language** (or **DBDL**).

Figure 6.2 shows sample DBDL documentation for the EMPLOYEE relation.

```
EMPLOYEE (EMPLOYEE_NUMBER, NAME, ADDRESS*, SOC_SEC_NUMBER,
          DEPARTMENT_NUMBER,...)
    CK    SOC_SEC_NUMBER
    SK    NAME
    FK    DEPARTMENT_NUMBER → DEPARTMENT DLT RSTR UPD CSCD
```

FIGURE 6.2a
DBDL for EMPLOYEE
relation (all choices
listed)

```
EMPLOYEE (EMPLOYEE_NUMBER, NAME, ADDRESS*, SOC_SEC_NUMBER,
          DEPARTMENT_NUMBER,...)
    CK    SOC_SEC_NUMBER
    SK    NAME
    FK    DEPARTMENT_NUMBER → DEPARTMENT
```

FIGURE 6.2b
DBDL for EMPLOYEE
relation (default
choices ommitted)

FIGURE 6.2c
Summary of DBDL

DBDL (Database Design Language)

1. Relations, attributes, and primary keys are represented in the usual way.

2. Attributes that are allowed to be null are followed by an asterisk.

3. Candidate keys are identified by the letters CK followed by the attribute(s) that comprise the candidate key.

4. Secondary keys are identified by the letters SK followed by the attribute(s) that comprise the secondary key.

5. Foreign keys are identified by the letters FK followed by the attribute(s) that comprise the foreign key.

   a. Foreign keys are followed by an arrow pointing to the relation identified by the foreign key.

   b. Delete rules are specified as
      DLT NLF _ DELETE NULLIFIES
      DLT RSTR _ DELETE RESTRICTED (default)
      DLT CSCD _ DELETE CASCADES

   C. Update rules are specified as
      UPD NLF _ UPDATE NULLIFIES
      UPD RSTR _ UPDATE RESTRICTED
      UPD CSCD _ UPDATE CASCADES (default)

In DBDL, relations and their primary keys are represented in the usual manner. Any field that is allowed to be null, such as the ADDRESS attribute in the EMPLOYEE relation, is followed by an asterisk. Underneath the relation, the various types of keys are listed. Each is preceded by an abbreviation indicating the type of key (CK — candidate key, SK — secondary key, FK — foreign key). It is sufficient to list the attribute or collection of attributes that forms a candidate or secondary key. In the case of foreign keys, however, additional restrictions must also be represented.

For each foreign key, we must represent the relation that is identified by the foreign key; i.e., the relation whose primary key the foreign key must match. This is accomplished in DBDL by following the foreign key with an arrow pointing to the relation that the foreign key identifies. (This is the same type of notation, incidentally, that we use for functional dependencies. A functional dependence of the primary key in this relation on the foreign key really does exist, and so this is an appropriate mechanism for documenting that fact.)

If a foreign key accepts nulls, the attribute will be followed by an asterisk. Delete restrictions are documented by following the foreign key description with DLT NLF (delete nullifies), DLT RSTR (delete restricted), or DLT CSCD (delete cascades). Update restrictions are documented by following the foreign key description with UPD NLF (update nullifies), UPD RSTR (update restricted), or UPD CSCD (update cascades). The choices that were described as the most common (update cascades and delete restricted) are considered the default choices. Since the representation in Figure 6.2a happens to utilize the default choices, the representation shown in Figure 6.2b. is equally valid.

Figure 6.2c summarizes the details of DBDL. Examples of DBDL will be presented in this chapter and later ones. The only feature of DBDL not listed is actually more of a tip than a rule. When several relations are listed, a relation containing a foreign key should be listed after the relation that the foreign key identifies, if possible.

In the example shown in Figure 6.2a and 6.2b, we are saying that there is a relation (table) called EMPLOYEE, consisting of fields EMPLOYEE_NUMBER, NAME, ADDRESS, SOC_SEC_NUMBER, DEPARTMENT_NUMBER, and so on. The ADDRESS field is the only one that can accept null values. The primary key is EMPLOYEE_NUMBER. Another possible key is SOC_SEC_NUMBER. We are interested in being able to retrieve information efficiently, based on the employee's name, so we have designated NAME as a secondary key. The DEPARTMENT_ NUMBER is a foreign key identifying the department to which the employee is assigned (it identifies the appropriate department in the DEPARTMENT relation). Each employee must be assigned to an actual department so DEPARTMENT_ NUMBER may not be null. We are not to be able to delete a department that contains any employees, so delete of DEPARTMENT is restricted. It is legitimate to change the DEPARTMENT_NUMBER in the DEPARTMENT relation provided that the DEPARTMENT_NUMBER of the employees who are in that department is also changed, and thus update cascades.

Note that we have just provided an example in which questions were answered in one particular way. With a different organizational policy, we would have a different example. For example, nulls might be allowed or update might be restricted.

4. DETERMINE ANY OTHER RESTRICTIONS

Determine and document any special restrictions in addition to the ones already documented that involve keys. For example, perhaps a department number must be less than 50 or employees with earnings greater than zero may not be deleted or the state must be Ohio, Michigan, or Indiana.

It may be that many of the restrictions documented in steps three and four cannot be enforced by the DBMS and that programs will have to assume the burden for enforcing them instead. It is still crucial and appropriate, however, to address these problems during the design phase. As we noted earlier, the information-level design, in this case, will produce a list of restrictions that must be enforced by programs which process the data in this database.

5. MERGE THE RESULT OF THE PREVIOUS STEPS INTO THE DESIGN

As soon as we have completed steps one through four for a given user view, we can merge these results into the overall design. If the view on which we have been working happens to be the first user view, then the cumulative design will be identical to the design for this first user. Otherwise, we add all the relations for this user to those that are currently in the cumulative design. We combine relations that have the same primary key to form a new relation containing all the attributes from both relations with the same primary key. In the case of duplicate attributes, we remove all but one copy of the attribute. We then check the new design to ensure that it is still in third normal form. If it isn't, we convert it to 3NF before proceeding. In addition, we add the list of restrictions that we encountered for this user to the list of restrictions in the cumulative design.

This process is repeated for each user view until all user views have been examined. At that point, the design is reviewed in order to resolve any problems that may remain and to ensure that the needs of all individual users can indeed be met.

Thus, the information-level design has been completed. The process is summarized in Figure 6.3.

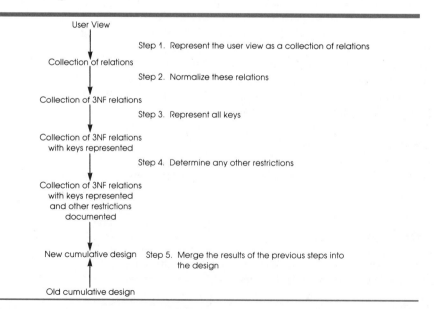

FIGURE 6.3
Information level
design methodology

.5 DATABASE DESIGN EXAMPLES

EXAMPLE 1:

For an initial example of the design methodology, let's complete an information-level design for a database that must satisfy the following constraints and requirements:

1. For a sales rep, store the sales rep's number, name, address, total commission and commission rate.
2. For a customer, store the customer's number, name, address, balance, and credit limit. In addition, store the number and name of the sales rep who represents this customer. Upon further checking with the user we determine that a sales rep can represent many customers but a customer must have exactly one sales rep (i.e., a customer *must have* a sales rep and cannot have more than *one*.)
3. For a part, store the part's number, description, units on hand, item class, the number of the warehouse in which the part is located, and the price.
4. For an order, store the order number, order date, the number, name, and address of the customer who placed the order, and the number of the sales rep who represents that customer. In addition, for each line item within the order, store the part number and description, the number of the part that was ordered, and the quoted price. The following information has also obtained from the user:
   a. Each order must be placed by a customer who is already in the customer file.
   b. There is only one customer per order.
   c. On a given order, there is at most one line item for a given part. For example, part BT04 cannot appear on several lines within the same order.
   d. The quoted price may be the same as the current price in the part master file, but it need not be. This allows the enterprise the flexibility to sell the same parts to different customers for different prices. It also allows us to change the basic price for a part without necessarily affecting orders that are currently on file.

What are the user views in the preceding example? In particular, how should the design proceed if we are given requirements that are not specifically stated in the form of user views? We might actually be lucky enough to be confronted with a series of well-thought-out user views in a form that can readily be merged into our design. On the other hand, we might only be given a set of requirements like the set we have encountered in this example. Or we might be given a list of reports and updates that a system must support. If we happen to be given the job of interviewing users and documenting their needs as a preliminary to the design process, we can make sure that their views are specified in a form that will be easy to work with when the design process starts. On the other hand, we may just have to take this information as we get it.

If the user views are not spelled out as user views per se, then we should consider each requirement that is specified to be a user view. Thus each report or update transaction that the system must support, as well as any other requirement, such as any of those just stated, can be considered an individual user view. In fact, even if the requirements are presented as user views, we may wish to split up a user view that is particularly complex into smaller pieces and consider each piece a user view for the design process.

Let us now proceed with the example.

Requirement 1: This requirement poses no particular difficulty. Only one relation is required to support this view:

SLSREP (SLSREP_NUMBER, NAME, ADDRESS, TOTAL_COMM, RATE)

This relation is in 3NF. Since there are no foreign, candidate, or secondary keys, the DBDL representation of the relation is precisely the same as the relational model representation.

You will notice we have assumed that the sales rep's number (SLSREP_ NUMBER) is the primary key to the relation. This is a fairly reasonable assumption. But since this information was not given in the first requirement, we would need to verify its accuracy with the user. In each of the following requirements, we shall assume that the obvious attribute is the primary key, i.e., CUSTOMER_NUMBER, PART_NUMBER, ORDER_NUMBER. Since this is the first user view, the "merge" step of the design methodology will produce a cumulative design consisting of this one relation.

Requirement 2: At first glance, it would appear that this user view would be represented by the single relation

CUSTOMER (CUSTOMER_NUMBER, NAME, ADDRESS, BALANCE,
          CREDIT_LIMIT, SLSREP_NUMBER, SLSREP_NAME)

A problem appears, however, when we examine the functional dependencies that exist in CUSTOMER. CUSTOMER_NUMBER determines all the other fields, as it should. But SLSREP_NUMBER determines SLSREP_NAME, yet SLSREP_NUMBER is not a candidate key. This relation, which is in 2NF since no attribute depends on a portion of the key, is not in 3NF. Converting to 3NF produces the following two relations:

CUSTOMER (CUSTOMER_NUMBER, NAME, ADDRESS, BALANCE,
          CREDIT_LIMIT, SLSREP_NUMBER)

SALES (SLSREP_NUMBER, SLSREP_NAME)

It is these two relations that we merge into the design. Besides the obvious primary keys, CUSTOMER_NUMBER for CUSTOMER and SLSREP_NUMBER for SALES, the CUSTOMER relation now contains a foreign key, SLSREP_ NUMBER. We need to determine the rules pertaining to this foreign key. Since the requirement for this user is that each customer must have a sales rep, this foreign key cannot be null. We would have to check with the user to determine whether a sales rep who represented customers currently on file could be deleted or could have his or her number changed. Let's assume for the purposes of this example that both of these possibilities are forbidden. Then CUSTOMER would be represented in DBDL, as shown in Figure 6.4. Both update and delete

```
CUSTOMER (CUSTOMER_NUMBER, NAME, ADDRESS, BALANCE,
          CREDIT_LIMIT, SLSREP_NUMBER)
     FK    SLSREP_NUMBER → SALES      UPD RSTR
```

FIGURE 6.4
DBDL for CUSTOMER
relation

are restricted for the foreign key, SLSREP_NUMBER. Note that UPD RSTR (update restricted) must be listed, since the default is UPD CSCD. DLT RSTR (delete restricted), on the other hand, is the default and thus does not need to appear.

Note that there are no candidate keys, nor did the requirements state anything that would lead to a secondary key. If there were a requirement to retrieve the customer based on his or her name, for example, we would probably choose to make NAME a secondary key. (Since names are not unique, NAME could not have been considered a candidate key.)

At this point, we could represent the relation SALES in DBDL in preparation for merging this collection of relations into the collection we already have. Looking ahead, however, we see that since this relation has the same primary key as the relation SLSREP from the first user view, the two relations will be merged. A single relation will be formed that has the common key SLSREP_ NUMBER as its primary key and that contains all of the other attributes from both relations without duplication. For this second user view, the only attribute in SALES besides the primary key is SLSREP_NAME. This attribute is the same as the attribute called NAME already present in SLSREP from the first user view. Thus, nothing will be added to the SLSREP relation that is already in place. The cumulative design now contains the two relations SLSREP and CUSTOMER, as specified. The foreign key CUSTOMER relation will now, of course, reference the SLSREP relation, not SALES.

Requirement 3: Like the first requirement, this one poses no special problems. Only one relation is required to support this view:

```
PART (PART_NUMBER, DESC, UNITS_ON_HAND, ITEM_CLASS,
      WAREHOUSE, PRICE)
```

This relation is in 3NF. The DBDL representation is identical to the relational model representation.

Since PART_NUMBER is not the primary key of any relation we have already encountered, merging this relation into the cumulative design produces a design with the three relations SLSREP, CUSTOMER, and PART.

Requirement 4: This requirement is a bit more complicated. An initial relation to satisfy this requirement could be

```
ORDER (ORDER_NUMBER, DATE, CUSTOMER_NUMBER,
          CUSTOMER_NAME, CUSTOMER_ADDRESS,
          SLSREP_NUMBER,

       PART_NUMBER, DESC, NUMBER_ORDERED, QUOTED_PRICE)
```

Since this relation is not even in 1NF, we would remove the repeating group and expand the key to produce:

```
ORDER (ORDER_NUMBER, DATE, CUSTOMER_NUMBER, CUSTOMER_
       NAME, CUSTOMER_ADDRESS, SLSREP_NUMBER, PART_NUMBER,
       DESC, NUMBER_ORDERED, QUOTED_PRICE)
```

In the new ORDER relation, we have the following functional dependencies:

```
ORDER_NUMBER → DATE, CUSTOMER_NUMBER, CUSTOMER_NAME,
          CUSTOMER_ADDRESS, SLSREP_NUMBER

CUSTOMER_NUMBER → CUSTOMER_NAME, CUSTOMER_ADDRESS,
          SLSREP_NUMBER

PART_NUMBER → DESC

ORDER_NUMBER, PART_NUMBER → NUMBER_ORDERED,
          QUOTED_PRICE
```

It should be noted, from the discussion of the quoted price in the statement of the requirement, that quoted price does indeed depend on *both* the order number and the part number, not the part number alone. Since some attributes depend on only a portion of the primary key, the ORDER relation is not in 2NF. Converting to 2NF yields:

```
ORDER (ORDER_NUMBER, DATE, CUSTOMER_NUMBER,
          CUSTOMER_NAME, CUSTOMER_ADDRESS,
          SLSREP_NUMBER)
```

ORDER_PART (PART_NUMBER, DESC)

ORDER_LINE (ORDER_NUMBER, PART_NUMBER,
            NUMBER_ORDERED, QUOTED_PRICE)

The relations ORDER_PART and ORDER_LINE are in 3NF. The ORDER relation is not in 3NF, since CUSTOMER_NUMBER determines CUSTOMER_NAME, CUSTOMER_ADDRESS, and SLSREP_NUMBER in the ORDER relation and since CUSTOMER_NUMBER is not a candidate key. Converting the ORDER relation to 3NF and leaving the other relations untouched produces the following design for this requirement:

ORDER (ORDER_NUMBER, DATE, CUSTOMER_NUMBER)

ORDER_CUSTOMER (CUSTOMER_NUMBER, CUSTOMER_NAME,
                CUSTOMER_ADDRESS, SLSREP_NUMBER)

ORDER_PART (PART_NUMBER, DESC)

ORDER_LINE (ORDER_NUMBER, PART_NUMBER,
            NUMBER_ORDERED, QUOTED_PRICE)

This is the collection of relations that will be represented in DBDL and then merged into the cumulative design. Again, however, we can look ahead and see that ORDER_CUSTOMER will be merged with CUSTOMER, and ORDER_PART will be merged with PART. In neither case will anything new be added to the CUSTOMER and PART relations already in place, so the ORDER_CUSTOMER and ORDER_PART relations can be eliminated from consideration. To represent ORDER and ORDER_LINE in DBDL, we need more information than was given concerning the foreign keys: CUSTOMER_NUMBER in ORDER and *both* ORDER_NUMBER and PART_NUMBER in ORDER_LINE. Let's assume that this needed information was obtained from the user and that Figure 6.5a is an accurate representation. The representation given in Figure 6.5b is identical to that in Figure 6.5a except that default choices are not listed. From this point on, we will follow the style shown in Figure 6.5b; i.e., we will not list default choices.

```
ORDER (ORDER_NUMBER, DATE, CUSTOMER_NUMBER)
       FK    CUSTOMER_NUMBER → CUSTOMER    DLT RSTR    UPD CSCD

ORDER_LINE (ORDER_NUMBER, PART_NUMBER, NUMBER_ORDERED,
            QUOTED_PRICE)
       FK    ORDER_NUMBER → ORDER    DLT CSCD    UPD CSCD
       FK    PART_NUMBER → PART      DLT RSTR    UPD CSCD
```

FIGURE 6.5a
DBDL for ORDER and
ORDER_LINE relations
(default choices listed)

```
ORDER (ORDER_NUMBER, DATE, CUSTOMER_NUMBER)
    FK    CUSTOMER_NUMBER → CUSTOMER

ORDER_LINE (ORDER_NUMBER, PART_NUMBER, NUMBER_ORDERED,
            QUOTED_PRICE)
    FK    ORDER_NUMBER → ORDER    DLT CSCD
    FK    PART_NUMBER → PART
```

FIGURE 6.5b.
DBDL for ORDER and
ORDER_LINE relations
(default choices
omitted)

The foreign key restrictions for ORDER state that no order can exist without a customer (since CUSTOMER_NUMBER cannot be null), that a customer with orders on file cannot be deleted (since delete is restricted), and that we can change a customer's number but that the change should cascade (since update cascades). Note that the foreign key restrictions in ORDER_LINE are a little different. Here we are saying that no ORDER_LINE can exist without both the order and the part existing. We cannot delete a part for which line items exist on some order. On the other hand, we can delete an order for which there are line items but we will automatically delete all these line items. We can change either an order number or a part number for which line items exist, provided these changes cascade.

At this point, we have completed the process for each user. We should now review the design to make sure that it will cleanly fulfill all of the requirements. If problems are encountered or new information comes to light, the design must be modified accordingly. Based on the assumption that we do not have to further modify the design here, the final information-level design is shown in Figure 6.6.

```
SLSREP (SLSREP_NUMBER, NAME, ADDRESS, TOTAL_COMM, RATE)

CUSTOMER (CUSTOMER_NUMBER, NAME, ADDRESS, BALANCE,
          CREDIT_LIMIT, SLSREP_NUMBER)
    FK    SLSREP_NUMBER → SLSREP  UPD RSTR

PART (PART_NUMBER, DESC, UNITS_ON_HAND, ITEM_CLASS,
      WAREHOUSE, PRICE)

ORDER (ORDER_NUMBER, DATE, CUSTOMER_NUMBER)
    FK    CUSTOMER_NUMBER → CUSTOMER

ORDER_LINE (ORDER_NUMBER, PART_NUMBER, NUMBER_ORDERED,
            QUOTED_PRICE)
    FK    ORDER_NUMBER → ORDER    DLT CSCD
    FK    PART_NUMBER → PART
```

FIGURE 6.6
Final information
level design for
example 1

Something further should be said concerning this example. First, as you may have spotted from the beginning, this set of requirements was leading to the design you have seen many times already for Premiere Products. This is so for three reasons. First, where we have previously encountered this example, it was used to illustrate concepts, definitions, and nondesign processes and it is worthwhile to see the path by which the design process would have produced this collection of relations from a set of user requirements. Second, using a design with which you were familiar for the first example probably helped you to focus better on the ideas of the design methodology and to be less concerned with the ramifications of various requirements. Third, in subsequent examples we are going to examine how changes in requirements for this familiar design will affect it.

EXAMPLE 2:

Imagine that the requirements of example 6.1 have been changed in such a way that a customer is not necessarily represented by a single sales rep but can be represented by several sales reps. Imagine further that when a customer places an order, the sales rep who gets the commission on the order *must* be one of the collection of sales reps who represent that customer. The other requirements remain the same. How would these changes affect the design? Let's consider each of the requirements in the first example in turn to arrive at the answer.

(Old) Requirement 1: No change would need to be made to the SLSREP relation as a result of to the new requirements.

(Old) Requirement 2: The CUSTOMER and SALES relations created in the previous example would have to be changed. The requirements previously resulted in a one-to-many relationship between sales reps and customers. The new requirements will result in a many-to-many relationship. Following the tip in the design methodology for many-to-many relationships, the relations necessary to support this user view would be:

CUSTOMER (<u>CUSTOMER_NUMBER</u>, NAME, ADDRESS, BALANCE,
        CREDIT_LIMIT)

SALES (<u>SLSREP_NUMBER</u>, SLSREP_NAME)

SALES_CUSTOMER (<u>CUSTOMER_NUMBER</u>, <u>SLSREP_NUMBER</u>)

As before, the SALES relation would be merged into the existing SLSREP relation without adding anything to the cumulative design. The relation CUS–TOMER would longer have any foreign keys, and thus its DBDL representation would be exactly the same as its relational model representation:

CUSTOMER (<u>CUSTOMER_NUMBER</u>, NAME, ADDRESS,
        BALANCE, CREDIT_LIMIT)

The relation SALES_CUSTOMER has two foreign keys, CUSTOMER_NUMBER and SLSREP_NUMBER. Let's assume that the rules for these foreign keys have been determined and that they lead to the DBDL representation shown in Figure 6.7.

FIGURE 6.7
DBDL for
CUSTOMER—SALES
relation

```
SALES_CUSTOMER (CUSTOMER_NUMBER, SLSREP_NUMBER )
      FK    CUSTOMER_NUMBER → CUSTOMER    DLT CSCD
      FK    SLSREP_NUMBER → SLSREP    DLT CSCD
```

(Old) Requirement 3: No changes are necessary here.

(Old) Requirement 4: The main change necessary in this requirement is due to the fact that CUSTOMER_NUMBER no longer functionally determines SLSREP_NUMBER. If we are given a customer number, we cannot now produce a unique sales rep number, since a customer can be represented by several sales reps. Consider the 2NF version of the ORDER relation in the first example:

```
ORDER (ORDER_NUMBER, DATE, CUSTOMER_NUMBER,
          CUSTOMER_NAME, CUSTOMER_ADDRESS, SLSREP_NUMBER)
```

The functional dependencies would now be:

```
ORDER_NUMBER → DATE, CUSTOMER_NUMBER, CUSTOMER_NAME,
          CUSTOMER_ADDRESS, SLSREP_NUMBER

CUSTOMER_NUMBER → CUSTOMER_NAME, CUSTOMER_ADDRESS
          (BUT NOT SLSREP_NUMBER)
```

so that converting to 3NF would now produce:

```
ORDER (ORDER_NUMBER, DATE, CUSTOMER_NUMBER,
          SLSREP_NUMBER)

ORDER_CUSTOMER (CUSTOMER_NUMBER, CUSTOMER_NAME,
          CUSTOMER_ADDRESS)
```

The other relations in the fourth requirement, ORDER_PART and ORDER_LINE, would not be affected by the change in requirements.

The preceding changes would take care of the new requirement that a customer could have several sales reps. What about the constraint that the sales rep who receives commission for an order must be one of the sales reps who actually represents the customer who placed the order? How do we build this constraint into the design? This is handled through an appropriate foreign key. If we say that the CUSTOMER_NUMBER in the ORDER relation is a foreign key matching CUSTOMER, and the SLSREP_NUMBER is a foreign key matching SLSREP, then we are requiring only that the customer and the sales rep recorded for a given order are both currently in the company file. We are *not* requiring that the sales rep actually represent that customer. Thus we would be totally ignoring the constraint.

What should be done to enforce this constraint?
Answer:
The solution is to use the concatenation of CUSTOMER_NUMBER and SLSREP_NUMBER as a foreign key which must match a tuple in the new SALES_CUSTOMER relation created for the second requirement in this example. A row exists in this relation only if the sales rep does indeed represent the customer. In DBDL, the ORDER relation is represented in the manner shown in Figure 6.8.

```
ORDER (ORDER_NUMBER, DATE, CUSTOMER_NUMBER, SLSREP_NUMBER)
    FK    CUSTOMER_NUMBER, SLSREP_NUMBER → SALES_CUSTOMER
```

FIGURE 6.8
DBDL for ORDER
relation in example 2

As before, the ORDER_CUSTOMER table would be merged into the CUSTOMER table and nothing new would be added, so we will not represent it here.
Let us briefly review the changes that were made to the design of the example 1.

1. Since the relationship between customers and sales reps is now many-to-many, the foreign key of SLSREP_NUMBER was removed from the CUSTOMER relation and a new relation, SALES_CUSTOMER, was created. The key to this relation was the concatenation of CUSTOMER_NUMBER and SLSREP_NUMBER. There were no other attributes in this relation. Note that if there had been an attribute that depended on both the customer number and the sales rep number, such as the date when a sales rep began representing a customer, it would have been included in this relation.

2. In the design for example 1, we could assume that the sales rep who received credit for an order was the only one representing the customer who placed the order. Since this is no longer the case, the sales rep number remains in the ORDER relation even after converting to 3NF. (Before, it depended on the customer number and was removed.) Thus, in the ORDER relation, both a customer number and a sales rep number are identified.

3. We needed to ensure that the sales rep who was recorded on an order was actually one who represented the indicated customer. So we made the concatenation of CUSTOMER_NUMBER and SLSREP_NUMBER a foreign key, which is required to match the primary key of some row in the SALES_CUSTOMER table. In this way we ensured that the combination was meaningful, that the sales rep did indeed represent the customer. Had we merely made CUSTOMER_NUMBER a foreign key identifying CUSTOMER and SLSREP_NUMBER a foreign key identifying SLSREP, we would have ensured only that both the customer and the sales rep were actually on record. It would not have ensured that that particular sales rep represented that particular customer.

4. Some comments about the foreign key constraints are in order. In the new relation, SALES_CUSTOMER, CUSTOMER_NUMBER is a foreign key identifying CUSTOMER and SLSREP_NUMBER is a foreign key identifying SLSREP. In both cases, NULLS are not allowed, so a row will be added to the relation only if we have both a customer number and a sales rep number. Also, delete cascades in both cases. For example, if we delete a customer, we will delete all rows from the SALES_CUSTOMER table that contain that customer number. This seems to make sense in general. We have no need for the information that a particular sales rep represents customer 123 if customer 123 is no longer in the database.

But what if customer 123 still has some orders on file? In this case we would probably not want to allow the deletion. When we defined the concatenation of CUSTOMER_NUMBER and SLSREP_NUMBER in the ORDER relation as a foreign key for access to SALES_CUSTOMER, we specified that delete of SALES_CUSTOMER was restricted. This meant that if order 11111 had been placed by customer 222 and sales rep 15, we could not have deleted the entry in the SALES_CUSTOMER relation for customer 222 and sales rep 15. As a consequence we would be prevented from deleting either customer 222 or sales rep 15.

So even though the SALES_CUSTOMER relation specifies cascading deletion of CUSTOMER and SLSREP, the foreign key rules in the ORDER relation prevent this from occurring when an order for that customer or sales rep exists.

EXAMPLE 3:

Suppose that the requirements of the original example have been changed in such a way that there is no relationship between customers and sales reps. When a customer places an order, it may be through any sales rep. On the order itself, we still need to identify both the customer placing the order and the sales rep responsible for the order. How would these changes affect the design?

(Old) Requirement 1: The new requirements would not necessitate that any change be made to the SLSREP table.

(Old) Requirement 2: In this case, there is no relationship between customers and sales reps. We need to remove the sales rep number from the CUSTOMER relation, since its inclusion implies a one-to-many relationship. A new relation as added in example 2 to imply a many-to-many relationship is not necessary here. To satisfy the new requirements of this example, the relation CUSTOMER should be:

CUSTOMER (CUSTOMER_NUMBER, NAME, ADDRESS,
          BALANCE, CREDIT_LIMIT)

(Old) Requirement 3: No changes are necessary here.

(Old) Requirement 4: As in example 2, CUSTOMER_NUMBER no longer functionally determines SLSREP_NUMBER. With these new requirements there is no direct relationship between customers and sales reps. Conversion to 3NF produces:

ORDER (ORDER_NUMBER, DATE, CUSTOMER_NUMBER,
        SLSREP_NUMBER)

ORDER_CUSTOMER (CUSTOMER_NUMBER, CUSTOMER_NAME,
        CUSTOMER_ADDRESS)

The difference for this requirement between this example and the previous one appears not in the relations themselves but in the foreign keys. In example 2, the concatenation of CUSTOMER_NUMBER and SLSREP_NUMBER was a foreign key that identified SALES_CUSTOMER. This ensured that the customer recorded for an order was actually represented by the given sales rep. In this example, we have no such constraint. We do, however, wish to ensure that the customer and the sales rep both exist. We accomplish this by making the CUSTOMER_NUMBER a foreign key that identifies CUSTOMER and the SLSREP_NUMBER a foreign key that identifies SLSREP. In DBDL, this would be represented in the manner shown in Figure 6.9.

```
ORDER (ORDER_NUMBER, DATE, CUSTOMER_NUMBER, SLSREP_NUMBER)
    FK    CUSTOMER_NUMBER → CUSTOMER
    FK    SLSREP_NUMBER → SLSREP
```

FIGURE 6.9
DBDL for ORDER
Relation in example 3

EXAMPLE 4:

As a final example of the effect that changes in requirements can have on a design, let's suppose that the third requirement of example 1 has been changed to the following:

> *For a part, store the part's number, description, item class, and price. In addition, for each warehouse in which the part is located, store the number of the warehouse, the description of the warehouse, and the number of units of the part stored in the warehouse.*

(Old) Requirement 3: It is now possible to store a part in more than one single warehouse. Suppose that all of the other requirements have remained the same. What changes would this bring about in the design?

The only relation in the design from example 1 that would be affected is the PART relation. The initial PART relation in this case would be:

PART (<u>PART_NUMBER</u>, DESC, ITEM_CLASS, PRICE,
       WAREHOUSE_NUMBER, WAREHOUSE DESC, UNITS_ON_HAND)

Removing the repeating group to convert to 1NF produces:

PART (<u>PART_NUMBER</u>, DESC, ITEM_CLASS, PRICE,
            <u>WAREHOUSE_NUMBER</u>, WAREHOUSE DESC,
            UNITS_ON_HAND)

In the 1NF version of the PART relation, we have the following functional dependencies:

PART_NUMBER → DESC, ITEM_CLASS, PRICE

WAREHOUSE_NUMBER → WAREHOUSE_DESC

PART_NUMBER, WAREHOUSE_NUMBER → UNITS_ON_HAND

Using these functional dependencies to convert to 2NF produces:

PART (<u>PART_NUMBER</u>, DESC, ITEM_CLASS, PRICE)
WAREHOUSE (<u>WAREHOUSE_NUMBER</u>, WAREHOUSE_DESC)
PART_WH (<u>PART_NUMBER</u>, <u>WAREHOUSE_NUMBER</u>, UNITS_ON_HAND)

These relations are also in 3NF. Note that PART_WH has a purpose comparable to that of SALES_CUSTOMER in example 2. It is used to implement a many-to-many relationship between parts and warehouses. Besides the attributes that make up the key, you will notice that UNITS_ON_HAND is an additional attribute stored in this relation. This attribute depends on both the part number and the warehouse. It is the number of units of a particular part stored in a particular warehouse.

The DBDL representation of these three relations is shown in Figure 6.10.

PART (<u>PART_NUMBER</u>, DESC, ITEM_CLASS, WAREHOUSE_NUMBER, PRICE)

WAREHOUSE (<u>WAREHOUSE_NUMBER</u>, WAREHOUSE DESC)

PART_WH (<u>PART_NUMBER</u>, <u>WAREHOUSE_NUMBER</u>, UNITS_ON_HAND)
         FK   PART_NUMBER → PART
         FK   WAREHOUSE_NUMBER → WAREHOUSE

FIGURE 6.10
DBDL for PART,
WAREHOUSE, and
PART_WH relations

Be aware that another approach could have been taken to determine the design for this requirement. We could have decided in the beginning of the process that two types of entities, warehouses and parts, would have a many-to-many relationship between them. Using the tips provided in the design methodology, we would be led to create a PART relation, a WAREHOUSE relation, and a third relation whose key would be the concatenation of the part number and the warehouse number. The PART relation would have part number as its primary key and also would contain the attribute description, item class, and price. The WAREHOUSE relation would have the warehouse number as its primary key and also would contain the attribute warehouse description. The function of the third relation would be to associate parts and warehouses. These decisions would lead to:

PART (<u>PART_NUMBER</u>, DESC, ITEM_CLASS, PRICE)

WAREHOUSE (<u>WAREHOUSE_NUMBER</u>, WAREHOUSE_DESC)

PART_WH (<u>PART_NUMBER</u>, <u>WAREHOUSE_NUMBER</u>,

We now would place any attribute that depends on both the part number and the warehouse number in the PART_WH relation. The single attribute units on hand would be the only one selected. The collection of relations now would be:

PART (<u>PART_NUMBER</u>, DESC, ITEM_CLASS, PRICE)

WAREHOUSE (<u>WAREHOUSE_NUMBER</u>, WAREHOUSE_DESC)

PART_WH (<u>PART_NUMBER</u>, <u>WAREHOUSE_NUMBER</u>, UNITS_ON_HAND)

We have obtained exactly the same set of relations as we did with the previous method. In this case, however, the initial collection is in 3NF. The more experience a designer has, the more likely he or she is to create 3NF relations initially: but as long as the initial collection of relations is a correct implementation of the user requirements, it is not so critical that this initial design be in 3NF. The second step in the methodology will still bring the design to this point.

In examples 1 through 4, many requirements leading to the foreign key decisions were not specified. We made certain assumptions and proceeded to list the foreign key rules. In an actual design problem, these assumptions would certainly need to be discussed with and approved by the user.

We also encountered in these four examples no special restrictions that had to be documented. Some of these we will encounter in the next section. There is one possible restriction we *might* wish to document in example 4. It concerns the number of units we have on hand of a particular part in a particular warehouse. If we have none on hand, then there really is not need to store a row in the relation to record this fact. The absence of a row will imply that no units of that part are on hand in that warehouse. Thus the restriction we would record for this user view would be that PART_WH.UNITS_ON_HAND cannot be zero.

6.6   A FURTHER EXAMPLE OF THE METHODOLOGY

As a fifth example of the application of the design methodology to an actual design problem, consider the following set of requirements that must be met by a database-oriented system at a college.

Update (transaction) requirements:

1. Enter/edit dormitory information (number and name).
2. Enter/edit faculty information (number, name, office number, phone, department number).
3. Enter/edit course information (course code, description, number of credits).
4. Enter/edit prerequisites for a given course.
5. Enter/edit sections of courses for current offerings (schedule code, course code and section letter, and the number of the faculty member who is teaching the course; e.g., schedule code 2345 is section A of course CS253 and is taught by the faculty member whose number is 3).
6. Enter/edit student information (student number, name, permanent address, status, dorm number). Note that status is a code indicating the type of student (full-time, part-time, continuing education, etc.) and the dorm number is the number of the dormitory in which the student resides, provided the student lives in a dorm.
7. Determine whether a student has the necessary prerequisites for a given course. If the answer is yes, enroll the student in the course.

Report requirements:

8. For each department, list its number and name and the number and name of each of its faculty members.
9. For each dormitory, list its number and name and the number and name of all the students living there.
10. For each course, list its code and description and the code and description of any of its prerequisites.
11. For each faculty member, list all sections of all courses that he or she is currently teaching.
12. For each student, list all courses he or she has taken and the grade received.
13. For each section of each course, list the schedule code, section letter, course code, and course description, the number and name of the professor who is teaching the course, and the number, name, and status of each student who is taking the course.
14. Given a student's name, list the student's number.

Each of the preceding requirements will be considered a user view in the terminology of the methodology.

User view 1: No particular problem is involved in the decision that this user view should be:

DORM (DORM_NUMBER, DORM_NAME)

This relation is in 3NF. The only key of any kind is the primary key of DORM_NUMBER. Note that this user view, like many others, does not specifically state anything about one property uniquely identifying any of the others. We will assume in each case that the appropriate users have been contacted and that in each case the obvious property, in this case the DORM_NUMBER, is indeed a unique identifier. The design for user view 1 is represented in DBDL exactly as it is represented in the relational model.

User view 2: User view 2 is similar to user view 1 in that there is an obvious relation:

FACULTY (FACULTY_NUMBER, NAME, OFFICE, PHONE,
          DEPARTMENT_NUMBER)

Let's assume we are not interested in the fact that OFFICE determines PHONE. Thus, this relation is in 3NF.

In reviewing the attributes in this relation, we discover the need for a further step. It certainly would seem that DEPARTMENT_NUMBER must be a foreign key identifying a row in some DEPARTMENT relation. So far, we have not encountered such a relation. The safest thing to do at this point is to assume that there will be a DEPARTMENT relation, whose key is DEPARTMENT_ NUMBER, with other attributes yet to be determined. If, by the time the design is completed, no other attributes have been filled in, we could consider dropping this relation from the collection. We also would have to determine from the user the assumptions concerning the relationship between faculty and departments so that we could make the appropriate decision concerning the foreign key rules. Let's assume that this has been done and that the decisions dictate the representation shown in Figure 6.11.

FACULTY (FACULTY_NUMBER, NAME, OFFICE, PHONE, DEPARTMENT_NUMBER)
    FK   DEPARTMENT_NUMBER → DEPARTMENT

FIGURE 6.11
DBDL for FACULTY
relation

In many of the following user views just the relation(s) that are involved will be described. It will be up to you to document these relations in DBDL.

User view 3: This view leads to the following single relation:

COURSE (COURSE_CODE, COURSE_DESCRIPTION,
         NUMBER_OF_CREDITS)

User view 4: In this user view a many-to-many relationship really does exist between courses and courses. A course could have many prerequisites and it could itself be prerequisite to many other courses. This is then the many-to-many relationship described earlier, except that the entities on both sides of the relationship are the *same type of entity*, namely, courses. The rules for many-to-many relationships described earlier still apply, however. This user view thus includes the following two relations:

COURSE (<u>COURSE_CODE</u>, COURSE_DESCRIPTION)

PREREQ (<u>COURSE_CODE</u>, <u>PREREQ_COURSE_CODE</u>)

For example, if CS151 and CS153 were prerequisites for CS253, then the two rows (CS253, CS151) and (CS253, CS153) would appear in the PREREQ table. If CS253 were a prerequisite for CS350 and CS353, then the two rows (CS350, CS253) and (CS353, CS253) would appear in the PRE-REQ table.

You will notice that this COURSE relation is not a new relation. It is contained in the relation already encountered in user view 3 and is not added to the cumulative collection of relations. The relation PREREQ *is* new, however, and its representation in DBDL, as shown in Figure 6.12, is worth examining .

PREREQ (<u>COURSE_CODE</u>, <u>PREREQ_COURSE_CODE</u>)
    FK   COURSE_CODE → COURSE   DLT CSCD
    FK   PREREQ_COURSE_CODE → COURSE   DLT CSCD

FIGURE 6.12
DBDL for PREREQ relation

User view 5: The relation necessary for this user view is:

SECTION(<u>SCHEDULE_CODE</u>, COURSE_CODE, SECTION_LETTER,
        FACULTY_NUMBER)

In this relation, FACULTY_NUMBER is a foreign key identifying FACULTY and COURSE_CODE is a foreign key identifying COURSE.

User view 6: The relation necessary for this user view is:

STUDENT(<u>STUDENT_NUMBER</u>, NAME, PERM_ADDRESS, STATUS,
        DORM_NUMBER)

Here, DORM_NUMBER is a foreign key identifying DORM. But we could have NULLS ARE ALLOWED for this foreign key to provide for the possibility of students not residing in dorms. (You will recall that this is indicated by placing an asterisk after DORM_NUMBER in the DBDL representation of this relation.) We would also indicate at this point that status is restricted to values of "F" for full-time, "P" for part-time, and "C" for continuing education.

User view 7: Given user view 4, we have the relations necessary to determine a course's prerequisites. In addition, we must be able to determine which courses are taken by a given student. Looking ahead to user view 12, we can see that this requires listing all the courses that each student has taken, along with the grade received. The combination of user view 4 and user view 12 provides the requirements for determining whether or not a student has the necessary prerequisites. (See the treatment of user view 12 for details concerning the relation that must be added to support this view.) The only new relation needed is one that will allow us to enroll a student in a course. The relation to support this is:

ENROLL (STUDENT_NUMBER, SCHEDULE_CODE)

where SCHEDULE_CODE is the code for the particular section of the course in which the student is to be enrolled. In the exercises, you will be asked why this relation is a better choice than the following, which would be another possibility:

ENROLL (STUDENT_NUMBER, COURSE_CODE, SCHEDULE_CODE)

Note that in this example we are assuming that a student will enroll in only one section of a given course, which means that a student number coupled with a course code would give us the schedule code. (Since student 123 can be enrolled in only one section of CS253, the combination of this student number together with this course code will allow us to determine the unique schedule code, for example.)

User view 8: The initial relation that we might try is:

DEPT_INFO (DEPT_NUMBER, NAME, FAC_NUM, FAC_NAME

In this relation, (FAC_NUM, FAC_NAME) is a repeating group. Converting this relation to 1NF yields:

DEPT_INFO (DEPT_NUMBER, NAME, FAC_NUM, FAC_NAME)

or does it? This is what the process gives us. Let's assume, however, we have determined that DEPARTMENT_NUMBER is functionally dependent on FAC_NUM. Then the primary key is not the combination of DEPARTMENT_NUMBER and FAC_NUM, but merely FAC_NUM. The correct normalization should be:

DEPT_INFO (DEPT_NUMBER, NAME, FAC_NUM, FAC_NAME)

This relation violates not 2NF, as we might have guessed, but 3NF. Converting to 3NF gives:

DEPT (DEPT_NUMBER, NAME)

FAC (FAC_NUM, FAC_NAME, DEPT_NUMBER)

You will notice that FAC is really a portion of the FACULTY relation encountered earlier; no new attributes have been added. The discrepancies in names can be resolved: FAC_NUM ←→ FACULTY_NUM, FAC_NAME ←→ NAME. If there were any new attributes (LENGTH_OF_SERVICE, for example), they would have been added to the relation already in place. You will also notice that we now have the DEPT relation that was discussed in user view 2.

User view 9, user view 10, and user view 11: All three user views are satisfied by relations already in place and will not be discussed here.

User view 12: This user view requires a many-to-many relationship between students and courses and adds the following relation to the collection already in place:

STUDENT_COURSE (STUDENT_NUMBER, COURSE_CODE, GRADE)

The description in DBDL of this relation would be similar to the description of PREREQ in user view 4.

User view 13: This user view can be satisfied with relations already in place and will not be discussed here.

User view 14: This user view would cause us to add NAME as a secondary key in the STUDENT relation of user view 6.

Having reached this point, we would review the entire collection of relations. We would match the relations against all user requirements to make sure that the requirements can all be met and that the final design is in 3NF.

6.7 SUMMARY

In this chapter, we began the study of database design, which we defined as the process of determining the structure of the underlying database that will support some collection of user requirements. This design is divided into two phases: information-level design and physical-level design. In the information-level design, we attempt to capture the essence of the requirements in as clean a structure as possible, without any regard for the DBMS that will actually be used to implement the final system. In fact, if the final system were to be implemented without using a DBMS, the design process would still be the same at the information level. In the physical-level design, we are concerned with transforming the information-level design to a design for the particular DBMS that will be used in the implementation of the system in such a way that the system will perform in an acceptable manner. Discussion of information-level design will be continued in greater detail in chapter 7, and the topic of physical-level design will be explained further in chapter 12.

We described the goals of database design. The design produced during the information-level phase should be complete and should enforce, as thoroughly as possible, the constraints imposed on the system by the user requirements. We also discussed the process of classifying the requirements for the system as user views.

We presented the basic information-level design methodology, which consists of repeating several steps for each user view.

These steps are as follows:

1. Represent the user view as a collection of relations.
2. Normalize these relations.
3. Represent all keys.
4. Determine any other restrictions.
5. Merge the result of the previous steps into the design.

Once these steps are completed for each user view, the final design is reviewed to ensure that each requirement can indeed be met. If problems are discovered, the design is altered as necessary to resolve them.

Finally, we presented a series of examples that were intended to illustrate the concepts of the methodology.

For examples of other database design methodologies, see [1], [2], [3], [5], [6], [7], and [8].

REVIEW QUESTIONS

1. Describe the inputs to the database design process. Which of these inputs are useful with regard to the information-level design? Which are useful with regard to the physical-level design?

2. Describe the outputs produced by the process of database design. What is the difference between the output produced during the information-level design phase and the output produced during the physical-level design phase?

3. Describe the goals of the information-level database design and the goals of the physical-level database design.

4. Define the term user view as it applies to database design.

5. What is the purpose of breaking down the overall design problem into the consideration of user views.

6. Under what circumstances would you not have to break down the overall design into a consideration of user views?

7. The information-level design methodology presented in this section contains a number of steps that are to be repeated for each user view. List the steps and briefly describe the kinds of activity that must take place at each step.

8. Describe the function of each of the following types of keys:
   a. primary
   b. candidate
   c. secondary
   d. foreign

EXERCISES

1. Suppose that a given user view contains information about employees and projects. Suppose further that each employee has a unique employee number and that each project has a unique project number. Explain how you would implement the relationship between employees and projects in each of the following scenarios:
   a. Many employees can work on a project but each employee can work only on a *single* project.
   b. An employee can work on many projects but each project has a *unique* employee who works on the project.
   c. An employee can work on many projects and a project can be worked on by many employees.

2. Suppose we have a foreign key called ADVISOR_NUMBER in a STUDENT relation. This foreign key identifies a relation called ADVISOR. In describing the foreign key, we have several options: in deciding how to treat NULLS, in determining restrictions for the deletion of an advisor, and in determining update restrictions for ADVISOR.ADVISOR_NUMBER. In each case, list the options and describe the significance of your the various possible choices.

3. A database is required to support the following requirements at a college:
   a. For a department, store its number and its name.
   b. For an advisor, store his or her number and name and the number of the department to which he or she is assigned.
   c. For a course, store the course code and the course description (e.g. MTH110, ALGE-BRA).
   d. For a student, store his or her number and name. For each course the student has taken, store the course code, course description, and grade received. In addition, store the number and name of the student's advisor. Assume that an advisor may advise any number of students but that each student has exactly one advisor.

Complete the information-level design for this set of requirements. Use your own experience to determine any assumptions you need that are not stated in the problem. Represent the answer in DBDL.

4. List the changes that would need to be made in your answer to exercise 3 if a student could have more than one advisor and an advisor could advise more than one student.

5. List the changes that would need to be made in your answer to exercise 3 if a student could have more than one advisor but an advisor could advise only one student.

6. List the changes that would need to be made in your answer to exercise 3 if a student could have at most one advisor but did not have to have an advisor.

7. Suppose that in addition to the requirements specified in exercise 3, we must also store the number of the department in which the student is majoring. Indicate the changes this would cause in the design for each of the following situations:

   a. The student must be assigned an advisor who is in the department in which the student is majoring.

   b. The student's advisor does not necessarily have to be in the department in which the student is majoring.

8. For the example given in section 6.6, write in DBDL the complete collection of relations in the final information-level design.

9. Discuss the significance of the foreign key decisions that were made in this design.

10. In user view 7, explain why the relation

ENROLL (STUDENT_NUMBER, SCHEDULE_CODE)

   is a better choice than

ENROLL (STUDENT_NUMBER, COURSE_CODE, SCHEDULE_CODE)

11. Determine the relations necessary to support user view 9, user view 10, and user view 11. Normalize them and merge the results into the cumulative design to demonstrate the claim made in the example that these three views can be satisfied with relations already in place.

12. Repeat exercise 11 for user view 13.

13. In the discussion of user view 7, reference was made to user view 4 and user view 12. Write up a complete discussion of user view 7 without reference to any other user views.

14. Explain why the relation DEPARTMENT_INFO of user view 8 violates the restrictions of 3NF rather than 2NF, as one might expect.

REFERENCES

1] Chen, Peter. *The Entity-Relationship Approach to Logical Data Base Design*. QED Monograph Series, 1977.

2] Date, C. J. *A Guide to DB2*. Addison-Wesley, 1984.

3] Date, C. J. *Database: A Primer*. Addison-Wesley, 1983.

4] Hammer, Michael, and McLeod, Dennis. ''Database Description with SDM: A Semantic Database Model.'' *Transactions on Database Systems* 6, no. 3 (September 1981).

5] Howe, D. R. *Data Analysis for Data Base Design*. Edward Arnold, 1983.

6] Kroenke, David. *Database Processing*, 2d ed. SRA, 1983.

7] Martin, James. *Managing the Database Environment*. Prentice-Hall, 1983.

8] Vetter, M., and Madison, R. N. *Database Design Methodology*. Prentice-Hall, 1981.

DATABASE DESIGN II ×

CHAPTER

7

I INTRODUCTION

In this chapter, we continue the study of the information-level of **database design** begun in chapter 6. In section 7.2, we discuss the process of obtaining **user views**, including the survey form as a vehicle for acquiring and documenting the various types of data needed to support a user view. We also discuss a process that can be used to obtain information on user views from existing documents. In section 7.3, we examine the process of representing user views as relations. This subject was initially discussed in chapter 6 and is reviewed and expanded here. The representation of other restrictions is covered in section 7.4. In section 7.5 we further discuss the process of merging individual user views into the collective design. Section 7.6 offers some general comments on design.

The remainder of the chapter is devoted to the most popular of the graphical approaches to database design, the **Entity-Relationship (E-R) model**, which was proposed in the mid 1970s by Peter Chen. This model is discussed as a graphical alternative to the nongraphical **DBDL (Database Design Language)**. We also examine the process of converting from DBDL to an E-R design as well as the process of converting from an E-R design to DBDL.

Some design examples are reviewed in this chapter, but Appendix B contains two design examples that are presented in considerably more detail. They illustrate the complete methodology, including both the information level and the physical level of design. Appendix B also includes design exercises.

2 OBTAINING USER VIEWS

Obtaining information on **user views** is a crucial task, but not an easy one. Procedures, documents, reports, screens, file layouts, and programs for the existing system must be reviewed. While all of these provide valuable information as a starting point, they are insufficient in themselves for three reasons. First, the underlying functional dependencies may often be obvious when we study the various aspects of the current system, but in many cases they are not. Second, they only provide information about the *existing* system, whether it be manual or computerized. Third, we need information about the data requirements of the *new* system. The only source for obtaining this information is the users who will be involved in the new system. It is they who decide what changes and improvements must be incorporated into the new system.

SURVEY FORM

To obtain the required information from users, some sort of survey form is helpful. This form may first be filled out by the user and then reviewed by the analysts involved in the project. Alternatively, it may be filled out by an analyst as part of an interview with the user. Before beginning the interview, the analyst may fill in the survey form for all existing data that can be determined by viewing various reports, documents, and so on. In any case, it is crucial that the completed survey form contain all of the information necessary for the design process.

To be truly valuable to the design process, the survey form must contain the following information:

1. ENTITY INFORMATION

For each **entity** (e.g., sales reps, customers, parts) a name and description should be recorded. Any synonyms for the entity should also be identified. If the user is aware, for example, that what he or she calls "parts" are referred to as "products" by other users within the organization, this information must be noted. Any general information about the entity, such as its use within the organization, should also be recorded. Finally, for the physical end of the design process, we need to know how many times this entity is expected to occur in the database.

2. ATTRIBUTE INFORMATION

For each **attribute** of an entity, its name, description, synonyms, and physical characteristics (e.g., twenty character alphanumeric, five-digit number), along with general information concerning its use, should be listed. Any restrictions on values (e.g., must be 300, 500, 800, or 1000; must be less than 0.25; must be greater than zero) must be listed. We should also list the place where values for the item originate (e.g., from time cards; from orders placed by customers; computed from values for other attributes, as in dividing honor points by number of credits to obtain grade point average). Finally, we should list any security restrictions that apply to the attribute.

3. RELATIONSHIPS

For each **relationship**, the survey form should include the entities involved, the type of relationship (one-to-one, one-to-many, many-to-many), and the meaning of the relationship. For example, we might list a one-to-many relationship between sales reps and customers in which each customer is related to the sales rep who represents that customer. Any restrictions on the relationship should also be listed. In the relationship between sales reps and customers, we might state that there can be no customer without a corresponding sales rep, and that no sales rep who represents any customers may be deleted from the database. We also need volume information. For example, on the average, how many customers will be related to an individual sales rep?

4. FUNCTIONAL DEPENDENCIES

We need information concerning the **functional dependencies** that exist among the attributes. The analyst would ask the user such questions as, For a given attribute, say, the customer number, if we know a particular customer number what else do we know? Do we know the name? (If so, the name is functionally dependent on the customer number.) Do we know the number of the sales rep who represents the customer? (If so, the sales rep number is functionally dependent on the customer number. If, on the other hand, a given customer can be represented by many sales reps, then we would not know the sales rep number and it would not be dependent on the customer number.) While we will probably not use the term functional dependency with the user, it is important to ask the right questions so that the functional dependencies can be identified. An accurate list of functional dependencies is absolutely crucial in the design process.

5. PROCESSING INFORMATION

The survey form should include a description of the manner in which the various types of processing are to take place (updates to the database, reports that must be produced, etc.). The analyst would pose such questions as, How exactly is the report to be produced? Where do the entries on the report come from? How are they calculated? When we enter a new order, where does the data come from? Precisely what entities and attributes must be updated, and how?

In addition, we must obtain estimates on processing volumes. To this end, the analyst would ask the user, How often is the report produced? On the average, how long is the report? What is the maximum length of the report? How many orders do we receive per day maximum and on the average? How many invoices do we print per day maximum and on the average?

OBTAINING INFORMATION FROM EXISTING DOCUMENTS

It is virtually impossible for an analyst to look at a document and complete a corresponding survey form without input from the appropriate user. But if the analyst makes a good start by partially completing the survey form before meeting with the user, he or she will have in hand something concrete with which to begin the interaction. The partially completed form can be nothing more than a starting point, however. The analyst cannot create the design merely be considering existing forms. Using Figure 7.1 on the following page, we illustrate a technique for drawing information from existing forms and also show why, after this initial step, user involvement is essential.

Date: 10/15/87

ALLIED DISTRIBUTORS
146 NELSON PLACE
ALLENDALE, MI 49401

Invoice 11025

Sold To: SMITH RENTALS
153 MAIN ST.
SUITE 102
GRANDVILLE, MI 49494

Ship To: A & B SUPPLIES
2180 HALTON PL.
ARENDVILLE, MI 49232

Customer	P.O. No.	Our Order No.	Order Date	Ship Date	Sls Rep
1354	PO335	12424	10/02/87	10/15/87	10 - SAM BROWN

Quantity			Item Number	Description	Price	Amount
Order	Ship	B/O				
6	5	1	AT414	LOUNGE CHAIR	42.00	210.00
4	4	0	BT222	ARM CHAIR	51.00	204.00
				FREIGHT		42.50
					Pay This Amount	456.50

FIGURE 7.1
Invoice for Allied Distributiors

FIGURE 7.2
List of attributes

INVOICE_NUMBER
INVOICE_DATE
CUSTOMER_NUMBER
CUSTOMER_SOLD_TO_NAME
CUSTOMER_SOLD_TO_ADDRESS_LINE_1
CUSTOMER_SOLD_TO_ADDRESS_LINE_2
CUSTOMER_SOLD_TO_CITY
CUSTOMER_SOLD_TO_STATE
CUSTOMER_SOLD_TO_ZIP
CUSTOMER_SHIP_TO_NAME
CUSTOMER_SHIP_TO_ADDRESS_LINE_1
CUSTOMER_SHIP_TO_CITY
CUSTOMER_SHIP_TO_STATE
CUSTOMER_SHIP_TO_ZIP
CUSTOMER_PO_NUMBER
ORDER_NUMBER
ORDER_DATE
SHIP_DATE
CUSTOMER_SLSREP_NUMBER
CUSTOMER_SLSREP_NAME
ITEM_NUMBER
ITEM_DESCRIPTION
ITEM_QUANTITY_ORDERED
ITEM_QUANTITY_SHIPPED
ITEM_QUANTITY_BACKORDERED
ITEM_PRICE
ITEM_AMOUNT
FREIGHT
INVOICE_TOTAL

The first step an analyst can take to obtain information from a document is to list all attributes that he or she can see and give them appropriate names. This process is demonstrated in Figure 7.2. Certainly, this list may not be perfect. In all likelihood the names chosen by the user for many of these attributes will be different from the names selected by the analyst. Attributes may be required that were not evident on the document the analyst saw. For example, the ship-to address for the customer on a particular invoice happened not to require a second line and so the analyst did not list the attribute CUSTOMER_SHIP_TO_ADDRESS_LINE_2. However, this attribute may be required in general. Some attributes may not be required. If SHIP_DATE, for example, will always be the same as INVOICE_DATE, a separate attribute is unnecessary. The user's help is essential in clarifying these issues.

Next, we need to identify functional dependencies. If the document we are examining is totally foreign to us, we may not be able to make much headway in determining the dependencies and may need to get all of the information directly from the user. On the other hand, we can often make intelligent guesses based on our general knowledge of the type of document we are studying. We may make mistakes, of course, and these should be corrected when we interact with the user. After initially determining the functional dependencies, as shown in

Figure 7.3, we may find out, for example, that the ship-to address for a given

---

```
CUSTOMER_NUMBER  →
            CUSTOMER_SOLD_TO_NAME
            CUSTOMER_SOLD_TO_ADDRESS_LINE_1
            CUSTOMER_SOLD_TO_ADDRESS_LINE_2
            CUSTOMER_SOLD_TO_CITY
            CUSTOMER_SOLD_TO_STATE
            CUSTOMER_SOLD_TO_ZIP
            CUSTOMER_SHIP_TO_NAME
            CUSTOMER_SHIP_TO_ADDRESS_LINE_1
            CUSTOMER_SHIP_TO_CITY
            CUSTOMER_SHIP_TO_STATE
            CUSTOMER_SHIP_TO_ZIP
            CUSTOMER_SLSREP_NUMBER
            CUSTOMER_SLSREP_NAME

ITEM_NUMBER  →
            ITEM_DESCRIPTION
            ITEM_PRICE

INVOICE_NUMBER  →
            INVOICE_DATE
            CUSTOMER_NUMBER
            ORDER_NUMBER
            ORDER_DATE
            SHIP_DATE
            FREIGHT
            INVOICE_TOTAL

INVOICE_NUMBER,  ITEM_NUMBER  →
            ITEM_QUANTITY_ORDERED
            ITEM_QUANTITY_SHIPPED
            ITEM_QUANTITY_BACKORDERED
            ITEM_AMOUNT
```

FIGURE 7.3
Tentative list of functional dependencies

---

customer will vary from one invoice to another, i.e., that it depends on the invoice number, not the customer number. (A general ship-to address may be defined for a given customer which serves as a default in case no ship-to address is entered with an order. This would depend just on the customer. The address that actually appeared on the invoice would depend on the invoice number, however.) We may also find out that a number of the attributes actually depend on the order that was initially entered. The order date, the customer, (perhaps the ship-to address), and the quantities ordered on each line of the invoice may all have been entered as part of the initial order. At the time of invoicing, further information, such as quantities shipped, quantities back-ordered, and freight, may be added. We may also find that the price is not necessarily the one stored with the item and that it can vary from one order to another. Given all these corrections, a revised list of functional dependencies might look like Figure 7.4 on the following page.

CUSTOMER_NUMBER →
    CUSTOMER_SOLD_TO_NAME
    CUSTOMER_SOLD_TO_ADDRESS_LINE_1
    CUSTOMER_SOLD_TO_ADDRESS_LINE_2
    CUSTOMER_SOLD_TO_CITY
    CUSTOMER_SOLD_TO_STATE
    CUSTOMER_SOLD_TO_ZIP
    CUSTOMER_SLSREP_NUMBER
    CUSTOMER_SLSREP_NAME

ITEM_NUMBER →
    ITEM_DESCRIPTION
    ITEM_PRICE

INVOICE_NUMBER →
    INVOICE_DATE
    ORDER_NUMBER
    SHIP_DATE
    FREIGHT
    INVOICE_TOTAL

ORDER_NUMBER →
    ORDER_DATE
    CUSTOMER_PO_NUMBER
    CUSTOMER_SHIP_TO_NAME
    CUSTOMER_SHIP_TO_ADDRESS_LINE_1
    CUSTOMER_SHIP_TO_ADDRESS_LINE_2
    CUSTOMER_SHIP_TO_CITY
    CUSTOMER_SHIP_TO_STATE
    CUSTOMER_SHIP_TO_ZIP

ORDER_NUMBER, ITEM_NUMBER →
    ITEM_QUANTITY_ORDERED   (filled in when ORDER entered)
    ITEM_QUANTITY_SHIPPED   (filled in during invoicing)
    ITEM_QUANTITY_BACKORDERED   (")
    ITEM_PRICE   (filled in when ORDER entered)

FIGURE 7.4
Revised list of
functional
dependencies

Once the functional dependencies have been determined, even if in a preliminary manner, we can begin to determine the entities and assign attributes to them; i.e., we can begin to create the relations. If the number of attributes is not too large, we may choose to initially combine all attributes into a single relation, replace this one relation with equivalent 3NF relations, and then create an entity that corresponds to each of the relations thus created. The attributes from the relation will become the attributes of the corresponding entity (many times, the entities will be reasonably apparent without having to resort to such a forced approach), and we may create the tentative list of entities shown in Figure 7.5a. Generally, applying normalization techniques to this list will expand the list of entities as relations are split. The new list might look like Figure 7.5b.

Thus, we can take initial steps toward listing entities, attributes, and functional dependencies. We can then also list relationships among the entities (they come from foreign-key-type restrictions, which can be discerned from the functional dependencies once entities and their keys have been identified). This kind of effort is certainly worthwhile; it gives us a better feel for the problem when we

ORDER
CUSTOMER
SALES REP
PART

FIGURE 7.5a
Tentative list
of entities

INVOICE
CUSTOMER
SALES REP
PART
ORDER
ORDER_LINE

FIGURE 7.5b
Expanded list of
entities

interact with the user and also a good solid starting point for both ourselves and the user. Much of what we have done may be changed during our interaction with the user. It is easy to miss things or reach false conclusions when studying a document in a vacuum. Even if our work proves to be accurate, more still needs to be added. What names does the user think are appropriate for the various entities and attributes? What synonyms are in use? What restrictions exist? What are the meanings of the various entities, attributes, and relationships?

If the organization has a computerized system, current file layouts can furnish further information on entities and attributes. Current file sizes can furnish information on volume. Examining both the logic in current programs and operational instructions can yield processing information. Again, however, this is just a starting point. We still need further information from the user. How many invoices does he or she expect to print? Exactly how are the values on the invoice calculated, or where do they come from? What updates must be made during the invoicing cycle of processing? What fields in the PART record must change? In the CUSTOMER record? In the SALESREP record?

For other information on obtaining user views, see [1], [2], [5], and [6].

.3 REPRESENTING VIEWS AS RELATIONS

The basic technique for representing user views as relations was discussed in chapter 6. In this section, we examine some of these ideas in greater detail and add some new concepts.

TYPES OF RELATIONSHIPS

Two types of relationships warrant further examination: one-to-one relationships and many-to-many relationships that involve more than two entities.

ONE-TO-ONE

One-to-one relationships may be implemented by including the primary key of each relation as a foreign key in the other relation. Suppose that each customer has a single sales rep and each sales rep represents a single customer. Applying the suggested technique to this one-to-one relationship produces two relations:

SLSREP(<u>SLSREP_NUMBER</u>, SLSREP_NAME, CUSTOMER_ NUMBER)

CUSTOMER(<u>CUSTOMER_NUMBER</u>, NAME, SLSREP_NUMBER)

These relations would, of course, contain any additional sales rep or customer attributes of interest in the design problem.

Sample extensions of these relations are shown in Figure 7.6. This design

SLSREP	SLSREP_NUMBER	SLSREP_NAME	CUSTOMER_NUMBER
	3	MARY JONES	124
	6	WILLIAM SMITH	256
	12	SAM BROWN	311

CUSTOMER	CUSTOMER_NUMBER	NAME	SLSREP_NUMBER
	124	SALLY ADAMS	3
	256	ANN SAMUELS	6
	311	DON CHARLES	12

FIGURE 7.6
One-to-one relationship implemented by including the primary key of each relation as a foreign key in the other

clearly forces a sales rep to be related to a single customer. Since the number of the customer represented by a sales rep is a column in the SLSREP table, there can be only one customer for each sales rep. Likewise, this design forces a customer to be related to a single sales rep.

What is the potential problem with this solution?

Answer:

There is no guarantee that the data will match. Consider Figure 7.7, for example. The data in the first table indicates that sales rep 3 represents customer 124. The data in the second table, on the other hand, indicates that customer 124 is represented by sales rep 6! This may be the simplest way of implementing a one-to-one relationship from a conceptual standpoint, but it clearly suffers from this major deficiency. The programs themselves would have to ensure that the data in the two tables agreed, a task that the design should be able to accomplish.

SLSREP	SLSREP_NUMBER	SLSREP_NAME	CUSTOMER_NUMBER
	3	MARY JONES	124
	6	WILLIAM SMITH	256
	12	SAM BROWN	311

CUSTOMER	CUSTOMER_NUMBER	NAME	SLSREP_NUMBER
	124	SALLY ADAMS	6
	256	ANN SAMUELS	12
	311	DON CHARLES	3

FIGURE 7.7
Problem with implementation of one-to-one relationship. Information does not match

To correct these problems, we will consider some alternative solutions. One alternative is to form a single relation, such as

SLSREP(SLSREP_NUMBER, SLSREP_NAME, CUSTOMER_NUMBER, NAME)

An extension of this relation is shown in Figure 7.8. What should be the key

SLSREP	SLSREP_NUMBER	SLSREP_NAME	CUSTOMER_NUMBER	NAME
	3	MARY JONES	124	SALLY ADAMS
	6	WILLIAM SMITH	256	ANN SAMUELS
	12	SAM BROWN	311	DON CHARLES

FIGURE 7.8
One-to-one
relationship
implemented in a
single table

of this relation? If it is the sales rep number, then there is nothing to prevent all three rows from containing the same customer number. On the other hand, if it is the customer number, the same would hold true for the sales rep number. The solution would be to choose either the sales rep number or the customer number as the primary key and make the other a candidate key. In other words, the uniqueness of both sales rep numbers and customer numbers should be enforced. Since each sales rep and each customer will then appear on exactly one row, we have indeed implemented a one-to-one relationship between them.

While this solution is workable, it has two facets that are not particularly attractive. First, it combines attributes of two different entities in a single table, although it certainly would seem more natural to have one table with sales rep attributes and a separate table with customer attributes. Second, if it is possible for one entity to exist without the other, e.g., if there is a customer who has no sales rep, this structure is going to cause problems. Would we leave the sales rep columns null? What about the sales rep number, which is supposed to be the key? We can't very well have a null sales rep number.

A better solution would be two separate tables, a sales rep table and a customer table; and the key of one of them included as a foreign key in the other. This foreign key would also be designated as a candidate key. Thus, we could choose either

SLSREP(SLSREP_NUMBER, SLSREP_NAME, CUSTOMER_NUMBER)
CUSTOMER(CUSTOMER_NUMBER, NAME)

or

SLSREP(SLSREP_NUMBER, SLSREP_NAME)
CUSTOMER(CUSTOMER_NUMBER, NAME, SLSREP_NUMBER)

Sample extensions of these two possibilities are shown in Figure 7.9. In either

SLSREP	SLSREP_NUMBER	SLSREP_NAME	CUSTOMER_NUMBER
	3	MARY JONES	124
	6	WILLIAM SMITH	256
	12	SAM BROWN	311

CUSTOMER	CUSTOMER_NUMBER	NAME
	124	SALLY ADAMS
	256	ANN SAMUELS
	311	DON CHARLES

or

SLSREP	SLSREP_NUMBER	SLSREP_NAME
	3	MARY JONES
	6	WILLIAM SMITH
	12	SAM BROWN

CUSTOMER	CUSTOMER_NUMBER	NAME	SLSREP_NUMBER
	124	SALLY ADAMS	3
	256	ANN SAMUELS	6
	311	DON CHARLES	12

FIGURE 7.9
One-to-one relationship implemented by including the primary key of one relation as foreign key (and candidate key) in the other

case, we must enforce the uniqueness of the key that we have included. In the first solution, for example, if customer numbers need not be unique, all three rows might contain customer number 124, and this would certainly violate the one-to-one relationship. We enforce the uniqueness by making these candidate keys. They will also be foreign keys, of course, since they must match an actual row in the other table.

How do we make a choice between the possibilities? In some cases, it really makes no difference which we choose. Suppose, however, that one of these entities can exist without the other. Suppose that a customer can exist without a sales rep. In this case, the first alternative would be preferable, since a customer without a sales rep merely appears as a row in the customer table. Since there is no sales rep column in the customer table, we wouldn't have to deal with null values, as we would in the second alternative.

Another situation might lead us to prefer one alternative to the other. Suppose we anticipate the possibility that this relationship may not always be one-to-one. Suppose we feel there is a real likelihood that in the future, sales reps may represent more than one customer but customers will still be represented by exactly one sales rep. The relationship would then be one-to-many, and it would be implemented with a structure similar to the second alternative. In fact, the structure would differ only in that the sales rep number in the customer table would *not* be a candidate key. Thus, to convert from the second alternative to the appropriate structure would be a simple matter (we would merely remove the restriction that the sales rep number in the customer table is a candidate key). This would lead us to favor the second alternative.

MANY-TO-MANY

Complex issues will arise when more than two entities are related in a many-to-many fashion. Let's consider some possible relationships between sales reps, customers, and parts.

Suppose initially that we want to know which sales reps sold which parts to which customers. There are no restrictions on which customers a given sales rep may sell to or on the parts that a sales rep may sell. We actually have what is termed a many-to-many-to-many relationship. The relation

SALES(SLSREP_NUMBER, CUSTOMER_NUMBER, PART_NUMBER)

is an appropriate way to model the situation. Figure 7.10 gives a sample extension

SALES	SLSREP_ NUMBER	CUSTOMER_ NUMBER	PART_ NUMBER
	3	124	AX12
	3	256	CB03
	6	124	CB03
	6	124	BZ66
	12	412	AX12
	12	256	AX12

FIGURE 7.10
Implementation of
a many-to-many-
to-many relationship

of this relation. Attempting to model this situation as two (or three) many-to-many relationships is not legitimate. Consider Figure 7.11, for example, in which the same data is split into three relations:

SLSCUST(SLSREP_NUMBER, CUSTOMER_NUMBER)

CUSTPART(CUSTOMER_NUMBER, PART_NUMBER)

SLSPART(PART_NUMBER, SLSREP_NUMBER)

FIGURE 7.11
Result obtained by
splitting SALES into
three relations

SLSCUST	SLSREP_ NUMBER	CUSTOMER_ NUMBER
	3	124
	3	256
	6	124
	12	412
	12	256

CUSTPART	CUSTOMER_ NUMBER	PART_ NUMBER
	124	AX12
	124	CB03
	124	BZ66
	256	AX12
	256	CB03
	412	AX12

SLSPART	PART_ NUMBER	SLSREP_ NUMBER
	AX12	3
	AX12	12
	CB03	6
	CB03	3
	BZ66	6

Figure 7.12 shows the result of joining these three relations together. It

SALES	SLSREP_ NUMBER	CUSTOMER_ NUMBER	PART_ NUMBER	
	3	124	AX12	
	3	124	CB03	! ! ! ! !
	3	256	AX12	! ! ! ! !
	3	256	CB03	
	6	124	CB03	
	6	124	BZ66	
	12	412	AX12	
	12	256	AX12	

FIGURE 7.12
Result obtained by
joining SLSCUST,
CUSTPART, and
PARTSLS. Second and
third rows are in error!

contains inaccurate information. The second row, for example, states that sales rep 3 has sold part CB03 to customer 124. Yet this row will be in the join, since sales rep 3 is related to customer 124 in SLSCUST, customer 124 is related to part CB03 in CUSTPART, and, finally, part CB03 is related to sales rep 3 in SLSPART. The problem is that this relationship really involves all three, sales reps, customers, and parts, and splitting it any further is inappropriate.

On the other hand, let's assume the following. A sales rep represents many customers and each customer is represented by many sales reps. A sales rep sells many parts and a part can be sold by many sales reps. If this is the information we wish to model (i.e., the relationship between sales reps and the customers they represent together with the relationship between sales reps and the parts they sell), the three-way many-to-many-to-many relationship implemented by

SALES(<u>SLSREP_NUMBER</u>, <u>CUSTOMER_NUMBER</u>, <u>PART_NUMBER</u>)

is inappropriate. The independence that exists between these entities was not present in the prior situation. In particular, this relation would not be in 4NF (see the discussion of 4NF in chapter 4). The correct method for modeling this situation would be as follows, with two relations:

SLSCUST(<u>SLSREP_NUMBER</u>, <u>CUSTOMER_NUMBER</u>)

SLSPART(<u>PART_NUMBER</u>, <u>SLSREP_NUMBER</u>)

If, in addition, there was a relationship between customers and parts that was of interest, we could include a third relation:

CUSTPART(<u>CUSTOMER_NUMBER</u>, <u>PART_NUMBER</u>)

The crucial issue in making the determination between a single many-to-many-to-many relationship and two (or three) many-to-many relationships is the independence. If all three entities are crucial in the relationship, then the three-way relationship (like SALES) is appropriate. If there is independence among the individual relationships, as in the second situation (where the relationship between sales reps and the customers they represent really had nothing to do with the relationship between sales reps and the parts they sell), then separate many-to-many relationships are appropriate. Incidentally, if a many-to-many-to-many relationship is created where it is not appropriate, the conversion to 4NF will correct the problem.

DOMAINS

A **domain** is a pool of possible values for a given column. For a DBMS to support domains, it must allow the database administrator to specify domains for each column of each table in the database. The DBA gives a name and description to the domain and then specifies the values within it. The specification may be broad, stating that the domain contains a thirty-character string. On the other hand, it may be so tightly specified that a specific set of values is actually listed (e.g., the domain CREDIT_LIMIT contains one of four values: 300, 500, 800, or 1000). Only values from the domains of columns are accepted in any updates to the database, and this must be enforced by the DBMS. Further, if users attempt to join on columns coming from two different domains, the system either should reject the join or, perhaps better, should warn the user that the join is suspicious at best. Without support for domains, for example, the system has no way of knowing that joining customers to sales reps where the customer's zip code matches the sales rep's social security number is not a meaningful join. Both fields are numeric. In fact, with nine-digit zip codes, both fields are even the same length. If domains are used, it is a simple matter for the DBMS to determine that the values for one of the fields are drawn from the domain SOCIAL_SECURITY_NUMBER and the values for the other are drawn from the domain ZIP_CODES. It does not matter that ultimately each domain is described as containing nine-digit numbers. They are still separate domains, and that is all the system needs to know.

We have described what it means for a system to support domains. At the present time, very few systems provide this support to any adequate degree, but this is changing, and the next few years should bring domain support to many of the leading systems. Even though this support may not be present on the DBMS we are using, domains are an important concept in the design process and are discussed for that reason.

Domains provide valuable documentation for the type of data that can be entered in any field or column. They offer a nice way to document certain constraints that are to be applied to the data. They also provide documentation as to which columns can be joined with which others. Thus, it is important to use them in the design process, and this is done as follows.

Each column must have an associated domain. The domain may have the same name as the column. In fact, this is desirable in general. The only time we should not use the same name is when that it is impractical to do so. In DBDL, we might represent domains as shown in Figure 7.13. Each domain is given a descriptive

FIGURE 7.13
Sample domain definitions

******************** **DOMAIN DEFINITIONS** ************************

DOMAIN	TYPE	DESCRIPTION	RESTRICTIONS
ADDRESS	C(20)	ADDRESSES	
DORMITORY_ NUMBER	D(2)	DORMITORY NUMBERS	
NAME	C(20)	NAMES	
STATUS	C(1)	STUDENT STATUS's	MUST BE "F" – FULL TIME, "P" – PART TIME, OR "C" – CONTINUING ED.
STUDENT_NUMBER	D(9)	STUDENT NUMBERS	

name. At a minimum, the domain entry contains format details and a brief description of the types of entries (e.g., the STUDENT_NUMBER row, indicates that

STUDENT_NUMBER is the domain of all possible student numbers and that these are nine-digit numbers; or the NAME row, indicates that NAME is the domain of all possible names and that these are twenty characters in length). ("D" Stands for DECIMAL and "C" stands for character.) If there are any restrictions that can be stated for the values in the domain (e.g., STATUS must be "F", "P", or "C"), they are also included in the domain entry. The domain entry can also include, when necessary, a more detailed description of the meaning of the domain.

After domains have been described in this manner, they are related to the attributes in the table definitions, as shown in Figure 7.14. Entering the domain

＊＊＊＊＊＊＊＊＊＊＊＊＊ TABLE AND COLUMN DEFINITIONS ＊＊＊＊＊＊＊＊＊＊＊＊＊＊＊＊＊＊＊＊＊

TABLE	COLUMN	DOMAIN	COMMENTS
DORM	DORMITORY_NUMBER	DORMITORY_NUMBER	
STUDENT			
	STUDENT_NUMBER NAME PERMANENT_ADDRESS	STUDENT_NUMBER NAME ADDRESS	A STUDENT'S PERMANENT ADDRESS. IT IS TO THIS ADDRESS THAT REPORT CARDS AND OTHER CRITICAL DOCUMENTS WILL BE SENT.
	STATUS DORMITORY_NUMBER . . .	STATUS DORMITORY_NUMBER . . .	

FIGURE 7.14
Use of domains in table definitions

for a given column is then sufficient to give a description of the meaning, format details, and any restrictions placed on the column. The only thing that might be added is any description of this particular column not covered by the description of the domain itself. The fact that PERMANENT_ADDRESS is defined on the domain ADDRESS, for example, tells us that it is an address and that it is twenty characters long, but it does not tell us anything about the significance of "PERMANENT". A description might be included for the column PERMANENT_ADDRESS that would relate the precise meaning of a "PERMANENT" address as far as the college is concerned.

NULLS AND ENTITY SUBTYPES

Potentially *serious* problems are involved with the use of "NULLS", so we will look at a method for avoiding them.

Let's consider a STUDENT relation in which one of the attributes is a foreign key, DORMITORY_NUMBER, that identifies a DORMITORY relation. We will assume that this foreign key is allowed to be null because some students do not live in a dormitory. This means that for some rows in the STUDENT relation, the DORMITORY_NUMBER column is empty. To avoid this use of null values, we could remove the DORMITORY_NUMBER attribute from the STUDENT relation and create a *separate* relation STU_DORM, which contains the two attributes STUDENT_NUMBER (the key) and DORMITORY_NUMBER. A student would have a row in this new table *only* if he or she was indeed living in a dorm. Students not living in a dorm would have their normal row in the STUDENT relation but *no* row in the STU_DORM relation.

This change is illustrated in Figure 7.15. Note that STUDENT_NUMBER, the

STUDENT	STUDENT_ NUMBER	NAME	PERMANENT_ADDRESS	STATUS	DORM_ NUMBER
	1253	ANN JOHNSON	123 1ST, ADA, MI	F	3
	1662	TOM ANDERSON	26 FOLKS, BENSON, MI	F	1
	2108	BILL LEWIS	95 108TH, HOLTON, MI	C	–
	2546	MARY DAVIS	514 PETE, SPARTA, MI	P	2
	2867	CATHY ALBERS	878 2ND, GRANT, MI	C	2
	2992	MARK MATTHEW	11 COLLEGE, IONIA, MI	F	–
	3011	TIM CANDELA	27 MARTIN, ERA, MI	P	3
	3574	SUE TALEN	434 RAYMOND, ADA, MI	F	–

STUDENT Relation including column with nulls allowed

STUDENT	STUDENT_ NUMBER	NAME	PERMANENT_ADDRESS	STATUS
	1253	ANN JOHNSON	123 1ST, ADA, MI	F
	1662	TOM ANDERSON	26 FOLKS, BENSON, MI	F
	2108	BILL LEWIS	95 108TH, HOLTON, MI	C
	2546	MARY DAVIS	514 PETE, SPARTA, MI	P
	2867	CATHY ALBERS	878 2ND, GRANT, MI	C
	2992	MARK MATTHEW	11 COLLEGE, IONIA, MI	F
	3011	TIM CANDELA	27 MARTIN, ERA, MI	P
	3574	SUE TALEN	434 RAYMOND, ADA, MI	F

STU_DORM	STUDENT_ NUMBER	DORM_ NUMBER
	1253	3
	1662	1
	2546	2
	2867	2
	3011	3

FIGURE 7.15
STUDENT Relation split to avoid use of null values

primary key of STU_DORM, will also be a foreign key that must match a student number in the STUDENT relation. We have created what is often termed an **entity subtype** (or sometimes a *subentity type*). In this case, we say that STU_DORM is a subentity of STUDENT. In other words, "students living in dorms" is a subentity (or subset) of "students". While some design methodologies have specific ways of denoting entity subtypes, this is really not necessary in **DBDL**. Entity subtypes will be recognized by the fact that the primary key is also a foreign key.

Two issues need to be addressed as we make the decision whether to create this type of relation. First, is it worth it? Perhaps the value of a given attribute being unknown will not cause a problem. If the attribute will never be used in any selection criteria and will never be used in joining this relation with any other, and if statistics will never be calculated on this attribute, allowing it to be null should never cause a problem. (We could still create a new relation, as we previously discussed, but it is probably unnecessary.) Another alternative might be to eliminate the problems with nulls by choosing a phony value to use in place of null. We might let a dormitory number of zero, for example, indicate that a student does not reside in a dorm. We might even store a dormitory 0, called "NONE", within our dormitory relation.

The second issue is a little trickier. Suppose several different attributes can be null and that we have a student relation

STUDENT(STUDENT_NUMBER, NAME, ..., DORMITORY_NUMBER,
    ..., THESIS_TITLE, THESIS_AREA, ...)

In this relation, the dormitory number either is the dormitory in which the student resides or null. In addition, students at this college must write a senior thesis. Once students attain senior standing, they must declare a thesis title and the area in which they will write their thesis. Thus seniors will have a thesis title and a thesis area, whereas other students will not. This can be handled by allowing the fields THESIS_TITLE and THESIS_AREA to be null.

We now have three different attributes, dormitory number, thesis title, and thesis area, that can be null. Dormitory will be null for students who do not reside in a dorm. Thesis title and thesis area, on the other hand, will be null for students who have not yet attained senior standing. It wouldn't make much sense to combine all three of these in a single relation. A better choice would be to create a relation

STU_DORM (STUDENT_NUMBER, DORMITORY_NUMBER)

for students living in dorms, and another relation

SENIOR_STUDENTS (STUDENT_NUMBER, THESIS_TITLE,
    THESIS_AREA)

for students who have attained senior status. Sample extensions of these relations are shown in Figure 7.16 (below and opposite page), and the DBDL for these relations are shown in Figure 7.17 on the opposite page. Both relations represent entity subtypes. In both, the primary key, student number, will also be a foreign key matching the student number in the main student relation.

FIGURE 7.16a
STUDENT Relation including columns with nulls allowed

STUDENT	STUDENT_NUMBER	NAME	PERMANENT_ADDRESS	STATUS	DORM_NUMBER	THESIS_TITLE	THESIS_AREA
	1253	ANN JOHNSON	123 1ST,ADA,MI	F	3	–	–
	1662	TOM ANDERSON	26 FOLKS,BENSON,MI	F	1	–	–
	2108	BILL LEWIS	95 108TH,HOLTON,MI	C	–	P.D.Q. BACH	MUSIC
	2546	MARY DAVIS	514 PETE,SPARTA,MI	P	2	CLUSTER SETS	MATH
	2867	CATHY ALBERS	878 2ND,GRANT,MI	C	2	RAD. TREATM.	MEDICINE
	2992	MARK MATTHEW	11 COLLEGE,IONIA,MI	F	–	–	–
	3011	TIM CANDELA	27 MARTIN,ERA,MI	P	3	–	–
	3574	SUE TALEN	434 RAYMOND,ADA,MI	F	–	–	–

STUDENT

STUDENT_NUMBER	NAME	PERMANENT_ADDRESS	STATUS
1253	ANN JOHNSON	123 1ST, ADA, MI	F
1662	TOM ANDERSON	26 FOLKS, BENSON, MI	F
2108	BILL LEWIS	95 108TH, HOLTON, MI	C
2546	MARY DAVIS	514 PETE, SPARTA, MI	P
2867	CATHY ALBERS	878 2ND, GRANT, MI	C
2992	MARK MATTHEW	11 COLLEGE, IONIA, MI	F
3011	TIM CANDELA	27 MARTIN, ERA, MI	P
3574	SUE TALEN	434 RAYMOND, ADA, MI	F

FIGURE 7.16b
STUDENT Relation split to avoid use of null values

STU_DORM

STUDENT_NUMBER	DORM_NUMBER
1253	3
1662	1
2546	2
2867	2
3011	3

SENIOR_STUDENTS

STUDENT_NUMBER	THESIS_TITLE	THESIS_AREA
1662	P.D.Q. BACH	MUSIC
2108	CLUSTER SETS	MATH
2867	RAD. TREATM.	MEDICINE

```
STUDENT (STUDENT_NUMBER, NAME, PERM_ADDRESS, STATUS)

STU_DORM (STUDENT_NUMBER, DORMITORY_NUMBER)
    FK    STUDENT_NUMBER → STUDENT      DLT CSCD
    FK    DORMITORY_NUMBER → DORMITORY

SENIOR_STUDENTS (STUDENT_NUMBER, THESIS_TITLE, THESIS_AREA)
    FK    STUDENT_NUMBER → STUDENT      DLT CSCD
```

FIGURE 7.17
Sample DBDL with entity sub-types

In general, attributes that can be null should be grouped functionally. If a given subset of the entity in question can have nulls in a certain collection of attributes, that fact should be noted. The option of splitting those attributes out in a separate relation (really an entity subtype) should be strongly considered. If we do create an entity subtype, it's a good idea to give it a name that is suggestive of the related entity type as well as its relationship to it, e.g., SENIOR_STUDENTS. In addition, the meaning of the entity subtype should be carefully documented, especially the conditions that will cause an occurrence of the entity itself to also be an occurrence of the entity subtype. If we do not create such an entity subtype, we must at least document precisely when the attributes might take on null as a value.

DERIVED DATA

Should we include an attribute in a relation that can be derived or computed from other attributes? For example, in an INVENTORY relation that contains attributes UNITS_ON_HAND and COST, should we include the attribute ON_HAND_VALUE, which is the product of the two? Should we include in the STUDENT relation the attribute TOTAL_NUMBER_OF_CREDITS (assuming, of course, that there is a need for such an attribute), which can be computed by summing the NUMBER_OF_CREDITS for each of the courses in which the student has a passing grade? In both cases, the answer is yes for the information-level design, but we must be sure to document the means of obtaining the results. The answer may very well be different in the physical-level design.

Note that including such a value means technically that the relation will not be in 3NF. (ON_HAND_VALUE is functionally dependent on the combination of UNITS_ON_HAND and COST, for example.) Since it is important that such an attribute be present and documented in the information-level design, we would disregard this type of functional dependency in our quest for 3NF relations.

ENCODED DATA

The encoding of data is another issue. This is not encyphering, which is used for security, but rather the assignment of codes to frequently used data values. In many cases, this is done quite naturally and without our being particularly aware that we are encoding data. If, for example, in maintaining information on students, we have an attribute, CLASS_STANDING, that is 1 if the student is a "FRESHMAN", 2 if a "SOPHOMORE", 3 if a "JUNIOR", and 4 if a "SENIOR", we have actually encoded data. We have replaced one of the words "FRESHMAN", "SOPHOMORE", "JUNIOR", or "SENIOR" with a one-digit code. In this case, these codes might have been determined long before the college was ever computerized.

To illustrate the process of deciding which data to encode and how, suppose the codes described in the previous paragraph had not already been determined. Suppose the users have told us that they need to know the standing of a student and that this standing could be "FRESHMAN", "SOPHOMORE", "JUNIOR", or "SENIOR". When we are confronted by a situation in which there is a limited set of possible values, we should consider encoding these values, i.e., developing a scheme whereby each possible value is replaced by a much shorter code. The users may have some ideas at this point concerning appropriate codes. There are all sorts of possibilities. We could use the numbers 1, 2, 3, and 4, or we could choose codes that are two characters long and use "FR", "SO", "JU", and "SE".

The use of encoding entails two basic advantages. First, a substantial saving in storage space can be realized. Storing the word "SOPHOMORE" requires nine bytes, whereas storing the number 2 requires only a single byte, for example. The second advantage is felt more directly by users. Typing the number 2 requires only a single keystroke, whereas typing the word "SOPHOMORE" requires nine.

On the other hand, there is one disadvantage: the codes, in general, will not be as readable or as easily recognizable as will the words that we are encoding. But there are exceptions to this, of course. One could certainly argue that the codes "FR", "SO", "JU", and "SE" *are* both readable and recognizable as the categories for class standing by anyone working in a college environment.

To overcome this disadvantage in general, it must be easy to substitute the actual values for the codes in reports that include this field. In addition, it should be easy for users to expand the list of codes when the need arises. We can address both of these requirements by creating a new relation with the code as the key and the value for which the code stands as the other attribute. The code in the original relation becomes a foreign key matching the key of the newly created relation. In the student example, we would replace

```
STUDENT(STUDENT_NUMBER, NAME, ...,
     CLASS_STANDING, ...)
```

with

```
STUDENT(STUDENT_NUMBER, NAME, ...,
     STANDING_CODE, ...)
```

```
STANDING_INFO(STANDING_CODE, CLASS_STANDING)
```

Figure 7.18 contains sample extensions of these relations. Note that in the new

STUDENT	STUDENT_ NUMBER	NAME	CLASS_STANDING
	1253	ANN JOHNSON	SOPHOMORE
	1662	TOM ANDERSON	SENIOR
	2108	BILL LEWIS	SENIOR
	2546	MARY DAVIS	FRESHMAN
	2867	CATHY ALBERS	SENIOR
	2992	MARK MATTHEW	FRESHMAN
	3011	TIM CANDELA	SOPHOMORE
	3574	SUE TALEN	JUNIOR

FIGURE 7.18a
Student information
before encoding

STUDENT	STUDENT_ NUMBER	NAME	STANDING_ CODE
	1253	ANN JOHNSON	2
	1662	TOM ANDERSON	4
	2108	BILL LEWIS	4
	2546	MARY DAVIS	1
	2867	CATHY ALBERS	4
	2992	MARK MATTHEW	1
	3011	TIM CANDELA	2
	3574	SUE TALEN	3

STANDING_INFO	STANDING_ CODE	CLASS_STANDING
	1	FRESHMAN
	2	SOPHOMORE
	3	JUNIOR
	4	SENIOR

FIGURE 7.18b
Student information
after encoding

version of STUDENT, STANDING_CODE is a foreign key that matches the primary key of the STANDING_INFO table. With this structure, obtaining the actual standing involves a join operation between the two tables. Adding a new standing involves adding a new row in the STANDING_INFO table. By making STANDING_CODE a foreign key, we are ensuring that no student may be stored with a code that does not match the code for an actual standing. Thus, at least during the information level of design, this is a clean way of encoding data.

(During the physical level of design, we may choose to do things differently for performance reasons.)

For additional discussion of the issues addressed in this section, see [1], [4], [5], and [6].

7.4   DETERMINE OTHER RESTRICTIONS

This category includes all restrictions not treated in some other way. Restrictions on uniqueness of certain fields may be handled by making the field or fields a primary key (or at least a candidate key). Restrictions on the existence of related records in other relations may be handled through foreign-key restrictions. Restrictions on permitted values for certain fields may be handled through the use of domains. It is the remainder of the restrictions that we are concerned with here.

The representation and documentation of all restrictions is, if anything, more important than the form used to document them. Any form that is easily understood and applied by programmers is acceptable for this documentation. The form of written communication varies from English prose to specific formal languages. In English prose we might list the following restrictions:

1. Credit limits in the customer relation must be $300, $500, $800 or $1000.
2. Commission rates in the sales rep relation must be less than or equal to 0.25.
3. Customers with nonzero balances may not be deleted.
4. Any order must have at least one order line.

(Note that restrictions one and two could also be handled through appropriate domain definitions.) The same restrictions could be formally listed through an ASSERT command, as follows:

```
1.
ASSERT RESTRICTION1 ON CUSTOMER:
CREDIT_LIMIT IN (300, 500, 800, 1000)

2.
ASSERT RESTRICTION2 ON SLSREP:
COMMISSION_RATE <= .25

3.
ASSERT RESTRICTION3 ON DELETION OF CUSTOMER:
BALANCE = 0

4.
ASSERT RESTRICTION4 ON ORDER:
EXISTS (SELECT *
          FROM ORDER_LINE
          WHERE ORDER.ORDER_NUMBER =
               ORDER_LINE.ORDER_NUMBER)
```

The first and second restrictions are self-explanatory. The third 3 says that in order to delete a customer, his or her balance must be zero. The fourth states that for an order to be in the database, the relation formed by selecting all rows from the ORDER_LINE relation whose order number matches the number of the order in question must actually have some rows in it (it must EXIST, in SQL terms). In other words, at least one order line must exist for this order.

The preceding ASSERT commands serve the purposes of documentation. This is not meant to imply that any such restrictions can be implemented in a given DBMS. The advantage of stating restrictions in this way is that the form is both concise and precise, which is not always the case when restrictions are stated as English prose.

For additional discussion of the ASSERT command, see [4].

.5   MERGE THE RESULT INTO THE DESIGN AND REVIEW

Once user views have been represented as relations and all appropriate restrictions have been documented, the results are merged into the cumulative design. The design is reviewed at various points along the way. When the design is finally complete, the subschemas for each user must be established. This section expands on these processes.

MERGE

The first step in merging is simply to add the list of relations for the user view in question to those relations already in the cumulative design. Next, relations with the same primary key are combined, i.e., two relations with the same (primary) key become a single relation, having the same primary key as the two originals and containing all of the attributes from the original relations but without duplication. If the cumulative collection of relations, for example, contained the relation

STUDENT(<u>STUDENT_NUMBER</u>, NAME, ADDRESS, STATUS)

and the relations in a user view contained the relation

STUDENT_INFO(<u>STUDENT_NUMBER</u>, NAME, GPA)

the two would be combined to form this single relation:

STUDENT(<u>STUDENT_NUMBER</u>, NAME, ADDRESS, STATUS, GPA)

The new relation is assigned a name that is descriptive of the entity in question. In all probability, it will be the same as the name of the relation that already existed in the cumulative design.

In one particular case, relations with identical primary keys should *not* be combined. If relations were split within an individual user view to form an **entity subtype**, combining them would destroy what we are trying to accomplish. The trick is to recognize when this has occurred so that we do not combine relations inappropriately. As we pointed out previously, such entity subtypes can be recognized by the fact that their primary key is also a foreign key. (In STU_DORM, the primary key, STUDENT_NUMBER, is also a foreign key that must match a student in the STUDENT relation, for example.) Again, such relations *should not be combined*. Further, we must be extremely careful about combining other relations with those relations that represent entity subtypes. Suppose we have the two relations, STUDENT and STU_DORM, in the cumulative design already and we have a new relation to add whose primary key is STUDENT_NUMBER. Should the new relation be combined with STUDENT or STU_DORM, or should it be left alone? If the new relation does not represent an entity subtype, it should be combined with STUDENT. STUDENT is the fundamental relation here, the one that other relations with a primary key of STUDENT_NUMBER must match. If the new relation does represent an entity subtype, it should probably be left alone, with its primary key listed as a foreign key matching the STUDENT relation.

INCLUDING DETERMINANTS

When two 3NF relations are combined, the result need not be in 3NF. While

CUSTOMER(<u>CUSTOMER_NUMBER</u>, NAME, SLSREP_NUMBER)

CUSTOMER_INFO(<u>CUSTOMER_NUMBER</u>, NAME, SLSREP_NAME)

are both in 3NF, this is the result obtained by combining them:

CUSTOMER(<u>CUSTOMER_NUMBER</u>, NAME, SLSREP_NUMBER,
      SLSREP_NAME)

This relation is not in 3NF. The relations created should be reviewed to ensure that they are in 3NF. Any that are not should be changed accordingly.

We can attempt to avoid the problem of obtaining a relation that is not in 3NF by being a little careful when representing user views. The problem occurs when an attribute, A, in one user view **functionally determines** an attribute, B, in a second user view. Thus A is a **determinant** for attribute B and yet A is not an attribute in the second user view. In the preceding example, the attribute SLSREP_NUMBER in the first relation determined the attribute SLSREP_NAME in the second relation, yet SLSREP_NUMBER was *not* one of the attributes in the second relation. If we always attempt to determine whether determinants exist and, if they do, include them in the relations, we will go a long way toward avoiding this problem.

For example, if when the second user indicates that the name of a sales rep is part of that user's view of data, we should ask whether any special way has been provided for sales reps to be uniquely identified within the organization. Even though this user evidently does not need the sales rep number, he or she might very well be aware of the existence of such a number. If so, we would include this number in the relation. Having done this, we would have a relation in this user view like the following:

CUSTOMER_INFO(<u>CUSTOMER_NUMBER</u>, NAME, SLSREP_NUMBER, SLSREP_NAME)

Now, the normalization process for this user would produce

CUSTOMER_INFO(<u>CUSTOMER_NUMBER</u>, NAME, SLSREP_NUMBER)

SLSREP_INFO(<u>SLSREP_NUMBER</u>, SLSREP_NAME)

When these two relations are merged into the cumulative design, we will not produce any non-3NF relations. Note that, effectively, the determinant SLSREP_NUMBER has replaced the attribute that it determines, SLSREP_NAME, in the CUSTOMER_INFO relation.

RESTRICTIONS

Basically, new foreign key restrictions as well as others are merely added to the cumulative design. We do need to be aware, however, of the potential for conflict. In the cumulative, design, for example, there may be a foreign key of SLSREP_NUMBER within the CUSTOMER relation that matches the SLSREP relation and for which delete is restricted. If we later encounter a user view that contains precisely the same foreign key but for which delete cascades, we have a problem. Which restriction is correct? Likewise, if a restriction in the cumulative design states that credit limits must be $300, $500, $800, or $1000 and and we later encounter a user view in which credit limits must be $500 or $1000, we have a problem.

At this point, we must go back to the users and try to obtain agreement on what the actual restriction must be. If we are unsuccessful, we must go to someone within the organization who has the authority to make a decision. We obviously cannot enforce conflicting restrictions at the same time.

REVIEW

Reviews of various portions of the design take place at several stages. Each user should review the information concerning his or her view of data. Naturally, this material should be presented to users in a format that is easily understood by them. The purpose of this review is to ensure that we have correctly understood the entities, attributes, relationships, dependencies, and restrictions necessary to support this user's needs.

As each new user view is merged into the design, the new cumulative design should be reviewed to ensure that it can indeed support this new user. The creation of a **subschema** for this user view often proves valuable. If we can create such a subschema, this user can indeed be supported by the cumulative design. These subschemas must be created eventually, anyway. Since the overall design might change before it has been completed, these subschemas might have to be changed before the final version is developed, but the work done in this direction will still prove valuable.

Once each user view has been merged into the cumulative design, the design is tentatively complete. At this point, each user view should be reviewed against the complete design to ensure not only that it can still be satisfied but that there is no better way it can be satisfied. Some user view that was merged into the design later may have caused a change to the cumulative design that provides a different (and better) way of supporting the user view in question. We make changes to the cumulative design as we encounter the need for them. If along the way we have actually made some changes, then we should make another pass through all of the user views. We repeatedly make these passes until there are no further changes to be made.

DETERMINE SUBSCHEMAS

A variety of methods can be used to specify the subschemas required for each user. Basically, we need to list the relations and the attributes within these relations that are necessary to support each user's view of data. Further, we should document how the user may employ the various relations and attributes. For example, are there certain attributes the user may retrieve but not update? It is perfectly appropriate to use SQL view definitions, if desired, within the representation of the subschema for a given user. The main difference between an SQL view and a subschema is that an SQL view is a single, derived table. It may well be derived from a combination of other tables, but it is still treated as a single table. For some user views, a single SQL view might be appropriate. Other users, however, may require several individual tables or perhaps a combination of tables and views.

Developing and documenting the subschema for a user as that user's view is merged into the cumulative design is a worthwhile undertaking. When the design is complete, all subschemas must be reviewed, however, to ensure that no change to the design has invalidated this subschema.

As we discussed earlier, if we wish to select the approach to documenting a subschema that will be the most consistent with the way the overall design mechanism is being documented, we will use SQL views. The simplest way is to create a view for each relation required by this user, listing only the fields the user needs. If any restrictions exist for this user view which can be expressed as part of any of the view definitions, they should be so expressed. If the user's view requires the joining of two tables and if this user is only going to be retrieving data, we can create a view that represents the join of the appropriate tables. If the user will be updating, however, it is better to represent a separate view for each table.

For example, consider the following user views from the first design example in chapter 6. The final DBDL representation of the information-level design is shown in Figure 7.19.

FIGURE 7.19
DBDL for first design
example in chapter 6

```
SLSREP (SLSREP_NUMBER, NAME, ADDRESS, TOTAL_COMM, RATE)

CUSTOMER (CUSTOMER_NUMBER, NAME, ADDRESS, BALANCE,
          CREDIT_LIMIT, SLSREP_NUMBER)
     FK    SLSREP_NUMBER → SLSREP  UPD RSTR

PART (PART_NUMBER, DESC, UNITS_ON_HAND, ITEM_CLASS,
      WAREHOUSE, PRICE)

ORDER (ORDER_NUMBER, DATE, CUSTOMER_NUMBER)
     FK   CUSTOMER_NUMBER → CUSTOMER

ORDER_LINE (ORDER_NUMBER, PART_NUMBER, NUMBER_ORDERED,
            QUOTED_PRICE)
     FK    ORDER_NUMBER → ORDER   DLT CSCD
     FK    PART_NUMBER → PART
```

1. For a sales rep, enter/edit his or her number, name, address, total commission, and commission rate.

   This user view can be satisfied with the single SLSREP relation. It is, in fact, the full SLSREP relation that is necessary. We would still represent it as a view, however, for the sake of consistency among subschemas, as in:

```
USER_1_SUBSCHEMA
     CREATE VIEW USER_1_SLSREP
          (SLSREP_NUMBER,
           NAME,
           ADDRESS,
           TOTAL_COMMISSION,
           COMMISSION_RATE)
          AS
     SELECT SLSREP_NUMBER, NAME, ADDRESS,
            TOTAL_COMMISSION, COMMISSION_RATE
          FROM SLSREP
```

2. For a customer, enter/edit his or her number, name, address, and credit limit, along with the number of the sales rep who represents him or her. In addition, when the number of the sales rep is entered, the name of the sales rep should be displayed. The name of the sales rep cannot be updated during this transaction, however.

   For this user, the subschema must contain all the fields within the CUSTOMER table except the balance. It must also contain the number and name of the sales rep from the SLSREP table. The fields within the customer table can all be updated. The fields within the sales rep table can only be retrieved. The subschema could be represented in this way:

```
USER_2_SUBSCHEMA
    CREATE VIEW USER_2_SLSREP
        (SLSREP.SLSREP_NUMBER,    /* RETRIEVE */
         SLSREP.NAME)             /* RETRIEVE */
        AS
    SELECT SLSREP_NUMBER, NAME
        FROM SLSREP
    CREATE VIEW USER_2_CUSTOMER
            CUSTOMER_NUMBER,              /* UPDATE */
            NAME,                         /* UPDATE */
            ADDRESS,   /* NULL */         /* UPDATE */
            CREDIT_LIMIT,                 /* UPDATE */
            SLSREP_NUMBER)                /* UPDATE */
            AS
    SELECT CUSTOMER_NAME, ADDRESS,
            CREDIT_ LIMIT, SLSREP_NUMBER
        FROM CUSTOMER
RELATIONSHIPS:
        CUSTOMER.SLSREP_NUMBER IDENTIFIES SLSREP
```

This documentation indicates that the sales rep number and name from the sales rep table and the customer number, name, address, credit limit, and sales rep number from the customer table are included in this user's subschema. All of the columns from the customer table may be updated by this user. The columns from the sales rep table may only be retrieved, not updated. The relationship between the two tables is achieved through the foreign key of CUSTOMER.SLSREP_NUMBER, which identifies the sales rep associated with each customer. Update and delete rules for this foreign key, if not listed specifically here, are those which are found in the schema. For the purposes of illustration, we have assumed that the ADDRESS column can accept null values. This is indicated by including "/* NULL */" on the same line as the word "ADDRESS".

3. For every customer, list his or her number, name, address, and credit limit, along with the number and name of the sales rep who represents the customer.

We could certainly use a subschema similar to the one used in the preceding example. In this case, however, access to all columns would be for retrieval only. Another approach is a little simpler and is appropriate for a user interested only in retrieval: it involves representing the user's view as a single table that is defined as a join. This is done as follows:

USER_3_SUBSCHEMA

```
    CREATE VIEW USER_3_SLSREPS_AND_CUSTOMERS
            (SLSREP.SLSREP_NUMBER,        /* RETRIEVE */
             SLSREP.NAME,                 /* RETRIEVE */
             CUSTOMER.CUSTOMER_NUMBER,    /* RETRIEVE */
             CUSTOMER.NAME,               /* RETRIEVE */
             CUSTOMER.ADDRESS,            /* RETRIEVE */
             CUSTOMER.CREDIT_LIMIT)       /* RETRIEVE */
            AS
SELECT SLSREP.SLSREP_NUMBER, SLSREP.NAME,
            CUSTOMER.CUSTOMER_NUMBER, CUSTOMER.NAME,
            CUSTOMER.ADDRESS, CUSTOMER.CREDIT_LIMIT
        FROM CUSTOMER, SLSREP
        WHERE CUSTOMER.SLSREP_NUMBER =
                SLSREP.SLSREP_NUMBER
```

In this case, the subschema is represented as a single view that is created by joining the sales rep table to the customer table. There is no problem with such a view for retrieval purposes.

4. For each sales rep, list his or her number and name as well as all the numbers and dates of all orders placed by any customers represented by the sales rep.

Since this user is interested only in retrieval, the same approach can be the same as for user 3, i.e., a single view that represents a join of existing tables. In this case, the view consists of the joining of the ORDER table and the SLSREP table. These tables, however, do not have a common column. Since each order is related to a customer, who in turn is related to a sales rep, we can accomplish the task by joining the three tables as follows:

USER_4_SUBSCHEMA

```
    CREATE VIEW USER_4_SLSREPS_AND_ORDERS
            (SLSREP.SLSREP_NUMBER,        /* RETRIEVE */,
             SLSREP.NAME,                 /* RETRIEVE */
             ORDER.ORDER_NUMBER,          /* RETRIEVE */
             ORDER.DATE)                  /* RETRIEVE */
            AS
SELECT SLSREP.SLSREP_NUMBER, SLSREP.NAME,
            ORDER.ORDER_NUMBER, ORDER.DATE
        FROM ORDER, CUSTOMER, SLSREP
        WHERE ORDER.CUSTOMER_NUMBER =
            CUSTOMER.CUSTOMER_NUMBER
                AND CUSTOMER.SLSREP_NUMBER =
                    SLSREP.SLSREP_NUMBER
```

This view represents the joining of the ORDER, CUSTOMER, and SLSREP tables. As it happens, the columns in which this user is interested are found in only two of the three tables. All three tables are required for the join operation, however.

If a similar user view had required update capabilities, then we would have had to represent three separate views, one drawn from the ORDER table, one from the CUSTOMER table, and one from the SLSREP table. The fields listed from the CUSTOMER table would be present only to enable the users to draw appropriate relationships.

5. List the number, name, balance, credit limit, sales rep number, and sales rep name of each customer whose balance exceeds his or her credit limit.

Since this user is also interested only in retrieval, we can again form the subschema as a single view. In this case, an added restriction is necessary beyond the restriction to accomplish the join. This view can be represented as:

```
USER_5_SUBSCHEMA
    CREATE VIEW USER_5_SLSREPS_AND_CUSTOMERS
        (SLSREP.SLSREP_NUMBER,       /* RETRIEVE */
        SLSREP.NAME,                 /* RETRIEVE */
        CUSTOMER.CUSTOMER_NUMBER,    /* RETRIEVE */
        CUSTOMER.NAME,               /* RETRIEVE */
        CUSTOMER.ADDRESS,            /* RETRIEVE */
        CUSTOMER.BALANCE,            /* RETRIEVE */
        CUSTOMER.CREDIT_LIMIT)       /* RETRIEVE */
        AS
SELECT  SLSREP.SLSREP_NUMBER, SLSREP.NAME,
        CUSTOMER.CUSTOMER_NUMBER, CUSTOMER.NAME,
        CUSTOMER.CREDIT_LIMIT
        FROM CUSTOMER, SLSREP
        WHERE CUSTOMER.SLSREP_NUMBER =
                SLSREP.SLSREP_NUMBER
            AND CUSTOMER.BALANCE >
                CUSTOMER.CREDIT_LIMIT
```

For additional information on developing subschemas, see [5], [6], and [7].

7.6 GENERAL DESIGN COMMENTS

Database design problems run the gamut from designs for complex systems, with large numbers of entities and relationships and large numbers of users with widely diverse needs, to designs for relatively simple, special-purpose systems, with small numbers of entities, relationships, and requirements. While the basic design principles are the same for both simple systems and complex ones, many of the information-level details discussed in this chapter as well as the physical-level details discussed in chapter 12 can be omitted in the case of simple systems. At the very least, these details will require far less attention than they would in a more complex system.

DATA DICTIONARY

While some forms of documentation produced during the design process have already been specified, one crucial form, the **data dictionary**, has not yet been mentioned. Every relation, every attribute, and every relationship should be described in great detail. To do justice to this process, an automated data dictionary is essential.

COMPUTERIZATION OF DATABASE DESIGN

No matter how straightforward the application of a methodology, the process of database design can be very time-consuming, particularly for large, complex systems. Some form of computer assistance for the design process is clearly desirable. One such form was mentioned earlier, an automated data dictionary that assists in the documentation process. In addition, such tools as Data Designer (see [3]) can assist in the actual process of database design. Each passing year sees further developments and enhancements in this area.

A computerized tool to assist in the information level design process will accept input concerning individual user views. The input can be in the form of 3NF (or 4NF) relations or functional dependencies or, perhaps, multivalued dependencies. The tool will then synthesize this input to create an information-level database design. After that, it will produce reports and graphical outputs describing various features of the overall design. To be truly valuable, the tool must allow for its users to override any decisions the tool might make. It also must be iterative; i.e., it must allow interaction with a user, permitting successive refinements to the design until the desired result is obtained.

SYNONYMS

In English, a synonym is a word or expression that has the same meaning as another word or expression, or at least a meaning that is very close to it. In computing, synonyms are two different names for the same entity, attribute, or relationship. It is absolutely critical to resolve any questions concerning possible synonyms before beginning the design process. If we do not know that the attribute one user called COURSE_CODE is called COURSE_NUMBER by another user, we will probably end up having two *separate* attributes in the database for the same thing and will *not even be aware of the problem we have created*.

If the attributes in question are primary keys, which is probably the case with COURSE_CODE and COURSE_NUMBER, the problem gets worse. We will create two separate relations that really should be merged, yet we won't realize what we have done. Before assigning the primary key COURSE_NUMBER for a relation necessary to support a particular user, we should carefully examine the keys of the relations already in place. If we spot a relation, COURSE, with a primary key called COURSE_CODE, which sounds like a potential synonym, we should consult the users to determine whether it is a synonym, or, in fact, a different attribute. Note that this process only helps resolve synonyms involving primary keys. While unrecognized synonyms for primary keys constitute the most serious problem, any case of unrecognized synonyms is a problem.

TOP-DOWN VS. BOTTOM-UP

The methodology presented here is an example of a bottom-up methodology, i.e., starting from specific user requirements, a design is ultimately synthesized. A top-down design methodology is one which begins with a general database design that models the overall enterprise and repeatedly refines the model until a design is achieved which will support all necessary applications. Both strategies have their advantages. The top-down approach lends a more global feel to the project; we at least have some idea where we are headed, which is not so with a strictly bottom-up approach.

On the other hand, a bottom-up approach provides a rigorous way of tackling each separate requirement and ensuring that it will be met. In particular, relations are created to satisfy precisely each user view or requirement. When these relations are merged into the cumulative design, provided the merge is done correctly, we can rest assured that each user view can indeed be satisfied.

The ideal strategy would combine the best of both approaches. With a simple modification, the methodology presented here can do this. Assuming that the design problem is sufficiently complicated to warrant the benefits of the top-down approach, we can begin the design process with the following steps:

1. After gathering data on all user views, review them without attempting to create any relations. In other words, try to get a general feel for the task at hand.
2. From this information, determine the basic entities of interest to the enterprise, e.g., customers, sales reps, orders, and parts. Do not be overly concerned that you might happen to miss an entity. If you do, it will show up in later steps of the design methodology.
3. For each entity, start a relation. For example, if the entities are customers, sales reps, orders, and parts, we will have:

CUSTOMER (

SLSREP (

ORDER (

PART (

4. Determine and fill in a primary key for each relation. In this example, we might have:

CUSTOMER(<u>CUSTOMER_NUMBER</u>,

SLSREP(<u>SLSREP_NUMBER</u>,

ORDER(<u>ORDER_NUMBER</u>,

PART(<u>PART_NUMBER</u>,

5. (Optional) For each one-to-many relationship that can be identified among these entities, create and document an appropriate foreign key. If there is a one-to-many relationship from SLSREP to CUSTOMER, for example, add the foreign key, SLSREP_NUMBER to the CUSTOMER relation. Again don't worry. If this is not done, or if any foreign keys are missed in the process, the situation will be rectified when we treat individual users views later.

We can now apply the methodology that has been discussed earlier for treating individual user views. We keep in mind the relations that we have created and their keys as we design each user view. When it is time to determine the primary key for a relation, for example, we find out whether such a primary key exists in our overall collection. When it is time to determine a foreign key, we find out whether the primary key it is required to match exists in the overall collection. In either case, if the primary key exists we give it the name that has already been assigned. This ensures that the relations will merge properly. If, at the end of the design process, there are any relations that were created initially and that have not had any other attributes added to them and have no foreign keys matching them, they may be removed.

The addition of this methodology to the process provides the benefits of the top-down approach. As we proceed through the design process for the individual user views, we do have a general idea of the overall picture.

7   THE ENTITY-RELATIONSHIP MODEL

The methodology that we have been studying using DBDL is not at all graphical. No diagrams are associated with the methodology at any point. Some methodologies, however, are totally graphical. Not only do they have diagrams associated with them but, in a very real sense, the diagram *is* the methodology. Some database design practitioners favor a graphical approach and others favor a nongraphical method. We will not debate the point here. Instead, in this section, we will study the most popular of the graphical methodologies, the **entity-relationship (E-R) model**. We will also investigate how a design using DBDL could be converted to an E-R design and how an E-R design could be converted to DBDL.

Knowledge of both a nongraphical and a graphical approach and the ability to move easily between the two is valuable background for anyone intending to practice database design. This is so for two reasons. First, certain design problems may lend themselves more readily to a nongraphical solution and just the opposite might be true for others. Designers who are comfortable with both approaches can choose whichever method better suits the problem at hand. Second, a given designer may be more comfortable with one of these two approaches and yet find that the company for which he or she works uses the other. A designer can use whichever system he or she prefers to do a design, provided he or she can communicate this design to others in the form expected by the organization.

The E-R model was proposed by Peter Chen of the M.I.T. Sloan School of Management in 1976 (see [2]) and has been widely accepted as a graphical approach to database design. The basic constructions in the E-R model are the familiar entities, attributes, and relationships, all of which are represented in E-R diagrams. Domains also can be represented.

In the E-R model, entities are drawn as rectangles and relationships as are drawn as diamonds, with lines connected to the entities involved. Both entities and relationships are named in the E-R model. The lines are labeled to indicate the degree of the relationship. In Figure 7.20, the relationship between sales reps and

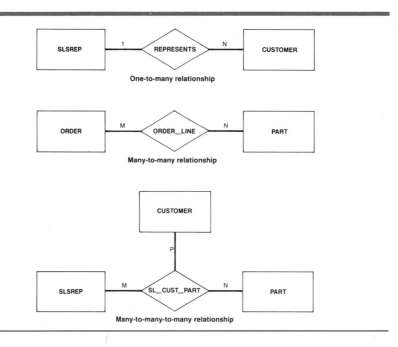

FIGURE 7.20
Representing entities and relationships in E-R model

customers is "1" to "N", or one-to-many. The relationship between orders and parts is "M" to "N", or many-to-many. Finally, the many-to-many-to-many relationship between sales reps, customers, and parts discussed earlier is referred to as "M" to "N" to "P".

In the E-R model, not only can entities have attributes, but relationships can as well. Attributes are indicated in a diagram by listing them near the entity or relationship to which they correspond. Domains can also be represented, if desired. They are termed value types and are represented by circles, grouped together, if possible, often at the bottom of the diagram. The attribute name is then attached to an arrow, which goes from the entity or relationship to the appropriate domain. An example of the use of domains is shown in Figure 7.21. The lower

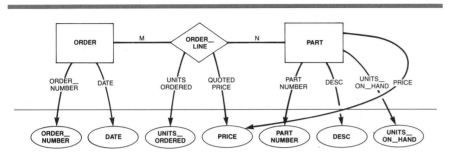

FIGURE 7.21
Representing attributes and value types (domains) in E-R model

portion of the diagram, sometimes called the **lower conceptual domain**, contains a bubble for each domain. The upper portion of the diagram, termed the **upper conceptual domain**, contains the entities, attributes, and relationships.

The ORDER entity, the PART entity, and the ORDER_LINE relationship all contain arrows to appropriate domains. Associated with each arrow is the name of the attribute. Thus, the ORDER entity contains two attributes, ORDER_NUMBER and DATE, each associated with a domain of the same name. The ORDER_LINE relationship contains two attributes, UNITS_ORDERED and QUOTED_PRICE. UNITS_ORDERED is associated with a domain of the same name. QUOTED_PRICE is associated with the domain of all prices. The PART entity contains attributes PART_NUMBER, DESC, and UNITS_ON_HAND, which are all associated with domains of the same name. It also contains an attribute PRICE, which is associated with the same domain as QUOTED_PRICE, a domain called simply PRICE.

Often, for the sake of simplicity, any reference to domains is documented separately from the diagram. In addition, if there are many attributes, these are also listed separately. Otherwise, the diagram can rapidly become cluttered and the nice, explicit visual rendering of the relationships can easily be obscured. Wherever the attributes are listed, the attribute (or collection of attributes) that forms the primary key for an entity must be specified. Often in sample E-R diagrams this is not done, but it is absolutely crucial to do so. The only possible justification for not doing it is that in certain simple diagrams, the keys may be obvious, but this is not a sufficient reason for overlooking this critical point. The simplest way to indicate the keys is by underlining them, as we have done with the relational model.

Two special types of dependencies are important in the E-R model: existence dependencies and ID dependencies. If the existence of one entity depends on the existence of another related entity, we have an **existence dependency**. Job history information will not be stored in the Marvel College database unless the corresponding faculty member exists. Thus, the existence of job history information *depends* on the existence of a corresponding faculty member. The relationship between faculty and job history is an existence dependency, indicated by placing an "E" in the relationship diamond, as shown in Figure 7.22. Further, an entity that depends on another entity for its existence is called a **weak entity type** and is indicated by being enclosed in a double rectangle, as shown in Figure 7.22.

If an entity cannot be uniquely identified through its own attributes but must be identified through its relationships with other entities, we have an **ID dependency**. The attributes for job history records are rank and starting date, neither of which uniquely determines a job history record. To uniquely identify a job history record also requires knowing the faculty member to whom the job history record is related. (The job history record for Betty Jones on which the rank is ASST PROF and the starting date is 6/15/75 is different from a job history record for Sam Martin that contains the same rank and starting date.) An ID dependency is indicated on an E-R diagram by including "ID" in the relationship diamond. It is possible to have a given relationship be *both* an existence dependency *and* an ID dependency, in which case the relationship diamond will contain "E & ID", as shown in Figure 7.23.

CONVERTING FROM DBDL TO AN E-R DIAGRAM

The following procedure can be used to convert a design represented in DBDL to an E-R diagram.

1. Create an entity (rectangle) for each relation in the DBDL design. The primary key for the relation will be the key for the entity. The attributes for the relation will be the attributes of the entity. If domains have been used in the DBDL design, they can be represented as value types in the E-R diagram.
2. For each foreign key in the DBDL design, create a one-to-many relationship between the corresponding entities in the E-R diagram. The relation containing the foreign key becomes the "many" portion of the relationship. The relation that the foreign key identifies becomes the "one" portion. The relationship can either be given a descriptive name or left blank.
3. If nulls are not allowed for the foreign key in the relationship just created, the relationship is an existence dependency and should be so labeled. If this is the case, the entity at the "many" end of the relationship is a weak entity type and may be so represented (although this is not essential).
4. If the primary key of the "many" entity type contains the primary key of the "one" entity type, the relationship is an ID dependency and should be so labeled.
5. Any foreign key restrictions for update and delete should be documented. Since these types of restrictions are not included in the E-R model, this documentation will be external to the diagram. It is important nonetheless.
6. Any other restrictions should also be documented. Again, this documentation will be external to the E-R diagram.

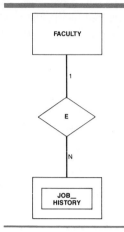

FIGURE 7.22
Existence
Dependency

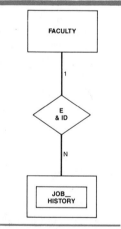

FIGURE 7.23
Existence
Dependency
and ID Dependency

7. (Optional) If an entity constitutes the "many" portion of two (or more) relationships, it can be converted to a many-to-many relationship. Instead of an entity type, it becomes a relationship type. The attributes remain. Now, however, they are attributes of a relationship rather than an entity.

Step seven warrants further explanation. The preceding discussion of the E-R model represents the original version of the model as proposed by Chen, and the version that is probably most commonly used today. In it, both entities and relationships can have attributes. In particular, the typical many-to-many relationship is represented as a relationship which, in turn, had attributes of its own. Some confusion has existed as to whether something like ORDER–L I NE, for example, should be an entity or a relationship. In other words, should the many-to-many relationship between orders and parts be represented by the diagram shown in Figure 7.24a. or the one shown in Figure 7.24b? The usual response to this question was that it didn't matter.

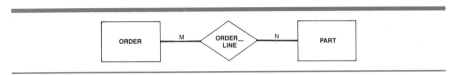

FIGURE 7.24a
ORDER–NUMBER as a many-to-many relationship

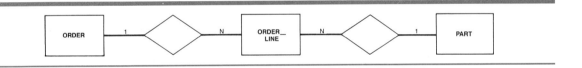

FIGURE 7.24b
ORDER_LINE as an entity

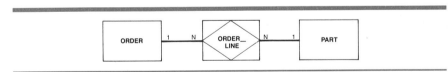

FIGURE 7.24c
ORDER_LINE as a composite entity

Then Chen proposed what really amounted to a slight change in the E-R approach, one which addressed this issue (see [7]). In this new version, relationships cannot have attributes; only entities can. Given this rule, Figure 7.24a. is not an appropriate implementation of the relationship, since ORDER–L I NE has attributes. However, Figure 7.24b. does not emphasize that the entity ORDER–L I NE is really implementing a many-to-many relationship between orders and parts. Chen gets around this problem by giving a special name to such an entity. It is called a **composite entity** and is represented on an E-R diagram by a diamond within a rectangle to emphasize that it is essentially both entity and relationship. Further, relations themselves no longer have special symbols. Thus, the representation that would most closely approximate Chen's most recent proposal would be Figure 7.24c. In each representation, the list of attributes would be the same as that shown in Figure 7.21.

As an example of this methodology, consider the DBDL shown in Figure 7.19. Note that domains are not used in this example. If they were, they would become domains (value types) in the E-R diagram.

1. Since there are five tables in the DBDL, there will be five entities, SLSREP, CUSTOMER, PART, ORDER, and ORDER_LINE.
2. Examining the foreign keys in the DBDL yields one-to-many relations from SLSREP to CUSTOMER, from CUSTOMER to ORDER, from ORDER to ORDER_LINE, and from PART to ORDER—LINE.
3. Since nulls are not allowed in any of these relationships, all relationships are existence dependencies.
4. Since the primary key of both ORDER and PART are included in the primary key of ORDER_LINE, the relationship between ORDER and ORDER_LINE and the relationship between PART and ORDER_LINE are both ID dependencies.
5. and 6. Foreign key restrictions and other restrictions must be documented. Since this documentation does not appear in the E-R diagram, we will omit it here.

FIGURE 7.25
Result of converting
DBDL to E-R diagram
with ORDER—LINE as
an entity

The design created in this fashion is shown in Figure 7.25. It is technically

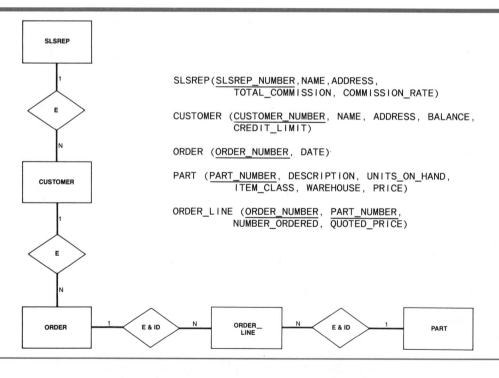

SLSREP(SLSREP_NUMBER,NAME,ADDRESS,
        TOTAL_COMMISSION, COMMISSION_RATE)

CUSTOMER (CUSTOMER_NUMBER, NAME, ADDRESS, BALANCE,
        CREDIT_LIMIT)

ORDER (ORDER_NUMBER, DATE)

PART (PART_NUMBER, DESCRIPTION, UNITS_ON_HAND,
        ITEM_CLASS, WAREHOUSE, PRICE)

ORDER_LINE (ORDER_NUMBER, PART_NUMBER,
        NUMBER_ORDERED, QUOTED_PRICE)

correct as it stands. We might choose to make two enhancements, however. If we apply step seven, we will convert ORDER_LINE to a many-to-many relationship, since it is the "many" end of more than one relationship. This solution is shown in Figure 7.26 and would be the closest to how the E-R approach is most commonly

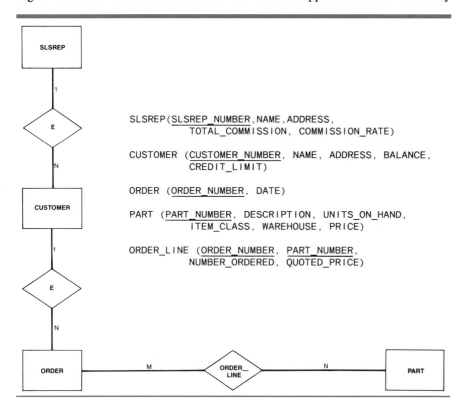

FIGURE 7.26
Result of converting
DBDL to E-R diagram
with ORDER_LINE as
a relationship

SLSREP(<u>SLSREP_NUMBER</u>,NAME,ADDRESS,
        TOTAL_COMMISSION, COMMISSION_RATE)

CUSTOMER (<u>CUSTOMER_NUMBER</u>, NAME, ADDRESS, BALANCE,
         CREDIT_LIMIT)

ORDER (<u>ORDER_NUMBER</u>, DATE)

PART (<u>PART_NUMBER</u>, DESCRIPTION, UNITS_ON_HAND,
     ITEM_CLASS, WAREHOUSE, PRICE)

ORDER_LINE (<u>ORDER_NUMBER</u>, <u>PART_NUMBER</u>,
           NUMBER_ORDERED, QUOTED_PRICE)

used. Another alternative is to make ORDER_LINE a composite entity and not to explicitly diagram other relationships. This approach is shown in Figure 7.27 on the following page and is the closest to the most recent proposals for the E-R model as specified by Chen.

CONVERTING FROM AN E-R DIAGRAM TO DBDL

The following procedure can be used to convert an E-R diagram to a DBDL representation.

1. For each entity, create a relation. The key for the entity will become the key for the relation. The attributes of the entity will become attributes in the relation.
2. For each one-to-many relationship in the E-R diagram, add the primary key of the "one" entity as a foreign key in the "many" entity. If the relationship is an existence dependency, nulls will not be allowed for this foreign key. Otherwise, they will be. If this is an ID dependency, the primary key of the "one" entity should be part of the primary key of the

"many" entity. If the relation in the E-R diagram has any attributes (which is unlikely) they should be added as attributes to the relation that corresponds to the "many" entity.

3. A many-to-many (or many-to-many-to-many) relationship in the E-R diagram becomes a relation in DBDL. Attributes of the relationship become attributes of the relation. The primary key of the relation will be the concatenation of the keys of all entities related by this relationship. Each of these keys individually will also be a foreign key matching the relation that corresponds to the entity for which it is the primary key Nulls will not be allowed for any of these foreign keys.

4. An E-R diagram does not contain enough information to allow some of the necessary foreign key decisions to be made. It is not possible to deduce from the diagram, for example, whether update cascades or is restricted. Unless some form of external documentation indicates how this decision is to be made, we will either need to check with appropriate users or make the decisions arbitrarily.

To illustrate the procedure, let's assume that we are given the E-R diagram, as shown in Figure 7.26. Note that value types (domains) are not shown in this example. If they do appear, setting up corresponding domains in DBDL is a simple matter. (The E-R diagrams shown in Figures 7.25 and 7.27 will also yield the same result in DBDL. If anything, they will lead us to the result more easily than

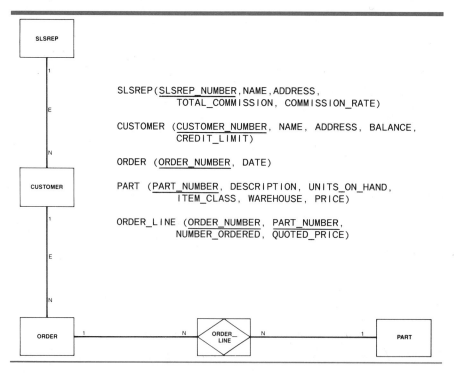

SLSREP (SLSREP_NUMBER, NAME, ADDRESS,
        TOTAL_COMMISSION, COMMISSION_RATE)

CUSTOMER (CUSTOMER_NUMBER, NAME, ADDRESS, BALANCE,
        CREDIT_LIMIT)

ORDER (ORDER_NUMBER, DATE)

PART (PART_NUMBER, DESCRIPTION, UNITS_ON_HAND,
        ITEM_CLASS, WAREHOUSE, PRICE)

ORDER_LINE (ORDER_NUMBER, PART_NUMBER,
        NUMBER_ORDERED, QUOTED_PRICE)

FIGURE 7.27
Result of converting DBDL to E-R diagram with represented as arrows ORDER_LINE as a composite entity and relationships only

will Figure 7.26 on page 301.)

1. For each entity, we create a relation. In this example, we would create four relations, SLSREP, CUSTOMER, ORDER, and PART. The primary key and the attributes in each relation will be the same as those of the entities in the E-R diagram. At this point, we would have:

```
SLSREP (SLSREP_NUMBER, NAME, ADDRESS,
        TOTAL_COMMISSION, COMMISSION_RATE)

CUSTOMER (CUSTOMER_NUMBER, NAME, ADDRESS,
        BALANCE, CREDIT_LIMIT)

ORDER (ORDER_NUMBER, DATE)

PART (PART_NUMBER, DESCRIPTION, UNITS_ON_HAND,
        ITEM_CLASS, WAREHOUSE, PRICE)
```

2. For each one-to-many relationship, we add the primary key of the "one" to the "many". We thus add a foreign key of SLSREP_NUMBER to the CUSTOMER relation, which must match the SLSREP relation. We also add a foreign key of CUSTOMER_NUMBER to the ORDER relation, which must match the CUSTOMER relation. Since these are existence dependencies, nulls are not allowed for any of the foreign keys.
3. The many-to-many relationship, ORDER_LINE, becomes a relation in DBDL. The attributes NUMBER_ORDERED and QUOTED_PRICE become attributes of the relation. The concatenation of the keys of the entities to which ORDER_LINE is related becomes the key of the ORDER_LINE relation. Since ORDER_LINE is related to ORDER and PART, the primary key is the concatenation of ORDER_NUMBER and PART_NUMBER. These will also be foreign keys matching the ORDER and PART relations, respectively, with nulls not allowed.
4. We must make decisions on foreign key rules and any other restrictions, but since we don't have enough information to indicate how the decisions should be made, we must make them arbitrarily.

Figure 7.19 shows the final DBDL representation.

.8 SUMMARY

In this chapter, we have concluded our study of the information level of database design begun in chapter 6. We have discussed the process of obtaining and documenting user views. We examined the use of a survey form containing information about entities, attributes, relationships, functional dependencies, and processing information. We also investigated how to obtain information concerning user views from existing documents.

We then expanded on the topic of representing user views as relations. An analysis of various methods for representing one-to-one relationships was presented, along with the concepts pertaining to many-to-many relationships that involve more than two entities. We looked at domains as a valuable tool in the documentation process as well as a mechanism for documenting them. We described the relationships between nulls and entity subtypes and proposed a method for treating nulls. We discussed the use of derived and encoded data.

A mechanism was provided for representing other restrictions. We investigated the process of merging relations for each user view into a cumulative design, including the process of creating subschemas for each user. We made some general design comments concerning the use of data dictionaries, the computerization of database design, and the resolution of synonyms. We proposed a means of bringing the advantages of both the top-down and bottom-up approaches to database design to the methodology proposed in this text.

The remainder of the chapter dealt with the most popular of the graphical approaches to database design, the Entity-Relationship (E-R) model, proposed by Peter Chen. The basic structure of the model, the use of E-R diagrams, and the types of restrictions that can be represented in such diagrams were discussed. We investigated the process of converting from DBDL to an E-R diagram and from an E-R diagram to DBDL.

REVIEW QUESTIONS

1. Why is it impossible to design a system just by looking at existing documents?
2. How may a survey form be used in the design process? What types of categories should appear on the survey form? Who should fill out the survey form?
3. Why is processing information included in the survey form? Isn't processing information used during the physical-level design phase rather than during the information-level design phase?
4. Why should domains be used in the design process? How are domains documented in DBDL?
5. What does it mean for a column to allow nulls? What is an entity subtype? What is the relationship between nulls and entity subtypes? How are subtypes documented in DBDL?
6. What is derived data? Should derived data be included in an information-level design? We have not yet discussed the physical level of design, but do you think derived data should be included in a physical-level design? Why or why not?
7. What is encoded data? What are the advantages of encoding data? What are the disadvantages?
8. List the steps involved in merging the relations into the cumulative design to satisfy a given user's view. When should relations *not* be merged? In what way can foreign key restrictions become a problem?

9. Describe the different points in the design process at which a review will take place. What is accomplished by each of these types of reviews? Who does the reviewing?

10. When can we use view definitions that include the join operation in defining subschemas? Why do some situations preclude the use of such view definitions?

11. What features would be desirable in a computer tool to assist in the database design process?

12. What are synonyms in the computing environment? What problems do synonyms cause?

13. What is the difference between a top-down and a bottom-up design methodology? Name advantages and disadvantages of each. Into which category does the methodology we have been studying using DBDL fall? How can we modify DBDL to include the advantages of both types of methodologies?

14. Describe the entity-relationship model. Describe how entities, attributes, and relationships are represented in the original E-R model. What term in the E-R model corresponds to domains? How are they represented pictorially?

15. Describe the changes to the E-R model that were proposed by Chen. How do these changes affect relationships?

16. Describe existence dependency. Describe ID dependency. Can a relationship be both an existence dependency and an ID dependency? What is a weak entity type? What is the relationship between weak entity types and either existence or ID dependency?

EXERCISES

1. Design a survey form of your own. Fill it out as it might have been filled out during the database design for Premiere Products. For any questions areas that you have too little information to answer, make a reasonable guess.

2. Consider Figure 7.28, a report card from Marvel College.
   a. List all of the attributes.
   b. List all of the functional dependencies.
   c. Create an appropriate collection of 3NF relations. If a functional dependency is not clear, make your best guess based on your knowledge of a college environment.

3. Fill out your survey form with the information obtained in exercise 2. For any additional information you require, use your knowledge of a college environment.

4. Describe two different ways

FIGURE 7.28
Report cards for Marvel College

DISCIPLINE	NUMBER	COURSE TITLE	GRADE	CREDITS	CREDITS EARNED	GRADE POINTS
COMP. SCI.	153	COBOL	A	4	4	16.0
MATH	201	CALCULUS	A	3	3	12.0

CURRENT SEMESTER TOTALS

CREDITS	CREDITS EARNED	GPA	TOTAL POINTS
7	7	4.00	28.0

ADVISOR: 57 - ELLEN ROBERTS
SEMESTER: WINTER
YEAR: 1987
STUDENT NUMBER: 4825
MAJOR: COMPUTER SCIENCE
EMPHASIS: INFORMATION SYS.

CUMULATIVE TOTALS

CREDITS	GRADE POINT CREDITS	CREDITS EARNED	GPA	TOTAL POINTS	TOTAL CREDITS EARNED
47	44	44	3.39	149.2	46

STUDENT NAME & ADDRESS	LOCAL ADDRESS (IF DIFFERENT)
BRIAN CONNORS 686 FRANKLIN HART, MI 48282	

of implementing one-to-one relationships. Assume that we are maintaining information on offices (office number, building, phone number) and faculty (number, name, etc.). No office houses more than one faculty member. No faculty member is assigned more than one office. Illustrate the ways of implementing one-to-one relationships using offices and faculty. Which approach would be best in each of the following situations?

   a. A faculty member must have an office and each office must be occupied by a faculty member.

   b. A faculty member must have an office, but some offices are not currently occupied. (We still need to maintain information about these unoccupied offices in an OFFICE relation, however.)

   c. Some faculty members do not have an office. All offices are occupied, however.

   d. Some faculty members do not have an office. Some offices are not occupied.

5. For each of the following collections of relations, give the assumptions concerning the relationship between students, courses, and faculty members which are implied by the collection. In each relation only the keys are shown.

A.   STU(STUDENT_NUMBER, COURSE_NUMBER, FACULTY_NUMBER)

B.   STU(STUDENT_NUMBER, COURSE_NUMBER)

    FAC(COURSE_NUMBER, FACULTY_NUMBER)

C.   STU(STUDENT_NUMBER, COURSE_NUMBER)

    FAC(COURSE_NUMBER, FACULTY_NUMBER)

    STUFAC(STUDENT_NUMBER, FACULTY_NUMBER)

D.   STU(STUDENT_NUMBER, COURSE_NUMBER, FACULTY_NUMBER)

E.   STU(STUDENT_NUMBER, COURSE_NUMBER)

    FAC(COURSE_NUMBER, FACULTY_NUMBER)

    STUFAC(STUDENT_NUMBER, FACULTY_NUMBER)

6. Assume that at Marvel College if a faculty member is also the chair of a department, his or her record should also contain the budget for that department. No other faculty members have budgets. Assume that if the faculty member has a special research grant, the type of grant and a description of the project should be stored. Any faculty member who does not have such a grant will not have this information.
   a. Give a design that would contain all of the above information in a single FACULTY relation in which certain columns have NULLS ALLOWED. Document this in DBDL.
   b. Modify the design to include appropriate subtypes. Document the modified design in DBDL.
7. How can other restrictions be represented? Is one method more advantageous? Represent the following restrictions to the design of Figure 7.19 using the ASSERT command:
   a. Commission rates are less than 20 percent.
   b. Parts cannot have a price of zero.
   c. No order line can be added for a part with zero units on hand.
   d. The credit limit for a customer cannot be changed if the balance is over the credit limit.
8. How is it possible to merge a collection of relations that is in 3NF into a cumulative design that is in 3NF and not obtain a collection of relations that is in 3NF? Give an example.
9. Create appropriate subschemas for user views 6, 7, and 8 in the design example in section 6.6.
10. Convert the DBDL for the design example in section 6.6 to an E-R diagram.
11. Convert the E-R design shown in Figure 7.29 on the following page to DBDL. Any decisions for which the diagram does not supply enough information may be made arbitrarily.

FIGURE 7.29
Sample E-R diagram

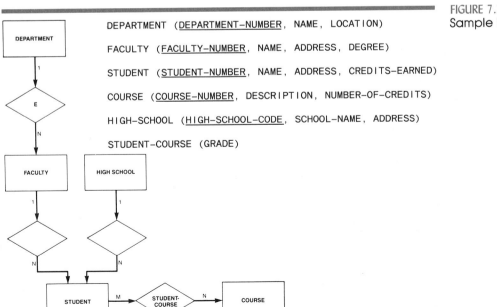

DEPARTMENT (DEPARTMENT-NUMBER, NAME, LOCATION)

FACULTY (FACULTY-NUMBER, NAME, ADDRESS, DEGREE)

STUDENT (STUDENT-NUMBER, NAME, ADDRESS, CREDITS-EARNED)

COURSE (COURSE-NUMBER, DESCRIPTION, NUMBER-OF-CREDITS)

HIGH-SCHOOL (HIGH-SCHOOL-CODE, SCHOOL-NAME, ADDRESS)

STUDENT-COURSE (GRADE)

REFERENCES

1] Atre, S. *Data Base: Structured Techniques for Design, Performance and Management*. Wiley-Interscience, 1980.

2] Chen, Peter. *The Entity-Relationship Approach to Logical Data Base Design*. Q.E.D. Information Sciences, Inc. Data Base Monograph Series, no. 6.

3] Database Design Inc. Information on DATA DESIGNER is available from Database Design Inc., 2020 Hogback Rd., Ann Arbor, MI, 48104.

4] Date, C. J. *Introduction to Database Systems, Volume II*. Addison-Wesley, 1983.

5] Kroenke, David. *Database Processing*, 2d ed. SRA, 1983.

6] McFadden, Fred R., and Hoffer, Jeffrey A. *Data Base Management*. Benjamin Cummings, 1985.

7] Yao, S. Bing. *Principles of Database Design*. Prentice-Hall, 1985.

CODASYL MODEL I – INTRODUCTION TO THE CODASYL MODEL

8.1 INTRODUCTION

In the mid 1960s, a few commercial DBMS's began to appear, and they were met with at least some acceptance within the computing community. Of these, IDS (Integrated Data Store) was probably the most influential. It was developed at General Electric by a team headed by Charles Bachman. This system, sometimes called the Grandfather of Database Management Systems, proved to be the forerunner of the CODASYL model, which we will study in this chapter.

CODASYL (COnference on DAta SYstems Languages) is a voluntary organization consisting of representatives from diverse areas within the computing community. Already known as the organization responsible for the development of COBOL, CODASYL turned its attention in the late 1960s to the problem of standardization of database management systems. The initial process of developing a standard was carried out by a task group within CODASYL called the **Data Base Task Group (DBTG)**. This group studied existing systems (most notably IDS) and prepared a preliminary report on specifications for languages that define and process data. This DBTG report, published by the Association for Computing Machinery in October 1969, drew widespread criticism, and the task group received a number of proposals from various groups suggesting changes and extensions. Many of these suggestions were accepted by the DBTG, which published an updated report in 1971 (see [8]).

The specifications detailed in the 1971 report were considered by the American National Standards Institute (ANSI) for establishment as a standard. ANSI did not accept the specifications as a standard (neither did they reject them), but a number of vendors developed systems that followed these guidelines. Such systems have come to be called CODASYL systems or DBTG systems (the terms are synonymous). The general approach to database management proposed in the 1971 report is termed the CODASYL model or the DBTG model.

The **CODASYL model** falls within the general category of the **network model**. A simple network is just a collection of records and one-to-many relationships. A system technically falls within the general network model if its underlying data structures are simple networks. Since this is true of the CODASYL model, it is technically a subset of the network model. There are non-CODASYL systems, most notably the systems TOTAL (a product of Cincom) and IMAGE (a product of Hewlett-Packard), which also must be deemed to fall within the network model. The vast majority of network model systems are also CODASYL systems, however, so to many people within the computing community, the term network model has also come to be synonymous with CODASYL. Thus, if various individuals refer to their system as a network system or a CODASYL system or a DBTG system, they are usually talking about the same thing.

More work has been done on the specifications. The DBTG became a permanent part of CODASYL and assumed a new name (Data Description Language Committee, or DDLC) in 1972. In 1973 the DDLC published another report, one which differed in some minor aspects from the 1971 report (see [6]). Another report, this one with more substantial changes, was published in 1978 (see [3] and [5]), and yet another one was published by ANSI in 1981 (see [4] and [7]). While the term DBTG model should technically be used only to refer to the 1971 specifications, many people use it to refer to any or all of the four versions published in 1971, 1973, 1978, and 1981.

Given four different reports and the lack of a national standard, the presence of differences between CODASYL systems is not surprising; but the similarities far outnumber the differences. A person who is proficient in one CODASYL system will have no difficulty mastering another. The version of the model that we will study in this chapter is the most typical of CODASYL systems commercially available. What this means, essentially, is that we will study the model that is based on the 1971–1973 specifications. At the end of the chapter, we will investigate some of the changes made in the 1978–1981 specifications.

A number of CODASYL systems are commercially available, including IDMS (Cullinet Software), IDS/II (the descendant of the original IDS and now a product of Honeywell Information Systems), DMS/1100 (Univac), DBMS 10 (DEC), DMS-170 (CDC), PRIME DBMS (PRIME Computer), and PHOLAS (Phillips Electrologica of Holland).

CODASYL systems are known to be powerful and capable of supporting applications with high-volume processing requirements. They are best suited to applications whose requirements can be well specified in advance. They are not particularly well suited to applications that cannot be so tightly specified. The latter really demand the flexibility that only relational model systems can truly provide.

In section 8.2 of this chapter, we will study the basic concepts and terminology of the CODASYL model. Section 8.3 covers the data definition language (DDL), and section 8.4 reviews the data manipulation language (DML). Both of these concepts will be illustrated with the Premiere Products database. Finally, in section 8.5, we will investigate some of the changes alluded to in the 1978–1981 reports. In chapter 9, we will examine in detail one of the major commercial CODASYL systems by Cullinet, called IDMS. We will also look at some of the more advanced features of the CODASYL model and compare the CODASYL and relational models.

2 BASIC CONCEPTS AND TERMINOLOGY

Since a database is a structure that houses not only information about different types of **entities** but also information about **relationships** between these entities, we will begin our study of the CODASYL model by investigating how these types of information are stored in CODASYL systems. We need to examine, of course, not only how the information is stored within a CODASYL database, but also how it is manipulated. In this section we will investigate the structures within CODASYL that are used to store information about entities and relationships between them as well as the basic facilities used within CODASYL systems to manipulate this information.

To illustrate the basic concepts, let's focus on two different entities, faculty and students, and on the one-to-many relationship between them, which we will call "advises". (A faculty member is related to the many students whom he or she advises. Each student is related to the one faculty member who advises him or her.) Thus, we need to be able to store faculty information and student information and to relate a faculty member to all of his or her advisees and a student to his or her advisor.

ENTITIES — RECORDS AND FIELDS

The terms **record** and **field** are used in the CODASYL model exactly as they are in ordinary file processing. Thus, if for the entity STUDENT, we are interested in the properties STUDENT_NUMBER, NAME, and NUMBER_OF_CREDITS, we would have a STUDENT record with fields STUDENT_NUMBER, NAME, and NUMBER_OF_CREDITS. In COBOL, this structure would be described as:

```
01     STUDENT.
       03    STUDENT-NUMBER          PIC 9(4).
       03    NAME                    PIC X(20).
       03    NUMBER-OF-CREDITS       PIC 9(3).
```

(Note the use in COBOL of hyphens rather than underscores.) We can picture it visually as:

STUDENT		
STUDENT- NUMBER	NAME	NUMBER-OF- CREDITS

It is often important to make a distinction between the structure itself, which is called the **type**, and a specific example of the structure, which is called an **occurrence**. Thus, what we have just looked at would be called a record type (we could speak of a record of type STUDENT, for example), whereas

1234	MARY JONES	14

is a record occurrence (technically an occurrence of the record of type STUDENT). This distinction is not always a necessary one, but some situations make it absolutely essential. As we encounter such situations, we will point out why the distinction is necessary, and, of course, we will use the appropriate term.

ONE-TO-MANY RELATIONSHIPS — SETS

Records and fields allow us to maintain information on entities and the properties of these entities, but it is another construction, called a **set**, that allows us to maintain relationships. Just as there are record types and record occurrences, there are set types and set occurrences. The set type is the general structure.

Def: A **set type** is a one-to-many association between record types.

In our example, we would have two record types, FACULTY and STUDENT. The one-to-many association between them would be represented by a set type, say, ADVISES. Figure 8.1 shows a pictorial way of representing these two records and the set between them. This type of diagram is called a **data structure diagram**. Some people refer to it as a **Bachman diagram** (named for Charles Bachman). In it, we represent each record type with a box and each set type as an arrow going _from_ the record type that is the "one" part of the association _to_ the record type that is the "many" part of the association. Since one faculty member is assigned to many students, the arrow goes from the record of type FACULTY to the record of type STUDENT. The record at the head of the arrow, in this case FACULTY, is called the **owner record type**. The record at the foot of the arrow, in this case STUDENT, is called the **member record type**.

Just as an occurrence of a record type is a specific example of that record type, an occurrence of a set type will be a specific example of that set type. But what would an example of a one-to-many association be in this case? It would be one occurrence of the owner record type (one faculty member) and many occurrences of the member record type (the many students whom this particular faculty member advises). Consider Figure 8.2, in which, for the sake of simplicity,

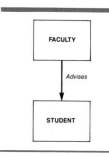

FIGURE 8.1
Data structure
diagram

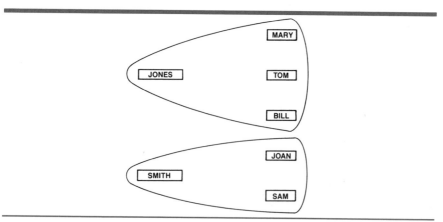

FIGURE 8.2
Occurrences of
ADVISES

last names represent occurrences of FACULTY and first names represent occurrences of STUDENT. The bubbles represent occurrences of ADVISES: one faculty member and the many students whom he or she advises. Thus, two occurrences of ADVISES are shown. In the first, JONES is the owner occurrence and MARY, TOM, and BILL are the member occurrences. In the second, SMITH is the owner occurrence and JOAN and SAM are the member occurrences.

The following questions are intended to illustrate the basic concepts just explained. Try to answer each question yourself before reading the answer. All the questions pertain to the example we are discussing.

How many records do you see in Figure 8.2?
Answer:
This is an ambiguous question. If, by records, we mean record types, there are two: FACULTY and STUDENT. If we mean record occurrences, there are seven: JONES, SMITH, MARY, TOM, BILL, JOAN, AND SAM.

How many sets do you see?
Answer:
Again, this is an ambiguous question. If we mean set types, there is one: ADVISES. If we mean set occurrences, there are two: the two bubbles.

If we add another faculty member, WILSON, who has *no* advisees, what would the picture look like?
Answer:
There would be an additional faculty member, WILSON, in the picture and an additional bubble containing only WILSON.

If BILL is advised by *both* JONES *and* SMITH, what would the picture look like? Would BILL have to be in an overlap of the two bubbles?
Answer:
The answer is that BILL cannot be advised by both JONES and SMITH, since this would violate the relationship. (Each student is advised by exactly one faculty member.) The diagram is inappropriate for a college that allows students to have more than one advisor.

These relationships are not actually implemented as "bubbles", as they are shown in Figure 8.2. For now, however, we do suggest that you visualize set occurrences as bubbles, each bubble containing exactly one occurrence of the owner record type and many occurrences of the member record type. In other words, each bubble will contain exactly one faculty member and the many students (possibly zero) whom this faculty member advises.

CURRENCY

Later in the chapter we will formally introduce a concept called **currency**, which is used in processing a CODASYL database. For now, let's picture that for each record type in our database, we are given a "finger" that we can use to point at a particular occurrence of the record type. At a given instant, for example, the FACULTY finger could be pointing at JONES and the STUDENT finger could be pointing at MARY. Also, for each set type, we are given a finger that we can use to point at a particular occurrence (bubble) of that set. Furthermore, this same finger will also be pointing at one of the record occurrences (owner or member) in this bubble, indicating our position within the set. These fingers are used by the system to keep track of our position within the database. Various commands utilize them in order to determine exactly what it is that needs to be accomplished. For example, let's consider the following scenario. The STATEMENT column indicates the action we are requesting the system to perform. The EFFECT column indicates the system's response. The FACULTY, STUDENT, and ADVISES columns indicate what the appropriate fingers will be pointing at *after* the action has been completed. Let's assume that initially none of the fingers are pointing at anything.

STATEMENT	EFFECT	FACULTY	STUDENT	ADVISES
1. Find faculty JONES	System locates JONES	JONES	—	bubble 1 JONES
2. Find next student in ADVISES set	System locates MARY	JONES	MARY	bubble 1 MARY
3. Find next student in ADVISES set	System locates TOM	JONES	TOM	bubble 1 TOM

STATEMENT	EFFECT	FACULTY	STUDENT	ADVISES
4. Find next student in ADVISES set	System locates BILL	JONES	BILL	bubble 1 BILL
5. Find next student in ADVISES set	System shows no more students in set. Fingers do not change	JONES	BILL	bubble 1 BILL
6. Find student JOAN	System locates JOAN	JONES	JOAN	bubble 2 JOAN
7. Find owner within ADVISES set	System locates SMITH	SMITH	JOAN	bubble 2 SMITH

Note that the type of commands illustrated in steps one through five would serve to find a faculty member and all of his or her advisees. The commands illustrated in steps six and seven would serve to find a student and his or her advisor.

MANY-TO-MANY RELATIONSHIPS — LINK RECORDS

So far, we have seen how the set construction within the CODASYL model handles the one-to-many relationship. What kind of structure is available to handle the many-to-many relationship? In particular, what about the relationship between students and the courses they have taken? Since a student has taken many courses (up to forty or so for a graduating senior; an incoming freshman, of course, has not yet taken any) and a course has been taken by many students, this is a many-to-many relationship. Figure 8.3 shows a diagram of this relationship.

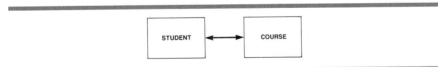

FIGURE 8.3
Many-to-many
relationship

Even though the many-to-many relationship is quite common, there is no facility within the CODASYL model to handle it directly. We can, however, use a little trick to change a single many-to-many relationship into two one-to-many relationships, which can then be implemented using sets. We introduce a third record type called a **link record** (in this example, named STUDENT_COURSE_ LINK), together with a one-to-many relationship from STUDENT to STUDENT_ COURSE_LINK and another one-to-many relationship from COURSE to STUDENT_COURSE_LINK. In this particular example, the STUDENT_COURSE_ LINK record contains a single field, GRADE. (After discussing the concepts involved in this procedure, we will examine which types of fields this new record type will contain in general.) The one-to-many relationship between STUDENT and STUDENT_COURSE_LINK will be represented by a set, RECEIVES, which relates a student to the grades he or she received. The one-to-many relationship between COURSE and STUDENT_COURSE_LINK will be represented by a set, GIVES, which relates a course to all of the grades given by that course. Figure 8.4 gives the data structure diagram for the new structure.

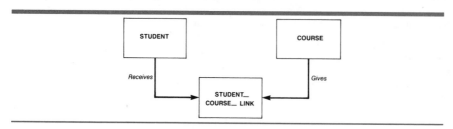

FIGURE 8.4
Link record used to implement many-to-many relationship

To demonstrate why the new structure is appropriate, we need first to examine exactly what is meant by the original structure (Figure 8.3). When we see this kind of diagram, we know we must be able to do two things:

1. Given a student, list all the courses he or she has taken.
2. Given a course, list all the students who have taken it.

If the new structure (Figure 8.4) is appropriate, we must be able to use it to accomplish at least the same two tasks. Let's see whether we can do this by examining some sample occurrences of the record types and set types.

Figure 8.5 shows sample occurrences of all three record types. If we inspect this figure, we can tell that five students (MARY, BOB, TOM, FRED, and SUE), five courses (ENG 100, MTH 110, HST 206, GEO 100, and PHY 120), and eleven grades (A, C, C, B, D, A, B, C, F, A, and B) are currently in the database. We have no idea, however, which students obtained which grades, nor do we know in which courses the grades were received.

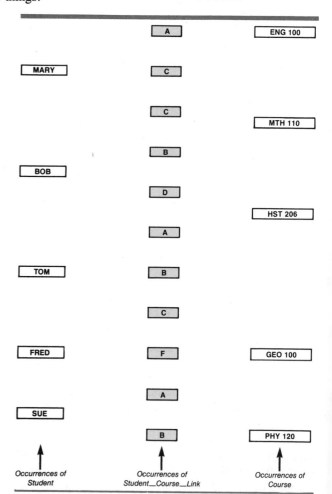

FIGURE 8.5
Occurrences of STUDENT, STUDENT_COURSE_LINK and COURSE

Suppose we look at occurrences of the set RECEIVES. These occurrences, shown in Figure 8.6, allow us to determine which grades were received by which

FIGURE 8.6
Occurrences of
RECEIVES

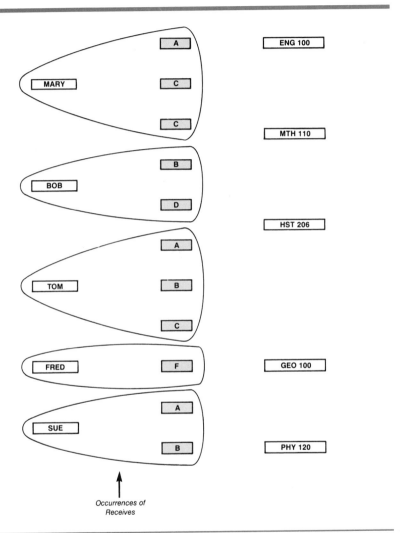

Occurrences of
Receives

students. We can see, for example, that MARY received an A and two C's, whereas TOM received an A, a B, and a C. We still cannot determine in which courses these grades were earned. If, on the other hand, we look at occurrences of the set GIVES, shown in Figure 8.7 on the next page, we can see that in ENG 100 an A was awarded, in MTH 110 a C, a B, and an A, in HST 206 a C, a D and another C,

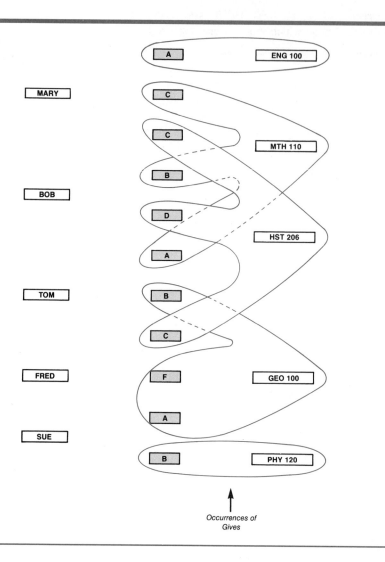

FIGURE 8.7
Occurences of GIVES

Occurrences of
Gives

and so on, but we cannot tell which students received these grades. What we need to do, of course, is to examine occurrences of both sets at the same time. Figure 8.8 on the opposite page, shows the complete picture, occurrences of all three record types and both set types. The occurrences of RECEIVES are shown in black, and occurrences of GIVES are shown in blue.

Now that we have access to all of the information, we can see that MARY received an A in ENG 100, a C in MTH 110, and a C in HST 206. We learn this by examining all of the grades that are in the RECEIVES bubble in which the student is MARY, and then, for each of these grades, determine the unique course that is in the same GIVES bubble as the grade in question. Specifically, after first finding MARY, we repeatedly find the next grade within the RECEIVES set and then find

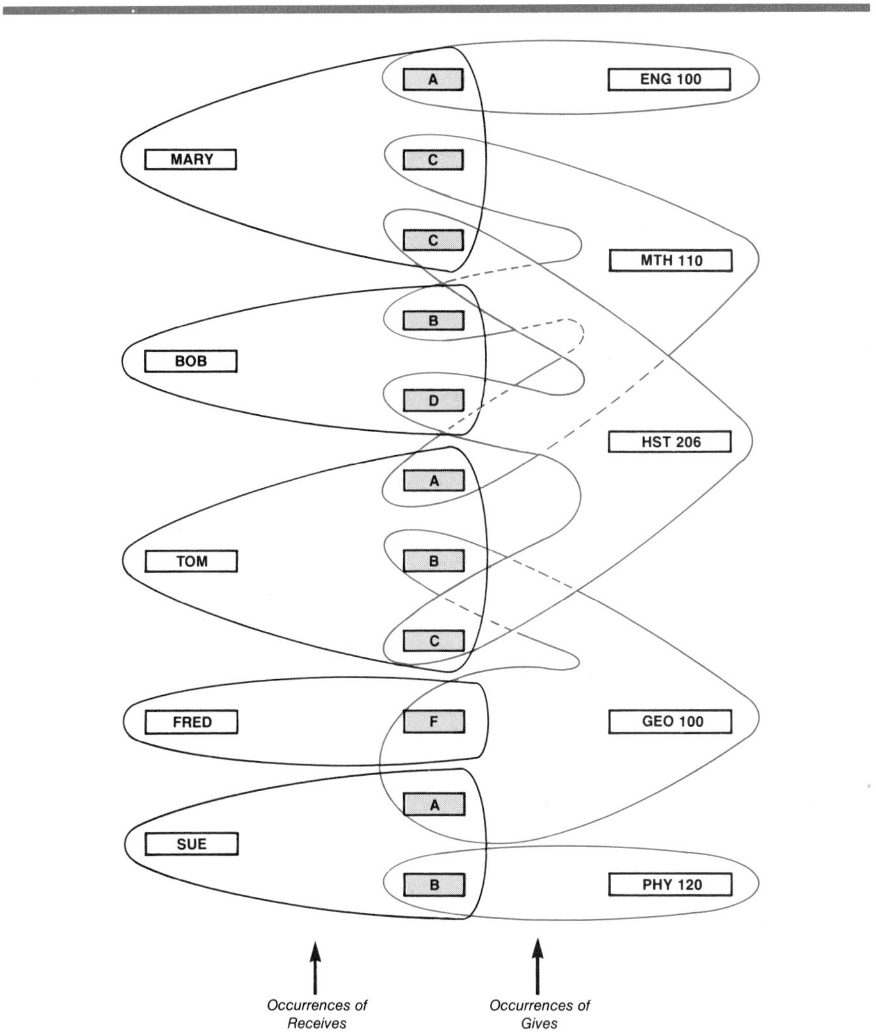

FIGURE 8.8
Occurrences of
RECEIVES and GIVES

this grade's owner within the GIVES set. This process continues until we run out of grades in Mary's set occurrence. (We will examine the exact syntax for these and other data manipulation commands, along with ways of using them, in section 8.4). We could obviously go through the same procedure for any other student. We can thus fulfill the first requirement listed above: for a given student, we can list all of the courses he or she has taken. We can actually do more than was originally required: we can give the grade the student received in the course. This is a nice bonus, but what is crucial is that we can meet the stated requirement.

In a similar fashion we can determine that MTH 110 gave a C to MARY, a B to BOB, and an A to TOM. Since we can do this for any course, we can fulfill the second requirement: for a given course, we can list all of the students that have taken the course. Again, we can actually do more: we can list the grades that these students received.

Since both of these requirements can be fulfilled by the new structure, it is a legitimate way of implementing the many-to-many relationship. It is a worthwhile exercise at this point for you to list for every student all of the grades received as well as the courses in which the grades were earned. Once you have done this, list for every course all of the grades given as well as the students to whom these grades were given. If you can get comfortable with the general concept here, things will be much easier when we look at a rigorous approach to processing CODASYL databases in section 8.4.

FIELDS WITHIN LINK RECORDS — INTERSECTION DATA

A natural question to ask at this point is, Where did GRADE come from? It was not mentioned in the original problem; we only had students and courses and a many-to-many relationship between them. In particular, suppose there was no such field. Suppose for example, that the relationship had been not between students and courses they had *taken* but rather between students and courses they were *taking*. In this case, the students would not yet have received a grade. So what could we use in place of a grade? Do we really need a grade? What if every grade were replaced with some unlikely symbol, such as an asterisk, as shown in Figure 8.9? We wouldn't be able to tell what grades students had received, since no grades would have been given, but couldn't we still tell which students were related to which courses and which courses were related to which students in exactly the same way we did before? In fact, we could even leave the boxes blank that contained the grades, as shown in Figure 8.10 (opposite), and still be able to determine the relationship between students and courses.

FIGURE 8.9
Link records containing "*" rather than grades

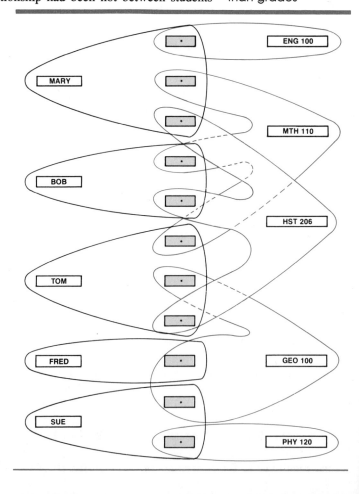

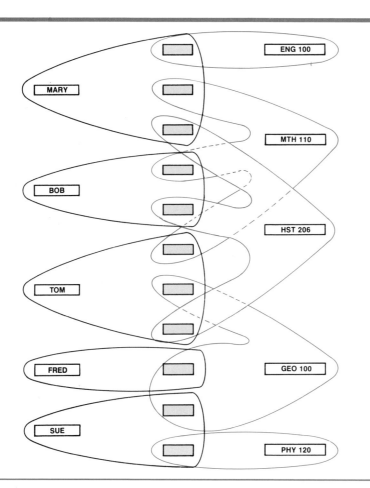

FIGURE 8.10
Link records
containing no data
fields

Now that we have seen why the GRADE field is not necessary to accomplish the many-to-many relationship, the question remains, Where did this field come from? This is a database design question, of course, and as such has essentially been answered in chapters 6 and 7. We will briefly review the general idea here, at least as it relates to the CODASYL model. This means that we will examine the way many-to-many relationships are handled within the model.

The basic approach to dealing with a many-to-many relationship, such as the one between students and courses, involves first creating a third record type and two set types. The new record type will be the member in both sets; the original two records will be the owners (see Figure 8.11). Various terms are used for the new record type that has been introduced. It is often called a **link**, since it "links"

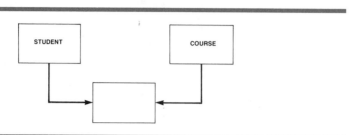

FIGURE 8.11
General link record

occurrences of one record type to occurrences of the other record type. (In Figure 8.8, for example, the first occurrence of GRADE linked Mary to English 100.) It is also sometimes called a **cross reference**, since it serves as a "reference" from records of one record type to records of the other type. Finally, the data that this new record type contains is called **intersection data**. Looking at Figure 8.8, we see the reason for this term: the occurrences of this record are in the *intersection* of a student bubble and a course bubble.

Generally speaking, the next step is to determine what type of intersection data we will have in this new record. In our example, this will be the data that is found in the intersection of a student and a course. We need to ask ourselves what sort of items pertain to *both* a student *and* a course. The student's address, for example, pertains only to the student; it has nothing to do with the courses he or she has taken. The description of a course has nothing to do with the student. These fields are not intersection data and do not belong in the link record. GRADE, however, pertains to both. To find an individual grade in the database, it is not enough to know that the student who received the grade was Mary or that the grade was earned by English 100. We need to know both the student and the course. Thus, GRADE is intersection data and should be one of the fields within the link record. (Note that this is essentially the same process discussed in chapter 6 for implementing many-to-many relationships. In that case, a new relation was created whose key was the concatenation of the keys of the original relations. The other attributes that were placed in this new relation were those which pertained to *both* of the original entities. These additional attributes are the intersection data.)

Where would each of the following fields go: in the STUDENT record, the COURSE record, or the link record?
1. A student's GPA (grade point average).
2. The number of credits awarded by a course.
3. The term in which a student took the course.

continued

Once the intersection data has been determined, we can give a name to the new record type. If the record type now has a special meaning, we could use the meaning as a guide to naming the record. We might also choose to name the record as we did in the example, STUDENT_COURSE_LINK, emphasizing its nature as a link between students and courses. Finally, we can name the two sets. In this case, we have used RECEIVES, since a student receives a grade, and GIVES, since a course gives a grade.

IMPLEMENTATION OF SETS

Before moving on to the specifics of the CODASYL model, we will briefly explain the actual implementation of these sets. Of course, they aren't actually implemented as bubbles, although this is a useful way to picture them. They are implemented as linked lists (you can consult appendix A for a discussion of linked lists if you are not already familiar with this topic). A pointer goes from the owner occurrence to the first member occurrence, from the first member to the second, from the second to the third, and so on. Finally, the last member occurrence points back to the owner. While the pointer is really a number, namely, the address or "database key" of the next member, it is often visualized as an arrow. Thus the set occurrences in Figure 8.2 are implemented in the fashion shown in Figure 8.12 and those in Figure 8.8 are implemented in the fashion shown in

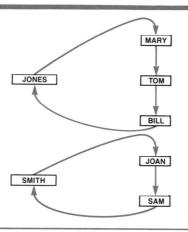

FIGURE 8.12
Implementation of
ADVISES set

Figure 8.13. The processing ideas that we discussed earlier still apply, however.

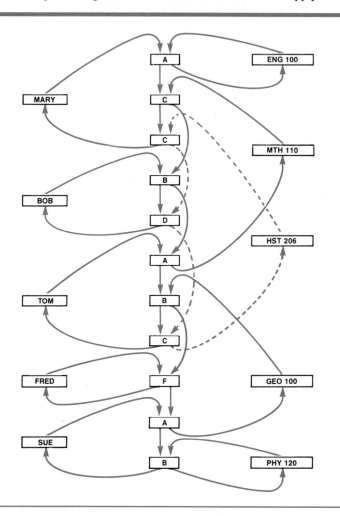

FIGURE 8.13
Implementation of
RECEIVES and GIVES

EXAMPLE DATABASE

As an example of the preceding points, consider the entities and relationships required for the Premiere Products database described in chapter 1. The basic entities are sales reps, customers, orders, and parts, and so we have four record types, say, SLSREP, CUSTOMER, ORDER, and PART. There is a one-to-many relationship from sales reps to customers (one sales rep represents many customers but each customer is represented by exactly one sales rep) and a one-to-many relationship between customers and orders (one customer may have many orders on file but each order was placed by exactly one customer). Thus we have two set types: one from SLSREP to CUSTOMER and another from CUSTOMER to ORDER.

A relationship also exists between orders and parts but it is many-to-many (one order can contain many parts and one part can be found on many orders). We thus create an additional record type, a link record, and two additional sets: one from ORDER to the link record and the other from PART to the link record. The fields in the link record will be the intersection data (if any), i.e., the properties that pertain to both an ORDER and a PART. In this case, two properties pertain to both: quantity ordered and quoted price. Putting this all together yields the data structure diagram shown in Figure 8.14. The fields within each record are listed to the right of the diagram.

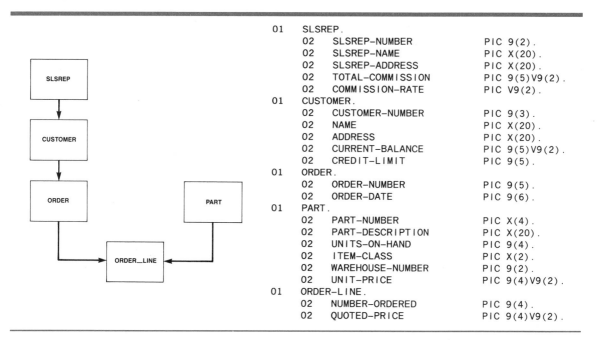

01	SLSREP.		
	02	SLSREP–NUMBER	PIC 9(2).
	02	SLSREP–NAME	PIC X(20).
	02	SLSREP–ADDRESS	PIC X(20).
	02	TOTAL–COMMISSION	PIC 9(5)V9(2).
	02	COMMISSION–RATE	PIC V9(2).
01	CUSTOMER.		
	02	CUSTOMER–NUMBER	PIC 9(3).
	02	NAME	PIC X(20).
	02	ADDRESS	PIC X(20).
	02	CURRENT–BALANCE	PIC 9(5)V9(2).
	02	CREDIT–LIMIT	PIC 9(5).
01	ORDER.		
	02	ORDER–NUMBER	PIC 9(5).
	02	ORDER–DATE	PIC 9(6).
01	PART.		
	02	PART–NUMBER	PIC X(4).
	02	PART–DESCRIPTION	PIC X(20).
	02	UNITS–ON–HAND	PIC 9(4).
	02	ITEM–CLASS	PIC X(2).
	02	WAREHOUSE–NUMBER	PIC 9(2).
	02	UNIT–PRICE	PIC 9(4)V9(2).
01	ORDER–LINE.		
	02	NUMBER–ORDERED	PIC 9(4).
	02	QUOTED–PRICE	PIC 9(4)V9(2).

FIGURE 8.14
Data structure diagram for Premiere Products

No set names were given in Figure 8.14 but these sets do need to have a name. Basically, we can use two methods in assigning names to sets. We can use a name that is descriptive of the set's meaning, as we did with the ADVISES, RECEIVES, and GIVES sets earlier. The advantage of this method is that anyone looking at the name can tell the meaning of the set, provided the name was well chosen. The disadvantage is that we cannot tell from the name which record is the owner record type and which is the member. We can guess that the owner of a set called ADVISES is the FACULTY record, but we can't be sure. The second method for naming sets doesn't require us to guess the owner and the member; we simply include the name of both the owner and the member in the set name, e.g., S_ FACULTY_STUDENT. The disadvantage of this method, of course, is that we now have to guess the meaning. As you can see, there are pros and cons to both methods. For the remainder of the text, we will use the second method unless a specific situation precludes the use of the method. (Obviously, if two sets have the same owner and member, they cannot both be named in this fashion.) One benefit of this method in a data structure diagram is that there is no real need to include the set names. We know, for example, that the set from SLSREP to CUSTOMER is called S_SLSREP_CUSTOMER. Omitting the names in the diagram tends to make the diagram a little less cluttered.

If you compare the list of fields within each record for the CODASYL version of the Premiere Products database with the columns in the corresponding tables in the relational model version (see Figure 3.1), you will note that for some columns which are present in the relational model version, there are no corresponding fields here. The reason is that in the relational model, relationships are determined by common columns, whereas in the CODASYL model they are determined by sets. For the relationship between sales reps and customers, for example, we needed to include the sales rep number as part of the customer table within the relational model implementation. In the CODASYL implementation, this is not necessary. We determine which sales rep is related to a given customer by finding the sales rep who *owns* that customer within the set S_SLSREP_CUSTOMER, not by looking at the sales rep number field within the customer record.

This brings up a question: Could we include the sales rep number in the CUSTOMER record even though it is not necessary? The answer is that we certainly could, although we usually don't. It is worth noting, however, that if we include the sales rep number in the customer record, the set S_SLSREP_CUSTOMER is technically not necessary. We could use the sales rep number in the customer record to find the given sales rep directly. Likewise, to find all of the customers for a given sales rep, we could examine *all* customers looking for those customers who have the given sales rep's number in their sales rep number field. In this case, the set S_SLSREP_CUSTOMER is called an **inessential set** (since we could live without it). On the other hand, if the sales rep's number is not stored within the CUSTOMER record, the only way to find the sales rep who represents a given customer is through the set. In this case, the set is called an **essential set**.

The database for Premiere Products will form the basis for our discussion of the details of the CODASYL model in the sections to come.

8.3   DATA DEFINITION

The **ANSI/SPARC model** of data includes three levels: internal (what is seen by the machine), conceptual (the global enterprise view of data), and external (the individual user view of data). Information about the internal level is defined in the **internal schema**, about the conceptual level in the **conceptual schema**, and about the external level in a number of **external schemas**, one for each separate user view. Although the recent CODASYL reports essentially support these three levels, the 1971-1973 reports and most commercial CODASYL DBMS's do not. Instead, the latter support two levels, referred to as the **schema** and **subschema**. (Actually, it is probably more accurate to refer to two and a half levels. As we will see, some of the physical details of the database are described in a third structure but many physical details are still included in the schema.)   The subschema does represent an individual user view in the sense described in the ANSI/SPARC model. The schema represents the global view of the database. However, it includes both the conceptual level and some aspects of the internal level. In section 8.5, we will examine the changes in the later CODASYL reports that bring the CODASYL model more in line with the ANSI/SPARC model.

SCHEMA DDL

We begin our discussion of data definition within the CODASYL model by examining the way in which **schemas** are defined. In particular, we will look at the schema DDL (data definition language) for Premiere Products. At each step, we will examine the various options and indicate why a particular option was chosen. The complete schema DDL is shown in Figure 8.15. We will now examine each of the components to the schema.

FIGURE 8.15a
Schema DDL for Premiere Products (continued on the following page)

```
SCHEMA NAME IS SCHEMA_DISTRIBUTION.

AREA NAME IS AREA_DISTRIBUTION.

RECORD NAME IS SLSREP
      LOCATION MODE IS CALC
            USING SLSREP_NUMBER
            DUPLICATES ARE NOT ALLOWED
      WITHIN AREA_DISTRIBUTION.

      02    SLSREP_NUMBER        PIC 9(2).
      02    SLSREP_NAME          PIC X(20).
      02    SLSREP_ADDRESS       PIC X(20).
      02    TOTAL_COMMISSION     PIC 9(5)V9(2).
      02    COMMISSION_RATE      PIC V9(2).

RECORD NAME IS CUSTOMER
      LOCATION MODE IS CALC
            USING CUSTOMER_NUMBER
            DUPLICATES ARE NOT ALLOWED
      WITHIN AREA_DISTRIBUTION.

      02    CUSTOMER_NUMBER      PIC 9(3).
      02    NAME                 PIC X(20).
      02    ADDRESS              PIC X(20).
      02    CURRENT_BALANCE      PIC 9(5)V9(2).
      02    CREDIT_LIMIT         PIC 9(5).

RECORD NAME IS ORDER
      LOCATION MODE IS CALC
            USING ORDER_NUMBER
            DUPLICATES ARE NOT ALLOWED
      WITHIN AREA_DISTRIBUTION.

      02    ORDER_NUMBER         PIC 9(5).
      02    ORDER_DATE           PIC 9(6).
```

```
RECORD NAME IS PART
      LOCATION MODE IS CALC
            USING PART_NUMBER
            DUPLICATES ARE NOT ALLOWED
      WITHIN AREA_DISTRIBUTION.

      02    PART_NUMBER          PIC X(4).
      02    PART_DESCRIPTION     PIC X(20).
      02    UNITS_ON_HAND        PIC 9(4).
      02    ITEM_CLASS           PIC X(2).
      02    WAREHOUSE_NUMBER     PIC 9(2).
      02    UNIT_PRICE           PIC 9(4)V9(2).

RECORD NAME IS ORDER_LINE
      LOCATION MODE IS VIA
            S_ORDER_ORDER_LINE
      WITHIN AREA_DISTRIBUTION.

      02    NUMBER_ORDERED       PIC 9(4).
      02    QUOTED_PRICE         PIC 9(4)V9(2).
```

FIGURE 8.15b

```
SET NAME IS S_SLSREP_CUSTOMER
     OWNER IS SLSREP
          SET IS PRIOR PROCESSABLE
          ORDER IS PERMANENT INSERTION IS SORTED BY
                    DEFINED KEYS
          DUPLICATES ARE LAST.

     MEMBER IS CUSTOMER
          INSERTION IS AUTOMATIC
          RETENTION IS OPTIONAL
          LINKED TO OWNER
          KEY IS ASCENDING NAME
          SET SELECTION FOR S_SLSREP_CUSTOMER
               IS THRU S_SLSREP_CUSTOMER
               OWNER IDENTIFIED BY APPLICATION.

SET NAME IS S_CUSTOMER_ORDER
     OWNER IS CUSTOMER
          SET IS PRIOR PROCESSABLE
          ORDER IS PERMANENT INSERTION IS LAST.

     MEMBER IS ORDER
          INSERTION IS AUTOMATIC
          RETENTION IS OPTIONAL
          LINKED TO OWNER
          SET SELECTION FOR S_CUSTOMER_ORDER
               IS THRU S_CUSTOMER_ORDER
               OWNER IDENTIFIED BY APPLICATION.

SET NAME IS S_ORDER_ORDER_LINE
     OWNER IS ORDER
          SET IS PRIOR PROCESSABLE
          ORDER IS PERMANENT INSERTION IS LAST.

     MEMBER IS ORDER_LINE
          INSERTION IS AUTOMATIC
          RETENTION IS OPTIONAL
          LINKED TO OWNER
          SET SELECTION FOR S_ORDER_ORDER_LINE
               IS THRU S_ORDER_ORDER_LINE
               OWNER IDENTIFIED BY APPLICATION.

SET NAME IS S_PART_ORDER_LINE
     OWNER IS PART
          SET IS PRIOR PROCESSABLE
          ORDER IS PERMANENT INSERTION IS LAST.

     MEMBER IS ORDER_LINE
          INSERTION IS AUTOMATIC
          RETENTION IS OPTIONAL
          LINKED TO OWNER
          SET SELECTION FOR S_PART_ORDER_LINE
               IS THRU S_PART_ORDER_LINE
               OWNER IDENTIFIED BY APPLICATION.
```

SCHEMA ENTRY

SCHEMA NAME IS SCHEMA_DISTRIBUTION.

The first line in the schema DDL gives the name for the schema. In this case, the name SCHEMA_DISTRIBUTION was chosen. The word SCHEMA was included so that anyone can readily determine that this is in fact a schema, and the word DISTRIBUTION was chosen as an abbreviation for the database, since it involves the distribution activities of Premiere Products. As you can see in this name, the underscore (—) is a legal character for use in names. Unlike COBOL, the DDL does not allow the use of hyphens. When we examine the manner in which the database is manipulated in COBOL programs, we will see that hyphens effectively replace all of the underscores (COBOL does not recognize the underscore as a legal character).

AREA ENTRY

AREA NAME IS AREA_DISTRIBUTION.

The area is the physical file that will house the database. This construction has been removed in the later CODASYL reports but is still found in commercial implementations. As we will see when we discuss processing the database, particularly in COBOL, there is another word, *REALM*, that is used in place of AREA. The two are synonymous. It is actually possible to have several different areas (or realms) and to indicate which record types are stored in which areas. For our purposes, one area will be sufficient.

RECORD ENTRY

```
RECORD NAME IS SLSREP
       LOCATION MODE IS CALC USING SLSREP_NUMBER
              DUPLICATES ARE NOT ALLOWED
       WITHIN AREA_DISTRIBUTION.
       02    SLSREP_NUMBER          PIC 9(2).
       02    SLSREP_NAME            PIC X(20).
       02    SLSREP_ADDRESS         PIC X(20).
       02    TOTAL_COMMISSION       PIC 9(5)V9(2).
       02    COMMISSION_RATE        PIC V9(2).
```

For each record in the database, there is a *record entry* in the schema. The record entry gives the name of the record as well as the name and physical characteristics of all of the fields within the record. This can be done with COBOL pictures, as shown here, or with what is termed a TYPE clause. (Instead of PIC 9(2), we could use TYPE DECIMAL 2; instead of PIC X(20), we could use TYPE CHARACTER 20, etc.)

There are two other aspects of a record which must be described: the area in which occurrences of this record type are to be placed, and the record's location mode. Even though we may only mention one area within our schema, as we have done in this case, leaving no choice in terms of where to place the record, we must still specify that the record will be in that one area.

LOCATION MODE

A **location mode** is really a two-part strategy, one part for placing records in a database and a companion part for finding those records at some later time. Naturally, these two parts go hand-in-hand. How we place records in the database will determine what options we have for finding them later. (For a general discussion of location mode and the variety of possibilities, see **access method** in Appendix A.) The location modes possible within a CODASYL system are as follows:

1. DIRECT

A location mode of DIRECT implies that the programmer will indicate exactly where in the database a record occurrence is to be placed. (Technically, the programmer will furnish the database key or address of the position to be occupied by the record.) When the programmer wants to locate the record later, he or she must know where it has been placed and ask for the record in that position. This means that the programmer must be involved at a very physical level with the database. One of the goals of DBMS is to *avoid* this kind of physical involvement. The moral of the story is, *do not use a location mode of DIRECT!*

2. CALC

The word CALC is short for calculation, and that is exactly what happens. A record with a location mode of CALC must have one or more of its items declared to be the *key* for the record. When an occurrence of this record is stored, the position at which the record will be placed is determined by *calculating* from the value of the key. When the item is later retrieved, the same calculation is repeated, indicating to the system where to look for the record. This process is also known as randomizing or hashing and is discussed in Appendix A.

3. VIA SET

The final location mode is VIA SET. The exact syntax is VIA set-name, where the set-name is the name of a set in which the record is a *member*. In this case record occurrences will be positioned in the database as close as possible to their owner (within the set that was named in the VIA clause). There are two ramifications of this scheme. First, in contrast to the location mode CALC, we will not be able to retrieve one of these record occurrences directly. Second, retrieving an owner occurrence and all of its member occurrences is a *very* efficient process if the members are stored via set. A database is divided into blocks, often called pages, which are retrieved when the disk is accessed. If the owner and member occurrences are close together, the number of pages that must be read will by minimized. For example, should an owner occurrence and its eighteen member occurrences all be placed on the same page, we will get all nineteen occurrences with a single disk access. If, on the other hand, the member record type has a location mode of CALC, the eighteen member occurrences will be distributed all throughout the database and the same operation could require nineteen disk accesses!

As a general rule of thumb, we will use CALC when we have a key for a record (like SLSREP_NUMBER for the SLSREP record) on which we need to do direct access. We will use via set either when there is no appropriate key or when direct access is not required. If we choose CALC, the syntax is

```
LOCATION MODE IS CALC USING data-name
    DUPLICATES ARE [NOT] ALLOWED
```

If we choose to allow duplicates, it will be possible to store in the database a second record with the same key value. If we do not allow duplicates (which is more common), a second record with the same key value will be rejected and the system will notify us of this fact. Note that even though the key is most often a single data item, it need not be; it could be a combination of several items.

In the complete schema (see Figure 8.15), you will note that ORDER_LINE is stored via the set from ORDER to ORDER_LINE. This means that ORDER_LINE occurrences will be positioned physically close to the ORDER to which they belong, and retrieving an order and all of the associated order lines will be an efficient operation. ORDER_LINE is a member in another set, the set from PART to ORDER_LINE. The fact that an order line is stored close to the order that owns it will not prohibit us from retrieving a part and all of the order lines associated with that part. The only difference is that this operation will be less efficient, since the order lines are not close to the part that owns them.

If a record type is a member in two or more set types and the record should have location mode VIA SET, how do we pick which set to use? We can use only one. As this is really a physical-design issue, it is discussed more thoroughly in chapter 12. In terms of a general guide, however, since processing along the set we pick will be more efficient, we try to determine the relative benefits from choosing one set as opposed to the other.

SET ENTRY

```
SET NAME IS S_SLSREP_CUSTOMER
    OWNER IS SLSREP
        SET IS PRIOR PROCESSABLE
        ORDER IS PERMANENT INSERTION IS SORTED BY
            DEFINED KEYS
        DUPLICATES ARE LAST.
    MEMBER IS CUSTOMER
        INSERTION IS AUTOMATIC
        RETENTION IS OPTIONAL
        LINKED TO OWNER
        KEY IS ASCENDING NAME
```

```
SET SELECTION FOR S_SLSREP_CUSTOMER
     IS THRU S_SLSREP_CUSTOMER
     OWNER IDENTIFIED BY APPLICATION.
```

For each SET in the database there is a SET entry in the schema. The SET entry consists of the name of the set followed by what is called an OWNER subentry and one or more MEMBER subentries. The basic form of a SET entry is very simple, as follows:

```
SET NAME IS S_SLSREP_CUSTOMER
     OWNER IS SLSREP
     MEMBER IS CUSTOMER.
```

The extra clauses for the various options are what create the appearance of complexity. The subject is less overwhelming if we take the clauses one at a time and discuss their meaning and options.

CLAUSES WITHIN THE OWNER SUBENTRY

I. *SET IS PRIOR PROCESSABLE*

This option requests the system to maintain prior pointers, i.e., each record will contain not only a pointer to the next record in the chain but also a pointer to 'he *previous* record in the chain (see Figure 8.16). These pointers take up extra space. Any operation that involves finding the prior record (such as a deletion, in which the record *prior* to the deleted record should point to the record that came *after* the deleted record) will be made more efficient, however. As a general rule, prior pointers are good things to have, and if they are to be used, this clause should be included in the schema. If not, the clause is omitted.

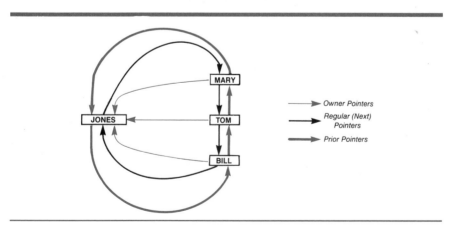

FIGURE 8.16
SET implementation illustrating prior and owner pointers

2. ORDER IS PERMANENT INSERTION IS ...

In the CODASYL specifications, the word PERMANENT is an option, the other choice being TEMPORARY. These options are usually not implemented and we will not discuss the difference between them here. The critical part of this clause is then the INSERTION portion. This describes what may be called the insertion mode. It does not affect where a record will be physically placed in the database; the location mode does that. Rather it indicates where the occurrence should be positioned within the appropriate set occurrence. To see the effect of each of the various possible insertion modes, consider Figure 8.17. Suppose that

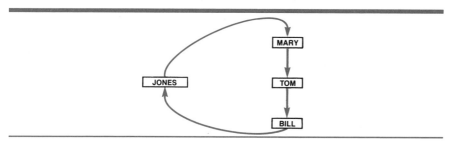

FIGURE 8.17
Set implementation
illustrating order

our current position within this set occurrence is TOM and we are adding a new student, ANN. The position in which the new student will be placed on the chain is determined by this insertion mode. The possibilities are as follows:

a. FIRST

   New occurrences become the first entry on the chain; they immediately follow the owner. Thus ANN would come between JONES (the owner) and MARY.

b. LAST

   New occurrences become the last entry on the chain; they immediately precede the owner. ANN would come between BILL and JONES.

c. NEXT

   New occurrences come immediately after the record at which we are currently pointing. ANN would come between TOM and BILL.

d. PRIOR

   New occurrences come immediately before the record at which we are currently pointing. ANN would come between MARY and TOM.

e. SORTED

   For this option, a sort key must be defined and as records are added, they are placed in such a position that the occurrences around the chain are positioned in order of this sort key. ANN would be placed in whatever position the sort key indicated.

f. IMMATERIAL

   Not all systems have this feature. Here we are allowing the system to place new occurrences in whatever position it chooses. This allows it the potential to place a new occurrence in the chain in the most efficient way. With this option, we have no idea where ANN would be placed.

If we indicate SORTED BY DEFINED KEYS, we must also indicate what should be done with duplicates. The possibilities are FIRST, LAST, and NOT ALLOWED. The duplication referred to, of course, is duplication on the sort key. If the set ADVISES were sorted by name and we attempted to add a second ANN to a set occurrence, this would be a duplicate. If we chose NOT ALLOWED, this addition would be rejected by the system. If we chose FIRST, the addition would be allowed and ANN would appear as the first of all of the ANNs in the chain. Likewise, if we chose LAST, ANN would appear as the last of the ANNs.

Which is more efficient, NEXT or PRIOR? If you think about the work the system must do, they seem fairly similar. In the one case the system must locate the next record, in the other the prior record. While locating the next record is easy (just follow the next pointer), locating the prior pointer may be a very lengthy process. If there are no have prior pointers, the only way to locate the prior record is to walk *all the way around* the chain. If the number of occurrences on the chain is large, this procedure may well be very impractical. On the other hand, if we do have prior pointers, NEXT and PRIOR are virtually identical; in the one case we follow the next pointer, in the other the prior pointer.

Is it useful to have sorted sets? The answer depends on many factors. Sorted sets are very convenient for the purpose of retrieval. If we are producing a report in which the required order matches the order in which the set was sorted, there is no extra work to do other than retrieving the data from the database. If this is not the case, we must first retrieve the data from the database and then sort it before producing the report. Thus, sorted sets allow us to skip a step we would otherwise have to take in the reporting process. On the other hand, they incur extra overhead when the database is updated, particularly if the number of occurrences in the set is large. If a faculty member advises one thousand students (a very busy person indeed) and we wish to add a new occurrence, PAUL, to this faculty member's set occurrence, the system must first locate the position in which to insert PAUL. In the normal procedure for storing sets, this would involve sequentially examining each student in the chain until we found the first student whose name came after PAUL. On the average, we would expect to examine *five hundred* records before finding the right position. More often than not, this would be a prohibitive effort.

Many CODASYL systems have made storing sorted sets more attractive through an alternative approach called POINTER ARRAYS. Conceptually, instead of a chain going from the owner occurrence through all of the member occurrences and back, pointers come out of the owner pointing to each record. This feature is usually implemented in a B-tree-like structure (see appendix A for a discussion of B-trees) which is more complex than the normal chain and does generate some added overhead of its own. Still, it does make the updating of sorted sets much more efficient, since we can use the structure itself to rapidly determine where to place a new occurrence.

CLAUSES WITHIN THE MEMBER SUBENTRY

1. INSERTION IS ...

This use of the word INSERTION differs from the previously described use. This clause determines a record's **storage class**. The two possibilities are *AUTO-MATIC* and *MANUAL*. If the choice is AUTOMATIC, the record will automatically be placed in the appropriate set occurrence as a result of the record being stored. No special action is required on the part of the programmer. If, on the other hand, the choice is MANUAL, the record will be placed in the appropriate set occurrence only when the programmer issues a special command, the CONNECT command, requesting the system to do this.

2. RETENTION IS ...

While the storage class determines whether or not a record is automatically placed in a set when the record is stored, the **removal class** determines whether a record that has already been placed in a set occurrence may be removed from the occurrence. The 1971 specifications and some commercial CODASYL DBMS's allow two choices here: MANDATORY and OPTIONAL. If the choice is MANDA-TORY, once a record has been placed in a set occurrence it may not be removed. It may be moved to another occurrence, however. If the choice is OPTIONAL, the record may be removed. Other systems allow three choices: MANDATORY, OPTIONAL, and FIXED. In these systems FIXED implies that a record may not be moved from a set occurrence once it has been stored. MANDATORY allows a record to be moved from one set occurrence *to another*; the record *must* belong to some occurrence of this set type. OPTIONAL allows a record to be removed from a set occurrence without requiring that the record then be placed in a different occurrence; the record could "float free," so to speak.

To illustrate the differences between MANDATORY, OPTIONAL, and FIXED, consider the set S_SLSREP_CUSTOMER, the set from SLSREP to CUSTOMER. If the removal class is FIXED and customer 123 has been placed in the set owned by sales rep 12, this customer must remain with this sales rep. The only way to switch the customer to another sales rep would be to delete him or her from the database and then add him or her back in, tied to the new sales rep. At the other extreme, if the removal class is OPTIONAL, the customer could be removed from the occurrence headed by sales rep 12 and *left without a sales rep*. In between these two is MANDATORY, in which a customer could be moved from sales rep 12's chain to another sales rep's chain, but *would have to have* a sales rep.

3. LINKED TO OWNER

This option requests the system to maintain pointers from each member record directly to the owner record (see Figure 8.16). Since it is always possible to find the owner of a given member record by following the chain until the owner is encountered, these pointers are not necessary. They do greatly facilitate the process of finding the owner, however. The tradeoff here is the added space occupied by the pointers versus the added efficiency in finding the owner.

4. KEY IS ...

If the sorted insertion mode has been specified, it is here that we define the sort key. After KEY IS we list the sort keys (there can be more than one) in order of importance. Each sort key is preceded either by the word ASCENDING or the word DESCENDING, indicating whether increasing or decreasing order is desired.

5. SET SELECTION IS ...

This clause is used to indicate how the system is to determine the "current" set occurrence, i.e., the one at which we are pointing. The most common approach, and the only one that will be discussed here, is shown in all set entries in this schema. It indicates that the application (the program) will take responsibility for ensuring that the system is indeed pointing at the desired set occurrence.

See Figure 8.15 for the complete schema for the Premiere Products database.

SUBSCHEMA DDL

Whereas the schema describes the complete database as it exists, a **subschema** describes an individual user's view of the database. It may contain all of the records, fields, and sets from the database, or it may contain only a portion. Fields may appear in a different order within a record than they did in the database itself. Names may be changed. Fields in the database may be treated as group items in a subschema and subdivided (e.g., a single field that is called NAME in the database may be subdivided into fields FIRST−NAME and LAST−NAME in a subschema). Conversely, fields in the database may be grouped in a subschema (e.g., if the database contained the fields FIRST−NAME and LAST−NAME, these fields might be grouped into a field called NAME in a subschema).

Since a subschema is by nature something that will be used in connection with a programming language, the form of a subschema designed to be used with one language may differ from the form of a subschema designed to be used with another language. We will focus on the form of the subschema that is appropriate for COBOL. Other forms will have similar objects within them but a structure that is more appropriate for another language.

FULL SUBSCHEMA

Figure 8.18 on the opposite page, is a COBOL subschema that encompasses all records, fields, and sets from the Premiere Products database with no changes to either name or format. If you are familiar with COBOL, you should definitely pick up a COBOL "flavor" in the syntax.

There are three divisions: TITLE, MAPPING, and STRUCTURE. In the title division, we indicate the name of this subschema and the schema with which it is associated. In the mapping division, we indicate any names that we wish to have changed. In Figure 8.18, since we have changed no names from the database

```
      TITLE DIVISION.
         SS  SUBSCHEMA-DISTRIBUTION WITHIN SCHEMA-DISTRIBUTION.
      MAPPING DIVISION.
      STRUCTURE DIVISION.
      REALM SECTION.
         RD  AREA-DISTRIBUTION.
      RECORD SECTION.
      01    SLSREP.
            02    SLSREP-NUMBER          PIC 9(2).
            02    SLSREP-NAME            PIC X(20).
            02    SLSREP-ADDRESS         PIC X(20).
            02    TOTAL-COMMISSION       PIC 9(5)V9(2).
            02    COMMISSION-RATE        PIC V9(2).
      01    CUSTOMER.
            02    CUSTOMER-NUMBER        PIC 9(3).
            02    NAME                   PIC X(20).
            02    ADDRESS                PIC X(20).
            02    CURRENT-BALANCE        PIC 9(5)V9(2).
            02    CREDIT-LIMIT           PIC 9(5).
      01    ORDER.
            02    ORDER-NUMBER           PIC 9(5).
            02    ORDER-DATE             PIC 9(6).
      01    PART.
            02    PART-NUMBER            PIC X(4).
            02    PART-DESCRIPTION       PIC X(20).
            02    UNITS-ON-HAND          PIC 9(4).
            02    ITEM-CLASS             PIC X(2).
            02    WAREHOUSE-NUMBER       PIC 9(2).
            02    UNIT-PRICE             PIC 9(4)V9(2).
      01    ORDER-LINE.
            02    NUMBER-ORDERED         PIC 9(4).
            02    QUOTED-PRICE           PIC 9(4)V9(2).
      SET SECTION.
         SD S-SLSREP-CUSTOMER.
         SD S-CUSTOMER-ORDER.
         SD S-ORDER-ORDER-LINE.
         SD S-PART-ORDER-LINE.
```

FIGURE 8.18
Full subschema for
Premiere Products

itself, this division is empty. In Figure 8.19 on the following page, we will see how names can be changed. The final division, the structure division, contains three sections: REALM, RECORD, and SET. In the realm section, we specify any realms (areas) that are to be included. In the record section, we specify the records and fields that we wish to include. We do not have to include all of the fields in a given record in our subschema, nor do the fields have to appear in the same order within the record. Here we could choose either to group fields or subdivide fields, as the next example will demonstrate. Finally, in the set section, all the sets that are to be included are listed.

PARTIAL SUBSCHEMA

Figure 8.19 represents a partial subschema that contains only portions of the SLSREP and CUSTOMER records and the set S_SLSREP_CUSTOMER. In addi-

```
TITLE DIVISION.
   SS   SUBSCHEMA-CUSTOMER WITHIN SCHEMA-DISTRIBUTION.
MAPPING DIVISION.
ALIAS SECTION.
   AD  = =CUSTOMER_NUMBER= =              BECOMES  CUST-NUMBER.
   AD  = =NAME= =                         BECOMES  CUST-NAME.
   AD  = =SLSREP= =  RECORD-NAME          BECOMES  REP.
   AD  = =S_SLSREP_CUSTOMER= =  SET-NAME  BECOMES  REPRESENTS.
   AD  = =AREA_CUSTOMER= =  REALM-NAME    BECOMES  CUSTOMER-REPS.
STRUCTURE DIVISION.
REALM SECTION.
   RD  CUSTOMER-REPS.
RECORD SECTION.
01    REP.
      02    SLSREP-NUMBER        PIC 9(2).
      02    SLSREP-NAME          PIC X(20).
      02    SLSREP-ADDRESS       PIC X(20).
01    CUSTOMER.
      02    CUST-NUMBER          PIC 9(3).
      02    CUST-NAME.
            03 FIRST-NAME        PIC X(8).
            03 LAST-NAME         PIC X(12).
      02    ADDRESS              PIC X(20).
SET SECTION.
   SD  REPRESENTS.
```

FIGURE 8.19
Partial subschema for
Premiere Products

tion, several things have been renamed. CUSTOMER_NUMBER is changed to CUST-NUMBER, NAME is changed to CUST-NAME, the record SLSREP is now called REP, and the set S_SLSREP_CUSTOMER is changed to REPRESENTS. Finally, the area is renamed CUSTOMER-REPS. The field whose name has been changed to CUST-NAME has been subdivided into two fields, FIRST-NAME and LAST-NAME.

The only difference between the title division here and in Figure 8.18 is that the subschema name is different; here it is called SUBSCHEMA-CUSTOMER. The mapping division contains all of the renaming information in a section called the ALIAS SECTION. The name enclosed in = =   = = is called pseudo-text, and it represents a name from the schema. It could be the name of the realm (area), a record, a set, or an item (field). The pseudo-text is followed by the word RECORD-NAME if it is a record, SET-NAME if it is a set, and REALM-NAME if it is a realm. If it is a field, it is not followed by any special word. Next is the word BECOMES, followed by the new name. It is this new name which will appear in the rest of the subschema and which will consequently be used in programs using this subschema. The only differences between the STRUCTURE DIVISION here and in Figure 8.18 are that a field, CUST-NAME, has been subdivided, and a number of records, fields, and sets have been omitted.

SCHEMA DMCL

The schema DDL and the subschema DDL form the major portion of the data definition facility within CODASYL systems, but we'll comment briefly on another component. In commercial systems, it is usually called the DMCL (Device Media Control Language). While the DMCL was mentioned in the CODASYL report, the form for this language as well as the specifics of what it must contain was not. It is used to specify the very physical aspects of the database. The following list represents some of the things usually specified:

1. Size of the database
2. Blocking factor (or page size)
3. Whether or not the database is to be encrypted
4. Whether or not journaling is to take place
5. Where in the database given records are to be located (ranges of pages on which records of a given type may appear)
6. Whether a given set is organized in a chain mode or uses pointer arrays (some systems include this within the schema DDL)

For further discussion of the CODASYL DDL, see [1], [2], [9], [10], [11], [12], and [13].

4   DATA MANIPULATION

In this section, we will investigate the **data manipulation language (DML)** of CODASYL DBMS's. The CODASYL DML consists of a number of commands that can be used within a programming language (called a **host language**) like COBOL. COBOL in fact, is by far the most common language used with a CODASYL system. This is why we chose to look at a COBOL subschema in section 8.3 and why we will base the examples in this section on COBOL. If you are not familiar with the COBOL language, viewing the algorithms presented as a form of pseudo-code should enable you to understand the concepts. We will not be delving deeply into the COBOL language itself, but merely using it as a vehicle for presenting the concepts. Please take note, however, that we will be using hyphens rather than underscores for the sake of consistency with the requirements of COBOL.

We will examine the DML by first discussing the *user work area (UWA)*, a holding area for data being loaded to or unloaded from the database, followed by an examination of the critical concept called **currency**. Next we will briefly look at the DML commands most likely to be encountered in practice. Finally, a number of examples using these commands will be presented. The same Premiere Products database that was presented in section 8.2 will be used in these examples.

USER WORK AREA (UWA)

Every program accessing a CODASYL database contains a user work area (UWA). All of the records (and thus all of the fields) in the subschema are a part of the UWA. According to the DBTG report (see [8]), "conceptually, the UWA is a loading and unloading zone where all data provided by the DBMS in response to a call for the data is delivered and where all data to be picked up by the DBMS must be placed." In a COBOL program, the records from the subschema are automatically inserted in a special section at the beginning of the data division by having the following:

```
DATA DIVISION.
SUB-SCHEMA SECTION.
DB    SUBSCHEMA-DISTRIBUTION WITHIN
         SCHEMA-DISTRIBUTION.
FILE SECTION.
```

The rest of the DATA DIVISION would not be changed.

The full subschema is effectively inserted during compilation at this point within the data division. (If a listing is being produced during compilation, you will actually see it here.) If you are familiar with COBOL, you will note that the records described in the subschema are identical in appearance to those described elsewhere in the DATA DIVISION. The fields and records within the subschema that have now been inserted in the program constitute the records and fields of the UWA. They may be used by the programmer just like records and fields in the other sections of the DATA DIVISION. When a record is stored or modified, the contents of the corresponding record in this subschema section are used to update the database. When information is retrieved from the database, it is placed in the appropriate records and fields within this section.

Besides the records from the subschema, the UWA contains other data: **currency indicators** and **special registers**. The currency indicators are used by the system and are normally not touched by the programmer (although it is possible to do so). The special registers are available to the programmer even though they are not explicitly listed within the subschema portion of the program. One of these, DB-STATUS, which is described later in this section, is absolutely crucial. It is through DB-STATUS that the system notifies us of any problems encountered during interaction with the database. Others, such as DB-SET-NAME and DB-RECORD-NAME, can be useful in telling us what set or record was being accessed at the time a problem arose. For the most part, however, DB-STATUS is the only one we will use, and it is the only one we will describe here.

CURRENCY INDICATORS

In section 8.2, we mentioned the fact that we have a variety of *fingers* that will point at various occurrences in the database. We said that we had a finger for each record type that would point at a single occurrence of that record and a finger for each set type that would point at a single occurrence of that set. The technical term for each of these fingers is *currency indicator*. In practice, a currency indicator is a variable that will be maintained and used by the system and will contain the address of the record occurrence most recently manipulated in a given category of records. The record whose address is contained in this variable is called the *current of record type* or simply the *current record*.

Def: A **currency indicator** is a conceptual pointer maintained by the DBMS to establish a current record of a run unit, record type, set type, or realm (area). A description of the various currency indicators follows:

1. CURRENT OF RUN UNIT
   The run unit is the program. There is only one current of run unit. This will be the last occurrence of any type of record that was found or stored.
2. CURRENT OF RECORD TYPE
   There is one of these for each record type in the subschema. The current of a given record type will be the last occurrence of that record type that was found or stored.
3. CURRENT OF SET TYPE
   There is one of these for each set type in the subschema. The current of a given set type will be the set occurrence most recently accessed. (You will recall that a set occurrence is actually a chain containing one owner occurrence and many member occurrences.) The pointer will actually point to the last occurrence of either the owner record type or member record type in this set type that was found or stored. Thus, this pointer establishes not only which occurrence of this set is the current of set type but also a position in the set.
4. CURRENT OF REALM
   There is one of these for each realm (or area) in the subschema. The current of a given realm will be the last record of any type that was found or stored *in* that realm. If there is only one realm, the current of realm will always be the same as the current of run-unit.

When we investigate the DML commands, we will see that these commands either use or update (or both) various currency indicators. This is how we **navigate** our way through the database.

For an example of this concept, we will expand on the discussion of currency given in section 8.2 by using the proper terminology and including the current of run unit in our comments. (The current of realm is used infrequently and we will ignore it here.) The statements that are described below are assumed to be processing the database shown in Figure 8.12. It is the same data that was used in the initial example of currency in section 8.2, but the set occurrences are represented realistically as chains instead of bubbles, as they were earlier.

STATEMENT	EFFECT	Current of Record Type FACULTY	Current of Record Type STUDENT	Current of Set Type ADVISES	Current of RUN_UNIT
1. Find faculty JONES	System locates JONES	JONES	—	JONES	JONES (faculty)
2. Find next student in ADVISES set	System locates MARY	JONES	MARY	MARY	MARY (student)
3. Find next student in ADVISES set	System locates TOM	JONES	TOM	TOM	TOM (student)
4. Find next student in ADVISES set	System locates BILL	JONES	BILL	BILL	BILL (student)
5. Find next student in ADVISES set	System shows no more students in set. Currencies do not change.	JONES	BILL	BILL	BILL (student)
6. Find student JOAN	System locates JOAN	JONES	JOAN	JOAN	JOAN (student)
7. Find owner within ADVISES set	System locates SMITH	SMITH	JOAN	SMITH	SMITH (faculty)

In these examples, you may have noticed that the current of run unit was maintained but never used. The reason for this is that we did not encounter any commands that used this indicator. As we study the commands, we will see that several of them do use it.

DB-STATUS

The special register DB–STATUS is really a code used by the system to inform us of any problems that were encountered as the database was being accessed. DB–STATUS is a seven-digit number that is best viewed as a two-digit number followed by a five-digit number. The first two digits indicate the type of statement that was being executed when a problem was encountered. The last five digits indicate the type of problem that occurred. A DB–STATUS of 0502400, for example, would indicate that in the execution of a FIND command no record was found to satisfy the record selection criteria. The following table is indicative of the manner in which the various possibilities for DB–STATUS can be presented. Bear in mind that this is a greatly abridged table showing just the general format. An actual table would have *many* more rows.

	CONNECT	DISCONNECT	ERASE	FIND	FINISH	GET	MODIFY	READY	STORE	
	02	03	04	05	06	08	11	13	15	
02100				X						End of realm or set has been reached.
02400				X						No record found to satisfy record selection.
05100	X						X		X	Contents of data items duplicated on database.
07200			X							Deletion of nonempty set specified.
–										
80200							X		X	Space in realm exhausted.

To read the table, we can go down the columns to see the two-digit codes for the various operations. We see that 05 is FIND and that 03 is DISCONNECT, for example. We read across the rows to see the codes and descriptions for the various problems. We see that 02100 is "End of realm or set has been reached" and 05100 is "Contents of data items duplicated on database," for example. If there is an X at the intersection of a row and column, it means that the combination is a legitimate one. Thus, 0502100 is a meaningful DB–STATUS, whereas 0202100 is not. Note also that some values of DB–STATUS represent conditions that might occur during normal processing and for which we would probably just include an error message on the report. The DB–STATUS 1505100 (Contents of data items duplicated on the database when executing a STORE operation) may mean only that the user tried to enter a customer whose number matched one already on file, for example. Others represent severe problems that would force processing to be terminated and some special action to be taken. Consider, for example, the DB–STATUS 1580200 (Space in realm exhausted)!

LIST OF COMMANDS

The following is a list of DML commands grouped by function. The exact syntax of these commands for use in COBOL will be demonstrated in examples given later in this section.

OPEN AND CLOSE DATABASE

READY   opens the area(s) required by the program. The basic options are RETRIEVAL (read operations only) and UPDATE (both read and write operations are permitted).

FINISH   closes the area(s).

RETRIEVAL

FIND   locates a record subject to some conditions. The record found becomes
current of run unit, current of record type, and current of set type for any set in
which it is either an owner or a member. There are several forms of the FIND
command, the most common of which are discussed at the end of the list of
commands. If no record can be found to meet the conditions, the program is
notified of this fact by an appropriate DB–STATUS and no currencies are
changed.

GET   retrieves the contents of the record identified as the current of run-unit
and places it into the UWA. Note that FIND does not place any data into the user
work area; it merely locates a record. The GET command is necessary to actually place the data in the appropriate fields in the UWA.

OBTAIN   is a combination of a FIND followed by a GET, i.e., data is actually
transferred at the same time the record is located. This command is not available
in all systems.

UPDATE

STORE   creates a new record occurrence at a position determined by the location mode of the record type using the data from the UWA. For any set in which
the record type is a member that has been declared AUTOMATIC, the occurrence
is inserted into the appropriate set occurrence at a position determined by the
set's insertion mode. This new occurrence becomes current of its record type,
current of run unit, and current of set type for any sets into which it has been
inserted. If storing the new occurrence would result in the violation of any
duplicates clause, then the store will *not* take place and the program will be
notified of the rejection by an appropriate DB–STATUS.

MODIFY   updates the current of run unit with data from the UWA.

ERASE   disconnects the current of run unit from occurrences of any set in
which it is a member and deletes the current of run unit, provided that the
current of run unit does not own any member occurrences in any set. (A customer who has orders, for example, would not be deleted.)

ERASE ALL   disconnects the current of run unit from occurrences of any set in
which it is a member and deletes the current of run unit and any members of set
occurrences owned by it. Note that any members deleted in this fashion that are
in turn owners in other set occurrences cause their member occurrences to be
deleted as well, and so on. Deleting a sales rep in the Premiere Products data

base causes all of the customers represented by that sales rep to be deleted. In turn, orders placed by any of these customers are deleted, and so on. A good description of the ERASE in this situation is LOOK OUT BELOW!!! (A customer who has orders, for example, would be deleted, as would all of the orders placed by this customer and all of the order lines on these orders.)

CONNECT   connects the current of run unit into a set occurrence. The record type of the current of run unit must, of course, be a member type for this set.

DISCONNECT   disconnects the current of run unit from a set occurrence. Again, the current of run unit must be a member type for this set. In addition, the set type must have RETENTION OPTIONAL.

RECONNECT   disconnects the current of run unit from one occurrence of a set of a given type and connects it to another occurrence of the same set type. This command is not available in all systems.

FORMS OF THE FIND COMMAND

ANY   locates a CALC record based on the contents of its CALC key. If duplicates have been allowed for this CALC key, the FIND ANY will find the first occurrence whose CALC key matches the value in the UWA. Another form of the same command, FIND DUPLICATE, can then be used to find the others.

NEXT   locates the next member in the indicated set occurrence. The command is actually FIND NEXT WITHIN set-name. The current of set is used to determine the present position and FIND NEXT then causes the next member occurrence within that chain to be located. If the current position happens to be the last member occurrence, no new record is located and the system notifies us of the fact via an appropriate DB-STATUS. Related options of this command are FIND FIRST (find the first member occurrence in the chain, i.e., the occurrence immediately following the owner); FIND LAST (find the last member occurrence in the chain); FIND PRIOR (find the member occurrence prior to the current position); FIND integer (finds the member occurrence in the position indicated by the integer); e.g., FIND 3 would find the third member occurrence in the chain and FIND identifier (identifier must be an integer variable whose contents then function as the integer in the FIND integer version of the command).

OWNER   locates the owner occurrence within the set occurrence of the indicated set. The syntax is FIND OWNER WITHIN set-name.

CURRENT   locates the current of record type. The syntax is F I ND CURRENT record-name. It may seem that this is a do-nothing command. If sales rep 12 is the current sales rep and we say F I ND CURRENT SLSREP, sales rep 12 will still be the current sales rep. It seems as though nothing has happened! Something very important has happened, however. In addition to being the current of record type, sales rep 12 is now also the *current of run unit*. In the examples to come, we will see that in certain situations the current of run unit is not the correct record type for the command that we wish to issue. We can correct this by using the F I ND CURRENT command. The procedure is a little tricky, but don't worry about it, since we will elaborate on the problem and its solution when we encounter it in the examples.

For further discussion of the CODASYL DML, see [1], [2], [9], [10], [11], [12], and [13].

EXAMPLES

We will now examine the use of the above commands through several examples, all of which refer to the database illustrated in Figures 8.14 (data structure diagram), 8.15 (schema DDL), and 8.18 (subschema DDL). For each of these examples, we will assume that the database has been opened in such a way that update is possible. This is accomplished with the following command:

    READY; USAGE-MODE IS UPDATE.

If only retrieval is required, then the syntax would be:

    READY; USAGE-MODE IS RETRIEVAL.

We will also assume that the database is closed when all processing has been completed. This is accomplished with the following command:

    FINISH.

In these the examples, we intentionally employ a greatly oversimplified approach to the use of the special register DB-STATUS. We assume that DB-STATUS is either zero indicating successful execution of the previous command, or not zero, indicating some obvious problem. If the previous command was STORE, for example, and DB-STATUS is not zero, we will assume that the occurrence we were attempting to store violated some duplicates clause, which would happen if we tried to store a second customer 124. As we saw earlier, there are a whole myriad of possibilities for DB-STATUS. In the case of a STORE, it may be that there was no space left in the database to accommodate the new occurrence. Thus, we really should check for a number of different possible values of DB-STATUS rather than just a nonzero value. Furthermore, the action that should be taken will differ, depending on the value of DB-STATUS. Rather than address these complications in the examples given in this chapter, we will defer discussion of them to chapter 9.

THE FIND COMMAND

Example 1: Find individual record occurrence.

STATEMENT: List the number and name of sales rep 12.

After moving 12 to the sales rep number, the CALC key, we attempt to find the sales rep. If the DB–STATUS is not zero, we have encountered an error and should print an error message. If it is zero, we have found the sales rep. The sales rep will now be current of run unit, so the GET command will place the data for that sales rep in the UWA. We now have the number and name of this sales rep and can display them. The code is thus:

```
MOVE 12 TO SLSREP–NUMBER.
FIND ANY SLSREP.
IF DB–STATUS NOT = 0
      print error message - "NO SUCH SALES REP"
   ELSE
      GET
      print SLSREP–NUMBER, SLSREP–NAME.
```

Before moving on to other examples, we need to make some general comments about the way in which the formulations to satisfy the requirements are presented. First of all, as indicated earlier, they are presented in COBOL. If you don't know COBOL, however, you should be able to treat them as just a form of pseudo-code and still obtain an understanding of the logic. Second, there may be some commands given in lowercase letters, such as "print error message". These are *not* COBOL but rather pseudo-code, indicating the task that must be accomplished at that point. It is our feeling that the actual COBOL statements to accomplish these tasks are not at all relevant to the problem at hand and would just tend to obscure the overall logic. If you are familiar with COBOL, the COBOL statements necessary to accomplish these tasks should be obvious to you. Finally, it is, of course, unrealistic to build a specific sales rep number, like 12, into the COBOL program. Were we to do so, it would mean that asking the same question about a different sales rep would require changing the code and recompiling the program. Rather, this sales rep number would be in a variable, say TR–SLSREP–NUMBER (transaction sales rep number), which would be read from a file of transactions or perhaps obtained directly from the user in some on-line session. In each example we will be dealing with specific data, but you should keep in mind that in actual practice we would be working with variables of the type just described.

Example 2: Find occurrences of a one-to-many relationship.

STATEMENT: List the number and name of all of the customers represented by sales rep 6.

We first attempt to find the sales rep, as we did in the previous example. If we are unsuccessful, we will again print an error message. If we are successful, we find all of the customers of this sales rep by repeatedly using the FIND NEXT command. This is accomplished with a priming FIND NEXT command, followed by a loop, which is performed until DB–STATUS is not zero, indicating that the end of the chain has been reached. As long as the DB–STATUS is not zero, we have found another customer. Since this customer would be the current of run unit (it is the last thing that has been found), the GET command will place the data for this customer in the UWA, where we can use it to display the desired information. Once this has been done, we can attempt to find the next customer with another FIND NEXT command. Thus:

```
MOVE 6 TO SLSREP-NUMBER.
FIND ANY SLSREP.
IF DB-STATUS NOT = 0
        print error message - "NO SUCH SALES REP"
ELSE
        FIND NEXT CUSTOMER WITHIN S-SLSREP-CUSTOMER
        PERFORM FIND-AND-DISPLAY-CUSTOMERS
                UNTIL DB-STATUS NOT = 0.
        .
        .
        .
FIND-AND-DISPLAY-CUSTOMERS.
        GET.
        print CUSTOMER-NUMBER, NAME.
        FIND NEXT CUSTOMER WITHIN S-SLSREP-CUSTOMER.
```

Example 3: Find occurrences of a many-to-many relationship.

STATEMENT: Find all of the orders for customer 522. For each order, list the number and date. In addition, for each order line within these orders, list the part number, the description, the quantity ordered, the quoted price, and the actual price.

Basically, the overall structure of this example is the same as that of example 2. In this case, we are finding all the orders related to a given customer instead of all the customers for a given sales rep. Since the overall problem is very similar, we would expect that the top level of logic should also be very similar, and it is. What's different in this example is what happens once we have found an order. Before moving on to another order, we will process all of its order lines by repeatedly using a FIND NEXT until reaching a DB–STATUS other than zero, which would indicate that there are no more order lines for the current order. Provided that we have found an order line, we will find the part that owns it by using the FIND OWNER command. Having done so, we will have gathered all of the required information for the order line: the part number, description, and price are in the PART record, and the number ordered and quoted price are in the ORDER–LINE record. Note that we also have to use the GET command appropriately. The code is:

```
MOVE 522 TO CUSTOMER-NUMBER.
FIND ANY CUSTOMER.
IF DB-STATUS NOT = 0
        print error message - "NO SUCH CUSTOMER"
    ELSE
        FIND NEXT ORDER WITHIN S-CUSTOMER-ORDER
        PERFORM FIND-AND-DISPLAY-ORDERS
            UNTIL DB-STATUS NOT = 0.
        .
        .
        .

FIND-AND-DISPLAY-ORDERS.
    GET.
    print ORDER-NUMBER, DATE.
    FIND NEXT ORDER-LINE WITHIN S-ORDER-ORDER-LINE.
    PERFORM FIND-AND-DISPLAY-ORDER-LINES
        UNTIL DB-STATUS NOT = 0.
    FIND NEXT ORDER WITHIN S-CUSTOMER-ORDER.
        .
        .
        .

FIND-AND-DISPLAY-ORDER-LINES.
    GET.
    FIND OWNER WITHIN S-PART-ORDER-LINE.
    GET.
    print PART-NUMBER, PART-DESCRIPTION,
            NUMBER-ORDERED, QUOTED-PRICE, UNIT-PRICE.
    FIND NEXT ORDER-LINE WITHIN S-ORDER-ORDER-LINE.
```

When the first line in the loop, FIND–AND–DISPLAY–ORDERS, is executed, the last record found is an order (from the FIND NEXT ORDER WITHIN S–CUSTOMER–ORDER). The GET command at the beginning of this loop will thus pull data for the current order into memory. Similarly, the GET command at the beginning of FIND–AND–DISPLAY–ORDER–LINES will pull data for the current ORDER–LINE into memory. The next command will find the part that owns this order line, so the GET command on the third line of FIND–AND–DISPLAY–ORDER–LINES will pull data for this part into memory.

Example 4: Sequentially scan the entire database.

STATEMENT: List the name and number of all customers.

We can find all customers by sequentially processing the entire database, using a version of the FIND NEXT command that allows us to repeatedly find the next customer within the realm. In attempting to find all the customers in the database, the system will encounter records of types other than CUS-

TOMER: sales reps, orders, order lines, and parts. It will skip over these, however, and only stop at customers. To get the process started, we find the first customer in the realm, using the FIND FIRST command. The formulation is:

```
FIND FIRST CUSTOMER WITHIN AREA-DISTRIBUTION.
IF DB-STATUS NOT = 0
        print error message - "NO CUSTOMERS EXIST"
    ELSE
        PERFORM FIND-AND-DISPLAY CUSTOMERS
                UNTIL DB-STATUS NOT = 0.
            .
            .
            .

FIND-AND-DISPLAY-CUSTOMERS.
        GET.
        print CUSTOMER-NUMBER, NAME.
        FIND NEXT CUSTOMER WITHIN AREA-DISTRIBUTION.
```

Note that since we already had located the first customer before beginning the loop, we began the loop with a GET. The final statement in the loop would then attempt to locate the next customer in the area and, if the attempt was successful, the next iteration of the loop would get the data for this customer, and so on.

Example 5: Use of system-owned sets.

STATEMENT: List the name and number of all customers.

There is another alternative to sequentially scanning the entire database to find all customers, and that is the use of a **system-owned set**. This set is described like any other except that the owner is not an actual record type but rather the special reserved word SYSTEM. Such a set is called a **singular set**. There will be only one occurrence of this set type. This occurrence will thus be a single chain that includes all member occurrences. Suppose that we have included such a set, called S-SYSTEM-CUSTOMER, where the owner is SYS-TEM and the member is CUSTOMER. We then have a chain that includes all customers. We could use this chain to answer the above query, as follows:

```
FIND FIRST CUSTOMER WITHIN S-SYSTEM-CUSTOMER.
IF DB-STATUS NOT = 0
        print error message - "NO CUSTOMERS EXIST"
    ELSE
        PERFORM FIND-AND-DISPLAY-CUSTOMERS
                UNTIL DB-STATUS NOT = 0.
            .
            .
            .
```

```
FIND-AND-DISPLAY-CUSTOMERS.
     GET.
     print CUSTOMER-NUMBER, NAME.
     FIND NEXT CUSTOMER WITHIN S-SYSTEM-CUSTOMER.
```

THE STORE COMMAND

Example 6: Store calc record with no owners.

STATEMENT: Store sales rep 14 (name "PAM WALL", address "41 CRANE, ADA, MI", total commission 0.00, commission rate 5 percent).

Since the sales rep record is not a member in any set type, we don't have to worry about establishing currency on any owner occurrence. The only potential problem here is that there might already be a sales rep 14 in the database. Since the sales rep record is CALC with DUPLICATES NOT ALLOWED, the system will not allow a duplicate record to be stored and will indicate through DB-STATUS that the record has been rejected. The code would thus be:

```
fill in all fields within SLSREP record.
STORE SLSREP.
IF DB-STATUS NOT = 0
     print error message - "DUPLICATE SALES REP".
```

Example 7: Store calc record with owners.

STATEMENT: Store customer 191 (name "PAUL SMITH", address "112 LONG, HART, MI", balance 0.00, credit limit $500, sales rep 3).

We do have to be concerned with storing a duplicate occurrence, as in example 6, but we have another problem here. The CUSTOMER record is the member record type in the set S-SLSREP-CUSTOMER. We thus have to ensure that we are current on the correct owner occurrence, in this case sales rep 3. We first attempt to establish this currency. If we are not successful, we will issue an error message and will not complete the transaction. If we are successful, we will then attempt to store the customer. If this is rejected as a duplicate, we will again issue an error message. Thus, the code is:

```
MOVE 3 TO SLSREP-NUMBER.
FIND ANY SLSREP.
IF DB-STATUS NOT = 0
     print error message "NO SUCH SALES REP"
   ELSE
     fill in all fields in CUSTOMER record
     STORE CUSTOMER
     IF DB-STATUS = 0
          print error message - "DUPLICATE CUSTOMER".
```

Storing an ORDER record is very similar to storing a CUSTOMER record since it, too, is the member record type within a set. Storing a PART record is similar to storing a SLSREP record since it is not the member type in any set. The link record, ORDER–LINE, is different in two ways: it is the member record type in two different set types and it is stored VIA SET instead of CALC. The fact that it is a member in more than one set type does not pose any special problem; we would merely establish currency on *all* of the appropriate owner occurrences. The fact that it is stored VIA SET (which is usually true of link records) does mean that our approach will be significantly different. The process for handling these link records is illustrated in examples 13 through 16.

THE MODIFY COMMAND

Example 8: Update data field.

STATEMENT: Change the name of customer 587 to "JUDY CLARK".

The command to change existing data, MODIFY, acts upon the current of run unit. We must thus establish customer 587 as the current of run unit. If we are successful, we can obtain the current data by using the GET command (which also acts upon the current of run unit), fill in any fields to be changed with new information, and then MODIFY the record. The formulation is:

```
MOVE 587 TO CUSTOMER-NUMBER.
FIND ANY CUSTOMER.
IF DB-STATUS NOT = 0
      print error message - "NO SUCH CUSTOMER"
    ELSE
      GET
      MOVE "JUDY CLARK" TO NAME
      MODIFY.
```

THE ERASE AND ERASE ALL COMMANDS

Example 9: Unconditional deletion.

STATEMENT: Delete order 12491 and any order lines within this order.

The ERASE command will delete a record occurrence. It acts upon the current of run unit, so we must establish order 12491 as current of run unit. In order to also have all members (in this case all of the corresponding order lines) deleted, we use the ERASE ALL MEMBERS form of the command. Thus, we have:

```
MOVE 12491 TO ORDER-NUMBER.
FIND ANY ORDER.
IF DB-STATUS NOT = 0
      print error message - "NO SUCH ORDER"
    ELSE
      ERASE ALL MEMBERS.
```

Example 10: Conditional deletion.

STATEMENT: Delete customer 405, provided he or she has no orders on file. If the customer does have orders on file, do not delete; print an error message indicating this fact.

The difference between this example and example 9 is that here, if there are any members (ORDERs), we do not want the owner (CUSTOMER) of the set (S–CUSTOMER–ORDER) to be deleted. This is exactly what will be accomplished by the ERASE command if we do *not* include the ALL MEMBERS clause. If a customer has orders, he or she will not be deleted, and the system will inform us of this through an appropriate DB–STATUS. Thus:

```
MOVE 405 TO CUSTOMER-NUMBER.
FIND ANY CUSTOMER.
IF DB-STATUS NOT = 0
      print error message - "NO SUCH CUSTOMER"
    ELSE
      ERASE
      IF DB-STATUS NOT = 0
            print error message - "CUSTOMER HAS ORDERS".
```

THE CONNECT AND DISCONNECT COMMANDS

Example 11: Disconnecting a record occurrence from a set occurrence.

STATEMENT: Change the sales rep for customer 124 to null, i.e., this customer no longer has a sales rep.

Since the RETENTION is OPTIONAL within the set S–SLSREP–CUSTOMER, it is indeed possible to disconnect the customer. The disconnect command acts upon the current of run unit, so we first establish customer 124 as current of run unit. We then attempt to disconnect the customer from the set occurrence in which the customer currently resides. If the customer has already been disconnected, we will receive an appropriate DB–STATUS. The code will be:

```
MOVE 124 TO CUSTOMER-NUMBER.
FIND ANY CUSTOMER.
IF DB-STATUS NOT = 0
      print error message - "NO SUCH CUSTOMER"
    ELSE
      DISCONNECT FROM S-SLSREP-CUSTOMER
      IF DB-STATUS NOT = 0
            print error message - "ALREADY DISCONNECTED".
```

Example 12: Connecting a record occurrence to a set occurrence.

STATEMENT: Assign customer 124 to sales rep 12.

To connect a record occurrence to a set occurrence, the desired set occurrence must be current of set type and the desired record occurrence must be current of run unit. Note that in the logic that follows, we first attempt to find the customer. If we are unsuccessful, we will issue an error message and will not complete the transaction. If we are successful, we will attempt to establish currency for the set type by finding the sales rep (the owner record type within S–SLSREP–CUSTOMER). If we are successful here, we will have put all of the pieces in place except for the fact that customer 124 is *no longer the current of run unit*. Sales rep 12 is. Customer 124, however, is still the current of record type for the CUSTOMER record. The FIND CURRENT command can be used to reestablish customer 124 as current of run unit. That having been done, we would be ready to issue the CONNECT command. The code for this is:

```
MOVE 124 TO CUSTOMER-NUMBER.
FIND ANY CUSTOMER.
IF DB-STATUS NOT = 0
      print error message - "NO SUCH CUSTOMER"
   ELSE
      MOVE 12 TO SLSREP-NUMBER
      FIND ANY SLSREP
      IF DB-STATUS-NOT = 0
           print error message - "NO SUCH SALES REP"
        ELSE
           FIND CURRENT CUSTOMER
           CONNECT TO S-SLSREP-CUSTOMER
           IF DB-STATUS NOT = 0
                print error message - "ALREADY CONNECTED".
```

PROCESSING LINK RECORDS

Example 13: Locating a link record.

STATEMENT: Find the number of units of part BZ66 that were ordered on order 12491.

Since the ORDER-LINE record has no key, we cannot find it directly and we must look for it. We can do this in one of two ways. We can first find order 12491 and then examine each order line it owns (within S–ORDER–ORDER–LINE) in turn, looking at the part that owns this order line (within S–PART–ORDER–LINE) to see whether it is BZ66. Alternatively, we can first find part BZ66, then examine each order line that it owns (within S–PART–ORDER–LINE) to see whether any of them are owned by order 12491 (within S–ORDER–ORDER–LINE). (You might want to look back at the example about students and courses earlier in this chapter and ask yourself how you would find the grade for Mary in MTH 110. The logic is the same.) In theory, it doesn't matter which of these approaches we choose; they will both work. In practice, however, it may very well be *much* more efficient to choose one over the other. If an average order contained three order lines but an average part were found on five hundred orders, for example, substantial benefits would accrue from employing the first alternative. We would have three member occurrences to examine as opposed to five hundred! This is the direction that has been chosen for the following:

```
MOVE 12491 TO ORDER-NUMBER.
FIND ANY ORDER.
IF DB-STATUS NOT = 0
        print error message - "NO SUCH ORDER"
    ELSE
        MOVE "NO" TO IS-THERE-A-MATCH
        FIND NEXT ORDER-LINE
            WITHIN S-ORDER-ORDER-LINE
        PERFORM FIND-ORDER-LINE
                UNTIL THERE-IS-A-MATCH
                OR DB-STATUS NOT = 0
        IF THERE-IS-A-MATCH
                FIND CURRENT ORDER-LINE
                GET
                print NUMBER-ORDERED.
                .
                .
                .

FIND-ORDER-LINE.
        FIND OWNER WITHIN S-PART-ORDER-LINE.
        GET.
        IF PART-NUMBER = "BZ66"
                MOVE "YES" TO IS-THERE-A-MATCH
            ELSE
                FIND NEXT ORDER-LINE
                    WITHIN S-ORDER-ORDER LINE.
```

Example 14: Adding a link record.

STATEMENT: Add an order line for order 12491 for part AX12 with ten units ordered and a quoted price of $16.95.

This process may seem to be a relatively simple one: find the order and the part that will own this order line and then (provided both order and part exist) fill in the order-line fields and store the record. There is a problem with this logic, however. In our example, if there already is an order-line occurrence with the same order number and part number, we should *not* store another. Could we just try to store the new occurrence and assume that the system will reject it if it is a duplicate, as we did with sales reps? In general, the answer is no. In order for the DBMS to reject a new occurrence as a duplicate, there must be a duplicates clause somewhere which states that duplicates are not allowed. As we have seen, there are two places where this can occur in the schema: in calc records, new occurrences that would duplicate the calc key of an existing record can be rejected, and in sorted sets, new occurrences that would duplicate the sort key of an existing record in the same set occurrence would be rejected. Is either of these possibilities relevant to our present discussion? To find the answers let's examine each one in turn.

In order to reject a record based on the calc key, there must be a calc key. In the case of ORDER–L I NE, the only two fields are NUMBER–ORDERED and QUOTED–PR I CE. It would certainly be strange if either of these were the calc key. Even if we chose to make one of these, say, NUMBER–ORDERED, as a calc key and reject duplicates, the record that was rejected would have the same NUMBER–ORDERED as an existing occurrence in the database! This is not the kind of duplication that concerns us.

In order to reject a record based on a sort key, some set in which the record is a member must be sorted. If we chose to sort the set S–ORDER–ORDER– L I NE, for example, the problem that arose in choosing a CALC key would be repeated: the only fields available would be NUMBER–ORDERED and QUOTED– PR I CE. If we chose to sort on NUMBER–ORDERED and reject duplicates, we would now reject a new ORDER–L I NE occurrence if its NUMBER–ORDERED value matched an existing record in the same set occurrence, i.e., another order line in the same order. This is not what we want either.

If the system will not detect duplicates, then the responsibility for doing so falls on our shoulders (unfortunately). This means that before we store a new order line, we must ensure that no order line for the same order and part combination already exists. In example 11, we found the number ordered and quoted price on an order line, given the order number and part number. The logic in that solution would also tell us if there were no such order line. In particular, if you examine the logic, you will see that the flag, I S–MATCH– FOUND, will be "NO" in the event that no such order line exists. This gives us the basis for the solution to the current problem.

We can use the same logic that we used in the solution to example 13 up to the point where we are attempting to find the number ordered and quoted price, i.e., the logic that reads

```
IF  THERE– I S–A–MATCH
        F I ND  CURRENT  ORDER–L I NE
        GET
        print NUMBER–ORDERED .
```

In the current problem we *do not* want a match. If there is a match, we have a duplicate and should reject the new occurrence. If there is no match, then we can store the new occurrence. We must first be current on the appropriate order and part. Since we found the correct order at the beginning of the process and never found another, we are current on the appropriate order. We are not current on the correct part, however; we are current on the part that owned the last of the line items. Thus we must establish currency on the correct part. Once this has been done, we can fill in the order-line fields and store the new order line. The logic for doing this would be:

```
IF THERE-IS-NOT-A-MATCH
       MOVE AX12 TO PART-NUMBER
       FIND ANY PART
       IF DB-STATUS NOT = 0
              print error message - "NO SUCH PART"
          ELSE
              fill in order line fields
              STORE ORDER-LINE.
```

Example 15: Modifying a link record.

STATEMENT: Change the number ordered on the order line for order 12491, part BZ66 to 3.

Now we have a problem similar to the one encountered in example 14. Since the order line has no key, we cannot find the desired order line directly. Instead, we must search for it ourselves. Again, the necessary logic is in the solution to example 13. There, if the desired order line existed, we merely wanted to get the number ordered and print the result. You will recall that to do the GET, the record had to be the current of run unit and it *was not* (the part that owned it was). So we first had to do a FIND CURRENT to establish the order line as current of run unit. The same problem faces us here, since the command to change data, MODIFY, also acts upon the current of run unit. Therefore, that portion of the solution to example 13 which reads as follows:

```
IF THERE-IS-A-MATCH
       FIND CURRENT ORDER-LINE
       GET
       print NUMBER-ORDERED.
```

would be changed to

```
IF THERE-IS-A-MATCH
       FIND CURRENT ORDER-LINE
       GET
       MOVE 3 TO NUMBER-ORDERED
       MODIFY.
```

Note that the GET is still necessary, since there is a field, QUOTED-PRICE, that is to retain its old value. If we did not have the GET, the quoted price for this occurrence in the database would be changed to whatever value was currently sitting in the field QUOTED-PRICE in the UWA.

Example 16: Deleting a link record.

STATEMENT: Delete the order line for order 12498, part BA74.

This problem is virtually the same as the one in example 13. Here, we want to delete a record (ERASE) instead of changing it (MODIFY), but we still have to find the record ourselves, and it still has to be the current of run unit. Thus, instead of:

```
IF THERE-IS-A-MATCH
      FIND CURRENT ORDER-LINE
      GET
      MOVE 3 TO NUMBER-ORDERED
      MODIFY.
```

we would have:

```
IF THERE-IS-A-MATCH
       FIND CURRENT ORDER-LINE
       ERASE.
```

Note that there is no need here for the GET, nor is there a need to fill in NUMBER-ORDERED, since the record is to be deleted.

DATABASE NAVIGATION

Example 17: Navigating the database.

STATEMENT: Determine whether part BT04 is included on an order placed by any customer represented by sales rep 3.

This request involves traveling through the entire database. We begin by locating part BT04. If the part does not exist, we will issue an error message and terminate our processing. If it does exist, we examine in turn each order line that it owns (within S-PART-ORDER-LINE). For each of these order lines we find first the order that owns it (within S-ORDER-ORDER-LINE), followed by the customer who owns the order (within S-CUSTOMER-ORDER), and finally the sales rep who owns the customer (within S-SLSREP-CUSTOMER). Once we have found the sales rep, we can use the GET command to pull the sales rep data into the UWA, where we can check to see whether the sales rep number is 3. If it is, we can terminate the process and print the answer "YES". If it is not, the process continues. When we have examined all of the order lines owned by the part without ever encountering sales rep 3, we can print the answer "NO". The code is thus:

```
MOVE "BT04" TO PART-NUMBER.
FIND ANY PART.
IF DB-STATUS NOT = 0
      print error message - "NO SUCH PART"
   ELSE
      MOVE "NO" TO IS-MATCH-FOUND
      FIND NEXT ORDER-LINE WITHIN S-PART-ORDER-LINE
      PERFORM FIND-AND-CHECK-ORDER-LINES
          UNTIL DB-STATUS NOT = 0
          OR MATCH-FOUND
      IF MATCH-FOUND
          print "YES"
        ELSE
          print "NO".
      .
      .
      .

FIND-AND-CHECK-ORDER-LINES.
      FIND OWNER WITHIN S-ORDER-ORDER-LINE.
      FIND OWNER WITHIN S-CUSTOMER-ORDER.
      FIND OWNER WITHIN S-SLSREP-CUSTOMER.
      GET.
      IF SLSREP-NUMBER = 3
          MOVE "YES" TO IS-MATCH-FOUND
          FIND NEXT ORDER-LINE
              WITHIN S-PART-ORDER-LINE.
```

UPDATING MULTIPLE OCCURRENCES

Example 18: Updating member occurrences.

STATEMENT: Change all credit limits to $800 for customers of sales rep 3 whose credit limit is now $500 and whose balance is not over their credit limit.

We first attempt to locate sales rep 3. If we are unsuccessful, we issue an error message. If we are successful, we can step through each customer owned by sales rep 3 (within S-SLSREP-CUSTOMER) until reaching the end of the chain, in which case DB-STATUS will not be zero. For each customer we encounter, we will check whether he or she meets the desired criteria: a credit limit of $500 and a balance that does not exceed the credit limit. If he or she does fulfill these conditions, then we move the new credit limit into the UWA and modify the record.

```
MOVE 3 TO SLSREP-NUMBER.
FIND ANY SLSREP.
IF DB-STATUS NOT = 0
      print error message - "NO SUCH SALES REP"
   ELSE
      FIND NEXT CUSTOMER WITHIN S-SLSREP-CUSTOMER
      PERFORM FIND-AND-MODIFY-CUSTOMERS
            UNTIL DB-STATUS NOT = 0.
          .
          .
          .

FIND-AND-MODIFY-CUSTOMERS.
      GET.
      IF CREDIT-LIMIT = 500
            AND BALANCE NOT > CREDIT-LIMIT
            MOVE 800 TO CREDIT-LIMIT
            MODIFY.
      FIND NEXT CUSTOMER WITHIN S-SLSREP-CUSTOMER.
```

Example 19: Updating all occurrences of a given record type.

STATEMENT: Change all credit limits to $800 for all customers whose credit limit is $500 and whose balance is not over their credit limit.

Example 3 demonstrated the logic of processing all customers within the database. Although in that example we only retrieved data, the same process could be used for update. The logic for the update would be:

```
FIND FIRST CUSTOMER WITHIN AREA-DISTRIBUTION.
IF DB-STATUS NOT = 0
      print error message - "NO CUSTOMERS"
   ELSE
      PERFORM FIND-AND-MODIFY-CUSTOMERS
            UNTIL DB-STATUS NOT = 0.
          .
          .
          .

FIND-AND-MODIFY-CUSTOMERS.
      GET.
      IF CREDIT-LIMIT = 500
            AND BALANCE NOT > CREDIT-LIMIT
            MOVE 800 TO CREDIT-LIMIT
            MODIFY.
      FIND NEXT CUSTOMER WITHIN AREA-DISTRIBUTION.
```

You will recall that example 4 demonstrated an approach to processing all customers in the event of a system-owned set in which the CUSTOMER record was the member record type. That same logic would apply equally well here.

5   CHANGES IN THE 1978-1981 SPECIFICATIONS

The 1971–1973 specifications and most commercial CODASYL DBMS's do not fully support the three levels of schema described in the ANSI/SPARC model; consequently, they do not attain the level of data independence that is the goal of that model. The later specifications (see [3], [4], [5], and [7]) pushed the CODASYL model further in the direction of ANSI/SPARC by removing some of the physical aspects from the schema DDL and placing them in a separate facility. Some additional facilities were defined in the later specifications as well.

The 1978 specifications called for a *DATA STORAGE DESCRIPTION LANGUAGE* (DSDL), which included the Device Media Control Language (DMCL) from the earlier specifications as well as many new options. This language is used to specify the internal schema (using the ANSI/SPARC terminology), i.e., to specify the mapping from the logical schema to physical storage. The portions of the 1971 schema DDL that were moved to the DSDL are some of those that described physical characteristics of the database, such things as the location mode of a record (CALC vs. VIA SET). In addition, more options are available than in the DMCL, including the ability to specify different types of indexes, the ability to split a record that is described as a single record in the DDL into two or more storage records in the physical database to improve performance, and so on.

The main changes that we will discuss here, however, concern the DDL. As we said before, the location mode of a record is no longer specified in the DDL. In addition, there is a new clause, the RECORD KEY clause, in the record entry which allows us to specify that one or more data items can be used as keys for the purpose of accessing record occurrences. A record key is specified as follows:

```
RECORD NAME IS SLSREP
     KEY SLSREP_NUMBER IS ASCENDING SLSREP_NUMBER
     DUPLICATES ARE NOT ALLOWED FOR SLSREP_NUMBER.
```

or just

```
RECORD NAME IS SLSREP
     DUPLICATES ARE NOT ALLOWED FOR SLSREP_NUMBER.
```

Basically, this indicates that no two occurrences of the SLSREP record will be allowed to have the same SLSREP–NUMBER. It also gives us the basis for using the SLSREP–NUMBER as a key to locate a specific occurrence. There is a corresponding DML command to do this:

```
FIND ANY SLSREP USING SLSREP-NUMBER.
```

Many of these keys can be declared within the same record type. We could choose to allow duplicates for some of them. We might state in the CUSTOMER record, for example, that

```
DUPLICATES ARE LAST FOR NAME.
```

This allows more than one customer to have the same name. It also allows us to find a customer rapidly, based on his or her name.

The STRUCTURAL CONSTRAINT clause is a new clause in the set entry that can be used when the member record type contains as one of its fields the key of the owner record type. In this instance, we can use the STRUCTURAL CON-STRAINT clause to ensure that the two match. If we include in the CUSTOMER record, for example, the number of the sales rep who "owns" that customer, we could use the STRUCTURAL CONSTRAINT clause to make sure that a customer who is owned by sales rep 6 will not have a 3 in the sales rep field on the customer's record. In this example, the clause would read:

```
STRUCTURAL CONSTRAINT
    SLSREP_NUMBER OF CUSTOMER EQUAL TO
    SLSREP_NUMBER OF SLSREP.
```

Two additional changes to the set entry are worth noting. The membership class FIXED is added as an option to the MANDATORY and OPTIONAL set membership classes. We have already discussed this, since it is a feature of some existing systems (even though it was not technically part of the 1971 specifications). The other change is that a record type can now be *both* an owner record type *and* a member record type *in the same set*. This type of set is called a **recursive set** and will be described in chapter 9 as one of the advanced topics within the CODASYL model. The earlier specifications did not allow this type of set.

While all of the preceding changes enhance the CODASYL model, it is unclear whether they will find their way into commercial systems. The level of data independence has certainly been improved by these changes, but it is still not on a par with that of relational model systems. A program still must navigate the database and thus must know all of the predefined paths (sets). A change of any substance to these predefined paths can require a major rewrite of the programs that access the database. Many CODASYL systems do offer query languages which are far less procedural than COBOL and which allow users to avoid much of the database navigation, but these languages are not standard (CODASYL did not propose specifications for a standard query language), nor are they appropriate for all applications.

8.6 SUMMARY

In this chapter, we have studied one of the major models for database management systems, the CODASYL model. CODASYL (COnference on DAta SYstems Languages) appointed a task group, called the Data Base Task Group (DBTG) to develop a set of specifications for DBMS's. The report of this task group was formally presented in 1971. While these specifications were not adopted as a national standard, a number of commercial systems developed which adhered to them. Such systems are usually called CODASYL systems or DBTG systems. They fall within the general network model for DBMS's, i.e., their underlying data structures are simple networks. Even though some network model systems definitely do not follow the CODASYL specifications, the term CODASYL has come to be synonymous with the network model for many people. Thus, if different people say they have a CODASYL system or a DBTG system or a network model system, they often mean the same thing.

The terms record and field are used within CODASYL systems just as they are used in ordinary processing. It is important to distinguish between a structure itself and a specific example of the structure, and we do this through the word *type* which refers to the structure, and the word *occurrence*, which refers to a specific example of the structure. Thus, we can speak of a record of type STUDENT, which contains fields of type STUDENT–NUMBER and NAME, and an occurrence of the STUDENT record, such as the following:

123	JOHN SMITH

Relationships are maintained in CODASYL systems by means of a construction called a set. A set type is a one-to-many association between record types. The record type that forms the "one" part of the association is called the owner record type, and the record type that forms the "many" part of the association is called the member record type. An occurrence of the set type is a single occurrence of the owner record type together with the many occurrences of the member record type that are related to it.

The schema is the overall logical structure of the database. It is conveyed to the computer through a language called the schema data definition language (or schema DDL). Physical aspects of the database are conveyed through the schema device/media control language (DMCL). A subschema is an individual user view of the database. It is conveyed through the subschema DDL. Since programs access the database through subschemas, various forms of the subschema DDL are tailored to different languages. The form presented here is tailored to COBOL.

Programs accessing the database do so through the normal commands present in the language in which the program is written and through additional commands specific to the processing of the database. These commands constitute the data manipulation language (DML). In CODASYL, these commands include CONNECT, DISCONNECT, ERASE, FIND, GET, MODIFY, STORE, and so on. The CODASYL DML is built around a concept called currency. A variety of currency indicators or conceptual pointers are used to keep track of our position within the database. There is a currency indicator for each record type that indicates the last record of the same type that was accessed. There is another for each set type which indicates not only which occurrence of that set type was last accessed but also its position within that set occurrence. There is also a currency indicator for the run unit (program) that indicates the last record of *any* type that was accessed. Various DML commands use and/or update these currency indicators.

While most commercial CODASYL systems follow the standards of the 1971 report (to which minor modifications were added in 1973), subsequent reports (1978, 1981) have proposed some significant changes to the model. Some physical characteristics have been moved from the DDL to the new Data Storage Description Language (DSDL), which also encompasses the DMCL from the earlier report. New clauses have been added to both the record and set entries. Whether these changes will find their way into existing commercial systems is uncertain.

In the next chapter, we will look at some advanced topics concerning the CODASYL model. We will also examine one of the major commercial CODASYL systems, IDMS, a product of the Cullinet Corporation.

REVIEW QUESTIONS

1. Define the following and explain the relationship between them: CODASYL, DBTG, and DDLC.
2. Explain the difference between a record type and a record occurrence. Give an example of each.
3. Define the term SET as it is used within the CODASYL model. What purpose does this construction serve? Explain the difference between a set type and a set occurrence.
4. Define owner record type. Define member record type. What is the relationship between the number of owner occurrences and the number of set occurrences, if any? What is the relationship between the number of member occurrences and the number of set occurrences, if any?
5. What is a schema?
6. What is a subschema? What is the relationship between a schema and a subschema?
7. Define and briefly describe DDL, DML, and DMCL.
8. Describe LOCATION MODE. What is the difference between a location mode of CALC and a location mode of VIA SET? What factors would we consider in determining which of these two location modes to choose for a given record type?
9. Describe the effect of the SET IS PRIOR PROCESSABLE clause within the SET ENTRY. What are the benefits of picking this clause? What are the drawbacks?
10. Describe the INSERTION mode. Describe the differences between insertions modes of FIRST, LAST, NEXT, PRIOR, SORTED, and IMMATERIAL.
11. Describe the storage class. Describe the difference between the storage classes AUTO-MATIC and MANUAL.
12. Describe the removal class. Describe the differences between the removal classes MANDATORY and OPTIONAL.
13. Describe the effect of the LINKED TO OWNER clause. What are the benefits of picking this clause? What are the drawbacks?
14. What purpose does the UWA serve when processing a CODASYL database? What does it contain?
15. Define DB-STATUS. How is this used within programs that access CODASYL databases?

16. Define currency indicator. Describe the various types of currency indicators that are available. How are they used?
17. What is the current of run unit? List the commands that act upon the current of run unit. List the commands that will change it.
18. Describe the DSDL of the 1978 specifications. What is its relationship to the DDL and DMCL of the earlier specifications?

EXERCISES

1. Suppose that a department may have many employees working in it and each employee may work in many departments. Draw a data structure diagram showing how we would implement this many-to-many relationship within the CODASYL model. In which of your record types would you place the following fields:
   a. Employee name
   b. Department number
   c Starting date (the date an employee began working for a department)
   d. Job description
2. A given user is concerned only with the ORDER and CUSTOMER records. Within the ORDER record, the only field required is the order number, which is to be called ORD–NUM. Within the CUSTOMER record, which is to be called CUST, the only fields required are the customer's number, name, and address. The set, S_CUSTOMER_ORDER, is also required for this user but is to be called "PLACED". Write the subschema for this user.
   Exercises 3 through 7 are based on the following information:
   A database is needed to satisfy these seven requirements:
   a. For a department, store its number (three digits) and name (twenty characters).
   b. For an employee, store his or her number (four digits) and name (twenty characters).
   c. For an insurance plan, store the plan number (four digits) and description (twenty characters).
   d. For a job history record, store the job classification (twenty characters) and the starting date.
   e. Each department can employ many employees but each employee works in exactly one department.
   f. Each insurance plan serves many employees but each employee is served by exactly one plan.
   g. Each employee can have several job history records but each job history record corresponds to exactly one employee.
3. Draw a data structure diagram for the database. Indicate the fields that would be a part of each record.
4. Write the schema DDL. Make whatever choices seem reasonable for LOCATION MODE, INSERTION, storage, and removal classes and indicate the effect of your choices.

5. What effect would the following four additional requirements have on the choices that you made?
    a. An employee does not have to have an insurance plan.
    b. An employee must be in a department but is allowed to change from one department to another.
    c. When employees are printed by department, the order in which they appear should be the reverse of the order in which they have been placed in the database.
    d. When employees are printed by insurance plan, they should be listed alphabetically.

6. Give a full subschema (a subschema encompassing all records, fields, and sets) for the above schema.

7. Give a partial subschema for a user needing the department record (called DEPT), the employee record (called EMP), and the set between them (called EMPLOYS).
    In exercises 8 through 23, write the code that will accomplish the required task. This code may be written in COBOL or pseudo-code. An appropriate error message should be displayed for any problems that may arise. (The questions refer to the Premiere Products database.)

8. List the description and the number of units on hand for part BT04.

9. List the order number and date for all orders placed by customer 124.

10. If customer 124 currently has part BT04 on order, print "YES". If not, print "NO".

11. List the part number and description of all parts.

12. Store part BT05 (description "RANGE", units on hand 12, item class "AP", warehouse number 2, price $450).

13. Store order 12506 (date — 9/05/87, customer — 412).

14. Change the description of part CA14 to "PAN".

15. Delete part CX11 only if there are no orders for this part.

16. Delete part CZ81 and any associated order lines.

17. Change the sales rep number for customer 256 to 12.

18. Add an order line for order 12491, part CA14 (number ordered 1, quoted price $19.95). If an order line for order 12491, part CA14 already exists, do *not* add this new order line.

19. Change the quoted price on the order line for order 12498, part AZ52, to $22.00.

20. Delete the order line for order 12504, part CZ81.

21. Determine whether sales rep 6 represents any customers who currently have any orders on file for any parts located in warehouse 2. If so, print "YES". If not, print "NO" (a highly useful query if there ever was one).

22. Change the quoted price on any order line for part BZ66 to $311.95.

23. Change the warehouse number for any part currently in warehouse 2 to 5.

24. ***** COMPUTER PROJECT *****
    If you have access to a CODASYL DBMS, do the following:
    a. Create a schema for your system for the Premiere Products database.
    b. Create a full subschema for your system for this database.
    c. Create the partial subschema described in the text for your system.

d. Using the full subschema, write a program to populate the database (i.e., load data into the database). The input to this program should come from five separate files: SLSREP, CUSTOMER, ORDER, ORDER_LINE, and PART. The record layouts for each of these files is shown in Figure 8.20. The program should first add all of the sales reps, followed by the customers, orders, parts, and order lines in this order.

```
01   SLSREP.
     02   SLSREP-NUMBER        PIC 9(2).
     02   SLSREP-NAME          PIC X(20).
     02   SLSREP-ADDRESS       PIC X(20).
     02   TOTAL-COMMISSION     PIC 9(5)V9(2).
     02   COMMISSION-RATE      PIC V9(2).

01   CUSTOMER.
     02   CUSTOMER-NUMBER      PIC 9(3).
     02   NAME                 PIC X(20).
     02   ADDRESS              PIC X(20).
     02   CURRENT-BALANCE      PIC 9(5)V9(2).
     02   CREDIT-LIMIT         PIC 9(5).
     02   SLSREP-NUMBER        PIC 9(2).

01   ORDER.
     02   ORDER-NUMBER         PIC 9(5).
     02   ORDER-DATE           PIC 9(6).
     02   CUSTOMER-NUMBER      PIC 9(3).

01   PART.
     02   PART-NUMBER          PIC X(4).
     02   PART-DESCRIPTION     PIC X(20).
     02   UNITS-ON-HAND        PIC 9(4).
     02   ITEM-CLASS           PIC X(2).
     02   WAREHOUSE-NUMBER     PIC 9(2).
     02   UNIT-PRICE           PIC 9(4)V9(2).

01   ORDER-LINE.
     02   NUMBER-ORDERED       PIC 9(4).
     02   QUOTED-PRICE         PIC 9(4)V9(2).
     02   ORDER-NUMBER         PIC 9(5).
     02   PART-NUMBER          PIC X(4).
```

FIGURE 8.20
Record layout for update files

Note that there are some additional fields that do not appear in the corresponding records in the schema and subschema. These are present for the purpose of identifying appropriate owner occurrences. In the CUSTOMER record, for example, the SLSREP_ NUMBER is present to allow us to identify the appropriate set occurrence within S_ SLSREP_CUSTOMER.

e. Create the files required for part d, using the data found in the tables for the relational model implementation of the Premiere Products database (see Figure 3.1). Using the program created in part d, add this data to the database.

f. Write a program (or programs) to do the queries and updates described in exercises 8 through 23.

g. If your system has a query language associated with it, write programs using this query language to accomplish as many of the queries described in exercises 8 through 23 as your system will handle.

REFERENCES

1] Bradley, James. *Introduction to Data Base Management in Business*. Holt, Rinehart & Winston, 1983.

2] Cardenas, Alfonso F. *Data Base Management Systems*, 2d ed. Allyn & Bacon, 1984.

3] CODASYL COBOL Committee. *Journal of Development*. 1978. Available from ACM.

4] CODASYL COBOL Committee. *Journal of Development*. 1981. Available from ACM.

5] CODASYL Data Description Language Committee. *DDL Journal of Development*. 1978. Available from ACM.

6] CODASYL Data Description Language Committee. *Journal of Development*. 1973. Available from ACM.

7] CODASYL Data Description Language Committee. *Journal of Development*. 1981. Available from ACM.

8] Data Base Task Group of CODASYL Programming Language Committee. *Report*. 1971. Available from ACM.

9] Date, C. J. *Introduction to Database Systems, Volume I*, 4th ed. Addison-Wesley, 1986.

10] Kroenke, David. *Database Processing*, 2d ed. SRA, 1983.

11] McFadden, Fred R., and Hoffer, Jeffrey A. *Data Base Management*. Benjamin Cummings, 1985.

12] Olle, T. W. *The CODASYL Approach to Data Base Management*. Wiley-Interscience, 1978.

13] Vasta, Joseph A. *Understanding Data Base Management Systems*. Wadsworth, 1985.

CHAPTER 9

CODASYL MODEL II — ADVANCED TOPICS AND IMPLEMENTATION

.1 INTRODUCTION

In this chapter, we continue our study of the CODASYL model. We will begin in section 9.2 by investigating some advanced concepts within the general model. We will look at the use of declaratives to facilitate handling errors in COBOL. We will examine multimember sets, i.e., sets with more than one member record *type*. We will expand on the discussion in chapter 8 of manual sets, system-owned sets, and sorted sets. We will see that it is possible to prevent currencies from being updated in the manner discussed in chapter 8, and we will learn how to save a position using the special ACCEPT command. We will examine two new options within the IF statement. We will also examine the bill-of-materials structure presented in chapter 5 to see how it is implemented within the CODASYL model.

Much of the remainder of chapter 9 will be devoted to IDMS, a major implementation of the CODASYL model which is marketed by Cullinet Software, Inc. In section 9.3, we present an overview of IDMS. In section 9.4, we discuss the data definition facilities of IDMS and the actual physical layout of an IDMS database. Data manipulation is covered in section 9.5. The current version of IDMS is actually called IDMS/R, with the "R" standing for relational. Relational capabilities have been added to IDMS; this is covered in section 9.6. Finally, in section 9.7, we discuss the way in which IDMS provides the capabilities of a DBMS described in chapter 2.

In section 9.8, we compare the CODASYL and relational models. We examine the strengths and weaknesses of each of these approaches, and we discuss the role each plays in today's computing and is likely to play in tomorrow's.

.2 ADVANCED TOPICS

DECLARATIVES

In the examples of data manipulation in chapter 8, we checked in a number of situations to see whether the DB−STATUS was zero. In example 1, after attempting to find sales rep 12, if the DB–STATUS was not zero we issued a message stating that the given sales rep did not exist in the database. In example 7, after attempting to store customer 191, if the DB–STATUS was not zero we issued a message indicating that a customer 191 already existed in the database. This approach is quite simplistic and it overlooks a number of other possibilities. While it is true that the nonzero DB–STATUS 1505100 would indicate the existence of a duplicate customer, the nonzero DB–STATUS 1580200 would indicate something entirely different, namely, that *there is no more space left in the database*. The nonzero DB–STATUS 1505200 would indicate that we are trying to store invalid data, e.g., a nonnumeric balance. Obviously, it is not appropriate to put out a message indicating that a customer with the same number already exists unless the DB–STATUS is specifically 1505100. Other action must be taken in the event that the DB–STATUS is different.

After each interaction with the database, we should check for all the possible errors that may have occurred and, if we find any, make sure we take appropriate action, depending on the type of error we encountered. In some cases, such action will mean displaying a simple error message; in other cases, it will mean actually terminating the program and displaying a message that indicates the reason for the termination. It would seem that our programs must be much more complicated than the examples in chapter 8 would indicate. Certainly, if every DML command had to be followed by a lengthy test that checked for a number of different values of DB–STATUS and took a number of different actions, we would be involved in a very cumbersome process indeed.

Fortunately, at least in COBOL, there is a simple way around the problem. The solution involves the use of declaratives. In general, declaratives are blocks of logic that are effectively set aside and executed only when some special event takes place. In interacting with a CODASYL database, the "special event" is a DB–STATUS other than zero. Figure 9.1 (opposite) illustrates this use of declaratives.

In WORKING-STORAGE, a flag called DATABASE-STATUS-FLAG has been described. This is *not* DB–STATUS, which is a special register controlled by the system, but rather our own flag. We will set this flag to "EOC" if the value in DB–STATUS indicates that we have reached the end of a chain ("0502100"), to "NOREC" if the value indicates that no record was found to match the desired conditions ("0502400"), or to "DUP" if the value indicates that we are attempting to store a duplicate ("1505100"). (The 88-level entries in COBOL are called condition names. They are used to make programs more readable by allowing us to replace conditions with condition names. The condition DATABASE-STATUS-FLAG = "EOC", for example, can now be replaced by the condition name END-OF-CHAIN.)

If declaratives are used, they must be placed at the beginning of the PROCE-DURE DIVISION. The beginning of the declaratives portion of the program is indicated by the word DECLARATIVES, and the end is indicated by the words END DECLARATIVES. Each declarative is a section that includes a USE command which indicates when the logic in the section is to be invoked. For database problems, the appropriate USE command is "USE FOR DB-EXCEPTION". The

FIGURE 9.1
Use of DECLARATIVES

```
01    STATUS-FLAGS.
      03   ...
      03   ...
      03    DATABASE-STATUS-FLAG              PIC X(5).
            88   DB-STATUS-OK                 VALUE "OK".
            88   END-OF-CHAIN                 VALUE "EOC".
            88   NO-SUCH-RECORD               VALUE "NOREC"
            88   RECORD-IS-A-DUPLICATE        VALUE "DUP"


PROCEDURE DIVISION.

DECLARATIVES.

DATABASE-ERROR-PROCESSING SECTION. USE FOR DB-EXCEPTION.

ERROR-PROCESSING-ROUTINE.
      IF DB-STATUS = "0502100"
            MOVE "EOC" TO DATABASE-STATUS-FLAG
         ELSE IF DB-STATUS = "0502400"
            MOVE "NOREC" TO DATABASE-STATUS-FLAG
         ELSE IF DB-STATUS = "1505100"
            MOVE "DUP" TO DATABASE-STATUS-FLAG
         ELSE
            DISPLAY "ABORTING"
            DISPLAY "ERROR STATUS ___ " DB-STATUS
            DISPLAY "ERROR RECORD ___ " DB-RECORD-NAME
            DISPLAY "ERROR SET _____ " DB-SET-NAME
            DISPLAY "ERROR AREA _____ " DB-REALM-NAME
            STOP RUN.

END DECLARATIVES.

(Beginning of regular procedure division code)
```

logic in this section will then be invoked whenever any command results in a DB–STATUS other than zero.

The way in which we prefer to structure this section is demonstrated in the figure. Using the IF ... ELSE IF ... ELSE IF structure, we test all values of DB–STATUS for which we will merely take some special action (such as an error message) and then continue processing. In this case, the values represent reaching the end of a chain during retrieval, attempting to locate a record that does not exist, and attempting to store a record that would violate some duplicates clause (e.g., trying to store a second customer 124). If the DB–STATUS indicates one of these conditions, we merely set our own flag, DATABASE–STATUS–FLAG, to an appropriate value and then continue processing. If, on the other hand, DB–STATUS contains some other value, we have a serious problem. This is handled within our declaratives by including a final ELSE followed by a statement that will cause the value of the DB–STATUS to be displayed as well as the values in the special registers, DB–RECORD–NAME , DB–SET–NAME , and DB–REALM–NAME, then a STOP RUN. (These values indicate which problem occurred as well as the record, set, and area being processed when the error occurred, all valuable information. We could, of course, also display any other information, such as values of certain data items, that might furnish additional assistance in the debugging process.) With this structure in the declaratives, we can begin the rest of the PROCEDURE DIVISION knowing that DATABASE–STATUS–FLAG will be set to the appropriate value automatically if one of the special conditions is encountered and knowing also that if something serious occurs, such as running out of space in the database, the program will terminate cleanly and, in the process, will display the value of DB–STATUS.

Assuming that we have included such declaratives in our program, we can restructure the examples given in chapter 8 in the manner shown in Figure 9.2. We

FIGURE 9.2a

```
MOVE 12 TO SLSREP-NUMBER.
MOVE "OK" TO DATABASE-STATUS-FLAG.
FIND ANY SLSREP.
IF NO-SUCH-RECORD
    print error message - "NO SUCH SALES REP"
  ELSE
    GET
    print SLSREP-NUMBER, SLSREP-NAME.
```

Example 1 — Chapter 8

```
MOVE 6 TO SLSREP-NUMBER.
MOVE "OK" TO DATABASE-STATUS-FLAG.
FIND ANY SLSREP.
IF NO-SUCH-RECORD
    print error message - "NO SUCH SALES REP"
  ELSE
    FIND NEXT CUSTOMER WITHIN S-SLSREP-CUSTOMER
    PERFORM FIND-AND-DISPLAY-CUSTOMERS
        UNTIL END-OF-CHAIN.
        .
        .
        .

FIND-AND-DISPLAY-CUSTOMERS.
    GET.
    print CUSTOMER-NUMBER, NAME.
    FIND NEXT CUSTOMER WITHIN S-SLSREP-CUSTOMER.
```

Example 2 — Chapter 8

can now test our own flag, DATABASE–STATUS–FLAG, using the condition names that we have assigned, and thus improve readability. In addition, we know that if some other problem occurs with regard to the database, the program will handle it cleanly. We do have to make sure that the DATABASE–STATUS–FLAG is initialized before each database command. If not, it will still contain the value to which it was set as a result of the previous database command. In the examples in this chapter, it is initialized to "OK" wherever necessary.

FIGURE 9.2b
Sample routines using
DATABASE-STATUS-
FLAG

```
MOVE 522 TO CUSTOMER-NUMBER.
MOVE "OK" TO DATABASE-STATUS-FLAG.
FIND ANY CUSTOMER.
IF NO-SUCH-RECORD
     print error message - "NO SUCH CUSTOMER"
   ELSE
     FIND NEXT ORDER WITHIN S-CUSTOMER-ORDER
          PERFORM FIND-AND-DISPLAY-ORDERS
              UNTIL END-OF-CHAIN.
     .
     .
     .


FIND-AND-DISPLAY-ORDERS.
   GET.
   print ORDER-NUMBER, DATE.
   FIND NEXT ORDER-LINE WITHIN S-ORDER-ORDER-LINE.
   PERFORM FIND-AND-DISPLAY-ORDER-LINES
          UNTIL END-OF-CHAIN.
   FIND NEXT ORDER WITHIN S-CUSTOMER-ORDER.
     .
     .
     .


FIND-AND-DISPLAY-ORDER-LINES.
   GET.
   FIND OWNER WITHIN S-PART-ORDER-LINE.
   GET.
   print PART-NUMBER, PART-DESCRIPTION,
        NUMBER-ORDERED, QUOTED-PRICE, UNIT-PRICE.
   FIND NEXT ORDER-LINE WITHIN S-ORDER-ORDER-LINE
```

Example 3 — Chapter 8

```
MOVE 3 TO SLSREP-NUMBER.
MOVE "OK" TO DATABASE-STATUS-FLAG.
FIND ANY SLSREP.
IF NO-SUCH-RECORD
     print error message "NO SUCH SALES REP"
   ELSE
     fill in all fields in CUSTOMER record
     STORE CUSTOMER
     IF RECORD-IS-A-DUPLICATE
          print error message - "DUPLICATE CUSTOMER".
```

Example 7 — Chapter 8

MULTIMEMBER SETS

Although sets usually contain only one member record type, this is not always
the case. The CODASYL model permits sets that contain multiple member record
types, called **multimember sets**. In certain cases, this type of set can be quite
advantageous.

Suppose, for example, that Marvel College were interested not only in the job history for each faculty member but also in the education history, i.e., all the degrees received by a faculty member as well as the date on which each degree was received. This new requirement would necessitate adding a new record type, DEGREE–HISTORY, which contains two fields, DEGREE and DATE–EARNED. To relate these degree history records to the appropriate faculty member, we could have a new set type with FACULTY as the owner and DEGREE–HISTORY as the member. The crucial portion of this database is shown in Figure 9.3.

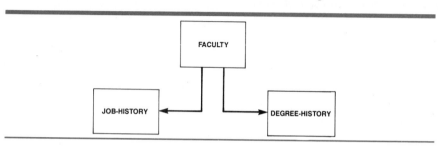

FIGURE 9.3
Two singlemember sets

Rather than use two separate sets, one from FACULTY to JOB–HISTORY and the other from FACULTY to DEGREE–HISTORY, we could use a multimember set in which the owner would be FACULTY and the members would be JOB–HISTORY and DEGREE–HISTORY. A common way to represent this structure is shown in Figure 9.4. Rather than possess two separate chains, one for job history

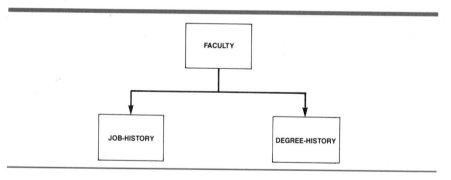

FIGURE 9.4
Multimember set

and another for degree history, as shown in Figure 9.5, each faculty member

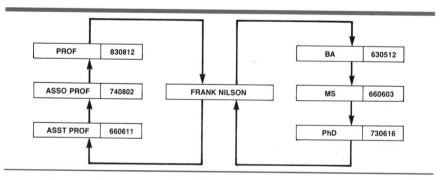

FIGURE 9.5
Occurrences of two singlemember sets

would possess a single chain containing both job history records and degree records. This chain could be sorted by record type, in which case all the occurrences of one of the member record types, say, DEGREE–HISTORY, would come before all the occurrences of the other member record type. This arrangement is shown in Figure 9.6. It is also possible to sort in some other fashion, for

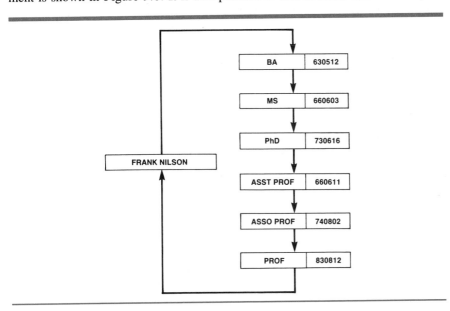

FIGURE 9.6
Occurrence of
multimember set
sorted by record type

example, by date, as demonstrated in Figure 9.7.

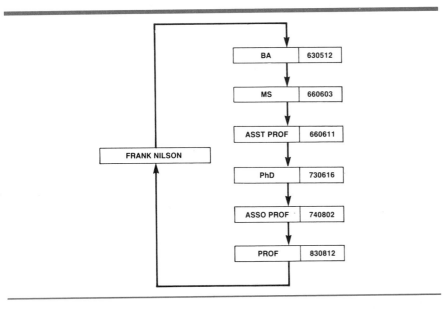

FIGURE 9.7
Occurrence of
multimember set
sorted by date

Is it better to have two separate sets or a single set with two different member record types? The answer depends on the type and volume of processing that will be done with this information. If a report listing both degree and job history information, sorted by date, were required with some regularity at Marvel College, then a multimember set would be preferable, sorted in the manner shown in Figure 9.7. If the job and degree history information were housed in two separate sets, complete data from both sets would have to be retrieved and then merged together to form the report. This would require additional complexity in the program as well as extra overhead for processing.

On the other hand, if the main requirements called only for job history information *or* degree information, two separate sets would probably be preferable. It would still be possible to retrieve only job history information from the multimember set (FIND NEXT JOB-HISTORY WITHIN ... would do it), but the process would be less efficient. The system would have to examine *all* member occurrences, both job history records and degree history records, searching only for those that were occurrences of the JOB-HISTORY record.

MANUAL SETS

By a **manual set**, we mean a set for which INSERTION IS MANUAL has been specified in the schema. We will now investigate two special uses of such sets.

LOOPS

The first use concerns a situation that does occur but is far from common: a loop in the database design. Consider, for example, Figure 9.8. In this design,

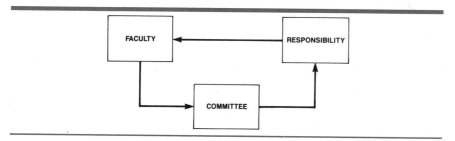

FIGURE 9.8
Loop in the database structure

there are three record types: FACULTY, COMMITTEE, and RESPONSIBILITY. Each committee is chaired by exactly one faculty member but each faculty member can chair several different committees. Each committee has several responsibilities (e.g., the curriculum committee must evaluate new course proposals, update catalog descriptions, investigate new programs, etc.). Each responsibility is assigned to exactly one committee. For each responsibility, there is a collection of faculty members assigned to carry out that responsibility. Each faculty member is assigned exactly one responsibility so that the work that needs to be accomplished will be evenly distributed. In the design of Figure 9.8, the set from FACULTY to COMMITTEE relates each faculty member to the committees he or she chairs. The set from COMMITTEE to RESPONSIBILITY relates each committee to its responsibilities. Finally, the set from RESPONSIBILITY to FACULTY relates each repon-sibility to the faculty members who are assigned to that responsibility (no faculty member is assigned more than one responsibility but each responsibility may have more than one faculty member assigned to it).

Could each of these three sets have INSERTION IS AUTOMATIC?
Answer:
   Suppose that all three are automatic sets and we try to store faculty member JONES, who happens to be the chair of the curriculum committee and who is assigned to the responsibility "update catalog descriptions", which is one of the responsibilities of the curriculum committee. Since Jones is owned by "update catalog descriptions" in the set from RESPONSIBILITY to FACULTY, this responsibility must exist in the database *before* Jones can be stored. This responsibility, however, is owned by the curriculum committee, and so the curriculum committee must be stored in the database before we store "update catalog descriptions" (can you guess what's coming?). Since Jones is the chair of the curriculum committee, the curriculum committee is owned by Jones, so Jones must exist in the database before the curriculum committee can be stored. Thus, before we can store Jones we must store "update catalog descriptions", but before we store "update catalog descriptions" we must store the curriculum committee, and before we store the curriculum committee we must store Jones. We are going to have an interesting time trying to get data into our database!

   The solution to the problem is to make one of these sets manual. Suppose, for example, that the set from RESPONSIBILITY to FACULTY were manual. We could then store all of the faculty members without any responsibilities existing in the database. After this, we could store all committees, automatically tying each one to the appropriate faculty member as it is stored. We could then store all responsibilities, tying each to the appropriate committee as it is stored. Finally, we could manually tie each faculty member to the responsibility to which he or she had been assigned.

NULLS

   Let's assume that each student is related to the dormitory in which he or she resides. To accomplish this relationship in a CODASYL system, we would have two record types, DORMITORY and STUDENT, and a set between them (see Figure 9.9). Let's assume further that a student does not have to reside in a dorm; i.e., the dormitory for a student can be **null**. How would this be handled in a CODASYL system?
   One solution is to avoid the problem. We could store a phony dorm, perhaps dorm number 0, with the name NONE. Then, any student who did not reside in a dorm would be tied to this nonexistent dorm. Another solution is to make the set from DORMITORY to STUDENT a manual set. In this way, if a student did reside in a dormitory, we could manually connect the student to the appropriate dorm after

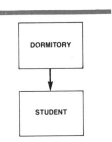

FIGURE 9.9
Dormitory-student relationship

storing the student. If, on the other hand, the student did not reside in a dorm, we would store the student but *not connect him or her to any dorm*. The student would effectively be "floating free", as far as that set were concerned. Incidentally, we would also want to make this set optional (RETENTION IS OPTIONAL) to allow for the possibility that a student residing in a dorm might leave it. In this event, we would disconnect the student from the dorm that currently owns the student and not connect the student to any other dorm.

Clearly, the solution involving a manual set represents the actual situation more accurately than creation of an artificial dormitory in our database.

Can you think of any ways in which the creation of a phony dorm might be more advantageous than the use of a manual set?

Answer:

The process of listing all students who do not reside in a dorm might very well be easier using a phony dorm than using nulls. It would simply entail listing all students related to dormitory 0. The logic would be *exactly* the same as listing all students who reside in dorm 3 (or any other dorm for that matter).

SYSTEM-OWNED SETS

A **system-owned set** (also called a **singular set**) is one in which the owner is specified as "SYSTEM". There is only one occurrence of such a set. It consists of a single chain through all of the member occurrences. If the member record type is CUSTOMER, this occurrence would be a single chain linking all customers. A requirement to list all customers could then be satisfied by retrieving all the member occurrences within this set, as example 5 of chapter 8 demonstrates. Otherwise, we might very well need to step through the entire database, picking up just the customers for our report, as example 4 of chapter 8 demonstrates.

Is stepping through the whole database just to retrieve customers a bad idea? From the standpoint of coding, the answer is no. The code in example 4 of chapter 8 is almost identical to the code in example 5. From the standpoint of efficiency, which approach is better depends on the size of the database and the number of occurrences of the record in question. Let's assume, for example, that the database consists of one hundred pages, that there are a thousand customers, and that the block size is one page (i.e., the DBMS will always read one page at a time).

How many disk accesses will be required if we retrieve all one thousand customers by sequentially scanning the entire database? In this case, the answer is one hundred. The DBMS would begin by reading the first page into memory. Each record on this page would be examined to determine whether or not it was a customer. Once a customer record had been found, the DBMS would return it to the program. If no customer was found on this page, the DBMS would then read the second page of the database, looking for a customer, and so on. When the program later asked the DBMS to retrieve the next customer, the DBMS would first examine the contents of the page currently in memory (this would *not* require another disk access). If a customer were found, the request could be satisfied. If not, another page would have to be read. In any case, once the complete database had been read once, we would have retrieved the complete set of customers. Since the database consists of one hundred pages, this process would require one hundred disk accesses.

How many disk accesses would be required if we were to retrieve all one thousand customers by using the system-owned set? In this case, the answer could be as many as a thousand. The DBMS would begin by reading the page on which the first customer is located. Assuming (as we naturally would) that the location mode for the customer record is CALC on the customer number, this customer would be on the page determined by applying the hashing function to the customer number. The request to retrieve the next customer would require another disk access unless, by chance, the hashing function happened to have produced the same page for both customers. Since it is highly unlikely that two consecutive customers would be placed on the same page, each request for another customer would probably require an additional disk access. Thus, we would expect close to a thousand disk accesses to retrieve the complete customer list.

With one thousand customers in a database that contains one hundred pages, the process of retrieving all customers was clearly accomplished with greater efficiency by sequentially scanning the entire database instead of using a system-owned set. On the other hand, suppose we wished to retrieve all sales reps and that there were only ten of them. The reasoning used previously would indicate that a sequential scan would require one hundred accesses, whereas following a system-owned set would require only ten.

Volumes clearly play an important part in determining whether system-owned sets should be used. Other concerns, however, also play a role. If a system-owned set is sorted in a fashion required for a report, then merely processing the set is all that is necessary. A sequential scan of the database, on the other hand, must be followed by a sort before the report can be produced.

SORTED SETS AND POINTER ARRAYS

A **sorted set** is a set in which the insertion is SORTED BY DEF I NED KEYS. If the set from SLSREP to CUSTOMER is sorted by customer name, then the member occurrences within each set occurrence will be ordered by name. Thus, for a report of all the customers of a given sales rep, merely following the chain will automatically give us an alphabetic listing. If a system-owned set in which the member is CUSTOMER is sorted by name, following this set will give us a list of all customers sorted alphabetically. Sorted sets can eliminate the need for sorting within a program. If the data required by a retrieval program can be obtained by processing a sorted set, the program will be both simpler and more efficient than if the set either did not exist or was not sorted.

Sorted sets sound like a very desirable feature. By having all our sets sorted in the appropriate fashion, we can greatly simplify and improve the efficiency of retrieval. There is a negative side to this, however, and it concerns update. Let's assume, for example, that there is a system-owned set, S–SYSTEM–CUSTOMER, in which the member record type is CUSTOMER, and let's assume further that this set is sorted by NAME. If a customer named PETERSON is added to the database, PETERSON must be positioned within the single occurrence of S–SYSTEM–CUSTOMER at the position dictated by the name. How does the system find this position? If the set is implemented in the fashion described in chapter 8, the only way is to follow the chain, examining the name of each customer sequentially until arriving at the position at which to insert PETERSON. We would expect the name PETERSON to occur a little more than halfway through the list. Consequently, if we currently had one hundred thousand customers in the database, we would probably have to examine between fifty-five and sixty-five thousand records in order to determine where to place PETERSON! Clearly, the same sorted sets that were attractive for retrieval can be very unattractive for update. In many cases, the update overhead would be prohibitive and would prevent us from using sorted sets.

Fortunately, however, many CODASYL systems offer an alternative implementation of sorted sets, called **pointer arrays**, which gives the same benefits for retrieval but does not suffer from the same update problems. Conceptually, the difference between the normal mode for implementing sets, usually called CHA I N, and pointer arrays is shown in Figure 9.10. In the chain implementation, the

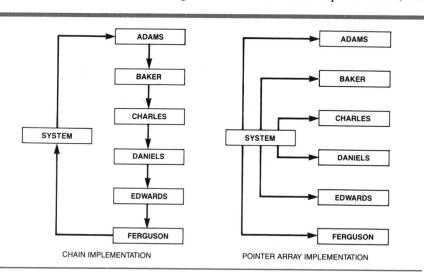

FIGURE 9.10
Chains vs. Pointer Arrays

CHAIN IMPLEMENTATION   POINTER ARRAY IMPLEMENTATION

owner points to the first member occurrence. Each member occurrence points to the next member occurrence except for the very last one, which points back to the owner. In the pointer array implementation, the owner points to all of the member occurrences with an "array of pointers". (The actual implementation usually involves a B-tree-like structure rather than an array of pointers, but the pictorial representation of it in Figure 9.10 gives the general idea.) While the pointer array implementation requires more storage space than the chain implementation, it permits the rapid location of the appropriate position within the set, based on the sort key. If the number of member occurrences within occurrences of a sorted set is at all large, the increased efficiency that pointer arrays provide is crucial. Without them, sorted sets may very well be ruled out, owing to the tremendous overhead associated with update.

RETAINING CURRENCY

Normally, successful execution of a F I ND command will update the current of realm, set, record, and rununit. By adding a special clause to any F I ND statement, however, we can request that a given type of currency not be updated. The necessary clause is

```
RETAINING CURRENCY FOR ...
```

where the FOR is followed by REALM, SETS, RECORD, or a specific list of sets, indicating which currencies are *not* to be changed after the F I ND command has been executed. If the word SETS is included, no SET currencies will be changed. On the other hand, if a specific list of sets is included, no currencies will be changed for these sets but any set not mentioned can have its currency updated.

Most of the time, having all currencies updated is not only not a problem, it is precisely what we want. Thus, the clause is not often used. Sometimes, however, it is essential. Consider the following:

List all of the items present on order 12491. For each item, determine whether enough units are on hand to fill all orders.

Does the following logic pose any difficulty as a solution to the problem?

```
MOVE 12491 TO ORDER-NUMBER.
FIND ANY ORDER.
IF NO-RECORD-WAS-FOUND
        print error message - "NO SUCH ORDER"
    ELSE
        PERFORM FIND-ORDER-LINE
            UNTIL END-OF-CHAIN.
        .
        .
        .
FIND-ORDER-LINE.
        FIND NEXT ORDER-LINE WITHIN S-ORDER-ORDER-LINE.
        IF NOT END-OF-CHAIN
```

continued

Q&A continued

```
        GET
        FIND OWNER WITHIN S-PART-ORDER-LINE
        GET
        MOVE 0 TO TOTAL-UNITS-ORDERED
        PERFORM FIND-UNITS-ORDERED
             UNTIL END-OF-CHAIN
        MOVE SPACE TO DATABASE-STATUS-FLAG
        IF UNITS-ON-HAND < TOTAL-UNITS-ORDERED
             print message PART NUMBER, "NOT ENOUGH ON HAND".
        .
        .
        .
FIND-UNITS-ORDERED.
     FIND NEXT ORDER-LINE WITHIN S-PART-ORDER-LINE.
     IF NOT END-OF-CHAIN
        GET
        ADD NUMBER-ORDERED TO TOTAL-UNITS-ORDERED.
```

The above routine begins by finding order 12491. Provided that the order actually exists, we successively examine each order line that corresponds to this order, i.e., each order line owned by this order within S-ORDER-ORDER-LINE. This is accomplished in the loop, FIND-ORDER-LINE. For each of these order lines, we first find the part that owns it by finding the owner within *S-PART-ORDER-LINE*. For this part, we determine the total units of it that are on order by looping through all of the order lines owned by that part and adding the number ordered to the total units ordered. When this loop has terminated, we compare the units on hand for the part with the total units ordered. If the number of units on hand is less than the total units ordered, a message is displayed. At this point, we have completely processed this order line and can move on to the next order line within the same order.

Answer:

A problem does exist. In the process of determining whether there were enough units on hand for the part that owned the first order line, we found a number of other order lines; in fact, we found all of the order lines owned by that part. Whenever a new order line was found, several currency indicators were updated, *including* the currency indicator for the set S-ORDER-ORDER-LINE, since the ORDER-LINE record is a member within this set type. Thus, when the loop, FIND-UNITS-ORDERED, was completed, the current of S-ORDER-ORDER-LINE would be the set occurrence in which the last order line owned by that part participated, and our position within this set would be at this order line. When we performed the next iteration of FIND-ORDER-LINE, we would find the *next* order line within this *new* order. The problem is that we have lost our original position within S-ORDER-ORDER-LINE.

The solution would be either to retain our position or to somehow save the position so that we could get it back when we needed it. Fortunately, both solutions are possible. It is possible to retain a given position by requesting that the system *not* update the currency indicator for S-ORDER-ORDER-LINE. This is accomplished by including a RETAINING CURRENCY clause.

Using this clause for solving the problem would produce the following:

```
MOVE 12491 TO ORDER-NUMBER.
FIND ANY ORDER.
IF NO-RECORD-WAS-FOUND
      print error message - "NO SUCH ORDER"
   ELSE
      PERFORM FIND-ORDER-LINE
            UNTIL END-OF-CHAIN.
      .
      .
      .
FIND-ORDER-LINE.
      FIND NEXT ORDER-LINE WITHIN S-ORDER-ORDER-LINE.
      IF NOT END-OF-CHAIN
         GET
         FIND OWNER WITHIN S-PART-ORDER-LINE
         GET
         MOVE 0 TO TOTAL-UNITS-ORDERED
         PERFORM FIND-UNITS-ORDERED
               UNTIL END-OF-CHAIN
         MOVE SPACE TO DATABASE-STATUS-FLAG
         IF UNITS-ON-HAND < TOTAL-UNITS-ORDERED
               print message PART NUMBER,
                  "NOT ENOUGH ON HAND".
      .
      .
      .
FIND-UNITS-ORDERED.
      FIND NEXT ORDER-LINE WITHIN S-PART-ORDER-LINE
 ----->       RETAINING CURRENCY FOR S-ORDER-ORDER-LINE.
      IF NOT END-OF-CHAIN
         GET
         ADD NUMBER-ORDERED TO TOTAL-UNITS-ORDERED.
```

The clause "RETAINING CURRENCY FOR S-ORDER-ORDER-LINE" prevents the currency indicator for S-ORDER-ORDER-LINE from being changed as it normally would. All other currency indicators affected by this statement (current of ORDER-LINE, current of S-PART-ORDER-LINE, current of realm, and current of run unit) will be changed in the usual manner.

ACCEPT

The other solution to the problem is to store the location of the given order line so that we could return to this position later. The user can store the data base key value of a given record and then, later in the program, use that value to find the record. If a record has a location mode of CALC, there is no need for this process, since the record can be found at a later point in the program simply by using the CALC key of the record. If we have retrieved a record, such as ORDER-LINE, whose location mode is VIA SET and we need to retrieve the record again at some later point in the program when it is no longer the current of record type, then we can use the following process.

In the example, after finding an order line within S-ORDER-ORDER-LINE, we store the database key of that order line in a special holding field that we have defined, say, ORDER-LINE-DBK. This field will be defined in WORKING-STORAGE and will be described as DB-KEY:

```
03  ORDER-LINE-DBK                DB-KEY.
```

To save the database key, we use the ACCEPT statement as follows:

```
ACCEPT ORDER_LINE_DBK FROM ORDER_LINE CURRENCY.
```

To later find this order line, using the database key that we have stored, we use the direct form of the find command:

```
FIND ORDER-LINE; DB-KEY IS ORDER-LINE-DBK.
```

Following is a solution to the problem using the ACCEPT command and the direct form of the find command:

```
        MOVE 12491 TO ORDER-NUMBER.
        FIND ANY ORDER.
        IF NO-RECORD-WAS-FOUND
            print error message - "NO SUCH ORDER"
          ELSE
            PERFORM FIND-ORDER-LINE
                UNTIL END-OF-CHAIN.
                .
                .
                .
FIND-ORDER-LINE.
        FIND NEXT ORDER-LINE WITHIN S-ORDER-ORDER-LINE.
        IF NOT END-OF-CHAIN
            ACCEPT ORDER-LINE-DBK FROM ORDER-LINE CURRENCY
            GET
            FIND OWNER WITHIN S-PART-ORDER-LINE
            GET
            MOVE 0 TO TOTAL-UNITS-ORDERED
            PERFORM FIND-UNITS-ORDERED
                UNTIL END-OF-CHAIN
            MOVE SPACE TO DATABASE-STATUS-FLAG
            FIND ORDER-LINE; DB-KEY IS ORDER-LINE-DBK.
            IF UNITS-ON-HAND < TOTAL-UNITS-ORDERED
                print message PART NUMBER,
                    "NOT ENOUGH ON HAND".
```

```
.
.
.
FIND-UNITS-ORDERED.
      FIND NEXT ORDER-LINE WITHIN S-PART-ORDER-LINE.
      IF NOT END-OF-CHAIN
            GET
            ADD NUMBER-ORDERED TO TOTAL-UNITS-ORDERED.
```

Assuming that we have found another order line within S-ORDER-ORDER-LINE and are not at the end of the chain, we save the database key using the ACCEPT statement. After having examined all of the order lines owned by the part in question, we refind this order line by using the direct form of the FIND command. This returns the currency indicator for S-ORDER-ORDER-LINE (among others) to the desired position.

Other forms of the ACCEPT are possible. We can ACCEPT from the current position in a set by using

```
ACCEPT ORDER-LINE-DBK FROM S-ORDER-ORDER-LINE CURRENCY
```

In our case, since the current position along the set was the order line in question, this statement would have had exactly the same effect. If we are accepting database keys from a set occurrence, however, there are other options. Instead of the word CURRENCY, we could use NEXT, PRIOR, or OWNER. If NEXT is used, we will accept the database key, not of the current position along the set but rather of the next position, i.e., the position where we would be if we issued a FIND NEXT WITHIN S-ORDER-ORDER-LINE command. Similarly, if PRIOR is used, we will accept the database key of the prior position, and if OWNER is used, we will accept the database key of the owner.

IF

Two special forms of the IF statement can be helpful when processing a CODASYL database. One is called a tenancy condition and the other is called a member condition.

The basic form of the **tenancy condition** is

```
IF set-name MEMBER ...
```

This statement can be used to determine whether the current of run unit is actually a member of the set that is named in the condition. Suppose that customers did not have to be represented by sales reps in the Premiere Products database. Suppose further that this were implemented by making the set S-SLSREP-CUSTOMER be INSERTION MANUAL and RETENTION OPTIONAL and by ensuring that any customer who did not have a sales rep would not be connected to any sales rep in the database. If we then found a customer and wished to determine his or her sales rep, it would not be appropriate to unconditionally use

```
FIND  OWNER  WITHIN  S-SLSREP-CUSTOMER
```

since customers might not have an owner within this set. Rather, we would need to use a structure similar to the following:

```
IF  S-SLSREP-CUSTOMER  MEMBER
     FIND  OWNER  WITHIN  S-SLSREP-CUSTOMER
     GET
  ELSE
     print "CUSTOMER NOT REPRESENTED BY SALES REP"
```

Additional forms of the tenancy statement are available. The word MEMBER can be replaced by OWNER, in which case the condition is true if the current of run unit is the owner of the named set type, or TENANT, in which case the condition is true if the current of run unit is either an owner or a member. The set-name may be omitted, in which case the test is applied to every set in the schema. In this case, the result is true if the current of run unit is a member (owner or tenant) in *any* set. Finally, the word NOT can be used with any of the preceding forms to reverse the test.

The basic form of the **member condition** is

```
IF  set-name  IS  EMPTY  . . .
```

This test is used to determine whether the current set occurrence of the named set has members. If no member occurrences exist, the result is true. Otherwise, the result is false. The condition may be reversed by using the form

```
IF  set-name  IS  NOT  EMPTY
```

Suppose we wished to determine whether sales rep 3 currently represented any customers. After finding sales rep 3, we could attempt to find the next customer within S-SLSREP-CUSTOMER and see whether we immediately hit the end of the chain. If we did, we would know that there were no customers related to this sales rep. Alternatively, we could use the member condition test:

```
IF  S-SLSREP-CUSTOMER  IS  EMPTY
     print "SALES REP DOES NOT REPRESENT ANY CUSTOMERS"
  ELSE
     print "SALES REP DOES REPRESENT CUSTOMERS"
```

BILL-OF-MATERIALS

The **bill-of-materials relationship** is the classic example of a special type of relationship, one that is found between occurrences of the same type of entity. In this case, it is the relationship between parts in which each part is related to its immediate components. Since in general a part can have many components and a part can be a component of many other parts, this is a many-to-many relationship.

PRODUCT_STRUCTURE	PARENT_ PART_NUMBER	COMPONENT_ PART_NUMBER	QUANTITY_ REQUIRED
	A	B	3
	A	C	2
	B	D	1
	B	E	1
	C	D	2
	C	E	1

FIGURE 9.11
Relational model
implementation of
bill-of-materials
relationship

Figure 9.11 shows the relational model implementation of this structure. Examining the data in this example, we see that part A, as a parent, has two immediate components: B and C. Three B's and two C's are actually required to assemble a single A. Further, we can see that as a parent, part B has components of its own, a D and an E. In addition, part C has components of its own, two D's and an E. We can also reverse the roles of parents and components to determine where a given part is used. We can see, for example, that part D is used in manufacturing both parts B and C. Part C actually requires two D's whereas part B requires only a single D.

How is such a structure implemented within the CODASYL model? If the many-to-many relationship were between two different record types, we would introduce a third record type as well as sets from each of the original record types to the third record type. If we tried to apply the same idea here, we would create an additional record type as well as two sets, both from the part record to the new record type. This would indeed be the appropriate structure and it is shown in Figure 9.12. In this case, the new record, which we would still call a link record, would be named PRODUCT_STRUCTURE. Fields within this record type would be fields that depended on *both* the parent part *and* its component part. In our example, the only such field is the QUANTITY_REQUIRED. The set that relates a part to its components is called BILL_OF_MATERIALS. The set that relates a component to its parents is called WHERE_USED.

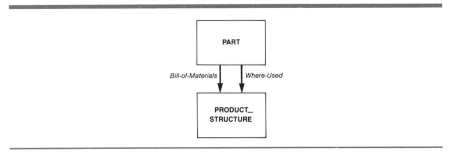

FIGURE 9.12
CODASYL
implementation of
bill-of-materials
relationship

To see how this structure works, consider Figure 9.13. Boxes containing letters are occurrences of the part record, and boxes containing numbers are occurrences of the PRODUCT_STRUCTURE record. Black arrows represent occurrences of the BILL_OF_MATERIALS set, and blue arrows represent occurrences of the WHERE_USED set. Neither prior pointers nor owner pointers are shown.

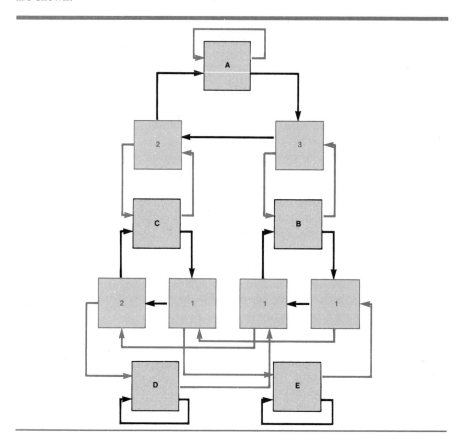

FIGURE 9.13
Example of bill-of-materials relationship

Beginning at part A and following the black arrows, we see that A has a product structure record for which the quantity required is 3. At this point, we have no idea what component this 3 corresponds to. To find it, we find the part that owns this 3 within the other set. Following the blue arrows from the 3 leads us to part B. Part A owns this 3 within the BILL_OF_MATERIALS set, and part B owns it within the WHERE_USED set. Thus, manufacturing a single part A requires three part B's. Following the black arrows from the 3 leads us to a product structure record for which the quantity required is 2. Using the same reasoning as before, we see that Part A owns this 2 within the BILL_OF_MATERIALS set and part C owns it within the WHERE_USED set. Thus, manufacturing a single part A also requires two part C's.

We could determine the components of part B in a similar manner. When we follow the black arrows from B, we encounter two product structure records, both containing the number 1. To find the owner of the first of these in the WHERE_ USED set, we follow the blue arrows until we arrive at a part record. In this case, the owner is part E. Similarly, we find that the owner of the other product structure record is part D. Thus, manufacturing a single part B requires a single part E and a single part D. Similarly, part C requires a single part E and two D's. If we attempt to locate the components of part D, we find there are no product structure records on the black arrow; i.e., it has no members within the set BILL_OF_MATERIALS and, thus, has no components.

By reversing the roles of the two sets in the preceding discussion, we can obtain what is usually called "Where Used" information; i.e., we can find the immediate parents of any part. Following the blue arrows from D shows that D owns two product structure records within the WHERE_USED set, one containing a quantity required of 1 and the other containing a quantity required of 2. By following the black arrows from each of these, we can determine that these records are owned by B and C, respectively, within the BILL_OF_MATERIALS set. Thus, a single part D is required in the manufacturing of part B, whereas two part D's are required in the manufacturing of part C. If we apply the same process to part A, we see that part A has no parents. It is evidently the final goal of the manufacturing process, what is termed an "End Item".

In other examples of this structure, the link record may not contain any fields. Consider the "prerequisite" relationship between courses, as shown in Figure 9.14. In the sample data, we can see that CS 453 has two prerequisites, CS 350

PREREQUISITE	COURSE_CODE	PREREQ_ COURSE_CODE
	CS 453	CS 353
	CS 453	CS 350
	CS 353	CS 153
	CS 353	CS 151
	CS 350	CS 153
	CS 350	CS 151

FIGURE 9.14
Relational model implementation of course — prerequisite relationship

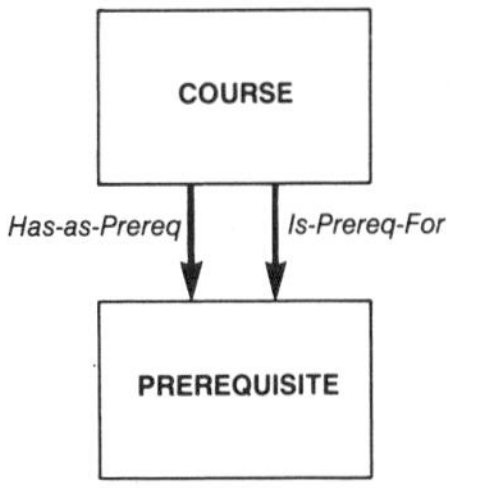

FIGURE 9.15
CODASYL implementation of course — prerequisite relationship

and CS 353. CS 353 has two prerequisites of its own, CS 153 and CS 151, as does CS 350. Further, we can see that CS 151 is prerequisite to both CS 350 and CS 353. Each of these in turn, is prerequisite to CS 453. The CODASYL version is shown in Figure 9.15.

This relationship is conceptually the same as the bill-of-materials relationship. Unless a college should choose to implement a requirement stating that a given prerequisite course must be taken a certain number of times before moving on to the next course, there is no need for a QUANTITY_REQUIRED field within the link record. Consider the sample database shown in Figure 9.16 on the following page. Notice the similarity between this and the sample database of Figure 9.13. The only differences are that we have courses instead of parts and the link records do not contain any data. Using the same logic as before, however, we can still determine the complete prerequisite relationships among all of the courses listed.

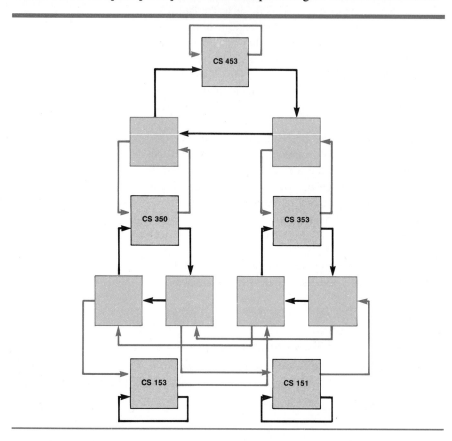

FIGURE 9.16
Example of course —
prerequisite
relationship

Occasionally, the relationship between an entity and itself will be one-to-many rather than many-to-many. Suppose that in a given organization, each employee had at most one manager. Then the relationship between the employee record and itself, in which each employee would be related to all of the employees that he or she managed is really a one-to-many relationship. A nice way to implement this relationship would be with a set in which the employee record would *both* the owner *and* the member. Such a set is called a **recursive set**. Recursive sets are supported in the later CODASYL standards but not in many commercial CODASYL systems. In the event that this kind of set is not supported, an approach similar to that used in the bill-of-materials relationship can be adopted; i.e. we can add a new record, a link record, and two sets, MANAGES and IS_MANAGED_BY. While it may not seem as clean a solution as the single set, MANAGES, in which the owner and member record types are both EMPLOYEE, this approach (or something similar to it) is our only choice in many cases.

For other perspectives on the CODASYL model, see [2], [4], [5], and [6]. For an additional discussion of the bill-of-materials structure and recursive sets, see [1].

.3 OVERVIEW OF IDMS

IDMS, which was developed originally by the Goodrich Tire Company, was acquired by the Cullinane Corporation in 1971. Cullinane, which is now called Cullinet Software, Inc., greatly improved the product and has sold it to thousands of companies worldwide. IDMS is a CODASYL DBMS, the prime CODASYL system available on IBM equipment. It essentially follows the 1971 guidelines except for some differences that we will explore in the next sections of this chapter.

IDMS is just a portion of the Cullinet product line. Cullinet offers a full **fourth-generation software environment** in which IDMS plays an important part. It offers a complete line of application software as well (accounts receivable, accounts payable, payroll, general ledger, and many more). IDMS has recently been renamed IDMS/R and and has been enhanced to include relational-type capabilities, which will be discussed in section 9.6.

One consequence of IDMS being a part of the fourth-generation environment is that it is integrated with an excellent **data dictionary**. Among other things, this data dictionary is where the output from compilation of schema or subschema DDL will be stored.

In many ways, IDMS represents a typical CODASYL system. In the sections that follow, we will describe the differences between IDMS and the general **CODASYL model**.

.4 DATA DEFINITION IN IDMS

SCHEMA DDL

We will examine only the ways in which IDMS differs from the general CODASYL model. The standard CODASYL schema DDL for Premiere Products is shown in Figure 9.17 on the following page. A corresponding IDMS schema is shown in Figure 9.18 (on pages 394 and 395). Some of the lines in both schemas are numbered for reference purposes.

FIGURE 9.17a

```
1    SCHEMA NAME IS SCHEMA_DISTRIBUTION.

2    AREA NAME IS AREA_DISTRIBUTION.

3    RECORD NAME IS SLSREP
          LOCATION MODE IS CALC USING SLSREP_NUMBER
               DUPLICATES ARE NOT ALLOWED
          WITHIN AREA_DISTRIBUTION.

          02   SLSREP_NUMBER          PIC 9(2).
          02   SLSREP_NAME            PIC X(20).
          02   SLSREP_ADDRESS         PIC X(20).
          02   TOTAL_COMMISSION       PIC 9(5)V9(2).
          02   COMMISSION_RATE        PIC V9(2).

4    RECORD NAME IS CUSTOMER
          LOCATION MODE IS CALC USING CUSTOMER_NUMBER
               DUPLICATES ARE NOT ALLOWED
          WITHIN AREA_DISTRIBUTION.

          02   CUSTOMER_NUMBER        PIC 9(3).
          02   NAME                   PIC X(20).
          02   ADDRESS                PIC X(20).
          02   CURRENT_BALANCE        PIC 9(5)V9(2).
          02   CREDIT_LIMIT           PIC 9(5).

5    RECORD NAME IS ORDER
          LOCATION MODE IS CALC USING ORDER_NUMBER
               DUPLICATES ARE NOT ALLOWED
          WITHIN AREA_DISTRIBUTION.

          02   ORDER_NUMBER           PIC 9(5).
          02   ORDER_DATE             PIC 9(6).

6    RECORD NAME IS PART
          LOCATION MODE IS CALC USING PART_NUMBER
               DUPLICATES ARE NOT ALLOWED
          WITHIN AREA_DISTRIBUTION.

          02   PART_NUMBER            PIC X(4).
          02   PART_DESCRIPTION       PIC X(20).
          02   UNITS_ON_HAND          PIC 9(4).
          02   ITEM_CLASS             PIC X(2).
          02   WAREHOUSE_NUMBER       PIC 9(2).
          02   UNIT_PRICE             PIC 9(4)V9(2).

7    RECORD NAME IS ORDER_LINE
          LOCATION MODE IS VIA S_ORDER_ORDER_LINE
          WITHIN AREA_DISTRIBUTION.

          02   NUMBER_ORDERED         PIC 9(4).
          02   QUOTED_PRICE           PIC 9(4)V9(2).
```

FIGURE 9.17b
Premiere Products
Schema DDL (General
CODASYL version)

```
8    SET NAME IS S_SLSREP_CUSTOMER
          OWNER IS SLSREP
               SET IS PRIOR PROCESSABLE
               ORDER IS PERMANENT INSERTION IS SORTED BY
                         DEFINED KEYS
               DUPLICATES ARE LAST.

          MEMBER IS CUSTOMER
               INSERTION IS AUTOMATIC
               RETENTION IS OPTIONAL
               LINKED TO OWNER
               KEY IS ASCENDING NAME
               SET SELECTION FOR S_SLSREP_CUSTOMER
                    IS THRU S_SLSREP_CUSTOMER
                    OWNER IDENTIFIED BY APPLICATION.

9    SET NAME IS S_CUSTOMER_ORDER
          OWNER IS CUSTOMER
               SET IS PRIOR PROCESSABLE
               ORDER IS PERMANENT INSERTION IS LAST.

          MEMBER IS ORDER
               INSERTION IS AUTOMATIC
               RETENTION IS OPTIONAL
               LINKED TO OWNER
               SET SELECTION FOR S_CUSTOMER_ORDER
                    IS THRU S_CUSTOMER_ORDER
                    OWNER IDENTIFIED BY APPLICATION.

10   SET NAME IS S_ORDER_ORDER_LINE
          OWNER IS ORDER
               SET IS PRIOR PROCESSABLE
               ORDER IS PERMANENT INSERTION IS LAST.

          MEMBER IS ORDER_LINE
               INSERTION IS AUTOMATIC
               RETENTION IS OPTIONAL
               LINKED TO OWNER
               SET SELECTION FOR S_ORDER_ORDER_LINE
                    IS THRU S_ORDER_ORDER_LINE
                    OWNER IDENTIFIED BY APPLICATION.

11   SET NAME IS S_PART_ORDER_LINE
          OWNER IS PART
               SET IS PRIOR PROCESSABLE
               ORDER IS PERMANENT INSERTION IS LAST.

          MEMBER IS ORDER_LINE
               INSERTION IS AUTOMATIC
               RETENTION IS OPTIONAL
               LINKED TO OWNER
               SET SELECTION FOR S_PART_ORDER_LINE
                    IS THRU S_PART_ORDER_LINE
                    OWNER IDENTIFIED BY APPLICATION.
```

FIGURE 9.18a

```
1    SCHEMA NAME IS SCHEMA-DISTRIBUTION.

2    AREA NAME IS AREA-DISTRIBUTION  RANGE IS 1 THRU 2000
                                     WITHIN FILE DSTFILE
                                     FROM 1 THRU 2000.

3    RECORD NAME IS SLSREP
            RECORD ID IS 101.
            LOCATION MODE IS CALC USING SLSREP-NUMBER
                    DUPLICATES ARE NOT ALLOWED
            WITHIN AREA-DISTRIBUTION AREA.

        02   SLSREP-NUMBER           PIC 9(2).
        02   SLSREP-NAME             PIC X(20).
        02   SLSREP-ADDRESS          PIC X(20).
        02   TOTAL-COMMISSION        PIC 9(5)V9(2).
        02   COMMISSION-RATE         PIC V9(2).

4    RECORD NAME IS CUSTOMER
            RECORD ID IS 102.
            LOCATION MODE IS CALC USING CUSTOMER-NUMBER
                    DUPLICATES ARE NOT ALLOWED
            WITHIN AREA-DISTRIBUTION AREA.
            CALL IDMSCOMP            BEFORE STORE.
            CALL IDMSCOMP            BEFORE MODIFY.
            CALL IDMSDCOM            BEFORE GET.

        02   CUSTOMER-NUMBER         PIC 9(3).
        02   NAME                    PIC X(20).
        02   ADDRESS                 PIC X(20).
        02   CURRENT-BALANCE         PIC 9(5)V9(2).
        02   CREDIT-LIMIT            PIC 9(5).

5    RECORD NAME IS ORDER
            RECORD ID IS 103.
            LOCATION MODE IS CALC USING ORDER-NUMBER
                    DUPLICATES ARE NOT ALLOWED
            WITHIN AREA-DISTRIBUTION AREA.

        02   ORDER-NUMBER            PIC 9(5).
        02   ORDER-DATE              PIC 9(6).

6    RECORD NAME IS PART
            RECORD ID IS 104.
            LOCATION MODE IS CALC USING PART-NUMBER
                    DUPLICATES ARE NOT ALLOWED
            WITHIN AREA-DISTRIBUTION AREA.

        02   PART-NUMBER             PIC X(4).
        02   PART-DESCRIPTION        PIC X(20).
        02   UNITS-ON-HAND           PIC 9(4).
        02   ITEM-CLASS              PIC X(2).
        02   WAREHOUSE-NUMBER        PIC 9(2).
        02   UNIT-PRICE              PIC 9(4)V9(2).
```

FIGURE 9.18b
Premiere Products
Schema DDL (IDMS
version)

```
7    RECORD NAME IS ORDER-LINE
          RECORD ID IS 105.
          LOCATION MODE IS VIA S-ORDER-ORDER-LINE
          WITHIN AREA-DISTRIBUTION AREA.

          02   NUMBER-ORDERED         PIC 9(4).
          02   QUOTED-PRICE           PIC 9(4)V9(2).


8    SET NAME IS S-SLSREP-CUSTOMER
          ORDER IS SORTED.
          MODE IS CHAIN          LINKED TO PRIOR.
          OWNER IS SLSREP        NEXT DBKEY POSITION IS 1
                                 PRIOR DBKEY POSITION IS 2.
          MEMBER IS CUSTOMER     NEXT DBKEY POSITION IS 1
                                 PRIOR DBKEY POSITION IS 2
                                 LINKED TO OWNER
                                    OWNER DBKEY POSITION IS 3.
                                 OPTIONAL MANUAL.
                  ASCENDING KEY IS NAME
                       DUPLICATES ARE LAST.


9    SET NAME IS S-CUSTOMER-ORDER
          ORDER IS LAST.
          MODE IS CHAIN          LINKED TO PRIOR.
          OWNER IS CUSTOMER      NEXT DBKEY POSITION IS 4
                                 PRIOR DBKEY POSITION IS 5.


          MEMBER IS ORDER        NEXT DBKEY POSITION IS 1
                                 PRIOR DBKEY POSITION IS 2
                                 LINKED TO OWNER
                                    OWNER DBKEY POSITION IS 3.
                                 OPTIONAL MANUAL.


10   SET NAME IS S-ORDER-ORDER-LINE
          ORDER IS LAST.
          MODE IS CHAIN          LINKED TO PRIOR.
          OWNER IS ORDER         NEXT DBKEY POSITION IS 4
                                 PRIOR DBKEY POSITION IS 5.

          MEMBER IS ORDER-LINE   NEXT DBKEY POSITION IS 4
                                 PRIOR DBKEY POSITION IS 5
                                 LINKED TO OWNER
                                    OWNER DBKEY POSITION IS 6.
                                 OPTIONAL MANUAL.


11   SET NAME IS S-PART-ORDER-LINE
          ORDER IS LAST
          MODE IS CHAIN          LINKED TO PRIOR.
          OWNER IS PART          NEXT DBKEY POSITION IS 1
                                 PRIOR DBKEY POSITION IS 2.


          MEMBER IS ORDER-LINE   NEXT DBKEY POSITION IS 1
                                 PRIOR DBKEY POSITION IS 2
                                 LINKED TO OWNER
                                    OWNER DBKEY POSITION IS 3.
                                 OPTIONAL MANUAL.
```

A minor difference between the two schemas concerns the hyphen. IDMS allows the use of hyphens, whereas the underscore is used in the straight CODA-SYL version. The general structure of both schemas is the same: a schema entry, area entries, record entries, and set entries. The schema entries (line 1) are identi-cal. The IDMS area entries (line 2) permit areas to be assigned to physical files (or portions of physical files) on disk. Two areas may be combined into a single file by mentioning the same file name in both area entries. In the sample database, the single area, AREA–DISTRIBUTION, consists of two thousand pages, numbered 1 through 2000, that will correspond to pages 1 through 2000 of the file, DSTFILE.

There are two differences in the record entries (lines 3 to 7). First, in IDMS, each record type is given an ID in the schema DDL. These IDs are numeric and must be unique. In the sample schema, the numbers 101, 102, 103, and so on are used for these IDs. The second difference is illustrated in the record entry found on line 4. In this entry there are three CALL statements, two using IDMSCOMP and the third using IDMSDCOM. Each CALL statement indicates a module together with the conditions under which the module will be invoked. The statement CALL IDMSCOMP BEFORE STORE, for example, indicates that the module IDMSCOMP, which compresses data, will be invoked immediately prior to the storing of a customer. The statement CALL IDMSDCOM BEFORE GET indicates that the mod-ule IDMSDCOM, which decompresses data, will be invoked immediately prior to retrieving customer data. The compression is accomplished by converting repeti-tive strings of characters to codes.

In addition to the IDMS-supplied modules, user-written modules can be invoked in a similar fashion. User-written modules allow users to develop error-checking routines, for example, that go beyond the built-in capabilities of IDMS. Unfortunately, no other IDMS calls are allowed within these modules, and thus error checking that involves any database accesses would not be possible.

Further differences are found within the set entries (lines 8 to 11). The clause "ORDER IS PERMANENT INSERTION IS ...." is merely "ORDER IS ..." in IDMS. The choices FIRST, LAST, NEXT, and PRIOR are identical. If sorted sets are required, the general CODASYL model uses the clause "SORTED BY DEFINED KEYS", whereas IDMS uses merely "SORTED". In both systems the key is described in the member portion of the set description. In IDMS, the dupli-cates clause is in the member portion, whereas in the general CODASYL system, it follows the "SORTED BY DEFINED KEYS" clause. The other difference con-cerns the placement of the ORDER clause itself. In IDMS, it precedes the owner portion of the set description; in the general CODASYL system, it is within the owner portion.

The clause MODE IS CHAIN is precisely the CHAIN mode for sets which was discussed in the material on SORTED SETS and POINTER ARRAYS in section 9.2. The other possible mode, MODE IS INDEX, is, for practical purposes, the same as the POINTER ARRAY mode discussed in that same section.

The clause to request prior pointers in the general CODASYL model is "SET IS PRIOR PROCESSABLE"; in IDMS, this is accomplished by including the clause "LINKED TO PRIOR" in the MODE statement. As with the ORDER clause, in IDMS this clause precedes the owner portion, and in the general CODASYL system it is within it.

The same connect options, AUTOMATIC and MANUAL, and disconnect options, MANDATORY and OPTIONAL, that are available in the general CODASYL system are also available in IDMS. The only difference in syntax here is that the phrases INSERTION IS and RETENTION IS are not used in IDMS.

Perhaps the most significant difference is the use in IDMS of DBKEY positions. Each of the possible pointers is assigned a DBKEY position within each record. This means that both owner and member records within a set need to have the NEXT pointer assigned a DBKEY position. If prior pointers are requested, they must be assigned a position in both the owner and member records. Finally, if owner pointers are requested, the owner pointer must be assigned a position within the member records (owner records do not have owner pointers). These pointers are physically stored at the beginning of each record and are numbered sequentially, beginning with 1. Thus, if a given record includes four pointers, the numbers to be assigned are 1, 2, 3, and 4.

If a record participates as a member in a number of sets and an owner in several others, we have many DBKEY positions to assign. As you can see in the sample IDMS schema, these assignments are made as part of the declarations of the sets themselves. In both the owner and the member subentries, a position must be given for the NEXT pointer. If prior pointers are requested, the position for the PRIOR pointer must be provided as well. In addition, if owner pointers are requested, the position of the owner pointer within the member record must be specified within the member subentry.

In the Marvel College database, the FACULTY record participates as a member in two sets and as an owner in two others. If prior and owner pointers are requested in all sets, the FACULTY record will contain next and prior pointers for the two sets in which it is the owner as well as next, prior, and owner pointers for the two sets in which it is a member, for a total of ten pointers. Since these pointers are specified with all the sets, determining the pointer assignments requires scanning through all of the set entries, looking for those sets in which FACULTY is either an owner or a member. In addition, the potential for error in making the pointer assignments is definitely there (assigning the same DBKEY twice or not assigning a DBKEY to position 3, for example). Thus, it is desirable to have a systematic way of assigning these positions. Cullinet suggests the following.

Using the graphical representation of the schema (the data structure diagram):

1. "Starting at top center (12 o'clock), circle the graphical representation of a record twice in a clockwise direction."
2. "On the first revolution, assign pointer positions for all sets in which the record participates as member in the order the sets are encountered."
3. "On the second revolution, assign pointer positions for all sets in which the record participates as owner in the order the sets are encountered."

For example, consider Figure 9.19. Part a demonstrates the use of the technique in assigning the pointer positions within the CUSTOMER record in the Premiere Products database. The record is circled twice, starting at the 12:00

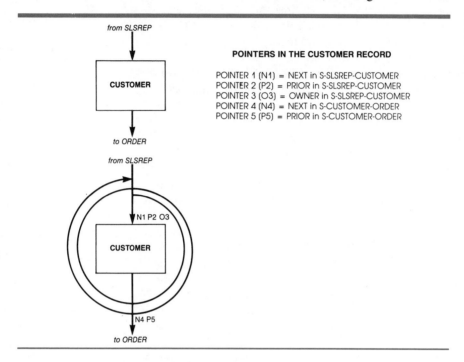

POINTERS IN THE CUSTOMER RECORD

POINTER 1 (N1) = NEXT in S-SLSREP-CUSTOMER
POINTER 2 (P2) = PRIOR in S-SLSREP-CUSTOMER
POINTER 3 (O3) = OWNER in S-SLSREP-CUSTOMER
POINTER 4 (N4) = NEXT in S-CUSTOMER-ORDER
POINTER 5 (P5) = PRIOR in S-CUSTOMER-ORDER

FIGURE 9.19a
Pointer assignment
for the CUSTOMER
record

position. On the first revolution, the only set encountered in which the CUSTOMER record is a member is S–SLSREP–CUSTOMER. Assuming that prior and owner pointers are both requested for this set, positions for the next, prior, and owner pointers must be assigned. As the diagram illustrates, the next pointer was assigned position 1, the prior position 2, and the owner position 3. As a shorthand representation, "N1 P2 O3" is used to indicate this pointer assignment. On the second revolution, the only set encountered in which the CUSTOMER record is the owner is S–CUSTOMER–ORDER. Since this is the owner record within the set type, a position for an owner pointer will not be assigned. We still need to assign positions for the next pointer and, assuming that prior pointers were requested in this set, for the prior pointer. Since positions 1, 2, and 3 are already taken, positions 4 and 5 are assigned to these pointers, respectively.

Part b illustrates the application of the technique to the ORDER–LINE record. In this case, since ORDER–LINE participates as a member in both S–ORDER–ORDER–LINE and S–PART–ORDER–LINE, both sets of pointers are assigned on the first revolution. The figure shows the results of these pointer assignments.

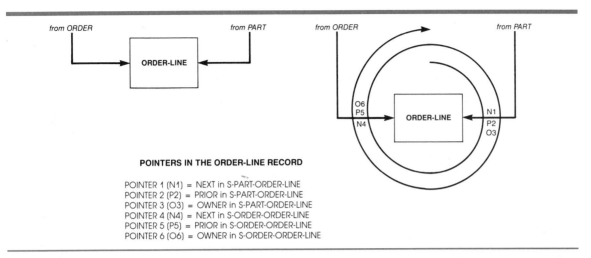

POINTERS IN THE ORDER-LINE RECORD

POINTER 1 (N1) = NEXT in S-PART-ORDER-LINE
POINTER 2 (P2) = PRIOR in S-PART-ORDER-LINE
POINTER 3 (O3) = OWNER in S-PART-ORDER-LINE
POINTER 4 (N4) = NEXT in S-ORDER-ORDER-LINE
POINTER 5 (P5) = PRIOR in S-ORDER-ORDER-LINE
POINTER 6 (O6) = OWNER in S-ORDER-ORDER-LINE

Finally, part c illustrates the application of the technique to the FACULTY record within the Marvel College database. During the first revolution, positions are assigned for the two sets in which it is a member, S–DEPARTMENT–FACULTY and S–PLAN–FACULTY. During the second revolution, positions are assigned for the two sets in which it is the owner, S–FACULTY–JOB–HISTORY and S–

FIGURE 9.19b
Pointer assignment for the ORDER-LINE record

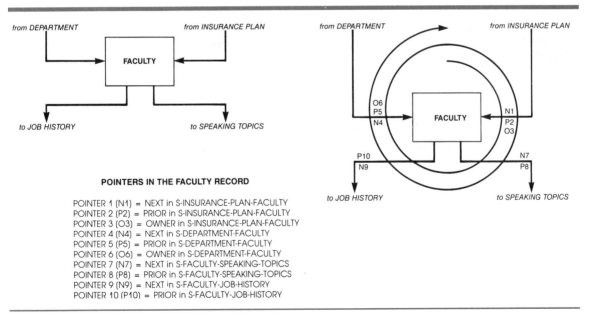

POINTERS IN THE FACULTY RECORD

POINTER 1 (N1) = NEXT in S-INSURANCE-PLAN-FACULTY
POINTER 2 (P2) = PRIOR in S-INSURANCE-PLAN-FACULTY
POINTER 3 (O3) = OWNER in S-INSURANCE-PLAN-FACULTY
POINTER 4 (N4) = NEXT in S-DEPARTMENT-FACULTY
POINTER 5 (P5) = PRIOR in S-DEPARTMENT-FACULTY
POINTER 6 (O6) = OWNER in S-DEPARTMENT-FACULTY
POINTER 7 (N7) = NEXT in S-FACULTY-SPEAKING-TOPICS
POINTER 8 (P8) = PRIOR in S-FACULTY-SPEAKING-TOPICS
POINTER 9 (N9) = NEXT in S-FACULTY-JOB-HISTORY
POINTER 10 (P10) = PRIOR in S-FACULTY-JOB-HISTORY

FACULTY–SPEAKING–TOPICS. The assignments shown here were based on the assumption that both prior and owner pointers were requested in all sets.

FIGURE 9.19c
Pointer assignment for the FACULTY record

DMCL

A sample of the IDMS DMCL (Device Media Control Language) is shown in Figure 9.20. The first entry indicates that the name of the DMCL is DISTRIBUTION–DMCL and that it corresponds to the schema called SCHEMA–DISTRIBUTION. In the buffer section, physical page size is indicated as well as

FIGURE 9.20
IDMS Device Media
Control Language

```
DEVICE_MEDIA NAME IS DISTRIBUTION_DMCL
                    OF SCHEMA_DISTRIBUTION.
BUFFER SECTION.
     BUFFER NAME IS DSTBUFF
     PAGE CONTAINS 1180 CHARACTERS
     BUFFER CONTAINS 5 PAGES.

AREA SECTION.
     COPY AREA_DISTRIBUTION.

      PREMIERE PRODUCTS SCHEMA DMCL (IDMS)
```

the number of pages that can be accommodated in memory at a time. In this example, the page size is 1,180 characters, and five such pages can be held in memory at any one time. Good choices for page size depend on both the particular application for which the database is designed and the characteristics of the device on which the database is located. The final entry shown here is the AREA SEC-TION, in which the information concerning the area or areas that make up the database are copied directly from the schema. (Not shown here is another section, the JOURNAL SECTION, in which the devices and files for journaling are described.)

PHYSICAL LAYOUT OF AN IDMS DATABASE

For the most part, it is not necessary for users of a DBMS to be concerned with the underlying physical layout of the database itself. After all, one of the advantages of database processing using a DBMS is that the DBMS handles all the physical activities. However, in the area of physical database design, it is impor-tant to have an understanding of the physical characteristics of the DBMS. Within physical database design, we must be able to determine the actual size of a data-base corresponding to a particular design as well as performance characteristics. To do this, we must know how the DBMS that we are using structures and manipu-lates data.

For these reasons, we will briefly examine the structure of an IDMS database. As we already mentioned, an IDMS database is divided into areas that are mapped into physical files in the schema. Each of these files is divided into pages, with the size of the pages specified in the DMCL.

The structure of these pages is shown in Figure 9.21. A page consists of a header, a footer, record occurrences, line index entries, and unused space. The header contains the number of the page, a calc header, and the number of bytes of space on the page that are still available. (As in other CODASYL systems, all of

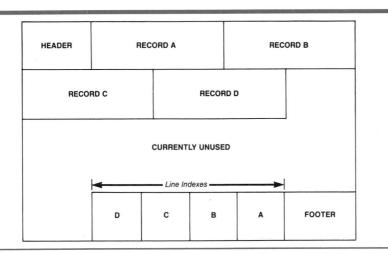

FIGURE 9.21
Physical Layout of an
IDMS Page

the records that are stored on a given page and whose location mode is calc are placed on a special chain called the calc chain. The calc header on the page points to the first of these calc entries.) The footer also contains the page number and the number of bytes used for the line index.

Record occurrences consist of a prefix area, which contains all of the appropriate pointers, and a data area. As Figure 9.22 demonstrates, occurrences of the

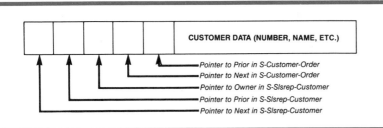

FIGURE 9.22
Physical Layout of the
CUSTOMER record

CUSTOMER record in the Premiere Products database contain a prefix area with five pointers (actually, there is a little more to the prefix area than just these pointers, but we will not get into that here) and a data area containing the actual customer data. The pointers appear within the prefix area in the order determined by the positions assigned within the schema. Each record in the database is assigned a DBKEY, which consists of the number of the page on which the record is located together with the record's line number within the page. If the page shown is page 157, the DBKEY of record C is 157/3. The pointers are really the DBKEYs of the records that are being pointed at.

The line indexes appear at the end of a page just prior to the footer, in reverse order. Thus, the line index for the *first* record on the page is the *last* line index. The line index contains the record ID, the location of the record within the page, the total length of the record, and the length of the prefix portion of the record.

The record ID corresponds to the ID assigned in the schema and indicates the type of record. If a line index in the Premiere Products database contains a record ID of 102, the system knows that this is a CUSTOMER record, since 102 is the ID assigned to the CUSTOMER record in the schema.

What should the system do if record C is deleted from the database shown in Figure 9.21? Certainly, record C could be removed from all the sets in which it participated as either owner or member by adjusting pointers appropriately. It could be physically removed from the page by moving the remaining records on the page up so that the unused space would be altogether in the middle of the page. In this case, record D would be moved to occupy the location formerly occupied by record C. What should be the DBKEY of record D after it has been moved? Should we change it from 157/4 to 157/3? We had better not make this change unless we want to make corresponding changes in all records that point to record D from anywhere in the database! The solution is to leave the DBKEY of record D alone, by removing record C from the database but *not its line index* (see Figure 9.23).

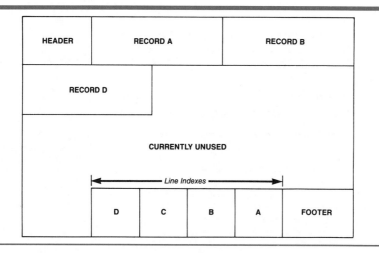

FIGURE 9.23
Physical Layout
after deletion of
RECORD C

Record D's line index will be updated to reflect its new location on the page, and record C's line index will be updated to reflect the fact that it is now unused. The next record to be added to this page will use this line index and will receive DBKEY 157/3.

SUBSCHEMA DDL

While IDMS does contain a subschema DDL that is similar but not identical to the CODASYL subschema DDL shown in chapter 8, subschemas may be specified in another way. A full subschema, SUBSCHEMA-DISTRIBUTION, that contains all of the records and sets of the Premiere Products database is shown in Figure 9.24. The first three lines of this subschema specify that the name of the subschema is SUBSCHEMA-DISTRIBUTION, that it is taken from the schema SCHEMA-DISTRIBUTION, and that the DMCL is specified in

```
ADD SUBSCHEMA NAME IS  SUBSCHEMA-DISTRIBUTION
    OF SCHEMA NAME SCHEMA-DISTRIBUTION
    DMCL IS DISTRIBUTION-DMCL.

ADD AREA NAME IS AREA-DISTRIBUTION.

ADD RECORD NAME   SLSREP
    ELEMENTS ARE ALL.
ADD RECORD NAME   CUSTOMER
    ELEMENTS ARE ALL.
ADD RECORD NAME   ORDER
    ELEMENTS ARE ALL.
ADD RECORD NAME   PART
    ELEMENTS ARE ALL.
ADD RECORD NAME   ORDER-LINE
    ELEMENTS ARE ALL.

ADD SET NAME      S-SLSREP-CUSTOMER.
ADD SET NAME      S-CUSTOMER-ORDER.
ADD SET NAME      S-ORDER-ORDER-LINE.
ADD SET NAME      S-PART-ORDER-LINE.
```

FIGURE 9.24
Full subschema for
Premiere Products
(IDMS)

DISTRIBUTION-DMCL. The next line indicates that there is only one area, AREA-DISTRIBUTION. The "ADD RECORD" lines indicate which record types are to be included. In addition, since ELEMENTS ARE ALL is specified in each record entry, all fields are to be included. Finally, the list of sets to be included is specified. If you check the list of records and sets against the full Premiere Products database, you will see that this subschema is indeed complete.

In contrast, the subschema shown in Figure 9.25, called SUBSCHEMA-CUSTOMER, contains only one set, S-SLSREP-CUSTOMER, and two records, SLSREP and CUSTOMER. Further, the list of fields available to this subschema is restricted. Within the SLSREP record the only fields (elements) available are SLSREP-NUMBER, SLSREP-NAME, and ADDRESS. Within the CUSTOMER record the only fields available are CUSTOMER-NUMBER, NAME, and ADDRESS.

```
ADD SUBSCHEMA NAME IS  SUBSCHEMA-CUSTOMER
    OF SCHEMA NAME SCHEMA-DISTRIBUTION
    DMCL IS DISTRIBUTION-DMCL.

ADD AREA NAME IS AREA-DISTRIBUTION.

ADD RECORD NAME   SLSREP
    ELEMENTS ARE SLSREP-NUMBER
                 SLSREP-NAME
                 ADDRESS.
ADD RECORD NAME   CUSTOMER
    ELEMENTS ARE CUSTOMER-NUMBER
                 NAME
                 ADDRESS.

ADD SET NAME      S-SLSREP-CUSTOMER.
```

FIGURE 9.25
Partial subschema for
Premiere Products
(IDMS)

For additional information on the data definition facilities of IDMS and for considerations regarding physical storage, see [3], [4], [5], and [6].

9.5   DATA MANIPULATION IN IDMS

For the most part, data manipulation in IDMS is the same as in the CODA-SYL model. Consequently, at this point, we will again focus only on differences between data manipulation within IDMS and within the general CODASYL model.

The primary difference in the available DML commands concerns the inclusion of the OBTAIN command. IDMS supports the various FIND commands. In each of those commands, the word OBTAIN can replace the word FIND, giving a legitimate OBTAIN command. The difference between the OBTAIN command and the FIND command is that the OBTAIN command is equivalent to the combination of a FIND and a GET. Thus, for example, the commands

```
FIND ANY CUSTOMER.
GET.
```

can be replaced with

```
OBTAIN ANY CUSTOMER.
```

and the commands

```
FIND OWNER WITHIN S-SLSREP-CUSTOMER.
GET.
```

can be replaced with

```
OBTAIN OWNER WITHIN S-SLSREP-CUSTOMER.
```

Other than this addition, the DML itself is very similar to the one discussed earlier.

Two other differences are found in the DATA DIVISION. It begins with a SCHEMA section rather than with a subschema section. The appearance of this section is identical to the SUBSCHEMA SECTION described in chapter 8. For the full subschema for Premiere Products, this section would be:

```
DATA DIVISION.
SCHEMA SECTION.
DB    SUBSCHEMA-DISTRIBUTION WITHIN SCHEMA-DISTRIBUTION.
FILE SECTION.
```

In addition, WORKING-STORAGE includes the statement

```
COPY IDMS SUBSCHEMA-DESCRIPTION.
```

During compilation, this statement causes the full subschema description to be inserted into the program. In addition to including all of the records, fields, and sets within the subschema, it includes the special registers as fields within a group item called SUBSCHEMA-CTRL. Among these special registers is ERROR-STATUS, which is used to detect error conditions in the same manner that DB-STATUS is used in other CODASYL systems. ERROR-STATUS is a four-character field. An ERROR-STATUS of "0000" indicates successful completion of a command, a value of "0307" indicates that the end of a set has been reached, and a value of "0326" indicates that no record was found to match the selection criteria. Within the SUBSCHEMA-CTRL, condition names may be associated with the various possible values for ERROR-STATUS, for example, DB-STATUS-OK with "0000", DB-END-OF-SET with "0307", and DB-REC-NOT-FOUND with "0326". Doing so allows us to replace

```
IF ERROR-STATUS = "0326" . . . .
```

with the more readable condition

```
IF DB-REC-NOT-FOUND . . .
```

and

```
PERFORM . . . .
      UNTIL ERROR-STATUS = "0307"
```

with

```
PERFORM . . . .
      UNTIL DB-END-OF-SET
```

We do not need to create our own flag to achieve this added readability. There are two apparent differences in the PROCEDURE DIVISION. The statement

```
COPY IDMS SUBSCHEMA-BINDS
```

appears in the startup portion of the PROCEDURE DIVISION. During compilation, this statement will cause code to be inserted which will tie, or *bind*, the subschema to the program at run time. In addition, the statement

```
COPY IDMS IDMS-STATUS
```

will appear someplace within the PROCEDURE DIVISION, probably somewhere near the end (although the placement is at the discretion of the programmer). This causes the following code to be inserted at compile time:

```
IDMS-STATUS     SECTION.
    IF DB-STATUS-OK GO TO ISABEX.
    DISPLAY "***************************"
             " ABORTING - "    PROGRAM-NAME
             ", "               ERROR-STATUS
             ", "               ERROR-RECORD
             " **** RECOVER  IDMS ****"
                UPON CONSOLE.
    DISPLAY "PROGRAM NAME        " PROGRAM-NAME.
    DISPLAY "ERROR STATUS        " ERROR-STATUS.
    DISPLAY "ERROR RECORD        " ERROR-RECORD.
    DISPLAY "ERROR SET -         " ERROR-SET.
    DISPLAY "ERROR AREA          " ERROR-AREA.
    DISPLAY "LAST GOOD RECORD _  " RECORD-NAME.
    DISPLAY "LAST GOOD AREA _    " AREA-NAME.
    CALL "ABORT".
ISABEX. EXIT.
```

The various fields that are displayed, PROGRAM-NAME, ERROR-STATUS, ERROR-RECORD, and so on, are all special registers within the SUBSCHEMA-CTRL that was mentioned earlier. With this section in place, the programmer will typically follow each IDMS command with logic that will first check to see whether some special condition (like DB-REC-NOT-FOUND) occurred and then, if the special condition did not occur, PERFORM IDMS-STATUS. In the process, if ERROR-STATUS is zero, indicating the lack of any problem, no special action will be taken. If, on the other hand, some other problem has occurred, then the values of the various special registers will be displayed for debugging purposes and the program will abort.

Figure 9.26 contrasts the IDMS versions of the solutions to some of the queries from chapter 8 with the general CODASYL solutions shown earlier in this chapter. Notice the following differences:

1. IDMS uses the term ERROR-STATUS rather than DB-STATUS. In some cases it is explicit (DISPLAY ERROR-STATUS), in others it is implicit (DB-REC-NOT-FOUND is really a condition name standing for ERROR-STATUS = "0306").
2. There are no GET statements in the IDMS version. Rather, all of the FIND commands are replaced by equivalent OBTAIN commands. Since the OBTAIN command is equivalent to a FIND followed by a GET, the GET commands are not necessary.
3. The function of the DATABASE-ERROR-PROCESSING section within the declaratives in the general CODASYL version is similar in one respect to that of the IDMS-STATUS SECTION in the IDMS version. Both will serve to display some data for debugging purposes in the event of a serious error and will then shut down the program. The IDMS-STATUS is invoked by means of strategically placed PERFORM statements, whereas the DATABASE-ERROR-PROCESSING SECTION is invoked automatically when any DML command results in a DB-STATUS other than zero.

4. The DATABASE–ERROR–PROCESSING section is also used in the general CODASYL version to set our own flag, the DATABASE–STATUS–FLAG. Since we were able to attach condition names to our own flag (NO–SUCH–RECORD, END–OF–SET, etc.), we were able to improve readability. In IDMS, condition names can be associated directly with ERROR–STATUS, and so this step is unnecessary.

FIGURE 9.26a
General CODASYL examples

```
                    GENERAL CODASYL VERSION

DECLARATIVES.

DATABASE-ERROR-PROCESSING SECTION. USE FOR DB-EXCEPTION.

ERROR-PROCESSING-ROUTINE.
      IF DB-STATUS = "0502100"
            MOVE "EOC" TO DATABASE-STATUS-FLAG
        ELSE IF DB-STATUS = "0502400"
            MOVE "NOREC" TO DATABASE-STATUS-FLAG
        ELSE IF DB-STATUS = "1505100"
            MOVE "DUP" TO DATABASE-STATUS-FLAG
        ELSE
            DISPLAY "ABORTING"
            DISPLAY "ERROR STATUS ___ " DB-STATUS
            DISPLAY "ERROR RECORD ___ " DB-RECORD-NAME
            DISPLAY "ERROR SET ____- " DB-SET-NAME
            DISPLAY "ERROR AREA ____ " DB-REALM-NAME
            STOP RUN.

END DECLARATIVES.

(Beginning of regular procedure division code)

        MOVE 12 TO SLSREP-NUMBER.
        MOVE "OK" TO DATABASE-STATUS-FLAG.
        FIND ANY SLSREP.
        IF NO-SUCH-RECORD
            print error message - "NO SUCH SALES REP"
          ELSE
            GET
            print SLSREP-NUMBER, SLSREP-NAME.
                                    Example 1 — Chapter 8
        MOVE 6 TO SLSREP-NUMBER.
        MOVE "OK" TO DATABASE-STATUS-FLAG.
        FIND ANY SLSREP.
        IF NO-SUCH-RECORD
            print error message - "NO SUCH SALES REP"
          ELSE
            PERFORM FIND-AND-DISPLAY-CUSTOMERS
                UNTIL END-OF-CHAIN.


FIND-AND-DISPLAY-CUSTOMERS.
      FIND NEXT CUSTOMER WITHIN S-SLSREP-CUSTOMER.
      IF DB-STATUS-OK
          GET
          print CUSTOMER-NUMBER, NAME.    Example 2 — Chapter 8
```

FIGURE 9.26b
Corresponding IDMS
examples

```
                    IDMS VERSION
       MOVE 12 TO SLSREP-NUMBER.
       OBTAIN ANY SLSREP.
       IF DB-REC-NOT-FOUND
            print error message - "NO SUCH SALES REP"
          ELSE
              PERFORM IDMS-STATUS
              print SLSREP-NUMBER, SLSREP-NAME.
```

Example 1 — Chapter 8

```
       MOVE 6 TO SLSREP-NUMBER.
       OBTAIN ANY SLSREP.
       IF DB-REC-NOT-FOUND
            print error message - "NO SUCH SALES REP"
          ELSE
              PERFORM IDMS-STATUS
              PERFORM FIND-AND-DISPLAY-CUSTOMERS
                    DB-END-OF-SET.


   FIND-AND-DISPLAY-CUSTOMERS.
          OBTAIN NEXT CUSTOMER WITHIN S-SLSREP-CUSTOMER.
          IF NOT DB-END-OF-SET
              PERFORM IDMS-STATUS
              print CUSTOMER-NUMBER, NAME.
```

Example 2 — Chapter 8

```
   IDMS-STATUS      SECTION.
          IF DB-STATUS-OK GO TO ISABEX.
          DISPLAY '**************************'
                   ' ABORTING - ' PROGRAM-NAME
                   ', '              ERROR-STATUS
                   ', '              ERROR-RECORD
                   ' **** RECOVER IDMS ****'
                   UPON CONSOLE.
          DISPLAY 'PROGRAM NAME ___ ' PROGRAM-NAME.
          DISPLAY 'ERROR STATUS ___ ' ERROR-STATUS.
          DISPLAY 'ERROR RECORD ___ ' ERROR-RECORD.
          DISPLAY 'ERROR SET ____- ' ERROR-SET.
          DISPLAY 'ERROR AREA ____ ' ERROR-AREA.
          DISPLAY 'LAST GOOD RECORD _ ' RECORD-NAME.
          DISPLAY 'LAST GOOD AREA __ ' AREA-NAME.
          CALL 'ABORT'.
   ISABEX. EXIT.
```

The DML commands within IDMS are actually implemented as a collection of subroutines. Technically, to store a sales rep in the Premiere Products database, the statement is

```
   CALL "IDMS" USING IDBMSCOM(42)
                 SR101.
```

and not the standard

```
STORE SLSREP
```

Fortunately, the code that programmers write uses the standard commands. Before compilation, the IDMS precompiler will convert the application program written with the standard DML commands to a program in which these commands have been replaced by appropriate call statements. It is this updated version that will then be compiled. In the updated version, the original form of the commands is retained but they are converted to comments; i.e.,

```
STORE SLSREP
```

is replaced by

```
*       STORE SLSREP
        CALL "IDMS" USING IDBMSCOM(42)
                          SR101.
```

For additional information on the data manipulation facilities of IDMS, see [3], [4], [5], and [6].

.6   IDMS/R

In 1983, an enhanced version of IDMS, called **IDMS/R (IDMS/RELATIONAL)**, was announced by Cullinet. All of the CODASYL facilities discussed earlier in this chapter were retained and new relational features were added. Since this chapter is concerned with advanced features of the CODASYL model as well as with an implementation of the model, a review of these added features technically does not belong here. We do include such a review for two reasons, however. The first is that IDMS is one of the dominant CODASYL systems currently available, and this new component is an important part of the system. The second is that this represents a direction in which many DBMS vendors are moving; i.e., the enhancement of existing systems with relational-like capabilities.

LOGICAL RECORD FACILITY (LRF)

Before discussing the feature that provides the relational capabilities themselves, we must examine the Logical Record Facility (LRF). The LRF allows specification of logical records; i.e., records that do not exist in the CODASYL database but can be derived from existing records and sets.

Suppose, for example, that a report were needed at Premiere Products which would list for a given sales rep his or her number and name as well as the number and name of all the customers represented by the sales rep, together with the order number and order date of all orders placed by each of these customers. Certainly this report could be produced by a program using a subschema that contained the SLSREP record, the CUSTOMER record, the ORDER record, and the sets S-SLSREP-CUSTOMER and S-CUSTOMER-ORDER. The program would, of course, need to navigate the database in an appropriate fashion to gather the required data. If, however, all of the data were stored in a single flat file whose records contained SLSREP-NUMBER, SLSREP-NAME, CUSTOMER-NUMBER, NAME, ORDER-NUMBER, and ORDER-DATE fields, no navigation would be required and the program would be much simpler. This is not to suggest that such a file would be appropriate. It would certainly suffer from a number of the update problems discussed in the chapter on normalization (chapter 4). It would be handy for the purpose of retrieval, though.

The LRF provides a mechanism for deriving such a record from data in the existing database. The subschema necessary for this particular record is shown in Figure 9.27. The record is called SALES-CUSTOMERS and contains the fields

FIGURE 9.27
Partial subschema
with logical record
(IDMS)

```
ADD SUBSCHEMA NAME IS  SUBSCHEMA-CUSTOMER
    OF SCHEMA NAME SCHEMA-DISTRIBUTION
    DMCL IS DISTRIBUTION-DMCL.

ADD AREA NAME IS AREA-DISTRIBUTION.

ADD RECORD NAME    SLSREP
    ELEMENTS ARE ALL.
ADD RECORD NAME    CUSTOMER
    ELEMENTS ARE ALL.
ADD RECORD NAME    ORDER
    ELEMENTS ARE ALL.

ADD SET NAME       S-SLSREP-CUSTOMER.
ADD SET NAME       S-CUSTOMER-ORDER.

ADD LOGICAL RECORD IS SALES-CUSTOMERS
    ELEMENTS ARE SLSREP-NUMBER, SLSREP-NAME, CUSTOMER-NUMBER
                 NAME, ORDER-NUMBER, ORDER-DATE.

ADD PATH-GROUP OBTAIN SALES-CUSTOMERS
    SELECT FOR FIELDNAME-EQ SLSREP-NUMBER
           OBTAIN SLSREP WHERE CALCKEY IS SLSREP-NUMBER OF REQUEST
           OBTAIN EACH CUSTOMER WITHIN S-SLSREP-CUSTOMER
           OBTAIN EACH ORDER WITHIN S-CUSTOMER-ORDER.
```

described earlier. It is termed a **logical record** (it does not actually exist physically in the database). The method for constructing such records is described in the PATH-GROUP. In Figure 9.27, the sales rep whose calc key matches the sales rep number of the request is found directly. Once this has been accomplished, each customer owned by this sales rep in the set S-SLSREP-CUSTOMER is obtained. For each of these customers, each order owned by the customer within the set S-CUSTOMER-ORDER is also obtained.

Notice that this data definition language contains data *manipulation* commands, something that is not true in general CODASYL systems. This feature more closely resembles relational systems in which views are typically defined through the regular data manipulation commands. In IDMS/R, however, the data manipulation commands used during data definition are different from those used in application programs.

An application programmer can treat logical records as though they exist physically. The system will create these records when needed, following the instructions specified in the subschema. The list of commands available when processing a logical record such as the SALES–CUSTOMERS record is:

```
OBTAIN FIRST SALES–CUSTOMERS RECORD WHERE condition
OBTAIN NEXT SALES–CUSTOMERS RECORD WHERE condition
MODIFY SALES–CUSTOMERS RECORD (the most recently
              obtained record)
ERASE SALES–CUSTOMERS RECORD (the most recently
              obtained record)
STORE SALES–CUSTOMERS RECORD
```

Actually, in order to use any of the above commands, a PATH–GROUP must be specified in the subschema for the command. In Figure 9.27, only a path group for OBTAIN has been specified, so only the OBTAIN operation would be valid. In fact, the example is more restrictive than that. It has only specified a procedure for obtaining a SALES–CUSTOMER record given a sales rep number. If elsewhere in the program we needed to obtain a SALES–CUSTOMERS record based on another field, say, ORDER–NUMBER, an additional procedure would be specified within the PATH–GROUP in a similar fashion. If, on the other hand, we needed to change a SALES–CUSTOMERS record, then an additional PATH–GROUP would have to be specified. In this case the PATH–GROUP command would begin with ADD PATH–GROUP MODIFY SALES–CUSTOMERS.

When processing logical records, the program need not concern itself with **database navigation**, which is a definite advantage. The system is still doing the navigation, however. In particular, it is maintaining appropriate currencies. Thus, mixing the processing of logical records and physical records in the same program can be very risky. If an access to a physical record updates one of the currency indicators the system is using in the processing of the logical records, the results will be unpredictable at best and potentially disastrous.

We could certainly view logical (or physical) records as relations. Since logical records can be specified that are effectively selections, projections, and/or joins of existing records in the network database, the LRF does provide some relational capabilities. It is not particularly dynamic, however, since a request for a selection, projection, or join that has not been previously defined necessitates the creation of a new subschema as well as a program to process this subschema. In addition, any optimization is done by the person or group that specifies the subschema, *not* by the system itself.

AUTOMATIC SYSTEM FACILITY (ASF)

While implementing the LRF on top of IDMS gives some relational flavor to the system, it is the Automatic System Facility (ASF) that really represents the "R" in "IDMS/R". The ASF adds many new capabilities to those of the LRF.

Relations (termed relational records, or tables, within the ASF) are treated as LRF logical records. A table can be a *stored* table, in which case it physically exists, or a **view**, in which case it is derived, when needed, from one or more existing tables. One interesting feature of the ASF is that stored tables can be derived; i.e., a query is defined along with the definition of the stored relation. Executing the POPULATE command within the ASF causes the results of the query to be physically placed in the table. (By contrast, views do not exist in any permanent physical sense.) At any time, the table may be repopulated, in which case the previous contents of the table will be deleted and the query reexecuted. This type of stored table is called a derived stored table. A stored table that does not have such a defining query is called a basic stored table.

BASIC STORED TABLES

The building blocks of an IDMS/R relational database are the basic stored tables. To define a basic stored table, the user specifies the names and attributes of the fields within the table as well as fields or combinations of fields that will serve as keys. The keys may be required to be unique, if so desired. The user then issues a GENERATE command. At this point, the ASF will:

1. Add a definition of the stored table to the "relational schema", which is the collection of the descriptions of all tables and indexes that have been defined to IDMS/R.
2. Add definitions of all indexes required for the keys that the user has specified to the relational schema.
3. Create and compile a subschema that defines the table as a logical record in the LRF. In this subschema are specified PATH-GROUPS for the OBTAIN, MODIFY, STORE, and ERASE that will make use of all the indexes described in step two.
4. Create code necessary to permit interactive update to the table through on-screen data entry forms. (The user does not create these forms. Other products within the Cullinet line allow users to create their own customized forms, if they so desire.)

Since at this point the user can begin to enter data into the table, update data within the table, and retrieve data from the table using simple queries, he or she has effectively created an application system, albeit a limited one, automatically. It is this fact that leads to the name "AUTOMATIC SYSTEMS FACILITY". The users can add further capabilities to this system and can customize it by using other components of the Cullinet line.

VIEWS

A user defines a **view** by specifying a **defining query**; i.e., by defining the view as an appropriate combination of the select, project, and join operations to be applied to existing basic stored tables. In addition, the user specifies whether updates are allowed for this view and, if they are, specifies what effect the updates are to have on the underlying basic stored tables. Once the view has been specified, the user issues the GENERATE command, at which time the ASF will:

1. Add a definition of the view to the relational schema.
2. Create and compile a subschema that defines the view as a logical record in the LRF, using the view definition to construct the appropriate PATH–GROUPS.
3. Create code necessary to permit interactive update to the table through on-screen data entry forms.

At this point, the user can operate on the view just as though it were a stored table. It is not stored, of course, but rather created dynamically by the system as needed.

DERIVED STORED TABLES

Both views and derived stored tables have defining queries. The only difference between specifying a view and a derived stored table is that an extra step is necessary for a derived stored table, the POPULATE step. This follows the "GEN–ERATE" and causes to be placed in the derived stored table the data obtained by applying the defining query to data currently existing in the appropriate basic stored tables.

It is important to note that once the data is placed in the derived stored table, it is static; i.e., a change to the data in the basic stored tables will not affect the data currently in the derived stored table. In order to make the data in the derived stored table current, it is necessary to repopulate the table. Derived stored tables are ideal for capturing snapshots of data in the actual database at a given point in time. These snapshots can then be manipulated in any way the user sees fit without affecting the users of the actual database.

RELATIONSHIP TO NETWORK DATABASES

One of the unique features of IDMS/R is the relational-like access to network databases that it offers. This is accomplished through views that are defined on an underlying network database. These views can then be manipulated in the same fashion as those views defined on relations (basic stored tables). In order to define views on network databases, the following steps are necessary:

1. The definitions of records and sets in the network schema must be copied to the relational schema. Any subsequent changes to the network schema *must also be made* to the relational schema. This will not happen automatically.

2. A network subschema must be created for each view, including all of the records *and sets* necessary to support the view.

3. An ASF view definition must be created for each view. This definition will involve the network records and sets necessary to support the view. It could also optionally involve basic stored tables. If sets exist in the network database to support a join operation, they may be specified in the view definition by using the condition "SET setname".

4. The GENERATE command must be issued for each view.

The ASF thus supports not only a relational approach to database management, where the relations are the basic stored tables, but also relational access to network databases, potentially achieving the extra efficiency for which network systems in general and IDMS in particular are known.

Suppose, for example Premiere Products were employing IDMS to process their database, using the network version of their schema that was shown earlier. Suppose further that there were a complete application system consisting of a number of COBOL programs that updated and reported on this database. These programs exist to satisfy well-known requirements. They efficiently support large numbers of users submitting large numbers of transactions. In other words, they do what CODASYL systems do best. They process with great efficiency a system whose requirements are well known and which do not tend to fluctuate drastically. If some users within Premiere Products had needs that were not so easy to anticipate and who required the flexibility afforded by the relational approach, their needs could be met as well. Views would be created that allowed them to access the database relationally. Further, wherever possible, joins would be effected through the use of the underlying sets.

If a view involved the joining of sales reps and customers, for example, it would be handled through the set S–SLSREP–CUSTOMER; i.e., the system would use this set to determine which customers were related to which sales reps rather than actually join on some common field. Note that this would be necessary here since there would be no sales rep field in the customer record. Even if there were such a field, however, we would still probably choose to accomplish the join through the set to achieve the increase in efficiency. (The set and all of its associated pointers are already being maintained. There is no need in this case to also maintain some sort of index to facilitate the join.)

In addition to the network database at Premiere Products, basic stored tables could also be defined for other needs within the enterprise. Some views could be defined that only included information from some of the stored tables. Other views might include only information from the network database. Still others might involve both. Thus, IDMS/R furnishes the capacity to mix the two, thus achieving the flexibility of the relational model while still having access to the power of IDMS when the extra efficiency is critical.

IDMS/R AS A RELATIONAL SYSTEM

When considered as a DBMS in its own right, the relational component of IDMS/R has the following characteristics:

1. Data is perceived by the user as collections of tables.
2. The select, project, and join operations are supported, although less dynamically than in relational systems like DB2, in which joins, for example, can be requested on the fly as part of an SQL query. In IDMS/R, joins are specified as part of a view definition, not as part of a true interactive query. In addition, when a select is requested as part of a view definition, duplicate rows are *not* eliminated as they technically should be in a fully relational system.
3. UNION and DIFFERENCE operations are not supported. Neither is dynamic ordering (like the SQL "ORDER BY") or update operations involving more than a single record (like the SQL "UPDATE WHERE").
4. *Referential integrity* is not supported directly. Any kind of support is done as part of the view definitions; e.g., by specifying the rules for update and the effects of the update on a view that involves sales reps and customers, users updating the database via this view could be prevented from entering a customer represented by a nonexistent sales rep. While this support for referential integrity is greater than that furnished by some relational systems, it is still not complete. There is nothing to prevent some other user with a different view from entering such a customer unless that user's view also carries exactly the same restrictions. Further, even if all user views carried these restrictions, any user entering data directly into the customer table would not be subject to these restrictions.

Owing in large measure to the popularity and power of IDMS, IDMS/R is an important and popular system. It does furnish a marriage of the relational and the network approaches to database management, providing for its users, it is hoped, the best of both.

For additional information on the relational component of IDMS/R, see [3], [4], and [5].

.7   IDMS and the FUNCTIONS OF A DBMS

Obviously, IDMS supports the storage, retrieval, and update of data. Through an integrated **data dictionary**, it furnishes a user-accessible **catalog** for data descriptions that far exceeds that of many of the other systems. It provides its own communications software (IDMS/DC), in addition to support for other communications control programs, such as IBM's CICS. It provides several utility services, including services to initialize and/or update the directory, print a variety of reports concerning the structure of the database, load records into the database according to user formats, and restructure the database. The remaining functions will be considered individually after we examine two crucial statements: **COM-MIT** and **ROLLBACK**.

COMMIT and ROLLBACK

There are two crucial commands within IDMS that relate to support for logical transactions, shared update, and recovery: COMMIT and ROLLBACK. The COMMIT command will cause all changes to the database that the run unit (program) currently has in process to be made permanent and all locks other than those on current records to be released. Another form of the COMMIT command, COMMIT ALL, will cause all changes to be made permanent, *all* locks to be released, and all currency indicators set to null. In either case, the state of the database and the log are synchronized and a clean checkpoint has been created. The ROLLBACK command causes all changes to the database made by the run unit since the last COMMIT to be undone, all locks to be released, and all currency indicators to be set to null. If the optional word CONTINUE is included (ROLLBACK CONTINUE), processing is allowed to continue from that point; otherwise, processing is terminated.

LOGICAL TRANSACTIONS

IDMS provides support for **logical transactions**. While there is no "BEGIN TRANSACTION" command, the COMMIT command effectively marks both the end of one logical transaction and the beginning of the next. The READY command marks the beginning of the first logical transaction and the FINISH command marks the end of the last one. If, for some reason, not all of the updates necessary for a single logical transaction can be completed, the ROLLBACK command, by undoing all of the updates since the last **checkpoint**, (i.e., all of the updates since the start of the current transaction) will ensure that none of them is completed.

SHARED UPDATE

IDMS uses the shared and exclusive locks in supporting **shared update**. When an application program retrieves a record, the program is granted a **shared lock**. When the program attempts to update a record, the system attempts to **promote the lock** to **exclusive** status. Once this has been done, the update can be completed and no other program can acquire any type of lock on the record. Locks may be released by the application program itself, using the COMMIT and ROLLBACK commands just described as well as the FINISH command. In addition, if a user is detected as having caused a deadlock, the system will cause an automatic ROLLBACK to be performed, in which case locks will be released.

RECOVERY

Basically, IDMS supports the type of **recovery** described in chapter 2. During the recovery process it uses a journal containing **before and after images** of all changes as well as information on **checkpoints**. These are not systemwide checkpoints but rather individual ones for each of the application programs processing the database. The various types of recovery proceed in the manner described in chapter 2.

IDMS does have a feature (not included in all systems) that can cause the necessity of a rollback. This feature is called *time-out*. When a program has been in a wait state for a predetermined amount of time (e.g., waiting for another program to release a lock), the program is timed out. In this case a ROLLBACK occurs.

SECURITY

Subschema authorizations provide the primary **security** features in IDMS. A given subschema may restrict users of that subschema to only retrieval within an area. Another may permit both retrieval and update. Each subschema can restrict its users to only certain operations on the records declared and sets described within the subschema. A given subschema for Premiere Products could, for example, allow users to OBTAIN any record, STORE, ERASE, and MODIFY ORDER records, STORE, ERASE and MODIFY ORDER-LINE records, MODIFY PART records, and ERASE CUSTOMER records. Programs accessing the database via this subschema could not issue any commands not in this list. They could not STORE a new customer, for example, since the STORE operation is not permitted for CUS-TOMER records.

Another security feature in IDMS is the database procedure mentioned earlier in this chapter. The use of procedures to compress and decompress data were illustrated in the example schema. We pointed out that the organization could supply procedures of its own. When DML commands are issued for which a procedure exists, IDMS will exit to this procedure prior to executing the DML command itself. Such procedures could be used to implement more sophisticated security features, perhaps even a dialogue with the user in which not one but several passwords must be given. Some of the passwords might be numbers calculated by a formula involving some always changing entity, like the date, for example. In the case of a date, a password that worked one day would not work the next. The user would need to know the formula.

Further security features are furnished by the integrated data dictionary.

INTEGRITY

IDMS provides some **integrity** support. It provides features to ensure that data values are of the right type (numeric, alphabetic, etc.), that key values are unique, and that an AUTOMATIC MANDATORY set member cannot exist in the database without being related to its owner. Other features can be added by the organization through user-defined procedures. These procedures, which will be invoked prior to the execution of certain DML commands, can be used to augment the integrity services of IDMS. A procedure could be written, for example, to ensure that a customer's credit limit would be $300, $500, $800, or $1000. These user-defined procedures suffer from an important limitation: they cannot contain any IDMS commands. Thus, if the validation of data within the CUSTOMER record requires accessing a SLSREP record for some reason, this validation cannot be accomplished through a user-defined procedure but instead must be enforced by the application programs themselves.

DATA INDEPENDENCE

Like many hierarchical and network systems, IDMS furnishes a moderate degree of **physical data independence**, i.e., many changes can be made to the physical structure of the database which do not need to affect application programs. In some ways, IDMS furnishes slightly less than some of the other network systems. If, for example, the database at Premiere Products were reorganized in such a way that the set S–SLSREP–CUSTOMER no longer had prior pointers, then the command FIND PRIOR WITHIN S–SLSREP–CUSTOMER would no longer be valid, and any program that contained such a command would have to be changed. In many systems this would not be the case. Although the command would not execute as rapidly as it did previously, it would still be legitimate in these systems.

Also, like most network and hierarchical systems, IDMS does not furnish a particularly high level of **logical data independence**, i.e., changes to the logical structure of the database do require changes to application programs. This is due to the navigational nature of such systems. The addition or removal of a relationship (SET) can drastically affect the way some of the application programs must navigate their way through the database.

IDMS/R, on the other hand, furnishes a much higher level of data independence through the LRF and, more specifically, the ASF. Defining logical records through the LRF removes navigational details from application programs and places these details in the subschema, specifically in the PATH–GROUP specifications. Thus, a change to the logical structure of the database may mean only a change to the access procedures specified in the PATH–GROUPS in the subschemas and not the application programs themselves. Since databases defined through the ASF are really relational in nature, they achieve, in general, the added logical independence furnished by the relational model.

For additional information on the manner in which IDMS furnishes the capabilities of a DBMS, see [3] and [5].

9.8 COMPARISON OF NETWORK AND RELATIONAL MODELS

Now let's compare the network model (specifically, the CODASYL model) to the relational model.

STRUCTURE

The tabular structure of the relational model is simpler than the records and sets structure of the CODASYL model, especially for the casual user. Although programmers who have worked on CODASYL systems do become quite comfortable with the model and with the process of database navigation, the necessity to continually navigate the database in an appropriate way in every program adds a level of complexity not present in the relational model.

The network structure is characterized by greater fragmentation of information than the relational structure. In the network version of the Premiere Products database, for example, the number of the sales rep who represents a given customer is not part of that customer's record, whereas in the relational model implementation, it is. Instead, in the network structure, we must find the sales rep who owns the customer within the set S–SLSREP–CUSTOMER.

There is only one construction in the relational model, and that is the relation. In the network model, there are two: records and sets. Computer professionals disagree as to whether having two constructions instead of one is an advantage or a disadvantage. Some argue that if the job can be done with a single construction, as in the relational model, the addition of a second unnecessarily increases complexity. Others claim that since, inherently, two facets of an organization, entities and relationships, need to be included in a database model, it is more natural to have two constructions. They would say it is desirable for the relationships to be explicit, as they are in the network model, rather than implicit, as in the relational model. They would further state that in the basic relational model, relationships are difficult to discern. Given a large collection of relations, discerning the relationships involves examining all of the tables for common columns. Since the names of these common columns can vary from one table to another, the task can be a complex one. The use of foreign keys can alleviate this problem. Current relational systems, however, are very weak in their support of foreign keys.

EFFICIENCY

At the present time, CODASYL systems are generally more efficient than those which support the relational model. Vendors of relational model systems are working hard to improve the level of efficiency in their systems, so the performance gap is going to narrow in years to come. No one knows just when the gap will finally be overcome, however.

The fact that CODASYL systems may be more efficient does not automatically guarantee that an application system that has been written using a CODASYL DBMS will provide better performance to the users of the system. To achieve high performance using a CODASYL DBMS, not only must the database be designed correctly, but the programmers themselves must choose the best way to process the database in order to satisfy the requirements they have been given. Optimization is accomplished by programmers in this case, not by the system. In contrast, good relational model systems contain efficient optimizers. A programmer or user of the system indicates the task to be done and the system determines the best way to accomplish the task, based on its own knowledge of the structure of the database and the presence or absence of various indexes.

The net result is that good, knowledgeable programmers working with a CODASYL system will probably produce an application system that performs better than the one produced by comparably skilled programmers using a relational model system. If the CODASYL programmers are not highly skilled, however, they may be less successful. There is another consideration, however. Let's assume that the CODASYL programmers have indeed done their job well. Let's assume further that after the system has been in place for some period of time, some change is made to the structure of the database. At this point, an approach to a given type of processing which previously was optimal may now be far less than optimal. Programs that formerly processed very efficiently may no longer be nearly as efficient. If programs in a CODASYL system are to retain their former efficiency, programmers must delve into the programs to reoptimize them. In contrast, in a relational model system, since the system itself does the optimization, programmers would not have to be concerned with the task of reoptimization. In some cases, this one factor alone outweighs the greater performance of the CODASYL model.

EASE OF USE

Because the structure and operations within the relational model are simpler than those of the CODASYL model, and because of the presence of relational model languages like SQL, relational model systems are easier to use. No complex database navigation is required. Complex queries can be formulated in a simple, straightforward manner.

Many CODASYL systems do achieve a comparable level of simplicity through query languages which are furnished along with the DBMS and which allow users to obtain reports and get answers to queries from the database. These languages are valuable, indispensable, tools, both to programmers, who benefit from the increased productivity, and to end users. There are two drawbacks, however, regarding the use of these languages compared to a relational model language like SQL. First, although in simple queries the users do not have to be concerned with database navigation, in more complex queries they do. This can present a large obstacle if the query language is being employed by a casual user and not by an experienced programmer who is familiar with the mechanics of navigating a CODASYL database. Second, these query languages are not standardized. Most of the query languages do offer roughly the same functionality, but the manner in which it is offered varies widely from one query language to another.

DATA INDEPENDENCE

There are two types of **data independence**: physical and logical. *Physical data independence* occurs when changes to the physical characteristics of the database do not affect application programs. *Logical data independence* occurs when changes to the logical structure of the database do not affect application programs.

Both CODASYL and relational model systems offer some degree of physical data independence. Programs are immune to many changes that can be made to the physical characteristics. In general, format details, field placement, and other storage characteristics can be changed in both types of systems without necessitating program changes. There are exceptions, of course. Within some CODASYL systems, like IDMS, the absence of prior pointers invalidates the FIND PRIOR command. Thus, any program using the FIND PRIOR command would need to be modified if the database were reorganized in such a way that prior pointers were no longer required. In other systems, however, the command would still be legitimate and, thus, the deletion of prior pointers would not cause this problem. Basically, though, it is fair to say that CODASYL and relational model systems both score well in the area of physical data independence.

Logical data independence is a different story, however. Commercially available CODASYL systems offer little, if any, logical data independence. Any change to the structure of the database that affects the manner of navigation necessary to satisfy a given requirement will affect all programs that were navigating the database in this way. (Suppose that customers at Premiere Products were assigned to territories and territories were in turn assigned to sales reps. To accommodate this, a new record type, TERRITORY, would be added and the set S–SLSREP–CUSTOMER would be replaced by two sets, S–SLSREP–TERRITORY and S–TERRITORY–CUSTOMER. Any program that previously located the sales rep for a given customer merely by finding the owner within S–SLSREP–CUSTOMER would have to be modified to first find the territory that owned this customer within S–TERRITORY–CUSTOMER and then find the owner of this territory within S–SLSREP–TERRITORY.) Cullinet, we might add, has made great strides in this direction with the LRF. If a logical record has been defined in a subschema and the logical structure of the database changes, a new subschema will be created, with the PATH–GROUPS modified to indicate how the record is to be constructed from the new schema. Since application programs access only these logical records and are not aware of how they are created, no program changes would need to be made.

Relational systems, in theory, offer a great deal of logical data independence. This is achieved through the view mechanism. Changes to the structure of the underlying relations are compensated for by corresponding changes to the view mechanism. In the hypothetical situation just referred to, the view definition would change from

```
CREATE VIEW SALES_CUSTOMER (SLSREP_NUMBER,
          SLSREP_NAME, CUSTOMER_NUMBER, NAME)
  AS     SELECT SLSREP.SLSREP_NUMBER, SLSREP.SLSREP_NAME,
             CUSTOMER.CUSTOMER_NUMBER, CUSTOMER.NAME
         FROM CUSTOMER, SLSREP
         WHERE CUSTOMER.SLSREP_NUMBER = SLSREP.NUMBER
to
  CREATE VIEW SALES_CUSTOMER (SLSREP_NUMBER,
          SLSREP_NAME, CUSTOMER_NUMBER, NAME)
  AS     SELECT SLSREP.SLSREP_NUMBER, SLSREP.SLSREP_NAME,
             CUSTOMER.CUSTOMER_NUMBER, CUSTOMER.NAME
         FROM CUSTOMER, TERRITORY, SLSREP
         WHERE CUSTOMER.TERRITORY_NUMBER
             = TERRITORY.TERRITORY_NUMBER
         AND TERRITORY.SLSREP_NUMBER
             = SLSREP.SLSREP_NUMBER
```

We say these systems offer a great deal of logical data independence *in theory* because of the restriction currently in many commercial relational systems that views which are constructed by using the join operation are not updatable. Suppose a change to a database necessitates a change to a view definition from one that did not involve a join to one that does. Users of this view will no longer be able to update the database! This should not be the case in order to have true logical data independence.

INTEGRITY

Rather than focus on integrity constraints that are theoretically possible in either model, we will focus on one particular type of constraint that presents a major problem in most relational model systems today: foreign keys. Most commercial relational systems do not provide adequate support for foreign keys. Most systems have no capability to ensure that the sales rep for a given customer must exist in the database before the customer is added, for example. In contrast, such facilities do exist in CODASYL model systems. While it might not be possible to implement all of the desired foreign key rules (such as UPDATE RESTRICTED or UPDATE CASCADES), by making the set S_SLSREP_CUSTOMER an AUTO-MATIC, MANDATORY set, we can at least ensure that no customer for whom no sales rep exists is permitted in the database.

MOMENTUM

As much of the previous discussion illustrates, relational model systems offer a number of advantages not provided by "pure" CODASYL systems. The only major disadvantage at the present time is their efficiency. When that problem has been corrected, there will be no reason to choose a "pure" CODASYL system over a relational system. This does not mean that CODASYL systems will disappear in the near future, however. They have a vast amount of momentum not yet enjoyed by relational model systems. A vast body of commercial application systems has been developed using some of the more popular, high-powered CODASYL systems. The investment that has been made in these systems will necessitate their continued use. Further, many future CODASYL systems will no longer be "pure" CODASYL systems. Like IDMS, they will be augmented with relational capabilities. When this happens, many of their former disadvantages will disappear.

For an additional discussion of the relative merits of the CODASYL and relational models, see [4] and [5].

9.9 SUMMARY

In this chapter, we have examined some advanced topics within the CODA-SYL model. We examined a method of using declaratives to improve readability and to handle unexpected errors that necessitated termination of the program. We examined multimember sets, i.e., sets with more than one member record type. Two special uses of manual sets, handling loops in the database design and implementing nulls, were discussed. We discussed the pros and cons of using system-owned sets. Another approach to sets in general and sorted sets in particular, called POINTER ARRAYS, was discussed. A method for causing certain currency indicators *not* to be updated, using the RETAINING CURRENCY clause, was discussed as well as a mechanism for saving a location of a record in the database using the ACCEPT statement. We reviewed two other conditions that can be used within the IF statement: the tenancy condition, in which we can test to see whether a record is a member within a specific set, and the member condition, in which we can test to see whether a given set occurrence contains any member occurrences.

We discussed the CODASYL implementation of the bill-of-materials structure. In this structure, each part is related to its immediate components. This many-to-many relationship between an entity, in this case PART, and itself can be handled with an additional record type, which we called PRODUCT_STRUCTURE, and two set types, which we called BILL_OF_MATERIALS and WHERE_USED. In both set types, PART is the owner record type and PRODUCT_STRUCTURE is the member record type. We discussed a similar structure that relates courses to their prerequisites. Finally, we discussed the possibility of implementing a one-to-many relationship between an entity and itself, using a recursive set, one in which the owner and member record types are both the same. Although the later CODASYL specifications permit such a structure, most commercial CODASYL systems do not. If this structure is not available, then a structure similar to the one in the bill-of-materials example is used to implement the relationship.

The CODASYL system IDMS, which is marketed by Cullinet Software, Inc., is the major CODASYL implementation running on IBM equipment. We examined the schema DDL for IDMS which, while differing slightly from that presented for the general CODASYL model, is essentially the same. We examined the DMCL as well as the actual physical layout of an IDMS database. The subschema DDL was also discussed. Except for the inclusion of the OBTAIN command, which is equivalent to a FIND followed by a GET, the DML is the same as the one discussed in chapter 8. We investigated the difference between the way in which errors are typically handled in a COBOL program processing an IDMS database and one processing a general CODASYL database.

The current version of IDMS is IDMS/R (IDMS/RELATIONAL). This system includes the full capabilities of the original IDMS plus relational capabilities. We examined the way this is accomplished, by looking first at the LRF (logical record facility) in which logical records can be defined in subschemas. When a program requests one of these records, it is created dynamically by the system. We then looked at the ASF (automatic system facility), which is the true relational portion of the system. Using the ASF, the user defines relations, which are then implemented by the system as logical records in the LRF. Using the operations of select, project, and join, views may be defined on these relations. In addition, views may be defined on network databases.

We discussed the ways in which IDMS furnishes the capabilities of a DBMS. IDMS supports the storage, retrieval, and update of data. It has an integrated data dictionary that furnishes a user-accessible catalog. It provides its own communication software as well as support for many other communications control programs.

It provides several utility services. It uses a single command, COMMIT, to mark the end of one logical transaction and the beginning of the next. The command ROLLBACK will undo any changes made since the last COMMIT. Together, these two commands provide support for logical transactions. IDMS uses the shared and exclusive locks, discussed in chapter 2, for control of shared update. If any user causes a deadlock, an automatic rollback is performed. Recovery is supported in the manner discussed in chapter 2. Security is provided through subschema authorizations as well as user-defined database procedures. It contains limited support for integrity, but the integrity services it furnishes can be augmented through user-defined database procedures. It furnishes an adequate level of physical data independence. Like most CODASYL systems, in its basic form it does not furnish much logical data independence. However, through the use of logical records within the LRF, as well as the use of the ASF, it furnishes a high level of logical data independence.

Finally, the network model (specifically the CODASYL model) and the relational model were compared in a number of areas. The structure of a CODASYL database is more complicated than that of a corresponding relational database, especially for the casual user. At the present time, CODASYL systems tend to be more efficient, provided database designers and programmers have done their job correctly. This efficiency may be outweighed, however, by the fact that a change to the structure of a CODASYL database may render totally unsatisfactory a program that formerly performed in a satisfactory manner. In order to re-optimize this program, programmers must make changes to the program code. On the other hand, in relational systems it is the system that does any re-optimization. In general, relational systems are easier to use. Many CODASYL systems include query languages that approach relational systems in ease of use. In some cases, however, many of these query languages require some database navigation on the part of the user. In addition, no standard has been determined for these query languages. Both CODASYL and relational systems get high marks for physical data independence. Compared to relational systems, however, CODASYL systems do not furnish an equal level of logical data independence. Most current relational systems do not provide adequate support for foreign keys. In contrast, CODASYL systems do, at least in part. Finally, with regard to the momentum of CODASYL systems, we noted that vast numbers of application systems have been developed using high-powered CODASYL systems, and we predicted that these application systems will be around for years to come.

REVIEW QUESTIONS

1. What is the advantage of using declaratives in a COBOL program in the manner shown in Figure 9.1?
2. What is a multimember set? When would it be advantageous to use one multimember set rather than of two or more single member sets? When would it be advantageous to use two single member sets?

3. What is a system-owned set? For what kind of processing is a system-owned set appropriate? If no system-owned set is present in the schema, how would the same kind of processing be handled? What are the advantages of using a system owned set? What are the disadvantages?

4. What are the advantages of having a set sorted? What are the disadvantages? What are pointer arrays? How do pointer arrays relate to sorted sets?

5. What does the RETAINING CURRENCY clause do?

6. How is the ACCEPT command used?

7. State two new conditions mentioned for the IF statement in this chapter.

8. What is the purpose of the line indexes in an IDMS database?

9. Why do we leave the line index for a deleted record in place?

10. Describe how the two functions performed by declaratives in this chapter are handled in a COBOL program accessing an IDMS database.

11. What is the advantage of using the logical records within a subschema, rather than physical records?

12. What is the relationship between the ASF and the LRF?

13. To what does the word "automatic" in Automatic Systems Facility refer?

14. Describe basic stored tables. Describe derived stored tables. What is the difference between the two?

15. Describe view (within IDMS/R). What is the difference between a view and a derived stored table?

16. Describe the relationship between IDMS/R and an IDMS network database.

17. How does IMDS/R compare with a straight relational system like DB2?

18. How do COMMIT and ROLLBACK relate to the support of logical transactions?

19. How do COMMIT and ROLLBACK relate to the support of shared update?

20. Describe how the LRF furnishes logical data independence.
   In questions 21 through 24 you are to compare network model systems (specifically CODASYL systems) with relational systems. For each category, indicate strengths and/or weaknesses of both types of systems.

21. Compare with respect to database structure.

22. Compare with respect to processing efficiency.

23. Compare with respect to "ease of use".

24. Compare with respect to physical data independence.

EXERCISES

1. Rewrite the COBOL code in exercise 9 of chapter 8, with the assumption that the declaratives shown in Figure 9.1 are present in the program.

2. The Presidential Database, presented in the March 1976 issue of the *ACM Computing Surveys*, includes a PRESIDENT record type, a STATE record type, and an ADMINISTRATION record type. Presidents are owned by the state in which they are considered a "native son." There will be exactly one such state. States are owned by the administration that was in office when the state was admitted to the Union. (Assume, for the sake of simplicity, that the original thirteen states were admitted when the first administration was

in office, even though they technically preceded it.) An administration is owned by the president who presided over it. (Administrations 1 and 2 are owned by George Washington, administration 3 by John Adams, and so on.) Draw a data structure diagram of this portion of the presidential database. Can all three set types be automatic? Why or why not?

3. Assume that a customer of Premiere Products does not have to be represented by a sales rep. Discuss a way this can be handled without using a manual set. Discuss a way this can be handled using a manual set. Name advantages and disadvantages of both approaches.

4. Assuming that to manufacture part M requires three of part N, six of part P, and twelve of part R; manufacturing part N requires two of part S and a single part T; manufacturing part P requires three of part S, two of part T, and a single part V; and manufacturing part R requires a single part T and a single part V:

   a. Diagram this structure.
   b. Write the code that will list all the immediate components of part M, along with the quantity of each component that is required.
   c. Write the code that will list all the immediate parents of part T.
      (***Note: In parts b and c, be careful with your currencies.)

5. Write an IDMS version of the schema from exercise 4 of chapter 8.

6. Write an IDMS subschema encompassing all records, fields, and sets for the schema of exercise 5.

7. Write IDMS solutions to exercises 8 and 9 of chapter 8.

8. IDMS uses a precompiler to convert DML commands to appropriate subroutine calls. In other systems, the COBOL compiler has been augmented to recognize the DML commands. Which approach is better? Why do you think the developer of IDMS has chosen to take the precompiler approach?

9. Write a subschema for the schema of exercise 5 that includes a logical record DEPT–EMP consisting of the department number, and department name together with the employee number and the employee name for all employees in a given department.

10. What command will find the first DEPT–EMP record for department 3? What command will find the next?

11. Give an example of how a database procedure could be used to increase security.

12. Describe how a database procedure could be used for integrity support.

13. The claim was made in this chapter that CODASYL systems do support foreign key restrictions. Do you agree or disagree? Justify your answer.

REFERENCES

1] Bradley, James. *Introduction to Data Base Management in Business*. Holt, Rinehart & Winston, 1983.

2] Cardenas, Alfonso F. *Data Base Management Systems*. 2d ed. Allyn & Bacon, 1984.

3] Cullinet Software, Inc., Westwood, Massachusetts. Information on IDMS/R.

4] Date, C. J. *Introduction to Database Systems, Volume I*, 4th ed. Addison-Wesley, 1986.

5] Kroenke, David. *Database Processing*. 2d ed. SRA, 1983.

6] Vasta, Joseph A. *Understanding Data Base Management Systems*. Wadsworth, 1985.

THE HIERARCHICAL MODEL

10.1 INTRODUCTION

In previous chapters the relational and CODASYL data models have been covered in detail. This chapter focuses on the hierarchical model to round out our study of the three data models. IBM's Information Management System (**IMS**) is one DBMS that is based on the hierarchical model. Since IMS has dominated the market for hierarchical model systems for the past two decades, it will be used to illustrate the concepts and implementation of the hierarchical model.

First released by IBM in 1968, IMS was the product of a joint venture with the aerospace company North American Aviation (now Rockwell International Corporation). Over the years IMS has been enhanced by additional features, improved performance, and the accommodation of developments in hardware. With thousands of enterprises relying on it to meet their database management needs, IMS remains a strong force in the marketplace.

IMS provides both database and data communications capabilities. The database access and manipulation component of IMS is called **Data Language/I (DL/I)**. DL/I is a separate component that can either be used stand-alone in a batch processing mode or can be connected with other data communications products for on-line processing. DL/I follows the fundamental rules and constraints of the hierarchical model while providing additional features to extend its flexibility and usefulness.

Relational model DBMSs are based on a strong theoretical foundation; extensive research predated their first production release. CODASYL model DBMSs are based on a number of published specifications. Hierarchical model DBMSs have no comparable research or publication base on which to draw. Instead, a DBMS is held to be based on the hierarchical model if it represents data relationships in terms of hierarchies. In the next section we will discuss the hierarchical model, introduce the terminology associated with this model, and present specific terminology and capabilities associated with DL/I.

In section 10.3 the data definition language of DL/I is discussed and illustrated; its data manipulation language is covered in section 10.4. In section 10.5, we contrast the three data models (hierarchical, CODASYL, and relational) in terms of their advantages and disadvantages.

In chapter 11, we will discuss the inverted file model and ADABAS, a DBMS that fits this model. At the end of chapter 11, we will discuss how well DL/I and ADABAS support the ten functions of a DBMS.

10.2 BASIC CONCEPTS AND TERMINOLOGY

Let's try a variation on Marvel College's requirements. This time we will use departments, faculty, majors, students, and the relationships between them to illustrate the basic concepts and terminology of the hierarchical model and of DL/I. Figure 10.1 shows the data structure diagram for these four entity types and for three one-to-many relationships. Each FACULTY member is employed by one

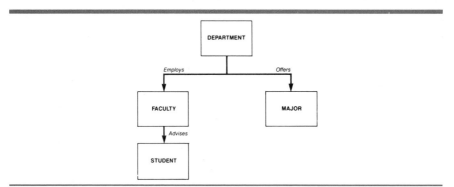

FIGURE 10.1
Data structure diagram of department, faculty, student, and major entity types with their relationships.

DEPARTMENT, and each DEPARTMENT has many FACULTY members. Each STUDENT is related to the one FACULTY member who advises the student, while each FACULTY member advises many STUDENTs. Finally, each MAJOR is offered by one DEPARTMENT, and each DEPARTMENT may offer many MAJORs.

Figure 10.2 shows one occurrence of this structure for the business department. Jones is a faculty member advising Tom, Smith is a faculty member advising

FIGURE 10.2
One occurrence of the department-faculty-student-major hierarchical structure.

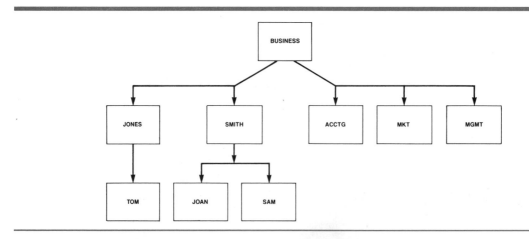

Joan and Sam, and accounting, marketing, and management are majors offered by the department.

HIERARCHICAL MODEL CONCEPTS AND TERMINOLOGY

The **hierarchical model** supports a **tree** structure. The tree structure, however, is inverted, with a single root at the top and its branches leading toward the bottom, so it looks like the organizational chart, or hierarchy chart, of a typical enterprise. The terminology used for genealogical, or family, trees is also associated with the general hierarchical model.

A tree consists of **nodes**, connected by **branches**. The **root** node is at the top, and its **descendants** are below it. A **parent** node appears immediately above its **children**. In Figure 10.1 DEPARTMENT, FACULTY, STUDENT, and MAJOR are nodes connected by the branches EMPLOYS, ADVISES, and OFFERS. DEPARTMENT is the root, has descendants FACULTY, STUDENT, and MAJOR, and is the parent of FACULTY and MAJOR. FACULTY is the parent of STUDENT. FACULTY and MAJOR are children of DEPARTMENT. Finally, STUDENT is the child of FACULTY. In the hierarchical model the branches are not named; these branches (i.e., EMPLOYS, OFFERS, and ADVISES) have been named merely for the sake of convenience in referencing the diagram.

In Figure 10.2, business is the root and the parent of faculty Jones and Smith and of the accounting, marketing, and management majors. Jones is the parent of Tom, and Smith is the parent of Joan and Sam. Jones, Smith, accounting, marketing, management, Tom, Joan, and Sam are children of their respective parents.

When viewing an occurrence of a tree structure like the one shown in Figure 10.2, *siblings*, or **twins**, are defined as children of the same node type with the same parent occurrence. Jones and Smith are siblings, sharing business as a parent. Accounting, marketing, and management are siblings, since they share business as a parent. Joan and Sam are siblings, sharing Smith as a parent. Though Smith and accounting share business as a parent, they are not siblings, since they belong to different node types. Likewise, though Tom is of the same node type as Joan and Sam, Jones and Smith are different parent occurrences, so Tom is not a sibling of Joan and Sam.

Each node contains one or more fields or attributes. The FACULTY node, for example, in addition to having faculty name, could also have the fields office location, phone number, and highest degree earned.

The following constraints apply to the hierarchical model:

1. There is a single root node, which is department in Figure 10.1. This restriction applies to the root node type, not to occurrences of the root. Business, biology, and psychology could exist as occurrences of the root node in the example database.
2. Each child node has a single parent node. Note that this is true for all children in Figure 10.1. If we needed additionally to represent a one-to-many relationship between MAJOR and STUDENT, we could not do it directly by simply adding a relationship between the two nodes. We could,

however, retain the tree as structured and add a second, separate tree, with MAJOR as the root and STUDENT as its child. Or we could retain the tree as structured and combine major and student data into the STUDENT node, so that major data would appear in both the MAJOR and STUDENT nodes. Either solution results in duplicate data being stored in two different nodes. Note that this restriction prohibits many-to-many relationships directly in one tree, since we normally construct two one-to-many relationships, or a node with two parents, to represent these types of relationships.

3. Each node is accessed through its parent. Thus, to get to student Tom, we must first access business, then Jones, then Tom. This also means that a child node cannot exist without its parent or other ancestors. We could not add Tom as a student until we knew his advisor. Also, if faculty member Jones left and we deleted her node, we also would delete her children. Access, in other words, is along a **hierarchical path** from top to bottom.

The most common access method, and storage approach, is called **preorder traversal**, in which node occurrences are retrieved from top to bottom and left to right for each occurrence. For Figure 10.2, the preorder traversal path starts at business and travels in order to Jones, Tom, Smith, Joan, Sam, accounting, mar-

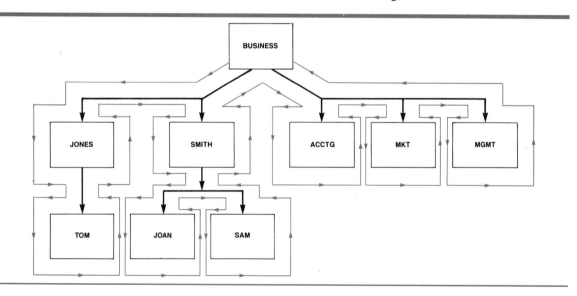

keting, and management. Figure 10.3 shows this preorder traversal path more clearly. We have traced the preorder traversal path by enclosing the segment occurrences with a circuit starting at the root segment occurrence, traveling down the left side of the structure, and continuing around each segment occurrence until once again reaching the root segment occurrence. A preorder traversal path always forms this type of pattern around a hierarchical structure occurrence.

FIGURE 10.3
One occurrence of the department-faculty-student-major hierarchical structure showing its preorder traversal path.

DL/I FUNDAMENTAL CONCEPTS AND TERMINOLOGY

DL/I TREE-RELATED TERMINOLOGY

The terminology used in **DL/I** differs in several ways from that of the general hierarchical model. Specifically, DL/I uses the following terminology:

- A node is called a **segment**, so segments consist of logically grouped fields. The equivalent CODASYL term is record, and the equivalent relational term is table or relation. The segment at the top of the tree is the **root segment**. In Figure 10.1 the segments are DEPARTMENT, FACULTY, STUDENT, and MAJOR, with DEPARTMENT as the root segment.
- One tree structure occurrence of the root segment and all its descendants is called a **physical database record (PDBR)**. Figure 10.1 is an example of one *PDBR type*, while Figure 10.2 shows a single *PDBR occurrence* of this PDBR type.
- The collection of all physical database records for a particular tree structure is called a **physical database**. So business and all its descendants from Figure 10.2, biology and all its descendants, and so on, constitute the physical database that is summarized in the tree structure of Figure 10.1.

A number of different physical databases can exist under DL/I. Figure 10.4 shows the tree structure for a second possible physical database, with BUILDING as the root segment, ROOM as a child segment to BUILDING and a parent segment for COURSE, and COURSE as a child segment for ROOM. Many different courses are offered at different times in a particular room, and a particular course is offered in a single, specific room, so this is a one-to-many relationship. And a particular building has many rooms, another one-to-many relationship.

In DL/I each physical database is defined separately in a single database definition. This is where all segments, all fields within each segment, and all hierarchial relationships between segments are defined. This database definition is called a **database description**, or **DBD**. The process of defining a DBD is called a **DBD generation**, or **DBDGEN**. There would be one DBDGEN for the physical database in Figure 10.1 and a second DBDGEN for the physical database in Figure 10.4. Each DL/I physical database can have a maximum of 255 different segment types, and a single hierarchical path from the root segment to the bottommost segment is limited to fifteen segments.

DL/I LOGICAL DATABASES

A **logical database** is an individual user's, or program's, view of the database. It can be different from the physical database or databases. For example, a logical database could be one entire physical database, like the one shown in Figure 10.1, or a subset of one physical database, like the DEPARTMENT and FACULTY segments from Figure 10.1, or portions from two or more physical databases. The last of these three possibilities will be covered more fully in the next topic, which

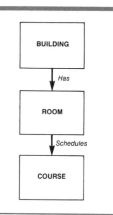

FIGURE 10.4
Data structure diagram for building, room and course entities.

covers logical relationships. The primary restriction on a logical database is that its root segment must also be a root segment of a physical database.

Each logical database is defined through a **program specification block generation**, or **PSBGEN**. Defined in the PSBGEN are the fields and segments that constitute the logical database. In a particular logical database, for example, we could allow the user to update fields in certain segments and to access but not update fields in other segments. For example, in Figure 10.1, one logical database could provide:

- access to all fields in the DEPARTMENT segment, but no update privileges.
- update privilege to all fields in the STUDENT segment. If neither access nor update privileges are to be permitted to the FACULTY segment, it would still need to be defined in the PSBGEN so that the user could retrieve a particular STUDENT segment occurrence by traveling the hierarchical path from DEPARTMENT to FACULTY to STUDENT. In this case, we would define the FACULTY segment as having no access or update privileges. The FACULTY segment would be defined as *key sensitive* to permit traveling the path from DEPARTMENT to STUDENT. If the user required access to only the STUDENT segment, then both the DEPARTMENT and the FACULTY segments would be defined as key sensitive.

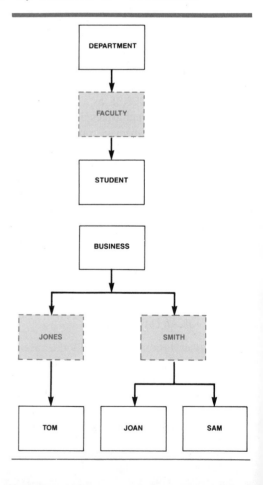

FIGURE 10.5
Data structure diagram for the business-student logical database and one logical database record occurrence.

One occurrence of a logical database is called a **logical database record (LDBR)**. Based on the preceding paragraph and on Figure 10.2, one LDBR would be business, Tom, Joan, and Sam. Figure 10.5 shows the data structure diagram for this logical database and the occurrence just described. FACULTY, Jones, and Smith are in blue boxes indicating that access is permitted to these segments only for the purposes of traveling the hierarchical path.

DL/I LOGICAL RELATIONSHIPS

In the general hierarchical model, each child node has a single parent. You will recall that if we need additionally to represent a one-to-many relationship between MAJOR and STUDENT in Figure 10.1, we cannot do it directly simply by adding a relationship between the two nodes.

DL/I, however, provides a facility called a **logical relationship** which overcomes this restriction through the use of **logical pointers**. There are several variations of logical relationships; we will discuss just two of them. The first variation is illustrated in Figure 10.6. This new data structure diagram has a logical relationship, shown with a blue line, between the MAJOR and STUDENT segments.

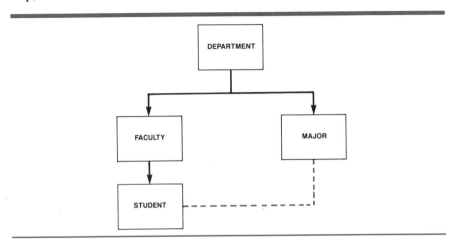

FIGURE 10.6
Logical relationship
between the major
and student segments.

A logical relationship is a physical connection between two segments, and it is established through the DBDGEN process. Actually, three segments are needed for a logical relationship. In Figure 10.6, FACULTY is the **physical parent**, MAJOR is the **logical parent**, and STUDENT is a **physical child** to FACULTY and a **logical child** to MAJOR. Note that there is no arrowhead on the blue line. This is because, depending on user requirements and the resulting database design, there are two different ways to define this first logical relationship variation.

- In the first case, suppose we needed to know only the student's major, given a particular student occurrence. Then we would define in the DBDGEN a **unidirectional** (or one-way) **logical relationship** from the STUDENT segment to the MAJOR segment. From this DBDGEN definition, DL/I adds a single pointer, actually the key of the MAJOR segment, to the STUDENT segment. Given a STUDENT occurrence, DL/I uses this logical pointer to retrieve the proper MAJOR occurrence. In Figure 10.7 on the following page, the blue lines traveling from the occurrences of STUDENT to the occurrences of MAJOR show that Tom has a management major and both Joan and Sam have accounting majors. If we wish to travel from MAJOR to STUDENT, we cannot do so with these unidirectional logical pointers. The only way of accessing a STUDENT occurrence is through its physical parent of FACULTY.

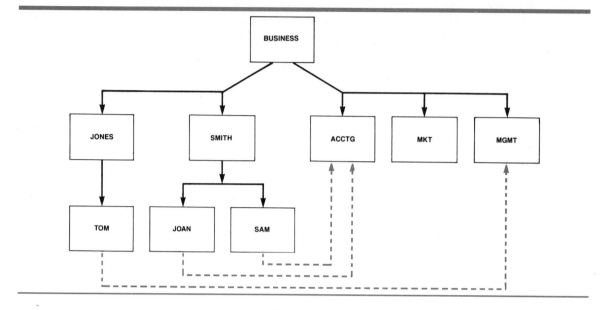

FIGURE 10.7
An unindirectional
logical relationship
occurrence between
major and student.

- In the second case, suppose we also needed to access all students having a particular major from an occurrence of the MAJOR segment. Then we would define in the DBDGEN a **bidirectional** (or two-way) **logical relationship** between the STUDENT segment and the MAJOR segment. Retained in the STUDENT segment is the pointer we just described. A pointer is now added to the MAJOR segment. DL/I uses this new pointer to retrieve the first STUDENT occurrence for a particular MAJOR. To retrieve all other STUDENT occurrences for that MAJOR, DL/I uses a second pointer in the STUDENT segment (the third pointer overall) that connects each of the STUDENT occurrences for that MAJOR.

Suppose that the STUDENT occurrences in Figure 10.2 were all accounting majors. Then in Figure 10.8 the first logical pointers for Tom, for Joan, and for Sam would all point to accounting, the logical parent to each of these STUDENT

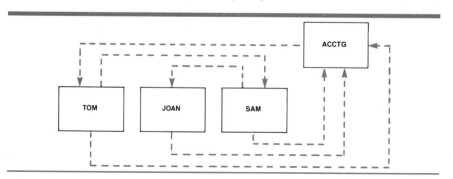

FIGURE 10.8
A bidirectional
logical relationship
occurrence between
major and student.

occurrences. If the logical pointer in the accounting occurrence pointed to Tom, then the second STUDENT segment logical pointer for Tom might point to Sam, the second logical pointer for Sam would point to Joan, and the second logical pointer for Joan would indicate the end of the chain.

The second logical relationship variation involves a method for defining a logical database that consists of portions of two physical databases using logical relationships. Suppose each department were assigned a block of rooms in which to hold its classes, and only classes for a given department were held in the assigned block of rooms. Suppose further that we had defined the two physical databases shown in Figures 10.1 and 10.4 and needed to retrieve all rooms for a given department and to know which department had been assigned a given room. Figure 10.9 shows the logical database we would like to define. The blue line

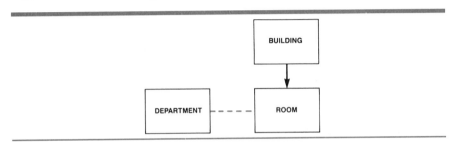

FIGURE 10.9
Logical relationship between the department and room segments in two different physical databases.

between the DEPARTMENT and ROOM segments again indicates that a logical relationship, defined in the DBDGEN, exists between the two segments. DEPART–MENT is the logical parent, and ROOM is the logical child. BUILDING is the physical parent of ROOM, and ROOM is the physical child of BUILDING. The possibilities for pointers discussed in the previous MAJOR–STUDENT example also pertain to this example.

It is important to emphasize that other variations are possible on the logical relationship capability. In summary, logical relationships allow a segment to have more than one parent segment and allow two or more physical databases to be considered part of the same logical database. DL/I, however, has a number of restrictions on the establishment of logical relationships. Following are a few that are of interest to us:

1. Every segment, except root segments, must have one physical parent segment.
2. A given segment can have at most one logical parent segment.
3. A root segment cannot be a logical child. However, it may be a logical parent.
4. A logical child segment cannot also be a logical parent segment.

Remember that both physical databases and logical relationships are defined explicitly in the DBDGEN process. A logical database, defined through a PSBGEN, must be defined in terms of existing physical databases and logical relationships already defined. In other words, the logical relationships, or user views, must be known in advance so that appropriate physical relationships can be established during the DBDGEN process.

Physical databases, logical databases, and logical relationships get very complicated when we study the full DL/I capabilities in these areas. We have chosen to touch on the main DL/I capabilities and to leave aside these areas of complexity.

DL/I PHYSICAL STORAGE STRUCTURES

For each segment stored in the database, DL/I stores the data fields for the segment, logical pointers if necessary, and various control and identification information about the segment. The specific method of storing segments and hierarchical relationships between segments depends upon the particular *physical storage structure* chosen. DL/I has four physical storage structures: hierarchical sequential, hierarchical indexed sequential, hierarchical direct, and hierarchical indexed direct. IBM refers to these physical storage structures as access methods, and a brief overview of each one follows.

HIERARCHICAL SEQUENTIAL ACCESS METHOD (HSAM)

An **HSAM (hierarchical sequential access method)** physical database stores segments sequentially in a **preorder traversal** structure. Figure 10.10 shows how the PDBR of Figure 10.2 would be stored using HSAM. The root segment is physically followed by its first child segment, which in turn is followed by its first child segment, and so on. This PDBR would be followed physically by the next PDBR, and so on. Stored in each segment is a segment identification field so that the segment type can be determined when segments are retrieved. This segment identification field is also present for each of the other DL/I access methods.

An HSAM database can be sequentially accessed only, and the database must be recreated if updates have to be made. Logical relationships cannot be defined. HSAM can be used either for disk or tape media; the other three access methods must be stored on disk. Since random access is not permitted under HSAM and since space requirements for HSAM are the least of the four access methods, HSAM is best suited to historical retention on tape of segments deleted from the production databases. These production databases are best stored using one of the other three access methods, since they permit random access.

HIERARCHICAL INDEXED SEQUENTIAL ACCESS METHOD (HISAM)

A **HISAM (hierarchical indexed sequential access method)** physical database provides sequential and random access through an index to root segment occurrences and provides sequential access to dependent segment occurrences. Depending on which IBM operating system is used, either an **ISAM** or **VSAM** file organization (see Appendix A) is employed for the root segment index.

Figure 10.11 shows the index entries for the root segment occurrences pointing to the start of their respective physical database records. Behind the scenes, the dependent segment occurrences may not necessarily be physically contiguous, as

BUSINESS
JONES
TOM
SMITH
JOAN
SAM
ACCTG
MKT
MGMT

FIGURE 10.10
HSAM storage of a physical database record in preorder traversal order.

depicted in Figure 10.11; but the figure does represent the order in which dependent segment occurrences would be retrieved once a given root segment occurrence had been retrieved.

HIERARCHICAL DIRECT ACCESS METHOD (HDAM)

An **HDAM (hierarchical direct access method)** physical database provides random access through a **hashing** technique to root segment occurrences. Access to dependent segment occurrences is through pointers stored in each segment. Either hierarchical or child-twin pointers may be used.

Figure 10.12 on the following page, pictures the way in which hierarchical and child-twin pointers techniques would be used with the physical database record from Figure 10.2. Note that sequential access to the root segments is not possible unless a secondary index, which will be discussed just ahead, is also used.

HIERARCHICAL INDEXED DIRECT ACCESS METHOD (HIDAM)

A **HIDAM (hierarchical indexed direct access method)** physical database provides sequential and random access through an index to root segment occurrences. This is similar to the method used by HISAM; refer to Figure 10.11. The difference is that access to dependent segment occurrences is through either hierarchical or child-twin pointers stored in each segment. This is similar to the method used by HDAM; refer to Figure 10.12.

DL/I SECONDARY INDEXING

To permit random access through any of the hashing or indexed schemes used with HISAM, HDAM, and HIDAM, each root segment must have a primary key field defined during the DBDGEN process. We can also define a key or **sequence field** for nonroot segments. If a sequence field is used, DL/I arranges occurrences of that segment in order by that field. Even when using sequence fields, however, we still must travel the hierarchical path to reach a particular nonroot segment. But placing segments in some sequence makes updating and retrieval easier, as we shall see when we get to the data manipulation section of this chapter.

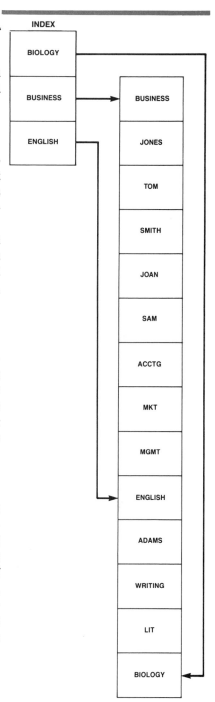

FIGURE 10.11
HISAM storage of physical database records using an index.

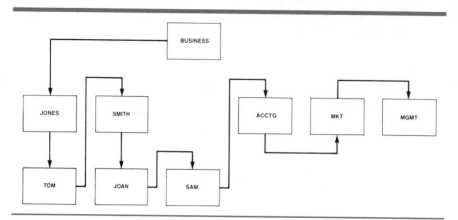

FIGURE 10.12a
HDAM hierarchical
pointers for one
occurrence of the
department-faculty-
student-major
hierarchical structure.

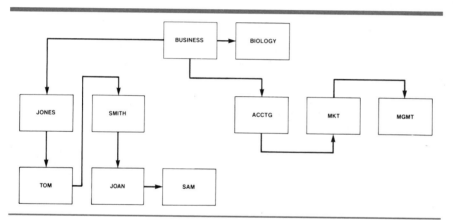

FIGURE 10.12b
HDAM child-twin
pointers for one
occurrence of the
department-faculty-
student-major
hierarchical structure.

If we also need to randomly access the database through a nonroot segment, DL/I provides this capability through its **secondary indexing** feature. Secondary indexing is an **inverted file structure**. Figure 10.13 on the opposite page, illustrates secondary indexing on the MAJOR segment. We are still able to randomly access, based on the root segment key values of biology, business and English. With secondary indexing on the MAJOR segment, we can randomly access further, based on the major segment key values of accounting, marketing, management, writing, and literature.

DL/I FAST PATH

Fast Path is a DL/I feature supporting applications that require faster processing than can be obtained using the standard DL/I structures already described. The Fast Path feature obtains its greater efficiency through special transaction processing facilities, through a special set of utilities, and through two special types of

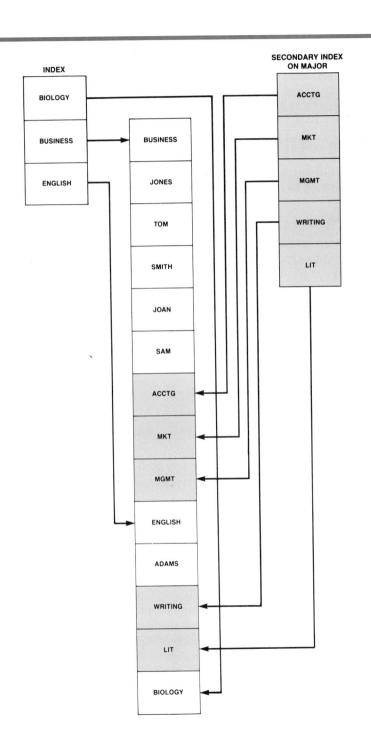

FIGURE 10.13
An example of the
use of a secondary
index on the major
segment.

databases: the **main storage database** (MSDB) and the **data entry database** (DEDB).

An MSDB is a memory resident database (the MSDB actually resides in virtual storage) consisting of root-only segments. It obtains its greater efficiency through this root-only restriction and through its memory-resident placement.

A DEDB resides on disk like normal DL/I databases but is restricted to a root segment and optionally up to seven child segment types. That is, a DEDB can be at most two hierarchical levels deep. Special storage techniques are used to assist in gaining greater efficiency in processing.

Both MSDB and DEDB have additional restrictions and characteristics. For more detail on the facets of Fast Path, see various IBM DL/I and IMS publications.

PREMIERE PRODUCTS DATABASE

For a further example of DL/I concepts, consider the entities and relationships required for the Premiere Products database described in chapter 1. The basic entities and relationships are as follows:

- a sales rep entity, called SLSREP
- a customer entity, called CUSTOMER
- a one-to-many relationship from SLSREP to CUSTOMER
- an order entity, called ORDER
- a one-to-many relationship from CUSTOMER to ORDER
- a part entity, called PART
- a many-to-many relationship between ORDER and PART

Designing a DL/I database to handle these requirements poses little difficulty except for the many-to-many relationship between ORDER and PART. A variety of approaches are available for handling a many-to-many relationship in a DL/I database design. The design strategy chosen, of course, depends upon both the processing requirements and the performance needs of the system.

Figure 10.14 on the opposite page, shows the data structure diagram for the DL/I design and the fields placed within each segment. There are two physical databases: SALESDB and PARTDB. The SALESDB physical database has SLSREP as the root segment, CUSTOMER as its child and the parent of ORDER, and ORDER as the child of CUSTOMER. The PARTDB physical database has PART as the root segment; there are no other physical segments in this database.

In this database design we have implemented the many-to-many relationship between ORDER and PART by defining an ORDER_LINE segment that contains **intersection data**, i.e., fields related to a specific PART for a specific ORDER. To form the connection between the two physical databases, we have defined a **bidirectional logical relationship** between ORDER_LINE and PART. ORDER is the physical parent of ORDER_LINE, which is the physical child of ORDER. PART is the logical parent of ORDER_LINE, which is the logical child of PART. ORDER_LINE is a segment serving a role similar to the CODASYL model link record

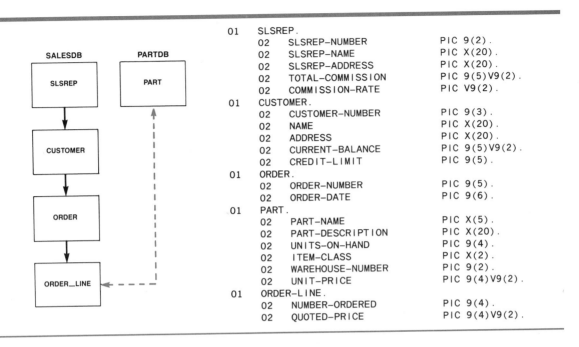

01	SLSREP.	
	02	SLSREP-NUMBER	PIC 9(2).
	02	SLSREP-NAME	PIC X(20).
	02	SLSREP-ADDRESS	PIC X(20).
	02	TOTAL-COMMISSION	PIC 9(5)V9(2).
	02	COMMISSION-RATE	PIC V9(2).
01	CUSTOMER.	
	02	CUSTOMER-NUMBER	PIC 9(3).
	02	NAME	PIC X(20).
	02	ADDRESS	PIC X(20).
	02	CURRENT-BALANCE	PIC 9(5)V9(2).
	02	CREDIT-LIMIT	PIC 9(5).
01	ORDER.	
	02	ORDER-NUMBER	PIC 9(5).
	02	ORDER-DATE	PIC 9(6).
01	PART.	
	02	PART-NAME	PIC X(5).
	02	PART-DESCRIPTION	PIC X(20).
	02	UNITS-ON-HAND	PIC 9(4).
	02	ITEM-CLASS	PIC X(2).
	02	WAREHOUSE-NUMBER	PIC 9(2).
	02	UNIT-PRICE	PIC 9(4)V9(2).
01	ORDER-LINE.	
	02	NUMBER-ORDERED	PIC 9(4).
	02	QUOTED-PRICE	PIC 9(4)V9(2).

approach. We have turned a many-to-many relationship, which DL/I cannot directly support, between ORDER and PART into two one-to-many relationships, which DL/I can support through the use of a logical relationship. As we will see in the next section, there is more to the database design than what is shown in Figure 10.14, but the data structure diagram does represent the general approach to the Premiere Products design.

FIGURE 10.14
Data structure diagram and fields in each segment for Premiere Products database.

These databases for Premiere Products will be used to discuss DL/I's data definition and data manipulation languages in the following sections.

0.3 DL/I DATA DEFINITION

We learned in the previous section that DL/I has physical databases and logical databases. A logical database is an application program's view of the physical databases. In this section we will discuss how to define physical and logical databases in DL/I.

PHYSICAL DATABASE DESCRIPTION

A physical database is defined with a **database description**, or **DBD**. The DBD consists of assembly language macro statements that are coded by the Database Administration group, assembled, and linked into an IMS load module library. This process is called a **DBD generation**, or **DBDGEN**, and occurs for each separate physical database required by the enterprise. A particular physical database goes through the DBDGEN procedure once, unless the physical structure of the database changes, in which case the macro statements would be changed and the DBDGEN procedure would be repeated.

The data structure diagram in Figure 10.14 shows two physical databases. Their corresponding DBDs are shown in Figure 10.15. We will refer to Figure 10.15 in explaining each DBD statement type. Note that ORDER_LINE has been renamed ORDLINE to conform to DL/I restrictions.

1	DBD	NAME = SALESDB , ACCESS = HDAM
2	SEGM	NAME = SLSREP , PARENT = 0 , BYTES = 51
3	FIELD	NAME = (REPNUM , SEQ , U) , BYTES = 2 , START = 1
4	FIELD	NAME = REPNAME , BYTES = 20 , START = 3
5	FIELD	NAME = REPADDR , BYTES = 20 , START = 23
6	FIELD	NAME = COMMISS , BYTES = 7 , START = 43
7	FIELD	NAME = COMRATE , BYTES = 2 , START = 50
8	SEGM	NAME = CUSTOMER , PARENT = SLSREP , BYTES = 55
9	FIELD	NAME = (CUSTNUM , SEQ , U) , BYTES = 3 , START = 1
10	FIELD	NAME = CUSTNAME , BYTES = 20 , START = 4
11	FIELD	NAME = CUSTADDR , BYTES = 20 , START = 24
12	FIELD	NAME = CURRBAL , BYTES = 7 , START = 44
13	FIELD	NAME = CREDLIM , BYTES = 5 , START = 51
14	SEGM	NAME = ORDER , PARENT = CUSTOMER , BYTES = 11
15	FIELD	NAME = (ORDNUM , SEQ , U) , BYTES = 5 , START = 1
16	FIELD	NAME = ORDDATE , BYTES = 6 , START = 6
17	SEGM	NAME = ORDLINE , POINTER = (LPARENT , LTWIN , TWIN) , PARENT = ((ORDER) , (PART , PHYSICAL , PARTDB)) , BYTES = 15
18	FIELD	NAME = (PARTNAME , SEQ , M) , BYTES = 5 , START = 1
19	FIELD	NAME = NUMORD , BYTES = 4 , START = 6
20	FIELD	NAME = QUOPRICE , BYTES = 6 , START = 10

FIGURE 10.15 a.
DBD for the SALESDB physical database.

21	DBD	NAME = PARTDB , ACCESS = HIDAM
22	SEGM	NAME = PART , BYTES = 39
23	LCHILD	NAME = (ORDLINE , SALESDB) , PAIR = PORDLINE , POINTER = SNGL
24	FIELD	NAME = (PARTNAME , SEQ , U) , BYTES = 5 , START = 1
25	FIELD	NAME = PARTDESC , BYTES = 20 , START = 6
26	FIELD	NAME = ONHAND , BYTES = 4 , START = 26
27	FIELD	NAME = ITEMCLAS , BYTES = 2 , START = 30
28	FIELD	NAME = WARENUM , BYTES = 2 , START = 32
29	FIELD	NAME = PRICE , BYTES = 6 , START = 34
30	SEGM	NAME = PORDLINE , POINTER = PAIRED , PARENT = PART , SOURCE = ((ORDLINE , SALESDB))
31	FIELD	NAME = (ORDNUM , SEQ , M) , BYTES = 5 , START = 1
32	FIELD	NAME = NUMORD , BYTES = 4 , START = 6
33	FIELD	NAME = QUOPRICE , BYTES = 6 , START = 10

FIGURE 10.15 b.
DBD for the PARTDB physical database.

DBD STATEMENT

For each DBD there is one **DBD** macro **statement**, which is the first entry in the DBD (see lines 1 and 21). Using this statement, we give a name to the database with the NAME parameter. The name of the first database is SALESDB, and PARTDB is the name of the second database. We also specify the physical storage structure in the DBD statement, using the ACCESS parameter. We have decided to use HDAM for the SALESDB database, and HIDAM for the PARTDB database.

SEGM STATEMENT

For each DBD there is one **SEGM statement** for each segment type in the database. We must start with the SEGM statement for the root segment (lines 2 and 22). The order of SEGM statements that follow the root determine the **hierarchical path** for the database (lines 8, 14, 17, and 30). So SEGM statement order is important.

We name each segment, using the NAME parameter, and specify the size of each segment, using the BYTES parameter.

The PARENT parameter indicates the parent segment for a given child. SLSREP is the parent of CUSTOMER (line 8), and CUSTOMER is the parent of ORDER (line 14). We can identify the root segment by coding PARENT = 0 (line 2) or by omitting the PARENT parameter (line 22).

The PARENT parameters for lines 17 and 30 are more complicated because these SEGM statements establish the **many-to-many** relationship between ORDER and PART by means of the **bidirectional logical relationship** between ORDER_LINE and PART, shown in Figure 10.14. We want to be able to access occurrences of ORDER_LINE through either ORDER or PART, access an occurrence of ORDER from ORDER_LINE, and access an occurrence of PART from ORDER_LINE.

Figure 10.16 shows a way of viewing the relationships among ORDER, PART, and ORDER_LINE (ORDLINE) in order to better understand the SEGM

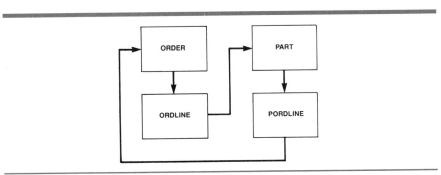

FIGURE 10.16
Conceptual view of the logical relationship for the ORDER, PART, and ORDER-LINE segments.

statements. ORDER is the physical parent of ORDLINE, and ORDLINE is the physical child of ORDER. PART is the logical parent of ORDLINE, and ORDLINE is the logical child of PART. The segment PORDLINE is called a **virtual segment** since to the user it appears to physically exist even though in point of fact it does not. Figure 10.14 shows what actually exists, and Figure 10.16 shows what appears to exist and what must be defined in the SEGM statements.

The SEGM PARENT parameter for ORDLINE (line 17) has ORDER as the physical parent segment and PART in the PARTDB database as the logical parent segment. The PHYSICAL subparameter means that PARTNAME, the key to the PART segment, will be stored in the ORDLINE segment. It is not required that we store PARTNAME in the ORDLINE segment, but we have chosen to do so. The POINTER parameter allows the database designer to specify the pointer types needed for that segment. In the case of ORDLINE, we have the following pointers:

- a logical parent pointer, subparameter of LPARENT, in each ORDLINE occurrence that points to its logical parent occurrence in the PART segment
- a logical twin pointer, subparameter of LTWIN, connecting the twin occurrences of ORDLINE for the same PART occurrence in PARTNAME sequence
- a physical twin pointer, subparameter of TWIN, connecting the occurrences of ORDLINE for the same ORDER occurrence in ORDNUM sequence

The SEGM PARENT parameter for PORDLINE (line 30) and its LCHILD statement (line 23) should be studied together. The LCHILD statement immediately follows the SEGM for PART and defines PORDLINE in the PAIR parameter as being paired with ORDLINE in the SALESDB database; i.e., they are one and the same. The POINTER parameter for the LCHILD statement creates in each PART occurrence a logical child pointer to the first ORDLINE occurrence in the logical twin pointer chain. The SEGM statement names this virtual segment as PORDLINE, specifies its virtual parent as PART, and identifies PORDLINE as being paired with the real segment of ORDLINE in the SALESDB database.

Since we are using HDAM and HIDAM, the two databases will have pointers connecting segment occurrences. We can choose to use hierarchical pointers for all segments or child-twin pointers for all segments or hierarchical pointers for some segments and child-twin pointers for the other segments. A given segment type can have only one of the two pointer types. The choice between these two pointer types is made in the SEGM statement, using the POINTER parameter. The default is child-twin pointers if the POINTER parameter is not explicitly coded. Except for the ORDLINE and PORDLINE segments, we have chosen to use the default pointer types.

FIELD STATEMENT

We use the **FIELD statement** to define all fields for a given segment. There is one FIELD statement for each field in the segment. The FIELD statements follow the SEGM statement that names and defines the segment. The BYTES parameter defines the size of the field, and the START parameter defines the byte position in the segment where the field starts.

The NAME parameter provides the field name. Additionally, we can name one field per record as a *sequence* (or key) *field* (lines 3, 9, 15, 18, 24, and 31) by using the SEQ subparameter. If a sequence field is defined, then the segment occurrences will be stored in order by the sequence field. If U is specified for the sequence field, then DL/I ensures that only one segment occurrence with that sequence field value exists for a given parent occurrence. If M is specified for the sequence field, then multiple occurrences of that segment can have the same sequence field value for a given parent occurrence.

LOGICAL DATABASE DESCRIPTION

A **logical database** is defined with a **program specification block**, or **PSB**. The PSB consists of assembly language macro statements that undergo a process similar to that undergone by the DBDGEN. The result of this process is called a PSB generation, or PSBGEN. In order for an application program to access the database, there must be a PSB defined for that program.

Figure 10.17a is an example PSB for the Premiere Products databases we have designed. Each PSB consists of one or more **program communication blocks** (**PCBs**). In each PCB (lines 1 and 7) we indicate that we are dealing with a database PCB, using the TYPE parameter, and give the name of the database,

1	PCB	TYPE = DB , DBNAME = SALESDB
2	SENSEG	NAME = SLSREP , PROCOPT = G
3	SENSEG	NAME = CUSTOMER , PARENT = SLSREP , PROCOPT = G
4	SENFLD	NAME = CUSTNUM , START = 1
5	SENFLD	NAME = CREDLIM , START = 51
6	SENSEG	NAME = ORDER , PARENT = CUSTOMER , PROCOPT = (G , I , R , D)
7	PCB	TYPE = DB , DBNAME = PARTDB
8	SENSEG	NAME = PART , PARENT = 0 , PROCOPT = G
9	PSBGEN	LANG = COBOL , PSBNAME = SAMPLE

FIGURE 10.17a.
PSB for a sample COBOL application program that will interact with a subset of the Premiere Products database.

using the DBNAME parameter. The database name matches the name given in a previously defined DBD.

We define the **sensitive segments** for this application program with **SENSEG statements**. In the NAME parameter we give the name of the sensitive segment. This name must match the name in the applicable DBD SEGM statement. We define the sensitive segments in hierarchical sequence and use the PARENT parameter to name the parent for the segment, as previously done in the DBD. Note that we can again indicate a root segment by coding PARENT = 0 or by omitting the PARENT parameter. We authorize the *processing options* allowable to the segment by using the **PROCOPT parameter**. A number of processing options can be chosen, among which are G for get or retrieval only, I for insert, R for replace, and D for delete.

The entire segment named in a SENSEG statement is accessible under the constraints of the PROCOPT parameter except for those segments having SENFLD statements defined. If used, the SENFLD statements define the specific fields accessible for the preceding SENSEG statement. In our example we have two SENFLD statements (lines 4 and 5) that permit us to get values of only the CUSTNUM and CREDLIM fields from the CUSTOMER segment. The other fields from the CUSTOMER segment, CUSTNAME, CUSTADDR, and CURRBAL, cannot be accessed, since SENFLD statements are not defined for them. On the other hand, all fields for the SLSREP, ORDER, and PART segments can be accessed, since their SENSEG statements are not followed by SENFLD statements.

We end the PSB with a PSBGEN statement (line 9), in which we specify the programming language, COBOL in this example, to be used with this PSB and give a name, SAMPLE, to the PSB. Other programming languages that can be specified are PL/I and Assembler.

Figure 10.17a is a PSB that allows the application program to access just the SLSREP, CUSTOMER, ORDER, and PART segments, while Figure 10.17b is a PSB that allows access to all segments of the SALESDB and PARTDB databases.

```
10    PCB        TYPE = DB , DBNAME = SALESDB
11    SENSEG     NAME = SLSREP , PROCOPT = (G , I , R , D)
12    SENSEG     NAME = CUSTOMER , PARENT = SLSREP , PROCOPT = (G , I , R , D)
13    SENSEG     NAME = ORDER , PARENT = CUSTOMER , PROCOPT = (G , I , R , D)
14    SENSEG     NAME = ORDLINE , PARENT = ORDER , PROCOPT = (G , I , R , D)

15    PCB        TYPE = DB , DBNAME = PARTDB
16    SENSEG     NAME = PART , PARENT = 0 , PROCOPT = (G , I , R , D)
17    SENSEG     NAME = PORDLINE , PARENT = PART , PROCOPT = (G , I , R , D)

18    PSBGEN     LANG = COBOL , PSBNAME = EXAMPLE
```

FIGURE 10.17b.
PSB for a sample COBOL application program that will interact with all segments of the Premiere Products database.

DL/I DATA DEFINITION IN AN APPLICATION PROGRAM

Once the DBDs and the PSBs have been defined and the databases have been loaded, application programs are written to manipulate the databases. How do the DBDs and PSBs interact with the application programs?

Briefly, if we are using COBOL, we define in the LINKAGE SECTION of the DATA DIVISION the PCBs from our authorized PSB and a number of status flags and control values. The COBOL program communicates with DL/I through CALL statements that access the data areas established in the LINKAGE SECTION. We also define within the WORKING–STORAGE SECTION the **function code** and **segment search arguments** (SSAs), both discussed in detail in the next section. The function code tells DL/I the database manipulation required, and the SSAs tell DL/I the specific segment occurrence, or occurrences, desired.

The exact details of how all this works are not critical for gaining an appreciation of the DL/I data definition process. What is critical is the process of creating DBDs and PSBs in preparation for manipulating the databases.

.4   DL/I DATA MANIPULATION

The Premiere Products SALESDB and PARTDB databases defined in the previous section will be used to describe the data manipulation capability of DL/I. The EXAMPLE PSB defined in Figure 10.17b will also be used. Figure 10.18 illustrates the occurrences of the SALESDB and PARTDB databases that will be used:

- There are three occurrences of the SALESDB database with Rep 1, Rep 2, and Rep 3 being occurrences of the root segment SLSREP.
- CUSTOMER segment occurrences are Cust A and Cust B for Rep 1, Cust Z for Rep 2, and Cust D, Cust E, and Cust F for Rep 3.
- Cust A, Cust Z, Cust D, and Cust F have no ORDER segment occurrences. Cust B has OR 11 as its single ORDER segment occurrence, while Cust E has OR 25 and OR 55 as its ORDER segment occurrences.
- There are two occurrences of the PARTDB database, with LOCK and GAUGE as occurrences of the root segment PART.
- ORDLINE has five occurrences: the physical child of OR 11 and the logical child of GAUGE, which is one and the same entity, has five units ordered; the physical child of OR 11 and the logical child of LOCK has two units ordered; the physical child of OR 25 and the logical child of LOCK has three units ordered; the physical child of OR 55 and the logical child of LOCK has six units ordered; and the physical child of OR 55 and the logical child of GAUGE has eight units ordered.

FIGURE 10.18
3 occurrences of the SALESDB database and occurrences of the PARTDB database.

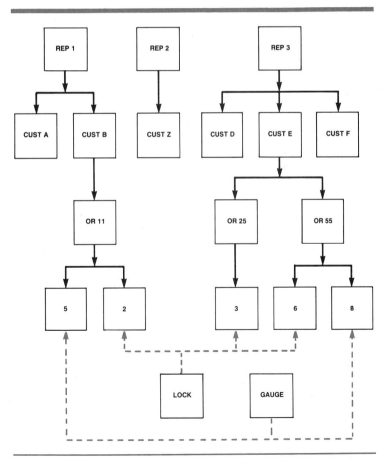

An application program in a host language like COBOL interacts with the data-bases by using DL/I DML requests. A request is expressed as a CALL statement with a parameter list. The parameter list communicates to DL/I the following:

- the function code, or specific DL/I request
- the PCB being used
- the program record area, where DL/I places a retrieved segment occurrence or obtains one to place into the database,
- segment search arguments, which describe the segment(s) of the PSB to be manipulated

After executing the CALL, DL/I returns a value in the PCB's status code field. The application program tests this status code to determine the success or failure of the CALL statement just completed.

A summary of the DL/I function codes is shown in Figure 10.19. Rather than use the actual DL/I CALL syntax, we will use a simplified syntax to illustrate and explain each of these DL/I function codes.

Function Code	Description
GET UNIQUE (GU)	Direct retrieval of a segment occurrence that satisfies a given SSA
GET NEXT (GN)	Sequential retrieval of the next segment occurrence using preorder traversal
GET NEXT WITHIN PARENT (GNP)	Sequential retrieval of the next segment occurrence under current parent
GET HOLD UNIQUE (GHU)	Same as GU, but allows subsequent DLET and REPL
GET HOLD NEXT (GHN)	Same as GN, but allows subsequent DLET and REPL
GET HOLD NEXT WITHIN PARENT (GHNP)	Same as GNP, but allows subsequent DLET and REPL
DELETE (DLET)	Delete an existing segment occurrence
REPLACE (REPL)	Replace an existing segment occurrence
INSERT (ISRT)	Add a new segment occurrence

FIGURE 10.19
DL/I function code summary.

GET UNIQUE (GU)

The **GET UNIQUE (GU)** function code is used for direct retrieval of a specific segment occurrence.

GU Example 1: Retrieving a Specific Root Segment

```
GU SLSREP (REPNUM = 3)
```

This DL/I request retrieves the Rep 3 SLSREP root segment occurrence. In this example, GU is the function code, SLSREP is the segment name, REPNUM is a field name within the SLSREP segment of the DBD, and SLSREP (REPNUM = 3) is the segment search argument (SSA). This SSA is a *qualified SSA*, since the condition REPNUM = 3 qualifies which specific segment occurrence is needed. After executing this request, the contents of the Rep 3 SLSREP segment occurrence are available for use by the application program. Since REPNUM was declared as a unique field in the DBD, there is only one SLSREP segment occurrence with REPNUM = 3. If, however, we had specified that SLSREP could have multiple occurrences with the same REPNUM value, then this GU request would have retrieved the first occurrence having that REPNUM value.

The **SSA** is a program data item whose value is "filled in" during execution of the program. For example, we would define the following:

```
03   SLSREP-SSA.
     05   FILLER               PIC X(19) VALUE
            "SLSREP  (REPNUM = ".
     05   SLSREP-SSA-NUMBER  PIC 9(2).
     05   FILLER               PIC X     VALUE ")".
```

Then during execution of the program:

```
MOVE 3 TO SLSREP-SSA-NUMBER.
GU SLSREP-SSA
```

In all the examples that use SSAs, the equal (" = ") relational operator is used. DL/I, however, allows the use of these other relational operators: " > = ", " < = ", " > ", " < ", and "NE".

GU Example 2: Retrieving a Specific Nonroot Segment

```
GU SLSREP    (REPNUM = 3)
   CUSTOMER (CUSTNUM = 'E')
   ORDER     (ORDNUM = 55)
```

For direct retrieval of a specific nonroot segment occurrence, SSAs are used to specify the hierarchical path to that segment occurrence. The three SSAs, SLSREP (REPNUM = 3), CUSTOMER (CUSTNUM = 'E'), and ORDER (ORDNUM = 55), provide the hierarchical path to the OR 55 segment occurrence. After executing this DL/I request, the contents of the OR 55 ORDER segment occurrence are available for use by the program. Only the ORDER segment occurrence is retrieved; neither the SLSREP nor the CUS–TOMER segment occurrences along the hierarchical path are retrieved.

Since the SALESDB is using HDAM, DL/I hashes on the REPNUM of 3, goes directly to the Rep 3 SLSREP occurrence, sequentially searches CUS-TOMER segment occurrences to find the one with CUSTNUM of 'E', and then sequentially searches ORDER segment occurrences to find the one with ORDNUM of 55.

GU Example 3: Retrieving a Specific Nonroot Segment Using Unqualified SSAs

```
GU  SLSREP
    CUSTOMER
    ORDER      (ORDNUM  =  55)
```

Here we have omitted conditions for the first two SSAs, so DL/I will sequentially search the database until it finds the first ORDER segment occurrence having an ORDNUM of 55. DL/I ends up retrieving the same ORDER segment, OR 55, that it did in the previous example. But since DL/I goes through the database sequentially, it typically takes more accesses and more time when we do not supply the SSAs. So SSAs should be provided for each segment, if possible, in order to reduce overall processing time.

An SSA without a condition is called an *unqualified SSA*. The two unquali-fied SSAs in the example could be eliminated and OR 55 would still be retrieved. Thus, the following DL/I request is equivalent in that it produces identical results:

```
GU  ORDER  (ORDNUM  =  55)
```

GU Example 4: Retrieving a NonRoot Segment Using All Unqualified SSAs

```
GU  SLSREP
    CUSTOMER
    ORDER
```

Since only unqualified SSAs are specified, DL/I sequentially searches from the first root segment occurrence and retrieves the very first ORDER segment, OR 11 in Figure 10.18.

It is also possible to issue a GU command with no SSAs:

```
GU
```

In this case DL/I retrieves the first root segment occurrence, Rep 1. In other words, this is a way to get to the start of the database at any time during processing.

GU Example 5: Root Segment With a Non-Sequence Field SSA

```
GU  SLSREP     (REPNAME  =  'MARY  JONES')
```

An SSA does not have to consist of a sequence, or key, field. The sequence field for SLSREP is REPNUM, and here REPNAME is being used for the SLSREP segment search field in the SSA. DL/I sequentially searches SLSREP segment occurrences until it finds the first one with a REPNAME of MARY JONES.

GU Example 6: Retrieving Multiple Segments with One Statement

```
GU  SLSREP     *D(REPNUM   =  3)
    CUSTOMER   *D(CUSTNUM  =  'E')
    ORDER       (ORDNUM   =  55)
```

In all previous GU examples, only the lowest-level segment occurrence was retrieved. In this example, one GU request is used to retrieve three segment occurrences: Rep 3, Cust E, and OR 55. An asterisk after the segment name indicates that one or more *command codes* will follow. In this case the D command code is a **path call** requesting DL/I to additionally retrieve the occurrence of the segment named preceding the asterisk, both the SLSREP and CUSTOMER segments in the example. DL/I has several other command codes, but we will not discuss them further.

GET NEXT (GN)

The **GET NEXT (GN)** function code retrieves the next segment occurrence sequentially in preorder traversal sequence. Typical use of the GN requires that a *current position* be established within the database prior to issuing the GN. The current position is the segment occurrence accessed by the most recently executed GU, GN, GNP, GHU, GHN, GHNP, or I SRT DL/I call.

There is one current position for each PCB. If the following requests were executed:

```
GU  SLSREP     (REPNUM  =  1)
    CUSTOMER   (CUSTNUM  =  'B')
    ORDER      (ORDNUM  =  11)
GU  PART       (PARTNAME  =  'LOCK')
```

then OR 11 would become the current position in the SALESDB database and LOCK would become the current position in the PARTDB database.

GN Example 1: Retrieval Without SSAs

```
GN
```

The effect of this DL/I request depends on the current position of the database. Let's assume that the parameter list for this request points to the SALESDB PCB. If this is the very first DL/I request executed, then Rep 1, the first root segment occurrence, is retrieved. Recall that a GU request issued at any time without SSAs yields the same result. A GU always goes back to the start of the database, while the GN goes from the current position.

If we continued issuing this GN request, DL/I would retrieve in sequence every database segment occurrence from the current position of Rep 1. That is, DL/I would retrieve Cust A, Cust B, Or 11, the two ORDLINE segment occurrences for OR 11, Rep 2, Cust Z, and so on.

What if the application program needed to retrieve all descendant segment occurrences for a given SLSREP segment occurrence, for example, Rep 2? The program could issue a GU SLSREP (REPNUM = 2) request to establish a current position at the needed root, followed by the execution of a loop issuing the GN request. But after Cust Z has been retrieved, there are no more descendant segments for Rep 2, so the next SLSREP segment occurrence of Rep 3 would be retrieved. How does the application program know this? A number of fields that are returned by DL/I, in addition to the status code and retrieved segment fields, can help. In particular, DL/I returns all sequence fields along the hierarchical path to the retrieved segment. So after each segment occurrence is retrieved, the application program could check the REPNUM–SEQUENCE–FIELD value and terminate the loop when it changed, as in the following:

```
GU SLSREP (REPNUM = 2)
GN
PERFORM PROCESS-AND-GET-SEGMENTS
    UNTIL REPNUM-SEQUENCE-FIELD NOT = 2.
    .
    .
    .
PROCESS-AND-GET-SEGMENTS.
    Process the segment occurrence.
    GN
```

GN Example 2: Retrieving All Occurrences of a Given Segment Type

To retrieve all root segments in the database, the program establishes a current position at the beginning of the database, using a GU request, and then successively retrieves root segments, using a GN SLSREP request. The program checks the status code after each request and continues until the status code equals 'GB', indicating the end of the database. The following illustrates the processing:

```
GU
PERFORM PROCESS-ROOT-SEGMENTS
     UNTIL STATUS-CODE = 'GB'.
     .
     .
     .
PROCESS-ROOT-SEGMENTS.
     Process the root segment.
     GN SLSREP
```

A similar process is followed to retrieve all occurrences of a nonroot segment type. For example, to retrieve all CUSTOMER segment occurrences:

```
GU CUSTOMER
PERFORM PROCESS-CUSTOMER-SEGMENTS
     UNTIL STATUS-CODE = 'GB'.
     .
     .
     .
PROCESS-CUSTOMER-SEGMENTS.
     Process the CUSTOMER segment.
     GN CUSTOMER
```

GN Example 3: Retrieving Selected Occurrences of a Given Segment Type

Let's assume for a moment that a customer can be serviced by more than one sales rep and that we want to retrieve all occurrences of Cust B in the database. The manner in which the program processes against the database is similar to that of the previous example, but it uses a qualified SSA to restrict retrieval to Cust B segment occurrences:

```
GU CUSTOMER (CUSTNUM = 'B')
PERFORM PROCESS-CUSTOMER-SEGMENTS
     UNTIL STATUS-CODE = 'GB'.
     .
     .
     .
PROCESS-CUSTOMER-SEGMENTS.
     Process the CUSTOMER segment.
     GN CUSTOMER (CUSTNUM = 'B')
```

GET NEXT WITHIN PARENT (GNP)

The **GET NEXT WITHIN PARENT (GNP)** function code retrieves segment occurrences under the current parent in preorder traversal sequence. When a segment occurrence for the next parent is encountered, DL/I sets the status code to a value of "GE" to indicate that there are no more segment occurrences for the current parent. Either a GU or GN preceding the GNP establishes the current parent.

GNP Example 1: Retrieval Without SSAs

```
GU SLSREP (REPNUM = 1)
GNP
PERFORM PROCESS-SEGMENTS
     UNTIL STATUS-CODE = 'GE'.
   .
   .
   .
PROCESS-SEGMENTS.
     Process the segment.
     GNP
```

The above retrieves all descendant segment occurrences under Rep 1 in hierarchical order: Cust A, Cust B, OR 11, and then the two ORDLINE occurrences. If GU SLSREP (REPNUM = 1) is changed to GU CUSTOMER (CUSTNUM = B), then OR 11 and the two ORDLINE occurrences are retrieved.

GNP Example 2: Retrieving Occurrences of a Given Segment Type

```
GU SLSREP (REPNUM = 3)
   CUSTOMER
PERFORM PROCESS-CUSTOMER-SEGMENTS
     UNTIL STATUS-CODE = 'GE'.
   .
   .
   .
PROCESS-CUSTOMER-SEGMENTS.

     Process the segment.
     GNP CUSTOMER
```

The above causes DL/I to retrieve the three CUSTOMER segment occurrences under Rep 3: Cust D, Cust E, and Cust F. The GNP does not limit retrieval to the immediate child of the current parent. The application program, for example, could establish the current parent as Rep 3 and retrieve all ORDER segment occurrences. OR 25 and OR 55 would be retrieved in the following example:

```
GU SLSREP (REPNUM = 3)
    ORDER
PERFORM PROCESS-ORDER-SEGMENTS
    UNTIL STATUS-CODE = 'GE'.
    .
    .
    .
PROCESS-ORDER-SEGMENTS.
    Process the segment.
    GNP ORDER
```

GET HOLD

The three function codes, GHU (GET HOLD UNIQUE), GHN (GET HOLD NEXT), and GHNP (GET HOLD NEXT WITHIN PARENT) work in precisely the same way as do their counterparts without the HOLD. These HOLD versions must be used whenever a segment occurrence is to be changed or deleted. That is, prior to the use of a replace (REPL) or delete (DLET) function code, the segment occurrence to be replaced or deleted must be retrieved, using an appropriate GET HOLD.

DELETE (DLET)

Deleting a database segment occurrence is a two-step process. First, the segment occurrence to be deleted must be retrieved using one of the three GET HOLD function codes. Then the **DELETE (DLET)** function code is issued to remove that segment occurrence from the database. There must not be any intervening DL/I requests between these two steps. The following requests would remove Cust A from the database:

```
GHU SLSREP    (REPNUM = 1)
    CUSTOMER (CUSTNUM = 'A')
DLET
```

If the segment occurrence to be deleted has descendant segment occurrences, these occurrences will also be deleted. In the following example not only is Cust B deleted, but OR 11 and its two ORDLINE occurrences are also deleted.

```
GHU SLSREP    (REPNUM = 1)
    CUSTOMER (CUSTNUM = 'B')
DLET
```

REPLACE (REPL)

Changing the field values within a segment occurrence is a three-step process: the segment occurrence to be changed must be retrieved, using one of the three GET HOLD function codes; the necessary changes are made to the field values within memory; and the **REPLACE (REPL)** function code is issued to replace the retrieved segment occurrence in the database. The following changes the ORD–DATE field value for OR 55 TO 870215:

```
GHU SLSREP (REPNUM = 3)
    CUSTOMER (CUSTNUM = 'E')
    ORDER    (ORDNUM = 55)
MOVE 870215 TO ORDDATE
REPL
```

There must not be any intervening DL/I requests between the GET HOLD and the REPL requests. Also, the value of a sequence field cannot be changed by using the REPL function code. Instead the segment occurrence must be deleted and then added back to the database by using the ISRT function code.

INSERT (ISRT)

The **INSERT (ISRT)** function code is used to add a new segment occurrence to the database. Unlike the other database update functions of DLET and ISRT, a GET HOLD request is not issued prior to an ISRT request. Before a given segment occurrence can be added, the parent of that segment occurrence must already exist in the database. The segment occurrence is added in proper order, based on its sequence field. In the following example, the new ORDER segment would be positioned under Cust E and between OR 25 and OR 55.

```
MOVE 40 TO ORDNUM.
MOVE 861105 TO ORDDATE.
ISRT SLSREP (REPNUM = 3)
     CUSTOMER (CUSTNUM = 'E')
     ORDER
```

10.5 COMPARISON OF THE THREE DATA MODELS

Now that the relational, CODASYL, and hierarchical data models have been described in detail, can we say which of the three is best suited to be the basis for a DBMS used to manage an enterprise's database? No universal answer is given by all database experts and by all enterprises utilizing a DBMS. Each data model has its proponents, and each enterprise can select from a large number of DBMS's conforming to each of the data models. A significant dollar investment has been made in each of the data models by vendors marketing DBMS's and by enterprises using these DBMS's.

Rather than abstractly decide which is the best data model, it is more instructive to contrast the various models in terms of their respective advantages and disadvantages. Some of the advantages and disadvantages are inherent in the data models themselves; others are relative. Those advantages and disadvantages that are covered in this section are summarized in Figure 10.20.

Hierarchical Data Model Advantages
 - Large current market penetration of IBM and of DL/I
 - Large number of available application packages
 - Simplicity of hierarchical data model
 - Performance is good
 - Integrity is good

Hierarchical Data Model Disadvantages
 - Difficulty of implementing non-hierarchical structures
 - Problems adding and deleting segments
 - Physical reorganization
 - Minimal data independence
 - Complexity
 - Potential inefficient processing

CODASYL Data Model Advantages
 - Longevity and availability of DBMSs for this model
 - All data relationships may be modeled
 - Standards exist for this model
 - Performance is good
 - Data independence

CODASYL Data Model Disadvantages
 - Complex navigation
 - Complexity

Relational Data Model Advantages
 - Simplicity
 - High level of data independence
 - Strong theoretical foundation

Relational Data Model Disadvantages
 - Performance needs to be improved
 - Referential integrity not supported

FIGURE 10.20
Advantages and disadvantages of the hierarchical, CODASYL and relational data models.

ADVANTAGES OF THE HIERARCHICAL DATA MODEL

- IBM is the dominant force in the computer industry, and it is committed to supporting the hierarchical data model through DL/I. IBM's continued support is based on the large number of enterprises using DL/I with large dollar investments in DL/I application systems. IBM's support means that enterprises can depend on future improvements in DL/I and can count on help in resolving current problems. DL/I is a proven DBMS in use since the late 1960s. The large base of knowledgeable enterprises, end users, programmers, and analysts for DL/I have formed organizations to address common problems and common needs and to interact as a common front with IBM in efforts to resolve them.

- A large number of application packages using DL/I are available, so an enterprise does not have to develop all of its application systems internally.
- The hierarchical data model itself is simple, with a small number of commands needed to navigate the database. There are forms of each command available that make this model more nonnavigational than the CODASYL data model. For those applications having natural hierarchical relationships, the hierarchical data model lends itself simply to a database design solution.
- For application systems that have fixed, predefined relationships that lend themselves to a hierarchical model or to an extended hierarchical model DBMS like DL/I, performance is better than that provided by the relational model and no worse than that provided by the CODASYL model.
- Since adding a segment occurrence requires that the parent segment occurrence and other ancestors already exist in the database, integrity in this situation is provided.

DISADVANTAGES OF THE HIERARCHICAL DATA MODEL

- Many data relationships are not hierarchical. The biggest disadvantages of the hierarchical data model are the difficulty of representing many-to-many relationships and the limitation of allowing no more than one parent for a given segment type. Even in DL/I, where two parents, one physical and the other logical, are allowed, these constraints turn database design and performance tuning into very challenging tasks. Solving these problems either creates unnatural data organization or introduces redundancy to the physical database.
- Even when the data relationships are hierarchical, the hierarchical data model can lead to problems. For example, if Premiere Products were to gain a new customer who was not associated with a sales rep, this customer could not be added to the database until he or she had been assigned to a sales rep. Or unintentional loss of data can occur when a segment is deleted, since all descendant segment occurrences are also automatically deleted.
- It is difficult to modify the structure of the physical database. Normally these modifications require reorganization and rebuilding of the physical database.
- There is minimal data independence. If a program is sensitive to segments that undergo physical restructuring either themselves or in relation to other hierarchical segments, then the program will normally require modification.
- Powerful hierarchical DBMS's such as DL/I are complicated to understand and to use. Premiums are paid to programmers, analysts, and designers who are competent in working effectively in a DL/I environment.
- Information requirements that do not follow the natural path of the hierarchy may be time-consuming to address. For example, if in Figure 10.1 a student were allowed to have more than one major and a report were needed for all students with their majors ordered by student number, then

all student segment occurrences would need to be retrieved and sorted before the report could be produced.

ADVANTAGES OF THE CODASYL DATA MODEL

- CODASYL data model DBMS's have been available since the late 1960s, so a number of proven, successful DBMS's follow this model.
- There are no limitations on the types of data relationships that can be represented, in contrast to the hierarchical data model.
- The CODASYL data model is supported by various specification reports published by the Data Base Task Group and Data Description Language Committee.
- Performance is better than that of the relational data model and no worse than that of the hierarchical data model.
- This model supplies a degree of data independence in that an application program whose subschema does not reference a new record type or a changed record type does not have to be changed.

DISADVANTAGES OF THE CODASYL DATA MODEL

- Application programs written to interact with CODASYL DBMS's are complex in that they have to provide for navigation through the records and sets of the subschema used by the program.
- The CODASYL data model is not as natural as the relational data model and thus not as easy to understand and use.

ADVANTAGES OF THE RELATIONAL DATA MODEL

- The simplicity of the relational data model makes it easy to understand and use. The end user need not be concerned with the physical structuring of the database, so user requests can be nonprocedural in nature.
- This model supplies a high level of data independence, so both the physical structure and the logical structure can be changed without affecting the application programs.
- The relational data model has a strong theoretical foundation. It is the focus of most database research today, which means that significant advances in database technology are most likely to occur with this model.

DISADVANTAGES OF THE RELATIONAL DATA MODEL

- Poor performance is the biggest disadvantage of this model. Performance has improved, however, and is expected to improve more.
- Unlike the hierarchical and CODASYL data models, most relational DBMS's do not currently provide for referential integrity. A table record can be deleted without deleting dependent table records, and a table record can be added without the records it depends upon in other tables being present. This is likely to be corrected in the near future.

10.6 SUMMARY

In this chapter, we examined the hierarchical data model. The hierarchical model represents data relationships in the form of a tree structure. Each tree has a single root node at the top, with its descendants below it. Each child node has one parent node; each parent node can have multiple child nodes. Twin node occurrences are children occurrences of the same node type with the same parent occurrence. Each node is accessed along a hierarchical path from top to bottom, beginning at the root node. Preorder traversal is an access method in which node occurrences are retrieved from top to bottom and left to right.

We discussed Data Language/I (DL/I), the database component of IBM's Information Management System (IMS). DL/I, in use since 1968, is an extended version of the hierarchical data model and is one of the most widely used DBMS's.

In DL/I a node is called a segment, and one tree structure occurrence is called a physical database record. The collection of physical database records for a given tree structure is called a physical database.

A DL/I logical database is an individual user view of the database. A logical database can be an entire physical database, a portion of one physical database, or portions of two or more physical databases.

DL/I permits the creation of linkages between segments called logical relationships, which allow a segment to have both a physical parent segment and a logical parent segment. These linkages are made through pointer fields that can form unidirectional or bidirectional logical relationships. The logical parent segment can be in the same physical database or in another physical database.

We studied DL/I's four physical database storage structures, called access methods. The hierarchical sequential access method (HSAM) stores segment occurrences sequentially in preorder traversal order. HSAM allows sequential access only and is used primarily for historical data retention. The hierarchical indexed sequential access method (HISAM) creates a separate index for the key field of the root segment. Both sequential and random access are permitted to the root segment, while access is sequential to dependent segments. The hierarchical direct access method (HDAM) uses a hashing technique for random access to the root segment. Either hierarchical or child-twin pointers provide access to dependent segments. The hierarchical indexed direct access method (HIDAM) allows sequential and random access through an index to the root segment and access to dependent segments through hierarchical or child-twin pointers. An inverted file structure, called secondary indexing, permits random access to nonroot segments.

A DL/I physical database is defined through a database description (DBD). The DBD defines all segments, fields, and hierarchical relationships, both physical and logical. A DL/I logical database is defined through a program specification block (PSB), in which program communication blocks (PCBs) define the sensitive segments accessible to a given program view.

DL/I segment retrieval is done through the GET UNIQUE, GET NEXT, GET NEXT WITHIN PARENT, and HOLD versions of these function codes. Segment updating is done through the DELETE, REPLACE, and INSERT function codes. These function codes can be used with or without segment search arguments

(SSAs). The segment search argument forms can be qualified or unqualified.

In the last section, we compared the hierarchical, CODASYL, and relational data models by describing the advantages and disadvantages inherent in each model and relative to the two other models.

REVIEW QUESTIONS

1. Define the following tree structure terms: node, branch, root, descendant, parent, child, and twin.
2. Explain the three constraints that apply to the general hierarchical model.
3. What is a hierarchical path? Compare it to preorder traversal access.
4. Explain the difference in DL/I between a physical database and a logical database.
5. Describe the method used by DL/I to allow a segment to have two parents. Include in your answer the name of this feature, the names of the parents, and an explanation of the unidirectional and bidirectional forms of this feature.
6. Explain the difference between the HSAM and HISAM access method.
7. Explain the difference between the HDAM and HIDAM access method.
8. What is a DBD? How does it differ from a DBD statement?
9. What is a virtual segment?
10. What is a PSB and how does it differ from a DBD?
11. How does a PCB relate to a PSB and to a DBD?
12. What is a SENSEG statement, and how does it relate to a SEGM statement?
13. Which six DL/I function codes are used for retrieval? Which three are used for updating?
14. What is a segment search argument (SSA)? Name two situations in which an SSA is not used.
15. Explain current position. Which DL/I function codes establish current position?
16. Why would a GNP function code be used instead of a GN?
17. When is a GHU function code used instead of a GU?
18. What problem can occur if the DLET is not used carefully?
19. Which data model would you recommend? Justify your answer by listing its advantages over the other two data models.

EXERCISES

1. Construct a data structure diagram that shows a virtual segment for the many-to-many relationship between STUDENTS and COURSES.
2. Construct an example of a qualified SSA and another example of an unqualified SSA, using the Premiere Products database. Use the DBD from Figure 10.15, the PSB from Figure 10.17b, and the occurrences in Figure 10.18.

Exercises 3 through 5 are based on the following information:

A database is needed to satisfy the following seven requirements:
a. For a department, store its number (three characters) and name (twenty characters).
b. For an employee, store his or her number (four characters) and name (twenty characters).
c. For an insurance plan, store the plan number (four characters) and description (twenty characters).
d. For a job history record, store the job classification (twenty characters) and the starting date (six characters).
e. Each department can have many employees, but each employee works in exactly one department.
f. Each insurance plan serves many employees, but each employee is served by exactly one plan.
g. Each employee can have several job history records, but each job history record corresponds to exactly one employee.

3. Draw a data structure diagram for the database. Indicate the fields that would be a part of each record.

4. Write the DBD for this physical database. Make logical choices for sequence fields. If more than one physical database is required and a logical relationship is needed, be sure to include the logical relationship properly in the DBDs.

5. Give a full PSB, permitting access to all segments for the DBDs defined.

Exercises 6 through 9 are based on Figure 10.21 (opposite), which consolidates the data structure diagram and one physical database record for the example database used earlier in this chapter.

6. Write the DBD for this physical database. Assume that there is one field per segment: DEPTNAME (fifteen characters), FACNAME (ten characters), STNAME (twelve characters), and MAJNAME (eight characters) for segments named DEPT, FACULTY, STUDENT, and MAJOR, respectively. Assume that each field is a sequence field.

7. Give a full PSB permitting access to all segments for the DBD defined.

8. Which segment occurrences are retrieved with the following:
   a.
   ```
   GU
   GN
   ```
   b.
   ```
   GU  DEPT
   GN  STUDENT
   ```
   c.
   ```
   GU  DEPT
       FACULTY  (FACNAME  =  "Smith')
   GN  STUDENT
   ```
   d.
   ```
   GU  DEPT
       FACULTY  (FACNAME  =  "Smith')
       STUDENT
   ```

e.
```
GU  STUDENT  (STNAME  =  "Sam')
GN
GN
```
f.
```
GU  DEPT
    FACULTY  (FACNAME  =  "Smith')
GNP  STUDENT
GNP  STUDENT
```

9. Show the DL/I statements needed to perform the following actions:
    a. Retrieve all major segment occurrences.
    b. Delete 'Sam'.
    c. Delete all segments related to 'Jones'.
    d. Add student 'Paulette' to faculty 'Jones'.
    e. Modify major 'Mkt' so that it is called 'Finance' instead.

FIGURE 10.21
Data structure
diagram and one
occurrence of the
department-faculty-
student-major
hierarchical structure.

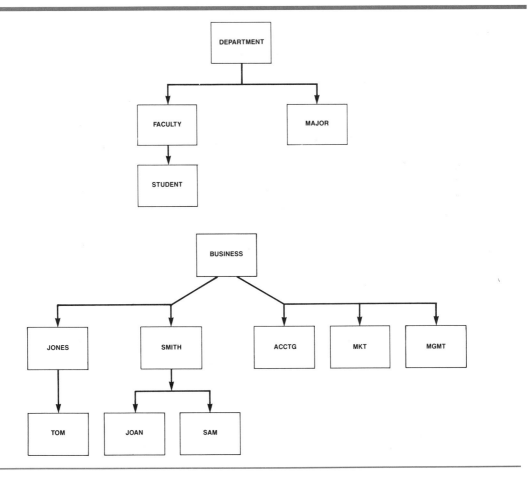

REFERENCES

1] Atre, S. *Data Base: Structured Techniques for Design, Performance, and Management*. John Wiley & Sons, Inc., 1980.

2] Date, C. J. *An Introduction to Database Systems, Volume I*, 4th ed. Addison-Wesley, 1986.

3] Hawryszkiewycz, I. T. *Database Analysis and Design*. SRA, 1984.

4] Hubbard, George U. "Computer-Assisted Hierarchical Database Design" In *Principles of Database Design Volume I: Logical Organizations*, S. Bing Yao. Prentice-Hall, 1985.

5] Kapp, Dan, and Leben, Joseph F. *IMS Programming Techniques: A Guide to Using DL/I*. Van Nostrand Reinhold, 1978.

6] McElreath, T. Jack. *IMS Design and Implementation Techniques*. Q.E.D. Information Sciences, Inc., 1979.

7] Tsichritzis, D. C. and Lochovsky, F. H. "Hierarchical Data-Base Management: A Survey" *ACM Computing Surveys* 8, no. 1 (March 1976).

8] Wiederhold, Gio. *Database Design*, 2d ed. McGraw-Hill, 1983.

INVERTED FILE MODEL

1.1 INTRODUCTION

In previous chapters we completed our coverage of the relational, CODA-SYL, and hierarchical data models. Experts in the field of database processing generally place each DBMS in one of these three categories, and a number of DBMS's conform closely to one particular model. However, there is nothing sacred about these three data models. Some DBMS's, while said to conform to a specific data model, deviate from it to some degree. For example, the hierarchical model restricts a child node to a single parent; but DL/I, though classified as a hierarchical DBMS, allows a child segment to have two parents through the logical child facility.

Then there are DBMS's which are difficult to classify. In some cases, they are **hybrid systems** that combine features of two or more of the models. For example, the IMAGE DBMS, marketed by Hewlett-Packard, combines some features of the CODASYL and hierarchical models. Also, in recent years many of the nonrelational DBMS's have added a relational component in order to take advantage of the benefits of the relational model. A book many times the size of this one would be required to discuss all the hybrid or combined-model systems.

Another reason for the classification difficulty is that some DBMS's do not fit any of the models. For example, ADABAS and DATACOM/DB are among the group of DBMS's that follow an inverted file structure. The inverted file structure and ADABAS are the subjects of this chapter. There are three important reasons for studying them:

- Some database experts believe there is a fourth data model, the **inverted file model**, which is based upon an inverted file structure.
- ADABAS and DATACOM/DB are two of the most widely used mainframe DBMS's. Each of these is at the core of leading-edge fourth-generation information processing environments. So an examination of the database component of one of these products is highly relevant.
- Even though they conform to one of the three main data models, many DBMS's use an **inverted file structure** for physically storing secondary keys.

In the next section we give an overview of the basic concepts and terminology of the inverted file model. Section 11.3 describes ADABAS in some detail. In section 11.4, we discuss the ways in which ADABAS, as a representative inverted file model system, and DL/I, as a representative hierarchical model system, support the functions of a DBMS.

11.2   BASIC CONCEPTS AND TERMINOLOGY

Before discussing the inverted file model, we need to note that there is no industry standard for this model. Furthermore, the inverted file model is not generally accepted as one of the standard models for database management systems. As a result, the terminology used for this model varies from expert to expert, and the method used to implement a DBMS conforming to this model varies from manufacturer to manufacturer. So rather than list an inventory of all the terminology and methods of implementation, we will describe the fundamentals of the inverted file structure, which is the basis of the inverted file model.

We will use the Premiere Products database as our example in explaining the inverted file model. Figure 11.1a shows the data structure diagram for the five entity types of SLSREP, CUSTOMER, ORDER, ORDER_LINE, and PART and the four one-to-many relationships among them.

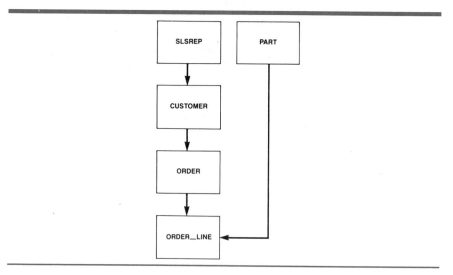

FIGURE 11.1a
Diagram for Premiere
Products database

In order to implement the database shown in Figure 11.1a with the inverted file model, we create five files, one for each of the five different entity types. The SLSREP file contains the five fields shown in Figure 11.1b: SLSREP-NUMBER, SLSREP-NAME, SLSREP-ADDRESS, TOTAL-COMMISSION, and COMMISSION-RATE. Likewise, the CUSTOMER file, ORDER file, PART file, and ORDER-LINE files contain fields as shown in Figure 11.1b.

```
01   SLSREP.
     02   SLSREP-NUMBER          PIC 9(2).
     02   SLSREP-NAME            PIC X(20).
     02   SLSREP-ADDRESS         PIC X(20).
     02   TOTAL-COMMISSION       PIC 9(5)V9(2).
     02   COMMISSION-RATE        PIC V9(2).
01   CUSTOMER.
     02   CUSTOMER-NUMBER        PIC 9(3).
     02   NAME                   PIC X(20).
     02   ADDRESS                PIC X(20).
     02   CURRENT-BALANCE        PIC 9(5)V9(2).
     02   CREDIT-LIMIT           PIC 9(5).
     02   SLSREP-NUMBER          PIC 9(2).
01   ORDER.
     02   ORDER-NUMBER           PIC 9(5).
     02   DATE                   PIC 9(6).
     02   CUSTOMER-NUMBER        PIC 9(3).
01   PART.
     02   PART-NUMBER            PIC X(4).
     02   PART-DESCRIPTION       PIC X(20).
     02   UNITS-ON-HAND          PIC 9(4).
     02   ITEM-CLASS             PIC X(2).
     02   WAREHOUSE-NUMBER       PIC 9(2).
     02   UNIT-PRICE             PIC 9(4)V9(2).
01   ORDER-LINE.
     02   ORDER-NUMBER           PIC 9(5).
     02   PART-NUMBER            PIC X(4).
     02   NUMBER-ORDERED         PIC 9(4).
     02   QUOTED-PRICE           PIC 9(4)V9(2).
```

FIGURE 11.1b
Fields for each entity
for Premiere Products
database

Note the similarity of the design so far to that of the relational model. Each of the five files corresponds to a relation from that design, and the fields in each of the files are equivalent to the attributes in those relations. Each file contains appropriate **primary key** field(s): SLSREP-NUMBER in the SLSREP file, CUSTOMER-NUMBER in the CUSTOMER file, ORDER-NUMBER in the ORDER file, PART-NUMBER in the PART file, and the combination of ORDER-NUMBER and PART-NUMBER in the ORDER-LINE file. There is no standard method associated with the inverted file model for physically placing and locating a record in the file based on a given primary key value. Instead, the use of an **index** or of a **hashing** scheme are two ways of handling primary keys. Each file in our example also contains fields that serve as **foreign keys** to allow the formation of relationships between files: SLSREP-NUMBER in the CUSTOMER file and CUSTOMER-NUMBER in the ORDER file.

The five files look no different than they would look if we used a non-DBMS **flat file structure**. To understand the difference between the flat file structure and the **inverted file structure**, we need to see how each structure permits access to records based on the value of a nonkey field. Consider the ORDER file and the necessity of retrieving all records for CUSTOMER_NUMBER = 522. For the flat file structure of Figure 11.2 on the following page, we would need to read sequentially all records in the ORDER file, each time testing to determine whether the CUSTOMER_NUMBER equaled 522. For a file with thousands of records, a considerable amount of time would be required to select the correct records. If access to the ORDER file based on a given value of CUSTOMER_NUMBER were a frequent requirement, retrieval performance would be a problem with this flat file structure.

ORDER File

ORDER	ORDER_NUMBER	DATE	CUSTOMER_NUMBER
	12489	90287	124
	12491	90287	311
	12494	90487	315
	12495	90487	256
	12498	90587	522
	12500	90587	124
	12504	90587	522

FIGURE 11.2
A sample ORDER flat file

Figure 11.3 shows the same ORDER file, but this time there is a second file associated with it. This second file is shown to the right of the ORDER file and has one entry or record for each different CUSTOMER_NUMBER. Along with the CUSTOMER_NUMBER each record has all the ORDER_NUMBERs from the ORDER file that belong to that particular customer. (Most implementations of the inverted

ORDER File

ORDER	ORDER_NUMBER	DATE	CUSTOMER_NUMBER
	12489	90287	124
	12491	90287	311
	12494	90487	315
	12495	90487	256
	12498	90587	522
	12500	90587	124
	12504	90587	522

Inverted File on CUSTOMER_NUMBER

CUSTOMER_NUMBER	ORDER_NUMBER
124	12489
	12500
256	12495
311	12491
315	12494
522	12498
	12504

FIGURE 11.3
A sample ORDER file inverted on CUSTOMER_NUMBER

file structure would store the addresses of the ORDER file records rather than the ORDER_NUMBERs. We are using the ORDER_NUMBERs in these examples so that we can present the concepts of the inverted file structure without getting lost in the details of actual implementations.) This second file is structured to permit random access (it may have a hashing scheme, or it may be indexed, etc.) and is in sequence by CUSTOMER_NUMBER. To retrieve all ORDER records for CUSTOMER_NUMBER = 522, we make use of this second file and find the record whose CUSTOMER_NUMBER equals 522. Once found, the list of ORDER_NUMBERs in the record for this CUSTOMER_NUMBER is used to randomly retrieve the two records from the ORDER file with ORDER_NUMBERs of 12498 and 12504. In contrast to the requirements for the flat file structure, we do not need to sequentially access all records in the ORDER file to satisfy the retrieval criterion. We do, however, have to process against this second file; but since we can randomly access against it, retrieval performance is considerably improved for files with large numbers of ORDER records.

The structure just described and shown in Figure 11.3 is what is known as an **inverted file structure**. What we have done is to take a nonkey field, CUSTOMER_NUMBER in our example, and make an **inverted file** on CUSTOMER_NUMBER (or *inverted on* CUSTOMER_NUMBER). That is, CUSTOMER_NUMBER normally serves as one of the fields of the ORDER file, and we have inverted that role, so it now serves as the key of a separate file, used when retrieval is required against the ORDER file based on specified values of CUSTOMER_NUMBER. CUSTOMER_NUMBER is also called a **secondary key**, which is a field other than the primary key that is used for random access to records in the file. Note that a secondary key does not need to be unique, as does the primary key.

A DBMS using the inverted file model automatically creates and maintains the extra inverted file once we specify a field as a secondary key. When we need to access records based on a specific value of that secondary key, the DBMS interacts with the inverted file to determine whether there is an entry for that value. If so, the DBMS then accesses the records from the primary file pointed to by the values in that inverted file entry. The user is not even aware that this extra inverted file exists, since the DBMS handles all interaction with it and shields the user from it. In one way, however, a user is aware that a field is a secondary key: retrieval is much more rapid when a field is inverted than when it is not.

Figure 11.3 is an example of a **partially inverted file**, where only some of the fields in the file are established as secondary keys. If all nonprimary key fields are declared to be secondary keys, then we have a **fully inverted file** (sometimes called a *totally inverted file*). Figure 11.4 shows the ORDER file fully inverted, with both CUSTOMER_NUMBER and DATE as secondary keys. If we need to access records from the ORDER file using a specific value for DATE, the DBMS

FIGURE 11.4
A sample ORDER file fully inverted on both CUSTOMER_NUMBER and DATE

ORDER File

ORDER NUMBER	DATE	CUSTOMER_ NUMBER
12489	90287	124
12491	90287	311
12494	90487	315
12495	90487	256
12498	90587	522
12500	90587	124
12504	90587	522

Inverted File on CUSTOMER_NUMBER

CUSTOMER_ NUMBER	ORDER_ NUMBER
124	12489 12500
256	12495
311	12491
315	12494
522	12498 12504

Inverted File on DATE

DATE	ORDER_ NUMBER
90287	12489 12491
90487	12494 12495
90587	12498 12500 12504

would interact with the inverted file on DATE in a manner similar to the way it interacted with the inverted file on CUSTOMER_NUMBER.

For more complicated accesses involving two or more secondary keys, the DBMS would interact with all necessary inverted files to find those records meeting the search criteria. For example, what if we needed to retrieve all ORDER records where the CUSTOMER_NUMBER = 522 and the DATE = 90287? The DBMS would process this query as follows:

1. Access the inverted file on CUSTOMER_NUMBER to find the entry with a value of 522. The two ORDER_NUMBERs 12498 and 12504 belong to this customer.
2. Access the inverted file on DATE to find the entry with a value of 90287. The two ORDER_NUMBERs 12489 and 12491 have this date.
3. Check to see whether there are any ORDER_NUMBERs in common from steps one and two. In this case there aren't any, so the DBMS informs the user that there are no ORDER records that meet the search criteria.

All this has occurred without ever accessing the ORDER file! And it has taken place with a minimal number of disk accesses. In fact, large portions of the inverted files may be memory resident to even further reduce disk interaction.

How many disk accesses would be required to retrieve all ORDER records where the CUSTOMER_NUMBER = 124 and the DATE = 90587?

Answer:

Three accesses would be required: the first to the inverted file on CUSTOMER_NUMBER to retrieve entry 124; the second to the inverted file on DATE to retrieve entry 90587; and the third to retrieve the ORDER_NUMBER 12500 record from the ORDER file.

With the speed of access in mind, why not always declare every field to be a secondary key when using an inverted file DBMS? That is, why not always have a fully inverted file? The two major drawbacks are the extra disk space required for each secondary key and the extra time required to update these secondary keys. In Figure 11.4, notice that in addition to the disk space needed for the ORDER file, disk space is needed for the inverted file on CUSTOMER_NUMBER and the inverted file on DATE. If there is little or no need for access using one or the other of these secondary keys, disk space is being wasted.

Even more importantly, notice what happens when we add a new order to the ORDER file, say, ORDER_NUMBER = 12499 with CUSTOMER_ NUMBER = 311 and DATE = 90687. The DBMS would take the following actions:

1. Check the ORDER file to see whether ORDER_NUMBER of 12499 already exists (we assume that ORDER_NUMBER is a unique primary key). Since it

does not exist, this record is added to the ORDER file.

2. Check the inverted file on CUSTOMER_NUMBER to see whether there is already an entry with CUSTOMER_NUMBER = 311. Since there is such an entry, add 12499 as the second ORDER_NUMBER for this entry.

3. Check the inverted file on DATE to see whether there is already an entry with DATE = 90687. Since such an entry does not exist, a new record must be added to this inverted file with DATE = 90687 and ORDER_ NUMBER = 12499.

Similar steps must be taken by the DBMS when changes and deletions occur. The larger the number of secondary keys, the more time the DBMS needs to complete an update action.

A fully inverted file with dozens of secondary keys will take considerable disk space and considerable time for updating. So normally only those critical fields against which random access frequently occurs should be made secondary keys. For example, the SLSREP file in Figure 11.1b may or may not have SLSREP_ NAME as a secondary key, but only under most unusual circumstances would the other three fields, SLSREP_ADDRESS, TOTAL_COMMISSION, and COMMISSION_RATE, be made secondary keys. For further details on the performance characteristics of the inverted file structure, see [5].

In the next section we describe the way that ADABAS implements the inverted file model.

1.3   ADABAS

ADABAS (Adaptable DAta BAse System) is an inverted file model DBMS offered by Software AG of North America, Inc. It was first installed in 1971 and has proven to be one of the most popular DBMS products available on IBM mainframe computers. ADABAS is also available on IBM-compatible mainframe computers and Digital Equipment Corporation's VAX line of processors.

ADABAS TERMINOLOGY AND PHYSICAL DATA STORAGE

As with a number of systems in the DBMS world, ADABAS has its own terminology, its own method of physically storing and retrieving data, its own data definition language, and its own data manipulation language. We will first describe ADABAS's terminology and its method of physically storing data. Then we will describe ADABAS's data definition and data manipulation languages.

FILE STRUCTURE

ADABAS can manage a database with a maximum of 255 files, each file having a maximum of 16.7 million records. To illustrate how ADABAS structures a database, we will again use the Premiere Products database, shown in Figure 11.1a and 11.1b. As we did with the inverted file model design in the previous section, we would create five different ADABAS files. To simplify the explanation of ADABAS's file structure, let's concentrate on how ADABAS would structure the ORDER file.

Figure 11.5 shows the ORDER file as structured by ADABAS. Records that constitute the ORDER file are stored in fixed-length blocks (physical records) on disk, using relative block addressing in an area called **data storage**. In this example, ADABAS stores the seven records of the ORDER file in two blocks: four records in block 1 and three records in block 2. In addition to the three data fields

ADABAS Data Storage
ORDER File

ISN	ORDER_NUMBER	DATE	CUSTOMER_NUMBER	
3	12489	90287	124	Block 1
1	12491	90287	311	
7	12494	90487	315	
5	12495	90487	256	
6	12498	90587	522	Block 2
8	12500	90587	124	
2	12504	90587	522	

ADABAS Associator

Address Converter

ISNs:	1	2	3	4	5	6	7	8
Block Numbers:	1	2	1	0	1	2	1	2

Inverted List on the
CUSTOMER_NUMBER Descriptor

CUSTOMER_NUMBER	NUMBER_OF_RECORDS	ISN
124	2	3
		8
256	1	5
311	1	1
315	1	7
522	2	2
		6

Inverted List on the
DATE Descriptor

DATE	NUMBER_OF_RECORDS	ISN
90287	2	1
		3
90487	2	5
		7
90587	3	2
		6
		8

Inverted List on the
ORDER_NUMBER Descriptor

ORDER_NUMBER	NUMBER_OF_RECORDS	ISN
12489	1	3
12491	1	1
12494	1	7
12495	1	5
12498	1	6
12500	1	8
12504	1	2

ORDER_NUMBER, DATE, and CUSTOMER_NUMBER, ADABAS stores an **internal sequence number (ISN)** in each data record. ADABAS automatically assigns a unique ISN to each record in the file. The records in block 1 have ISNs of 3, 1, 7, and 5; and the records in block 2 have ISNs of 6, 8, and 2.

FIGURE 11.5
An ADABAS database for the ORDER file and its three descriptor fields

While the data records themselves are stored in data storage, the **associator** is where ADABAS stores all other information concerning the database. The associator is simply an area on disk allocated for the exclusive use of ADABAS. Within the associator, ADABAS maintains tables that provide database, file, and field definitions (in effect this is a primitive form of data dictionary, though ADABAS does have a full data dictionary capability; the data dictionary is stored as another ADABAS file) and tables for storage management of data storage and the associator.

More importantly for purposes of discussing the structure of the ORDER file, the associator also contains an **address converter** for each file in the database and inverted files for each primary key and each secondary key, both of which are called **descriptors** in ADABAS terminology. A descriptor may be declared to be unique, and ADABAS will ensure that duplicate values do not occur for this descriptor. A primary key defined as a descriptor would typically be declared to be a unique descriptor. However, ADABAS does allow the user to specify that the primary key should use a hashing approach to storage of records instead of defining the primary key as a descriptor.

ADABAS calls its inverted files **inverted lists**, another common term for this structure. Each inverted list is in sequence by the value of the descriptor. In Figure 11.5 there are three inverted lists, one for the primary key of ORDER_NUMBER, the other two for the secondary keys of CUSTOMER_NUMBER and DATE. Each entry in an inverted list has the value of the descriptor, the number of records in data storage that have this particular descriptor value, and the ISNs of the data storage records with this particular descriptor value. For example, the first entry in the inverted list on CUSTOMER_NUMBER has a CUSTOMER_NUMBER value of 124. There are two data records having a CUSTOMER_NUMBER value of 124. The ISNs for these two records are 3 and 8. If you check back to the records in data storage with ISNs of 3 and 8, you will see that these do in fact have a CUSTOMER_NUMBER value of 124. Note that ADABAS employs higher-level indexes to speed up processing; we have not shown these higher-level indexes so as to not overly complicate the essential ADABAS structure.

ISNs do not directly relate to where in data storage a data record with that ISN can be found. The **address converter** is used for this purpose. The address converter is a compact list of block numbers. The first block number in the address converter refers to which relative block in data storage is used to store the data record with an ISN value of 1; the second block number points to the relative block for the data record with an ISN value of 2; and so on. The inverted list on CUSTOMER_NUMBER has ISN values of 3 and 8 for CUSTOMER_NUMBER 124. The third entry in the address converter has a relative block number of 1, and the eighth entry has a relative block number of 2. Checking back to data storage in block 1 and block 2, we see that these blocks do in fact have the two data records for CUSTOMER_NUMBER 124. The address converter in Figure 11.5 shows the block numbers for all seven ORDER file records. If you're wondering about the block number of 0 for ISN equal to 4, the data record with ISN of 4 has been physically deleted from the database, and this ISN is available for reuse, as is the data storage area formerly occupied by the data record.

What needs to change if the database is physically reorganized and ADABAS must move a data record from one block to another? Let's assume, for example, that ADABAS relocates the first record in block 1 with an ISN of 3 to block 100. The data record is moved but none of the values within the data record are changed. Also, none of the inverted lists need to change at all, since the ISN is still the same value. The third block number in the address converter is simply changed from its current value of 1 to a value of 100. This is clearly an improvement over storing the block numbers in the inverted lists, a method used by some inverted file model DBMS's. Storing the block numbers in the inverted lists would require each inverted list connected to that data record to change if the physical location of the data record changed.

STORAGE AND COMPRESSION OF FIELDS

Each ADABAS record may contain a maximum of five hundred fields. ADABAS allows a field to be stored in a data record as an elementary field or as a multiple-value field. An **elementary field** has one value per record. A **multiple-value field** is permitted to have multiple values per record up to a maximum of 191 values. In other words, a multiple-value field is a repeating data item, which means that ADABAS records are allowed to be **unnormalized** if desired. Consecutive fields, both elementary and multiple-value, can be combined into a **group**. Groups can also repeat within a record; in this case they are called **periodic groups**.

ADABAS compresses fields and records in data storage automatically. ADABAS's **compression** algorithm removes from fields trailing spaces on alphanumerics and leading zeros on numerics, automatically packs numeric data, and replaces null-value fields with a single byte. Software AG claims a minimum 30 percent savings in data storage using this compression algorithm. Even with the extra space required for storage of the associator, the overall amount of space required for an ADABAS database is typically less than that required for a flat file approach. This is unusual for a DBMS.

FILE COUPLING

ADABAS forms a relationship between two files through a process called **coupling**. The only constraint is that each of the two files must have a descriptor field in common.

In the Premiere Products database, both the ORDER file and the CUSTOMER file have the CUSTOMER_NUMBER field in common. If CUSTOMER_NUMBER is declared to be a descriptor in both the ORDER file and the CUSTOMER file, then these two files may be coupled on the common descriptor of CUSTOMER_NUMBER. Data storage records for the ORDER file and the first two fields in the CUSTOMER file are shown at the top of Figure 11.6 on the following page; block numbers have been omitted for the sake of simplicity.

The inverted lists pertaining to CUSTOMER_NUMBER are shown in the associator at the bottom of Figure 11.6; both the address converters and other inverted

ADABAS Data Storage

ORDER File

ISN	ORDER_ NUMBER	DATE	CUSTOMER_ NUMBER
3	12489	90287	124
1	12491	90287	311
7	12494	90487	315
5	12495	90487	256
6	12498	90587	522
8	12500	90587	124
2	12504	90587	522

CUSTOMER File

ISN	CUSTOMER_ NUMBER	NAME
30	256	ANN SAMUELS
35	124	SALLY ADAMS
50	522	MARY NELSON
40	311	DON CHARLES
66	315	TOM DANIELS

ADABAS Associator

ORDER File Inverted List on the
CUSTOMER_NUMBER Descriptor

CUSTOMER_ NUMBER	NUMBER_OF_ RECORDS	ISN
124	2	3 8
256	1	5
311	1	1
315	1	7
522	2	2 6

CUSTOMER File Inverted List on the
CUSTOMER_NUMBER Descriptor

CUSTOMER_ NUMBER	NUMBER_OF_ RECORDS	ISN
124	1	35
256	1	30
311	1	40
315	1	66
522	1	50

CUSTOMER File Inverted List Coupled
with the ORDER File

ISN (CUSTOMER File)	NUMBER_OF_ RECORDS	ISN (ORDER File)
30	1	5
35	2	3 8
40	1	1
50	2	2 6
66	1	7

ORDER File Inverted List Coupled
with the CUSTOMER File

ISN (ORDER File)	NUMBER_OF_ RECORDS	ISN (CUSTOMER File)
1	1	40
2	1	50
3	1	35
5	1	30
6	1	50
7	1	66
8	1	35

lists for these two files have also been omitted. The top two inverted lists are for the CUSTOMER_NUMBER descriptor for the ORDER file and the CUSTOMER file. These are similar to the ADABAS inverted lists already discussed. The bottommost two inverted lists are created and maintained by ADABAS when we define the ORDER file and CUSTOMER file as being coupled on the common descriptor of CUSTOMER_NUMBER. Given a particular ORDER file ISN, ADABAS finds this

FIGURE 11.6
ADABAS file coupling between the ORDER file and the CUSTOMER file on the CUSTOMER_NUMBER descriptor

ISN entry in the coupled ORDER file inverted list and uses the CUSTOMER file ISN in this entry to access the related CUSTOMER record. In a similar fashion, given a particular CUSTOMER file ISN, ADABAS finds this ISN entry in the coupled CUSTOMER file inverted list and uses the ORDER file ISNs in this entry to access the related ORDER record(s).

Thus, coupling establishes a **bidirectional relationship** between two files. One file may be coupled with up to eighty other files. ADABAS utilities are available to couple and uncouple files at any time.

Software AG claims that users can select either a relational, CODASYL, or hierarchical structure for their ADABAS databases. It is through the coupling feature that these models can be partially simulated. However, the data definition and data manipulation languages of ADABAS do not fully support any of these three models.

ADABAS DATA DEFINITION

ADABAS has a simple data definition language. This language defines each file separately by describing the fields within the file and the characteristics of each field. Relationships between files may also be established.

The ORDER file for Premiere Products could be defined as follows:

```
FILE 1
     01, ON, 5, A, DE
     01, OD, 6, P, DE
     01, CN, 3, P, DE
```

The first line supplies a unique number to the ORDER file. This number is used in ADABAS's data manipulation language and utilities.

Each of the next three lines defines the ORDER_NUMBER, ORDER_DATE, and CUSTOMER_NUMBER, respectively. The "01" is a **field level number** similar to the COBOL language's level number. If we wanted to define ORDER_DATE as a group with components of month, day, and year, we could substitute the following for the "01, OD, 6, P, DE" ORDER_DATE definition:

```
     01, OD, DE
          02, MO, 2, P
          02, DA, 2, P
          02, YR, 2, P
```

The next parameter in each field definition is a two-character user-supplied **field name** with "ON" representing ORDER_NUMBER, "OD" representing ORDER_DATE, and "CN" representing CUSTOMER_NUMBER. When using ADABAS's data manipulation language, these two-character field names are used. More descriptive aliases may be employed when using ADABAS's query languages and other user-oriented processors.

The third parameter in this example is the field's **standard length** prior to any automatic field compression.

The fourth parameter defines the field's **format**: "A" for alphanumeric, "P" for packed decimal. Other formats available are "U" for unpacked decimal, "B" for binary, "F" for fixed point, and "G" for floating point.

The final parameter, "DE", defines the field as a descriptor. If the field is not to be a descriptor, the "DE" parameter is simply not entered.

Other features of ADABAS's data definition language allow one to declare the field to be a multiple-value field and to override the automatic field compression feature. ADABAS's cryptic data definition language takes some getting used to, but it certainly is not overly complicated, in contrast to the data definition languages of some other DBMS's.

Once a file and its fields have been defined and records have been loaded into this database file, fields can be added or removed, and characteristics of a given field can be modified using ADABAS utilities without having to reload the database or the individual file. Thus, as user requirements or system performance changes, the database may be modified and tuned with minimal disruption to programs and users.

ADABAS DATA MANIPULATION

Standard subroutine calls are used to communicate with ADABAS files at a program level. Programming languages that can be used are COBOL, FORTRAN, PL/1, and Assembler. Figure 11.7 shows a summary of the ADABAS data manipulation commands that can be issued. These are further explained in the following paragraphs.

Command	Description
FIND	Search associator retrieving ISNs of records satisfying search criteria.
– normal	Return ISN list in no particular order.
– sorted	Return ISN list in sorted order.
– coupled	Return ISN list from coupled files.
READ	Retrieve data storage records.
– random	Retrieve a single record.
– physical sequential	Retrieve file records in physical storage sequence.
– logical sequential	Retrieve file records in sequence by descriptor value.
– descriptor value	Retrieve all values of a descriptor value & number of their occurrences.
UPDATE	Modify values of existing fields within a record.
ADD	Insert a new record into an existing file.
DELETE	Delete a record from a file.

FIGURE 11.7
ADABAS command summary

FIND COMMAND

The **FIND command** does not retrieve data storage records. Rather, it retrieves a list of ISNs satisfying the search criteria specified as part of the command. The search criteria consist of descriptor values, so only the associator's inverted lists are used. A count of the number of ISNs and the ISNs themselves are placed in a program communication buffer by ADABAS. If the record count is the only purpose for issuing the FIND command, then no further database accesses are needed. This would be the case, for example, if we wished to know how many ORDER records existed for CUSTOMER_NUMBER 522. However, if we wished to retrieve all the ORDER records for this customer, then we would have to issue successive ADABAS READ commands to obtain them.

Different forms of the FIND command allow the program to retrieve the ISNs in no special order or in sorted order by descriptor value. The sort can be performed on one, two, or three different descriptors. The descriptors used as sort criteria can be different from those used as selection criteria.

The FIND command can be used with coupled files, wherein the search criteria are based on descriptors from both of the files. The ISNs retrieved are those from the one file defined as the primary file for purposes of the given FIND command. Either of the two files may be the primary file for different commands.

READ COMMAND

The **READ command** retrieves from the specified file either an entire data storage record or selected fields within the record. The retrieved fields can then be processed in a normal fashion. Though the program receives one record, entire blocks are actually read. And since fields and records are as compressed as possible, the actual number of physical file accesses are kept to a minimum when successive READ commands are processed.

For a random READ command, the ISN of the desired record must be supplied. Normally, therefore, this command follows a FIND command that returns a list of one or more ISNs. The result of the READ command is the reading of the single record having that ISN.

If an entire file must be read and the order of the records is not important, then the physical sequential READ is the fastest possible method of reading the records. This is because the associator is not used at all; data storage records are retrieved in the exact order in which they are physically located. Successive READs obtain the next records in physical order.

If the order of reading records is important, then the logical sequential READ is used. This command reads records in the order of the values of one of the descriptors. Since the associator is used and the inverted lists are in order by descriptor value, no actual sorting takes place.

The last form of the READ command, the descriptor value READ, retrieves all unique values of any descriptor and the number of occurrences of each of the values in data storage. Both the descriptor values and their number of occurrences, as you recall, are stored in the associator, so data storage is not accessed for this READ command.

UPDATE COMMAND

The **UPDATE command** is used to modify fields in existing records. The ISN of the record to be updated must be specified. Only those fields specified are updated with the values supplied. The new values can be different in length than they presently are; and their lengths can be different, either shorter or longer, than the standard length given at data definition time. ADABAS automatically updates any required inverted lists.

ADD COMMAND

The **ADD command** adds a new record to a file. Only those fields with known values need to be supplied. All inverted lists are automatically updated by ADABAS through this command.

DELETE COMMAND

The **DELETE command** eliminates the record with a given ISN from the specified file. The inverted lists and address converter are appropriately updated at this time. The space formerly occupied by the deleted record in both data storage and the associator is made available for immediate reuse.

MISCELLANEOUS DATA MANIPULATION

An ADABAS database may be manipulated through means other than program interaction. ADABAS offers a large number of utilities and languages for alternative means of interaction.

Some of the utilities allow for initial loading of a file and for bulk additions to a file once it has been created. Among the languages are ADAMINT, ADASCRIPT +, and NATURAL.

ADAMINT is a high-level data manipulation language interface to ADABAS that allows programmers to productively accomplish the same types of data manipulation we have just covered. **ADASCRIPT +** is an end-user query language. **NATURAL** is a fourth-generation language.

1.4 FUNCTIONS OF A DBMS: ADABAS AND DL/I

In chapter 2 we discussed ten different functions of a DBMS. In this section we discuss how well ADABAS, as a representative inverted file model DBMS, and DL/I, as a representative hierarchical DBMS, support each of these ten functions.

Both ADABAS and DL/I adequately support the following functions: a user-accessible catalog for data description; logical transactions; record-locking features to allow a shared update environment; full recovery services in the event of failure; and full utility services. These functions essentially operate as described in chapter 2, so they will not be discussed any further here.

In the remainder of this section, we will briefly describe how well ADABAS and DL/I support the following functions: storage and retrieval, security, data communications, integrity, and data independence.

STORAGE AND RETRIEVAL

Both ADABAS and DL/I allow users to store, update, and retrieve data in a database. With both systems, although users do not need to know the exact internal structure of the database, some knowledge of the current structuring of the database is required by programmers and nontechnical end users for efficient processing.

In the case of ADABAS, it is important for users to know which fields are descriptors and which files are coupled and on what descriptors. Most commands and queries will work only through the use of descriptors, so if retrieval is required against a nondescriptor field, it may not be achievable except by physically reading all data storage records in the appropriate file(s). Fortunately, current descriptor and coupling information is obtained from ADABAS's data dictionary system, and fields easily may be made descriptors by the database administrator through the use of an ADABAS utility.

In the case of DL/I, users must be able to navigate the database through knowledge of the segments' hierarchical relationships and of key field and secondary indexing declarations. Structure changes are accomplished easily in ADABAS but not in DL/I. Normally a reorganization of a DL/I database is required.

SECURITY

ADABAS has several **security** facilities. First, it provides an encryption technique called **ciphering**. The user supplies a cipher key when records are stored and the same cipher key when retrieving the records in unencrypted form. Without the cipher key, retrieved records remain in encrypted form.

Although ADABAS has what it calls a **userview** feature, this is not the true subschema capability described in chapter 2, since only a single file is involved in a given userview. An ADABAS userview is defined in the data dictionary system as an arrangement of selected fields from a single file. There may be multiple userviews per file.

True security is provided by ADABAS through the userview feature and a password protection system. Passwords may exist at both the file and field levels. Authorizations for both files and fields may be limited to access only or may be for full update privilege. Field value passwords are also available. These restrict users to selection of records from a file based on individual field values.

DL/I provides subschema and view capability through the program communication block (**PCB**). Access and update are limited to those segments and fields specified in the PCB.

DL/I also provides a full authorization system that restricts access to the system to authorized users. It also checks to make certain that a particular user can use a given transaction, and it can restrict transactions to specified terminals.

DATA COMMUNICATIONS

ADABAS can operate either in a batch or on-line mode. In the on-line mode, ADABAS interfaces with Software AG's COM-PLETE **teleprocessing monitor** or with any of the following teleprocessing monitors from other companies: CICS, IMS/DC, INTERCOMM, TASK/MASTER, TSO, WESTI, and SHADOW II.

DL/I can also operate either in a batch or on-line mode. In the on-line mode, IMS/DC and CICS are the two teleprocessing monitors almost exclusively used.

INTEGRITY

ADABAS handles data-type checking and uniqueness of primary keys (if defined as unique descriptors), but it lacks the more sophisticated **integrity** services as automated functions. For example, users must create their own procedures to handle data verification and **referential integrity**.

DL/I also handles data-type checking and uniqueness of primary keys (if defined as unique sequence fields). Also, because of its hierarchical structure, DL/I ensures that a child segment does not exist without its parent segment. However, if a parent segment is deleted, then all descendant segments are also deleted, so users must handle this situation themselves if this is not a proper action to be taken. Finally, users must create their own procedures to handle data verification.

DATA INDEPENDENCE

ADABAS has a fair degree of **data independence**. Files and fields may be added, changed, or deleted, and the users are not affected unless they need access to the changed files and fields. The same is true for changes to the physical database structure.

To a lesser degree, DL/I has logical and physical data independence. Since the hierarchical structure of DL/I forces the user to navigate the database, changes within the hierarchical path used often necessitate procedural change by the user. For example, the addition of a new segment within the hierarchical path would require user procedural change. The addition of a new field to an existing segment within the hierarchical path would not require user procedural change unless the user needed access to the field. Logical and physical database changes outside the hierarchical path of the user obviously do not require user procedural change.

1.5 SUMMARY

In this chapter, we examined the inverted file model, often considered to be the fourth DBMS data model. The inverted data model is based on the inverted file structure, in which a field in a primary file becomes the key to an inverted file that relates back to the primary file. We call such a key a secondary key. Primary files are similar in concept to non-DBMS flat files and to relations in the relational data model.

If only some of the fields in the primary file are secondary keys, we have a partially inverted file. If all fields in the primary file are secondary keys, we have a fully inverted file.

Inverted files allow rapid access to records based on secondary keys, at the expense of additional storage space requirements and additional update time.

We described ADABAS, an inverted file model DBMS, in some detail. ADABAS stores separate files in an area called data storage. Each file consists of one or more records consisting of one or more fields. Each record in a file also contains an internal sequence number (ISN), which is a unique sequence number for that record within the given file.

The inverted files, called inverted lists within ADABAS, are stored in an area called the associator, which is separate from data storage. The secondary keys within ADABAS are known as descriptors. In addition to the descriptor values, the inverted lists contain a count of the number of records and a list of the ISNs having that descriptor value. The actual physical block location of a data storage record is not stored in the inverted lists. These addresses are stored in a portion of the associator called the address converter, which relates each ISN to the address of the data storage block that contains the record having that ISN value. Thus, only the address converter needs to change if the physical location of the data storage record changes.

ADABAS allows for elementary fields that have a single value and multiple-value fields that have from 1 to 191 values. Consecutive fields can be combined into a group; if the group can be repeated within the record, it is called a periodic group. ADABAS automatically compresses fields, so total disk space requirements overall are often less than those for comparable flat files.

ADABAS allows two files to be coupled, or related, on a common descriptor. Coupling is bidirectional between the files. Files may be coupled and uncoupled at any time after the files are created.

We looked at the simple data definition language used by ADABAS to define files, fields, and relationships. File, field, and relationship structures may be changed easily in response to user requirements or performance analysis.

We saw that ADABAS has a full complement of data manipulation commands to add, update, and delete records and to retrieve stored records. The database may be accessed through several high-level languages and through query and other supported languages.

Finally, we reviewed the ability of both ADABAS and DL/I to support the functions of a DBMS. We saw that both of these systems are, by and large, competitive with other current products on the market today.

REVIEW QUESTIONS

1. How does the inverted file model relate to the relational, CODASYL, and hierarchical data models?
2. Give three reasons for studying the inverted file model.

3. Define the following terms: inverted file, secondary key, partially inverted file, and fully inverted file.

4. What are the advantages and disadvantages of a fully inverted file?

5. What does ADABAS store in data storage, and what does it store in the associator?

6. What is an ISN? Name and describe the three places in data storage and the associator where the ISN plays a role.

7. What is a descriptor? How is a descriptor value related to the address converter?

8. Explain what changes when a record in data storage is physically moved to a different block.

9. Define the following field-related ADABAS terms: elementary field, multiple-value field, group, and periodic group.

10. What is coupling, and what constraints exist for this feature?

11. How do the ADABAS F I ND and READ commands differ?

12. Describe ADABAS's security features. Describe DL/I's security features.

13. What are some integrity shortcomings of ADABAS? What are some integrity shortcomings of DL/I?

EXERCISES

1. Let's assume that Figure 11.5 represents the current status of data storage and the associator for the ORDER file. Show what changes would take place in the associator if a new ORDER record were added to block 2. Assume that this new record would have the following values: ISN of 4, ORDER_NUMBER of 12345, DATE of 91087, and CUSTOMER_NUMBER of 311.

2. Let's assume that Figure 11.6 represents the current status of data storage and the associator for the ORDER file and the CUSTOMER file.

   a. Show what changes would take place in the associator if a new ORDER record having the following values were added: ISN of 4, ORDER_NUMBER of 12200, DATE of 91087, and CUSTOMER_NUMBER of 311.

   b. Show what changes would take place in the associator if the DATE field were to become a descriptor.

REFERENCES

1] Atre, S. *Data Base: Structured Techniques for Design, Performance, and Management.* John Wiley & Sons, Inc., 1980.

2] Date, C. J. *An Introduction to Database Systems, Volume II.* Addison-Wesley, 1983.

3] Kroenke, David. *Database Processing,* 2d ed. SRA, 1983.

4] Software AG of North America, Inc. *ADABAS Introduction.*

5] Teorey, Toby J. and Fry, James P. *Design of Database Structures.* Prentice-Hall, 1982.

DATABASE DESIGN III PHYSICAL DATABASE DESIGN

.1 INTRODUCTION

Database design takes place in two phases, **information-level design** and **physical-level design**. The goal of the information level is to produce a DBMS-independent design for a given set of user requirements. The design must be complete; i.e., all user views must be included and all user requirements must be able to be satisfied. The design must also be correct. User views must be modeled correctly. All user restrictions must be present in the design and must be stated accurately. Some user restrictions, for example, "sales rep numbers are unique," will be implemented through primary keys. Others, such as "each customer in the database *must* have a sales rep," will be implemented through foreign keys. Still others, such as "credit limits are either 300, 500, 800, or 1000," may be implemented through domain definitions or through stating them in the category "other restrictions." The crucial point is that they must all be there and must accurately reflect the actual restrictions of the organization. Finally, the information-level design must be clean. It must not contain any of the kinds of problems associated with non-3NF relations.

When the information-level design is complete, the physical-level design process, which is the subject of this chapter, can begin. The final information-level design is the input to the physical design process together with volume and usage figures, security requirements, recovery requirements, and characteristics of the DBMS that will be used to implement the system. Additionally, restrictions on data in the database form an important type of input to the physical process. If an information-level design does not include such restrictions, they must be listed separately as input to the physical design process. Since these restrictions are included in our information-level design, we do not need such a separate list.

The output of the process contains, at a minimum, a DBMS-processable schema; i.e., a schema that can be implemented on the DBMS that will be used for the application. In addition, the output of this step may contain subschemas, program design information, and information for the database administration and database operation functions. The subschemas produced will be subschemas necessary to support the individual user views. Program design information may contain tips for processing the database in the most efficient way to satisfy the requirements. It also *must* contain information concerning any restrictions that programs must enforce. (You will recall that any restriction that is not enforceable by the DBMS must be enforced by the individual programs. Programmers must be aware of these restrictions.) Description of records, fields, relationships, domains, restrictions, program requirements, and so on, will be furnished to the database administration group for inclusion in the central data dictionary. Processing requirements and constraints will be furnished to operations.

One of the most important criteria for a physical-level design is adequate performance. We are concerned with such things as response time, system throughput, and utilization of disk space. It may very well be the case that some of the cleanness of the final information-level design is compromised in order to achieve adequate performance. Any such compromise must, of course, be thoroughly documented, and the data in the database must be closely monitored to ensure that it does not become inconsistent as a result of the compromise. (If the data is no longer in 3NF, inconsistencies are possible. Since programs must now enforce consistency, the possibility of a program error allowing inconsistent data in the database is very real.)

While some may treat the physical level of design as a single step, it usually works better to make it a two-step process. With this approach, the first step is to create a clean design for the particular type of DBMS that will be used. The result of the first step will be a legitimate implementation of the information-level design. No compromises will have been made, other than those forced upon us by the DBMS we are using. (If a portion of the information-level design contains foreign keys and our relational DBMS does not support foreign keys, for example, a compromise must be made. Likewise, if a portion of the information-level design could best be implemented using a recursive set and our CODASYL system does not support recursive sets, a compromise must be made.) However, we do not make any compromises that force our design to be in anything less than 3NF.

At this point, we have a legitimate design that can be implemented using our DBMS. The only remaining concern is adequate performance. If performance is not a major issue, we may not have to make any changes. If the database is relatively small, the demands may be light enough that spending more time in this portion of the design process to improve the expected performance of the system would not be worthwhile. Often, however, this is not the case and a second step is necessary. In this step, we make changes to the design created in the first step to improve the performance of the overall application system that is being developed. This process is called **tuning**. Ideally, we want to *tune* the design so that performance is optimal, i.e., so that no other version of the design will produce better performance. In practice, this is almost an impossible task and we settle for tuning the design in such a way that the system will perform in an acceptable manner.

Finally, subschemas are created, program design information is created, and documentation is prepared for the various groups mentioned earlier. Once the system is in production, its performance will be periodically reviewed and some retuning may be necessary. The ideas and techniques used in the retuning are the same as those we will discuss in this chapter. In a way, retuning is easier than the initial tuning, in that statistics on actual usage of the system can be gathered and used. In the original design process, we have no such statistics; rather, we have to deal with *predicted* usage patterns, and these are often very imprecise.

We begin this chapter by discussing the process of creating an initial design for the type of DBMS we are interested in. The process of creating such a design from our final information-level design is called **mapping**. In section 12.2, we focus on mapping to a relational model system and in section 12.3 on mapping to a CODASYL system. (These are the two types of systems most likely to be encountered in practice in the years to come). In section 12.4, we *briefly* discuss mapping to a hierarchical system and to an inverted file model system. We then discuss, in section 12.5, the tuning step, the process of changing the design to improve performance. In section 12.6, we discuss the problem of evaluating various alternative designs to determine the one whose performance is "best." (As mentioned earlier, it is extremely difficult to pick *the* best design. We are willing to settle for the one that we feel is closest.) Finally, in section 12.7, we discuss the process of creating subschemas (or views), and providing guidance for programmers.

Appendix B contains two detailed design examples. These illustrate both the information level and the physical level of design. Design exercises are also included.

.2   MAPPING TO THE RELATIONAL MODEL

An ideal **relational model** DBMS would include support for **primary keys** and **foreign keys**. **Nulls** would also be supported. In addition, there would be facilities to enforce restrictions on data in the database that were not merely consequences of primary and foreign key restrictions.

If we possess an ideal relational model DBMS, the mapping will be easy. Our final information-level design will effectively also be our physical-level design. The only potential difference between the two will be syntactical. Thus, the problem is merely to convert from the syntax of our information-level design to the syntax required for the DBMS.

Unfortunately, there is no ideal DBMS at this point in time. Much developmental activity is being devoted to moving systems in this direction, but it will undoubtedly be some time before the advent of a truly ideal relational DBMS. Thus, the methodology must address deficiencies in the DBMS.

METHODOLOGY

The general methodology for mapping to a relational model DBMS is as follows:

1. Create the relations.
2. Implement the keys.
3. Implement nulls.
4. Implement other restrictions.

Each of these steps will now be addressed.

CREATE THE RELATIONS

The relations in the physical design will be precisely those relations in the final information-level design. If the system supports domains, they should be used. If not, they should still be represented in the form of commentary for purposes of documentation in the physical design.

IMPLEMENT THE KEYS

Whatever facilities are present in the DBMS should be used. If the DBMS provides support for primary keys, primary keys should be implemented by the DBMS; if the DBMS provides support for foreign keys, foreign keys should be implemented by the DBMS; and so on. We need a way to implement these keys, however, in the event that they are *not* supported by the DBMS. If the DBMS does not provide the necessary support, that support must come from the programs that will access the database. This fact must be documented at this point, and this documentation must be furnished to any programmer who writes any program to access this database. It must indicate the restrictions that are to be enforced by the program as well as tips on how most efficiently to implement them. With this in mind, we will discuss how each of the different types of keys should be treated in the event that support from the DBMS is lacking.

PRIMARY KEYS

Programs must enforce the uniqueness of the **primary key**. They should also support efficient direct access, given a value for the primary key. The best way to accomplish both of these is to have the system create and maintain an index on the field or fields that constitute the primary key.

If the system allows indexes to be specified as "unique," this should be done. The system will then at least enforce the uniqueness. If the system does not, then even this responsibility will fall on the shoulders of programmers. To enforce uniqueness, programmers must attempt to find an existing record with a given key value before storing a new one, (e.g., before storing sales rep 4, the program should try to find sales rep 4 to determine if one already exists). Most mainframe systems do provide the option of specifying an index as unique, but many micro-computer systems do not.

CANDIDATE KEYS

Since **candidate keys** by definition, are also unique, programs must enforce this uniqueness. The process described for the primary key also applies here.

SECONDARY KEYS

Since **secondary keys** are fields or combination of fields that are of interest for retrieval purposes, the prime concern is supporting efficient retrieval given a value of the secondary key. The best way to do this is to create an index (not unique) on the fields that make up the secondary key.

FOREIGN KEYS

The process of supporting **foreign keys** in programs is much more involved than the processes required to support the other types of keys. To understand this process, consider the foreign key of SLSREP_NUMBER within the CUSTOMER relation that must match the number of an actual sales rep in the SLSREP relation. Since SLSREP_NUMBER is the primary key of the SLSREP relation, this primary key will be supported either through features of the DBMS or by programs, as described earlier. In addition, an index (not unique) will be built on the SLSREP_NUMBER within the CUSTOMER relation.

When customer information is entered or modified, the program must check the SLSREP relation, using the primary key, SLSREP_NUMBER, to ensure that the sales rep number entered for the customer is the number of a sales rep who actually exists in the database (unless it is null and nulls are allowed, of course).

When an attempt is made to change the number of a sales rep in the SLSREP relation, the index on SLSREP_NUMBER in the CUSTOMER relation will be used to determine whether there are any customers represented by this sales rep. If there are no such customers, the change is allowed. If there are customers represented by this sales rep, the action to be taken depends on the update restrictions for this foreign key. If update is restricted, the change is not allowed. If update cascades, the change is allowed, but then we must make a corresponding change for each customer represented by this sales rep. If update nullifies, the change is allowed, and then the sales rep number for each customer currently represented by this sales rep is set to null.

When an attempt is made to delete a sales rep in the SLSREP relation, the index on SLSREP_NUMBER in the CUSTOMER relation will again be used to determine whether there are any customers represented by this sales rep. If there are no such customers, the deletion is allowed. If there are customers represented by this sales rep, the action to be taken depends on the delete restrictions for this foreign key. If delete is restricted, the deletion is not allowed. If delete cascades, the deletion is allowed, but then each customer of this sales rep must also be deleted. If delete nullifies, the deletion is allowed, but then the sales rep number for all customers currently represented by this sales rep is set to null.

It should be pointed out that the above processing may not be particularly complicated from a programming standpoint, particularly if a language like SQL is used. When it is time to change all of the sales rep numbers of all customers currently represented by a given sales rep to the sales rep's new number, for example, all that is required is a single SQL command like:

```
UPDATE CUSTOMER
     SET SLSREP_NUMBER = NEW_SLSREP_NUMBER
     WHERE SLSREP_NUMBER = OLD_SLSREP_NUMBER
```

It is important that an index exists to make this process efficient, particularly if this operation is done with any frequency and if the number of customers is large.

Given a language like SQL, in which the processing just specified need not be overly cumbersome, and given the ability to create appropriate indexes to make the process reasonably efficient, it may seem as though the lack of support for foreign keys is not all that bad. The prime concern, however, is not the additional complexity in programs but rather the fact that all programs must enforce these restrictions. If a single program does not, then the possibility of having data that violates our integrity constraints is very real. Further, we must disable the features of the system that allow users to enter data directly into the various tables, since this bypasses all of the foreign key restrictions built into programs. (Incidentally, it is often desirable to disable these features anyway, since they allow the updating of data in the database without appropriate audit trails that the programs should be producing.)

IMPLEMENT NULLS

No problem exists in this area if any fields that allow nulls were removed during the information-level design process to create entity subtypes. If, however, the final information-level design contains fields that are allowed to be null and if the DBMS does not support nulls, then we must take special action. This action consists basically of two types. One type is to put the fields that are allowed to be null in separate tables, together with the key of the original relation (such as a table with student number and dormitory number as its only fields, student number being the key). This is really just the process of creating entity subtypes. In the preceding instance, we have created an entity subtype, namely, students who reside in dorms, which is a subentity of students. In many situations, this is exactly the action that is appropriate. Often, this very process will lead us to the realization that we do, in fact, have true entity subtypes. (You will note that this is an action that is usually taken during the information-level design. Sometimes, however, it can occur here.)

The other type of action is to support null fields by setting aside a certain value that will be treated as null by the programs accessing the database. An obvious choice would be space for character fields and zero for numeric fields. Sometimes these choices are, indeed, appropriate. Often, however, they are not. The value null is not really a space or a zero. It really means *unknown*. No real value can totally represent it. Further, in certain situations, zero might be a legitimate value for a given field. A customer might have a zero balance, whereas a null balance would mean that, for some reason, the customer's balance was not known, certainly a very different situation. The best we can do is to determine a value that the field can never legitimately assume. In one situation, zero might be appropriate; in another, -1 might be a better choice; in still another, we might choose -999999. The main concerns are, first, the ability to find such a "null" value and, second, the certainty that all programs accessing the database are aware of the meaning of this value and act upon it appropriately.

IMPLEMENT OTHER RESTRICTIONS

Any restrictions not already handled in other ways must be documented for programmers. The choice of style of documentation is not as important as the fact that these restrictions are all clearly documented in a fashion that will be useful to the programmers who must enforce them. They should be so organized that programmers can rapidly determine *all* the restrictions they must enforce.

EXAMPLE

Suppose we were given the **DBDL** design shown in Figure 12.1. For the sake of simplicity, we have omitted format details for the various attributes. Neither are domains represented in this design. If they were, they would be used directly in a system that supports domains. Otherwise, they would appear only for documentation purposes. If a domain definition held any restrictions (e.g., credit limit must be 300, 500, 800, or 1000), these would become other restrictions. In fact, this same restriction is represented as another restriction in Figure 12.1. In addition, there is a second restriction which states that customers with nonzero balances may not be deleted.

```
SLSREP (SLSREP_NUMBER, SLSREP_NAME, SLSREP_ADDRESS,
        TOTAL_COMMISSION, COMMISSION_RATE)

CUSTOMER (CUSTOMER_NUMBER, NAME, ADDRESS, CURRENT_BALANCE,
        CREDIT_LIMIT, SLSREP_NUMBER)
    FK   SLSREP_NUMBER → SLSREP  UPD RSTR

PART (PART_NUMBER, PART_DESCRIPTION, UNITS_ON_HAND, ITEM_CLASS,
        WAREHOUSE_NUMBER, PRICE)

ORDER (ORDER_NUMBER, DATE, CUSTOMER_NUMBER)
    FK   CUSTOMER_NUMBER → CUSTOMER

ORDER_LINE (ORDER_NUMBER, PART_NUMBER, NUMBER_ORDERED,
        QUOTED_PRICE)
    FK   ORDER_NUMBER → ORDER   DLT CSCD
    FK   PART_NUMBER → PART

RESTRICTIONS:
        ASSERT RETRICTION1 ON CUSTOMER;
            CREDIT_LIMIT IN (300, 500, 800, 1000)
        ASSERT RESTRICTION2 ON DELETION OF CUSTOMER;
            CURRENT_BALANCE = 0
```

FIGURE 12.1
Sample DBDL

Let us now create an appropriate physical design for a relational DBMS that corresponds to this information-level design. Let's assume that we have a relational DBMS that does not support either primary or foreign keys but that does allow indexes to be specified as "unique", i.e., the system will prevent two rows in the table from having the same values in the columns on which the index is built.

1. *Create the relations*. Each relation in the DBDL representation becomes a relation in the design. These relations will be communicated to the DBMS, using whatever facilities are provided for this purpose.
2. *Implement the primary keys*. An index (unique) will be created for each primary key. In addition, enforcement of the primary keys will be listed in the set of restrictions that must be enforced by programmers.
3. *Implement the candidate keys*. In this example, there are none. If there were any, we would create an index (unique) on the candidate key and list the candidate key in the set of restrictions that must be enforced by programmers.
4. *Implement the secondary keys*. In this example, there are no secondary keys. If there were some, we would create an index (nonunique) on the secondary key. We would also document the existence of such an index for use in retrieval based on this secondary key.
5. *Implement the foreign keys*. For each foreign key, an index will be created. The foreign key will be listed in the set of restrictions that must be enforced by programmers.
6. *Implement nulls*. There are no fields within this design for which nulls are allowed; thus, the issue does not occur in this design. If it did, we would follow the steps given earlier.
7. *Implement other restrictions*. None of the other restrictions listed in the DBDL design can be supported directly by the DBMS. Thus, they must be included in the list of restrictions to be enforced by programmers. They can be listed in exactly the same form in which they are listed in DBDL.

The overall design is shown in Figure 12.2 on the opposite page. Note that primary and foreign key restrictions are listed in separate categories. This is owing to the special character and importance of these restrictions. It is certainly not wrong to list them as other restrictions. In fact, we can actually represent them with the same kind of ASSERT command that we have used for other restrictions. For example, to indicate that delete is restricted for the foreign key CUSTOMER.SLSREP_NUMBER, we could use the ASSERT command

```
ASSERT ASSERTION3 ON DELETION OF SLSREP:
     NOT EXISTS
           (SELECT *
                 FROM CUSTOMER
                 WHERE CUSTOMER.SLSREP_NUMBER =
                          SLSREP.SLSREP_NUMBER)
```

While this example represents a relatively simple design problem that does not encompass all of the issues we are discussing it is representative of the process that is applied to produce the legitimate relational model design. Two examples that are considerably more complex are presented in Appendix B.

For additional information on creating physical designs for relational model systems, see [1], [2], [3], [4], [5], and [6].

FIGURE 12.2
Relational model
design (Each primary
key requires a unique
index. Each foreign
key requires a
non-unique index.)

```
_____ LIST OF RELATIONS _____

SLSREP (SLSREP_NUMBER, SLSREP_NAME, SLSREP_ADDRESS,
        TOTAL_COMMISSION, COMMISSION_RATE)

CUSTOMER (CUSTOMER_NUMBER, NAME, ADDRESS, CURRENT_BALANCE,
          CREDIT_LIMIT, SLSREP_NUMBER)

PART (PART_NUMBER, PART_DESCRIPTION, UNITS_ON_HAND, ITEM_CLASS,
      WAREHOUSE_NUMBER, PRICE)

ORDER (ORDER_NUMBER, DATE, CUSTOMER_NUMBER)

ORDER_LINE (ORDER_NUMBER, PART_NUMBER, NUMBER_ORDERED,
            QUOTED_PRICE)


      _____ LIST OF FOREIGN KEY RESTRICTIONS _____

CUSTOMER
     FK    SLSREP_NUMBER  →  SLSREP      UPD RSTR

ORDER
     FK    CUSTOMER_NUMBER  →  CUSTOMER

ORDER_LINE
     FK    ORDER_NUMBER  →  ORDER        DLT CSCD
     FK    PART_NUMBER  →  PART


          _____ OTHER RESTRICTIONS _____

ASSERT RETRICTION1 ON CUSTOMER;
     CREDIT_LIMIT IN (300, 500, 800, 1000)

ASSERT RESTRICTION2 ON DELETION OF CUSTOMER;
     CURRENT_BALANCE = 0
```

.3 MAPPING TO THE CODASYL MODEL

By a CODASYL system, we mean the general type that is commercially available. The methodology presented in this section is geared to such a system. Applying it to a specific commercial system might involve some slight adjustments.

The general methodology for mapping to a CODASYL model DBMS is as follows:

1. Create records.
2. Determine keys.
3 Determine sets.
4. Determine location modes.
5. Implement nulls.
6. Implement other restrictions.

Each of these steps will now be addressed.

CREATE RECORDS

The initial records in the physical design will be precisely the relations in the final information-level design. The fields will be the attributes. At this point, all fields will be included. In later steps some of them might be removed. The system probably does not support the concept of domains, but, if they had been used, they should still be represented as commentary for documentation purposes.

DETERMINE KEYS

At this step, only three of the types of primary, candidate, and secondary keys will be treated. Foreign keys are treated at the next step.

PRIMARY KEYS

The **primary key** becomes, at least for now, the CALC key of the record, with duplicates *not* allowed. This may be changed in later steps.

CANDIDATE KEYS

For any **candidate keys**, uniqueness must be ensured. We cannot make these CALC keys of the record in that this role has already been filled by the primary key. We must use some other features of the system. One of the two primary options would be to have the system maintain a unique index on this field (some systems designate such a field as a unique *alternate* key field). The other would be to create a system-owned set with this record as the member record type, sorted on this field. Duplicates must not be allowed within this set.

SECONDARY KEYS

By designating a field as a **secondary key** during the information-level design process, we are indicating that rapid retrieval based on a value in this field will be important. At this point, therefore, our task is to optimize retrieval on the field or fields that constitute this secondary key. The possibilities here are the same as those for candidate keys. The only difference is that we will not be ensuring uniqueness. The two main possibilities would thus be to have the system maintain an index (not unique) on this field. The second would again be to create a system-owned set with this record as the member record type, sorted on this field. In this case, duplicates must be allowed.

DETERMINE SETS

Sets within the CODASYL design are determined by the **foreign keys**. Let's assume that record A and record B in a CODASYL design correspond to relation A and relation B, respectively, in the final information-level design. Let's assume further that relation B contains a foreign key identifying relation A. Then we remove the field corresponding to the foreign key in record B and create a set from

A to B. If a CUSTOMER relation contains a field SLSREP_NUMBER that is a foreign key identifying SLSREP, the SLSREP_NUMBER will be removed from the CUSTOMER record and, instead, a set will be created in which the owner is SLSREP and the member is CUSTOMER. The process thus consists of removing foreign keys and replacing them with sets from the record that is being identified to the record that contained the foreign key.

There is one possible exception to this. If the foreign key identifies the relation itself (such as a foreign key within an EMPLOYEE relation identifying the manager of the employee, which happens to be another employee), a set created in the manner just described would be a recursive set; i.e., the owner and member record types would be the same. Such a set is shown in Figure 12.3a. There is no problem if the chosen DBMS supports recursive sets. If not, we have to make a change to the structure.

We could use the same approach taken in the bill-of-materials structure discussed in chapter 9, as shown in Figure 12.3b. A slightly cleaner approach is demonstrated in Figure 12.3c. If we use the bill-of-materials method, we are really implementing a many-to-many relationship between employees and the managers of these employees. In the event that the relationship is really one-to-many (one manager manages many employees, and each employee is managed by exactly one manager), this structure is inappropriate.

The structure shown in part c of Figure 12.3 implements a one-to-many relationship between managers and employees. Since, the employee record is owned by the link record in the IS_MANAGED_BY set, each employee corresponds to exactly one link record. In the MANAGES set, the roles are reversed, with the EMPLOYEE record being the owner and the link record being the member. Thus each link record is owned by a single employee, the manager. (Actually, in this set each manager will own exactly one occurrence of the link record and each non-manager will own zero occurrences.) To find all of the employees managed by a given manager, we first find the single link record that this manager owns in the MANAGES set and then find all of the employees owned by this link record in the IS_MANAGED_BY set. Conversely, to find the manager for a given employee, we first find the link record that owns this employee in the IS_MANAGED_BY set and then find the employee who owns this link record in the MANAGES set. In the sample database shown in Figure 12.4 on the following page, Smith owns a single link record in the MANAGES set which, in turn, owns Brown, Jones, Adams, and Fox in the IS_MANAGED_BY set. Thus, Smith manages Brown, Jones, Adams, and Fox. Brown is owned by the link record in the IS_MANAGED_BY set that is owned by Smith in the MANAGES set, so Jones is managed by Smith. Brown owns the link record that owns Lewis and Cook, so Brown manages Lewis and Cook.

If each employee works on a single project which, in turn, is assigned to a single manager, the same structure would suffice. The only difference is that project details (such as the name of the project) would be placed in the link record.

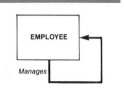

FIGURE 12.3a
(Recursive set)

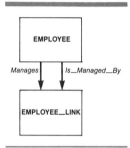

FIGURE 12.3b
(Using a link record)

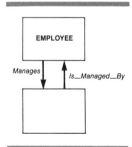

FIGURE 12.3c
(Using a link record)

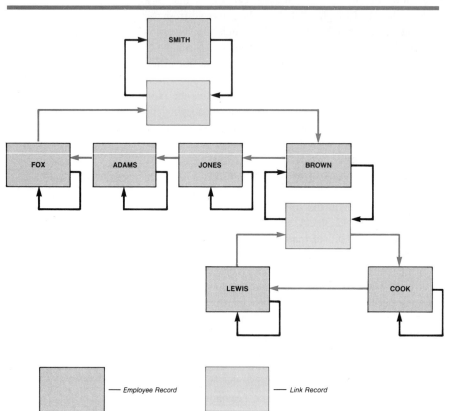

FIGURE 12.4
Sample occurrences
of MANAGES and
IS_MANAGED_BY
sets

In Figure 12.5 (opposite), Smith manages two projects, PROJ 1 and PROJ 2. Brown and Jones are assigned to PROJ 1; Adams and Fox are assigned to PROJ 2. All four employees are actually managed by Smith, but on different projects. (Actually, a structure such as this would have been created during the information-level design phase and not as a result of trying to remove a recursive set, as we are doing here. During the information design phase, we undoubtedly would have created a PROJECT relation with employees related to the projects to which they were assigned and projects related to the employees who manages the project. The set structure shown in Figure 12.5 would then have been created directly, not as a result of an attempt to remove a recursive set from the CODASYL structure.)

At this point, we have used the foreign keys to determine the sets in the CODASYL design. For each foreign key, however, there were a number of restrictions indicated during the information-level design phase: whether the foreign key could be null or not, restrictions on update, and restrictions on deletion. Thus, we need to implement these restrictions within our design.

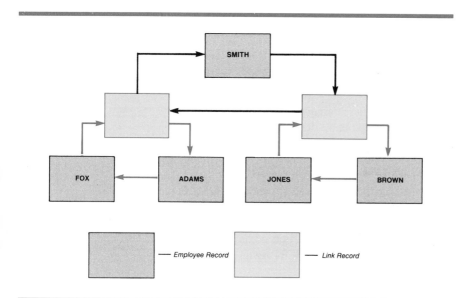

FIGURE 12.5
Sample occurrences
of MANAGES and
IS—MANAGED—BY
sets with data in the
link record

NULLS

If a foreign key can be null, then the corresponding set should be INSER-TION MANUAL and RETENTION OPTIONAL. (With these options, a customer whose SLSREP_NUMBER is null will not be connected to any occurrence of SLSREP.) Another possibility is to create a phony sales rep called "NONE", or perhaps "UNKNOWN", and tie any customer whose sales rep number is null to this phony sales rep. We will generally use the first method, the manual set, unless there is a good reason to use the second.

UPDATE

The three possibilities are nullifies, cascades, and restricted. Again we use sales reps and customers in the example. If update nullifies, it is legitimate to change the number of a sales rep, but all the customers of that sales rep must have their sales rep number set to null. We would first disconnect all the customers from that sales rep and then allow the change of the sales rep number. Since this is not something that the DBMS can enforce, this type of processing must be listed among the restrictions that the programs must enforce.

Since the number of the sales rep who represents a given customer is obtained by finding the sales rep who owns the customer in the set, S_SLSREP_CUSTOMER, changing the number of the sales rep automatically changes the sales rep number for each customer represented by that sales rep. Thus, update cascades is easy to implement. We simply allow sales rep numbers to be changed.

On the other hand, if update is restricted, we must not allow the sales rep number of any sales rep for whom there are members within S_SLSREP_ CUSTOMER to be changed. Since the system will not enforce this, we must document this fact as something programs must enforce.

DELETE

The three possibilities are again nullifies, cascades, and restricted. If delete nullifies, it is legitimate to delete a sales rep but all the customers of that sales rep have their sales rep number set to null. Thus, we must first disconnect all of the customers from that sales rep and then allow the deletion. This type of processing must be listed among the restrictions that the programs must enforce.

If delete cascades, then the presence of any customers owned by the sales rep does not prevent deletion; rather, these customers must also be deleted. This fact, too, must be documented.

If delete is restricted, we must not allow the deletion of any sales rep for whom there are members within S_SLSREP_CUSTOMER. Again, this fact must be documented.

Can we simply instruct programmers to use the ERASE command if delete is to be restricted and the ERASE ALL MEMBERS command if delete is to CASCADE? That would certainly make for a simple way of implementing these restrictions. This approach has some validity. The difficulty is that the owner record might participate as an owner in some other sets, thus rendering this approach inappropriate.

DETERMINE LOCATION MODES

If a record has the primary key intact after the removal of foreign keys, then its **location mode** will be CALC on this primary key. If all or a portion of the primary key has been removed, then the location mode will be VIA SET. If the record participates as a member in more than one set, one of these will be chosen as the "VIA" set. At this point, it doesn't really matter which one. Factors influencing the choice will be discussed in the section on tuning the design for performance.

IMPLEMENT NULLS

Primary keys, by definition, cannot be null and thus do not have to be treated as part of this step. Foreign keys can potentially be null, but the treatment of null foreign keys has already been discussed. The treatment of nulls for any other fields is identical to that described in section 12.2, "Mapping to a Relational Model."

IMPLEMENT OTHER RESTRICTIONS

Some restrictions that involve enforcing foreign key rules have already been encountered and must be documented. Any other restrictions in the information-level design must also be documented. Several means of documenting these restrictions are appropriate. In fact, using SQL is perfectly appropriate here even though we are dealing with a CODASYL system. All that matters is that agreement is reached on the style for documenting these restrictions and that all of them are, indeed, documented.

EXAMPLE

Let's suppose, again, that we have been given the DBDL design shown in Figure 12.1. Now let's create an appropriate physical design for a CODASYL DBMS that corresponds to this information-level design. We will assume that we have a general CODASYL system.

1. *Create records*. Each relation in DBDL becomes a record in the CODASYL design. The attributes of the relations become the fields in the records. The records and fields are listed in Figure 12.6.

FIGURE 12.6
Initial list of CODASYL records (primary keys underlined)

```
SLSREP (SLSREP_NUMBER, SLSREP_NAME, SLSREP_ADDRESS,
        TOTAL_COMMISSION, COMMISSION_RATE)

CUSTOMER (CUSTOMER_NUMBER, NAME, ADDRESS, CURRENT_BALANCE,
        CREDIT_LIMIT, SLSREP_NUMBER)

PART (PART_NUMBER, PART_DESCRIPTION, UNITS_ON_HAND, ITEM_CLASS,
        WAREHOUSE_NUMBER, PRICE)

ORDER (ORDER_NUMBER, DATE, CUSTOMER_NUMBER)

ORDER_LINE (ORDER_NUMBER, PART_NUMBER, NUMBER_ORDERED,
        QUOTED_PRICE)
```

2. *Determine keys*. Primary keys are taken directly from the DBDL version at this point. There are no candidate or secondary keys in this example. If there were, they would be handled as discussed above.
3. *Determine sets*. Foreign keys are removed from records and replaced by sets. The owner will be the record identified by the foreign key; the member will be the record that contained the foreign key. When the sets are documented, the foreign key restrictions should be listed as well, since these form restrictions that programmers must enforce in regard to these sets. The list of sets, together with the appropriate foreign key restrictions, is shown in Figure 12.7.

FIGURE 12.7
List of sets

_____ CODASYL SETS _____

SET	OWNER	MEMBER	COMMENT
S_SLSREP_CUSTOMER	SLSREP	CUSTOMER	
S_CUSTOMER_ORDER	CUSTOMER	ORDER	
S_ORDER_ORDER_LINE	ORDER	ORDER_LINE	
S_PART_ORDER_LINE	PART	ORDER_LINE	

4. *Determine location modes*. Any record whose primary key is intact after step three will have a location mode of CALC based on the primary key. Any record whose primary key has been either partially or completely removed will have a location mode of VIA SET. If there is more than one set to choose from, then one must be chosen. If there is not enough information to make an informed choice for the set, one may be chosen arbitrarily at this point. The result of this step is shown in Figure 12.8.

```
_____ CODASYL  RECORDS _____


SLSREP  (SLSREP_NUMBER,  SLSREP_NAME,  SLSREP_ADDRESS,
        TOTAL_COMMISSION,  COMMISSION_RATE)

CUSTOMER  (CUSTOMER_NUMBER,  NAME,  ADDRESS,  CURRENT_BALANCE,
        CREDIT_LIMIT)

PART  (PART_NUMBER,  PART_DESCRIPTION,  UNITS_ON_HAND,  ITEM_CLASS,
        WAREHOUSE_NUMBER,  PRICE)

ORDER  (ORDER_NUMBER,  DATE)

ORDER_LINE  (NUMBER_ORDERED,  QUOTED_PRICE)
        VIA S_ORDER_ORDER_LINE
```

FIGURE 12.8
Updated list of records (CALC keys underlined)

5. *Implement nulls*. Nulls are not permitted in this example. If they were, they would be treated in the manner discussed above.
6. *Implement other restrictions*. Other restrictions must be listed. Even though we are not dealing with a relational model system, they can still be listed in the same manner they were in the relational model example.

Again, this example represents a relatively simple design problem that does not encompass all of the issues previously discussed. It is, however, representative of the process that is applied to produce a design for a general CODASYL DBMS.

For additional information concerning mapping to a CODASYL model, see [1], [3], [5], [6], and [7].

12.4 MAPPING TO THE HIERARCHICAL AND INVERTED FILE MODELS

The main thrust of this chapter, as we noted, involves the process of physical design for a relational model DBMS or for a CODASYL DBMS. In this section, we will briefly touch on the process for systems following either the hierarchical or inverted file models.

HIERARCHICAL SYSTEMS

When mapping to a hierarchical model system, the same rules discussed in the network model can also be applied to yield a network structure. This network must then be converted to a hierarchy or a collection of hierarchies. In a system like IMS, for example, which supports logical child relationships between physical databases, the overall network could be replaced by physical databases together with logical child relationships between them. Record types become segment types and sets become parent-child relationships. If a record type requires direct access (a CALC record in the CODASYL version), then either the corresponding segment should be the root of a physical database (which gives direct access capabilities), or some other feature should be used to provide the access.

INVERTED FILE SYSTEMS

When mapping to an inverted file system, the same rules discussed in mapping to a relational system can be applied. Each relation becomes a separate file. At various points in the methodology, we discussed the need to create indexes on fields or combinations of fields. We would create the same indexes within the design for an inverted file system (the technical term is that we will "invert on" these fields). If the system supports some sort of coupling between files based on matching fields (as does ADABAS, for example), we would use this feature wherever the relational design contained foreign keys. We would "couple" the foreign key in one file to the primary key in the file that it matched.

In designs for both hierarchical and inverted file model systems, the same final rule applies that applied to the models covered earlier: whatever the DBMS won't support must be handled by the application programs themselves and this fact *must* be documented.

For additional information concerning mapping to the hierarchical or inverted file models, see [1], [3], [5], and [6].

2.5 TUNING FOR PERFORMANCE

By applying one of the techniques described in the previous sections, we have created a legitimate, clean design that can be implemented using the DBMS that has been chosen. At this point, we begin the process of **tuning** the design, i.e., making changes to improve the performance of the final system. To effectively accomplish this tuning, we must know the kinds of changes that we can make to a design, the advantages and disadvantages associated with each type of change, and, finally, a way to choose between alternative designs created in this process. In this section, we will discuss the types of changes that can be made, together with the associated advantages and disadvantages. In the next section, we will examine the problem of choosing from among various alternative designs that we might produce.

The changes discussed will be grouped according to whether they apply to a relational model system, a CODASYL system, or any system.

RELATIONAL MODEL

SPLITTING RELATIONS

A relation may be split into two or more relations that each have the same key as the original relation and that collectively contain all the columns of the original relation. For example, the relation

CUSTOMER(<u>CUSTOMER_NUMBER</u>, NAME, ADDRESS, BALANCE,
        CREDIT_LIMIT, SLSREP_NUMBER)

could be split into the two relations

CUST_ADDRESS(<u>CUSTOMER_NUMBER</u>, NAME, ADDRESS)

and

CUST_FINANCIAL(<u>CUSTOMER_NUMBER</u>, NAME, BALANCE,
        CREDIT_LIMIT, SLSREP_NUMBER)

Figure 12.9 below, shows a sample extension of the relation CUSTOMER with data from the Premiere Products database. Figure 12.10 on the opposite page shows sample extensions of the relations CUST_ADDRESS and CUST_FINANCIAL with the same data. The original relation could be reconstructed, when needed, by joining these two relations on the customer number.

CUSTOMER	CUSTOMER_NUMBER	NAME	ADDRESS	CURRENT_BALANCE	CREDIT_LIMIT	SLSREP_NUMBER
	124	SALLY ADAMS	481 OAK, LANSING, MI	418.75	500	3
	256	ANN SAMUELS	215 PETE, GRANT, MI	10.75	800	6
	311	DON CHARLES	48 COLLEGE, IRA, MI	200.10	300	12
	315	TOM DANIELS	914 CHERRY, KENT, MI	320.75	300	6
	405	AL WILLIAMS	519 WATSON, GRANT, MI	201.75	800	12
	412	SALLY ADAMS	16 ELM, LANSING, MI	908.75	1000	3
	522	MARY NELSON	108 PINE, ADA, MI	49.50	800	12
	567	JOE BAKER	808 RIDGE, HARPER, MI	201.20	300	6
	587	JUDY ROBERTS	512 PINE, ADA, MI	57.75	500	6
	622	DAN MARTIN	419 CHIP, GRANT, MI	575.50	500	3

Advantages: Even if a user accesses only certain columns within a relation, the remaining columns must still be transported from disk to memory. If the relation contained only the columns required by this user, his or her processing would be more efficient (less data to transport for each occurrence of the relation, more occurrences of the relation placed in a block on disk). If this user has very heavy processing requirements, the whole system may benefit through the creation of a relation tailored to his or her needs and a separate

FIGURE 12.9
CUSTOMER relation
for Premiere Products

FIGURE 12.10
Result of splitting
CUSTOMER relation

CUST_ADDRESS

CUSTOMER_ NUMBER	NAME	ADDRESS
124	SALLY ADAMS	481 OAK,LANSING,MI
256	ANN SAMUELS	215 PETE,GRANT,MI
311	DON CHARLES	48 COLLEGE,IRA,MI
315	TOM DANIELS	914 CHERRY,KENT,MI
405	AL WILLIAMS	519 WATSON,GRANT,MI
412	SALLY ADAMS	16 ELM,LANSING,MI
522	MARY NELSON	108 PINE,ADA,MI
567	JOE BAKER	808 RIDGE,HARPER,MI
587	JUDY ROBERTS	512 PINE,ADA,MI
622	DAN MARTIN	419 CHIP,GRANT,MI

CUST_FINANCIAL

CUSTOMER_ NUMBER	NAME	CURRENT_ BALANCE	CREDIT_ LIMIT	SLSREP_ NUMBER
124	SALLY ADAMS	418.75	500	3
256	ANN SAMUELS	10.75	800	6
311	DON CHARLES	200.10	300	12
315	TOM DANIELS	320.75	300	6
405	AL WILLIAMS	201.75	800	12
412	SALLY ADAMS	908.75	1000	3
522	MARY NELSON	49.50	800	12
567	JOE BAKER	201.20	300	6
587	JUDY ROBERTS	57.75	500	6
622	DAN MARTIN	575.50	500	3

relation containing all the other columns. Additionally, splitting can be used for security purposes. In the preceding example, financial details have been separated from address details. The financial relation may not even be available to users who are not authorized to access financial data, in which case an added measure of security is provided.

Disadvantages: Any user requiring data from both relations needs to do a join operation to obtain the required data. Since the relations in questions will be joined on their primary keys, this type of join will be fairly efficient. It still requires extra activity, however, that would not be required if the relations had not been split. In many cases, any benefits obtained by the splitting are negated by the additional overhead experienced by this type of user. Another disadvantage is that the primary key must appear in both relations and an index must be created on this primary key for both relations. Thus, there is a potentially significant increase in the space that is required for the database.

COMBINING RELATIONS

Combining relations is exactly the opposite of splitting them. If two or more separate relations exist that have the same primary key, they may be combined into a single relation. For example, we could combine

CUST_ADDRESS(<u>CUSTOMER_NUMBER</u>, NAME, ADDRESS)

and

CUST_FINANCIAL(<u>CUSTOMER_NUMBER</u>, NAME, BALANCE,
    CREDIT_LIMIT, SLSREP_NUMBER)

producing

CUSTOMER(<u>CUSTOMER_NUMBER</u>, NAME, ADDRESS, BALANCE,
    CREDIT_LIMIT, SLSREP_NUMBER)

Since this process is exactly the opposite of the previous one, the same discussion of advantages and disadvantages applies here, only with the roles reversed.

DENORMALIZING

Even though relations in 3NF are desirable to prevent the types of problems discussed in chapter 4, we will occasionally make compromises in this area for the sake of performance. By "denormalizing", we mean converting relations that are in 3NF to something less than 3NF. This process introduces the problems alluded to previously, but it can decrease the number of disk accesses required by certain types of transactions, thus potentially increasing the overall efficiency of the system. The advantages of this increased efficiency must, of course, be weighed against the disadvantages associated with not being in 3NF.

FIGURE 12.11
ORDER and
ORDER_LINE relations
for Premiere Products

1NF

We might choose to convert relations into non-1NF relations. As an example, consider the combination of ORDER and ORDER_LINE within the Premiere Products database, as shown in Figure 12.11. If we have a system that will support repeating groups in some fashion (many will not), we could choose to combine these into a single ORDER relation with repeating groups for the order lines, as shown in Figure 12.12 on the opposite page. Since each row in this new relation represents an order, together with all of the order lines for the order, by accessing this single row we might have all the information about the order that we need. If we need to find any further information about the parts on each of the order lines, we would require further disk accesses, but, even in this case, we wouldn't need to go through the ORDER_LINE relation to get there.

ORDER	ORDER_NUMBER	DATE	CUSTOMER_NUMBER
	12489	90287	124
	12491	90287	311
	12494	90487	315
	12495	90487	256
	12498	90587	522
	12500	90587	124
	12504	90587	522

ORDER_LINE	ORDER_NUMBER	PART_NUMBER	NUMBER_ORDERED	QUOTED_PRICE
	12489	AX12	11	14.95
	12491	BT04	1	402.99
	12491	BZ66	1	311.95
	12494	CB03	4	175.00
	12495	CX11	2	57.95
	12498	AZ52	2	22.95
	12498	BA74	4	4.95
	12500	BT04	1	402.99
	12504	CZ81	2	108.99

ORDER	ORDER_NUMBER	DATE	CUSTOMER_NUMBER	PART_NUMBER	NUMBER_ORDERED	QUOTED_PRICE
	12489	90287	124	AX12	11	14.95
	12491	90287	311	BT04	1	311.95
				BZ66	1	402.99
	12494	90487	315	CB03	4	175.00
	12495	90487	256	CX11	2	57.95
	12498	90587	522	AZ52	2	4.95
				BA74	4	22.95
	12500	90587	124	BT04	1	402.99
	12504	90587	522	CZ81	2	108.99

FIGURE 12.12
Result of combining ORDER and ORDER_LINE relations for Premiere Products (creating a non-1NF relation)

Advantages: As discussed before, the advantage is that certain kinds of retrieval are more efficient. In this case, the retrieval of an order and all of the associated order lines will be more efficient than it would be with a separate ORDER_LINE relation.

Disadvantages: One disadvantage of the non-1NF structure is that many systems do not support repeating groups. Even if a system does support them, there are problems that make them unattractive. Usually, a fixed number of occurrences of the repeating group (in this case a fixed number of order lines) must be specified. Once this has been done, any order with fewer order lines is wasting space and any order with more order lines than this maximum number causes a real problem. In addition, certain types of processing, e.g., listing for a given part all of the orders on which it is present, become considerably more complex.

2NF

We might choose to convert relations into non-2NF relations. If, in the Premiere Products database, the only part information that we needed when processing all of the order lines for a given order were the part description, we might choose to include the part description in the ORDER_LINE relation, as shown in Figure 12.13 on the following page. This relation is not in 2NF, since part description depends only on the part number, which is just a portion of the key for the ORDER_LINE relation. This procedure would, however, permit us to obtain the description of the part on a given order line without requiring that we access the PART relation.

ORDER_LINE	ORDER_NUMBER	PART_NUMBER	PART_DESCRIPTION	NUMBER_ORDERED	QUOTED_PRICE
	12489	AX12	IRON	11	14.95
	12491	BT04	STOVE	1	402.99
	12491	BZ66	WASHER	1	311.95
	12494	CB03	BIKE	4	175.00
	12495	CX11	MIXER	2	57.95
	12498	AZ52	BASEBALL	2	22.95
	12498	BA74	SKATES	4	4.95
	12500	BT04	STOVE	1	402.99
	12504	CZ81	WEIGHTS	2	108.99

FIGURE 12.13
Including description in ORDER_LINE relation (creating a non-2NF relation)

Advantages: Again, certain types of retrieval become more efficient. In the example, the process of listing for a given order all of the order lines within the order, giving the part number, description, number ordered, and quoted price, is more efficient, since this query will no longer involve the PART relation as it would with the original design.

Disadvantages: The fact that the relation is not in 2NF creates redundancy and update problems.

3NF

We might choose to convert relations into non-3NF relations. If, in the Premiere Products database, we frequently need to retrieve both the number *and the name* of the sales rep who represents a particular customer, we might choose to store the sales rep's name as part of the CUSTOMER relation, as shown in Figure 12.14. This relation is not in 3NF. It would, however, allow us to obtain the name of the sales rep who represents a customer at the same time we retrieve the customer without requiring any further accesses.

FIGURE 12.14
Including SLSREP NAME in CUSTOMER relation (creating a non-3NF relation)

CUSTOMER	CUSTOMER_NUMBER	NAME	ADDRESS	CURRENT_BALANCE	CREDIT_LIMIT	SLSREP_NUMBER	SLSREP_NAME
	124	SALLY ADAMS	481 OAK, LANSING, MI	418.75	500	3	MARY JONES
	256	ANN SAMUELS	215 PETE, GRANT, MI	10.75	800	6	WILLIAM SMITH
	311	DON CHARLES	48 COLLEGE, IRA, MI	200.10	300	12	SAM BROWN
	315	TOM DANIELS	914 CHERRY, KENT, MI	320.75	300	6	WILLIAM SMITH
	405	AL WILLIAMS	519 WATSON, GRANT, MI	201.75	800	12	SAM BROWN
	412	SALLY ADAMS	16 ELM, LANSING, MI	908.75	1000	3	MARY JONES
	522	MARY NELSON	108 PINE, ADA, MI	49.50	800	12	SAM BROWN
	567	JOE BAKER	808 RIDGE, HARPER, MI	201.20	300	6	WILLIAM SMITH
	587	JUDY ROBERTS	512 PINE, ADA, MI	57.75	500	6	WILLIAM SMITH
	622	DAN MARTIN	419 CHIP, GRANT, MI	575.50	500	3	MARY JONES

Another type of change that would create non-3NF relations is the inclusion of the number of the sales rep who represents the customer in the ORDER relation, as shown in Figure 12.15. Since customer number determines sales rep number but is not a candidate key for the ORDER relation, this relation is no longer in 3NF. If, given an order, there is a need to find the sales rep who corresponds to the order without finding the customer, or if, given a sales rep, there is a need to find all the orders that correspond to that sales rep without finding the corresponding customers, retrieval will be more efficient with this new structure. Without it, we would have to go through the CUSTOMER record to get from the ORDER record to the SLSREP record (or vice versa), even though customer data was not needed for the retrieval.

ORDER	ORDER_NUMBER	DATE	CUSTOMER_NUMBER	SLSREP_NUMBER
	12489	90287	124	3
	12491	90287	311	12
	12494	90487	315	6
	12495	90487	256	6
	12498	90587	522	12
	12500	90587	124	3
	12504	90587	522	12

FIGURE 12.15
Including SLSREP__NUMBER in ORDER relation (creating a non-3NF relation)

Advantages: Once again, certain types of retrieval become more efficient. In the first example, the process of listing for a given customer data that includes the name of the customer's sales rep will be more efficient, since this query will no longer involve the SLSREP relation as it would with the original design. In the second example, listing information that involves the relationship between sales reps and orders without requiring any customer data will be more efficient, since no customer data need be retrieved along the way.

Disadvantages: The fact that the relation is not in 3NF creates redundancy and update problems.

CREATING INDEXES

Processing that involves finding occurrences of relations based on values in certain columns can be enhanced if there is an index on these columns. This type of processing includes accessing the database based on a primary key (finding information about a sales rep given the sales rep's number), accessing the database based on some secondary key (finding the name of all customers who have a $500 credit limit), and joining two relations together (joining the sales rep and the customer relations based on matching sales rep numbers). If we anticipate the need for such processing, we should strongly consider creating an appropriate index.

Advantages: The existence of such an index will greatly expedite the database retrieval that must take place.

Disadvantages: An index involves overhead. The index itself occupies space on the disk. Further, any change made to the database that affects the index (adding new rows, deleting old rows, changing a value in a column on which the index is built) requires updating the index. Trying to build indexes on all combinations of columns, as some people have tried to do, will create a system that works wonderfully for retrieval purposes but disastrously when it comes to update.

CODASYL MODEL

SPLITTING OR COMBINING RECORDS

The same discussion of splitting or combining relations applies equally well to the CODASYL model. Records could be split or combined for exactly the same reasons. The same discussion of advantages and disadvantages applies.

DENORMALIZING

The discussion concerning denormalizing also applies as well to the CODASYL model as it does to the relational model. The same discussion of advantages and disadvantages applies.

SPECIAL SET OPTIONS

The uses of **system-owned sets, sorted sets, pointer arrays,** and **multimember sets** were discussed in chapter 9 along with their associated advantages and disadvantages. The discussion will not be repeated here. The possible use of these structures, however, should be considered during the process of tuning the design for performance.

ADDING SETS

In the discussion on changes to a relational database, an example was given in which it was necessary to retrieve data on sales reps and related orders but not on the customers in between. A change to the structure to make this retrieval more efficient was discussed. A similar change can be made to a CODASYL database by adding an extra set, in this example a set in which the owner is SLSREP and the member is ORDER. The new structure is shown in Figure 12.16.

Advantages: Retrieval of sales rep data and related order data that does not require intermediate customer data will be more efficient, since less data must be retrieved.

FIGURE 12.16
Including an
additional set

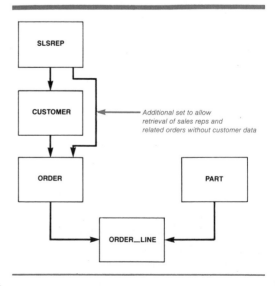

Additional set to allow retrieval of sales reps and related orders without customer data

Disadvantages: There is an extra set to maintain. Added pointer space is required in the database which is technically unnecessary (all required processing could still be done in the absence of this set). There may also be a problem with consistency of data. If order 12489 is owned by customer 124 in S_CUSTOMER_ORDER and customer 124 is, in turn, owned by sales rep 3 in S_SLSREP_CUSTOMER, but order 12489 is owned by sales rep 6 in S_SLSREP_ORDER, the data is inconsistent.

INCLUDING KEY OF OWNER IN MEMBER RECORD

Including the key of an owner record in a member record (e.g., including the number of the sales rep in the customer record in the Premiere Products database) is unnecessary in a CODASYL system. The relationship between sales reps and customers is accomplished through the set S_SLSREP_CUSTOMER, not by having the sales rep number as a field within the customer record. It is only within the relational model that such an inclusion would be necessary.

There is a reason why we might choose to make such an inclusion, however. A given type of transaction that requires directly retrieving customer data *and* the customer's sales rep's number, but no other sales rep data, would be more efficient. In processing such a transaction there would then be no need to find the owner within S_SLSREP_CUSTOMER after retrieving the customer. (The set would now be termed "inessential".) If the volume of this type of transaction is sufficiently large, such a change might be warranted.

Advantages: The advantage has already been discussed. The processing of certain types of transactions becomes more efficient.

Disadvantages: Since including the presence of the key of the owner within the member record is technically unnecessary, it is a waste of space. Further, the value in this field had better agree with the value of the key in the owner record. This makes the update of the key of the owner record a more complex process. Not only would the sales rep number in the SLSREP record need to be changed, but also the sales rep number in the customer records of those customers whom the sales rep represents would need to be changed. Also, most CODASYL systems will not enforce consistency in values between the owner record and the member records, although the later CODASYL specifications do include a CHECK clause within the SET definitions that will cause the system to enforce such consistency.

CHANGING CALC RECORD TO VIA SET

If the primary key of a record was left intact after removing the foreign keys, the methodology indicated that the location mode of the record was to be CALC on this primary key. If there is a need to access records of this type, which are directly based on the foreign key, with any frequency, this is probably an appropriate choice. If, however, records of this type are usually accessed some other way, we might consider changing the location mode from CALC to VIA SET. In the Premiere Products database, for example, if orders are usually accessed through the customer who placed the order rather than directly, we could make the location mode of the ORDER record as VIA S_CUSTOMER_ORDER. This will then cause each order to be placed as close as possible to the customer who placed the order. In turn, retrieving a customer and all of the orders placed by the customer becomes a very efficient process. However, we have lost the ability to directly retrieve an order based on the order number alone.

Advantages: One advantage has already been mentioned. Retrieving a customer and all associated orders becomes more efficient. Another advantage is that since the order record is no longer CALC, there is no need for the CALC chain pointer and, thus, less storage space is required for each order.

Disadvantages: The disadvantage has also already been mentioned. Retrieving an order directly based on the order number is no longer possible. Any transaction that requires such a retrieval will have to include some type of search of the database rather than a simple FIND ANY command. This not only makes the logic involved in the transaction more complicated, but it also makes processing such a transaction less efficient.

CHANGING VIA SET RECORD TO CALC

Consider the link record, ORDER_LINE, within the CODASYL version of the Premiere Products database. As discussed in example 13 of chapter 8, the process of finding the order line for order 12491, part BZ66, entails more than a simple FIND command. Rather, it requires a search routine, as shown in the example. Further, the attempt to store a second order line for order 12491, part BZ66, will *not* be rejected by the DBMS, since no duplicates clause is being violated. Thus, the burden of ensuring that duplicate order lines are not stored in the database falls to the programmers, something that we would like to avoid.

A change to the design can be made that will both simplify the direct retrieval of an order line and allow the DBMS to reject duplicates. To accomplish both of these objectives requires two changes. First, we include the keys of both owner records, ORDER and PART, within the ORDER_LINE record. Second, instead of a location mode of VIA SET, the ORDER_LINE record will be CALC on the concatenation of ORDER_NUMBER and PART_NUMBER, with duplicates not allowed. With this change to the design, filling in both the order number and the part number and then executing the command

FIND ANY ORDER-LINE

allows us to directly find a specific order line. In addition, an attempt to store a second order line for order 12491, part BZ66, will be rejected by the DBMS as a duplicate.

The general process entails including the keys of one or more owner records in the member record, as discussed earlier, and making the location mode of the member record CALC on these included keys.

Advantages: Advantages include both those discussed previously for including keys of owner records within member records and those just discussed. With this change, it will be possible to find a given order line directly, and the DBMS will be able to reject duplicate order lines.

Disadvantages: Those disadvantages presented in the discussion of including keys of owner records within member records also apply here. The problem of wasted space tends to be even worse in this case, however. We are probably including the keys of *two* owner records, not just one. In addition, since the record is now CALC rather than VIA SET, each record occurrence must also include a calc chain pointer. If Premiere Products happened to have six character order numbers and twelve character part numbers, and if pointers were three bytes long, each order line record would now contain an extra twenty-one bytes. Multiply this by the number of order lines in the database, which can be sizable, and we may have more wasted space than we can tolerate.

Another disadvantage concerns the characteristics of the CALC location mode as opposed to those of VIA SET. If the ORDER_LINE record is stored VIA S_ORDER_ORDER_LINE, order lines will be clustered as closely as possible to the orders that own them. This will make transactions that retrieve first an order and then all of the associated order lines very efficient. It may be, for example, that a given order and its six order lines are all stored on the same page and thus can all be retrieved with a single disk access. This clustering is lost if the ORDER_LINE record is CALC, since order line occurrences will then be distributed around the database in positions determined by application of the hashing function to the calc key.

CHANGING THE SET IN THE VIA SET

If the procedure explained earlier for producing a CODASYL design has indicated that the location mode of a particular record is to be VIA SET, the set mentioned must be one in which the record participates as a member. If there is more than one such set, one of them must be chosen. The procedure indicates that we may pick any of them. At this point, we might decide not to use the one we chose earlier and instead pick another possibility.

The important thing to keep in mind in making such a decision is that occurrences of the record will be placed as closely as possible to the owner occurrence *within the set that we choose*. If we choose, for example, to use VIA S_ORDER_ORDER_LINE as a location mode for the ORDER_LINE record, order lines will be placed near the order that owns the order line. If we choose to use VIA S_PART_ORDER_LINE, they will instead by placed near the part that owns them. Thus, the real question is, Which arrangement will be more beneficial to the overall processing of the system?

Processing that uses the set we choose will be more efficient than processing that uses the other set. If we choose to use S_ORDER_ORDER_LINE, then processing an order and all of the associated order lines will be much more efficient than processing a part and all of its associated order lines. Thus, one factor to consider in the decision is which type of processing to make more efficient. Another factor to consider is the average number of member occurrences in each of these sets. If the number in one set is much larger than the number in another, we might want to avoid this set. If the average number of member occurrences in S_ORDER_ORDER_LINE is five, for example, and the number of member occurrences in S_PART_ORDER_LINE is one thousand, we might choose to use S_ORDER_ORDER_LINE. Trying to cluster one thousand order lines near a part can cause problems. Not only will such a large number of order lines require several pages of the database to house them, thus causing much of the benefit of the clustering to be sacrificed, but it also tends to fill several pages, thus causing problems the next time something needs to be stored in this portion of the database.

PRIOR POINTERS

In any set, we might choose to include prior pointers. Prior pointers occupy space and constitute another field that must be updated whenever data in the database is changed. On the other hand, prior pointers make the process of finding the prior occurrence within a set efficient. This process is used not only when a FIND PRIOR WITHIN set-name command is executed, but also during a deletion. If customer 405 is deleted in Figure 12.17, for example, the prior customer, 311, must point to the next customer, 522. Since any set has to contain next pointers, finding customer 522 is a simple matter for the DBMS. On the other hand, if the system does not contain prior pointers, finding customer 311 is not a simple matter at all, particularly if the number of member occurrences is large. It requires searching sequentially all the way around the chain. Thus, deletion is also more efficient.

The vast majority of the time, prior pointers are a good choice. Some systems even require their use, in which case we don't even have to address this issue during database design. Even if the DBMS does not require their use, some designers consider them so valuable that they always automatically include them in the design.

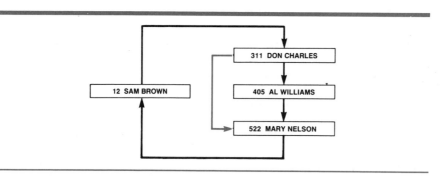

FIGURE 12.17
Deleting customer
405

OWNER POINTERS

In any set, we might also choose to include owner pointers. Owner pointers also occupy space and also constitute another field that must be updated whenever data in the database is changed. On the other hand, owner pointers lend efficiency to the process of finding the owner occurrence within a set. For any set in which we need to find the owner with any frequency, we should probably choose owner pointers. In addition, some systems require the presence of owner pointers in order to find the owner. While the inclusion of owner pointers is perhaps not as universally appropriate as the inclusion of prior pointers (if prior pointers are the right choice 95 percent of the time, owner pointers would be the right choice 75 percent of the time), some database designers automatically include owner pointers in their designs. In addition, some systems require owner pointers in all sets.

ANY SYSTEM

ENCODING DATA

In the information level of design, we may have decided to encode certain data items. There are only two real decisions to make here:

1. Do we really want to encode the data?
2. If so, will we store the codes in the database or elsewhere?

The advantage of encoding data is that it saves space. The disadvantage is that an extra step is necessary to retrieve any encoded data. First of all, the code itself is retrieved along with all the other data that is being retrieved. After this has taken place, the value for which the code stands must also be retrieved. If the data had not been encoded, this second step would be unnecessary. At this point, we may decide not to encode after all because of the additional overhead incurred during retrieval, choosing, instead, to put up with the additional storage cost incurred by not encoding.

Assuming that we decide to encode, the next question is, Where will the codes themselves be stored? They might be stored in the database, and, in general, this would probably be appropriate. If the codes are more global to the enterprise than the data in this database, however, they should probably be external to the database, perhaps in a keyed file in which the key is the code and the record contains the value that has been encoded. By saying the code is more global to the enterprise, we mean that these codes are, or will be, used in other applications that do not use the database we are designing.

INCLUDING DERIVABLE DATA

In the information level of design, we said we would include attributes that could be derived from other attributes. For example, in an INVENTORY relation that contains attributes UNITS_ON_HAND and COST, we would include the attribute ON_HAND_ VALUE (UNITS_ON_HAND * COST). In the STUDENT relation, the attribute TOTAL_NUMBER_OF_CREDITS, which can be computed by summing the NUMBER_OF_CREDITS for each of the courses in which the student has a passing grade, would be included. We must be sure we document the manner in which the result is to be obtained, of course.

In the actual implementation, however, there are other considerations. If we store an attribute that is computable from other attributes, we are creating redundancy, update problems, and the possibility of inconsistency in the database. This would certainly argue against storing the attribute. (If UNITS_ON_HAND = 10 and COST = 15.00, but ON_HAND_VALUE = 125.00, the information is inconsistent. The reason we have this problem is that a relation containing such derived data is technically not in 3NF. In this example, the concatenation of UNITS_ON_HAND and COST determines ON_HAND_VALUE. Yet, creating a separate relation containing UNITS_ON_HAND, COST, and ON_HAND_VALUE does not seem to be a particularly attractive alternative.)

In spite of these arguments, there are two situations in which we really should include the attribute. If the DBMS we are using supports the notion of VIRTUAL attributes (i.e., an attribute is not physically stored but rather the formula for computing it is applied whenever the attribute is requested), then the problems mentioned previously disappear. The second situation arises when the computation is complicated, i.e., when it involves processing a large number of occurrences in the database. In this case we may decide to store the result for the sake of efficiency. Suppose that every time we needed the TOTAL_NUMBER_OF_CREDITS for a given student we had to sum the NUMBER_OF_CREDITS for all the courses he or she had successfully completed. We would have introduced a great deal of overhead, perhaps more than we can endure. As an aside, if we do decide to store the TOTAL_NUMBER_OF_CREDITS as a part of the STUDENT relation, we should create a UTILITY program that periodically will verify that these numbers are correct, e.g., that we didn't inadvertently update the TOTAL_NUMBER_OF_CREDITS for a particular student in such a way that it no longer matches the figure obtained by summing the NUMBER_OF_CREDITS from the individual courses.

GENERAL PHYSICAL CHARACTERISTICS

Depending on the DBMS, it may be possible to make other changes to the physical characteristics of the database. We may be able to adjust the blocking factor and/or the page size; we may be able to choose different access methods or a different hashing function. A complete treatment of all the possibilities is beyond the scope of this text. To determine which things can be changed as well as the physical implications of the various options, it is necessary to have a thorough knowledge of the DBMS that is being used.

For additional information concerning tuning for performance, see [1], [3], [5], [6], and [7].

.6 ANALYZING SPACE AND PROCESSING REQUIREMENTS

The previous section included many choices that could be made to change the database design in such a way as to affect the performance characteristics of the overall application. With so many different choices to make in so many areas, the number of possible physical designs that can be derived from a single information-level design is extremely large (seemingly almost infinite). How can we possibly determine which design is best?

In many cases, knowing the advantages and disadvantages associated with certain compromises will make the appropriate choice obvious. It may well be clear that the advantages will be beneficial to our application and the disadvantages will be something that we can easily live with. By making these choices early in the physical design process, we can drastically reduce the overall number of possible alternatives that we must consider. In some cases, however, it will not be clear which choice is the most beneficial. When that happens, we will need some kind of mechanism that will allow us to choose from among the remaining possibilities.

If we must choose from two or more physical designs, two distinct factors must be considered. The first is storage space. How much space will be needed by a database using this design if it is to support the required volume of data? The second factor is performance. How well will the system perform if this design is chosen? Both factors are important. Since computations on storage space and performance are totally dependent on the characteristics of the DBMS that will be used, we cannot offer one exclusive technique that will always work. Rather, we will give some general guidelines to follow. Before applying these guidelines to a given situation, however, it is essential to be very familiar with the characteristics of the DBMS.

SPACE REQUIREMENTS

Several different components must be considered when we are determining the size of a database. We must consider the space occupied by the data itself; the space occupied by pointers and/or indexes; the space occupied by system data; the space wasted by the DBMS; and the space intentionally wasted by the users of the system. In making these determinations, we should include not only the volumes given to us as current requirements by the users but also volumes for projected growth.

SPACE OCCUPIED BY THE DATA ITSELF

For each record in the database, the record length can be calculated. It is the sum of the lengths of the individual fields. We must, of course, take into account the storage characteristics of the DBMS we are using in order to determine how much space an occurrence of a specific field will occupy. Character data will occupy one byte per character unless the system supports special compression techniques. There are so many different ways to store numeric data that we really need to consult the manual for the given DBMS to determine which alternatives we might specify and the amount of storage each would require.

Once the total record length for a given record type has been calculated, this figure can be multiplied by the number of occurrences that are expected to be stored in the database in order to arrive at the total storage required by all occurrences of records of this type. When these figures have been calculated for each record type in the design, they are added together to give the total storage requirements for data in the database.

POINTERS (CODASYL ONLY)

In CODASYL systems, pointers embedded within records are used to maintain set relationships unless the pointer array option is chosen. (Since pointer arrays behave more like indexes, they will be discussed along with them.) To calculate the amount of pointer space required for a given record type, we need to know how many pointers will be embedded in this type of record and how much space is occupied by each pointer. We find the amount of space occupied by a pointer in the manual. Four bytes is a relatively common size, although three bytes is also common for databases that are not tremendously large. To calculate the number of pointers that are embedded we need to understand the following:

1. For any set in which the record participates as either an owner or member, there will be a pointer to the next member occurrence within the set.
2. For any set in which the record participates as either an owner or member and for which prior pointers are requested, there will be a pointer to the prior member occurrence within the set.
3. For any set in which the record participates as a member and for which owner pointers are requested, there will be a pointer to the owner occurrence within the set.
4. If the location mode of the record is CALC, the record will have a pointer for the CALC chain.

We can thus calculate the number of pointers embedded in a given record type. Multiplying this figure by the size of these pointers will give the amount of space devoted to pointers within a single occurrence of this record type. This number can be multiplied by the number of occurrences of this record type that we expect to store in the database in order to get the total amount of pointer space for all records of this type. When we have made this calculation for each type of record in the database, we can add these numbers together to obtain the total amount of pointer space required in the database.

INDEXES

Indexes are sometimes built on various fields or combinations of fields. When this is the case, the index, even though it is external to the database itself, takes up space and must be included in our computation of the total space requirements. The same type of computations are made for sets whose mode is POINTER ARRAY as opposed to the normal CHAIN. In this case, however, the structure is actually stored within the database.

The ability to make a precise computation really depends on knowledge of the structure of the index used by the given DBMS. We can make a good guess at the total space required, however, even if we don't have knowledge of this precise structure. We add the length of the field (or the combined lengths of the fields) on which the index is built to the length of a single pointer. This figure is then multiplied by the number of occurrences of the record in question. The final result should be a reasonable guess for the space required by the index. (This computation is based on the very simple index structure illustrated in Figure 12.18 in which each entry is simply a value for the field or fields on which the index is built together with a pointer to the record on which the value occurs. In reality, the index structure will be much more sophisticated than this, usually some type of B-tree.)

FIGURE 12.18
Sample index

CUST_NUMBER INDEX	CUST NUMBER	RECORD LOCATION
	124	1
	256	2
	311	3
	315	4
	405	5
	412	6
	522	7
	567	8
	587	9
	622	10

field on which   pointer to
index was built   corresponding
record in database

SYSTEM DATA

By system data, we mean data stored within the database that contains special information about a page or a record. We do not mean schema, subschema, or data dictionary information, which occupy a negligible amount of space compared to the amount of space occupied by the actual database. In IDMS, for example, this data would include the header and footer (one per page) and the line indexes (one per record occurrence).

SPACE WASTED BY SYSTEM

The database structure supported by the DBMS will, in general, cause some space to be "wasted" at any point in time. For example, if a page has only fifty bytes of available space remaining and the shortest record that can be stored on that page is seventy bytes long, the fifty bytes cannot be used and this space will be wasted.

SPACE INTENTIONALLY WASTED BY USERS

Often, during the creation of a design, wasted (unused) space will be built in intentionally. Sometimes, extra space will be assigned as a safety factor in case the requirements have been underestimated. If hashing is to be used, extra space must be assigned or system performance will suffer drastically (see the discussion of hashing in Appendix A for elaboration on this point). As a general rule of thumb, if hashing is used, the database should be no more than 80 to 85 percent full.

EXAMPLE

To illustrate the process, let's assume we have a CODASYL system on which we are implementing the schema shown in Figure 12.19. An examination of the manual for this DBMS has produced the following pertinent information:

1. A database is divided into pages of 4,096 bytes each.
2. Any record occurrence must be totally contained within a single page.
3. Eight bytes per page are devoted to system data. An additional four bytes per page are devoted to the header of the CALC chain.
4. Four bytes per record occurrence are devoted to system data.
5. Pointers for a database of the size we are implementing are three bytes each.
6. Numeric data occupies one byte per digit. Alphanumeric data occupies one byte per character.

```
1     SCHEMA NAME IS SCHEMA_DISTRIBUTION.

2     AREA NAME IS AREA_DISTRIBUTION.

3     RECORD NAME IS SLSREP
          LOCATION MODE IS CALC USING SLSREP_NUMBER
              DUPLICATES ARE NOT ALLOWED
          WITHIN AREA_DISTRIBUTION.

          02   SLSREP_NUMBER          PIC 9(2).
          02   SLSREP_NAME            PIC X(20).
          02   SLSREP_ADDRESS         PIC X(20).
          02   TOTAL_COMMISSION       PIC 9(5)V9(2).
          02   COMMISSION_RATE        PIC V9(2).

4     RECORD NAME IS CUSTOMER
          LOCATION MODE IS CALC USING CUSTOMER_NUMBER
              DUPLICATES ARE NOT ALLOWED
          WITHIN AREA_DISTRIBUTION.

          02   CUSTOMER_NUMBER        PIC 9(3).
          02   NAME                   PIC X(20).
          02   ADDRESS                PIC X(20).
          02   CURRENT_BALANCE        PIC 9(5)V9(2).
          02   CREDIT_LIMIT           PIC 9(5).
```

FIGURE 12.19a
Premiere Products schema DDL (General CODASYL version) (continued on the following pages)

FIGURE 12.19b

```
5    RECORD NAME IS ORDER
          LOCATION MODE IS CALC USING ORDER_NUMBER
                DUPLICATES ARE NOT ALLOWED
          WITHIN AREA_DISTRIBUTION.

          02   ORDER_NUMBER            PIC 9(5).
          02   ORDER_DATE              PIC 9(6).


6    RECORD NAME IS PART
          LOCATION MODE IS CALC USING PART_NUMBER
                DUPLICATES ARE NOT ALLOWED
          WITHIN AREA_DISTRIBUTION.

          02   PART_NUMBER             PIC X(4).
          02   PART_DESCRIPTION        PIC X(20).
          02   UNITS_ON_HAND           PIC 9(4).
          02   ITEM_CLASS              PIC X(2).
          02   WAREHOUSE_NUMBER        PIC 9(2).
          02   UNIT_PRICE              PIC 9(4)V9(2).


7    RECORD NAME IS ORDER_LINE
          LOCATION MODE IS VIA S_ORDER_ORDER_LINE
          WITHIN AREA_DISTRIBUTION.

          02   NUMBER_ORDERED          PIC 9(4).
          02   QUOTED_PRICE            PIC 9(4)V9(2).


8    SET NAME IS S_SLSREP_CUSTOMER
          OWNER IS SLSREP
                SET IS PRIOR PROCESSABLE
                ORDER IS PERMANENT INSERTION IS SORTED BY
                          DEFINED KEYS
                DUPLICATES ARE LAST.

          MEMBER IS CUSTOMER
                INSERTION IS AUTOMATIC
                RETENTION IS OPTIONAL
                LINKED TO OWNER
                KEY IS ASCENDING NAME
                SET SELECTION FOR S_SLSREP_CUSTOMER
                     IS THRU S_SLSREP_CUSTOMER
                     OWNER IDENTIFIED BY APPLICATION.

9    SET NAME IS S_CUSTOMER_ORDER
          OWNER IS CUSTOMER
                SET IS PRIOR PROCESSABLE
                ORDER IS PERMANENT INSERTION IS LAST.

          MEMBER IS ORDER
                INSERTION IS AUTOMATIC
                RETENTION IS OPTIONAL
                LINKED TO OWNER
                SET SELECTION FOR S_CUSTOMER_ORDER
                     IS THRU S_CUSTOMER_ORDER
                     OWNER IDENTIFIED BY APPLICATION.
```

FIGURE 12.19c

```
10    SET NAME IS S_ORDER_ORDER_LINE
              OWNER IS ORDER
                    SET IS PRIOR PROCESSABLE
                    ORDER IS PERMANENT INSERTION IS LAST.

              MEMBER IS ORDER_LINE
                    INSERTION IS AUTOMATIC
                    RETENTION IS OPTIONAL
                    LINKED TO OWNER
                    SET SELECTION FOR S_ORDER_ORDER_LINE
                          IS THRU S_ORDER_ORDER_LINE
                          OWNER IDENTIFIED BY APPLICATION.


11    SET NAME IS S_PART_ORDER_LINE
              OWNER IS PART
                    SET IS PRIOR PROCESSABLE
                    ORDER IS PERMANENT INSERTION IS LAST.

              MEMBER IS ORDER_LINE
                    INSERTION IS AUTOMATIC
                    RETENTION IS OPTIONAL
                    LINKED TO OWNER
                    SET SELECTION FOR S_PART_ORDER_LINE
                          IS THRU S_PART_ORDER_LINE
                          OWNER IDENTIFIED BY APPLICATION.
```

Also, an interview with the users has produced the following information concerning volumes:

1. There are twenty sales reps.
2. There are a thousand customers.
3. There are two thousand orders on file at any one time.
4. On the average each order has four order lines.
5. There are five thousand parts.

Note that we have not been given the specific number of order lines to expect. It is quite common for users to think in the terms indicated in the preceding list. They have the feeling that an average order has a certain number of order lines. All that we need to do, of course, is to multiply the number of orders (two thousand) by the average number of order lines per order (four) to determine that there are eight thousand order lines. It is this figure that we will use in our computations.

How many pages should be devoted to this database? The first step is to compute the amount of space occupied by records of each type. To do this, we calculate the total length of the record and multiply this figure by the number of occurrences of the record that we expect will be in the database. It doesn't matter whether we do the computations for data and pointers separately and then combine at the end or combine at the beginning. In this case, we will combine at the beginning. The following are the computations for each record type.

Determine Record Lengths

SLSREP: The SLSREP record is CALC, so it contains a CALC chain pointer. It participates as the owner in S_SLSREP_CUSTOMER, in which prior pointers are requested. It participates as the member in no sets. There are thus three pointers in each occurrence of the record: CALC chain, next within S_SLSREP_CUSTOMER, and prior within S_SLSREP_CUSTOMER. The data fields total fifty-one bytes (two for SLSREP_NUMBER, twenty for SLSREP_NAME, twenty for SLSREP_ADDRESS, seven for TOTAL_COMMISSION, two for COMMISSION_RATE).

CUSTOMER: The CUSTOMER record is CALC, so it contains a CALC chain pointer. It participates as the owner in S_CUSTOMER_ORDER, in which prior pointers are requested. It participates as the member in S_SLSREP_CUSTOMER, in which prior and owner pointers are requested. There are thus six pointers in each occurrence of the record: CALC chain, next within S_CUSTOMER_ORDER, prior within S_CUSTOMER_ORDER, next within S_SLSREP_CUSTOMER, prior within S_SLSREP_CUSTOMER, and owner within S_SLSREP_CUSTOMER. The data fields total fifty-five bytes.

ORDER: The ORDER record is CALC, so it contains a CALC chain pointer. It participates as the owner in S_ORDER_ORDER_LINE, in which prior pointers are requested. It participates as the member in S_CUSTOMER_ORDER, in which prior and owner pointers are requested. There are thus six pointers in each occurrence of the record: CALC chain, next within S_ORDER_ORDER_LINE, prior within S_ORDER_ORDER_LINE, next within S_CUSTOMER_ORDER, prior within S_CUSTOMER_ORDER, and owner within S_CUSTOMER_ORDER. The data fields total eleven bytes.

PART: The PART record is CALC, so it contains a CALC chain pointer. It participates as the owner in S_PART_ORDER_LINE, in which prior pointers are requested. It participates as the member in no sets. There are thus three pointers in each occurrence of the record: CALC chain, next within S_PART_ORDER_LINE, prior within S_PART_ORDER_LINE. The data fields total thirty-six bytes.

ORDER_LINE: The ORDER_LINE record is not CALC, so it does not contain a CALC chain pointer. It participates as the owner in no sets. It participates as the member in S_ORDER_ORDER_LINE and S_PART_ORDER_LINE. In both of these sets, prior and owner pointers are requested. There are thus six pointers in each occurrence of the record: next, prior, and owner within S_ORDER_ORDER_LINE, and next, prior, and owner within S_PART_ORDER_LINE. The data fields total ten bytes.

Determine Total Space Required

The preceding figures are used in calculating space requirements. The calculations are shown in Figure 12.20 on the next page. The first column gives system data per record occurrence. In all cases, this is four bytes. The second column, which lists the total of the data fields, and the third column, which lists the number of pointers within a record occurrence, have been discussed. The fourth column gives the space occupied by the pointers. It is obtained by multiplying the number of pointers by the length of a pointer, in this case three bytes. The total amount of space is figured by adding the system data, user data, and space for pointers, and is given in bytes. Multiplying the total space for a single record by the expected number of occurrences gives the space required for all occurrences of the record type. Finally, adding all of these numbers together gives the total space required to store the data and associated pointers, in this case 645,280 bytes.

RECORD TYPE	SYSTEM DATA	USER DATA	# OF PTRS	SPACE PTRS	TOTAL SPACE	# OF OCCUR.	SPACE REQUIRED
SLSREP	4	51	3	9	64	20	1,280
CUSTOMER	4	55	6	18	77	1,000	77,000
ORDER	4	11	6	18	33	2,000	66,000
PART	4	36	3	9	49	5,000	245,000
ORDER_ LINE	4	10	6	18	32	8,000	256,000

Determine Number of Pages Required

FIGURE 12.20
Space calculations

We now have all of the information we need in order to calculate the number of pages to reserve for this database. It may seem that all we need to do is divide the total number of bytes required by 4,096, the number of bytes per page. If we go ahead and do this, however, we are overlooking three crucial points.

First, as we discussed earlier, eight bytes per page are devoted to system data and another four to the header for the CALC chain. Thus, only 4,084 (4,096 - 8 - 4) bytes are actually usable for data.

Second, since any record occurrence must be totally contained within a single page, we will have some wasted space. If, for example, we attempt to store a customer record on a page on which fewer than seventy-seven bytes remain available, we will be unsuccessful. If fewer than thirty-two bytes (the length of the shortest record) remain on a page, we will be unable to store records of any type and the space will be totally wasted. How should we calculate the amount of space on a page that is truly available?

A valid but conservative method is to subtract from the 4,084 bytes one less than the length (in bytes) of the longest record. In this example, the longest record is the customer record, which is seventy-seven bytes in length. Thus, we subtract seventy-six from 4,084, which yields 4,008. The rationale is that this much of the page will be totally usable. If fewer than 4,008 bytes are currently used, we will be able to store any occurrence of any type record on the page. This is a conservative approach because even if more than 4,008 bytes are stored, records of some types may still fit on the page. If, for example, 4,020 bytes were used on a particular page, we could still store a SLSREP record (sixty-four bytes), an ORDER record (thirty-three bytes), a PART record (forty-nine bytes), or an ORDER_LINE record (thirty-two bytes). Thus, on many pages, more than 4,008 bytes may be used. Rather than use the longest record, we could attempt to use some kind of average record length, for example, to obtain a slightly more realistic picture. Let's assume for now, however, that we do adopt this conservative technique. Thus, the practical amount of data that will fit on a page for this database is 4,008 bytes.

We still have a problem. If we divide 645,280 bytes by 4,008 bytes/page, we obtain 161 pages. If we reserve only 161 pages, however, and we try to store the amount of data that the users indicate they require, the database will effectively be 100 percent full. This figure would be pure disaster for the hashing that takes place for all CALC records. Ideally, for hashing, the database should be no more than 80 to 85 percent full. Thus, as a final step, we solve the equation

$$161 = .80 \times$$

for $\times$, yielding about 200. If we indeed have 161 pages worth of data and we reserve 200 pages, then the database will be about 80 percent full, and satisfactory performance from the hashing routines should be achieved.

Now let's summarize the process. Once the total number of bytes has been calculated, the following steps are applied:

1. Subtract the amount of space occupied on a page by any system data from the total amount of space for a page. In the example, this gave a figure of 4,084 bytes.
2. Subtract from this figure one less than the length (in bytes) of the longest record. In the example, this gave a figure of 4,008 bytes. This is a conservative approach. A slightly more realistic approach would be to use an average (or possibly a weighted average) of the record lengths of all types of records.
3. Divide the total number of bytes needed for the database by this figure. This result gives the number of pages necessary for a database that is totally full (in our example, 161 pages).
4. Calculate the number of pages needed so that this figure represents about 80 percent (or potentially as much as 85 percent, but no more) of the total.

Plan for Growth

This completes the example. The only crucial aspect not covered in the algorithm itself is growth. The calculations here do not build in any growth factor. We don't change the procedure to accommodate growth, however. The easiest way to ensure that the database will support both current needs *and* a certain growth rate for some period of time is to increase the initial requirements to cover the projected growth.

PERFORMANCE

Estimating the relative performance of two different designs is not a simple task. We will investigate one methodology for attempting to do so. We will also discuss the limitations of this methodology and suggest other factors that might be considered to improve the picture. For an example, we will use the CODASYL database represented in Figure 12.19, together with the volume requirements given in the example on calculating space requirements.

LOGICAL RECORD ACCESSES

This methodology relies heavily on **logical record accesses** (LRAs) and was proposed by Teorey and Fry in [7]. Each time a record from the database is retrieved, even if the record already happens to be in main memory, a logical record access occurs. Thus, LRAs do not take into account any buffering that might take place. If a record to be read is already in main memory, a logical record access occurs, but not a **physical record access**. It is, of course, the physical record accesses that really give the picture. Measuring physical record accesses involves difficulties, however, which will be addressed after the discussion of the methodology. By calculating LRAs, we are effectively simulating a system in which there is no buffering at all; every time a record is retrieved from the database, another disk access is required.

Calculate the Number of LRAs Required

The first step in the methodology is to calculate the number of LRAs required for each application. We consider each transaction or report in the system and calculate the number of LRAs it requires. To do this, it is necessary to know the structure of the database, the number of occurrences of various types of records in the database and the algorithm that will be used to satisfy the request. The algorithms can be documented in different ways (discussed in section 12.7). For now, what is important is not how the algorithms are documented but rather how we determine LRAs, once we have determined the algorithm to process a given transaction or produce a given report.

Once we have this information, we can calculate the number of records that must be read in order to satisfy the request. To illustrate the process, consider the following transactions and reports.

1. For a given customer, list his or her number, name, and address.
2. For a given sales rep, list his or her number and name, together with the number, name, and address of each customer he or she represents.
3. For a given customer, list his or her number and name, the number and name of the sales rep who represents the customer, and the number and date of each order placed by the customer. In addition, for each order line on each of these orders, list the part number, description, number of units ordered and quoted price.

4. For each customer, list his or her number and name, and the number and name of the sales rep who represents the customer.

5. Store a new customer. In this transaction, the user will enter a customer number. At this point, the system will verify that no customer with this number currently exists. The user will then enter the number of the sales rep who is to represent this customer. The system will ensure that such a sales rep does exist. In addition, the name of the sales rep will be displayed. Finally, the user will enter the remaining data (name, address, etc.) for this customer. At this point, the system will store the new customer.

Actually, it is useful to break down by record type the LRAs required for each application. That is the way we will proceed in the example. We will now discuss the mechanics of calculating LRAs for each of the five types of applications.

1. Since the CUSTOMER record is calc, we should be able to retrieve information about a given customer directly. Thus, this application requires one LRA for the CUSTOMER record type and none for all of the others.

2. Since the SLSREP record is also calc, retrieving information about a given sales rep requires one LRA for the SLSREP record type. At this point, however, we must retrieve information about all customers represented by this sales rep. The appropriate way to do this is to find all the member occurrences in S_SLSREP_CUSTOMER that are owned by this sales rep. There will be one LRA for each customer in this chain. Thus, we need to determine, on the average, how many customers are owned by a given sales rep. Since there are twenty sales reps and a thousand customers, an average sales rep would represent fifty (1,000/20) customers. Thus, this application will also require fifty LRAs for the CUSTOMER record type.

3. For reasons mentioned earlier, retrieving the given customer requires one LRA for the CUSTOMER record type.

Calculating the number of LRAs required to find the sales rep who owns this customer is a little trickier. The answer depends on whether or not the set S_SLSREP_CUSTOMER contains owner pointers. If it does, as in our example, the answer is simple. Since there is a pointer directly to the desired sales rep, one LRA for the SLSREP record type is all that is required. If not, then to find the sales rep the system must work its way around the remainder of the chain, starting with the given customer until encountering the sales rep. To determine the number of LRAs required in this case, we assume, as stated before, that an average occurrence of S_ SLSREP_CUSTOMER contains fifty customers. We also assume that the customer we are processing will be, on the average, about halfway around this chain. Thus, twenty-five LRAs of the CUSTOMER record type and finally, one LRA of the SLSREP record type would be required to determine the sales rep who represents the customer in this case.

Retrieving all the orders for this customer requires processing a complete occurrence of S_CUSTOMER_ORDER. Since there are one thousand customers and two thousand orders, we would expect a customer to own, on the average, two orders. Thus we must add two LRAs for the ORDER record type. For each order, we are to retrieve all order lines. Since the average order contains four order lines and we are retrieving two orders, we will ultimately retrieve eight (two times four) order lines. Finally, since the part description is required along with the data for each order line, when we have retrieved an order line we must also retrieve the part that owns it in S_PART_ORDER_LINE. Since this set includes owner pointers, this process requires one LRA for the PART record. Since we have eight LRAs for the ORDER_LINE record type, we will also have eight LRAs for the PART record type. If S_PART_ORDER_LINE did not include owner pointers, the procedure explained earlier for finding the sales rep who represents a customer would apply.

4. Since the set S_SLSREP_CUSTOMER contains owner pointers, retrieving the sales rep who represents the customer, once we have retrieved a customer, requires a single LRA for the sales rep record type. How do we retrieve all customers, however? If there were a system-owned set in our schema in which the member was CUSTOMER, we could retrieve all of the members in this set. Since this would entail retrieving each customer and there are a thousand customers, this would give a thousand LRAs of the customer record type.

   In the absence of such a set, we must scan the entire database, looking for customers. (Even though we use the command FIND NEXT CUS-TOMER WITHIN AREA–DISTRIBUTION), the system must still retrieve each record occurrence.) Thus, the process requires twenty LRAs of the SLSREP record type, 1,000 LRAs of the CUSTOMER record type, 2,000 LRAs of the ORDER record type, 8,000 LRAs of the ORDER_LINE record type, and 5,000 LRAs of the PART record type. (A system-owned set would certainly have benefited this application!) Additionally, for each of the thousand customers, an additional LRA of the SLSREP record will then be required to obtain the sales rep who represents the customer. There will then be 1,020 LRAs for the sales rep record (20 LRAs during the sequential scan plus an LRA of a sales rep record whenever a customer is encountered).

5. When the customer number is initially verified, there will be a single LRA of the CUSTOMER record type. When the sales rep number is verified, there will be a single LRA of the SLSREP record type. Finally, when the customer is added, there will be another LRA of the CUSTOMER record type (in this case for output) to add the customer to the database.

   At this point, the customer must be placed in the occurrence of S_SLSREP_CUSTOMER. Since the order of this set is sorted, the member occurrences along the chain must be examined sequentially to determine the location at which to insert the new customer (unless the set is stored using the pointer array mode, in which case the analysis would take that into account). Since the average occurrence of S_SLSREP_CUSTOMER contains fifty customers, and we would expect to have to search about half the chain, we would expect to require about twenty-five LRAs to determine the position at which to insert this customer. Finally, the customers on either side of the new customer must have their pointers updated, requiring two additional LRAs for the CUSTOMER record type. In total, this application requires one LRA for the SLSREP record type and twenty-nine LRAs for the CUSTOMER record type (one to attempt to read the customer initially, one to add the customer to the database, twenty-five to find a position at which the customer should be inserted into the occurrence of S_SLSREP_CUSTOMER, and two to adjust the pointers of the customers on either side of the new customer in the set occurrence).

This scenario depicts the customer being added before the position in the chain is known. If things truly happened in this fashion, the customer's record would have to be updated later, once the position had been determined to make the customer point to the correct next and prior occurrences in the set. In reality, the customer would not be added until this information was known. This fact does not alter any of the numbers listed in the previous paragraph, however.

The numbers just calculated are shown in Figure 12.21. As you can see, the computations depend on numbers of occurrences of the various record types, the structure of the database, options chosen within the schema (set insertion, for example), and knowledge of the algorithm used in each application. A change to the structure of the database, a change in the options within the schema, or a change in the algorithms used will affect the results. In particular, the addition of a system-owned set in which the member is the customer record type will greatly improve the number of LRAs required for application four. In the exercises at the end of this chapter, you will be asked to redo the computations on the assumption that some of these changes have been made.

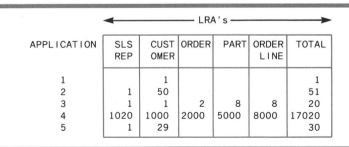

APPLICATION	SLS REP	CUST OMER	ORDER	PART	ORDER LINE	TOTAL
1		1				1
2	1	50				51
3	1	1	2	8	8	20
4	1020	1000	2000	5000	8000	17020
5	1	29				30

FIGURE 12.21
Calculation of number of Logical Record Accesses (LRA's)

Assign Weights

Now that LRAs have been calculated, we attach a weight, or measure of importance, to each application. This weight might be simply the number of times a given application occured in a set period of time, such as a day. Suppose, for example, that application one occured once every ten minutes; application two occured once a week; application three occured once every hour; application four occured once every month; and application five occured five times a day. Suppose also that the company were operating five days per week, eight hours per day. Figure 12.22 incorporates these figures.

APPLICATION	SLS REP	CUST OMER	ORDER	PART	ORDER LINE	TOTAL	WEIGHT	WEIGHTED TOTAL
1		1				1	48	48
2	1	50				51	.2	10.2
3	1	1	2	8	8	20	8	160
4	1020	1000	2000	5000	8000	17020	.05	851
5	1	29				30	5	150

← LRA's →

1219.2

FIGURE 12.22
Weighting the LRA calculations

The weights assigned in this case represent the frequency per day that an application is run. For applications that are not run every day, we still calculate the frequency. Application four runs once a month. Figuring a month as twenty working days yields a weight of 1/20, or .05. The higher an application's weight, the more we are going to prefer a design that reduces the number of LRAs it requires. Occasionally, an application that runs infrequently needs extremely rapid response time. If this is the case, the weight just calculated will be inappropriate. The needs of this application will be given a much lower priority in the choice of a design than will the needs of the jobs that run more frequently. The simplest solution is to increase the weight given to this application. This is why we intentionally call the column "WEIGHT" and not "FREQUENCY" or "FREQUENCY PER DAY".

Obtain Comparison Figures

The critical column in Figure 12.22 is the weighted total. This is the number of LRAs for each application, multiplied by the weight. It is the total at the bottom of this column that we will compare with totals from other designs.

The process then involves performing computations similar to those performed previously for each design alternative, and then comparing the final figures. If one alternative design has a figure substantially lower than that of another, we can be reasonably confident that it is a better design. Many times this will be the case. Some pitfalls await us, however, if we rely totally on this approach.

Potential Problems

The first potential problem concerns record length. If we are concerned only with LRAs, a design in which we have combined several record types and relaxed the requirement for 3NF may be unfairly rewarded by this methodology. There are bound to be substantially fewer LRAs. If we have such designs in the collection that we are analyzing, we can include another factor, called **transport volume**, meaning the volume of data that is *actually* transported. As with the use of LRAs, in calculating this figure we assume that when a record is retrieved, it requires a disk access. We further assume that this record, and this record alone, is transported to main memory. With this in mind, we multiply the LRAs required for a given record type by the length of the record (including pointers). Since the customer record is 77 bytes long (see Figure 12.20), the 50 LRAs for the customer record required by application two will cause 3,850 (77 times 50) bytes of data to be transported. These figures are then added in the same fashion as LRAs and multiplied by the appropriate weights. This gives us an additional check on the design process. If one design is substantially better in terms of the total number of LRAs, we should ensure that it will not be substantially worse in terms of total transport volume.

A second concern was mentioned earlier. It is not logical record accesses but physical record accesses that really tell the story. Ideally, we would like to apply the same procedure but replace LRAs with PRAs. Unfortunately, it is not that simple.

Consider, for example, the process of retrieving an order and the four order lines associated with the order. If the order line record is stored V I A S_ORDER_ORDER_L I NE, these order lines will be clustered as closely to the order that owns them as is possible. If, in fact, they end up on the same page as the order, one PRA will suffice to retrieve the order and all four order lines. On the other hand, if the page on which the order is located is full before all of the order lines have been stored, they will not be on the same page and more than one PRA will be required. Thus, we have to take a probabilistic approach to analyzing the storage of data within the database. We need to determine the likelihood of all order lines being on the same page as the order, or, if this is not likely, how many order lines we expect to find on the same page, how many on the next page, and so on. Further, there may well be enough buffers in memory to hold not just a single page of the database but, perhaps, twenty pages. To analyze whether another retrieval request actually necessitates another PRA, we need to determine the probability of the required data being on one of the twenty pages currently held in memory. If so, no PRA is required.

A detailed discussion of these issues is beyond the scope of this text; for further information on the subject, see [7].

A third problem concerns the methodology itself. While it seems ideally suited to CODASYL or hierarchical systems that are inherently navigational, what about inverted file systems or relational systems that are inherently nonnavigational? The methodology can be used fruitfully with such systems if the LRAs analyzed included indexes; the index in this case will be considered just another type of record.

For other information concerning the analysis of space and performance requirements, see [1], [3], [5], [6], and [7].

12.7 SUBSCHEMA AND APPLICATION DESIGN

In this section, we will discuss the generation of **subschemas** from the information gathered earlier. We will also discuss the design of applications as well as methods for representing algorithms. In the example in the previous section, the database and the associated algorithms were simple enough that we did not bother to represent the appropriate algorithms explicitly. We just assumed that we would satisfy the applications in the obvious way, and then we made our calculations. In many cases, of course, the database and the algorithms are not nearly so simple. To effectively analyze design alternatives requires applying the correct algorithms. For each design alternative, the algorithms must be created and carefully documented. When the final design alternative is chosen, this documentation will then be given to programmers along with an appropriate subschema, documentation of the data in the database, and a list of restrictions that the programs must enforce.

SUBSCHEMAS

General subschemas necessary to support each user view are often created during the information-level design. The information obtained during this phase is used to create actual subschemas for users. Creating a subschema from the documentation produced in the information-level design is not difficult. The form of these subschemas will depend, of course, on which DBMS is used.

In determining subschemas, it is important to keep in mind the role the subschema plays in furnishing data independence as well as the role it plays in security. Any features of the DBMS that can be used to promote data independence should be used. This means making maximum use of views in a relational system or using logical records in IDMS/R, for example. It means not including data in a subschema that is not necessary for that user. Exceptions should be made only for very good reasons. If, for example, the use of the most natural **view** in a relational DBMS will prohibit updating the database for a user who needs to do so, an exception must be made. If the performance associated with the use of a particular given logical record is inadequate, an exception must be made. The overall goal, however, must be to develop subschemas that promote as much data independence as possible.

The subschemas documented in the information-level design also contain security information. Subschemas can and should be used to restrict users from data that they cannot access. Not including unnecessary entities, attributes, and/or relationships in a subschema not only helps promote data independence but also furnishes a measure of security. Subschemas cannot, in general, restrict users to only retrieval-type access to certain fields. This requires other features of the DBMS, such as passwords in CODASYL systems and GRANT authority in many relational systems. These features should be used at this time and in conjunction with the assignment of subschemas to enforce the restrictions documented along with the subschemas in the information level design.

APPLICATION DESIGN

During the analysis of various possible database designs, the calculation of LRAs depended on knowledge of the algorithms that would be used to satisfy the required applications. Once a design is complete, programmers need to be given documentation on the algorithms. Many professionals prefer to use pseudo-code to document these algorithms, and this is a perfectly valid approach. Others, however, prefer more graphical methods. In this section, we will briefly discuss two related diagrammatic approaches to this documentation, **logical access maps** (LAMs) and **database action diagrams** (DADs). Our discussion represents an overview of the topic. If you are interested in further information, Martin offers an excellent discussion of LAMs, DADs, and the relationship between them (see [5]). Application three of the design example will be used to illustrate the basic ideas of these tools:

For a given customer, list his or her number and name, the number and name of the sales rep who represents the customer, and the number and date of each order placed by the customer. In addition, for each order line on each of these orders, list the part number, description, number of units ordered, and quoted price.

LOGICAL ACCESS MAPS

A **logical access map** (LAM) describes the sequence in which records are accessed to satisfy a given application. In the preceding example, the sequence would be

1. Access the CUSTOMER record.
2. Access the SLSREP record that owns the customer record within S_SLSREP_CUSTOMER.
3. Access each order owned by the customer within S_CUSTOMER_ORDER.
4. For each order, access each order line owned by the order within S_ORDER_ORDER_LINE.
5. For each order line, access the part that owns it within S_PART_ORDER_LINE.

This sequence can be represented on a data structure diagram, as shown in Figure 12.23. A LAM shows essentially the same information but is often drawn in a vertical fashion, as shown in Figure 12.24 on the following page. This figure indicates that we first access the CUSTOMER record; we next access a single SLSREP record; we then access many ORDER records (indicated by the double-headed arrow). After this, we access many ORDER_LINE records (again a double-headed arrow). Finally, we access a single PART record (indicated by the single-headed arrow).

FIGURE 12.23
Representing access sequence on data structure diagram

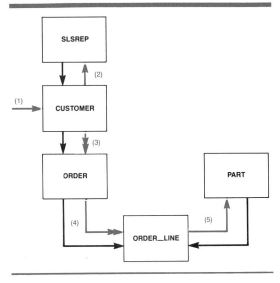

Other helpful information can be indicated on the LAM. In Figure 12.25, the fields to be accessed are indicated on the right. The numbers to the left of the arrows indicate the expected numbers of records to be accessed. Thus, we expect to access a single CUSTOMER record, a single SLSREP record, two ORDER records, followed by four ORDER_LINE records *for each order*, and finally one PART record *for each order line*. Note that this implies we will access eight ORDER_LINE records and eight PART records altogether.

DATABASE ACTION DIAGRAMS

Once a logical access map has been created, design of the algorithms can begin. Martin suggests that the designer begin with the LAM and ask three questions for each step in the LAM as follows (see [5]):

1. Under what conditions should we proceed?
2. What is to be done to the data?
3. What other operations are to be performed?

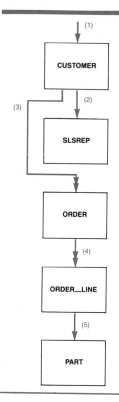

FIGURE 12.24
Sample Logical
Access Map (LAM)

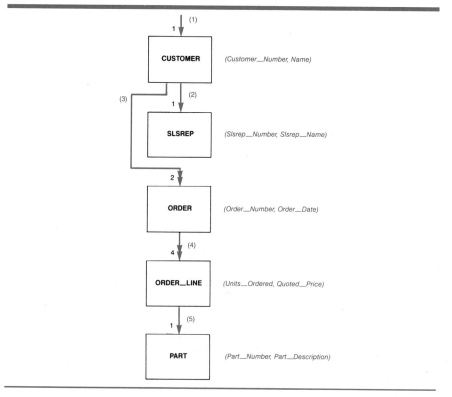

FIGURE 12.25
Expanded LAM

The designer uses the response to these questions to create a **database action diagram** (DAD). The DAD is composed of appropriate combinations of the special symbols shown in Figure 12.26. Figure 12.27 shows the DAD for application three. Note that in addition to the symbols it displays, Figure 12.27 contains two arrows, one from RETRIEVE GIVEN CUSTOMER to RETRIEVE ORDER RECORD and another from RETRIEVE ORDER RECORD to RETRIEVE ORDER LINE. These arrows indicate one-to-many relationships (SETS, if this is a CODASYL DBMS) between these record types. There are also commands that are not contained in the bubbles, such as "Print customer number and name". These are non-database-related commands. Finally, you will notice that the bubbles are labeled with the name of the record type upon which the given action will take place. If

FIGURE 12.26a
List of symbols for
Database Action
Diagrams (DAD's)
(continued on the
following page)

DATABASE ACTION DIAGRAM SYMBOLS

1. ACTION – An operation (add, change, delete, retrieve) that is applied to a single record.

   The symbol for an action is an oblong:

   Examples: (Add sales rep)   (Change customer address)

2. COMPOUND ACTION – An action that is applied to multiple occurrences of a record type.

   The symbol for a compound action is an oblong with a double bar:

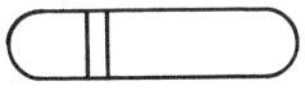

   Examples: [| SORT SALES REP RECORDS BY NAME]

   [| SELECT CUSTOMER WHERE CREDIT LIMIT = 300]

3. SELECTION – (IF/THEN structure)

   The symbol is a bracket with a partition:

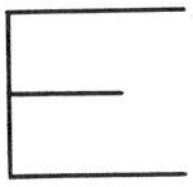

   Example:

   IF CURRENT_BALANCE > CREDIT LIMIT
   print "CUSTOMER",CUSTOMER–NUMBER "OVER CREDIT LIMIT"
   ELSE
   (CHANGE CREDIT LIMIT TO CREDIT LIMIT + 100)

FIGURE 12.26b

4. ITERATION — (Looping)

The symbol is a double bracket:

Example:

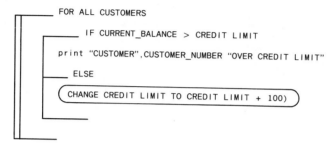

FOR ALL CUSTOMERS

IF CURRENT_BALANCE > CREDIT LIMIT

print "CUSTOMER",CUSTOMER_NUMBER "OVER CREDIT LIMIT"

ELSE

CHANGE CREDIT LIMIT TO CREDIT LIMIT + 100)

FIGURE 12.27
Sample Database
Action Diagram (DAD)

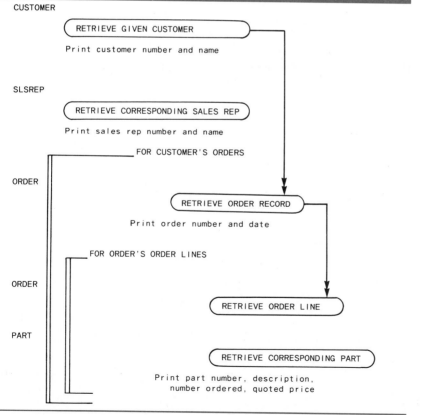

CUSTOMER

RETRIEVE GIVEN CUSTOMER

Print customer number and name

SLSREP

RETRIEVE CORRESPONDING SALES REP

Print sales rep number and name

FOR CUSTOMER'S ORDERS

ORDER

RETRIEVE ORDER RECORD

Print order number and date

FOR ORDER'S ORDER LINES

ORDER

RETRIEVE ORDER LINE

PART

RETRIEVE CORRESPONDING PART

Print part number, description,
number ordered, quoted price

you compare this DAD with the LAM given for the same application, you will see that it is effectively an elaboration of the LAM, i.e., it explains the actions that are required to support it.

For additional information on subschema and application design, see [1], [3], [5], [6], and [7].

2.9 SUMMARY

In this chapter, we studied the physical level of database design, the process of designing the database that will be implemented on a particular DBMS. Before this phase of design can begin, the information level of design, studied in chapters 6 and 7, must be completed. The final information-level design provides the input for the physical design. Whereas the goal of the information level was a clean design, free of problems and capable of satisfying each individual user's needs, during the physical design another criterion is added: satisfactory performance.

We saw that physical design is best done in two phases. The first phase consists of creating a legitimate design for the DBMS that will be used, one that retains as much of the character of the information-level design as possible. We discussed in detail how to accomplish this for a relational model system and for a CODASYL system and briefly indicated how it would be done with a hierarchical or inverted file system. The second phase consists of tuning this design to achieve optimum (or close to optimum) performance. This process consists of making changes to the design to improve it. We discussed the types of changes that could be made at this point to produce other possible designs, together with their advantages and disadvantages of the changes. A thorough understanding of the pros and cons will often make decisions concerning some of the possible changes obvious.

After making all of the obvious changes, however, we will often be faced with a number of possibilities where it is not clear whether the change is wise or not. We are thus faced with a number of potential alternative designs. We discussed how to attempt to choose the best design from among them. To this end, we examined the process of calculating the size of a database given an actual design and projected volumes of occurrences of various entities. We discussed the process of acquiring estimates on performance through the use of logical record accesses (LRAs) as well as the strengths and weaknesses of this approach. We reviewed some ways of overcoming the weaknesses of this approach when necessary.

Finally, we briefly discussed the use of logical access maps (LAMs) and database action diagrams (DADs) as tools for the development and documentation of algorithms.

REVIEW QUESTIONS

1. Describe the process of mapping an information-level design to a design for a relational model system. Describe in detail how the relations and keys are determined. Describe

how other restrictions will be handled.

2. Describe the process of mapping an information-level design to a design for a CODASYL system. Describe how records, fields, and sets are determined. Describe how location modes are assigned.

3. Describe the general process of mapping to a hierarchical system.

4. Describe the general process of mapping to an inverted file system.

5. What factors should be considered when calculating the total space required by a database?

6. Define logical record access (LRA). What is the difference between a logical record access and a physical record access? Which one gives a more accurate picture of the true performance that might be expected from a system? Why do we choose to use LRAs? What is meant by a weighted total of LRAs? What is transport volume? Why is transport volume sometimes considered in the process of choosing a design?

7. What is a logical access map (LAM)? How is it used?

8. What is a database action diagram (DAD)? What is the relationship between a LAM and a DAD?

EXERCISES

1. Illustrate mapping to the relational model by mapping the design you created in exercise 3 of chapter 6 to the relational model.

2. Illustrate mapping to the relational model by mapping the design given in section 6 of chapter 6 to the relational model.

3. Illustrate mapping to the CODASYL model by mapping the design you created in exercise 3 of chapter 6 to the relational model.

4. Illustrate mapping to the CODASYL model by mapping the design given in section 6 of chapter 6 to the relational model.

In exercises 5 through 10, illustrate each suggested change to a relational model design, using your solution to exercise 2 as an example. Give an example of such a change, together with a reason you might consider for making the change and a reason for which you might choose not to make the change. If no example in the design illustrates such a change, discuss the change in general terms.

5. Splitting relations.

6. Combining relations.

7. Creating non-1NF relations.

8. Creating non-2NF relations.

9. Creating non-3NF relations.

10. Creating indexes.

In exercises 11 through 23, illustrate each suggested change to a CODASYL model design, using your solution to exercise 4 as an example. Give an example of such a change together with a reason for which you might consider making the change and a reason for which you might choose not to make the change. If no example in the design illustrates such a change, discuss the change in general terms.

11. Splitting records.
12. Combining records.
13. Using system-owned sets.
14. Using sorted sets.
15. Using pointer arrays.
16. Using multimember sets.
17. Adding sets.
18. Including the key of the owner in a member record.
19. Changing a CALC record to V I A SET.
20. Changing a V I A SET record to CALC.
21. Changing the set in the V I A SET.
22. Requesting prior pointers.
23. Requesting owner pointers.

In exercises 24 and 25, illustrate the suggested change to any model design, using your solution to exercise 2 as an example. Give an example of such a change, together with a reason for which you might consider making the change and a reason for which you might choose not to make the change. If no example in the design illustrates such a change, discuss the change in general terms.

24. Encoding data.
25. Including derivable data.

Exercises 26 through 28 pertain to the CODASYL schema shown in Figure 12.19. In each exercise, you are to make the indicated change to the schema and then redo the calculations shown in Figures 12.20 and 12.21 concerning the size of the database and the weighted total of LRAs.

26. Add a system-owned set in which the member is the CUSTOMER record and in which prior pointers are requested.
27. Include the number and name of the sales rep who represents a customer in the CUS–TOMER record.
28. Include the number and description of the part in the ORDER_L I NE record.

REFERENCES

1] Atre, S. *Data Base: Structured Techniques for Design, Performance and Management*. Wiley-Interscience, 1980.

2] Date, C. J. *A Guide to DB2*. Addison-Wesley, 1984.

3] Hawryszkiewycz, I. T. *Database Analysis and Design*. SRA, 1984.

4] Kroenke, David. *Database Processing*. 2d ed. SRA, 1983.

5] Martin, James. *Managing the Data Base Environment*. Prentice-Hall, 1983.

6] McFadden, Fred R., and Hoffer, Jeffrey A. *Data Base Management*. Benjamin Cummings, 1985.

7] Teorey, Toby J., and Fry, James P. *Design of Database Structures*. Prentice-Hall, 1982.

THE FOURTH-GENERATION ENVIRONMENT

3.1 INTRODUCTION

Since the early 1950s firms have been using computers to handle both common business applications, such as payroll, accounts receivable, and inventory control, and more specialized applications, such as airline reservations and the computer-aided design of new products, in more productively and more cost effective ways. It is only during the past few decades, which is a relatively short period of time, that firms have been using computers, yet computer applications have already undergone significant improvements in terms of speed, cost, capability, reliability, and ease of use. These improvements are due to the advances in both hardware and software technology. Let's very briefly trace the progression of these advances.

HARDWARE GENERATIONS

Computer experts usually characterize each major hardware advance by its primary electronic component, and each major advance is commonly referred to as a generation. The first generation of computers used vacuum tube components. A switch to transistor components in the late 1950s led to the second computer generation, which lasted until the mid-1960s. Through the remainder of the 1960s, the third computer generation relied upon integrated circuits. Since the beginning of the 1970s, we have been in the fourth computer generation, in which thousands of circuits are placed on a single chip using large-scale integration (LSI) or very-large-scale integration (VLSI) technology. Improvements continue to occur as chip circuitry becomes more densely packed and as the functions performed by the hardware components become more sophisticated.

Each successive hardware generation has brought an increase in speed as the circuits have become more densely packed and more sophisticated. The reduction in size, improved manufacturing methods, and increased competition have additionally led to successive reductions in cost.

At the same time, peripheral devices have matured from the punched-card and simple printer configurations of the early generations to the terminal and laser printer technology of today. Magnetic disk has become the predominant secondary storage device for storing a firm's data.

SOFTWARE GENERATIONS

Major developments have also occurred in the software available to interact with advancing hardware technology. Each major software development is also referred to as a generation, though the time spans of the software and hardware generations do not exactly overlap.

FIRST AND SECOND SOFTWARE GENERATIONS

Machine language was the single programming language available for use with the earliest computers. This first software generation was replaced in the 1950s by assembly language, a more productive and less error-prone symbolic programming language that was equivalent to machine language. Both these first two generations of programming languages were executed on computers either with simple operating systems or with no operating system at all. Only one program at a time could be processed by the computer in a batch-processing mode. There were no database management systems, and data communications was in its infancy. Compared with the software environments of today, the first two software generations were primitive; but they did offer definite improvements over the alternative of manual processing.

THIRD SOFTWARE GENERATION

The introduction of high-level programming languages such as FORTRAN in 1957 and COBOL in 1960 (and hundreds of others over the years) signaled the start of the third software generation. These languages have command structures that are closer to English in syntax than are machine and assembly languages, and so they are considered to be at a higher level than the first- and second-generation programming languages. In addition, a single third-generation command translates to many machine-language instructions. This feature, plus the English-like syntax, led to significant productivity gains in the development and maintenance of application programs. In addition, industrywide standards for languages like COBOL allowed programs in these languages to be *portable*, meaning that the same program could run on various brands of computers with a minimal amount of alteration.

Programs in high-level languages do not execute as rapidly as those written in machine and assembly language. But the enormous demand for new programs and changes to existing programs would have required larger numbers of programmers than could be supplied. Also, the continued increase in programmer salaries combined with the continued decrease in hardware cost and increase in hardware speed made the use of high-level languages more cost effective.

The third-generation software environment saw the development of mature operating systems with multiprogramming capabilities (two or more programs executing concurrently) which, together with data communications, provided alternatives to batch processing. *Transaction processing*, for example, allows users to enter their own data and to query the database through terminals.

Database management systems got their start and flourished during this third software generation. Vendors of these DBMS products eventually added capabilities in such areas as query languages, report writers and data dictionaries.

New methods of developing software appeared during the 1970s. Structured analysis and design, top-down methodologies, structured programming, and other software engineering techniques helped improve the quality and maintainability of programs and helped increase programmer productivity. Also, top-quality packaged software became more readily available for common business functions. Thus, packaged software became a viable alternative to the in-house development of common application systems.

FOURTH SOFTWARE GENERATION

Within the past few years we have entered the fourth software generation. A DBMS that manages a firms's database is at the heart of this environment. Several other components are integrated with the DBMS. Functioning together, the DBMS and these other components constitute the **fourth-generation environment**. Since the DBMS is the foundation of this environment, the fourth-generation environment and its components are worthy of study in this book on database and are covered in this chapter. In section 13.2 we investigate some of the fundamental motivations for this environment, provide an overview of its components, and discuss the information center concept. The data dictionary component is covered in section 13.3. In section 13.4 we describe fourth-generation environment components such as program generators, report writers, screen generators, and query languages. Fourth-generation languages are covered in section 13.5. In addition, the technique of prototyping an application system through the use of fourth-generation components is discussed. Finally, we present in section 13.6 some of the emerging innovations in the fourth-generation environment that are leading us into the fifth-generation environment.

.2 OVERVIEW OF THE FOURTH-GENERATION ENVIRONMENT

Both traditional forms of application languages and the traditional system development life cycle used during the first three software generations are undergoing fundamental changes as we emerge into the fourth-generation environment. Before discussing the fourth-generation environment and its components, we will first explore the reasons why these changes are occurring.

MOTIVATION FOR THE FOURTH GENERATION ENVIRONMENT

Of course, change has been the only constant in the computer field since its inception. Innovative developments occur almost daily in hardware and software technology. This innovation is being shaped more by the demands of the marketplace now than ever before. Several factors have forced development of the fourth-generation environment.

PROGRAMMER SHORTAGE

First, the effective use of programming languages from the first three software generations requires well-trained programmers. This has posed a chronic problem, as there have never been enough such programmers to meet the demand. Additionally, this demand has edged salaries for programmers higher and higher. As a result, firms in need of programmers have been seeking alternate means for developing application systems.

INCREASED DEMAND FOR PROGRAMS

Second, the demand by firms for application programming work has increased consistently over the years. Long-time users of computers experience an ongoing need for maintenance and enhancement changes to existing programs. And these users have a constant backlog of new application system requests as they find more and more practical uses for their computers.

The demand for application programming work has accelerated over the past few years with the proliferation of computers, especially the low-cost microcomputers used by smaller firms and individuals. Interestingly enough, it was the development and continued improvement of the electronic *spreadsheet* capability that has been one of the principal causes of growth in the microcomputer area. The spreadsheet is a fourth-generation software tool that lends itself well to use by nontechnical users. So a software innovation has been fueling the sales of microcomputer hardware. This is a recurring phenomenon, as advancing hardware has made possible innovative types of software and as advancing software has extended the research and development boundaries of hardware technology.

The shortage of programmers and the consistent, increased demand for computerization by firms have combined to force more and more nontechnical people to develop their own applications. This in turn has led to a need for easier-to-use software. Both hardware manufacturers and software vendors have a vested interest in this development. The third-generation environment matured to the point where it could no longer sustain the significant sales and profit increases these companies had grown used to. So a low-cost, easy-to-use fourth-generation environment has provided a means of selling new products to existing computer users and a way to exploit new computer markets. Frequently, however, it has been new, start-up companies that have taken the lead in developing innovative capabilities in the fourth-generation environment; VisiCorp's VisiCalc spreadsheet (the first electronic spreadsheet ever developed) is just one example.

SYSTEM DEVELOPMENT PROBLEMS

The problems inherent in the traditional way of developing computer application systems are the third major cause of the transition to the fourth-generation environment. Usually called the *system development life cycle*, the traditional software development approach is a multiphased methodology in which analysis of the users' requirements is followed up with the design and eventual implementation of a computer solution that satisfyies these requirements. The major problems with the system development life cycle center around the time it takes to develop a system, the quality of the delivered system, and the degree to which the delivered system satisfies user requirements.

First, using third-generation programming languages, it takes much too long to develop a system of even moderate complexity. Many months or a year or two can elapse between the start of system development and the production use of the system. Users become impatient, and requirements often change during development. Meanwhile, the backlog of other developmental work increases. And users have been known to postpone requesting new developmental work because of the large backlog; this unrequested work is often referred to as the *invisible backlog*.

Second, it is virtually impossible to create error-free systems using conventional third-generation languages. Though systems of exceptional quality are occasionally developed, they are rare indeed. Errors can range from ones that are irritating nuisances to ones that can compromise the database by allowing unacceptable values to occur or by altering values illegally. And most systems suffer from a variety of errors across this range. Systems are simply too complex to be developed error-free with traditional approaches. Various structured methodologies do help to minimize errors, but they do not eliminate them.

Third, when systems are completed and installed, they more often than not fall short of the users' desires. Even if a system has been perfectly developed according to the written specifications prepared during the analysis phase, the user often finds the result less than satisfactory.

"Users don't know what they want until you give them what they asked for" is a famous comment that describes this user satisfaction problem. Though the statement may appear on the surface to be accusatory, there is justification for it. Imagine what it would be like if you were a user trying to picture how a future system would operate, and all you had to go on was a document consisting of written specifications filled with charts and diagrams. You would have to approve these specifications at the end of the analysis phase. It would be similar to what you would have to go through if the builder for your new home required you to approve construction on the sole basis of a written description of what was needed in the home, without any blueprints or a model home to review at the same time. The house would be bound to turn out differently in many ways from the way you pictured it.

WHAT IS THE FOURTH-GENERATION ENVIRONMENT?

In order to overcome these problems, the computer industry has worked to develop a hardware/software environment that is easier to use and more productive than that of preceding generations. The new environment has also become more integrated as software vendors have tied together more and more tools to work in concert with one another. The software now handles a great deal of the procedural work, so that the programmer and user can concentrate on the problems being solved instead of having to come up with the method of solution. As a result, the quality of the developed system is better, there are fewer errors, and the interface between the user and the computer is much improved.

If the first three software generations can be called the age of the programmer, then the fourth software generation is the age of the user and the analyst. Although programmers are still integral to the functioning of the information systems department, more and more software tools are simple enough to be used both by users and analysts. In the following paragraphs of this section, we will give an overview of the fourth-generation tools, from the perspective first of the programmer and then of the user. In later sections of this chapter, each of the tools will be covered in greater depth.

THE PROGRAMMER'S FOURTH-GENERATION ENVIRONMENT

Figure 13.1 shows a fourth-generation, multi-user environment from the perspective of the programmer. The programmer sits at an interactive workstation, which is either a terminal or a personal computer serving as a terminal. From this single workstation the programmer performs all the work required to develop and maintain an application system. For example, the programmer can key in a high-level language program written in COBOL, test the program, document it, and request that the completed program be migrated from the test environment to the production environment.

Or the programmer can use any of the fourth-generation software tools shown in Figure 13.1 to develop a program solution for a particular problem. The core components of this environment are a DBMS and a **data dictionary**. Although the DBMS may conform to any of the data models we have studied, it is becoming more and more common for the DBMS to follow the relational model. The data dictionary component permits the programmer to fully define all relations and the characteristics of all attributes.

The other components interact with the data dictionary and the DBMS in carrying out their functions. Either a **fourth-generation language (4GL)**, a **program generator**, a **report writer**, or a **screen generator** can be used to rapidly create an application program. Or combinations of these tools may be used in solving a given problem. For example, the functions of a 4GL, a report writer, and a screen generator can be combined to perform integrated functioning in order to achieve a solution to a given problem. The tools, in other words, are intended to be used with ease either together or singly, according to the requirements of any particular situation.

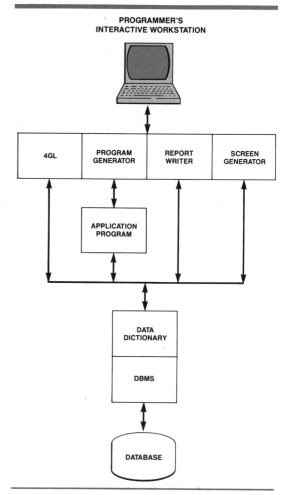

FIGURE 13.1
The programmer's fourth-generation environment

THE USER'S FOURTH-GENERATION ENVIRONMENT

Easier-to-use, more productive, and more highly integrated software products for use by programmers and other computer experts represent part of the fourth-generation environment. The other part of the environment consists of tools for use by nontechnical people, that is, the users themselves.

Figure 13.2 shows a typical fourth-generation environment for a user connected to a mainframe computer. The user's personal computer acts as a terminal to the host mainframe computer. Programmer-created application programs are managed by a **teleprocessing monitor**, which also manages the use of the terminals connected to the production mainframe environment. The user can create ad

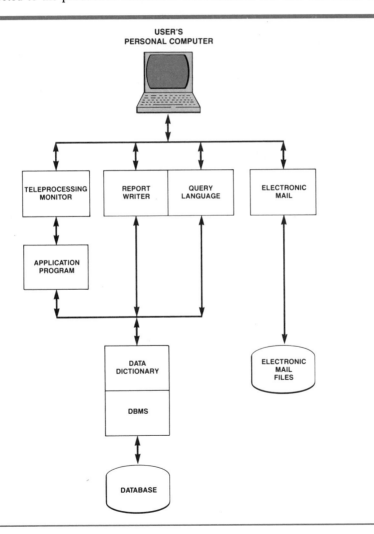

FIGURE 13.2
The user's mainframe
fourth-generation
environment

hoc reports, using either the report writer or query language facilities. All these software capabilities are again interfaced through the core components of the data dictionary and a DBMS. Additionally, the user can communicate with other mainframe users through an electronic mail software capability.

The software tools shown in Figure 13.2 are just a few of those that are available to users in today's fourth-generation environment. The full complement of tools is best explained in the context of the **information center** concept.

THE INFORMATION CENTER

There are two general categories of user computer-processing requirements. The first category consists of those requirements which are best handled by programs created and maintained by the information systems department. These programs interact with databases that require central control or must be shared by multiple users. Also in this first category are those requirements which have complex functions; these are best handled through programs constructed by an experienced computer programmer.

The second category of user computer-processing requirements consists of simple reports and queries or simple stand-alone information systems. Though these requirements can be handled by programmers, more and more firms today are having the users themselves handle them. Users have the best understanding of their total business requirements, their problems, and their information-processing needs. If easy-to-use software products are available for their use, it is most productive for the firm to have users solve their simplest information needs.

The **information center** serves as an adjunct to the information systems department and is designed to allow users to productively satisfy their own needs for information. An information center is typically staffed by information systems personnel who are expert in the use of the tools (i.e., software products) of end user computing. The function of the information center is to make these software tools available to users and to train users to use the tools effectively. Users are encouraged to solve their own information needs with the tools and to use the information center as a resource for assistance whenever necessary.

The information center was first introduced by IBM Canada in 1972 as a way to help overcome the various third-generation problems described earlier in this section. The great majority of firms now use the information center concept, though it is not always referred to in this way by every firm. Some firms have multiple information centers. For example, if there are large numbers of users at several decentralized locations, each location may have its own information center. Or a large university may have one information center for academic end user computing and one for administrative end user computing. Or a large corporation may have one specialized information center for use by the marketing and production staffs and another one for use by financial analysts and accountants.

If a user had access to the mainframe environment shown in Figure 13.2, the information systems department staff who developed the application program would be responsible for training the user in its use and for creating the user manual for the program. On the other hand, the information center staff would be responsible for training the user in the use of the report writer, query language, and electronic mail facilities.

The responsibilities of the information center, however, extend beyond the mainframe environment. The use of the personal computer is widespread throughout most firms today, and the information center provides training and support for a full line of personal computer software tools.

Frequently, the data that the user wants to manipulate on a personal computer already exists in the mainframe central database. The data does not have to be reentered manually on the personal computer; Figure 13.3 shows an alternate method that is gaining in popularity. The required data is extracted from the central database into a flat file on the mainframe computer through the use of a normal DBMS capability such as a report writer, query language, or utility. Special *uploading/downloading* software is then used to transfer the flat file from disk storage on the mainframe computer to hard disk or floppy disk storage on the personal computer. This process of transferring data from a mainframe computer to a personal computer is called **downloading**. Finally, the batch-loading facility of the microcomputer DBMS can be used to place the file onto the local database for processing by the user. If data exists on the local database and is needed on the central database, the entire process shown in Figure 13.3 can be reversed; the uploading/downloading software can be used to transfer data from the personal computer to the mainframe computer. This process is called **uploading**.

Once the user has the required data on the personal computer either through downloading or data entry, a large number of software tools can be used to manipulate the data. Figure 13.4 on the following page, shows a typical complement of tools. Again, the core components consist of a DBMS and a data dictionary integrated with the DBMS. The other tools are available as stand-alone products or can be bundled together as one integrated product. All these software tools (graphics, spreadsheet, word processing, fourth-generation language, screen generator, report writer, and query language) will be discussed further in later sections of this chapter.

As you can see, the information center staff must be fluent in a wide variety of hardware, software, and data communications functions. Increasingly, information centers are establishing guidelines and policies for the proper management of user computing within the firm. For example, it may be that only specific brands and models of personal computers are recommended for purchase by user departments. Likewise, users may be required to make their choice of specific software tools from among those recommended by the information center staff. In this way, a degree of compatibility between user-developed application systems is guaranteed.

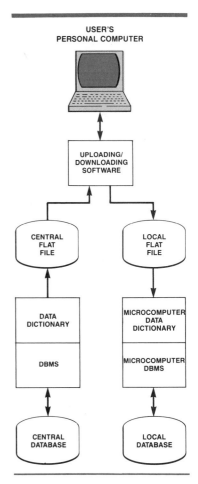

FIGURE 13.3
Downloading from
the central database
to a local database.

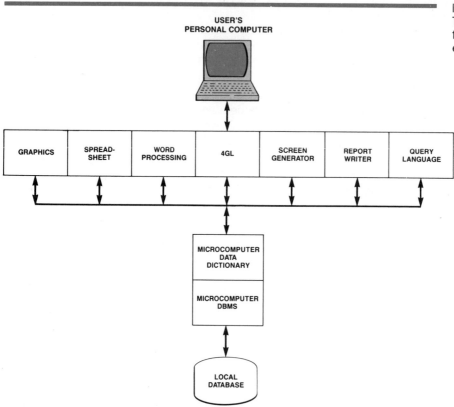

FIGURE 13.4
The user's local
fourth-generation
environment

13.3   THE DATA DICTIONARY

Most database management systems today have a data dictionary component. A **data dictionary** is a central storehouse of data about the entire firm's data. It is a database, or set of files, containing the definition, characteristics, structure, and usage of data within a firm. Often the word *metadata* is used as a synonym for "data about data," so that a data dictionary can be viewed as a storehouse of a firm's metadata.

A distinction is frequently made between a data dictionary and a data directory. In this context, a data dictionary contains the fundamental definitions, characteristics, and uses of data, i.e., it describes what the data is; and a data directory contains additional information about the data, such as where it is stored and how it is stored. For our purposes, this distinction is not necessary, and we will consider the data dictionary to be the comprehensive storehouse about a firm's data.

A **data dictionary system** is a system that stores, maintains, and reports on the contents of the firm's data dictionary. It is a set of programs to manage the data dictionary capability. This is the **catalog** function of a DBMS described in chapter 2.

As we proceed through this section, we will see that the data dictionary system provides information both to the users of the database environment and to the database environment itself. A data dictionary system may be a manual system or a computer-based system. Since most firms today use computer-based data dictionary systems, we will restrict our discussion to them.

DATA DICTIONARY CONTENT

The data dictionary is capable of storing a wide variety of documentation about a firm's data. Figure 13.5 lists a representative range of information that is stored in a comprehensive data dictionary. A data dictionary documents not only the firm's data but also the processes acting on the data and the environment in which the data exists.

DATA DICTIONARY FIELD ENTRIES

The data itself is documented from the field level to the database level. For each level the data dictionary entities (note that entity is used in this section to refer to each of the items shown in Figure 13.5; for example, field, group, file, program, report, system) and the relationships between entities at that level are defined, as well as the relationships between entities at different levels. For example, for each field we would store the following information:

- name of the field and any synonyms or aliases. For example, we might have a field in the data dictionary named "Customer Current Balance." Users within the firm might refer to this same field by using synonymous names, such as "Outstanding Balance," "Customer Outstanding Balance," "Current Balance," "Customer's Receivable Balance," and "Amount Owed." All these alternative names should be documented in the data dictionary. In addition, the names by which the field is known within programs (CURRENT–BALANCE within a COBOL program or CURBAL within an Assembler program, for example), within database entities (CURRBAL within a DL/I DBD or CURRENT_BALANCE within a DB2 relation), or anywhere else within the firm should appear in the data dictionary.
- description and definition.
- type (e.g., character, alphabetic, or numeric).
- representation (e.g., integer, zoned decimal, or packed decimal).
- length (e.g., number of bytes, number of characters, or number of decimal positions).
- output format for printing and display purposes.
- default value.
- validation rules (e.g., discrete or continuous range of values and cross-validation with other fields).
- derivation formula if a calculated value.
- number of occurrences if a repeating field.
- responsible users (which department or user(s) are primarily responsible for initial entry of the field value and for maintenance of the field value).

```
Data
     Field
     Group
     Record
     File
     File Relationships
     User Views
     Database
Processes
     Program
     Report
     Screen
     Transaction
     Job
Environment
     System
     Department (People)
     Terminal
     Communication Line
     Disk Storage
     Processor
     Operating System
```

FIGURE 13.5
A representative range of information stored in the data dictionary

- security (security codes for updating versus retrieval).
- key information (Is this a primary, candidate, foreign, or secondary key? If so, for which relations? What are the rules for nulls, update, deletion, and other restrictions?).
- If multiple or decentralized databases are used, where specifically is this field located?
- frequency of use and frequency of update.

In addition, a large number of relationships must be documented for the field. For example, which groups, records, user views, and databases contain this field? Which programs retrieve or update this field? Which reports, screens, and transactions include this field? Where specifically is this field located, that is, what medium is used to store this field and where exactly within the record is it stored?

DATA DICTIONARY REPORT ENTRIES

So for a given field there is a great deal of information that must be stored in the data dictionary. And fields are just one of the entities from Figure 13.5 that are documented in the data dictionary. Rather than explain everything that would be placed in the data dictionary for each entity in Figure 13.5, we will select one other entity, reports, as an illustration. For each report we would store in the data dictionary the following information:

- the report name
- frequency of print
- number of copies and report distribution
- any special form required for production of the report
- the report format, including the sequence of fields, their exact positioning and format, subtotals and grand totals required
- all calculations
- rules for excluding or including records and fields
- the program name that produces the report and the job name that includes that program's execution
- transactions used or created by the report program
- the system that includes this report

ENTRY AND MAINTENANCE OF DATA DICTIONARY INFORMATION

For each of the other entities shown in Figure 13.5, and for each entity's relationships to other entities, the data dictionary would contain information that is relevant and important. A considerable amount of information has to be entered into the data dictionary, too much, it may seem; however, all this information and more must be collected during the development and maintenance lifetime of an information system. Prior to the advent of the data dictionary capability, all this information appeared in written documents that were difficult to correct and maintain. Consequently, the documentation of an information system was often suspect and, therefore, seldom referenced during the system's production life.

Storing all documentation in the automated data dictionary rather than in written documents means that the documentation of an information system can be more easily and more accurately maintained. The entry of documentation into the data dictionary for an information system begins during its conceptual level design, continues through the external and internal level designs, and is modified as necessary during its production life. Most firms will not enter all the data for all their information systems into the data dictionary. Instead, only those information systems whose data is stored in the firm's database are normally documented in the data dictionary. The database administration group is the department within the firm responsible for managing the data dictionary capability and for making this type of decision.

TYPES OF DATA DICTIONARIES

Data dictionaries can be categorized in a number of ways. First, a data dictionary that is **free-standing** runs independent of a specific DBMS. This type is sometimes also called an *independent*, or a *stand-alone*, data dictionary. Most data dictionaries are not free-standing; rather, they are **integrated** (sometimes called *dependent*) data dictionaries that run only in conjunction with specific DBMS product(s).

The trend is toward the integrated data dictionary, and many database management systems have one. However, most integrated data dictionaries do not handle all the items shown in Figure 13.5. Fields and files are usually documented, but not to the extent described previously.

Another way of categorizing data dictionaries is to distinguish between the active data dictionary and the passive data dictionary. A **passive** data dictionary is simply a documentation tool for users of the environment. Information can be entered and maintained and then reported in a variety of ways. There is no interaction between the data dictionary and other environmental components such as programs and the database.

An **active** data dictionary likewise serves as a documentation tool for users of the environment, but it also interacts with the other software components in the environment. The DBMS, programs, and query languages, for example, will not function unless the proper information is stored in the data dictionary and then funneled to these other software components. That's why a data dictionary of this type is described as active: it is actively involved in driving the other software components. The trend is for most of the newer data dictionaries to be active, integrated data dictionaries.

FUNCTIONS OF DATA DICTIONARY SYSTEMS

Data dictionary systems typically support a number of functions. The most common functions, which are described in the following paragraphs, are entry and maintenance, control and management, reporting, and software environment interaction.

ENTRY AND MAINTENANCE

First, a data dictionary system must allow for the entry and maintenance of entities and their characteristics. This capability is implemented in some systems with a keyword language through batch-processed programs. In other, more prevalent systems the entry and maintenance are accomplished through menus and data entry screens in an on-line mode of processing.

Some data dictionary systems permit users to extend the standard capabilities of the system. One way of doing this is by having the system handle additional entities and their characteristics and relationships. Imagine, for example, that a given data dictionary system does not permit the entry and maintenance of user views as a standard part of its functions. If the system allows us to extend its data maintenance capabilities, then we can define the user view and determine what data about user views we want maintained. From this point forward, we could enter and maintain this additional data within the data dictionary system.

CONTROL AND MANAGEMENT

A data dictionary that is integrated with the DBMS most often has its data structured as a part of the database. Granted, this is a special part of the database. However, the normal authorization and recovery services of the DBMS are used to protect the data dictionary against unauthorized update and access and to recover the data in the event of damage. Also, ad hoc questions can be answered through normal query facilities and all other standard capabilities of the DBMS are available for use.

A free-standing data dictionary system normally has built-in security features. The degree to which concurrency control, recovery services, and other management and control functions exist in a free-standing system depends upon the particular data dictionary system.

REPORTING

The data dictionary system must also be able to provide a wide range of reports to the users of the environment. These users represent a wide cross section of the firm. They include the members of the database administration group; programmers, analysts, designers, and others within the information systems department; users; and auditors. Each user group requires reports that address their particular viewpoint and informational needs. Though some reports can be helpful to multiple user groups, each group also has unique reporting needs.

To meet these varying user needs, a data dictionary system should be capable of producing a combination of standard reports and user-defined reports. The standard reports are a fixed part of the system, while the user-defined reports are generated through a report writer component within the data dictionary system.

Some of the standard reports that can be produced by most data dictionary systems are as follows:

- lists of all fields in the database, alphabetized by field name. Particularly useful versions are lists of field names with their descriptions, lists of field names with their synonyms, and lists of field names along with the user area responsible for maintenance of the field within the database.
- reports by user area of the fields for which the user area has entry and maintenance responsibility. Information that often appears includes field name, length, default values, derivation formula, validation rules, and the names of the other user areas that have access to the field.
- reports showing relations and the fields contained within each relation. These reports could be ordered by application system or alphabetically by relation or for selected relations. Normally, the primary key field(s) will be identified.
- detail reports showing all characteristics of fields, records, user views, programs, or any other selected item stored in the data dictionary.
- cross-reference reports showing, for example, all the relations, screens, reports, programs, systems, and users using a field. These reports are especially helpful to programmers involved in the task of performing maintenance on a production application system.
- cross-reference reports that show for each user department the fields, user views, reports, screens, and transactions that it uses.

Other reports besides these may be created as standard informational output from the data dictionary system. Also, most data dictionary systems permit screen output of information similar to that already described, either through standard on-line options or through query facilities. Finally, if a powerful enough report writer capability functions in conjunction with the data dictionary, any type of report at all can be generated, as long as it is based on the data stored in the data dictionary. These user-defined reports are limited only by the imagination of the users working with the report writer capability.

SOFTWARE ENVIRONMENT INTERACTION

If we are working with a passive data dictionary, then entries made to the data dictionary do not cascade to the other software components in the environment; also, entries made to the other software components have no effect on the data dictionary. This means, for example, that the field-level documentation placed in the data dictionary also must be directly entered into the programs and database DDL in an appropriate form. This is not a productive use of the database administrator's time and the programmer's time. Furthermore, inconsistencies may exist between the data dictionary documentation and the data definitions in the other software components. When they do, users rely on the data definitions in the programs and the database and learn to mistrust the documentation in the data dictionary. Often, as a result, the data dictionary system eventually becomes obsolete.

The most exciting data dictionary function involves the interaction of the data dictionary system with the rest of the software environment. This interaction can occur in a variety of ways.

With some data dictionary systems, the interaction occurs by means of output generated by the data dictionary system. This output then serves as input to the other software components. Figure 13.6 illustrates such a data dictionary system. The data dictionary system is shown creating a file of extracted data definitions.

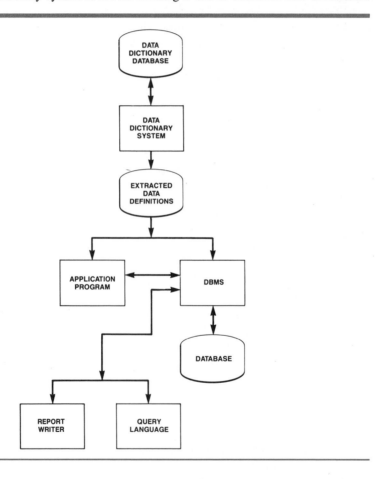

FIGURE 13.6
An interface between the data dictionary and the other software components occurring prior to execution

Actually, this file is more likely to be multiple files. For example, one file would consist of data definitions in a form that could be directly copied into a COBOL or fourth-generation language program. Another file would contain the schema that directly feeds into the DBMS. Still another file would contain a subschema, user view, DL/I PSB, or some other DBMS control data appropriate to the specific DBMS. The report writer and query language facilities would interact with the DBMS and use the control data and parameter information supplied by the data dictionary system. Users could even execute reports and queries that were created by the data dictionary system, fed to the DBMS, then stored in a user library on disk.

This form of interaction is called a **bridge facility** or a **static interface**, since the interaction occurs prior to the execution of the DBMS. The files created by the data dictionary system must be integrated with the appropriate software component, i.e., the COBOL program must be compiled with its supplied data definitions; the fourth-generation language program must be compiled or interpreted with its supplied data definitions; the DL/I PSB must be assembled; and so on.

Some data dictionary systems have a bridge facility that goes in the opposite direction. In this case, the data dictionary system extracts data definitions from application programs and from existing databases and on the basis of these definitions constructs entries in the data dictionary. This is a useful feature if databases and programs exist in the production environment prior to the installation of the data dictionary system; it saves considerable data entry time and ensures consistency.

One of the problems with the bridge facility is that it can be bypassed by users. Entries can be made directly into the data dictionary, and duplicate entries can be made directly into the other software components. When this occurs, there is no guarantee of consistency.

The problem of inconsistency is overcome by another type of data dictionary system, one that furnishes what is called a **dynamic interface** or a **runtime interface**. Such a system is shown in Figure 13.7. This is a true active data dictionary system that is fully integrated with a DBMS. All entries for data definitions and other system documentation are made in one place only, in the data dictionary. The

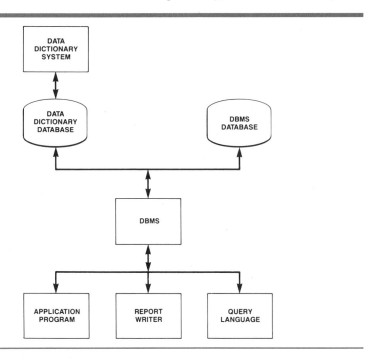

FIGURE 13.7
An interface between the data dictionary and the other software components occurring during execution

DBMS obtains its database definitions directly from the data dictionary database. Since the interaction between the DBMS and the data dictionary occurs during the execution of the DBMS, any data definition changes made to the data dictionary are automatically reflected in the executing DBMS. Software components that interact with the DBMS, such as application programs and the report writer and query language facilities, can obtain their data definitions as late as the time of their execution. This ensures the consistency of data definition throughout the entire software environment.

The tradeoff for this high degree of consistency is the extra time it takes during execution for the DBMS to interact with the data dictionary database. We are actually trading off consistency for productivity. In another sense, however, people are *more* productive as a result of the gain in consistency, even though the DBMS is less productive during its execution. A reduction in the productivity of the computer environment versus an increase in the productivity of the people interacting with it is a common tradeoff.

It is impossible for the creators of data dictionary systems to anticipate all the types of processing that a particular firm might like its data dictionary system to perform. Therefore, some data dictionary systems have an *exit capability* that allows users to program their own routines to interact with the system. This is another way in which the standard capabilities of the data dictionary system may be extended to meet the specific requirements of a firm. There are various applications of the exit capability. It may be used, for example, by the database administrator to create a routine that extends the standard security facility of the data dictionary system. This can make the system more secure or can make the security control approach compatible with the approach already used by the firm. It may also be used to create a routine that provides more complex validity in checking for a field than is ordinarily provided by the data dictionary system.

There is one other important way in which a data dictionary system may interact with the software environment, and that is when a firm ends up having more than one data dictionary system. This can occur when a firm has multiple database management systems, each with its own data dictionary. For example, on the mainframe computer there might be a central DBMS and several application packages, each using its own unique DBMS and data dictionary. Or the firm might be shifting from one DBMS to another or might be introducing a fourth-generation language containing its own data dictionary.

Ideally, in such instances, one of the data dictionaries is targeted as the central dictionary that interfaces with all the other data dictionaries. The interface can be handled in one of two ways. Entries containing all the required information can be made to the central dictionary, then fed to each of the other dictionaries; or entries can be made primarily to one of the subsidiary dictionaries, with a notation made in the central dictionary indicating in which dictionary the detailed definitions of that entity can be found.

COMMERCIAL DATA DICTIONARY SYSTEMS

Hundreds of data dictionary systems are available on the market today. Each DBMS discussed in detail in this book has a data dictionary system that can be purchased or leased from the vendor selling the system. In addition, a number of data dictionary systems can be procured from third-party software companies for use with each DBMS.

Since the number of data dictionary systems is large and constantly growing, it would be impractical to try to provide a survey of these systems here. For a good background on commercially available systems, see [1]. Also, companies like Datapro and Auerbach are good sources of more current descriptions and evaluations of data dictionary systems.

.4 FOURTH-GENERATION ENVIRONMENT COMPONENTS

The data dictionary and DBMS are the core components of the **fourth-generation environment**. What are the other components? You will get different answers to this question depending on which expert you ask. There is even disagreement over what software generation we are currently in, though most experts believe we are in the fourth and on our way to the fifth.

Besides a lack of agreement on what constitutes this environment, there are no standards for its components. Even some of the terminology is not standardized. Multiple terms may apply to the same component or concept, and a single term may be used in different ways by different people. This is to be expected, since the components are undergoing constant refinement and improvement. The establishment of standards at this point would only constrain the creative research and development efforts currently under way.

The lack of standardization does cause problems, however. Different products are difficult to compare and evaluate, since there is nothing to use as a benchmark. Also, if a firm develops a large number of application systems using a given set of products and then decides to switch to another line of products, the process is a costly and difficult one, since the applications have to be redeveloped using the different languages of the new components.

Despite the lack of agreement on fourth-generation environment components, there is a general consensus that several components are part of the environment, and it is these components and their capabilities that we will describe. We will use a generic approach, since the lack of standardization, the large number of available products, and the list of new products being released almost continually prohibit us from an examination of specific software products. For further information on specific products, see [9] and [12] as well as many popular computer periodicals.

In this section we are going to describe report writers, query languages, screen generators, program generators, and teleprocessing monitors. In the next section, we will cover fourth-generation languages and the process of prototyping.

REPORT WRITER

A **report writer** is a nonprocedural language for producing formatted reports from data in a database. A **nonprocedural language** specifies what it is that has to be accomplished but not how to accomplish it. Contrast this with a **procedural language**, in which the programmer, or other user, must specify in detail how to accomplish the solution to the problem. Languages like COBOL, Pascal, Assembler and FORTRAN are procedural.

In most cases, the report generated by the report writer is printed on paper, but it can also be output to a terminal screen or to a disk file. A report writer is sometimes called a *report generator*.

Let's take a look at the two relations, SLSREP and CUSTOMER, shown in Figure 13.8. The attribute names are listed at the top of each column. These are

FIGURE 13.8
The SLSREP and
CUSTOMER relations

SLSREP	SLSREP_NUMBER	SLSREP_NAME	SLSREP_ADDRESS	TOTAL_COMMISSION	COMMISSION_RATE
	3	Mary Jones	123 Main,Grant,MI	2150.00	.05
	6	William Smith	102 Raymond,Ada,MI	4912.50	.07
	12	Sam Brown	419 Harper,Lansing,MI	2150.00	.05

CUSTOMER	CUSTOMER_NUMBER	NAME	ADDRESS	CURRENT_BALANCE	CREDIT_LIMIT	SLSREP_NUMBER
	124	Sally Adams	481 Oak,Lansing,MI	418.75	500	3
	256	Ann Samuels	215 Pete,Grant,MI	10.75	800	6
	311	Don Charles	48 College,Ira,MI	200.10	300	12
	315	Tom Daniels	914 Cherry,Kent,MI	320.75	300	6
	405	Al Williams	519 Watson,Grant,MI	201.75	800	12
	412	Sally Adams	16 Elm,Lansing,MI	908.75	1000	3
	522	Mary Nelson	108 Pine,Ada,MI	49.50	800	12
	567	Joe Baker	808 Ridge,Harper,MI	201.20	300	6
	587	Judy Roberts	512 Pine,Ada,MI	57.75	500	6
	622	Dan Martin	419 Chip,Grant,MI	575.50	500	3

the same names used in the data dictionary for each attribute. Figure 13.9 (opposite), shows a report writer request that we want to execute against the data contained in these two relations. Each request statement has been numbered for convenience of reference; numbering of statements is not normally required. The generated report is shown below the request. Note that there is information in the generated report that was not specified in the request. For example, both the date and page number appear on the first line of the report. These are examples of the defaults inherent in the report writer. Since the majority of reports need the date and page number printed, they will appear on the first line of each page unless suppressed by the requester. If necessary, they may be repositioned elsewhere on the page.

Statement one in the request specifies which attributes should be printed on a detail level. CUSTOMER NAME is a synonym for the attribute NAME used in the relation and defined in the data dictionary. SALES REP is a synonym for SLSREP_NAME, CUSTOMER # is a synonym for CUSTOMER_NUMBER, and

BALANCE is a synonym for CURRENT_BALANCE. Because these synonyms are all stored in the data dictionary, they can be used without further definition.

```
1   PRINT SALES REP, CUSTOMER NAME, CUSTOMER #, BALANCE
2   PRINT GRAND TOTAL RESERVE (CURRENCY)
3       MATCH ON REP NUMBER
4       IN ORDER BY ASCENDING SALES REP, CUSTOMER NAME
5       ALL TOTALS FOR BALANCE
6       COUNT BY SALES REP
7       CALCULATE RESERVE = 2.5% * BALANCE
8       TITLE "CLIENT LIST BY SALES REPRESENTATIVE"
```

FIGURE 13.9
Report writer request and the report it produces based on the SLSREP and CUSTOMER relations

```
11/27/87       CLIENT LIST BY SALES REPRESENTATIVE          PAGE 1

                                     CUSTOMER     CURRENT
       SALES REP      CUSTOMER NAME    NUMBER     BALANCE

       Sam Brown      Don Charles        311      $200.10
                      Mary Nelson        522        49.50
                      Al Williams        405       201.75

       SALES REP TOTAL:   3                       $451.35

       Mary Jones     Sally Adams        124       418.75
                      Sally Adams        412       908.75
                      Dan Martin         622       575.50

       SALES REP TOTAL:   3                     $1,903.00

       William Smith  Joe Baker          567       201.20
                      Tom Daniels        315       320.75
                      Judy Roberts       587        57.75
                      Ann Samuels        256        10.75

       SALES REP TOTAL:   4                       $590.45

       GRAND TOTALS:                            $2,944.80

              RESERVE    $73.62
```

Statements two and seven are closely related. In statement seven we define a temporary field named RESERVE that is calculated during the generation of the report. In statement two we specify that the calculated grand total RESERVE value should be printed at the end of the report and should be formatted in normal currency form. The formats of the other values printed are based on the defaults established in the data dictionary.

Since we are obtaining data from two different relations, statement three specifies the manner in which the two relations should be joined. REP NUMBER is a synonym for SLSREP_NUMBER.

Statement four indicates the sequence for the report. Statement five specifies that subtotals and a grand total should be printed for the CURRENT_BALANCE attribute. Statement six states that a count of the number of detail lines printed for a given sales rep should appear on the report whenever the SALES REP changes in value. The last statement provides the report title.

Notice that the SALES REP name prints on the report only when it changes in value. This is another example of the default concept employed in the report writer. The column headings are another set of defaults built into the data dictionary; these would be the output-heading characteristics for their respective attributes.

It would take a few hundred statements in a procedural high-level language to produce this same report. In our example we have let the nonprocedural report writer and the DBMS determine how to produce the report. We only need to describe the report we want; both the report writer and the DBMS work in conjunction with the data dictionary to accomplish the task we define. A report writer can easily handle more complex processing than we have indicated.

The language is easy to read and to learn. Either a programmer or an end user can create the report writer request. Most firms train their end users to produce ad hoc reports using this capability. In order to obtain greater machine efficiency, however, most predefined reports are still generated by high-level language programs written by programmers.

Report writers are not a recent innovation; they have been around for the past twenty years. As they have evolved along with the software environment, report writers have become easier to use and have been better integrated with the data dictionary and the DBMS.

QUERY LANGUAGE

A **query language** is a nonprocedural language for retrieving information from a database. The retrieved information is typically displayed on a screen but may also be printed on paper or output to a disk file. Query language is a misleading term, since many query languages allow nonretrieval manipulation of the database by way of addition, deletion, and change commands.

Structured Query Language (SQL) and Query By Example (QBE) are two examples of query languages. Chapter 3 offers numerous examples of queries using each of these languages, so we will not provide further examples of them here.

A query language is similar in many ways to a report writer. Both are firmly integrated with the data dictionary capability. Both are intended for nontechnically oriented end users and thus are easy to learn and to use. Both are nonprocedural; a very small number of statements can accomplish a great deal. The report writer example request and SQL are *command driven languages*, which means that language commands, or statements, must be entered according to the precise syntax of the language. Some of the newer report writers and query languages are *menu driven languages*, which means that the user is prompted to respond to choices presented on a screen in a menu- or form-oriented manner. Though both are frequently used for ad hoc processing, either a report writer request or a query may be stored in a library file and executed repeatedly over a period of time.

Many report writers and many query languages can be processed in batch or on-line modes. However, the main objective of a report writer is to produce a hard-copy report, while that of a query language is to display retrieved information on a screen. Consequently, report writers tend to be more compatible with batch processing, and query languages are more on-line oriented. Report writers tend to have more sophisticated output-formatting capabilities, while query languages are built for rapid response.

Other differences between a report writer and a query language are more subtle. Often a product is advertised by a software vendor as a query language when it might be advertised more appropriately as a report writer, and vice versa.

FIGURE 13.10
A data entry screen to be created through use of a screen generator

SCREEN GENERATOR

A **screen generator** is an interactive facility for creating and maintaining display and data entry formats for screen forms. The screen generator allows you to define how the screen is to be *painted*, i.e., how literals are displayed on the screen and how color and other visual attributes are handled. It permits you to define the placement of variable data that the user is to enter or that is to be displayed. Through its interaction with the data dictionary, the screen generator performs validation on values entered by the user. Table lookups, calculations, interaction with the DBMS, and a user exit facility are other functions handled by the screen generator. *Screen painter* and *screen mapper* are two other names for a screen generator.

A screen generator should be easy to use. Some of the older screen generators are batch oriented, but almost all the newer ones are interactive. To illustrate an interactive screen generator, let's suppose we wanted to use one to create the Customer Maintenance data entry form shown in Figure 13.10. The areas in boxes are for values to be entered or displayed as necessary. The literals outside the boxes will be painted on the screen when the form first appears.

Figure 13.11 is the main menu for the interactive screen generator. Choice one for element maintenance lets us define the literal and variable value areas on the screen. Choice two lets us define color blocks on the screen and manipulate these blocks once they have been defined. Choice three allows us to move an entire form on the screen, store the form in a library, combine separate forms together, and otherwise manipulate entire forms. Choice four terminates the screen-generator session.

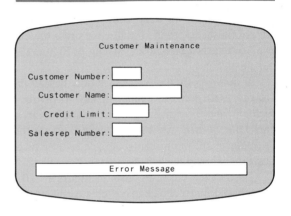

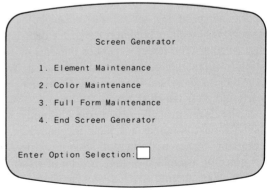

FIGURE 13.11
The main menu for the screen generator.

We start building the Customer Maintenance form by selecting choice one for element maintenance. The element maintenance menu shown in Figure 13.12 is then displayed by the screen generator. We are building a new form, so we select choice one to create a new element.

A similarly formatted menu appears next. On this menu we choose to define a literal on the screen. A blank screen then appears. On the blank screen we use the cursor control keys on the keyboard to move the cursor to the exact position where we want to begin the placement of the literal "Customer Maintenance". Once the cursor has been properly positioned, we enter this literal. We continue to alternate repositioning the cursor and entry of literals until we have fully defined the literal values we want painted on the screen. When we are finished with the literals, we press the enter key and are returned back to the screen in Figure 13.12 for our next choice.

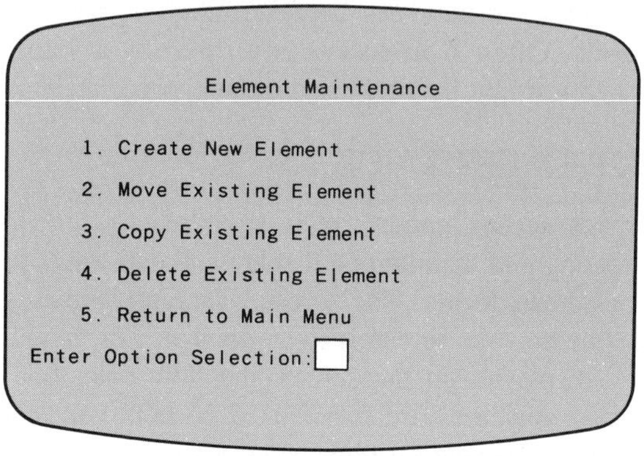

If at any point we aren't sure how best to proceed, we can use a keyboard function key to invoke a *help facility* that will explain our options and the actions we can take. When we have finished using the help documentation, the screen generator returns us back to the exact spot we were at prior to invoking the help facility.

Each of the boxed-in areas in Figure 13.10 is defined separately in a similar fashion. We make choice one ("create new element") in Figure 13.12 and specify that we are defining a variable area on the form, in this case for the boxed-in area for Customer Number. We are then prompted by the screen generator to enter the data dictionary field name or the calculation or our exit routine name for the variable field area we are defining. We also have the option of specifying special screen attributes for the screen area, such as blinking, reverse video, underlining, or color. The screen generator presents us with the screen with the literals we have defined on it. We position the cursor where the variable Customer Number starts and press the enter key.

The creation of the rest of the Customer Maintenance form follows in a similar manner. The screen generator creates a "program" that may need to be compiled or assembled or that may be in a form ready for execution. Figure 13.13 shows the generated screen form with sample user-entered data filled in.

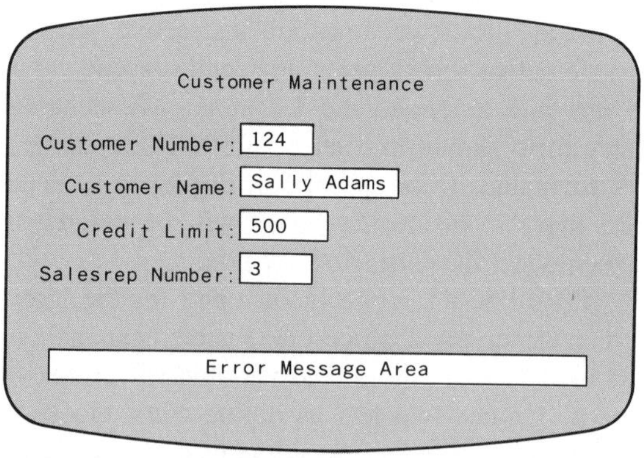

This screen generator approach is easy to use, and we can see our progress each step of the way. We can define the form in a matter of minutes, whereas it takes hours to create a program to handle the same processing. Testing time is

FIGURE 13.12
The element maintenance menu for the screen generator

FIGURE 13.13
A data entry screen filled in with user-entered data

minimal, compared to the length of time it takes to debug a high-level language program. Overall, the screen-generated process is considerably more productive than traditional methods of creating screen forms.

PROGRAM GENERATOR

A **program generator** is a language facility that generates a second- or third-generation language program. The objective of a program generator is to allow a programmer to more productively create and maintain programs written in traditional languages.

A *precompiler* language is one type of program generator. It combines its own unique language features with those of the target language. Another reason for its name is that it is compiled, and the output of the compilation is a source program in the target language.

There are a number of precompiler languages that generate COBOL programs. In these cases, the program is coded in the precompiler language, which is then compiled to create a COBOL program. Either the original precompiler language version of the program or the generated COBOL program can be maintained. The precompiler language increases productivity partly through the use of abbreviated names for data definitions, paragraphs, and so on. When it is compiled into COBOL, fuller names are substituted for the abbreviated names. Another way these languages save time is by automatically providing the standard portions of a COBOL program that remain the same from program to program. Yet another productivity aid is the use of precoded modules with parameters for commonly encountered routines.

One alternative to a program generator is the *skeletal program*. A skeletal program is the skeleton of a high-level language program. High-level languages like Pascal and COBOL have language statements that are fixed from program to program. These statements are already provided in the skeleton program. Normally, a number of different skeleton programs exist for the different common types of programs that need to be created. For example, there may be skeleton programs to produce a report from a file, to update a file in batch mode, to update a file in on-line mode, and so on. Each of these skeletons would have the standard routines already included for programs of that type.

The skeleton serves as the starting point for the program to be created. The skeleton is copied, and then an editor is used to manipulate the language statements in order to tailor them for the specific problem solution. Statements are added as necessary to complete the solution. The skeleton eliminates the bother of a great deal of the program coding that is repetitive from program to program.

TELEPROCESSING MONITOR

One of the functions of a DBMS is to provide integration with support for data communication. It is the purpose of a teleprocessing monitor to handle this function. A **teleprocessing (TP) monitor** is a system software product that controls a host computer's terminal communications and the application programs executed by the terminal users. The type of processing managed by a TP monitor is called **transaction processing**.

All major mainframe DBMS's have a TP monitor component. In addition, most DBMS's work with a number of other TP monitors. IBM's CICS (Customer Information Control System) is the dominant TP monitor in the marketplace today.

Figure 13.14 provides an overview of the relationship of the TP monitor to the DBMS. The TP monitor and the DBMS are placed in their own main memory areas when the production system is started up. The TP monitor scans the terminal

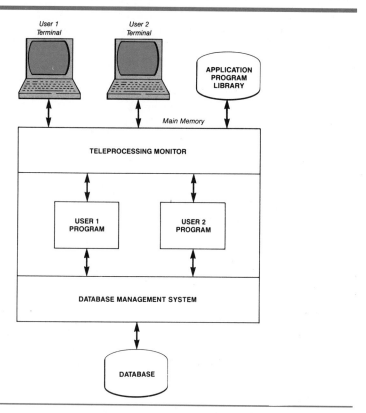

FIGURE 13.14
The use of a teleprocessing monitor to manage terminals and application programs

network, asking one terminal after the other if it has a transaction to submit. This process is called *polling*. (Sometimes a *front-end processor*, which is a mini- or microcomputer connected to the terminal network, handles this polling function instead.) The TP monitor queues the transaction and schedules the application program that handles that transaction type. When main memory becomes available, the program is loaded from the application program library and the program processes the transaction. All database program requests are handled by the DBMS. When the application program completes its execution, program output back to the terminal is passed to the control of the TP monitor. The TP monitor then communicates the output back to the proper terminal.

To perform its functions, the TP monitor must have a great deal of knowledge about the environment it is managing. For example, it must know which communication lines it controls, the type of terminal that is attached to each line, which application program handles each specific type of transaction, and which users are authorized to use specific terminals and transactions. These facts are stored in tables that are under the control of the TP monitor.

Since multiple users may be authorized to use the same type of transaction, the TP monitor must allow for concurrent use of the same application program and must have an authorization services function to control access. Also, it must provide recovery services for the terminal network and the application programs it manages. The TP monitor handles other functions as well, but the functions already mentioned should give you an appreciation for the complexity of the job it does.

Earlier we said that most DBMS products work with a number of different TP monitors. But not just any DBMS and TP monitor will function together properly. Both are complicated software products, and there is some overlap in the functions performed by each. Each must be specifically programmed to interface and function in synchronization with the other.

.5 FOURTH-GENERATION LANGUAGES AND PROTOTYPING

The fourth-generation environment consists of a DBMS, a data dictionary, and the components described in the previous section. Other components, such as spreadsheets, graphics, application generators, modeling tools, and decision-support systems, are also included in the fourth-generation environment as well, but we will not discuss them here.

We have to discuss one other major component of this environment. It is called a **fourth-generation language**, or **4GL**, and is discussed in this section along with the prototyping process.

FOURTH-GENERATION LANGUAGES

Each of the other components of the fourth-generation environment is easily defined, and software products can be categorized according to whether or not they have the characteristics of a given component. It is a different story with 4GLs. There is no common agreement as to what a 4GL is and is not. Let's review two of the more popular definitions and descriptions.

A definition frequently encountered is similar to one presented by Paquette and Sardinas (see [13]). According to them, a 4GL is a complete family of components rather than a single programming language. These components must be easy and productive to use, since end users have to be able to work with them comfortably.

James Martin (see [9]) implies that it should take approximately one-tenth the amount of time to develop a 4GL program as it does to develop an equivalent high-level language program. Martin also places all current nonprocedural languages and some other types of products in the category of 4GL and suggests that *high-productivity language* be used instead of 4GL to more clearly describe these languages.

Many software vendors tout as 4GLs products that range from fairly simple report writers, query languages, and programming languages to extremely comprehensive families of products that handle every conceivable function. 4GL, or fourth-generation language, has a nice state-of-the-art sound, and probably helps market a vendor's product.

But calling a particular software product a 4GL does not tell us anything about what the product does. It would be more helpful if a product were given a category name like Vendor A's ADA compiler, Vendor B's report writer, Vendor C's nonprocedural programming language, Vendor D's teleprocessing monitor, Vendor E's DBMS, or Vendor F's data dictionary. The categorization of each of these products would then give a clue as to its general functional capabilities.

Though we will not attempt to give a precise definition for a 4GL, it may be helpful to talk about what we think should be in one. A 4GL should be a programming language that integrates all the other fourth-generation environment components and complements them by providing any functions not already contained in them. From this description, it is clear that a 4GL has both procedural and nonprocedural aspects.

For an example of what we mean by a 4GL's integration capability, let's suppose we needed to use a TP monitor and a relational DBMS, both integrated with a data dictionary, to process a user's terminal transaction. We would create a screen form using a screen generator. The 4GL program would contain a nonprocedural statement to handle the input from the terminal by way of the TP monitor, an SQL statement to access the database, and another nonprocedural statement to send the output back to the terminal, again under the control of the TP monitor. So the 4GL would be integrating into one program the functions performed by the other components.

As an example of how the 4GL would complement the other components by providing additional functionality, let's suppose data validation were required beyond what the data dictionary and screen generator could provide. Then the previous scenario would need to include some procedural statements to perform these validity checks through a user exit from the screen-generator component.

Some products considered to be 4GLs function approximately along the lines we have just described. But we are not endorsing these products just because they follow our concept of what a 4GL should do. Products, and families of products, should be evaluated by what they do, not by what they are called. For more information on 4GLs, see [4], [8], [9], [10], [11], [12], [13], and [14].

PROTOTYPING

More and more frequently, the collection of components that constitute the fourth-generation environment is being called an *application development system*, while the environment itself is being called the *integrated development environment*. Though these terms may be more descriptive, "fourth generation" is still the phrase most in favor today.

When we put all the fourth-generation components together into an integrated package, the result is a set of high-productivity tools for developing and maintaining application systems. Some firms use these tools in place of traditional languages within the programming phase of the system development life cycle, thus realizing a dramatic decrease in the amount of time needed to program the information system.

However, firms may encounter two major problems when they use these tools simply as a replacement for traditional languages. First, the fourth-generation tools typically are less efficient when executing on the computer. That is, programs take longer to execute and may result in more database accesses and higher usage of other system resources. The lowered machine efficiency makes sense when you consider that some of the tools are interpretive languages rather than compiled languages. Also, these tools are still in their embryonic stage, so they are not as efficient as they eventually will be. Some application systems require a performance level higher than that which can be obtained through the fourth-generation tools, so they are still developed with traditional languages. Even assembly language is used in some cases to gain the highest performance level possible.

The second problem centers on the degree of user satisfaction with the developed production system. If we follow the system development life cycle by continuing to use written specifications as the basis for user requirements, this problem will be maintained; the user must continue to picture the final information system by means of the abstract written specifications. Earlier in this chapter we discussed the difficulties inherent in this approach.

Rather than use the fourth-generation tools as a replacement for traditional languages during the programming phase, many firms have begun using them as an aid in determining the user requirements during the analysis phase. So in place of written specifications as an abstract model for the information system, the fourth-generation tools are used to build an actual working version of the system. The system is constructed in an iterative fashion: The system developers first build an initial system that they feel satisfies user requirements. This is done rapidly, using the highly productive fourth-generation tools. This initial system is then given to the users to work with, which provides feedback on the system's functioning with respect to the user's particular needs. Users are encouraged to be highly critical of the system, and the system undergoes repeated change and critique until they are completely satisfied with it.

When the iterative cycle is completed, the result is a complete, functioning system. The working version of the system is called a **prototype**, and the process of creating the system in this manner is called **prototyping**. This process resembles the procedure used in the engineering world, where a less expensive prototype is created to eliminate the bugs before the final product is designed and produced.

When we prototype an application system, we end up with an application system that satisfies user requirements. People can more easily visualize what they will be getting when they work with a functioning system than they can by reading a written document. Developing a system that satisfies the needs of the users is the ultimate aim of any system development life cycle methodology, and prototyping is very successful in attaining this goal.

If the application system does not demand high performance, then the prototype can serve as the final version of the system and subsequent steps of the system development life cycle can be bypassed. If one of the fourth-generation components available is an *automatic documentation* component, then the user and operations manuals can be generated directly from the completed prototype. All in all, the process results in significant savings in time, money, and frustration.

If the system demands a performance level higher than can be obtained from the fourth-generation tools, then the prototype serves as the definition of the users' requirements. The remaining steps of the system development life cycle are then followed in order to design, develop, and implement the information system through the use of traditional programming languages.

Bernard Boar, in his landmark book on prototyping (see [3]), gives an example of the quantity of work that can be accomplished quickly by using fourth-generation tools. In only six weeks two prototypers were able to create a medium-sized application system. Using traditional programming languages, it would have taken many multiples of the six weeks to develop this same application system.

The high productivity components of the fourth-generation environment have made it possible to prototype application systems. For further details on the benefits, problems, and process of prototyping, see [3], [4], [9], and [10].

13.6 EMERGING SOFTWARE TOOLS

Much of the research and development effort in software technology continues to center around improvements and advancements in fourth-generation and earlier-generation concepts and tools. But there are software tools already available that are considered to be part of the fifth-software generation. **Fifth-generation software** is characterized chiefly by concepts and methods from the field of artificial intelligence. **Artificial intelligence** is the capability of a computer-based system to perform functions normally associated with intelligent human behavior. Examples of these functions include the ability to learn, to reason, and to draw inferences in solving problems.

Natural languages are one such example of fifth-generation software. A **natural language** allows a user to communicate with a computer in human language form by using ordinary English words. The user is not bound by an artificial computer language that has its own syntax and vocabulary. In section 7 of chapter 3, we listed some questions that might be asked by a fictitious natural language called NL:

- What is the name of customer 256?
- Give me the names of the customers of sales rep 6.
- Which ones have a credit limit of $300?

Natural languages rely upon the entries in the data dictionary and on an auxiliary dictionary of common words the language understands. They are not typically built to recognize every conceivable English-like communication a user might enter. Too much processing overhead would be incurred, owing to today's technology, and in many cases there would be great uncertainty on the part of the natural language processor as to the intent of the user. Furthermore, for repetitive processing requests, it is more efficient to use more productive language techniques.

While we are on the subject of more natural interfaces with computers, it should be pointed out that some users interact with computers through pictures and voice input. Picture-oriented input involves the use of special screen symbols, called *icons*, that serves as representations of the functions they perform. The use of a *mouse* or *touchscreen* to select the desired function is popular with this form of interface. Because of processing inefficiencies and vocabulary limitations, however, *voice input* and *output* are principally used in specialized applications.

Another area associated with fifth-generation software is knowledge-based software. A **knowledge-based system** consists of a knowledge database of both data and rules, and it can draw inferences from the stored knowledge. Many natural language systems are actually knowledge-based systems, according to this definition.

One special type of knowledge-based system is the expert system. An **expert system** is a knowledge-based system dedicated to a specific field of expertise. One example of an expert system is Mycin, which was developed by the Stanford University Medical Experimental Computer Facility to diagnose and prescribe treatments for meningitis and bacteremia infections. Mycin has been highly successful in diagnosing these types of infectious diseases and in prescribing treatment for them.

Expert systems are being used to store the knowledge and reasoning rules of an expert in a given specific field. The system is then used by a novice in the field to ask the same questions the expert would ask and to explain to the novice how the conclusions are reached. Thus, expert knowledge and reasoning can be transferred to those who are less expert in a specific field.

In the next few years we will see some stabilization in fourth-generation environment components as well as the continued emergence of fifth-generation products. These developments should make computers easier to use, and the job of developing and maintaining application systems more productive and more accurate. For more details on the topics in this section, see [9].

13.7 SUMMARY

We discussed hardware and software generations and saw that we are currently in the fourth generation for both hardware and software. We pointed out that there is considerable interest in developing improved fourth-generation software tools. A shortage of programmers, the increased demand for programs, and the problems inherent in the traditional system development life cycle are the major factors fostering this interest. The life cycle problems include the large amount of time required, the imperfections in the developed system, and the failure of the developed system to completely satisfy user requirements.

We discussed the large number of diverse products have been developed to improve the productivity of the developers and users of information systems. Some of the fourth-generation tools are intended primarily for the use of programmers, while other tools are excellent aids to user interaction with the computer environment.

We discussed the manner in which the information center provides user-oriented software tools and training for users in their operation both initially and on an ongoing basis. The tools exist on central mainframe computers and on personal computers. The downloading of data from the mainframe to the personal computer and the uploading from the personal computer to the mainframe aid the user in productively moving from environment to environment.

We then investigated the data dictionary, a central storehouse of data about all the firm's data. It contains a wealth of data that is of interest to the users of the software environment and to the environment itself. A data dictionary system stores, maintains, and reports on the contents of the firm's data. Data dictionaries may be free-standing or integrated, and they may be active or passive. Most newer data dictionaries are active and integrated. The data dictionary system must handle entry and maintenance of its data; contol and management of its functioning; reporting; and integration with the software environment. It can interact with the software environment either with a bridge facility or with a runtime interface.

The data dictionary and the DBMS are the core components of the fourth-generation environment. The other components of this environment that we discussed include report writers, query languages, screen generators, program generators, teleprocessing monitors, and fourth-generation languages, all of which tend to be nonprocedural, highly productive, and easy to use. When used together in the prototyping process, these integrated tools can help to rapidly develop an information system. The prototype may end up being the final product, or it may be the basis for the design phase of the system development life cycle.

Finally, we pointed out that, while work proceeds on the fourth-generation environment components, fifth-generation products based on artificial intelligence research are also being released. Natural languages, knowledge-based systems, and expert systems are three examples of fifth-generation components.

REVIEW QUESTIONS

1. What programming language was used during the first software generation? During the second software generation?
2. Name two benefits of high-level programming languages that were not offered by the earlier languages.
3. Name three principal factors that motivated the development of fourth-generation environment components.
4. What is an information center?
5. What is uploading? What is downloading? Sketch the manner in which data flows during these processes.
6. What is a data dictionary? What is metadata?
7. What is a data dictionary system?
8. Name at least five entities maintained in a data dictionary.
9. What data is maintained in a data dictionary for each field?
10. What is the difference between a free-standing and an integrated data dictionary? What is the difference between an active and a passive data dictionary?
11. What four functions does a data dictionary system perform?
12. What is a data dictionary bridge facility? How does this compare with a runtime data dictionary interface?
13. How does a procedural language differ from a nonprocedural language?
14. What is a report writer?
15. What is a query language?
16. What is a screen generator? What does "painted" mean in this context?
17. Name and describe two types of program generators.
18. What two areas are controlled by a TP monitor?
19. What is prototyping?
20. What is artificial intelligence?
21. How do icons fit in with user data entry?
22. What is an expert system?

EXERCISES

1. If the computer system you use for this course has fourth-generation environment tools, draw a diagram showing the relationships between them. Use Figures 13.2 and 13.4 as guidelines.
2. If your DBMS has a data dictionary capability, briefly describe its type (free-standing or integrated, active or passive) and say which field characteristics can be documented.
3. Figure 13.9 shows a generic report writer request and the report it produces. Use the report writer (or query) capability on your computer system to produce this same report.

4. After completing exercise 3, create the same report using a high-level language with which you are familiar. What time savings did you experience using the two different methods?

5. Use your computer system's screen generator capability to produce a data-entry screen similar to the one in Figure 13.13.

REFERENCES

1] Allen, Frank W.; Loomis, Mary E. S.; and Mannino, Michael V. "The Integrated Dictionary/Directory System." *ACM Computing Surveys* 14, no. 2, (June 1982).

2] Atre, S. *Data Base: Structured Techniques for Design, Permance, and Management.* John Wiley & Sons, Inc., 1980.

3] Board, Bernard H. *Application Prototyping: A Requirements Definition Strategy for the 80s.* John Wiley & Sons, Inc., 1984

4] Codd, E. F. "Codd Stresses Importance of Shared Data and Sublanguages." *ComputerWorld* (24 February 1986).

5] Garcia, Beatrice. "The Information Center Adapts to Corporate America." *ComputerWorld* (28 October 1985).

6] Mark L. *Database: Step-by-Step.* John Wiley & Sons, Inc., 1985.

7] Horwitt, Elizabeth. "Redefining the Information Center." *Business Computer Systems* (September 1985).

8] Leavitt, Don. "Fourth-Generation Programming: The End-User Environment." *Software News* (April 1985).

9] Martin, James. *Fourth-Generation Languages, Volume I, Principles.* Prentice-Hall, 1985.

10] Martin, James. *Fourth-Generation Languages, Volume II, Representative 4GLs.* Prentice-Hall, 1986.

11] Mimmo, Pieter. "4GL Part One: Power to the Users." *ComputerWorld* (8 April 1985).

12] Mimmo, Pieter. "4GL Part Two: Power from the Products." *ComputerWorld* (15 April 1985).

13] Paquette, Laurence R., and Sardinas, Joseph L. "Productivity Tools Past, Present and Future." *Data Management* (June 1985).

14] Rowe, Lawrence A. "Tools for Developing OLTP Applications." *Datamation* (1 August 1985).

DATABASE ADMINISTRATION

CHAPTER

.1 INTRODUCTION

You have come a long way in your study of database management. You have studied a large number of technical concepts, issues, strategies, and choices. By taking them a step at a time, you should now feel comfortable with database principles. We need to discuss next how database capabilities are managed and controlled within an enterprise.

The resources of an enterprise include money, materials, machines, and personnel. You are probably familiar with the enterprise's need to manage these resources. Data and information are other resources of an enterprise. Data represents facts and figures about the first four resources and about external entities, such as customers/clients and suppliers. Information, on the other hand, is data organized in a manner that provides specific meaning to executives of the enterprise about all the other resources and about the external entities. Many executives have little direct contact with all these resources and external entities; their view of the enterprise is acquired primarily from information they receive about them. To these executives, information about the enterprise and the enterprise itself are often one and the same.

Recognizing data and information as resources leads naturally to the conclusion that they must be managed in a way similar to that in which the other resources of the enterprise are managed. Data must be gathered and processed into meaningful information in an accurate, cost-effective, and controlled manner in order for the enterprise to meet its goals and objectives in producing goods and services. Where does data come from, and where is information used? Data originates from many sources, both internal and external to the enterprise. Likewise, many people and organizations, internal and external to the enterprise, make use of the information produced. Figure 14.1 on the following page, lists just a few of the many sources of data and destinations of information. Just as many departments within the enterprise play a role in the management and control of money, materials, machines, and personnel, so do many departments participate in the management and control of data and information.

INTERNAL: Budgeting	EXTERNAL: Shareholders
Research and Development	Lenders
Purchasing and Receiving	Suppliers
Inventory Control	Marketing
Production	Customers
Distribution	Competitors
Order Entry	Unions
Sales Analysis	Community Relations
Billing	Local Government
Accounts Receivable	State Government
Cash Receipts	Federal Government
Accounts Payable	Governmental
Fixed Assets	Agencies
Payroll	
General Ledger	

FIGURE 14.1
Sources of data and destinations of information

Though many departments fit into the flow of resources, an enterprise gives primary responsibility for the management and control of particular resources to specific departments. The finance and accounting departments administrate money, while the human resources department administrates personnel, for example. In this chapter we will study database administration, the department that has primary responsibility for the management and control of the data and information resources of an enterprise.

In section 14.2, we will discuss the background of database administration. We will explain why it is an important part of the organization and why it is necessary for optimal use of a DBMS. We also need to review how it has evolved from the time of its inception in order to gain a perspective on typical organizational concerns and on problems involved with the central management and control of data. Finally, we will describe a few of the ways in which an enterprise positions database administration in the organizational structure. The remaining sections of the chapter describe the functions performed by database administration: administrative functions, in section 14.3; application functions, in section 14.4; and technical functions, in section 14.5.

14.2 BACKGROUND OF DATABASE ADMINISTRATION

EARLY DEVELOPMENT

Prior to the use of computers, and even in the early days of their use, each department in an organization was responsible for its own data. Though corporate policies and procedures dictated the manner in which expenses, budgets, and other data should be processed, it was nonetheless left to each department to handle its own data. No central group was responsible for the overall data-processing rules. If specific procedures were required for the capture, storage, processing and retention of data relating to expenses, it was the job of the accounting department to establish them. Likewise, it was up to the payroll department to formulate the procedures for the capture, storage, processing, and retention of the hours worked by each employee within a department. But once these procedures had been established and standardized, there was no further centralization of data processing; each department was on its own.

You will recall from earlier chapters that when database management systems were introduced and used by companies for the first time in the 1960s and 1970s, several advantages were highlighted to justify their use. Among these were the minimization of data duplication; the economies of scale inherent in large, shared, centralized bases of data; the ability to easily form relationships among data elements and records; and the comprehensive reporting capabilities available, given these other advantages. But with these benefits came new responsibilities: additional considerations of security, disaster recovery, efficient data access, and user education, to name just a few. Though accounting and payroll, for example, continued to be responsible for the formulation of standard procedures for processing data under their jurisdiction, central databases necessitated central management and control of the stored data. The standard procedures now had to be updated to reflect this comprehensive, central data storage.

So along with the introduction of DBMS into the enterprise came the creation of a group of personnel referred to as **database administration (DBA)**, which was given the responsibility for the maintenance and control of the DBMS environment. Since the DBMS was a product of the technical world of computers, DBA was placed within the data processing department. The exact positioning of this group was based on the company's management philosophy, its then existing organizational structure, its maturity in the use of computers, its size, and the specific responsibilities and authority placed in the hands of DBA (some books say "the DBA," but they mean database administration as an individual, while we mean it as a group; others use DBA to refer to the database administrator, the individual who has chief responsibility for this group).

The formation of DBA under the data processing department was a natural development, since the responsibilities of the group were initially viewed as technical in nature. For example, DBA handled physical database design; security; backup and recovery; database reorganization; and the creation and enforcement of application programming standards and documentation related to database processing. In the execution of these technical functions, DBA functioned reasonably well. As with any new technology, however, there were the normal false starts and problems to be resolved. As experience with the new DBMS technology increased and as DBA recovered from these initial problems, it proved to be a necessary and important function of the organization for the purpose of managing the technical aspects of the DBMS environment.

MATURING OF DATABASE ADMINISTRATION

Many of the first applications developed in the new DBMS environment were stand-alone systems, such as general ledger, fixed assets, inventory control, purchasing, and payroll. A stand-alone system is not integrated with other application systems. This meant that one of the most powerful features of a DBMS, the ability to form relationships between the enterprise's data groups, was not being utilized. So the next step in the use of DBMS was to integrate applications by forming relationships between records of different applications. By attempting to integrate applications, data processing and the DBA group were also addressing the problem of redundant data storage, which is an inefficient, costly, and inconsistent way for an enterprise to manage its information.

The integration of applications requires that data processing and each user area look upon data and information as a corporate resource. This view of data and information was a novel concept back in the early 1970s. Each user had been taking a proprietary view of data: "This is my data, that is your data." And each programmer and systems analyst within data processing had a similar viewpoint: "This is my program, that is your program"; and "This is my application, that is your application." Now DBA was asking the enterprise to look at data, programs and applications on a more global, enterprise level. The results were as you might expect: inconsistencies between users in their views of data meanings, and conflicts in resolving these differences; lack of cooperation by some users in working with data processing; the inability of some programmers and systems analysts to make the transition from the application view of data to an enterprise view of data; and frustration over the inability to make rapid progress on data integration.

At this critical stage, some enterprises successfully overcame the problems of data integration and made the transition to true DBMS environments, while other enterprises continued to struggle. What were the factors that enabled some enterprises to succeed? They are, in fact, the same factors that determine which enterprises will succeed today.

ACHIEVING A SUCCESSFUL DBMS ENVIRONMENT AND DBA GROUP

Several factors influence the degree of success an enterprise achieves in its use of DBMS technology. Very important is the ability of the DBA group to perform the functions for which it is responsible. These functions will be discussed in subsequent sections of this chapter. For now, let's focus on the organizational factors that establish the proper climate for the DBMS environment and for the DBA group. The factors necessary for success are summarized in Figure 14.2; the following paragraphs explain them.

---

1. Top-level management commitment and involvement.

2. Data and information requirements planning

3. Authority vested in DBA.

4. Proper selection of people to staff DBA.

5. Realistic, flexible view of DBMS and DBA.

6. Action-oriented and results-oriented approach.

7. Improved information to users.

FIGURE 14.2
Organizational factors necessary for DBMS success

TOP-LEVEL MANAGEMENT COMMITMENT AND INVOLVEMENT

The first factor is top-level management commitment and involvement, and it is the most important one. Enterprises that have a successful DBMS environment take the concept of DBMS very seriously. Besides supporting the viewpoint that data and information are resources of the entire enterprise, top-level management gets involved, educates itself about the benefits of database technology, endorses the database concept with all its implications, and communicates its belief in database to the rest of the organization. Though top-level management commitment and involvement do not guarantee success (no single factor or combination of factors can), their absence does guarantee at best an ineffective DBMS environment and at worst (and more commonly), failure.

DATA AND INFORMATION REQUIREMENTS PLANNING

Top-level management also has a key role to play with regard to the second factor, data and information requirements planning. It is important for top-level management to oversee the creation of a plan that documents the data and information needs for the entire enterprise. This should be done prior to implementing applications into the DBMS environment. The plan provides the overall framework that will guide subsequent application development. It ensures that the overall requirements of the enterprise are always kept in mind as each application is developed. The DBA group normally acts as the developer of this plan, as we will see in the next section. But the support of top-level management is crucial to the success of the planning process. Top-level management must initiate, review, and approve the plan. It must also make certain that the plan is kept current by the DBA group, since business requirements change over time.

AUTHORITY VESTED IN DBA

The third factor is a strong DBA group, and it is essential to the success of the DBMS environment. It must administer the appropriate set of functions, or responsibilities. But the DBA group can derive its true strength only by being given full authority over these functions by top-level management. For example, when the DBA group institutes standards and procedures under management approval, it must be allowed to enforce them fully. If any dispute arises, management must intervene on the side of the DBA group to reinforce the authority granted to it. In other words, in order to function properly, the DBA group needs as much muscle as any other functioning group within the organization. Though this may seem obvious, it is frequently ignored in the everyday life of the enterprise. The placement of the DBA group organizationally within the enterprise affects its clout, as we will discuss further in the last portion of this section.

PROPER SELECTION OF PEOPLE TO STAFF DBA

DBA plays the leading role in the administration of the data and information resources of an enterprise. This is a complex responsibility. Accordingly, DBA needs a talented blend of people who can do the job effectively. The proper selection of people to staff DBA is the fourth factor necessary for the success of the DBMS environment and the DBA group. Most carefully chosen must be the head of DBA, who must have credibility within the organization and must command the respect of the others. This person takes the leading role in interactions with top and middle management and directs the functions of DBA while dealing with complex technical decisions. A most difficult, and necessary, person to find.

REALISTIC, FLEXIBLE VIEW OF DBMS AND DBA

The fifth factor for success is the need for the enterprise to take a realistic, flexible view of both DBMS and DBA. Though computers are sometimes thought of as miracle workers, it is best to think of a DBMS as just another tool to aid the organization in meeting its goals and objectives. As such, a DBMS should be called upon to do some things and not others. One misconception held by many experts in the late 1960s and early 1970s was the belief that all data of an enterprise would eventually reside within a single, central, corporate database. Instead of a single, central corporate database, successful enterprises recognize that common organizational data is best stored centrally, while other data may be stored in satellite databases, or under traditional file-processing techniques, or through totally manual means.

Taking a realistic, flexible view of both DBMS and DBA pays off in a number of other ways. For example, application software packages are an economical and practical solution to many business problems. The best package solution in a given situation may require the use of a database model different from the one currently used by the enterprise. Successful enterprises weigh the difficulties and costs of additional technical tools against the benefits that will be derived from the desired package and make decisions on a case-by-case basis. Likewise, the trends toward distributed data processing and increased use of microcomputers require a realistic, flexible approach.

ACTION-ORIENTED AND RESULTS-ORIENTED APPROACH

The sixth factor for success is an action-oriented and results-oriented approach to data and information processing. Successful enterprises plan properly, but they get the job done. Having selected and installed a DBMS, successful enterprises develop applications in small, manageable chunks. They use appropriate productivity tools, like 4GLs, and take advantage of prototyping to ensure accurate requirements definition. They take the necessary steps to ensure that the DBMS will enhance, rather than intrude on, the data and information resources. Getting the job done goes a long way toward providing both the user and the technical staffs with a sense of excitement and satisfaction about their work.

IMPROVED INFORMATION TO USERS

Finally, successful enterprises use DBMS technology to provide improved information to users. This, in the end, is the principal objective, and attaining it in a cost-effective manner is the true measure of success.

DBA ORGANIZATIONAL PLACEMENT AND STRUCTURE

As we mentioned earlier, when DBA was first introduced each enterprise determined its exact positioning, based on the management philosophy of the enterprise, its then existing organizational structure, its maturity in terms of computer utilization, its size, and the specific responsibilities and authority placed in the hands of DBA. These same factors still form the basis for DBA's positioning. Though DBA fits into the organizational structure of an enterprise in many ways, the size of the data processing (or information systems) department generally is a major determinant in its placement. A brief study of a few common placements based on the size of the data processing department will illustrate some of the possibilities.

In the smallest installations, the DBA technical functions are spread over the entire data processing department. Usually, there is no separate DBA group. Figure 14.3 shows a representative organization chart for a small installation. The director of data processing is the chief executive over the data processing area.

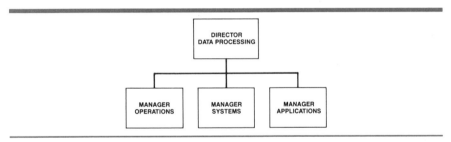

FIGURE 14.3
Organization chart
for a typical small
enterprise

Three managers report to the director and lead groups that handle different functional responsibilities. The operations group runs the computer and such peripheral devices as line printers. It also schedules the execution of batch jobs, distributes printed output, and serves as the first line of contact when users have problems with their operational computer applications. The systems group installs and supports systems software, such as the operating system, language and editor processors, and the DBMS. The applications group analyzes, designs, programs, tests, installs, and maintains application software, such as payroll and inventory control.

In this small installation, the management and control responsibilities for the DBMS environment are distributed among the three groups. The operations group coordinates the use of the DBMS, schedules batch database jobs, and monitors throughput and response times. The systems group handles performance improvements and physical database reorganizations. The applications group does database design and creates standards for testing, documentation and programs.

Administrative and application functions normally handled by DBA in larger installations are either not done at all or are the responsibility of the applications group along with either a user coordinator of data processing activity or a steering committee of users. We will describe these administrative and application functions in detail in the next two sections.

When the data processing department is slightly larger, or if a small organization does form a DBA group, the DBA group consists of a single individual called the **database administrator**. The database administrator reports to the director of data processing either in a line capacity on a level with the other three groups or from a staff-level position, as shown in Figure 14.4. It is impossible for a single individual to be responsible for all the DBA functions. Consequently, the other three groups continue to perform a number of database management and control functions, while the database administrator serves in a consulting or advisory capacity. He or she establishes standards and serves as a control point to ensure conformance to these standards. Users interact with the database administrator with regard to database planning, security, and performance, for example.

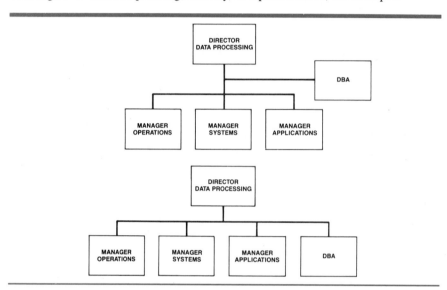

FIGURE 14.4
DBA placement: top in a staff position, bottom in a line position

In larger enterprises the DBA group consists of the database administrator in a manager position along with a number of other personnel. Either one of the two organizational structures shown in Figure 14.4 is a common placement of the DBA group. It is at this point that all the typical administrative, application, and technical functions associated with DBA become the responsibility of this group and are no longer handled by the other data processing groups. Specialization occurs as individual experts within DBA concentrate on separate areas, such as documentation and standards, performance, user interaction, database design, and security administration. The database administrator position is a varied, challenging, and important one. Figure 14.5 on the opposite page, lists some suggested qualifications for the database administrator position in a typical enterprise. Note that the position demands a combination of management, technical, and interpersonal skills.

In the past several years some of the largest enterprises have expanded the role of DBA to give it responsibility for all the data of the enterprise, not just the data under the control of the DBMS. The expanded function continues to be called DBA in some cases but has also been named *data administration* or *information resource management*, and it is placed higher in the organizational structure to reflect its increased importance. The head of the group may hold a director position that places him or her on an equal level with the head of data processing, or may be placed at an even higher level of the organization. This is to ensure that the group has sufficient authority to match its more significant role.

Formal Education:

    M.S. in Information Systems, Computer Science, or Accounting; MBA; or equivalent experience.

Skill Prerequisites:

    Must be able to work well with people at all levels of management.
    Must be capable of thorough investigation of implications of database changes.
    Must have mature judgment.
    Must be able to communicate effectively orally and in writing.
    Must thoroughly understand the business and its data needs.

Experience:

    Minimum of 5 years experience as a system designer and programmer; at least 2 years on large-scale integrated systems.
    Experience in large database systems.
    Minimum of 2 years supervisory experience of 5 or more subordinates.
    Application oriented background.

FIGURE 14.5
Suggested position qualifications for the database administrator position from a typical enterprise

In some of these larger enterprises, there continues to be a DBA group within data processing to perform the technical DBA functions, while the data administration, or information resource management, group performs the majority of the administrative functions. The application functions are then appropriately allocated between the two groups. Just as a single, central database has usually proved unworkable, a single group that carries out all DBA functions is not necessarily the best approach in these larger enterprises.

So there is no one standardized placement in an enterprise for the DBA function. What is right for one enterprise may be wrong for another. The factors for success mentioned earlier in this chapter should be kept in mind when organizing and staffing DBA; they must be satisfied no matter what its organization and placement.

Since a DBA group within the data processing department is still the most common placement, we will use this structure as the basis for our discussion of the

DBA functions in the next three sections. We will assume that there is no additional data administration group and that all functions are handled by the DBA group. You will notice as we discuss each function that there is overlap between some of the functions and that some functions could be placed equally well in one of the other categories. We will first discuss the administrative functions of DBA, followed by the application functions, and then finally the technical functions. We will concentrate on the most prevalent and most important responsibilities of DBA. Not all DBA groups deal with all these responsibilities, but some other DBA groups go well beyond them.

14.3 DBA ADMINISTRATIVE FUNCTIONS

Before the introduction of a DBMS, an enterprise does not have a database administrator or a DBA group. Ideally, in the transition to a DBMS environment, the database administrator, or chief candidate for that position, is involved in the transition process. This is not always the case. Many enterprises involve the data processing department in the initial stages of the decision-making process but give no thought to the need for a database administrator or DBA group or for the management and control activities necessary in a DBMS environment; instead, they evaluate and select the DBMS by means of a task force consisting of executives, key users, and representatives from the data processing department. It is only after the DBMS has been selected that the functions of DBA begin to be shaped and the position of database administrator is created and staffed. The development of the first application under the new DBMS environment may already be under way or may even have been completed before the database administrator begins functioning.

Again, this is not ideal. Fewer mistakes are likely to be made if a functioning database administrator is involved at the beginning of the DBMS evaluation and selection process. At the very least, a number of the administrative functions typically handled by the DBA should be identified and assigned to existing data processing personnel. We will assume that a database administrator or DBA group is in place from the very beginning of the DBMS evaluation and selection process as we discuss DBA functions in this section and in the following two sections.

In this section we will focus on the administrative functions performed by the DBA group. Functions of a planning or policy nature have been placed in the administrative category. Figure 14.6 is a summary of these functions. At the end of

1. Top-level education and commitment

2. Enterprise planning

3. Hardware/software requirements

4. Policy formulation

FIGURE 14.6
DBA administrative functions

this section, we will give an example of the type of requirements that frequently arise to complicate the job of DBA and make the DBMS environment a most challenging one.

TOP-LEVEL EDUCATION AND COMMITMENT

As we saw earlier in this chapter, the most important factor for a successful DBMS environment is top-level management commitment and involvement. The database administrator (we will use DA, a nonstandard acronym, for the individual who heads the database administration, or DBA, group) must take the lead in educating these executives about the major functions of a DBMS (see chapter 2). These functions are best explained in nontechnical business terms. It isn't necessary to turn the executives into technical experts, but they have to appreciate what a DBMS can do for the enterprise. And they must be familiar with the complexities of a DBMS. These complexities should be equated with the policies and procedures required to control and minimize their impact.

The DA should justify the proposed new database technology on a cost-benefit basis. Only in this way can top-level management be supplied with a realistic understanding of the price to be paid for shifting to the database technology. Progress has a price, and there is a price to be paid in managing and controlling the data and information resources. Not only is there an initial outlay, there are also recurring costs. The initial costs of database include the following:

1. DBMS software itself
2. DBMS software tools, such as query languages, 4GLs, and performance monitors, if they are not bundled with the DBMS software
3. Teleprocessing monitor, if they are not included with the base DBMS software
4. Additional hardware, especially disks, terminals, and additional memory
5. Technical and user training
6. Planning and start-up activities.
7. Facility preparation charges for additional hardware
8. DBMS installation and integration
9. Overhead for developing the first application

The recurring costs of database include:

1. Software maintenance
2. Hardware maintenance and depreciation
3. Ongoing training
4. DBA personnel
5. Teleprocessing/communications maintenance
6. Supplies
7. Computer system overhead

The costs associated with a database processing environment must be balanced by the benefits derived from its utlization. Benefits are often more difficult to quantify than costs. But since database represents significant capital and operating expenses to the enterprise, the benefits must be carefully identified and quantified in order to justify the investment. The benefits typically obtained through the use of database include:

1. Reduced program development costs
2. Reduced program maintenance costs
3. Reduced user costs in obtaining ad hoc information through queries
4. Ease of providing integrated information
5. More accurate data and information, i.e., improved integrity
6. Improved security
7. Information that users need rather than information that data processing can provide

Even if the known costs exceed the quantifiable benefits, the move to database proves to be a sound, economical choice in the long run because of improved information and improved control over the data and information resources, factors which make the enterprise more competitive and better able to provide employee and customer satisfaction. Though not easily quantified, these are usually things that count most to an enterprise.

Once the DA has educated top-level management and has justified the use of a DBMS on a cost-benefit basis, it is crucial for him or her to obtain a solid commitment for DBMS use. This commitment has to be ongoing, so the DA must continue to educate, inform, communicate to, and sell top-level management as improvements and refinements are made to the DBMS environment and to the administration of the data and information resources. Any serious problems that arise should be quickly and completely reported to the appropriate executives so that the communication line remains accurate and unbiased. If the DA is honest, considerate, enthusiastic, competent and professional in dealing with management and with others in the organization, the successes of database will overshadow any unavoidable difficulties.

ENTERPRISE PLANNING

Another administrative function of DBA is planning on an enterprise-wide basis. Successful use of database technology depends at least as much on skilled planning as on technical sophistication.

Action in the absense of planning is certain to result in failure. On the other hand, conducting planning effort after planning effort without taking any action also produces poor results. Obviously, planning must be completed before installing a DBMS, but how much planning and what kind of planning? Much depends upon the management philosophy of the organization. The planning process can be a lengthy and formal one, involving all functional areas and organizational levels of the enterprise. Or it can be short and informal, involving just a few key members of the enterprise. Both extremes work when handled properly.

An example of a popular, widely used planning methodology is *Business Systems Planning (BSP)*, created by IBM and offered for the first time in the mid-1970s. BSP provides a step-by-step process for developing a comprehensive plan of an organization's information requirements. For more information about BSP, see [7], [11], and [12].

No matter what approach is used for planning, the DA must produce at a minimum a plan that documents the following:

1. Overall goals and objectives of the enterprise
2. Primary business functions
3. General data and information requirements
4. Application system priorities

OVERALL GOALS AND OBJECTIVES OF THE ENTERPRISE

The overall goals and objectives of the enterprise should already be available from the organization's business plan. If a business plan does not exist, then the DA must meet with top-level management to determine these goals and objectives. Their importance lies in the fact that they help the DA understand the direction of the enterprise and help identify potential new business functions that may be necessary in the future. For example, Premiere Products may be planning to use excess warehouse capacity to stock super gizmos for Red Robin, Inc., starting a year from now. And when the company starts this new venture, it wants to be able to segregate the inventory data of Red Robin from its own inventory data. If a study of current data and information needs were conducted with lower-level management, this requirement would most likely not be uncovered. Interaction with top-level management is necessary in order to discover these types of plans.

Another reason for knowing the enterprise's goals and objectives is that they give an indication of planned future growth. It would be important to know that an enterprise planned to double its number of customers over the next three years or to start construction of its first satellite production plants in two years. In the former case, plans would have to be made for sufficient storage capacity in the new DBMS environment. In the latter case, meetings would have to be held to discuss the need for distributed processing of data.

By focusing on the executives of the enterprise, the DA is taking a top-down approach to planning. A top-down approach provides perspective in terms of where the enterprise is now and where it will be going in the future. The insight, knowledge and perspective of top-level management is important for creating a proper plan and for obtaining the support of the enterprise's executives.

PRIMARY BUSINESS FUNCTIONS

The DA needs to identify and document the primary business functions of the enterprise. For example, the DA for Marvel College would find that among the school's many business functions were general ledger, accounts payable, admissions, student records processing, and alumni processing. Knowledge of the primary business functions is necessary to provide the list of possible application systems under the DBMS. Some of these business functions may already be processed with a computer, while others may not. It is important to know the scope of the enterprise in preparation for the transition to database.

GENERAL DATA AND INFORMATION REQUIREMENTS

The DA must start to develop the **conceptual data level**, or global enterprise view of data. How thorough a job is done will depend on the individual organization. But based on the DA's determination of the primary business functions, he or she will at least document the principal entities, which would be students, faculty, and classes, for example, in the case of Marvel College. If using BSP, for example, the DA would ideally completely define all entities and all data elements for the enterprise; but time constraints, organizational philosophy, and shortage of personnel may preclude such thoroughness.

APPLICATION SYSTEM PRIORITIES

The enterprise must evaluate each business function and then decide which functions should be developed under the DBMS and when. Often a user committee is formed to do the preliminary evaluation and the results are presented to top-level management for their review. These executives make necessary modifications based on their strategic perspective. The DA takes this approved priority list and creates an implementation timetable. Unless a thorough plan has been created by means of a methodology like BSP, the timetable is tentative; the data processing department must analyze the detailed requirements of each application as it is developed, and only then can the timetable be definite.

The first application to be implemented under the DBMS must be carefully selected. The choice should be influenced by the fact that the transition to the DBMS environment is a learning experience for everyone in the enterprise. The application should be of small to medium size, but under no circumstances should it be any larger. If the application is of some significant size, then it is best to develop it a piece at a time, using a phased approach. Mistakes may be made with the new technology, and it is easier to recover from any mistakes or misunderstandings with a smaller, less complex application. Many experts claim you should plan to throw away the first application developed, since you will end up throwing it away whether you planned to do so or not.

Quick-payback applications are good first choices. These are applications of a manageable size whose benefits far exceed their costs, both developmental and ongoing. The decision to select them is not only smart and economical, it also gets the database environment initiated on a positive note.

HARDWARE/SOFTWARE REQUIREMENTS

If at all possible, the DA should be involved before the evaluation and selection of the DBMS occurs. In addition, all administrative steps previously discussed in this section should have been completed. The DA should make a thorough evaluation of available DBMS's, based on the enterprise's data and information requirements and on the constraints of the existing computer hardware environment. A complete checklist of desired features should be developed prior to the start of the evaluation process. The functions of a DBMS discussed in chapter 2 should be the starting point for this checklist; any special requirements should be added to it. For example, it will probably be necessary to add requirements for such software tools as 4GLs, application generators, and user-oriented query languages and report writers. See [10] for a comprehensive checklist of evaluation and selection criteria.

Standard software tools should be used throughout the enterprise for managing data and providing information. If a mainframe DBMS will be used as well as DBMS's on personal computers, now is the time to select the DBMS's and compatible, standard tools.

Once the DBMS and software tools have been selected, the DA can solidify the hardware requirements for database processing. The applications to be implemented under the DBMS will provide additional requirements for the hardware selection.

POLICY FORMULATION

The final administrative function of DBA is the creation of policies that set the stage for effective, controlled, and safe database processing. The DA must consider the capabilities of the selected DBMS in order to formulate these policies. These policies deal with security, disaster and contingency planning, and user billing, and a number of standards and procedures must be developed in support of them; these will be discussed next, along with other standards and procedures.

SECURITY

The provision for **security** facilities is one of the functions of a DBMS that we discussed in chapter 2. The protection of data in the database against intentional or accidental access, modification, and destruction is a key function of the DA. The DA takes advantage of facilities available within the DBMS and supplements them with non-DBMS facilities, as necessary, to secure the data and information resources of the enterprise. No protection system is foolproof, so the objective is to minimize the enterprise's exposure to possible security violations and to maximize its ability to discover and recover from security violations. The benefits obtained from elaborate security measures must be weighed against the degree of difficulty in their implementation.

Security considerations are important to all enterprises, even those which have neither a DBMS nor computers. Security is a complex area. The amount of publicity in the popular media concerning security violations demonstrates the importance of security to business, the public and the government, as well as the fact that it is an imperfect science at best. We will highlight several of the most important facets of security. The discussion of disaster and contingency planning which follows is closely related.

First, data processing personnel who require access to the database must be barred from incurring either inadvertant or intentional security violations. Operations personnel who tend the computers and peripheral devices do not need to access the database directly through normal DBMS methods. However, they are responsible for both scheduling and executing backups of the database, so they must be in physical contact with the equipment. Failure to properly back up the database can jeopardize database integrity and can result in loss of critical data in the event that recovery must occur. Also, uninformed or disgruntled employees may cause physical harm to the equipment. With regard to the former, DBA should review computer logs to ensure that scheduled backups are occurring according to schedule; with regard to the latter, close supervision minimizes the potential for physical harm.

Application programmers do need to interact directly with the database as they develop and maintain programs, as do systems programmers as they install and maintain systems software. Software bugs, deletion of production programs, and the intentional introduction of fraudulent or destructive code into programs are representative of potential security problems. DBA must enforce strict testing of programs. Testing and production environments should exist apart from one another, and application programmers should have access only to the test environment. DBA should transfer tested versions of programs into the production environment only after both DBA and the users have verified the quality of the software test results.

Separation of functions within data processing is most important. One person should not be responsible for too many functions, and each person's work should be subjected to a system of checks and balances. In smaller data processing departments where full separation of functions may not be feasible, careful selection and supervision of each employee and frequent reviews of emloyees' work by an audit group from outside the data processing department can serve the same purpose.

A second important facet of security is the proper control of user access and modification of data. Access should be given only to those users who require it, and each user's privileges should be limited according to what he or she needs to accomplish. Procedures and documentation that explain how to gain access to the database environment and to specific data should be issued only to authorized personnel and should be safely stored away when not in use.

Many elaborate methods have been devised to restrict access to authorized users. Voice recognition devices, fingerprint verification devices, and badge readers are three of the successfully used techniques. To control remote access to the total computer environment, some organizations require the user to call into the computer center and give a special user code. Using this code, the security clerk then contacts the registered location of that user and makes the connection between the user terminal and the computer from the computer center end of the communications link. This approach minimizes the chance of a hacker or other unauthorized person gaining access on a remote processing basis.

The most widely used approach to user security remains user entry of special codes to gain access. The DA gives a unique user identification code to a given user. This code is tied to a profile for that user that indicates which programs, records, and data elements he or she is permitted to access. In certain cases the user will be allowed read-only access; in other instances the user will be able to change specific data. Besides supplying an identification code, the user typically must enter a password. The user creates the password and changes it periodically. Together, the user identification code and password link the user to his or her profile for subsequent authorized processing. Since the DA knows the user identification code, the use of the password, which is known only to the user, protects somewhat against security violations by the DA and the DBA staff. It is important for the user to select a nonobvious password, to keep the password secret, and to change it periodically.

Subschemas and active data dictionaries provide controls over what users can and cannot access. Encryption of data disguises data in the event that someone is able to gain unauthorized access to the database. These controls have been discussed in previous chapters. Another control is the use of data change logs, or activity logs, employed by DBA to audit activity against the database. It has been proven many times that any security system can be circumvented by individuals who are smart enough and who wish to do so. After-the-fact reviews of these logs can minimize tampering with the security system and with data. The importance of audits conducted by both internal and external auditors cannot be overemphasized. The system of checks and balances should be as comprehensive as possible.

Though the DA and the DBA staff fall neither in the data processing nor in the user category, limitations should also placed on their ability to interact with the DBMS environment. Because of the number of critical duties alloted to it, DBA ends up having a great deal of access and control over the database. In many enterprises it has primary responsibility for security in the DBMS environment, but it would be better to assign this responsibility to a separate security officer who would report to someone outside the data processing department and outside the DBA group. It would be the security officer's job to create and distribute user identification codes. The security officer would also review the activity logs and perform other security tasks but would not perform any of the other normal duties of DBA. This separation of functions would better provide a more secure DBMS environment.

The third facet of security that we will discuss is physical security. Physical security is a concern not just in database processing but also non-DBMS and non-computer environments, and the steps taken on behalf of physical security there are just as important in a DBMS environment. User areas need to control access to terminals, to important source documents, and to reports. Locks can be placed on terminals so that only users with keys can use them. Critical source documents, which contain confidential data or which must be legally retained for audit or governmental purposes, should be locked away in fire-resistant, bomb-proof safes or storage vaults. The same is true for critical reports.

In the early days of computers, enterprises often liked to showcase their computer facilities. Few limitations were imposed on who could walk through rooms where hardware was located. If there were restrictions, then the computers might be located in glass-enclosed rooms. Many buildings were constructed before computers were purchased, so no planning had gone into safe placement of the computers. Computers would be situated wherever there was room: in the basement, near the reception area, or in an open, high-traffic area. These various choices of locale left organizations vulnerable to problems with physical security. Sabotage, theft of hardware, fire, and such natural disasters as floods and tornados are a few examples of problems that have occurred.

Today organizations carefully plan their computer facilities so as to eliminate or minimize such threats to physical security. The computer hardware is placed away from high-traffic areas and away from the threat of flood and other natural disasters, in rooms that provide strict access control. Only authorized employees are allowed entry, and entry is obtained through the use of badge readers, access codes, voiceprints, fingerprints, and other personal forms of identification. The computer room is provided with excellent fire and humidity protection and is isolated from the threat of sabotage.

In the absence of a separate security officer, DBA must always take the lead in formulating workable policies that take advantage of the security facilities built into a given DBMS. These policies must undergo reviews and approvals by appropriate executives of the enterprise. For further details on this subject, see [5].

DISASTER AND CONTINGENCY PLANNING

Closely related to security issues is disaster and contingency planning. Taken together, security and disaster and contingency planning help protect the organization from accidental and intentional damage to data. In the event that damage does occur, procedures for recovery and reconstruction must be part of the disaster and contingency plans. Owing to its management and control responsibilities for the database, DBA must take an active role in the formulation of these plans.

A key element in any such plan is redundancy. In chapter 2 we discussed the functions of a DBMS. Among these functions were recovery from failure plus certain utility services, such as journaling and backup/recovery. These are all integral parts of disaster and contingency planning, and they provide a degree of redundancy to database activity. Given a failure, backups of the database permit reconstruction and limit the damage. Journals can then make the database current with the most recent transactional activity. Care must be taken with the database backups. If the backups are stored near the computers and a catastrophe in the form of a fire or bomb occurs, for example, destroying or severely damaging the data storage devices (disks), there is a chance that the backups also will be damaged. Thus, backups should be stored outside the computer room itself, either in the same building in a fire/bomb-proof vault, or off the premises in another facility.

Some enterprises need to keep their computers functioning no matter what problems occur. Airlines, for example, can switch quickly to duplicate backup computers in the event of a malfunction in the main computer. Other companies contract with firms using hardware and software similar to their own so that in the event of a catastrophic problem they can temporarily use these other facilities.

Total loss of an enterprise's data or computers can have a crippling effect, so proper attention to disaster and contingency planning is a major function of DBA.

USER BILLING

Investment in computer hardware and software is a capital investment; so is the purchase of a DBMS. An enterprise also expends funds during the development of applications to run under the DBMS and on a continual basis once the application becomes functional. In a number of enterprises, the costs of developing and maintaining an application are charged back to the user areas served by that application. Database processing environments that provide the capability for integration, user queries, and other sophisticated functions complicate the billing process; the DA must help formulate fair user billing schemes in these instances.

A number of charge-back billing methods are feasible for operational applications. One method involves charging the user a fixed amount per month independent of the amount of computer resources used by the application in that same month. This fixed amount is determined in advance on a periodic basis, most often annually, and holds for the entire period as determined. A review is conducted of charges versus resources used and adjustments are proposed and renegotiated going into the next billing period. This method is simple to implement, and the negotiation process is an interesting exercise, as you might expect.

A second billing method involves charging a variable amount per month, based on the computer resources used during that month. This method is often called **resource utilization billing**. Computer resources are used as factors in devising a formula. The computer's operating system continuously tracks, captures, and files away the computer resources used by each application. Some of the computer resource factors used in the billing formula are the amount of permanent disk used for the part of the database associated with the application; the amount of temporary disk used for transaction and sort files, for example; the total amount of time during which terminals are connected to and in active use with the computer system; the amount of CPU time used by executing programs; the number of tapes mounted on drives for use with the application; the amount of main memory used during the period; and the number of lines of printed output for that application. Many other factors may be considered; the preceding list is typical.

On the surface this second method appears to be the most equitable way of billing for services that are provided to a given user area for its applications. There is a major drawback, however: resources used will vary from day to day and even from hour to hour, given equivalent work accomplished. For example, a heavier load on the computer system, i.e., more users and more complicated processing needs, will require more terminal connect time and more temporary disk accesses to page a program in and out of main memory for a given amount of work.

Therefore, the user is charged more when there is a heavier load on the computer system, even if the same amount of work is accomplished. One school of thought suggests that this method is fair because users who perform their work during heavy-use periods may force the enterprise to spend more in upgrades to accommodate the heavier system load. So these users should pay more, according to the proponents of resource-utilization billing. Others feel that this is unfair. Unless the formula automatically adjusts for this type of variation, resource-utilization billing varies too much to suit its opponents. Automatic adjustment, however, complicates the formula and makes it incomprehensible to all but selected experts. Much research and applied work continues to be done in this area.

A third approach to billing for operational applications is also a formula method. The user area is billed for the month on the basis of user-related volume factors. Marvel College, for example, may charge its alumni office for its alumni processing system on the basis of the number of alumni records, the number of queries made, and the number of output lines printed. These factors are simple and clear both to users and technical personnel. There is a correlation between the number of alumni records, the number of queries made, and the number of output lines printed versus the amount of work done by the computer environment, so this method appears to be a reasonable approximation of the resource-utilization method. It is not exact, however, since five queries could be simple and take just moments to complete or could be complex and require many hours of computer resources. In either case, the user would be billed the same amount with this method. On the other hand, one query executed under a light system load would result in the same charges as the same query executed an hour later under a much heavier system load.

Before leaving the subject of user billing, we should say something about charging users who sponsor the first few projects to develop applications under the new DBMS environment. Charges to these pioneers should be equitable but not overly burdensome. There are fixed costs associated with a computer environment. When there are few users, the proportionate share of the costs will be considerably higher than they will be when there is a full complement of users and applications. A certain portion of these fixed costs could be allocated to overhead expense and distributed across the enterprise in order to lessen the penalty for being a pioneer.

COMPLICATIONS TO DBMS PROCESSING

There is a particular type of user requirement that can complicate the job of DBA, and that is twenty-four-hour-a-day processing. We are discussing this here because it affects the administrative, application, and technical functions of DBA. There are other complicating requirements as well, such as distributed databases, which will be discussed in the next chapter. We will limit our discussion of twenty-four-hour-a-day processing to a review of its impact on database backups.

Making a complete backup of a database requires users to stop update activity under normal circumstances. Otherwise, transactions that update multiple database records may update one record prior to its being copied, while a related record may be updated after it has been copied. This will cause those records to be out of synch with one another. Extremely large databases need several hours to complete the backup cycle. This means that users cannot perform any update processing during the time required for the backup. For an enterprise whose update activity occurs over a limited geographical area and whose database is not very large, finding the necessary few hours of time overnight to do the backups is not a problem.

Multinational enterprises with worldwide offices often need access to their centralized database twenty-four hours a day, since some office or offices are always open and need to access the database. For such an enterprise there is no window of time during which overnight backups can be done. Doing backups only on the weekend is a solution; the tradeoff is that if recovery is needed, the most recent backup could be a week old. The amount of time to recover from that backup and all journals for the week would make the database unavailable for a long, possibly prohibitive, period of time.

Even if this potential outage does not cause a problem, many legal requirements force an enterprise to keep a backup copy of their database as of the end of each month. More often than not, month end occurs in the middle of the week, so we are now back to our original problem of making a backup at a time when the enterprise needs access to the database. There are two solutions to this problem. One is to make the system unavailable to users until backups have been completed when month end occurs in the middle of the week. A second solution is to factor the need for twenty-four-hour-a-day processing into the design of the database. This can be a tricky design problem, but it is not an unsolvable one. For example, the database design might end up being structured predominantly on an office basis. Then, instead of using the standard DBMS utility backup facility against the entire database, a special backup program would be written to selectively back up individual offices as they closed.

Every enterprise is different, and each one's overall application requirements will be unique. Interesting problems of the type just discussed are encountered frequently enough to make DBA's job most interesting and challenging.

4.4 DBA APPLICATION FUNCTIONS

DBA has to perform a number of application functions. We include in the application category those functions directly related to DBA's interaction with users and with data processing personnel. Figure 14.7 shows a summary of the application functions we will discuss in this section.

1. Standards and procedures	4. Overall coordination
2. Data dictionary management	5. Database loading
3. Training	

FIGURE 14.7
DBA application functions

STANDARDS AND PROCEDURES

Related to the policy formulation role of DBA is its responsibility for standards and procedures. DBA must create, publish, and enforce standards and procedures that control and enhance database processing and that conform to established policies. These standards and procedures must be developed in a nondisruptive manner. The ability of users to get their job done must not be adversely affected. The standards and procedures must not become a bottleneck to data processing's development and maintenance tasks and must not place an inordinate burden on system designers.

Standards and procedures are already in place when an enterprise acquires a DBMS. So the task of DBA is to develop new ones, or to modify existing ones, which integrate DBA functions and database processing into the functioning enterprise. These standards and procedures should be communicated to all departments and personnel that will be impacted by them. Most importantly, they must be enforced. They must also be periodically evaluated and revised as necessary.

An example of a user-related procedure is the process a user must follow to obtain a user identification code to access the database. The procedure should specify who is eligible; what forms need to be filled out; what authorizations are required; who receives and approves the request; how a rejected request is handled; how an approved request is communicated back to the requester; and how the user identification code is to be handled.

An example of a standard is the naming standard for data items, records, and files defined in the data dictionary. This standard describes the conventions used for naming and gives examples of them.

Other standards and procedures that need to be created include those for:

- program testing
- application program coding and design
- performance, e.g., terminal response time and report distribution
- change control - both user requests for change and the procedure programmers follow in making program changes
- documentation, including user, operations, program, and database

In large enterprises certain members of DBA would handle standards and procedures on a full-time basis. In smaller organizations the responsibility would be spread out among a number of DBA staff members.

DATA DICTIONARY MANAGEMENT

In chapter 13 we covered the concept and role of the **data dictionary** in the DBMS environment. The management and control of the data dictionary is another application function of DBA and is one of its primary responsibilities.

DBA must create naming convention standards and procedures for using the data dictionary. It creates the data definitions, including, for example, the data validation rules. It defines the user views, which describe access to and ownership of data. It handles entry into and maintenance of the data dictionary. Documentation of the data dictionary and the creation and distribution of informational reports from the data dictionary are other responsibilities of DBA. Finally, DBA must establish procedures for auditing the content, standards, and procedures associated with the data dictionary environment.

Whether data not stored in the database should be defined in the data dictionary is a question that has to be addressed and formulated into policy by DBA and the enterprise. Most companies aim for inclusion of all data definitions, but concentrate initially on defining only that data which is stored in the database.

TRAINING

A third application function of DBA is training. DBA will conduct training on the use of the data dictionary, on how to access the database, and even in some technical areas, such as how database users and programmers can efficiently use the database. In addition, DBA coordinates vendor training of data processing and user areas. DBA also ensures that applications programmers and analysts properly train users and data processing operations personnel.

OVERALL COORDINATION

A fourth application function of DBA is the overall coordination of the database environment. There are a number of database management and control functions that are handled by personnel outside DBA and that have to be coordinated by DBA; we will highlight a few of them.

The data processing operations group performs database backup and recovery processing, but DBA decides how often and when these functions should be scheduled and verifies that they have been executed properly. If recovery has to be undertaken, DBA ensures that operations notifies all users of the fact and of how long the recovery process will take. DBA also periodically ensures that backup and journal tapes are created safely and are stored properly, in case they need to be used in recovery.

When a problem occurs, DBA must be sure that the right people are involved in the solution. If it is a hardware or systems software problem, DBA helps coordinate the involvement of the hardware or software vendors and the data processing systems group. If it is an application software problem, DBA coordinates the involvement of the users and the data processing applications group. If application software corrections are necessary, DBA coordinates the user review of the test results and transfers the correction to the production environment.

When users have special one-time processing needs or have extensive query requirements against the database, DBA coordinates the users so that their needs are satisfied without unduly affecting the performance of the database environment.

When the data processing applications group develops a new application system or enhances an existing one, conflicting needs may arise if multiple users are involved. DBA helps to resolve these user conflicts. It also helps the applications group determine whether data already exists in the database to satisfy new informational requirements.

These are just a few examples of the extensive coordination role played by DBA.

DATABASE LOADING

Database loading is a fifth application function of DBA. DBA has a major role to play in the initial loading of data into the database for a new application. DBA must verify that everything is ready, i.e., that sufficient hardware is available to store the data and to handle the additional system load; that software has been tested and transferred from the test to the production environment; that documentation has been published and distributed; that training has taken place; that the data dictionary reflects the new data definitions; and so on.

If everything is in place, existing data must now be loaded into the database. If the application is a conversion from a nondatabase computer environment, special programs created by the data processing applications group must be ready to automatically convert the data to its proper database form. These programs must be executed and their results verified before users can begin processing against the database. Often extremely long periods of time are required to execute these programs, so DBA must fit them into the schedule, frequently over a weekend. Should problems occur, they must be rapidly resolved or, failing this, the former application must be ready to be resumed as a contingency measure until the problems can be corrected.

Even when the data is converted from another computerized form, new data items and records may be present and must now be added to the automatically converted data. The users will complete this entry of new data using the normal transactions of the new application or transactions specially created for this purpose. Because of the volume of data entry involved, it may be necessary to hire temporary help and to loan extra terminals to users from other areas of the enterprise in order to shorten the elapsed time required for data entry. The problem becomes even more severe when the former application was a manual one and all data must be entered manually through terminals.

If the project being completed is for an enhancement to an existing database application, there may be new data requirements. It may be necessary to reorganize the database to accommodate these new data requirements. All activities described for a new application may then need to be performed.

14.5   DBA TECHNICAL FUNCTIONS

We finish this chapter with a discussion of the technical functions performed by DBA. Figure 14.8 on the opposite page, shows a summary of the technical functions we will examine. These are no less important than the administrative and application functions discussed in the previous two sections. In fact, the technical functions must be performed extremely well to set the stage for smooth database functioning and for satisfied users and data processing personnel. If this is done, DBA usually does not hear from the users of the database environment. If it is not, you can be sure that DBA will receive many communications, none favorable, from the users.

1. DBMS support
2. Test/production environments
3. Database design
4. DBMS performance
5. Keep current with technology

FIGURE 14.8
DBA technical functions

DBMS SUPPORT

DBA is responsible for the DBMS. This responsibility includes the evaluation and selection activities already discussed under administrative functions. Once the DBMS has been selected and delivered to the enterprise, DBA continues to have primary responsibility for it.

DBA installs the DBMS, with vendor assistance. Should options be available, such as which DBMS features should be memory resident and which should be paged in from disk, the DBA chooses them. If these options must be changed in the future, DBA makes the changes.

If there is a separate teleprocessing monitor or separate communications packages or protocols, DBA ensures that the DBMS is properly connected to them. If the enterprise uses both a mainframe computer and micros, **downloading** of data from the mainframe to the micros and **uploading** of data from the micros to the mainframe may be required, in which case DBA selects the appropriate hardware and software links to enable this data transfer to occur.

When a new version of the DBMS is released by the vendor, DBA reviews the corrections and improvements it contains, determines whether the organization should install it, and when, and coordinates its implementation. If intermediate corrections are sent by the vendor, DBA handles their inclusion into the DBMS.

A DBMS, both the software itself and the database it manages, is ever changing. DBA makes sure that change takes place in a progressive, controlled manner.

TEST/PRODUCTION ENVIRONMENTS

The actual database and hardware/software environment for the users is called the production environment. This environment should be strictly controlled by DBA. With just two exceptions, only authorized users should have access and modification rights to the database. When problems occur, corrections or reconstructions must take place; and sometimes loading of new applications or reorganizations to the database must take place. In the case of these exceptions, DBA should handle the database activity or should closely control another area's inter-action with the database.

Programmers should not have access to the production environment. A sec-ond, totally separate, environment, called the test environment, should be used by programmers for developing new programs and for maintaining existing pro-grams. All programs should be completely tested in the test environment. When they are ready, the test results and documentation should be reviewed and approved by the user and by DBA. If they are acceptable, DBA notifies affected users that new or corrected features will now be available and then transfers the programs to the production environment.

There are enough complexities in a DBMS environment; controlling the pro-duction environment should not be one of them. A separate test environment reduces the complexity of the production environment by providing an extra mea-sure of control.

DATABASE DESIGN

In earlier chapters we covered logical and physical database design thor-oughly. You will recall that the **ANSI/SPARC** model has three levels: **conceptual** (the global enterprise view of data), **external** (the individual user view of data), and **internal** (what is seen by the machine). DBA takes on the primary design responsibility for two of these levels, the conceptual and internal, and a major advisory role for the external level.

DBA is responsible for the conceptual design. As part of its administrative planning function, DBA analyzes the enterprise's requirements and creates the conceptual design. This should be done before application development begins. When the job is done thoroughly, the conceptual design contains all entities, data elements, relationships, and keys representing the data and information require-ments of the enterprise. This becomes the model for all subsequent application development. The requirements for each individual application are measured against the conceptual model so that the external and internal level designs will be compatible with long-term data and information needs.

Taking into consideration the requirements of each user involved with the application, the systems analysts and designers within the data processing applica-tions group develop the external level design during system development. DBA reviews this design and recommends change when necessary. Design changes may be necessary to avoid redundancy with data already in the database or to allow for future database requirements, for example. Following the approval of the external level design, DBA creates the data dictionary entries and communicates these user views to the appropriate users and data processing personnel.

DBA uses the existing production database structure and the additional requirements from the new external level design to create the internal level, or physical, design. The issues, problems, tradeoffs, and steps involved in this phys-ical design were discussed in chapter 12. In summary, DBA determines the physi-cal access methods to be used and allocates physical storage for the database.

It is not just new or revised user views that may force a change to the existing physical design. Performance problems, new versions of the DBMS, new hardware, new programming languages, unforeseen growth, and better DBA understanding of DBMS capabilities are some of the other reasons for changing the physical design. Physical design changes should not cause changes to the external level design. If an extreme situation occurred and the external level design did have to be changed, it would have to be done carefully so that users could still enter and maintain their data productively and could continue to easily obtain the information they needed.

Many DBA groups use automated software aids and system software tools during design activities. For example, Data Designer was the first powerful computerized tool to assist in the design process. Given a number of user views, Data Designer produces a consolidated, normalized design and generates reports on its results. This eliminates a considerable amount of manual work on the part of DBA. See [3], [10], and [11] for more details on the Data Designer processor. Some of the physical design aids are discussed in the next topic.

DBMS PERFORMANCE

DBMS performance deals with the ability of the total hardware and software environment to serve the users in a timely, responsive, and cost-effective manner. Funding normally is a constraint, so the challenge involves getting the best possible performance from the available funds. Part of DBA's performance function is planning for optimal performance. The other part is monitoring performance and taking corrective action to enhance service to users.

PERFORMANCE PLANNING

DBMS performance begins with proper sizing of the hardware environment. By **sizing** we mean the process of evaluation that determines whether the enterprise has, for example, adequate CPU speed, adequate memory, sufficient disk capacity, sufficient printer capacity, and enough communications ports to meet the workload demands that the total DBMS environment will encounter. DBA bases the sizing on estimates for a large number of factors, such as the number of records of each entity type, the number of terminal users, the number of on-line transactions to be processed per day, the amount of work each terminal user needs to accomplish per day, the number of batch jobs and transactions per batch job, and the length of scheduled and ad hoc reports. These factors are then matched against terminal response and batch throughput expectations to obtain the proper system sizing.

Sizing may sound like a simple process, but it is very complex, and there is no guarantee that the resulting environment will optimally meet the enterprise's expectations. To understand some of the complexity, let's consider the load placed on the system over time. In sizing the system, consideration must be given to the average versus peak system loads. For example, printer capacity must be sufficient to handle the daily report volumes, but how much excess capacity would be required if daily, weekly, monthly, quarterly, semiannual, and annual reports all had to be produced the same day? Most enterprises allow these peak load reports to be printed over several days, or have the reports printed by a service company. In this way, excess printer capacity can be kept to a minimum, and so can costs.

Another issue involved in sizing complexity is expectations for terminal response during peak loads. Should the system be sized under the assumption that response time will be allowed to degrade substantially during peak loads? That is, if an average number of terminal users expect a response to a transaction within two seconds, should the system be allowed to take twenty seconds to give the same response when all terminal users are interacting with the system? Should it be allowed ten seconds? Five? Two? Questions like these must be answered before adequate sizing plans can be completed.

PERFORMANCE MONITORING AND TUNING

Once an operational DBMS environment has been established, the enterprise must be able to add new applications with minimal disruption to the applications already functioning. **Prototyping** can be used to help identify the impact of the new application and to provide a benchmark of its expected performance. But only when the new application becomes fully operational in the production environment can its performance be truly evaluated.

Another concern is the changing nature of applications as they mature in a DBMS environment. As the volume of business increases, so does the transactional and print load on the system. As users become more knowledgeable about capabilities, they want to schedule additional reports and enter more queries of a more complex variety. What was once the predicted usage pattern against the database changes as users request different information. In other words, change is inevitable. And change may cause performance problems: poorer transactional response, the delivery of reports later than scheduled, and so on.

Waiting for complaints from users is one way of discovering performance problems, but it is not the best method. Users experiencing these problems become dissatisfied, and a problem may take a long time to solve even after the user has complained. It is far better for DBA to anticipate potential problems.

So DBA must monitor system performance and tune the system to maintain a proper level of performance. A number of software tools are available with operating systems and with DBMS's to assist DBA in measuring performance. Some enterprises develop additional software tools to supplement available performance-monitoring tools. All these tools provide DBA with volume and performance statistics on both an average and a peak load basis.

These statistics include:

- the number of terminal users
- the number of transactions per transaction type
- the time it takes an application transactional program to execute
- the number of database accesses per transaction
- the number of database accesses per database record type
- the number of database accesses per disk pack

- the database pages having high access rates
- the transactional response time
- the user terminal connect time
- the number of ad hoc queries processed and their characteristics in terms of number of database accesses, record types accessed, response message lengths, and response time
- the time it takes an application batch program to execute
- the number of database accesses per batch program

The preceding list will give you an understanding of the wide range of statistics that need to be reviewed for potential performance problems. A variety of actions can be taken, depending on the nature of the problem.

The most extreme solution is to buy hardware, either additional or replacement, that is faster or has more capacity than the present configuration. A faster CPU, additional main memory, an additional processor, an added disk pack, and an extra channel for the secondary devices are a few examples of possible hardware enhancements.

Procurement of more hardware is just one way to change a DBMS environment. Data can be taken from the database that is accessed the most and distributed among several disks and channels to balance the data transfer more evenly, thus minimizing channel contention and improving performance. Also, if many terminals are connected through low-speed communication lines, upgrading to faster lines will improve response times.

The database itself can be tuned to improve performance. It may need to be redistributed so that records which are frequently accessed at the same time by given transactions can be clustered. It may be necessary to change the access methods to introduce redundancy in order to improve performance. Any of these database tuning techniques may require reorganization of the physical database, a task which must be carefully planned and executed. Any logical database changes that result from database restructuring must be coordinated along with the physical database changes.

If specific application programs are causing problems, they should be reviewed for potential redesign and rewrite. Streamlining the most frequently used, most inefficient programs can produce a marked improvement in overall system performance. Reviewing groups of programs for possible redesign can also be helpful. If, for example, two batch application programs are both accessing the same data to produce two separate reports, combining their functions into one program that makes one pass against the data can improve performance twofold. Further, it may be possible to reschedule batch jobs so that they will either run less frequently or will run at times of low user transactional activity.

At some point, data becomes obsolete, and if it isn't periodically purged from the database and placed in archival storage, it can interfere with system performance. Users typically are provided with transactional capabilities to remove obsolete data, but they often assign these transactions a low priority. DBA needs to periodically review database usage patterns and see to it that obsolete data is transferred to archival storage. The data can always be reconstructed from the archives, should it be needed at some future time.

Other performance tuning options are available. The options described here should give you an idea of the complex nature performance monitoring and tuning can be.

KEEP CURRENT WITH TECHNOLOGY

DBA needs to stay current with hardware and software innovations that could positively affect the DBMS environment. DBA must keep abreast of current industry efforts in database development. For example, recent strides in database design and in the use of 4GLs and prototyping should be studied for possible use by the enterprise. New features of the DBMS that are offered by the vendor should be evaluated by DBA and implemented as required. Since change is inevitable, DBA must keep alert to those changes that will improve the technical DBMS environment.

14.6 SUMMARY

In this chapter, we examined the role database administration (DBA) plays in managing and controlling the database for an enterprise. We briefly traced the historical development of DBA and its importance in a DBMS environment. We considered the factors that make for a successful DBMS environment and DBA group and explored some of the possible placements and structures for the DBA function.

In discussing the functions of DBA, we divided them into three categories: administrative, application, and technical functions.

A summary of the administrative functions, those involving overall, top-level management and control of the DBMS environment, that we examined is as follows:

- top-level education and commitment
- enterprise planning
- hardware/software requirements
- policy formulation

We then covered the application functions of DBA, those involving direct interaction with the database users and with personnel from the data processing department. They include:

- standards and procedures
- data dictionary management
- training
- overall coordination
- database loading

Finally, we examined the technical functions of DBA. These functions directly involve management and control of the technical aspects of the database environment. They include:

- DBMS support
- test/production environments
- database design
- DBMS performance
- keeping current with technology

REVIEW QUESTIONS

1. What are six resources an enterprise needs to manage?
2. Give definitions for data and for information that clearly distinguish the difference between the two.
3. List five internal sources of data for an enterprise and five external destinations of information.
4. In which department was the DBA function usually placed in the early days of DBMS's? Why?
5. Discuss the factors that influenced an enterprise's placement of DBA in the organization during the early days of DBMS's.
6. List the seven organizational factors required for DBMS success.
7. Which of the seven organizational factors required for DBMS success is the most critical, and why?
8. Who normally develops the data and information requirements plan?
9. Is the development of a single, central corporate database a realistic goal? Justify your answer.
10. A typical data processing department is divided into operations, systems, and applications groups. What are the functions of each group?
11. Name five skills a database administrator must possess.
12. What is the difference between database administration and data administration? What is another name for data administration?
13. What are four administrative functions of DBA?
14. Name nine of the initial costs in preparing a DBMS environment.
15. Name seven recurring costs of a DBMS environment.
16. Name eight benefits typically considered in justifying a DBMS on a cost/benefit basis.
17. What is Business Systems Planning?
18. What four areas must a plan cover at a minimum?
19. Name two reasons for DBA needing to know the overall goals and objectives of an enterprise.
20. Of the conceptual, external, and internal data level designs, which is a DBA administrative function?
21. What are attractive choices for the first application to be developed in a DBMS environment?

22. With which three areas does DBA concern itself in the formulation of policies?
23. What is meant by separation of functions?
24. Name four means employed by users to gain authorized access to a database.
25. What is the function of a security officer?
26. Name three different charge-back billing techniques.
27. What are some of the factors used in a resource-utilization billing formula?
28. What are the positive and negative aspects of resource-utilization billing?
29. What are five application functions of DBA?
30. List five standards and procedures for which DBA is responsible.
31. What are five technical functions of DBA?
32. Why should an enterprise have separate test and production environments?
33. What role does DBA play in each of the conceptual, external, and internal data levels?
34. What is meant by sizing?
35. What types of performance statistics are received and reviewed by DBA?

EXERCISES

1. Interview a database administrator in your local area and determine how the functions performed by this DA compare with those discussed in this chapter.
2. If your school has a data processing department or a computer center, diagram its organization and determine which functions covered in this chapter are handled by the different groups or individuals.

REFERENCES

1] Atre, S. *Data Base: Structured Techniques for Design, Performance, and Management*. John Wiley & Sons, 1980.
2] Cardenas, Alfonso F. *Data Base Management Systems*, 2d ed. Allyn & Bacon, 1985.
3] Database Design Inc. Information on Data Designer is available from Database Design Inc., 2020 Hogback Rd., Ann Arbor, MI 48104.
4] Date, C. J. *An Introduction to Database Systems, Volume II*. Addison-Wesley, 1983.
5] Fernandez, Eduardo B.; Summers, Rita C.; and Wood, Christopher. *Database Security and Integrity*. Addison-Wesley, 1981.
6] Gore, Marvin, and Stubbe, John. *Elements of Systems Analysis*, 3d ed. William C. Brown Co. Publishers, 1983.
7] IBM Corporation. *Business Systems Planning, Information Systems Planning Guide*, 2d ed. IBM Corporation, 1978.

8] Kroenke, David. *Database Processing*, 2d ed. SRA, 1983.

9] Lyon, John K. *The Database Administrator*. John Wiley & Sons, 1976.

10] Martin, James. *Managing the Data-Base Environment*. Prentice-Hall, 1983.

11] Martin, James. *Strategic Data-Planning Methologies*. Prentice-Hall, 1982.

12] McFadden, Fred R., and Hoffer, Jeffrey A. *Data Base Management*. Benjamin Cummings, 1985.

13] Tsichritzis, Dionysios C., and Lochovsky, Frederick H. *Data Base Management Systems*. Academic Press, 1977.

14] Vasta, Joseph A. *Understanding Data Base Management Systems*. Wadsworth, 1985.

15] Wiederhold, Gio. *Database Design*, 2d ed. McGraw-Hill, 1983.

ALTERNATIVES: DISTRIBUTED SYSTEMS, DATABASE COMPUTERS, AND MICROCOMPUTER SYSTEMS

.1 INTRODUCTION

During the 1970s database processing typically consisted of a mainframe computer that supported users through terminals connected directly to the mainframe. The mainframe would run a DBMS, which would manage databases on disk. In many organizations today, this is still the way database processing occurs, and it is perfectly appropriate. There are, however, three main alternatives to this scenario: distributed databases, database machines, and database systems for microcomputers. While each of these is a major topic in itself and a complete treatment is beyond the scope of this text, we will examine the basic ideas involved here.

The centralized approach to data processing, by which users access a central computer through terminals, was cost effective in the 1970s. But the advent of reasonably priced minicomputers and microcomputers facilitated the placement of computers at various locations within an organization, which meant that users could be served directly at those various locations. These computers were hooked together in some kind of network that allowed users to access data not only in their local computer but anywhere along the entire network. Thus, distributed processing was born. In section 15.2, we will examine the issues involved in **distributed databases**, the database component of distributed processing.

It has been common practice for some time to use special front-end computers to off-load communications functions from a host mainframe computer. Recently, **back-end machines** have appeared to off-load database access functions from a host computer. Such computers, often called **database computers** or **database machines**, form the subject of section 15.3.

The third alternative is database management systems for microcomputers. For some time now, such systems have been available, running the gamut from very limited capability systems to systems that furnish a number of the standard DBMS functions. Sometimes such systems are used in a stand-alone fashion; i.e., complete applications are developed using such tools. In other situations, data from the mainframe database is **downloaded** to a **microcomputer DBMS**, which users can then employ to manipulate the data in whatever way they see fit. These systems will be discussed in section 15.4.

15.2 DISTRIBUTED SYSTEMS

DESCRIPTION

Suppose that Premiere Products has many locations (or sites) around the country. For the most part, each location has its own sales reps and its own customer base, and each location maintains its own inventory. Instead of using a single, centralized mainframe computer that is accessed by all of the separate locations, Premiere Products is considering installing a computer at each site. If it did so, each site would maintain its own data concerning its sales reps, customers, parts, and orders. However, occasionally an order at one site might involve parts from another site. Also, customers from one site might occasionally place orders at another site. Thus, the computer at each site would have to be able to communicate with the computers at all the other sites. The computers would have to be connected in some kind of **communications network** (see Figure 15.1).

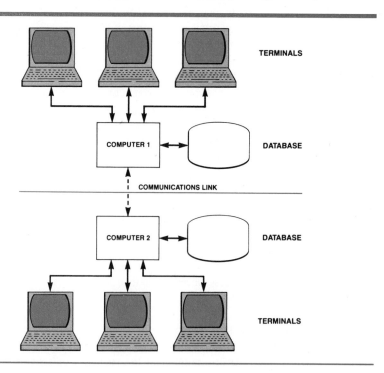

FIGURE 15.1
Communications
network

Distributed databases fall within the realm of database management and are involved in the networks just described. While there is some disagreement on a precise definition for distributed databases, the following is a good, general description:

> *Def:* A **distributed database** is a database that is stored on computers at several sites of a computer network and in which users can access data at any site in the network.

On the basis of this definition, we can go on to describe a distributed database management system:

> *Def:* A **distributed database management system** (DDBMS) is a DBMS capable of supporting and manipulating distributed databases.

Communication between computers in the network is achieved through **messages**; i.e., one computer sends a message to another. The word "message" is used in a fairly broad way here. It could mean a request for data. It could be used to indicate a problem. For example, one computer could send a message to another computer indicating that the requested data was not available. Finally, a message could be the data itself. Although we are not going to discuss the mechanics of sending a message, it is important to be aware that the length of time required to send one message depends on the length of the message together with the characteristics of the network. There will be some fixed amount of time, sometimes called the access delay, required for every message. In addition, the time for each message must include the time it takes to transmit all of the characters. The formula is as follows:

Communication time = access delay + (data volume / transmission rate)

We will discuss an example a little later in this section that is similar to one given by Date (see [3]) in which he assumes an access delay of one second and a transmission rate of ten thousand bits per second. Assuming that a message consists of one thousand records, each of which is a hundred bits long, the communication time would be as follows:

Communication time = 1 + (1,000 * 100) / 10,000
$$= 1 + 100,000 / 10,000$$
$$= 1 + 10$$
$$= 11 \text{ seconds}$$

To transmit a ten-byte message would take:

Communication time = 1 + 10 / 10,000
$$= 1 + .001$$
$$= 1.001 \text{ seconds or, for practical}$$
$$\text{purposes, 1 second}$$

As you can see, in short messages the access delay can become the dominant feature. Thus, in general, a small number of lengthy messages is preferable to a large number of short messages.

This form of communication is substantially slower than accessing data on a disk. In a centralized system, design decisions are made in order to minimize disk accesses, but, in general, in a distributed system, it is more important to minimize messages.

LOCATION TRANSPARENCY

The definition of a distributed database says nothing about the *ease* with which users access data that is stored at another site. Still, systems that support distributed databases should enable a user to access data at a **remote site** (a site other than the one at which the user is currently operating) just as easily as he or she accesses data at the **local site** (the site at which the user is working). Response times for accessing data stored at a remote site may be much greater, but except for this difference, it should feel to a user as though the entire database is stored at his or her location. This property is called **location transparency** and is one of the major objectives of distributed systems.

REPLICATION TRANSPARENCY

Sometimes, in a distributed database, data will be duplicated (technically called **replicated**) at more than one site, for performance reasons. (Accessing data at the local site is much more efficient than accessing data at remote sites because it does not involve the added communication discussed earlier.) If, for example, the sales reps at Premiere Products have customers at all locations and sales rep information must be accessed frequently, the company might very well choose to store sales rep data at all its locations.

While this replication of data can improve the efficiency of certain types of processing, it creates update problems and causes associated problems with data consistency. If we increase the total commission of one of the sales reps at Premiere Products, the update must be made at each of the locations at which data concerning this sales rep is stored. Not only does this make the update process more cumbersome, but should one of the copies of data for this sales rep be overlooked, there would be inconsistent data in the database.

Ideally, the DBMS should handle this problem for us. Any work to keep the various copies of data consistent should be done behind the scenes; the user should be unaware of it. This property is called **replication transparency**.

FRAGMENTATION TRANSPARENCY

When customers at each Premiere Products site are stored at that site, we have what is termed **data fragmentation**. A system supports data fragmentation if a logical object, such as the collection of all records of a given type, can be divided among the various locations. The main purpose of data fragmentation is to place data at the site where it is most often accessed.

Fragmentation can occur in a variety of ways. Let's assume, for example, that Premiere Products has four sites called S1, S2, S3, and S4. Let's also assume that an additional column in the CUSTOMER table, called SITE_NUMBER, identifies the primary site with which a customer is associated.

Using a SQL-like language illustrated by Date (see [3]), we could define the following fragments:

```
DEFINE FRAGMENT F1 AS
     SELECT CUSTOMER_NUMBER, NAME, ADDRESS,
          CURRENT_BALANCE, CREDIT_LIMIT, SLSREP_NUMBER,
          SITE_NUMBER
          FROM CUSTOMER
          WHERE SITE_NUMBER = 'S1'
DEFINE FRAGMENT F2 AS
     SELECT CUSTOMER_NUMBER, NAME, ADDRESS,
          CURRENT_BALANCE, CREDIT_LIMIT, SLSREP_NUMBER,
          SITE_NUMBER
          FROM CUSTOMER
          WHERE SITE_NUMBER = 'S2'
DEFINE FRAGMENT F3 AS
     SELECT CUSTOMER_NUMBER, NAME, ADDRESS,
          CURRENT_BALANCE, CREDIT_LIMIT, SLSREP_NUMBER,
          SITE_NUMBER
          FROM CUSTOMER
          WHERE SITE_NUMBER = 'S3'
DEFINE FRAGMENT F4 AS
     SELECT CUSTOMER_NUMBER, NAME, ADDRESS,
          CURRENT_BALANCE, CREDIT_LIMIT, SLSREP_NUMBER,
          SITE_NUMBER
          FROM CUSTOMER
          WHERE SITE_NUMBER = 'S4'
```

Each of these fragment definitions indicates what is to be selected from the global CUSTOMER relation that will be included in the fragment. Note that the global CUSTOMER relation will not actually exist in any one place. Rather, parts of it will exist in four pieces. These pieces, or fragments, will be assigned to locations. Here, fragment F1 is assigned to site S1, fragment F2 is assigned to S2, and so on. The effect of this assignment is that each customer is stored at the site at which he or she is a customer.

The Premiere Products data shown in Figure 15.2 is used as the basis for the

CUSTOMER	CUSTOMER_NUMBER	NAME	ADDRESS	CURRENT_BALANCE	CREDIT_LIMIT	SLSREP_NUMBER	SITE_NUMBER
	124	SALLY ADAMS	481 OAK,LANSING,MI	418.75	500	3	S1
	256	ANN SAMUELS	215 PETE,GRANT,MI	10.75	800	6	S1
	311	DON CHARLES	48 COLLEGE,IRA,MI	200.10	300	12	S4
	315	TOM DANIELS	914 CHERRY,KENT,MI	320.75	300	6	S2
	405	AL WILLIAMS	519 WATSON,GRANT,MI	201.75	800	12	S3
	412	SALLY ADAMS	16 ELM,LANSING,MI	908.75	1000	3	S1
	522	MARY NELSON	108 PINE,ADA,MI	49.50	800	12	S3
	567	JOE BAKER	808 RIDGE,HARPER,MI	201.20	300	6	S2
	587	JUDY ROBERTS	512 PINE,ADA,MI	57.75	500	6	S2
	622	DAN MARTIN	419 CHIP,GRANT,MI	575.50	500	3	S4

FIGURE 15.2
Customer data for
Premiere Products
including
SITE_NUMBER

fragmentation illustrated in Figure 15.3. Creation of the complete CUSTOMER relation entails taking the union of these four fragments.

FRAGMENT F1

CUSTOMER	CUSTOMER_NUMBER	NAME	ADDRESS	CURRENT_BALANCE	CREDIT_LIMIT	SLSREP_NUMBER	SITE_NUMBER
	124	SALLY ADAMS	481 OAK,LANSING,MI	418.75	500	3	S1
	256	ANN SAMUELS	215 PETE,GRANT,MI	10.75	800	6	S1
	412	SALLY ADAMS	16 ELM,LANSING,MI	908.75	1000	3	S1

FRAGMENT F2

CUSTOMER	CUSTOMER_NUMBER	NAME	ADDRESS	CURRENT_BALANCE	CREDIT_LIMIT	SLSREP_NUMBER	SITE_NUMBER
	315	TOM DANIELS	914 CHERRY,KENT,MI	320.75	300	6	S2
	567	JOE BAKER	808 RIDGE,HARPER,MI	201.20	300	6	S2
	587	JUDY ROBERTS	512 PINE,ADA,MI	57.75	500	6	S2

FRAGMENT F3

CUSTOMER	CUSTOMER_NUMBER	NAME	ADDRESS	CURRENT_BALANCE	CREDIT_LIMIT	SLSREP_NUMBER	SITE_NUMBER
	405	AL WILLIAMS	519 WATSON,GRANT,MI	201.75	800	12	S3
	522	MARY NELSON	108 PINE,ADA,MI	49.50	800	12	S3

FRAGMENT F4

CUSTOMER	CUSTOMER_NUMBER	NAME	ADDRESS	CURRENT_BALANCE	CREDIT_LIMIT	SLSREP_NUMBER	SITE_NUMBER
	311	DON CHARLES	48 COLLEGE,IRA,MI	200.10	300	12	S4
	622	DAN MARTIN	419 CHIP,GRANT,MI	575.50	500	3	S4

FIGURE 15.3
Fragmentation of customer data by site

While this type of fragmentation is certainly common, there are other possibilities. The following illustrates another type:

```
DEFINE FRAGMENT F1 AS
     SELECT CUSTOMER_NUMBER, NAME, ADDRESS,
          SLSREP_NUMBER, SITE_NUMBER
          FROM CUSTOMER
          WHERE SITE_NUMBER = 'S1'
               OR SITE_NUMBER = 'S2'
DEFINE FRAGMENT F2 AS
     SELECT CUSTOMER_NUMBER, CURRENT_BALANCE,
          CREDIT_LIMIT,
          SITE_NUMBER
          FROM CUSTOMER
          WHERE SITE_NUMBER = 'S1'
               OR SITE_NUMBER = 'S2'
```

```
DEFINE FRAGMENT F3 AS
     SELECT CUSTOMER_NUMBER, NAME, ADDRESS,
            SLSREP_NUMBER
            SITE_NUMBER
            FROM CUSTOMER
            WHERE SITE_NUMBER = 'S3'
                  OR SITE_NUMBER = 'S4'
DEFINE FRAGMENT F4 AS
     SELECT CUSTOMER_NUMBER, CURRENT_BALANCE,
            CREDIT_LIMIT,
            SITE_NUMBER
            FROM CUSTOMER
            WHERE SITE_NUMBER = 'S3'
                  OR SITE_NUMBER = 'S4'
```

This fragmentation is illustrated in Figure 15.4. In this case, to create the complete CUSTOMER relation, fragments F1 and F2 should be joined on CUSTOMER_NUMBER, fragments F3 and F4 should be joined on CUSTOMER_NUMBER, and, finally, the union of these two intermediate results should be taken.

FRAGMENT F1

CUSTOMER	CUSTOMER_NUMBER	NAME	ADDRESS	SLSREP_NUMBER	SITE_NUMBER
	124	SALLY ADAMS	481 OAK,LANSING,MI	3	S1
	256	ANN SAMUELS	215 PETE,GRANT,MI	6	S1
	315	TOM DANIELS	914 CHERRY,KENT,MI	6	S2
	412	SALLY ADAMS	16 ELM,LANSING,MI	3	S1
	567	JOE BAKER	808 RIDGE,HARPER,MI	6	S2
	587	JUDY ROBERTS	512 PINE,ADA,MI	6	S2

FRAGMENT F2

CUSTOMER	CUSTOMER_NUMBER	CURRENT_BALANCE	CREDIT_LIMIT	SITE_NUMBER
	124	418.75	500	S1
	256	10.75	800	S1
	315	320.75	300	S2
	412	908.75	1000	S1
	567	201.20	300	S2
	587	57.75	500	S2

FRAGMENT F3

CUSTOMER	CUSTOMER_NUMBER	NAME	ADDRESS	SLSREP_NUMBER	SITE_NUMBER
	311	DON CHARLES	48 COLLEGE,IRA,MI	12	S4
	405	AL WILLIAMS	519 WATSON,GRANT,MI	12	S3
	522	MARY NELSON	108 PINE,ADA,MI	12	S3
	622	DAN MARTIN	419 CHIP,GRANT,MI	3	S4

FRAGMENT F4

CUSTOMER	CUSTOMER_NUMBER	CURRENT_BALANCE	CREDIT_LIMIT	SITE_NUMBER
	311	200.10	300	S4
	405	201.75	800	S3
	522	49.50	800	S3
	622	575.50	500	S4

Again, users should not be aware of the underlying activity, in this case the fragmentation. They should feel as if they are using a single central database. If users are unaware of fragmentation, we say the system has **fragmentation transparency**.

FIGURE 15.4
Alternative fragmentation of customer data

HOMOGENEOUS VS. HETEROGENEOUS

Since a distributed database management system (DDBMS) effectively contains a local DBMS at each site, an important property of such systems is that they are either homogeneous or heterogeneous. A **homogeneous DDBMS** is one that has the same local DBMS at each site. A **heterogeneous DDBMS** is one that does not; i.e., there are at least two sites at which the local DBMS's are different. There are, of course, many more problems associated with heterogeneous systems than with homogeneous ones. This important subject is the focus of much research activity. No completely heterogeneous systems exist at this point, but advances are being made in this direction.

ADVANTAGES AND DISADVANTAGES

As compared with a single centralized database, distributed databases offer some advantages (shown in Figure 15.5) as well as some disadvantages (shown in Figure 15.6).

1. Local control of data

2. Increasing capacity

3. System availability

4. Added efficiency

FIGURE 15.5
Advantages to distributed databases

1. Update of replicated data

2. More complex query processing

3. More complex treatment of concurrency

4. More complex recovery measures

5. More difficult management of data dictionary

6. Database design is more complex

FIGURE 15.6
Disadvantages to distributed databases

ADVANTAGES

LOCAL CONTROL OF DATA

Since each location can retain its own data, it can exercise greater control over that data. With a single centralized database, on the other hand, the central data processing center that maintains the database will usually not be aware of all the local issues at the various sites served by the database.

INCREASING CAPACITY

In a properly designed and installed distributed database, the process of increasing system capacity is often simpler than in a centralized system. If the size of the database at a single site becomes inadequate, potentially only the local database at that site needs to be changed. Further, the capacity of the database as a whole can be increased by merely adding a new site.

SYSTEM AVAILABILITY

When a centralized database becomes unavailable for any reason, *no* users are able to continue processing. In contrast, if one of the local databases in a distributed database becomes unavailable, only users who need data in that particular database are affected; other users can continue processing in a normal fashion. In addition, if the data has been replicated (i.e., another copy of it exists in other local databases) potentially all users can continue processing. (Processing for users at the site of the unavailable database will be much less efficient, since data that was formerly obtained locally now must be obtained through communication with a remote site.)

ADDITIONAL EFFICIENCY

As we saw earlier, the fact that data is available locally means that the efficiency with which that data can be retrieved is much greater than with a remote centralized system.

DISADVANTAGES

UPDATE OF REPLICATED DATA

It is often desirable to replicate data, both for the sake of performance and to ensure that the overall system will remain available even when the database at one site is not. Replication can cause severe update problems, most obviously in terms of overhead. Instead of one copy being updated, several must be, and since most of these copies are at sites other than the site instigating the update, communication overhead must be added to the update overhead.

There is another, slightly more serious problem, however. Let's assume that data at five sites must be updated and that the fifth site is currently unavailable. If all updates must be made or none at all, the whole update fails. Thus, data is unavailable for update if even one of the sites that is the target of the update is not available. This certainly contradicts earlier remarks about *additional* availability. On the other hand, if we do not require all updates to be made, the data will be inconsistent.

There is a compromise strategy that is often used. One copy of the data is designated the **primary copy**. As long as the primary copy is updated, the update is deemed complete. It is the responsibility of the primary copy to ensure that all of the other copies are in sync. The site holding the primary copy sends update transactions to all other sites to accomplish the update and notes whether any sites are currently unavailable. If it discovers an unavailable site, the primary site must try to send the update again at some later time and continue trying until successful. This strategy overcomes the basic problem, but it obviously incurs more overhead. Further, if the primary site itself is unavailable, the problem remains unresolved.

MORE COMPLEX QUERY PROCESSING

The issues involved in processing queries can be much more complex in a distributed environment. The role of an efficient optimizer becomes even more crucial than in a single centralized database. The problem stems from the difference between the time it takes to send messages between sites and the time it takes to access a disk. As we saw earlier, the minimizing of message traffic is extremely important.

To illustrate the problems involved, we will consider two queries. The first query is: List all parts that are in item class "SG" and whose price is more than $100.00.

For this query, we will assume that (1) the PART table contains a thousand rows and is stored at a remote site; (2) there is no special structure, such as an index, which would be useful in processing this query; and (3) only ten of the one thousand rows in the PART table satisfy the conditions. How would we process this query?

One solution would involve retrieving each row from the remote site and examining the item class and price to determine whether or not the row should be included in the result. For each row, this solution would require two messages: a message from the local site to the remote site requesting a row, followed by a message from the remote site to the local site containing either the data or, ultimately, an indication that there is no more data. Thus, in addition to the database accesses themselves, this strategy would require two thousand messages.

A second solution would involve sending a single message from the local site to the remote site requesting the complete answer, followed by a single message from the remote site back to the local site containing all of the rows in the answer. The second message might be quite lengthy, especially where many rows satisfied the conditions, but this solution would still be a vast improvement over the first one. (Remember, a small number of lengthy messages is preferable to a large number of short messages.)

The net result is that systems that are only record-at-a-time oriented can create severe performance problems in distributed systems. If the only choice is to transmit every record from one site to another as a message and then examine it at the other site, the communication time can become intolerable. Systems which permit a request for a set of records as opposed to an individual record will inherently outperform record-at-a-time systems. This includes both a relational system in which the message sent could be an SQL query, for example, and a relational-like system, such as IDMS/R with its logical record facility.

A second query that illustrates the importance of an efficient optimizer is: List the order number of all orders placed on 9/02/87 which contain any parts in item class "SG" whose unit price is more than $100.00.

This time let's assume that (1) the PART table contains a thousand rows and is stored at a remote site; (2) the ORDER table contains one hundred orders, ten of which were placed on 9/02/87; (3) the ORDER_LINE table contains a thousand order lines, one hundred of which correspond to orders placed on 9/02/87 (both are stored at the local site); and (4) only two of these order lines correspond to parts that meet the conditions. What strategies can we use to satisfy this query? In what follows, we will concentrate on the factors that affect the time it takes to send the required messages, not on factors affecting disk accesses.

1. Move the PART relation from the remote site to the local site and process the query at the local site. This entails moving a thousand rows (and potentially some indexes) over a communications line before processing begins.
2. Move the ORDER and ORDER_LINE relations from the local site to the remote site, process the query there, and send the result back to the local site. This entails moving one hundred orders, one thousand order lines, and perhaps some index records, then processing the query, and finally moving the two rows in the result back to the local site.
3. Join the ORDER and ORDER_LINE relations at the local site and select only those rows in which the ORDER_DATE is 9/02/87. For each row selected, determine whether the part meets the given conditions by sending a message to the remote site. For each row this process involves two messages, a message to the remote site requesting data and a message back containing the response. Thus, two hundred messages will be required altogether.
4. Select all parts that meet the conditions at the remote site. For each row selected, examine all order lines for the part at the local site to determine whether any are for orders placed on 9/02/87. For each row this will entail two messages, a message from the remote site to the local site requesting that order lines for the given part be examined to see which ones were placed on 9/02/87, followed by a message carrying the response back to the remote site. Twenty messages will be required. (Actually, there would be two more messages in this example, an initial one from the local site to the remote site to request that the indicated processing begin and a final message sending the results from the remote site back to the local site.)
5. Select all parts that meet the conditions at the remote site. Move the result to the local site. Complete processing at the local site. This involves moving ten records from the remote site to the local site. This could be done with a single message, however.

In [3], Date gave a similar example and calculated the time it would take for each formulation, given the figures discussed earlier in this section (a one-second access delay and a transmission rate of ten thousand bits per second). The example he gave involved suppliers, parts, and shipments, which correspond to orders, parts, and order lines in our example. The volumes used in his example correspond to ten thousand orders, one hundred thousand parts, ten of which meet the indicated conditions, and one million order lines, one hundred thousand of which corresponded to orders placed on 9/02/87.

Using these volumes, Date obtained the following requirements for communication time for the strategies listed earlier:

Strategy	Communication Time
1	16.7 minutes
2	2.8 hours
3	2.3 days
4	20 seconds
5	1 second

Quite a variation! Yet each strategy is a legitimate way to process the query. Since the optimizer should choose the strategy, an efficient optimizer is absolutely critical to the success of a distributed system.

MORE COMPLEX TREATMENT OF CONCURRENCY

Concurrency in a distributed system is treated in basically the same way as it is treated in nondistributed systems: **shared** and **exclusive locks** are acquired; locking is **two-phase** (locks are acquired in a **growing phase**, during which no locks are released, and then all locks are released in the **shrinking phase**); **deadlocks** must be detected and broken; and offending transactions must be **rolled back**. The primary distinction lies not in the kinds of activities that take place but rather in the additional level of complexity created by the very nature of a distributed database.

If all of the records to be updated by a particular transaction occur at one site, the problem is essentially the same as in a nondistributed database. However, the records may be stored at a number of different sites, and, if the data is replicated, each individual occurrence may be stored at several sites, each requiring the same update to be performed. Assuming that each record occurrence has replicas at three different sites, an update that would affect five record occurrences in a nondistributed system might effect twenty different occurrences in a distributed system (each occurrence together with its three replicas). Further, these twenty different occurrences could conceivably be stored at twenty different sites.

The fact that there are more occurrences to update is only part of the problem. Assuming that each site keeps its own locks, several messages must be sent for each record to be updated: a request for a lock; a message indicating that either the record is already locked by another user or that the lock has been granted; a message indicating the update to be performed; an acknowledgment of the update; and, finally, a message indicating that the record is to be unlocked. Since all these messages must be sent for each record and the number of records can be much larger than in a nondistributed system, the total time for an update can be substantially longer in a distributed environment.

There is a partial solution to this problem. It involves the use of the primary copy mentioned earlier. You will recall that one of the replicas of a given record occurrence was designated as the primary copy. If this is done, then locking merely the primary copy rather than all copies will suffice. This will cut down the number of messages concerned with the process of locking and unlocking records. The number of messages may still be large, however, and the unavailability of the primary copy can cause an entire transaction to fail. Thus, even this partial solution presents problems.

As in a nondistributed system, deadlock is a possibility. Here there are two types, **local deadlock** and **global deadlock**. Local deadlock can be totally detected at one site. If two transactions are each waiting for a record held by the other at the same site, this fact can be detected from information internal to the site, i.e., the waiting-for information only at that site. Another possibility is that one transaction might require a record held by another transaction at one site while the second transaction required a record held by the first at a different site. In this case, neither site would contain information individually to allow this deadlock to be detected; this is a global deadlock, and it can be detected only through global waiting-for information. Maintaining such global waiting-for information, however, necessitates many more messages.

As you can see, the various factors involved in supporting shared update greatly add to the communications overhead in a distributed system.

MORE COMPLEX RECOVERY MEASURES

While the basic **recovery** process is the same as the one described in chapter 2, there is a potential problem. You will recall that each transaction should be either **committed** and made permanent or aborted and **rolled back**, in which case *none* of its changes will be made. In a distributed environment, with several local databases being updated by an individual transaction, the transaction may be committed at some sites and rolled back at others, thereby creating an inconsistent state in the global database. This *cannot* be allowed to happen.

This possibility is usually prevented through the use of the principle of **two-phase commit**. The basic idea of the two-phase commit is that one site, often the site initiating the transaction, will act as **coordinator**. In the first phase, the coordinator sends messages to all other sites requesting that they prepare to commit the transaction; in other words, they prepare all resources required to commit the transaction. They do not commit at this point, however, but rather send a message to the coordinator that they are ready to commit. If for any reason they cannot secure the necessary resources, or if the transaction must be aborted at their site, they send a message to the coordinator that they must abort. The coordinator waits for replies from all of the sites involved before determining whether or not to actually commit the transaction. If all replies are positive, the coordinator then sends a message to each site to commit the transaction. At this point, each site *must* proceed with the commit process. If any reply is negative, the coordinator sends a message to each site to abort the transaction and each site *must* follow this instruction. In this way, consistency is guaranteed.

While a process similar to the two-phase commit is essential to the consistency of the database, there are two problems associated with it. For one thing, as you may have noticed, many messages are sent in the process. For another, during the second phase, each site must follow the instructions from the coordinator; otherwise, the process will not accomplish its intended result. This means that the sites are not as independent as we might like them to be.

MORE DIFFICULT MANAGEMENT OF DATA DICTIONARY

The distributed environment introduces further complexity to the management of the **data dictionary** or **catalog**. Where should the data dictionary entries be stored? There are several possibilities:

1. Choose one site and store the complete data dictionary at this site and this site alone.
2. Store a complete copy of the data dictionary at each site.
3. Distribute (possibly with replication) the dictionary entries among the various sites.

While storing the complete dictionary at a single site is a relatively simple approach to administer, retrieval of information in the dictionary from any other site will suffer because of the communication involved. Storing a complete copy at every site solves the retrieval problem, since any retrieval can be completely satisfied locally. Since this approach involves total replication, i.e., since every occurrence is replicated at every site, it suffers from severe update problems. If the dictionary is updated with any frequency, the update overhead will probably be intolerable. Thus, some intermediate strategy is usually implemented.

One fairly obvious partitioning of the dictionary involves storing dictionary entries at the site at which the data they describe is located. Interestingly enough, this approach also suffers from a fairly severe problem. If a user is querying the dictionary in an attempt to access an entry not stored at the site, the system has no way of knowing where the data is. Satisfying this user's query may well involve sending a message to every other site, which involves a considerable amount of overhead.

A modification of this idea is actually used in the system called R*, a distributed system developed by IBM. Dictionary entries are stored at each site for all data items currently stored there as well as data items that were originally stored there. If the PART table was originally stored at site A but has now been moved to site B, dictionary entries concerning the PART table will be stored at site A (as the originating site) and site B (as the site at which the data is currently located). When a data item is originally defined, R* creates a unique name for it that includes, among other things, the identification of the site at which the item was created. (Users may assign local names to these items that are more convenient than the system-generated name.) When the dictionary is queried, if the query cannot be satisfied locally, the system-generated name is used to determine the site at which the item originated. A message is then sent to that site requesting the appropriate dictionary entry. This entry *will be* at this site even though the data may have been moved to another site, since the site of origination always maintains a dictionary entry for such an item. This strategy overcomes some of the problems discussed in the previous paragraph.

DATABASE DESIGN IS MORE COMPLEX

The distributed environment adds another level of complexity to database design. The information level of design is unaffected by the fact that the system is distributed, but, during the physical level phase of design, an additional factor must be considered, and that is communication. In a nondistributed environment, one of the principal concerns during the physical design is disk activity, both numbers of disk accesses and volumes of data to be transported. While this is also a factor in the distributed environment, there is another important factor to consider: communication activity. Since transmitting data from one site to another is *much* slower than transferring data to and from the disk, in many situations this will be the most important factor of all.

In addition to the standard issues encountered for nondistributed systems, possible fragmentation and/or replication must be considered during the physical level of database design. The process of analyzing and choosing among alternative designs must include any message traffic necessitated by each alternative. While much has been done concerning database design for distributed systems, much work remains to be done. See [1] for a discussion of distributed database design issues.

For other information on distributed systems, see [1], [2], [3], [4], and [6]. In addition, [5] and [7] contain a number of important papers concerning various aspects of distributed systems. Among other things, [5] contains a set of case studies investigating a number of existing systems.

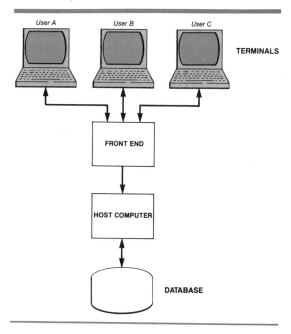

5.3 DATABASE COMPUTERS

GENERAL DESCRIPTION

Your computer may very well have a *front-end*. This is a computer that handles communication with terminals for the main computer, which is often called the host computer. This computer sits between the user and the host computer, hence the term front-end (see Figure 15.7). Without a front-end (see Figure 15.8 on the following page), every character you type on your terminal is acted upon by the main computer, and every response you see on your screen is received directly from the main computer. Much of this work can be handled by the front-end, thus freeing the host computer for other activities.

FIGURE 15.7
Host computer with front-end

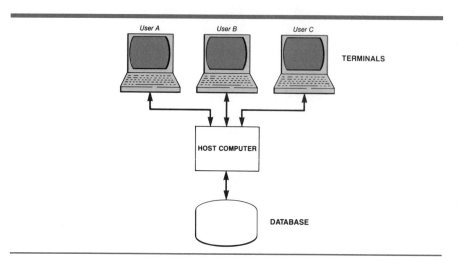

FIGURE 15.8
Host computer without
front-end

Within the past few years, vendors have developed specialized computers called **database computers**, or **database machines**, whose sole purpose is handling database accesses. One of the best known of these is the Intelligent Database Machine (IDM) developed by Britton-Lee.

Since these computers sit between a host computer and the disk on which a database resides, they have come to be called **back-end computers** (see Figure 15.9 on the following page). When a database computer is used, the host computer will communicate with it whenever access to a database is required. The database computer then begins the task of retrieving data from the database or updating data in the database to satisfy the request received from the host computer. While this activity is taking place, the host computer is free to accomplish other tasks or to serve other users. When the database computer has finished its job, it notifies the host computer. In addition, it will send any data that was retrieved to the host computer.

ADVANTAGES AND DISADVANTAGES

For every advantage obtained by using database computers, there is a corresponding disadvantage. Both are listed in Figure 15.10.

PERFORMANCE

Since the host computer can perform other operations while the database computer is performing some database operation, parallel processing is possible and improvements in overall system performance can be achieved. Further, since the database computer exists *only* to perform database operations, this computer, together with its operating system, can be tailored specifically to optimize these operations, potentially achieving still further improvements in performance.

On the other hand, every database operation that must be performed requires not only disk accesses on the part of the database computer but also communication between the host computer and the database computer. This communication

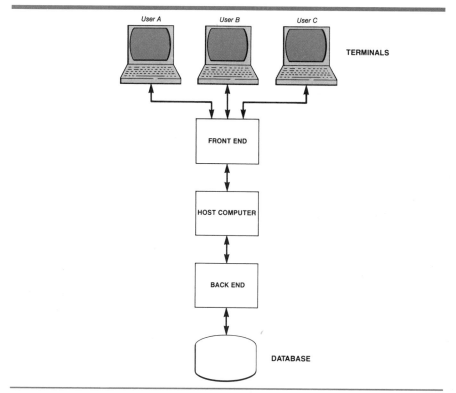

FIGURE 15.9
Host computer with
front-end and
back-end (database
computer)

would not be required if the host computer were performing all of the database accesses itself. In some cases, this additional communication will negate the performance benefits mentioned earlier. This is especially true if the request to the database computer entails retrieving or updating only a single row or record in the database. For this reason, a record-at-a-time oriented DBMS is not particularly well suited for use in a database computer.

SECURITY

If the host computer is maintaining the database, the potential exists for bypassing the DBMS and other facilities within the operating system in order to gain access to the database. Certainly there will be operating system facilities to protect the database and the database can be **encrypted**, but the possibility of this type of access still exists. If a database computer is used, it stands between users and the database (see Figure 15.9). It is not a computer on which users can run any programs directly, nor can they directly access its operating system, so it is much more difficult for a user to bypass the controls.

Users can, however, attempt to fool the database computer into believing that they are legitimate users making a database request. The database computer is an obvious point of attack, and this presents a potential weakness in security.

1. Performance

2. Security

3. Flexibility

4. Simplicity

5. Reliability

FIGURE 15.10
Advantages (and
disadvantages) of
database computers

FLEXIBILITY

Figure 15.9 illustrates a single host computer connected to a single database computer, but the approach is really much more flexible. Several host computers can be connected to a single database computer, permitting sharing of the database and database operations among the several hosts. The database computer, however, can easily become a bottleneck in the whole process. In addition, if the database computer fails, so does the entire system.

Another alternative is to connect a single host computer to several database computers. This permits an even higher degree of parallelism, which may dramatically improve performance in systems that are heavily database oriented. This structure becomes essentially a distributed system, so many of the problems associated with distributed systems also apply here.

SIMPLICITY

Unlike a host computer, a database computer exists for one purpose: to satisfy database requests. The hardware and operating system of such a computer can thus be totally dedicated to this purpose. Most functions that a host computer operating system must support do not need to be present in a database computer operating system. The database computer is thus much simpler than the host computer. Among other things, this means that there is less to go wrong.

On the other hand, the overall system is more complex than one in which a database computer is not used. Extra hardware is connected together in a fairly sophisticated fashion. One of the challenges in a configuration in which one component is handling one specialized function is to balance the load appropriately. While the host computer is processing at peak capacity, the database computer may be almost idle, if too little of the work requires elaborate database accesses. On the other hand, while the host computer is working far short of capacity, if most of the work requires heavy database accesses the database computer may be saturated, thus creating a bottleneck.

RELIABILITY

Because of the simplicity of a database computer and its operating system, database computers are potentially more reliable than host computers; fewer things can go wrong in the operating system. But this reliability may, in some cases, be offset by the potential for things to go wrong on account of the additional hardware and software!

For additional information concerning database machines, see [3], [4], and [6].

5.4 MICROCOMPUTER SYSTEMS

GENERAL DESCRIPTION

Database management systems for microcomputers have existed for some time now. The caliber of these systems improves every year with regard to functionality or ease of use, and sometimes with regard to both. The vast majority of such systems are relational. Most of them support the use of indexes to improve processing efficiency, and the indexes are usually implemented with a **B-tree** structure.

Some systems that are described as "database management systems" are misnamed. They should be termed file managers rather than database managers. They provide support for very flexible manipulation of a single file (or relation) but do not support manipulation involving more than one file. These systems are useful in some situations but certainly do not provide the full benefits we would expect to reap from a database management system. In the discussion that follows, we will not review file management systems but rather systems that do, at a minimum, provide support for manipulating several files or relations at the same time.

FIGURE 15.11
System-generated
form

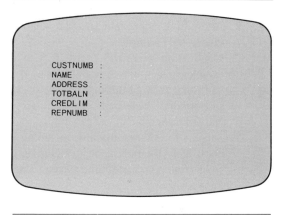

STANDARD FEATURES

The following are typical features in the database management systems found on microcomputers today:

1. Users can define tables (or files or relations, depending on the terminology used by the system) to the system in an easy way. The ease of definition is comparable to the use of the SQL CREATE statement.
2. Users can later modify the definition of these tables. Columns may be added, or deleted, or the physical characteristics of columns may be changed. This is currently more than many mainframe systems allow.
3. The system furnishes an easy way to enter data into these relations as well as to modify existing data. This will often be accomplished through a form on the screen in which the fields are stacked one above another, as shown in Figure 15.11.
4. The user can create custom forms in some easy fashion. These forms can be used in place of the system-generated forms just mentioned (see Figure 15.12).
5. Users can create reports that include related data from several files or

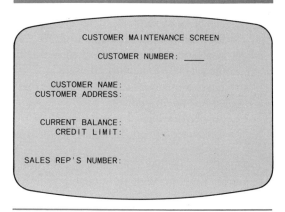

FIGURE 15.12
User-created form

tables in some fashion. The ease of defining such reports is roughly equivalent to formulating an SQL query.

6. Users can write application programs in a full **procedural language**, which can access the database. In some systems, such programs are written using conventional languages like BASIC, COBOL, FORTRAN, or Pascal, in which database commands may be embedded. Other systems contain their own full programming languages in which database commands may be embedded.

OPTIONAL FEATURES

The following optional features are possessed by some of the database management systems found on microcomputers today:

1. Integration with other utilities, such as spreadsheets, graphics, and word processors.
2. Alternative approaches to data manipulation and retrieval, such as **Query-by-Example**.
3. **Application generation** tools that allow users to develop flexible and complete menu-driven applications. If necessary, these applications can be further tailored through the use of whatever programming language is supported by the system.
4. **Natural language** query capabilities.
5. Support for **shared update**, including **locking** at various levels. This is not usually the full support, including deadlock detection, rollback, and so on, found on mainframe systems, but it is useful nevertheless.
6. Support of SQL.
7. Some rudimentary data dictionary support.
8. A micro-mainframe link. In systems that offer this feature, data can be transferred from a mainframe database to the microcomputer (called **downloading**) and can then be manipulated through the use of the microcomputer system. Data can also be shipped from the microcomputer to the mainframe (called **uploading**).
9. Sophisticated **password** schemes that limit access to various portions of the database to authorized users.
10. Easy-to-use menu-driven interfaces that allow casual users access to much of the system's power.
11. Support for **logical transactions**.
12. **Recovery** support, including sophisticated **journaling** facilities.

This list of options represents the direction in which database management systems are heading. With each passing year, existing systems will be incorporating more of these (and other) features. The development and enhancement of such systems is one of the hottest areas in computing today.

For additional information on microcomputer database management systems, see [2] and [6]. Also, see current publications like Infoworld that actively review such systems. Infoworld periodically publishes a collection of its reviews of database products.

15.5   SUMMARY

Conventional database processing consists of a single mainframe computer which supports several users and accesses a database through a DBMS stored and designed to operate on that computer. In this chapter, we have briefly examined three alternative modes of database processing: distributed systems, database computers, and microcomputer database management systems.

We saw that a distributed database is a database that is stored on several computers which are hooked together in some kind of network. A user at any site can access data at any site. A distributed database management system is a DBMS capable of supporting and manipulating distributed databases. We investigated some of the advantages and disadvantages associated with the use of distributed databases and contrasted them with a single mainframe computer that services many sites.

We examined database computers. A database computer, or database machine, is a computer designed to handle the database operations for some mainframe, called the host computer. When the host computer requires access to a database, this request is sent to the database computer. While the database computer is acting on this request, the host computer can accomplish other tasks. Once the database computer has completed its task, the host is notified and any data retrieved is sent to the host. We also investigated the advantages and disadvantages associated with the use of database computers.

Finally, we examined database management systems designed for microcomputers. Some systems that use the term database management system are more properly called file management systems; they permit the manipulation of only a single file. For systems that do permit the simultaneous use of several related tables (or files or relations), we saw that they had certain standard features. We also investigated some optional features that many of the systems possess.

REVIEW QUESTIONS

1. How does the area of database management relate to computer networks?
2. What is a distributed database? Can we use this name to describe a system in which each location has only its own private database that cannot be accessed by anyone else?
3. What is a distributed database management system? How does it differ from database management systems discussed earlier in the text?
4. What is a message? Why are messages important in designing distributed databases and in optimizing queries? Give examples of three different types of messages.
5. What is meant by a local site? By a remote site?
6. What is location transparency?

7. What is replication? Why is it used? What benefit is derived from using it? What is the biggest potential problems?

8. What is replication transparency?

9. What is data fragmentation? What purpose does it serve?

10. What is fragmentation transparency?

11. Explain why each of the following features of distributed systems is advantageous:
    a. Local control of data
    b. Ability to increase system capacity
    c. System availability
    d. Increased efficiency

12. Why is query processing more complex in a distributed environment? Why are record-at-a-time systems not particularly well suited to query processing in a distributed environment?

13. Why is the treatment of concurrency more complicated in a distributed environment? What is meant by local deadlock? By global deadlock?

14. Describe the principle of two-phase commit. How does it work? Why is it necessary?

15. Describe the various possible approaches to storing data dictionary entries.

16. What additional factors must be considered during the information-level design process if the design is for a distributed database?

17. What additional factors must be considered during the physical-level design process if the design is for a distributed database?

18. What is meant by a front-end? What purpose does it serve? What is meant by a back-end? What purpose does it serve? What other terms are used to describe a back-end?

19. Describe the positive and negative aspects of database computers in each of the following areas:
    a. Performance
    b. Security
    c. Flexibility
    d. Simplicity
    e. Reliability

20. What is the difference between a file management system and a database management system?

21. List six standard features found on microcomputer database management systems today.

22. List twelve additional features that are possessed by some microcomputer database management systems today.

EXERCISES

1. If the access delay is one second and the transmission rate is ten thousand bits per second, how long would it take to send five hundred records if each record were one hundred bits long and:
   a. Each record were sent in a separate message?
   b. All five hundred records were sent in a single message?

2. Let's assume that orders are to be stored at the same site (or sites) where the customers who placed those orders are stored. Define appropriate fragments to match the first fragmentation scheme for customers shown in the text.

3. If you have access to a microcomputer database management system, determine which of the standard features it possesses. Determine which of the optional features it possesses. Does it possess any other noteworthy features not listed in this chapter?

4. If you have access to any literature reviewing current microcomputer database management systems, attempt to determine how many of the features listed in this chapter are included by each system in the literature. In some cases, the reviews will not give enough information to make a complete determination, but do the best you can. (*Note: Infoworld* periodically publishes collections of reviews of various types of products. This is one excellent source for the kind of material required to answer this question.)

REFERENCES

1] Ceri, Stefano, and Pelagatti, Giuseppe. *Distributed Databases Principals and Systems*. McGraw-Hill, 1984.

2] Date, C. J. *Introduction to Database Systems, Volume I*, 4th ed. Addison-Wesley, 1986.

3] Date, C. J. *Introduction to Database Systems, Volume II*. Addison-Wesley, 1983.

4] Goldstein, Robert C. *Database Technology and Management*. John Wiley & Sons, 1985.

5] Larson, James A., and Rahimi, Saeed. *Tutorial: Distributed Database Management*. IEEE Computer Society Press, 1985.

6] McFadden, Fred R., and Hoffer, Jeffrey A. *Data Base Management*. Benjamin Cummings, 1985.

7] Mohan, C. *Tutorial: Recent Advances in Distributed Database Management*. IEEE Computer Society Press, 1984.

APPENDIX A
FILE AND DATA
STRUCTURES FOR
DATABASE PROCESSING

APPENDIX

A.1 INTRODUCTION

Data independence is one of the functions of a DBMS. Data independence means that users in a database environment should be unaffected by changes to the logical and physical structures of the database. The DBMS should shield users from these changes. In theory, users should not be concerned with the internal or physical level of the database. Instead, they should be concerned with data on the conceptual and external levels of the **ANSI/SPARC** model.

It is true that the DBMS and the operating system file access routines handle the job of storing and retrieving data from the physical database. It is not true, however, that users, particularly programmers and other technical personnel, do not need to be knowledgeable about the logical and physical structures of the database. Programmers, for example, need to know the logical structure of CODASYL and hierarchical model database management systems in order to navigate their way around the database. And database administrators need to know both the logical and physical structures available with their particular DBMS and must choose appropriate options if they wish to obtain optimal performance and flexibility from the database.

In Appendix A we will discuss the fundamentals of file and data structures for database processing. The appendix can serve as a refresher for those students who have taken a data structures course as a prerequisite to this database course. Other students will be able to gain a sufficient level of understanding to appropriately apply these fundamentals to the rest of the book.

We assume that the student is familiar with the fundamentals of disk storage and access. Furthermore, we do not attempt to exhaustively cover file and data structure topics; there are books of several hundred pages each devoted to these topics. Rather, we will concentrate on general concepts and on some commonly encountered data structures in database processing.

In section A.2 we will discuss the fundamental concepts of file and data structures as they relate to database processing. Section A.3 focuses on the three basic file organizations of sequential, direct, and indexed. In section A.4 we turn our attention to data structures, specifically, inverted files, linked lists, and the B-tree structure.

A.2 FUNDAMENTAL CONCEPTS

The database we will use throughout this appendix is shown in Figure A.1. It consists of a CUSTOMER file and an ORDER file. Both files are stored on a secondary storage device; we assume this device to be a disk unit throughout this appendix.

CUSTOMER File

CUSTOMER_ NUMBER	NAME	CURRENT_ BALANCE	CREDIT_ LIMIT
124	SALLY ADAMS	418.75	500
256	ANN SAMUELS	10.75	800
311	DON CHARLES	200.10	300
315	TOM DANIELS	320.75	300
405	AL WILLIAMS	201.75	800
412	SALLY ADAMS	908.75	1000
522	MARY NELSON	49.50	800
567	JOE BAKER	201.20	300
622	DAN MARTIN	575.50	500

ORDER File

ORDER_ NUMBER	DATE	CUSTOMER_ NUMBER
12489	90287	124
12491	90287	311
12494	90487	315
12495	90487	256
12498	90587	522
12500	90587	124
12504	90587	522

FIGURE A.1
Sample CUSTOMER and ORDER files

The sample CUSTOMER file contains nine records; "124, SALLY ADAMS, 418.75, 500" is the first record, "256, ANN SAMUELS, 10.75, 800" is the second record, and so forth. Each record in the CUSTOMER file contains four fields: a CUSTOMER_NUMBER that has a unique value for each record, the NAME of that customer, and the CURRENT_BALANCE and CREDIT_LIMIT for that customer.

The sample ORDER file contains seven records; "12489, 90287, 124" is the first record. Each record in the ORDER file contains three fields: an ORDER_NUMBER that has a unique value for each record, the DATE of the order, and the CUSTOMER_NUMBER of the customer who placed the order.

We begin this section by describing the steps that must be taken to access data in the database. This is followed by discussions of blocking, clustering, record access alternatives, page addresses, and keys.

ACCESSING DATA

LOGICAL TRANSACTION

A user at a terminal interacts with the environment through the use of logical transactions. A **logical transaction**, or, simply, a transaction, is a user request to accomplish a single task such as adding a customer, deleting an order, or increasing a customer's credit limit. Though the user pictures the transaction as a single interaction with the database, many more interactions typically are occurring behind the scenes.

Suppose the user enters an order with an ORDER_NUMBER of 12505 for CUSTOMER_NUMBER 522 with a DATE of 91387 and for an amount of $200.00. This constitutes one transaction to the user, who wants the new order added to the ORDER file only if this customer has sufficient remaining credit. The transaction is submitted to an application program, as shown in Figure A.2.

LOGICAL RECORD

The application program processes the transaction by interacting with the DBMS on a logical record basis. A **logical record** represents an individual application program's (or user's) view of a data record in the database. For the sample database shown in Figure A.1, we will assume that each of the nine CUSTOMER records and each of the seven ORDER records is a logical record, though this is not always the case. The application program does not directly access the database; instead, it requests that the DBMS store and retrieve data for it within the database.

To continue with our sample transaction, the application program performs the following logical record accesses in processing the single order transaction against the database:

1. Retrieve the CUSTOMER_NUMBER 522 logical record from the CUS-TOMER file and verify that the remaining credit of 750.50 (CREDIT_LIMIT of 800 minus CURRENT_BALANCE of 49.50) covers the 200.00 for this order.
2. Add a new logical record with ORDER_NUMBER of 12505, DATE of 91387, and CUSTOMER_NUMBER of 522 to the ORDER file.
3. Change the CURRENT_BALANCE to 249.50 and store this changed CUSTOMER logical record in the CUSTOMER file.

So the single transaction results in three logical record accesses to the database. A given transaction could result in fewer or more logical record accesses, depending on the work to be accomplished. Most of the time in this appendix we will simply say *record* when we are referring to a logical record.

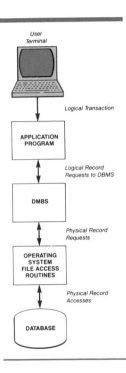

FIGURE A.2
Software component interaction to access physical database records

PHYSICAL RECORD

Each logical record request from the application program is submitted to the DBMS. The DBMS determines which physical record or records need to be accessed and then submits appropriate physical record requests to the operating system file access routines. A **physical record** is one unit of data transferred between memory and disk. It is the function of these operating system file access routines to transfer the data to and from disk and memory.

The number of physical record accesses required for the sample order transaction depends upon the characteristics and the current status of the database. The attempt to resolve the question of how many physical record accesses are required would be premature at this point, so we will come back to it later.

One significant point can be made now, however. One of the most important goals of a database environment is to minimize the number of physical record accesses required against the database. Transferring physical records between memory and disk is a time-consuming task, and keeping processing time to a minimum is an important consideration. The greater the number of physical record accesses needed, the worse the performance of the database environment. Keep this in mind as we probe deeper into file and data structures for database processing.

BLOCKING

Suppose a user submits a logical transaction to display all customers by name with their current balances in the same sequence in which they exist in the CUS-TOMER file. To satisfy this request, the application program needs to request that the DBMS retrieve all CUSTOMER records from the database. However, the application program requests these records one at a time, asking for the first record and then for each succeeding one until the end of the CUSTOMER file is reached.

Each request for a record would require a separate access to the CUSTOMER file if each logical record were a separate physical record. In this case, the display of all CUSTOMER records shown in Figure A.1 would require nine separate accesses to the database by the DBMS and operating system file access routines.

But a physical record can be larger than one logical record and, with rare exceptions, always is. Suppose each physical record is sized large enough so that it can contain three CUSTOMER records or seven ORDER records, as shown in Figure A.3. Each separate group of three CUSTOMER records and each separate group of seven ORDER records is treated as a unit, or **block**. Block and physical record are treated synonymously, so that an entire block of data is transferred as a single unit between memory and disk. What this means is that only three disk accesses are required instead of the previous nine. We say that the **blocking factor**, or number of logical records in a block, is three for the CUSTOMER file and seven for the ORDER file.

When the application program requests the first logical record, the entire first block is transferred from disk to memory. When it requests the second and third logical records, disk accesses are not required; the DBMS simply does a transfer within memory of the next logical record to the application program.

CUSTOMER File

CUSTOMER_ NUMBER	NAME	CURRENT_ BALANCE	CREDIT_ LIMIT	Block
124	SALLY ADAMS	418.75	500	
256	ANN SAMUELS	10.75	800	1
311	DON CHARLES	200.10	300	
315	TOM DANIELS	320.75	300	
405	AL WILLIAMS	201.75	800	2
412	SALLY ADAMS	908.75	1000	
522	MARY NELSON	49.50	800	
567	JOE BAKER	201.20	300	3
622	DAN MARTIN	575.50	500	

ORDER File

ORDER_ NUMBER	DATE	CUSTOMER_ NUMBER	Block
12489	90287	124	
12491	90287	311	
12494	90487	315	
12495	90487	256	4
12498	90587	522	
12500	90587	124	
12504	90587	522	

Figure A.4 demonstrates this process. The operating system file access routines transfer an entire block to a data buffer area under the control of the DBMS. A **buffer** is a memory area holding one or more blocks of data. When the application program requests the next CUSTOMER record, the DBMS transfers that record

FIGURE A.3
Blocking of the sample CUSTOMER and ORDER Files

FIGURE A.4
Data movement between the physical database and the logical components in memory

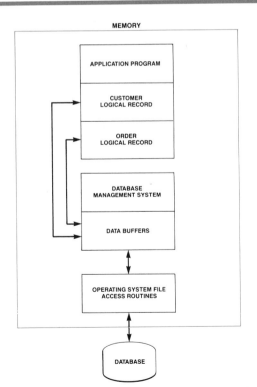

from its data buffers to the CUSTOMER logical record area in the application program. If the application program also processes ORDER records, it would have an additional ORDER logical record area, as shown in the figure.

The important consideration is that the number of disk accesses has been reduced to a third of its former level, and system performance has been proportionately improved. If the blocking factor for the CUSTOMER file is nine, then only one physical disk access is required and a further speedup in file processing has been achieved. The larger the blocking factor, the fewer the number of disk accesses required.

Also, the database administrator can normally control the number of blocks held in the DBMS data buffers. The larger this number is, the greater is the likelihood that the next logical record is already in memory. If so, then no disk access is required and performance is again improved.

For larger blocking factors and for a larger-sized buffer, there is a tradeoff: more memory is required. As the cost of memory has decreased and as memory sizes have increased, it has become more practical to manage increasingly larger sized blocks and buffers.

CLUSTERING

When dealing with a file processing environment, it is appropriate to talk about different block sizes and different blocking factors for each separate file. A DBMS, however, manages data in a more general way. All blocks are the same size, regardless of the data contents of the block. In a database environment a block is frequently referred to as a **page**, so that page, block, and physical record all mean the same thing.

Also, in a file processing environment, each block contains only logical records from the same file. A single block contains CUSTOMER records or ORDER records, but not both. (We will not deal with those cases in which one file contains records of various types differentiated by application programs through record type codes, nor will we deal with variable length records. Though important subjects, they are not relevant here.)

In a database environment, on the other hand, each page can contain different types of logical records. A single page can consist of CUSTOMER records only, ORDER records only, or a combination of CUSTOMER and ORDER records. The database administrator who configures the physical DBMS should have control over how records are grouped into pages, and most DBMS's do permit this type of control. Essentially, you want to place into the same page on disk, or in a page close by, those records that are frequently used together in order to minimize the number of pages accessed and the time needed to access them. This grouping process based on usage patterns is called **clustering**.

If CUSTOMER records are most frequently processed in CUSTOMER_NUMBER sequence and ORDER records in ORDER_NUMBER sequence, then the clustering shown in Figure A.5a on the following page, is appropriate. This figure is identical to Figure A.3 except that it has been redrawn with less detail in order to focus on the concept of record clustering. To process all CUSTOMER records, only

```
CUSTOMER    124  record     Page
CUSTOMER    256  record      1
CUSTOMER    311  record

CUSTOMER    315  record
CUSTOMER    405  record      2
CUSTOMER    412  record

CUSTOMER    522  record
CUSTOMER    567  record      3
CUSTOMER    622  record

ORDER  12489  record
ORDER  12491  record
ORDER  12494  record
ORDER  12495  record      4
ORDER  12498  record
ORDER  12500  record
ORDER  12504  record
```

FIGURE A.5a
Intrafile clustering
based on logical
record type

three pages need to be accessed. To process all ORDER records, only one page is accessed. This is an example of *intrafile clustering*: the clustering applies to individuals files. What if CUSTOMER records are most frequently processed in NAME sequence? It would then be appropriate to cluster the CUSTOMER file in NAME order rather than CUSTOMER_NUMBER order.

The usage pattern, on the other hand, might be that a given CUSTOMER record and its ORDER records are frequently processed together. Then the clustering method shown in Figure A.5b would be selected. This is called *interfile clustering*:

```
CUSTOMER    124  record     Page
ORDER  12489  record
ORDER  12500  record         1
CUSTOMER    256  record

ORDER  12495  record
CUSTOMER    311  record       2
ORDER  12491  record
CUSTOMER    315  record

ORDER  12494  record
CUSTOMER    405  record       3
CUSTOMER    412  record
CUSTOMER    522  record

ORDER  12498  record
ORDER  12504  record          4
CUSTOMER    567  record
CUSTOMER    622  record
```

FIGURE A.5b
Clustering based on
an interrecord
relationship

the clustering applies to multiple files. Now only four pages are accessed to process all CUSTOMER records in CUSTOMER_NUMBER sequence, along with their individual ORDER records.

Show why the intrafile clustering of Figure A.5a could require as many as eighteen page accesses to accomplish the same results just described.

Answer:

If the DBMS buffer is big enough to hold only one page at a time, then the retrieval of CUSTOMER pages would alternate with the retrieval of the ORDER page. This is necessary to determine whether a given CUSTOMER has any ORDERs on file.

We cannot simultaneously cluster the same file in two or more ways. We have to choose either the intrafile clustering of Figure A.5a or the interfile clustering of Figure A.5b. If our sample database had a third file, however, it could be clustered on an intrafile basis while the CUSTOMER and ORDER files were clustered on the interfile basis of Figure A.5b. In other words, separate files can be clustered in different ways but a given file cannot be clustered in two different ways.

If usage patterns change so that performance suffers, clustering changes may correct this problem. The database administrator needs to continually review this area for potential change. If clustering changes must occur, it is best if individual programs do not have to be changed, i.e., if true data independence exists within the DBMS.

For more details on clustering, see [9].

RECORD ACCESS ALTERNATIVES

There are two different ways of accessing records in a file: sequentially and randomly. **Sequential access** requires that records be stored or retrieved in a predetermined order, while random access does not.

SEQUENTIAL ACCESS

Physical sequential access is one type of predetermined order. For the CUSTOMER file in Figure A.1, CUSTOMER_NUMBER 124 is the first physical record and CUSTOMER_NUMBER 622 is the last physical record. Using physical sequential access to retrieve records from this file, we need to start at the physical beginning of the file and proceed in physical order, record by record. If we are using physical sequential access and need to retrieve just a single record from the file, all records physically preceding the needed record must be retrieved before we can reach the desired record.

Logical sequential access is a second type of predetermined order. An example of this for the CUSTOMER file shown in Figure A.1 is accessing the records in

NAME sequence by starting at SALLY ADAMS (CUSTOMER_NUMBER 124), then accessing SALLY ADAMS (CUSTOMER_NUMBER 412), then JOE BAKER, and so on, until ending with AL WILLIAMS. Notice that this file is in physical order by CUSTOMER_NUMBER so that access by NAME could not represent physical sequential access.

RANDOM ACCESS

With **random access**, the storage and retrieval of records is not based on any predetermined order. Records are stored in the file as they occur, in such a way that they can later be retrieved directly, without the necessity of accessing other records in the file. Since records are directly accessed, random access is also frequently called *direct access*. If we were to randomly access records from the CUSTOMER file, for example, we might first need to access MARY NELSON, then ANN SAMUELS, and then DAN MARTIN.

CHOICE OF ACCESS

Sequential access is appropriate when we need to access all or most of the records in a file. Also, if a file contains few enough records to fit in one page or a very few pages, then sequential access may be acceptable, since the file's pages very probably already reside in the memory buffers. In all other cases, random access is the appropriate access technique.

Random access and logical sequential access techniques are available only because there are special ways of structuring files and databases to accommodate them. These structures are the topics in all remaining sections in this appendix. Before ending this section on fundamental concepts, we need to discuss page addresses and keys.

PAGE ADDRESSES AND KEYS

In a file processing environment, the operating system keeps track of each file in terms of its size, its starting position on disk, its block size, its locations on disk, and a number of other factors. In a database environment, the operating system keeps track of the pages on disk allocated to the database, while the DBMS controls what data is located where within these allocated pages. Each page (or block) on disk has a unique address, which we call the *page number*, that can be used to store or retrieve the data in that page. In addition to the use of the page number, there are a number of other possible addressing techniques. The use of a relative record number is one of them. The **relative record number** is the number of a record relative to the start of the file. All the examples in this appendix use either the page number or the relative record number as the address for storing and retrieving a logical record on disk. When the page number is used, multiple logical records will be stored in each page.

In order to use random access to store and later retrieve a particular record, we need some mechanism for transforming the value of a field (or group of fields) within the record into a page address. In most cases, a primary key is used as the basis for this transformation. A **primary key** is a field (or group of fields) that has a unique value for each record. Therefore, it can uniquely distinguish one record in the file from any other record in the file. For example, CUSTOMER_NUMBER could serve as a primary key for the CUSTOMER file, and ORDER_NUMBER could be a primary key for the ORDER file.

Frequently, we need to randomly retrieve records in a file through the value of a field other than the primary key. For example, we might want to retrieve all customers whose CREDIT_LIMIT is 800. A field that allows access in this fashion is called a **secondary key**.

A third type of key in file and database processing is a sequence key. A **sequence key** is a field (or group of fields) within a record that determines the order of records within the file. From the appearance of the CUSTOMER file in Figure A.1, CUSTOMER_NUMBER serves as the sequence field, since the records are in physical order on the basis of this field. If this file also allowed logical sequential access based on the NAME field, then NAME would also be a sequence field for the file. Some DBMS's refer to a sequence key as a *sequence field*.

A.3 FILE ORGANIZATION

File organization refers to the physical structure of a file on disk. The three available file organization techniques are **sequential**, **direct**, and **indexed**, and they will be discussed in this order.

Each of these file organizations is used by a DBMS in some form. Sequential organization is used for journal files; for backup copies of the database; for certain extract files passed to batch application programs; for batch transaction files; and for certain forms of data storage within the database. Both direct and indexed organization are techniques used by a DBMS for storage of data within the database.

A file organization together with the set of possible access techniques for that organization constitute an **access method**. Each access technique defines the steps involved in storing and retrieving specific records through either sequential or random access. As we discuss each file organization, we will describe the access techniques possible for that organization, thereby describing the complete access method.

SEQUENTIAL ORGANIZATION

For **sequential organization**, records are stored in physical sequence as they occur during processing. Two different types of sequential organization are possible. If records are stored in no special sequence except chronological (that is, time occurrence or arrival sequence), the file is called a *pile*. Figure A.6a shows the CUSTOMER file organized as a pile. Note that the records are not in order by CUSTOMER_NUMBER, nor are they in order by any other field. Journal files, backup copies, batch

CUSTOMER	405	record	Page
CUSTOMER	256	record	1
CUSTOMER	311	record	
CUSTOMER	622	record	
CUSTOMER	124	record	2
CUSTOMER	567	record	
CUSTOMER	522	record	
CUSTOMER	412	record	3
CUSTOMER	315	record	

FIGURE A.6a
Sequential organization showing record arrival sequence: a pile

transaction files, and certain types of archive files would typically call for the use of a pile.

The second type of sequential organization is applicable with certain kinds of database storage and with master files in a file processing environment, where a large percentage of the records usually need to be accessed. This type is usually implied when sequential organization is indicated for a file. A file with this type of sequential organization has all its records stored in sequence key order. The sequence key is normally a primary key. Figure A.6b illustrates the CUSTOMER file with this type of sequential organization. The sequence key is CUSTOMER_NUMBER, which is also the primary key for the file.

Only sequential access can be used with a sequentially organized file; random access is not possible. (*Caution:* the word "sequential" describes both a type of file access and a type of file organization. We will be careful in this appendix to make clear which meaning of the word we are using.) If one specific record needs to be retrieved from the file, all records physically preceding that record must be retrieved first to get to it. Thus, sequential organization is not suited for an on-line environment, which requires rapid access.

When records are sequentially accessed in a sequentially organized file, records can be added to the end of the file. If changes need to be made to an existing record, that record can be updated and rewritten to the same physical location. But if a new record must be inserted anywhere in the middle of the file, the entire file must be recopied to a new physical location, with the new record properly positioned. Physically deleting an existing record also requires that the file be recopied to a new physical location; the deleted record would not be output to the new version of the file. Figure A.6c demonstrates the addition and deletion process: CUSTOMER records 256 and 522 from Figure A.6b have been deleted; CUSTOMER record 600 has been added. Additions, deletions, and changes to a sequentially organized master file are normally collected in a transaction file in the form of a pile. The transaction file is sorted and processed against the current version of the master, thereby creating the new version of the master, which incorporates the effects of the additions, changes, and deletions.

Sequential organization is extremely useful in terms of storage on disk, since only the logical records themselves need be stored. No additional physical structure fields need be stored, so the file is as compact as possible in disk usage.

CUSTOMER	124	record	Page
CUSTOMER	256	record	1
CUSTOMER	311	record	
CUSTOMER	315	record	
CUSTOMER	405	record	2
CUSTOMER	412	record	
CUSTOMER	522	record	
CUSTOMER	567	record	3
CUSTOMER	622	record	

FIGURE A.6b
Sequential organization showing the more typical primary key value order

CUSTOMER	124	record	Page
CUSTOMER	311	record	1
CUSTOMER	315	record	
CUSTOMER	405	record	
CUSTOMER	412	record	2
CUSTOMER	567	record	
CUSTOMER	600	record	
CUSTOMER	622	record	3

FIGURE A.6c
The previous file after deleting records 256 and 522 and adding 600

DIRECT ORGANIZATION

Direct organization gives exceptional performance in an on-line environment where random access is required. For **direct organization**, each record is stored and retrieved at a disk address on the basis of a formula that is applied to the value of a field in the record. (If the field used for the formula is alphanumeric, we assume that it is converted to a number before being used in the formula.) Two different types of direct organization are possible, one using key-addressing techniques and the other using hashing techniques.

KEY-ADDRESSING TECHNIQUES

With **key-addressing** techniques, the formula is applied to the primary key field and results in a unique **relative record number**. Figure A.7a provides an example of this technique. We have now given CUSTOMER_NUMBER, the primary key field, values 1 through 9, respectively, for each of the nine CUS-TOMER records. The value of CUSTOMER_

			Relative Record Number	Page
CUSTOMER	1	record	1	
CUSTOMER	2	record	2	1
CUSTOMER	3	record	3	
CUSTOMER	4	record	4	
CUSTOMER	5	record	5	2
CUSTOMER	6	record	6	
CUSTOMER	7	record	7	
CUSTOMER	8	record	8	3
CUSTOMER	9	record	9	

FIGURE A.7a
Direct organization using a key-addressing technique: the relative record number equals the CUSTOMER_NUMBER

NUMBER is used to store the record in the same-valued relative record position in the file. Retrieving a record, say, CUSTOMER_NUMBER 8, simply means reading the record whose relative record number is 8. The formula in this example uses the primary key field value without any change.

Figure A.7b provides a second example of the key-addressing technique. In this case a true formula is used. For CUSTOMER_NUMBER 19, we subtract 3 from the CUSTOMER_NUMBER value of 19 and divide the resulting value of 16 by 2, giving 8 as the relative record number to be used. Again, each primary key value results in a unique relative record number used for file access. Notice that it takes just one file access to store and retrieve a specific record. Increased speed of file access is a distinct advantage of the key-addressing technique for direct organization.

In these first two examples, the primary key values behave nicely; the pattern maps the records to file storage locations without any wasted space. Usually, it is impossible to establish such a pattern. Our original CUSTOMER file example is typical of what we find in actual practice. Figure A.8 on the following page, shows this file stored with the key-addressing technique, using the CUSTOMER_NUMBER value as the relative record number. Once again, only one

			Relative Record Number	Page
CUSTOMER	5	record	1	
CUSTOMER	7	record	2	1
CUSTOMER	9	record	3	
CUSTOMER	11	record	4	
CUSTOMER	13	record	5	2
CUSTOMER	15	record	6	
CUSTOMER	17	record	7	
CUSTOMER	19	record	8	3
CUSTOMER	21	record	9	

FIGURE A.7b
Direct organization using a key-addressing technique: the relative record number determined from the formula (CUSTOMER_NUMBER - 3) / 2

access is required to manipulate a given record. However, you will notice that only 9 out of the first 622 storage locations are used in the figure. The unused storage locations, called *gaps*, must be reserved, even though they are not being used. There is usually a tradeoff between speed of access and wasted disk storage space when the key-addressing technique is applied.

Unless we have a primary key that can be directed into a very compact mapping to relative record numbers, the key-addressing technique is not a wise choice for direct organization. Though it is a fast access method, it leaves many gaps, which wastes disk storage. In our three examples the records end up stored in sequence by primary key, but sequential access is time-consuming, owing to the necessity of retrieving and bypassing the gaps in order to reach the actual records. Finally, if we were to decide to change the key-addressing formula we were using, the file would most certainly need to be reorganized and might no longer be in primary key sequence.

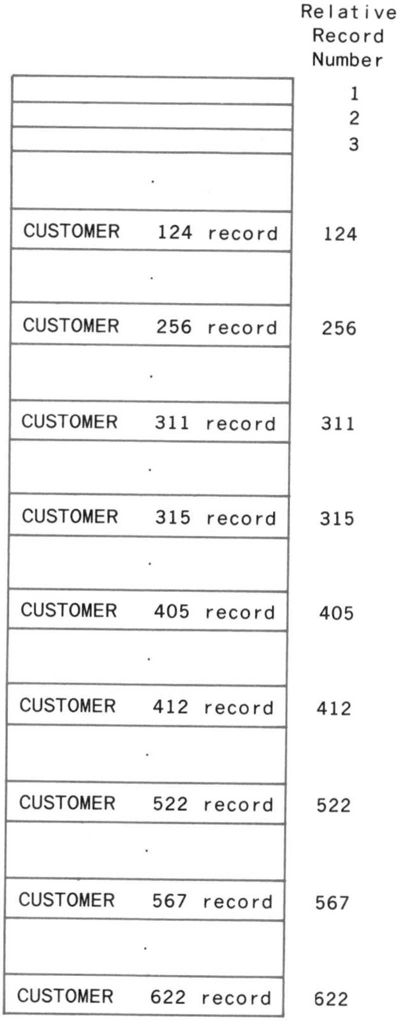

	Relative Record Number
	1
	2
	3
CUSTOMER 124 record	124
CUSTOMER 256 record	256
CUSTOMER 311 record	311
CUSTOMER 315 record	315
CUSTOMER 405 record	405
CUSTOMER 412 record	412
CUSTOMER 522 record	522
CUSTOMER 567 record	567
CUSTOMER 622 record	622

FIGURE A.8
Direct organization using a key-addressing technique: the relative record number equals the CUSTOMER_NUMBER

For example, instead of using the CUSTOMER_NUMBER value as the relative record number, let's use a formula in which the first digit of CUSTOMER_NUMBER is added to the last two digits. Figure A.9 on the following page, shows the results of this change to our formula. The file requires reorganization to place the nine CUSTOMER records into 72 storage locations, rather than the 622 we had before. Programs have to be changed to use the new formula, and the records are no longer stored in primary key sequence. Finally, what happens if a record with a CUSTOMER_NUMBER of 553 is added to the file? It should be stored using a relative record number of 58, but the CUSTOMER 256 record is already stored there! Direct organization is still possible, but now we must switch from a key-addressing technique to a hashing technique.

	Relative Record
	1
	2
	3
.	
CUSTOMER 405 record	9
.	
CUSTOMER 311 record	14
	15
CUSTOMER 412 record	16
	17
CUSTOMER 315 record	18
.	
CUSTOMER 124 record	25
	26
CUSTOMER 522 record	27
CUSTOMER 622 record	28
.	
CUSTOMER 256 record	58
.	
CUSTOMER 567 record	72

FIGURE A.9
Direct organization using a key-addressing technique: the relative record number determined from the formula (last two digits of CUSTOMER_NUMBER + first digit of CUSTOMER_NUMBER)

HASHING TECHNIQUES

Hashing techniques are similar to key-addressing techniques in that a formula is applied to a field in the record (again usually the primary key field), resulting in a value that is used as the disk address for storing and retrieving the record. The difference is that hashing does not guarantee a unique storage address. The formula can produce two or more records with the same resulting value. Also, the stored records are normally not in primary key sequence. So why use a hashing technique? The answer is that this technique allows us to efficiently utilize disk storage while attempting to retain the fastest possible random access (no more than one disk access) for on-line processing. Fast random access is possible only if we can minimize the effects of duplicate results from the formula.

Hashing techniques are sometimes called *randomizing techniques*. The formula used to transform the primary key into a disk address is also known as a *hashing algorithm*, a *hashing routine*, a *randomizing routine*, or, simply, a **hash function**. The hash function is chosen so that the records are spread as evenly as possible throughout the file, but the stored records usually end up stored in no particular sequence.

When we attempted to add a new record having CUSTOMER_NUMBER 553 to the CUSTOMER file in Figure A.9, we saw that the result of the hash function yielded a relative record number of 58. Since the CUSTOMER_NUMBER 256 record already is stored there, we now have two records that need to be stored in the same disk location. When two or more records end up with the same hash function value, we have what is called **collision**. And the two records, the ones with CUSTOMER_NUMBER 256 and 553, are called **synonyms**, since they have the same hash function value. Before we discuss different methods of managing the collision problem, we will review two commonly used hashing techniques.

FOLDING HASHING TECHNIQUE

The hash function used in Figure A.9 is an example of the **folding method**. This method involves taking the primary key value, dividing the digits of it into two or more groups, and adding these groups of digits together. The resulting sum is used as the disk address. In effect, we take a somewhat large primary key value and transform it into a smaller number, used as a disk address. This is true of all hashing techniques because we are dealing with large primary key values, such as social security numbers and bank account numbers. Our objective is to map each primary key value into as small a disk address space as possible while minimizing the collision problem. Note that none of the nine records in Figure A.9 has a synonym; however, we are utilizing only 12.5 percent (9 out of 72) of the available space. This percentage is frequently referred to as the *packing density*, or *load factor*, of the file.

What would be the packing density of the nine records in Figure A.9 if we changed the hash function to be the sum of the first two digits of CUSTOMER—NUMBER and the last digit of CUSTOMER—NUMBER? Would any collisions occur with this new folding method?

continued

Answer:

The packing would be 14 percent (9 out of 64), and no collisions would occur. The transformations would be:

CUSTOMER_NUMBER	Relative Record Number
124	16
256	31
311	32
315	36
405	45
412	43
522	54
567	63
622	64

DIVISION-REMAINDER HASHING TECHNIQUE

The **division-remainder method** employes a formula in which the primary key value is divided by a fixed, preselected number and the remainder of this division is used as the disk address. Research has proven that the number selected for the division should be a prime number and that the division-remainder method is one of the very best hashing techniques. Since the remainder could be zero, we will add 1 to the remainder in our examples of this method.

Figure A.10 on the following page, demonstrates the division-remainder method, using the same CUSTOMER file records and a divisor of 29. We have added 1 to the results of the formula to produce the relative record number. The nine CUSTOMER records fit into twenty-nine storage locations, a 31 percent packing density.

There are no collisions in this example, but that does not guarantee that there will be none in the future. For instance, if we attempt to add the record whose CUSTOMER_NUMBER was 625, the hash function produces a value of 17. Thus, the CUSTOMER 567 record is a synonym for this new record, so collision results.

COLLISION MANAGEMENT

No matter how well we choose our hashing algorithm, we are going to have to face the problem of collisions and how best to manage them. A variety of techniques are used to minimize the number of collisions and to minimize the effects of collision when it does occur.

You will recall that a DBMS stores records in pages holding multiple records and that each page has a unique page number, or address. Rather than use a relative record number for storing and retrieving records, hashing techniques use

	Relative Record Number
CUSTOMER 522 record	1
	2
	3
.	
CUSTOMER 412 record	7
	8
CUSTOMER 124 record	9
.	
CUSTOMER 622 record	14
.	
CUSTOMER 567 record	17
.	
CUSTOMER 311 record	22
.	
CUSTOMER 256 record	25
CUSTOMER 315 record	26
.	
CUSTOMER 405 record	29

FIGURE A.10
Direct organization with a hashing technique using the division-remainder method and a divisor of 29

the page number for locating records. With this approach, a page is often called a *bucket*, and each record location within a page is called a *slot*.

In Figure A.11 on the following page, seven pages have been allocated, and each page can store three CUSTOMER records. The division-remainder method is used with a divisor of 7 (and again we add 1 to the result to obtain the page number). The CUSTOMER 315 and 567 records both hash to page 1, but both records can be stored with room for one additional record in the future. What we have done is to minimize the effects of collision, since it will now cause a problem only when we attempt to store an additional record in a page that is full with three records.

If we enlarge the size of each page so that it will hold more records, then the effects of collision will be reduced further. The file in Figure A.11 has a packing density of 42 percent (9 out of 21, the maximum number of records that can be stored). If we enlarge each page so that it will hold four records and keep the number of pages and our hash function the same, the packing density reduces to 32

percent (9 out of 28). This demonstrates that the more we try to eliminate collision, relying strictly on larger page sizes, the less efficiently we are utilizing disk
space.

			Page
CUSTOMER	315	record	1
CUSTOMER	567	record	
			2
			3
CUSTOMER	311	record	4
CUSTOMER	256	record	5
CUSTOMER	522	record	
CUSTOMER	124	record	6
CUSTOMER	405	record	7
CUSTOMER	412	record	
CUSTOMER	622	record	

FIGURE A.11
Collision resolution
using page addresses

When a page becomes full and a further collision occurs on that page, there
are a number of methods for dealing with the new record. One method involves
the use of a **linear search** for storing and later retrieving the record. If we find that
the page is full when we attempt to add a new record to it, we place the record in
the next page that has an available record slot.

Let's assume that we need to add two new records to those shown in Figure
A.11. These records are for CUSTOMER_NUMBERs 623 and 630, both of which
hash to page 1. The CUSTOMER 623 record is placed into page 1, since there is
room for one more record, and the CUSTOMER 630 record is placed into page 2,
the next page having an available record slot. Figure A.12 on the following page,
shows the result of these additions. When later retrieving the CUSTOMER 630
record, we employ the division-remainder hash function and get a value of 1. Page
1 is retrieved, and when we find that the CUSTOMER 630 record is not located
there, page 2 is retrieved and the record is found.

The advantage of the linear search method is that records that hash to the same
address will end up clustered together in the same page or in nearby pages. But
what happens if there are many records that hash to the first three pages, so that
when we store the CUSTOMER 630 record, it must be stored in page 4 or even a

later page? Multiple file accesses are required to obtain the requested record. This procedure is inefficient but does not affect performance too badly if only a few accesses are required.

FIGURE A.12
Collision resolution
using a linear search

But what happens when we are asked to retrieve the CUSTOMER 616 record, which hashes to page 1, and the first five pages are filled with CUSTOMER records? We have to retrieve each of these pages and check each record before we will know for sure that this record does not exist. And the problem can be even worse for large-sized files with high packing densities. We may have to search through thousands of pages before we store or retrieve the correct record or find that such a record does not exist.

There is another method of managing collision that helps overcome these problems. It involves the use of a separate **overflow area** for storing records that cannot be placed in the exact page specified by the hash function. Figure A.13 demonstrates the use of a separate overflow area consisting of pages 8 and 9. These two pages are in addition to the seven pages, normally called the *prime area*, that we have been using in our examples. Rather than store the CUSTOMER 630 record in page 2, as we did with the linear search method, we store this record in page 8, the first of the two overflow pages. Now when we retrieve the CUSTOMER 630 record, we employ the division-remainder hash function, getting a value of 1. Page 1 is retrieved, and when we find that the CUSTOMER 630 record is not located there, page 8 is retrieved and the record is found.

FIGURE A.13
Collision resolution using overflow pages

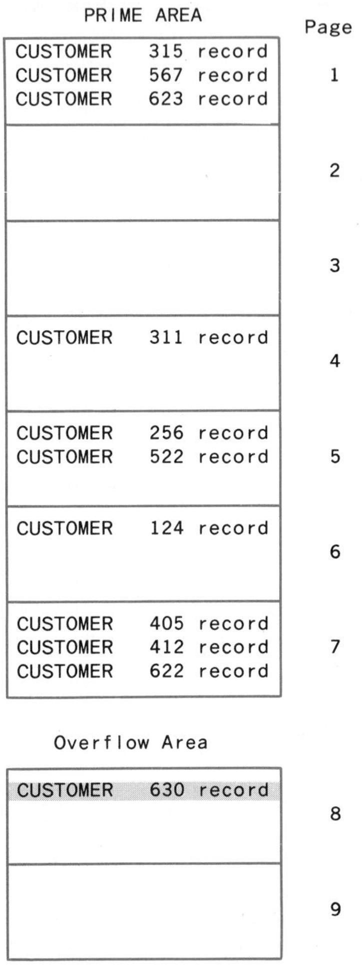

Both with the linear search and the overflow area method, exactly two accesses were required to retrieve the CUSTOMER 630 record. So both methods appear to be equally efficient. However, the overflow area method proves to be more efficient in the long run. When collision occurs with the linear search method, the record is placed in the closest nearby page. This may tend to cause collision for a future record that hashes to that same page. Also, if we can keep the number of collisions to a minimum, it will be faster to search through a smaller overflow area than to search through the prime area, where records that properly hash to a given page are intermingled with records placed in that page because of collision management.

The efficiency of both the linear search and the overflow area method can be improved through the use of a **pointer chain** (also known as a *synonym chain* or a *collision chain* when using direct organization). Each page has a field called a pointer that serves as an indicator of whether collision has occurred on that page. In Figure A.14, pages 2 through 6 have a pointer value of zero, meaning that no collision has occurred on any of these pages. Both pages 1 and 7 have a pointer value of 8, meaning that collision has occurred on both these pages and that the synonym records for both pages have been stored in page 8 in the overflow area.

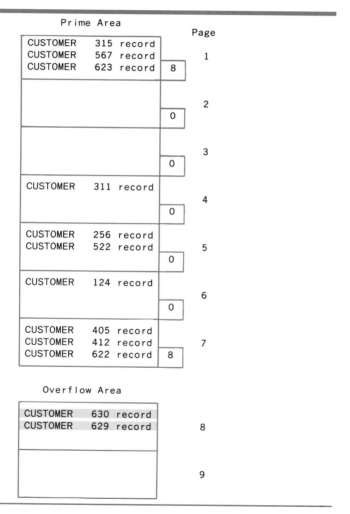

FIGURE A.14
Collision resolution using overflow pages and a pointer chain

The use of a pointer chain helps to minimize the number of pages that have to be searched when collision occurs.

A number of other collision management techniques and variations are available; for further details, see [2], [7], [9], and [10].

DIRECT ORGANIZATION SUMMARY

Direct organization provides fast random access, but sequential access is inefficient and does not normally return records in primary key sequence. Key-addressing techniques which require only one disk access are most efficient, but are also impractical in most situations, owing to low packing densities and the need for large amounts of disk space.

Hashing techniques provide a reasonable tradeoff between very fast access and efficient use of disk space. Because of collisions, hashing techniques require on an average more than one disk access to store or retrieve a given record. The precise performance of a given hashing technique in a given application depends upon a number of factors, including the following:

1. The characteristics of the primary key used as the basis for the hash function.
2. The hash function that is chosen.
3. The collision management technique that is chosen.
4. The page size that is chosen, since larger page sizes tend to reduce the likelihood of a record needing to be placed outside its proper page.
5. The packing density, since higher densities will result more frequently in the need to place a record outside its proper page. Experts claim that the packing density should be no higher than 80 percent. On the downside, very low packing densities result in greater waste of disk storage, so that 40 percent to 80 percent is the typical range for effective packing density.

See [2], [5], and [7] for analyses of these performance factors.

INDEXED ORGANIZATION

Indexed organization provides efficient access to records both sequentially and randomly; the logical records are stored in one file, called the *data file*, and there is a separate **index file** (or simply *index*) that contains records consisting of the key value and the address of the logical record having that key value. We say that the data file is *indexed by* the index file. Most operating systems restrict the type of indexed organization covered in this section to keys having unique values, or to primary keys. As a result, this type of index is often called a **primary index**. However, methods permitting the data file to be indexed by a non-unique secondary key will be discussed in the next section. In this case we would have what is called a **secondary index**. Two general types of indexed organization are possible, one called indexed random organization and the other called indexed sequential organization.

INDEXED RANDOM ORGANIZATION

An example of indexed organization is shown in Figure A.15a on the following page. The nine records of the CUSTOMER file are stored in the data file, and the index has one record, or entry, for each of the nine data file records. Each index record contains a CUSTOMER_NUMBER, which is the primary key, and the page number that indicates where the record having that CUSTOMER_NUMBER value is located in the data file.

```
      Index File              Data File
      Key Address

                                                   Page
       124    2      CUSTOMER   405   record
       256    1      CUSTOMER   256   record          1
       311    1      CUSTOMER   311   record
       315    3
       405    1      CUSTOMER   622   record
       412    3      CUSTOMER   124   record          2
       522    3      CUSTOMER   567   record
       567    2
       622    2      CUSTOMER   522   record
                     CUSTOMER   412   record          3
                     CUSTOMER   315   record
```

The index file obviously places additional space requirements on record storage. So why incur this additional overhead? One purpose is to allow sequential retrieval of the logical records. The logical records in the data file in Figure A.15a are not stored in primary key sequence, but the index records are stored in primary key sequence. By retrieving CUSTOMER records in the order specified by the index, we end up accessing them in logical sequence by CUSTOMER_NUMBER. This form of indexed organization is called **indexed random organization** (also known as *indexed nonsequential organization*), since the data file records are in random sequence. Since the logical records are not in sequence, there must be one index record for each logical record when we are using indexed random organization.

A second benefit of indexed organization is that we can randomly access records much faster than we could without the use of the index. Without it, we would have to sequentially access data file records if we wanted to randomly retrieve a specific record. Though we have to sequentially access the index to achieve the same result, the overall search time is substantially reduced. One reason for the more rapid random access is the relative sizes of data file records and index records. Data file records are usually large; in many applications, each logical record is hundreds or thousands of bytes in size. In the absence of an index, a considerable amount of time is required to sequentially retrieve each page and scan each logical record in order to find the one record needed randomly. On the other hand, each index record is very small. Typically the address is four bytes, so with the addition of the primary key length of three bytes in our example, we have a record size of seven bytes. Many index records can fit in one page of the index file, so fewer disk accesses are needed and the overall search time is considerably reduced.

Furthermore, if a large proportion of the index can fit into memory, the sequential search proceeds at memory speeds and requires a minimal number of disk accesses. And even faster search methods, such as a binary search, can be used to further reduce the search time to a very small fraction of a second.

Another advantage of using an index for random access applies to data files containing large numbers of records. As the number of logical records grows, the number of records in the index grows at the same rate. Index search time increases, but even more time would be spent searching through the data file. Additionally, once the index has grown to a point where it can no longer reside in memory, we can treat it as if it were a data file and create an index to the index.

Figure A.15b illustrates this process. The "level 2 index" is our original index, and the "level 1 index" is the new index to the original index. We now have a two-level index, more generally called a *multilevel index*. We call level 1 index a

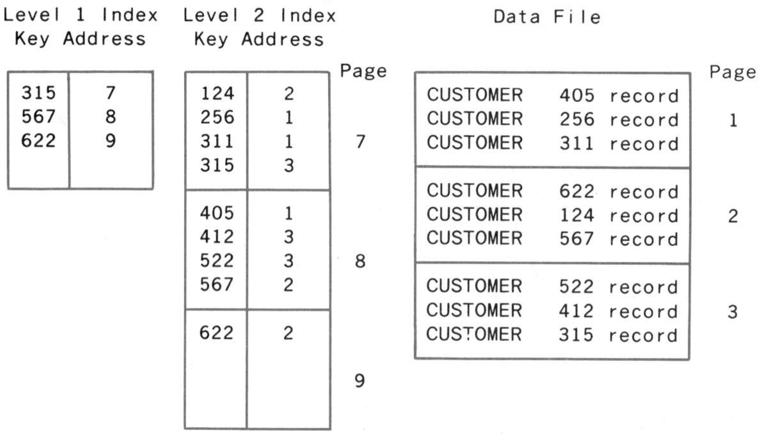

FIGURE A.15b
Indexed random organization using a 2-level index

Level 1 Index		Level 2 Index		Page	Data File			Page
Key	Address	Key	Address					
315	7	124	2		CUSTOMER	405	record	
567	8	256	1		CUSTOMER	256	record	1
622	9	311	1	7	CUSTOMER	311	record	
		315	3					
		405	1		CUSTOMER	622	record	
		412	3		CUSTOMER	124	record	2
		522	3	8	CUSTOMER	567	record	
		567	2					
		622	2		CUSTOMER	522	record	
					CUSTOMER	412	record	3
				9	CUSTOMER	315	record	

high-level index, and level 2 index a low-level index. Since the key values in our original index are in sequence, we only need to have one record in the high-level index for each page in the low-level index, with the key being the highest-valued key in that low-level index page. This is called a *sparse index*, since it does not contain a record for each record in the low-level index, while the low-level index is called a *dense index*, since it has one record for each record in the data file. Now we can fit the high-level index in memory, search it, and retrieve the proper low-level index page, search the low-level index page in memory, and finally retrieve the data file page containing the record we need to randomly access. Two accesses to randomly retrieve a logical record! We have only nine records and three pages in our data file, so this may not seem too impressive; to fully appreciate the benefits of using an index for random access, picture a data file and low-level index requiring thousands of pages of disk storage. If necessary, the indexing structure can expand to many more levels than we have shown.

An additional advantage of indexed random organization is that we do not need to access the data file if all we need to know is whether a logical record having a specific primary key value exists. This question can be answered by restricting the search to the index. As a result, one less disk access is required.

A final advantage of indexed random organization is that the data file records do not need to be in sequence. When records are added and deleted, the data file update process is fairly simple. However, the programming to handle the indexes can become complicated. Fortunately, indexed organization is a standard feature on most computers. This means that index management is the responsibility of the operating system file access routines, not of the programmer.

INDEXED SEQUENTIAL ORGANIZATION

If indexed organization is being used and the data file records are in primary key sequence, we have **indexed sequential organization**. In Figure A.16a the CUSTOMER records are in sequence by the primary key of CUSTOMER_NUMBER. The index looks the same as before. But must we continue to have one index record for each data file record? No! Since the data file records are in sequence, we need only one index record for each data file page. The index, therefore, is reduced in size and is stored as a sparse index. Figure A.16b depicts the index for indexed sequential organization.

Index File		Data File		Page
Key	Address			
124	1	CUSTOMER	124 record	
256	1	CUSTOMER	256 record	
311	1	CUSTOMER	311 record	1
315	2			
405	2	CUSTOMER	315 record	
412	2	CUSTOMER	405 record	2
522	3	CUSTOMER	412 record	
567	3			
622	3	CUSTOMER	522 record	
		CUSTOMER	567 record	3
		CUSTOMER	622 record	

FIGURE A.16a
Indexed sequential
organization

Fewer index records means a smaller-sized index, faster search times, and the need for fewer levels to the index as the data file grows in size. On the other hand, we can no longer determine the existence of a specific primary key value by searching only through the index, as we could with indexed random organization. Now the data file must be accessed with one additional disk access. But since fewer index pages and levels are required overall, in practice fewer disk accesses are required to the index, so in the end, indexed sequential organization turns out to be more efficient.

Since indexed sequential organization takes less space and performs better than indexed random organization, why would we ever want to use the latter? The answer is that it allows us to have the data file indexed by as many fields as we need. In other words, we can have a number of **secondary indexes**. Since the data file is in one sequence only, usually by the primary key, all secondary indexes must use indexed random organization or some other structure for relating a secondary key value to the record(s) containing that particular value.

If we need to sequentially retrieve records from an indexed sequential file by its primary index, it is not necessary to use the index. Since the data file is in primary key sequence, we simply retrieve data file pages in order. The index is

Index File		Data File		Page
Key	Address			
311	1	CUSTOMER	124 record	
412	2	CUSTOMER	256 record	1
622	3	CUSTOMER	311 record	
		CUSTOMER	315 record	
		CUSTOMER	405 record	2
		CUSTOMER	412 record	
		CUSTOMER	522 record	
		CUSTOMER	567 record	3
		CUSTOMER	622 record	

FIGURE A.16b
Indexed sequential
organization with one
index entry per page

used for random access retrieval only. But what happens to the primary key sequence of the data file when we attempt to add a new logical record to a page that is full? Where does the system insert the record, and what happens to the index? To answer these questions, we need to look into the data file management alternatives available under indexed sequential organization.

INDEXED SEQUENTIAL ORGANIZATION DATA FILE MANAGEMENT

One method for managing data file insertions under indexed sequential organization is the use of an **overflow area** and a **pointer chain**. Suppose we need to add the CUSTOMER 350 record to the example shown in Figure A.16b. Since all data file pages are full, a record must be placed in an overflow page, and a means must be established for locating the record placed in the overflow page. As Figure A.17a demonstrates, a separate overflow area and two new fields in each data file page have been added. One of the new fields is an overflow location pointer,

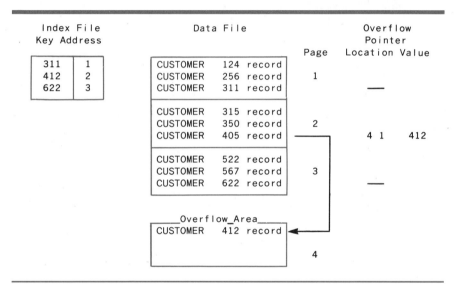

FIGURE A.17a
Indexed sequential organization using an overflow area with a pointer

which links the data file page to the next logical record in sequence located in the overflow area. The overflow location pointer consists of a page number and relative record number within that overflow page. The expression "4 1" for page 2 means that the next logical record can be found in the overflow area in relative record position 1 of page 4. The other new field represents the highest key value associated with the given data file page that can be found in the overflow area, the CUSTOMER 412 record in our example. Note that the new CUSTOMER 350 record has been positioned in proper sequence in page 2, and the CUSTOMER 412 record is the one that has been relocated to the overflow area. The "——" for data file pages 1 and 3 represents the fact that overflow has not occurred for these pages. Finally, this logical record insertion has resulted in no change to the index file.

When the CUSTOMER 410 record is now added, it must be stored in the overflow area, as shown in Figure A.17b. Since this record precedes the CUS-TOMER 412 record already in the overflow area, the page 2 location pointer must be changed to indicate where the CUSTOMER 410 record is located, and a pointer chaining the CUSTOMER 410 record to the CUSTOMER 412 record must be added. The records in the overflow area are kept in arrival sequence, not logical sequence, and thus pointer chaining is required for the overflow area. The pointer associated with the CUSTOMER 412 record in the overflow area would be "—".

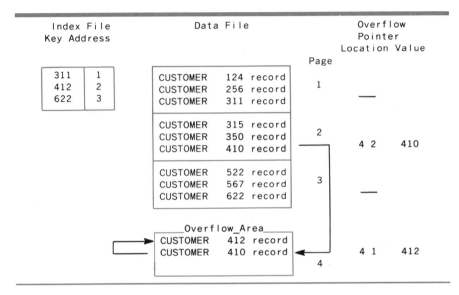

FIGURE A.17b
Indexed sequential organization using an overflow area with a pointer chain after CUSTOMER 350 and 410 have been added

As you can guess, performance degrades as more and more records are added to the overflow area and the pointer chains become longer and longer. Periodically, the indexed file needs to be reorganized so that all records are placed in the data file in correct logical sequence and the index file is appropriately reconstructed.

When the overflow area technique is used with indexed sequential organization, usually the data file is initially built with gaps in each page. That is, each data file page is only partially filled with logical records, leaving empty record slots for use for future additions to the file. These gaps are called **distributed free space**. The use of distributed free space reduces the problem of overflow area chaining but does not eliminate the problem entirely. Low packing densities reduce the need for placing records in the overflow area and for chaining within the overflow area, but they do increase the size of the index and the number of levels to the index.

IBM's *indexed sequential access method* (ISAM) uses the overflow area technique on a more complicated basis that relies on the physical characteristics of disk. For details on the ISAM approach, see [2], [4], and [7].

A second method for managing data file insertions under indexed sequential organization is the use of the **block-splitting** technique. To demonstrate this technique, we will again add the CUSTOMER 350 record to the file shown in Figure A.16b. Page 2 is where this new record should be stored, but there is no room left there. So page 4, the next available empty page, is used, and the CUSTOMER 350 record plus the three records in page 2 are divided between the two pages. Figure A.18a shows the result. We have split the contents of the full page, or block, into two pages; and thus the term block splitting for this technique.

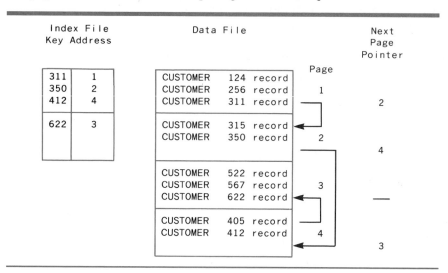

FIGURE A.18a
Indexed sequential organization using block splitting after adding the CUSTOMER 350 record

Adding the CUSTOMER 410 record presents no difficulty, as you can see in Figure A.18b. It is simply stored in page 4, since there is room for one additional record. But now the page is full. It may seem that this technique would require us

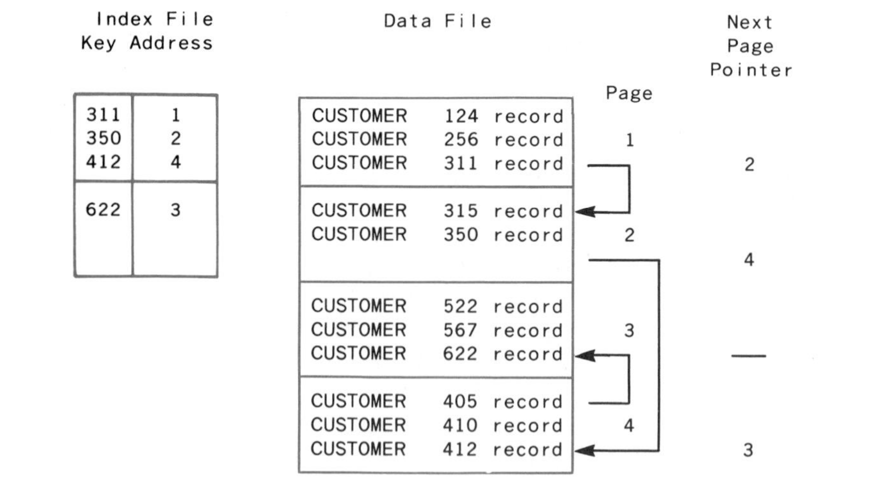

FIGURE A.18b
Indexed sequential organization using block splitting after CUSTOMER 350 and 410 records have been added

to split pages quite frequently. However, our examples are structured small in order to illustrate concepts; in reality, we would be storing a larger number of logical records in each page. If we were to store twenty CUSTOMER records in each page, then when we split the contents of one full page into two pages, there would be enough room to accommodate ten more records in each of the two pages.

The index file has to change to reflect the added page in the proper sequence. This is shown both in Figure A.18a and A.18b. Although the logical records are no longer in logical sequence by page number, the index can be used as a guide for sequentially accessing data file records. Another technique that is frequently employed to avoid the necessity of using the index for sequential access is the addition of a field to each data file page. This field serves as a pointer to the next logical page in sequence. It is shown in the two A.18 figures as the "next page pointer," and arrows have been drawn to indicate the correct sequence of records by primary key.

Distributed free space can be used with the block-splitting technique when the indexed file is first created to delay the initial need to redistribute records. IBM's *virtual storage access method* (VSAM) uses both distributed free space and the block-splitting technique to manage its type of indexed sequential organization. For details on the VSAM approach for managing the data file, see [2], [4], and [7].

INDEXED ORGANIZATION SUMMARY

Indexed organization provides an efficient means of both sequentially and randomly accessing records. Random retrieval of records is faster than with sequential organization, though not as fast as with the best forms of direct organization. Extra disk storage space is required to store the index and possible pointers, and additions and deletions to the data file can be time-consuming.

We will investigate some further index structures in the next section when we discuss inverted files and tree structures.

A.4   DATA STRUCTURES

The file organizations discussed in the previous section are sufficient to support traditional file processing environments. They fall short, however, of totally supporting DBMS environments that in effect are managing many files and many relationships among these files. A DBMS, for example, has to be able to form relationships between records from different files, to handle secondary indexes having multiple records for each secondary key value, and to provide rapid response to both predefined and ad hoc requests. The DBMS must provide more sophisticated data structures for dealing with these common requirements. In this section we will discuss three of the data structures that are frequently utilized by DBMS's. They are inverted files, linked lists, and B-trees.

INVERTED FILES

We've mentioned a number of times that secondary key access is important to users in a database environment. One file structure that can be used to represent secondary keys is **indexed random organization**, which was reviewed in the previous section. When indexed random organization is used in this way on a secondary key, we have what is called a **secondary index**. Figure A.15b shows indexed random organization applied to the CUSTOMER_NUMBER field, but this organization works in the same way for any secondary key that has unique values for each record in the data file.

When we use an index on a secondary key field in this fashion, we say that we have *inverted on* that field, and the index formed to support that secondary key is known as an **inverted file**, or *inverted list*. We have inverted the normal role of a field in the record, since we find the record based on the field value instead of finding the field value after locating the record.

We can use an inverted file structure (or index) on any secondary key in a logical record. Figure A.15b, however, is not sufficiently complex to illustrate how the index is structured when the secondary key has nonunique values across the data file. Our original CUSTOMER file, for example, consisted of CUSTOMER_NUMBER, NAME, CURRENT_BALANCE, and CREDIT_LIMIT. What if we need to randomly access CUSTOMER records, using CREDIT_LIMIT as a secondary key? CREDIT_LIMIT cannot serve as the primary key for the CUSTOMER file, since a given value appears in more than one record. Therefore, the index structure in Figure A.15b is not appropriate for handling the CREDIT_LIMIT situation.

What we need is an index structure that handles secondary key values pointing to multiple data file records. The inverted file structure in Figure A.19 does exactly this. We now show both CUSTOMER_NUMBER and CREDIT_LIMIT for each of the nine logical records in the CUSTOMER file. The page numbers we have been using have been changed back to relative record numbers to simplify the discussion of this form of inverted file structure.

FIGURE A.19
Inverted file structure
on CREDIT_LIMIT

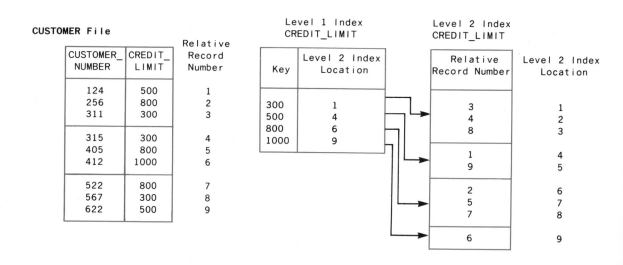

The inverted file for this example is a two-level index. The level 1 index consists of one record for each different secondary key value, CREDIT_LIMIT in this example. Since CREDIT_LIMIT has four different values (300, 500, 800, and 1000), there are four records in the level 1 index, which is in sequence by CREDIT_LIMIT value. Stored in each level 1 index record, along with the CREDIT_LIMIT value, is a pointer to the level 2 index. This pointer indicates the position in the level 2 index that starts the list of relative record numbers with that secondary key value. For example, the CREDIT_LIMIT value of 300 in the level 1 index points to location 1 in the level 2 index. The first three entries in the level 2 index, which are 3, 4, and 8, give the relative record numbers for the three CUSTOMER records having a CREDIT_LIMIT of 300.

If we have inverted files for all fields in the CUSTOMER file, then we have a *fully inverted file*. If only some of the fields in the CUSTOMER file have inverted files, then we have a *partially inverted file*.

Inverted files can be used to answer certain queries without the need to access the data file. Examples of queries of this type are:

1. How many customers have a CREDIT_LIMIT of 800?
2. How many customers have a CREDIT_LIMIT between 500 and 800?
3. How many orders are there for CUSTOMER_NUMBER 405?
4. How many orders having a DATE more recent than 90587 are there for CUSTOMER_NUMBERs 256 and 567?
5. Are there any records that have a CURRENT_BALANCE greater than 750.00?

The retrieval of records is very efficient with an inverted file structure; such is the case with most indexing techniques. The tradeoffs are the space required to store the multilevel index and the extra time required to update the inverted files. Therefore, inverted files are created only for those fields critically needed for retrieval. For further information on inverted files, see [2], [7], and [9].

LINKED LISTS

There are methods other than inverted files for managing secondary keys. Among them is the use of linked lists. Before considering how linked lists can be used in secondary key and other situations, we need to examine the basic concepts and terminology of the linked list structure and processing techniques.

A **linked list** consists of a field added to each logical record that has as a value the location of the next logical record in sequence. This field is called a link field or *pointer*, and the linked list is also known as a **pointer chain**, since pointers are used to chain records together. Suppose we take the CUSTOMER file from Figure A.19 and form a linked list to allow sequential access of the logical records based on increasing values of the CREDIT_LIMIT field. Figure A.20a on the following page, has the new pointer field added to each CUSTOMER record. There is an additional field external to the CUSTOMER records which serves the function of pointing to the start of the linked list. This field is a *head pointer* and has a value

CREDIT_LIMIT Head Pointer: 3

CUSTOMER File

CUSTOMER_ NUMBER	CREDIT_ LIMIT	Pointer	Relative Record Number
124	500	9	1
256	800	5	2
311	300	4	3
315	300	8	4
405	800	7	5
412	1000	—	6
522	800	6	7
567	300	1	8
622	500	2	9

FIGURE A.20a
Linked list with
pointers for
CREDIT_LIMIT

of 3 in Figure A.20a. The value 3 represents the relative record number of the first
CUSTOMER record in sequence. This record has a CREDIT_LIMIT value of 300
for CUSTOMER_NUMBER 311. The pointer field for this record links to relative
record number 4, which is the next record in CREDIT_LIMIT sequence. You can
follow the chain of pointers until reaching CUSTOMER_NUMBER 412, which has a
CREDIT_LIMIT value of 1000 and is the last record in the chain. The pointer
value of "——" signifies the end of the chain.

What happens if we start in the middle of the linked list, say, at the CUS-
TOMER 622 record, and want to retrieve every CUSTOMER record in the order
specified by the pointer field? We would not be able to do so, since the CUSTOMER
412 record does not point to any other record. Once we reached the end of the
chain, however, we could use the value of the external head pointer to continue our
circuit of the chain. Another more common approach is to have the last link field
point to the first record in the chain, as shown in Figure A.20b. The pointer for the

CREDIT_LIMIT Head Pointer: 3

CUSTOMER File

CUSTOMER_ NUMBER	CREDIT_ LIMIT	Pointer	Relative Record Number
124	500	9	1
256	800	5	2
311	300	4	3
315	300	8	4
405	800	7	5
412	1000	3	6
522	800	6	7
567	300	1	8
622	500	2	9

FIGURE A.20b
Circular linked list
with pointers for
CREDIT_LIMIT

CUSTOMER 412 record now points to relative record number 3, which is the start of the chain. This refinement is called a *circular linked list* or *ring*.

We can have as many linked lists as we need in the data file, just as we can have as many indexes as we need. In addition to the linked list for CREDIT_ LIMIT, we could create one for NAME and one for CURRENT_BALANCE in the CUSTOMER file. Each additional linked list takes additional storage space and requires extra time to update.

A linked list can be used as an alternative to the inverted file to represent **secondary keys** through a structure called a *multilist*. Figure A.21 shows a multilist constructed on the CREDIT_LIMIT field as the secondary key. There is one index similar to the level 1 index we needed for the inverted file structure in Figure A.19. The multilist index has one record for each different secondary key value and is in order by the secondary key. Instead of pointing to a level 2 index, as with the inverted file, each multilist record has a head pointer that starts the chain for records having that particular CREDIT_LIMIT value. For example,

FIGURE A.21
Multilist with
CREDIT_LIMIT as
secondary key

CUSTOMER File

CUSTOMER_ NUMBER	CREDIT_ LIMIT	Pointer	Relative Record Number
124	500	9	1
256	800	5	2
311	300	4	3
315	300	8	4
405	800	7	5
412	1000	—	6
522	800	—	7
567	300	—	8
622	500	—	9

CREDIT_LIMIT Index

Key	Relative Record Number
300	3
500	1
800	2
1000	6

CREDIT_LIMIT 500 in the index points to relative record number 1 for CUSTOMER_NUMBER 124, whose pointer of 9 links to CUSTOMER_NUMBER 622, which is the end of the chain.

If we have multiple secondary keys, we can use a separate multilist structure for each one. Each multilist would have its own index and its own linked list. Compared to the inverted file, the multilist's index is easier to create and to maintain, since the level 2 index for the inverted file has a variable number of entries. On the other hand, the multilist pointers must be maintained, while there are no pointers within the logical records with the inverted file. Overall, the multilist is easier to maintain.

A major disadvantage of the multilist list approach as compared to the inverted file is that answering the queries we posed earlier at the end of the inverted file discussion is more difficult and takes more time. The response to the query "How many customers have a CREDIT_LIMIT of 800?" could be determined by means of the level 1 and level 2 index of the inverted file structure. To answer the same query with a multilist, we have to "walk" the chain from the multilist index through all the records that are linked together. And for more complicated queries, such as "How many customers have a CURRENT_BALANCE over 500.00 and a CREDIT_LIMIT of 800 or 1000?" we have to traverse two separate multilist chains with multiple paths. With the inverted files, we can take the intersection of the indexes without having to access the data file.

The linked lists so far have been *singly linked lists* or *one-way linked lists*; the chains travel in one direction only. We can also have *doubly linked lists* or *two-way linked lists*. These have two sets of chains, one traveling in the forward direction we've seen so far, and the other traveling in a backward direction. Figure A.22 illustrates a doubly linked list on the CREDIT_LIMIT field. The forward pointers are next pointers and the backward pointers are prior pointers. The additional external tail pointer is needed to start the prior pointer chain. Doubly linked lists make the job of maintaining the chains easier for additions and deletions, at the expense of additional space requirements.

FIGURE A.22
Doubly linked list on CREDIT_LIMIT

CREDIT_LIMIT Head Pointer: 3
CREDIT_LIMIT Tail Pointer: 6

CUSTOMER File

CUSTOMER_ NUMBER	CREDIT_ LIMIT	Next Pointer	Prior Pointer	Relative Record Number
124	500	9	8	1
256	800	5	9	2
311	300	4	6	3
315	300	8	3	4
405	800	7	2	5
412	1000	3	7	6
522	800	6	5	7
567	300	1	4	8
622	500	2	1	9

Linked lists can be used to establish a relationship between records from two different files. There is a **one-to-many relationship** between the CUSTOMER file and the ORDER file. Each CUSTOMER record can have zero, one, or more ORDER records, while a given ORDER record is owned by only one CUSTOMER record. Figure A.23 on the following page shows the use of a doubly linked list to tie together the records in this one-to-many relationship. Beginning with a CUS-TOMER record, the head pointer starts the chain in a forward direction to the ORDER records and the tail pointer starts the chain in a backward direction to the ORDER records. The next and prior pointers in the ORDER file link together ORDER records for the same CUSTOMER. Note that we have included the CUS-TOMER records with the ORDER records in the pointer chains.

We could add another linked list to the ORDER file which would provide a pointer for each ORDER record back to the CUSTOMER file. These pointers are called *parent pointers* or *owner pointers*. These pointers would allow us to get directly back to the CUSTOMER record for a given ORDER record without having to travel around the chain back to the CUSTOMER record. This can be a considerable time saver if the chain tends to be very long.

CUSTOMER File

CUSTOMER_ NUMBER	CREDIT_ LIMIT	Head Pointer	Tail Pointer	Relative Record Number
124	500	10	15	1
256	800	13	13	2
311	300	11	11	3
315	300	12	12	4
405	800	5	5	5
412	1000	6	6	6
522	800	14	16	7
567	300	8	8	8
622	500	9	9	9

ORDER File

ORDER_ NUMBER	CUSTOMER_ NUMBER	Next Pointer	Prior Pointer	Relative Record Number
12489	124	15	1	10
12491	311	3	3	11
12494	315	4	4	12
12495	256	2	2	13
12498	522	16	7	14
12500	124	1	10	15
12504	522	7	14	16

FIGURE A.23
Doubly linked list forming the relationship between CUSTOMERs and their ORDERs

As with any file organization or data structure, our main concern is to minimize disk accesses. So in addition to the use of linked lists for the CUSTOMER to ORDER relationship, it would be ideal if ORDER records were clustered in the same page as the owner CUSTOMER record. Some DBMS's permit this as an option at the time the database is defined.

For further details on linked lists, see [2], [7], and [9].

TREES

We now turn to a discussion of one final data structure, called the **B-tree**. The B-tree is one of the most widely used data structures in database processing today. Its chief use is for the storage and management of indexes. The B-tree is a special form of the general tree structure, so we will begin our discussion by reviewing some of the terminology and concepts of trees.

GENERAL TREE TERMINOLOGY

A **tree** is a structure that resembles the organizational, or hierarchy, chart of a business enterprise. It also resembles a genealogical, or family, tree. The tree is inverted, with a single root at the top and the tree's branches leading toward the bottom. Tree terminology is a mixture of botanical and genealogical tree terms.

A tree consists of *nodes* that are connected by *branches*. The single *root* node is at the top, and its *descendants* are below it. In Figure A.24, nodes appear in boxes, and branches are the connecting lines between boxes. Node A is the root, and all other nodes are its descendants. A node other than the root, together with all its descendants, comprises a *subtree* of the original tree. There are several subtrees in Figure A.24; nodes D, J, and K represent one subtree, as does node J by itself.

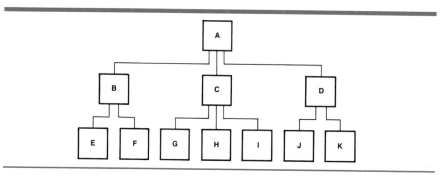

FIGURE A.24
Tree structure

A *parent* node appears immediately above its *children*. Every node has exactly one parent, except for the root, which does not have a parent. In Figure A.24 the root is the parent to its children B, C, and D. Node D is the parent of J and K, both of which are its children and only descendants. A node's *ancestors* consist of all nodes, including the root, which connect that node by branches directly back to the root. The ancestors of node G are nodes A and C, while node B has just the root as its ancestor.

A *leaf* node has no children. The leaves in Figure A.24 are E, F, G, H, I, J, and K. A *twin*, or *sibling*, is a node related to other nodes by virtue of its having the same parent. In Figure A.24 there are four sets of siblings: B, C, and D; E and F; G, H, and I; and J and K.

The root is defined to be at *level* 0, the root's children (B, C, and D in Figure A.24) are level 1, and so on down the tree. The *height*, or *depth*, of a tree is the maximum number of levels in the tree. Figures A.24 and A.25a show trees of height 3, while the tree in Figure A.25b on the following page, is of height 4.

A *balanced tree* is one in which the height of each node's subtrees differs at most by 1. Balanced trees are shown in Figures A.24 and A.25a, but Figure A.25b is an unbalanced tree, since the subtree starting from node B differs by 2 levels from the subtree starting from node C.

FIGURE A.25a
A balanced
tree structure

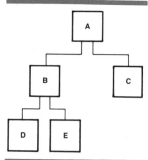

The **order**, or *degree*, of a tree is the maximum number of children a node can have. Figure A.24 has a tree of order 3 (node C has three children), whereas both trees in Figure A.25 are of order 2. A tree of order 2 is called a *binary tree*. A *multiway tree* is one in which a node may have more than two children, or a tree of order greater than 2.

You may be wondering about the purpose of all this tree terminology. Picture each node as a page of disk storage and each branch as a pointer forming a relationship between the pages. This is exactly what an index is. A tree structure is the overwhelming choice for the representation of index structures in file and database processing environments today.

Whatever organization or data structure is used for the index, our objective in randomly accessing a data file record is to minimize the number of disk accesses. If we use a tree structure for our index and each tree node is a page of disk storage, what we want to achieve is a balanced tree with as few levels as possible under the circumstances. One tree structure that does well with this constraint is the B-tree.

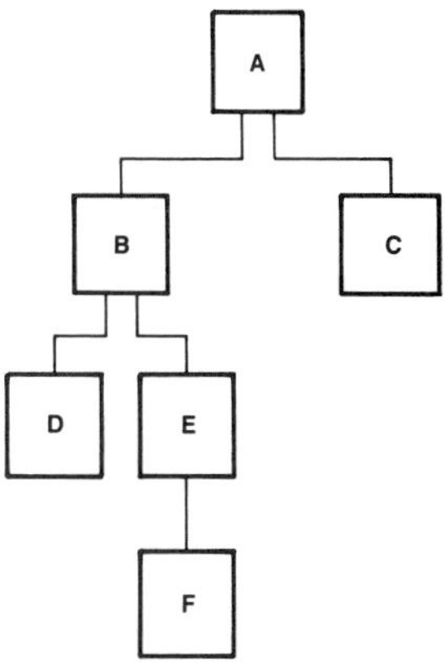

FIGURE A.25b
An unbalanced
tree structure

B-TREE

The **B-tree** was first described in a paper by Bayer and McCreight in 1972 (see [1]). It is a multilevel index, and each of its nodes is an index page having the following general format:

Pointer	Key	Address	Pointer	Key	Address	Pointer	...
1	1	1	2	2	2	3	...

Each "pointer" points to an index page at the next lowest level, each "key" is the value of a logical record key in the data file, and each "address" is the location in the data file of the logical record that has that "key" value. A key value/address combination will appear exactly once in some node of the B-tree for each key that exists in the data file. The maximum number of pointers in the page is the **order** of the B-tree, since the number of pointers determines the maximum number of children the node can have. A B-tree can be of any order, and a B-tree of order n has the following properties:

1. The root is either a leaf or has at least two children.
2. Each node, except for the root and the leaves, has between $n/2$ and n children.
3. All leaves appear on the same level.
4. A nonleaf node with k children has k-1 keys.

Figure A.26 shows an example of a B-tree index of order 5. The root node is shown below:

With reference to the first property in the list, this root has two children, pointed to by the root entries with a "*", which would actually be index page numbers. The other three pointers have a "−" entry to indicate (for illustrative purposes only) that they do not point anywhere. The "425" is a shorthand way of representing both the key value of 425 and its location in the data file. Any key value less than 425 can be found in the root's left subtree (pointed to by the leftmost root pointer), and any key value greater than 425 can be found in the root's right subtree (pointed to by the pointer to the right of "425" in the root).

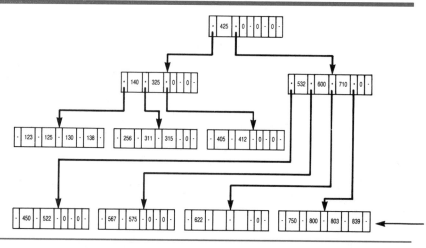

FIGURE A.26
B-tree of order 5

NOTE: These leaves are placed here due to space limitations. They are actually on the same level as the other leaves.

The three "0" entries have been inserted where key value/address combinations would be placed as needed. The root would be a leaf only if the data file contained zero through four logical records, since four is the maximum number of key value/ address combinations that can be stored in the root without needing children node storage.

With reference to the second property, every node has between three (5 divided by 2) and five children. Leaves have no children within the index structure, and that is why the property is worded the way it is. The root node will always have between two and five children, except when the root is a leaf and has no children at all.

All leaves are on the same level, in concordance with the third property. Therefore, the B-tree is a balanced tree.

Each node with two children has one key (key value/address combination); each node with three children has two keys; each node with four children has three keys; and each node with five children has four keys, though no example of the latter appears in Figure A.26. Each node can contain a maximum of four keys.

The key values are in sequence within each node. This is important to the way B-trees operate. Let's assume we wished to randomly access the record whose key value is 622. Starting at the root, we determine that 622 is greater than 425 and retrieve the node at the next level down within the right subtree. Comparing 622 to the keys in this node, we find that it is between 600 and 710 and retrieve the child node indicated by the third pointer. Retrieving this leaf node, we find a match on the first key value and use the address associated with it to retrieve the page containing the logical record with a key of 622.

If we had wanted to randomly access the record whose key value is 623, we would have completed the exact same steps and found no such key value in the leaf node. This would have signified the absence of any record having this key value.

Finally, if the record we needed had a key value of 532, we would find its location after two accesses, one to the root and the other to the right subtree node directly beneath it. Most of the time only one access would be required, since the root would reside in memory with almost no exceptions.

The great advantage of B-trees is not evident from the order 5 example in Figure A.26. It becomes apparent only when we look at B-trees of a realistic size. Before we do so, determine how many keys can be contained in a B-tree of order 5 in its first three levels, counting the root as one level.

Answer:

The root can contain four keys and can have five children. Each of these five children can have four keys, for an additional total of 20 keys, and each child can have five children, for a total of twenty-five children on the third level (level 2, in tree terminology). Each of the twenty-five level 2 children can have four keys, for a final total of 100 keys. Adding 4, 20, and 100 gives a grand total of 124 keys that can be represented at a maximum.

A more realistically sized B-tree on a mainframe would probably use a page size of at least 4,096 bytes. Using 4,096 as the page size, let's determine the number of keys that can be represented in each page, the order of the B-tree, and the number of keys that can be represented at a maximum in the first three levels. We will assume that each index page pointer and each key address requires 4 bytes and that the key value itself requires 9 bytes.

If we add together the 4-byte index pointer, the 4-byte key address, and the 9-byte key, getting 17, we can use this value to divide into the 4,096 page size for a close approximation to the number of keys that can be stored in one page. We must realize that an additional 4 bytes will be consumed by the one additional index pointer (there is always one more index pointer than key value/address combination) and that the operating system or DBMS may need to use some of the bytes in the page for control purposes. Dividing 17 into 4,096, we have 240 keys for each node in the B-tree. The order of this B-tree is 241.

The root can hold 240 keys and can have 241 children. Each of these 241 children can hold 240 keys, for a total additional 57,840 keys. Since each of the 241 children on level 1 can have 241 children, there can be a maximum of 58,081 children on level 2. Each of these children can hold 240 keys, for a total of 13,939,440 level 2 keys. Adding 240 to 57,840 and the result of that to 13,939,440 gives a grand total of 13,997,520 keys that can be contained in our order 241 B-tree. This is the theoretical maximum. In practice, not all nodes would be full, and the number of keys would be smaller than our calculation.

If we again assume that the root resides in memory, what we are saying is that we can randomly access one record in a data file having up to 13,997,520 records with no more than three accesses (one to the level 1 index, one to the level 2 index, and one to retrieve the record from the data file). Three accesses is the worst case; some of the data file records could be retrieved with one or two. In common applications, more than three B-tree levels are seldom required.

B-trees have other advantages besides rapid access. First, insertions and deletions are reasonably efficient. Second, disk utilization is acceptable, with packing densities of at least 50 percent, since each node is at least half full. And third, the data file is maintained in sequence by primary key, so that sequential access by primary key is both possible and efficient.

Many variations of the B-tree and other multiway tree structures have been researched and implemented in DBMS environments. For further examples and details, see [2], [3], [5], [6], [8], [9], [10], and [11].

A.5   SUMMARY

In this appendix, we focused on fundamental file processing concepts and on the file and data structures important in the study of a DBMS environment. A logical transaction, which is a user request to accomplish a single task, is processed by a program on a logical record basis against the physical records of a file or database. Logical records are grouped into blocks, which are also called pages or physical records.

We saw that grouping records based on usage patterns in the process called clustering allows control over the DBMS's responsiveness to the more common user requests. Clustering can be applied to records within a single file (intrafile) or to records from multiple files (interfile).

We next studied sequential and random access. Sequential access necessitates the storage and retrieval of records in a predetermined order, while random access permits the storage and retrieval of records in a direct fashion. Random access is used for rapid response in an on-line environment.

We examined the three major file organizations: sequential, direct, and indexed. Sequential organization permits sequential access only. The pile and the ordering of records by primary key value are the two common physical arrangements of records for sequential organization.

We saw that direct organization uses an algorithm to store and later retrieve records randomly in the file. Key-addressing techniques produce a unique physical storage location, but they are difficult to construct in practice and usually leave storage gaps which waste disk storage. Hashing techniques use a hash function algorithm that does not guarantee a unique disk storage location. When two or more records hash to the same storage location, they are called synonyms and we have collision. Different methods for resolving collision include the linear search and overflow area techniques; pointer chains are usable with both.

We discussed indexed organization which provides an efficient means of sequentially and randomly accessing records. The logical records are stored in a data file and a separate index is used to locate records in the data file. Both primary and secondary indexes are possible. Indexed random and indexed sequential are two different forms of this type of organization. Indexed sequential organization must work at keeping records in sequence through the use of overflow areas and pointer chains, distributed free space, and block splitting.

The three data structures we covered were inverted files, linked lists, and B-trees. An inverted file is an index on a secondary key, which can have unique or nonunique values. Linked lists use pointers to chain together records within a single file or to establish a relationship between two files. The B-tree is widely used as an multilevel index structure and provides fast and efficient random and sequential processing.

REVIEW QUESTIONS

1. Explain the difference between a logical transaction, a logical record, and a physical record.
2. What is blocking? Explain the tradeoffs involved in large blocking factors.
3. Explain the difference between intrafile and interfile clustering.
4. What is the difference between physical sequential and logical sequential access?
5. Define primary key, secondary key, and sequence key.
6. What is a pile? Name three situations in which a pile would be an appropriate organization.
7. What is the difference between the key-addressing and hashing techniques?
8. Describe two different hash function techniques. In general, which technique is better? Why?
9. How can a pointer chain be used for collision management?
10. How are both sparse and dense indexes used with indexed random organization?
11. Describe the use of distributed free space with the block-splitting technique.
12. What is the difference between a fully and a partially inverted file?
13. How does the multilist structure differ from an inverted file?
14. Define subtree, height, balanced tree, and order.
15. For a B-tree of order 7, how many children per node can there be at a maximum? For a two-level B-tree of order 7, how many keys can be stored at a maximum?
16. What are the advantages of the B-tree structure?

EXERCISES

1. A hash function using the division-remainder method and a divisor of 37 is used to store records with these key values into a direct file with forty pages: 112, 186, 195, and 225. Which pages does each of these keys hash to? Does collision occur? If so, for which key values?

2. If a file with direct organization has twenty-five buckets and five slots per bucket, what is the packing density if seventy-five records are stored?

3. Imagine a data file of ten records with primary key values of 5, 10, 20, 25, 30, 50, 60, 70, 80, and 90. Construct an indexed sequential file for these records with a two-level index and two data records and three index records stored per page. Add one record that requires block splitting, and show the changes caused by its addition.

4. Imagine a data file of ten records with secondary key values of 10, 10, 20, 30, 30, 50, 60, 60, 60, and 60. Construct an inverted file to allow access to the data records.

5. Picture a data file of ten records with secondary key values of 10, 10, 20, 30, 30, 50, 60, 60, 60, and 60. Construct a multilist to allow access to the data records.

6. For a B-tree of order 7 that has three levels, calculate how many keys can be stored at a maximum. How many index pointers would there be at a maximum?

REFERENCES

1] Bayer, R., and McCreight, E. M. "Organization and Maintenance of Large Ordered Indices." *Acta Informatica* 1, no. 3 1972.

2] Bradley, James. *File and Data Base Techniques*. Holt, Rinehart & Winston, 1981.

3] Ellzey, Roy S. *Data Structures for Computer Information Systems*. SRA, 1982.

4] Gillenson, Mark L. *Database Step-by-Step*. John Wiley & Sons, 1985.

5] Knuth, Donald E. *The Art of Computer Programming* Vol. 3, *Sorting and Searching*. Addison-Wesley, 1973.

6] Lewis, T. G., and Smith, M. Z. *Applying Data Structures*, 2d ed. Houghton Mifflin, 1982.

7] Martin, James. *Computer Data-Base Organization*. 2d ed. Prentice-Hall, 1977.

8] Merrett, T. H. *Relational Information Systems*. Reston Publishing Co., 1984.

9] Teorey, Toby J., and Fry, James P. *Design of Database Structures*. Prentice-Hall, 1982.

10] Wiederhold, Gio. *Database Design*, 2d ed. McGraw-Hill, 1983.

11] Wirth, Niklaus. *Algorithms and Data Structures*. Prentice-Hall, 1986.

APPENDIX B
DATABASE DESIGN
EXAMPLES

B
APPENDIX

1 INTRODUCTION

This appendix consists of two examples of database design, one for Marvel College and one for Premiere Products. In section B.2, we will examine the information requirements for Marvel College. In section B.3, the information-level design will be completed. In sections B.4 and B.5, this design will be mapped to a legitimate relational model implementation and a legitimate CODASYL model implementation. In section B.6, we will examine some of the physical constraints for the Marvel College system and will calculate the corresponding size of the CODASYL database to demonstrate the calculation of space requirements. Finally, in section B.7, we will discuss the process of calculating LRAs and transport volume for a particular application. We will also illustrate the process of making a change to the design to improve performance and then recalculating space requirements, LRAs, and transport volume.

In the exercises, you are presented with a change in requirements and/or assumptions at Marvel College and asked what effect the changes would have on the design. The last exercise is a special project: you are provided with requirements and assumptions for Premiere Products and then asked to complete the design process on your own.

2 MARVEL COLLEGE REQUIREMENTS

Now that Marvel College has entered the database age, the administration has decided to computerize more of the school's operations. Following is an explanation of the requirements that the system must satisfy.

GENERAL DESCRIPTION

Marvel College is organized by department (e.g., math, physics, English). A department may offer more than one major (e.g., the math department might offer majors in mathematics education, applied mathematics, and statistics). Each major, however, is offered by only one department. Each faculty member is assigned to a single department. Students can have more than one major, but most have only one. Each student has a faculty member as an advisor for his or her major; students who have more than one major have a faculty advisor for each one. The faculty member may or may not be assigned to the department offering the major.

Each department is identified by a three-character code (e.g., MTH for math, PHY for physics, ENG for English). Each course is identified by the combination of this code and a three-digit number (e.g., MTH 201 for calculus, ENG 102 for creative writing). The number of credits offered by a particular course does not vary; i.e., all students who pass the same course receive the same amount of credit.

Each semester is identified by a two-character code for the term combined with two digits that designate the year (e.g., FA87 for the fall semester of 1987). For a given semester, each section of each course is assigned a four-digit schedule code together with a section letter (schedule code 1295 for section A of MTH 201, 1297 for section B of MTH 201, and 1302 for section C of MTH 201). For a different semester, the schedule codes will be entirely different. The schedule codes are listed in the time schedule, and students use them to indicate the sections in which they wish to enroll. (The enrollment process is described in detail later in this section.)

After the enrollment process has been completed for a given semester, each faculty member receives a class list for each section he or she is teaching. In addition to listing the students who are in that particular section, the class list provides space to indicate the grade each student has earned in the course. At the end of the term, the faculty member will place the student's grades on this list and will return a copy of the list to the records office, where the grades will be entered into a computer. (At some point in the near future, the college hopes to automate this part of the process.)

Once the grades have been posted, report cards are generated and sent to students. The grades become part of the student's permanent record and will appear on the student's transcript, which is generated by the computer upon request.

The preceding description of the requirements is general; the specific information requirements of the college follow.

REPORT REQUIREMENTS

1. REPORT CARD

At the end of each semester, report cards must be produced. A sample report card is shown in Figure B.1.

FIGURE B.1
Sample report card for Marvel College

MARVEL COLLEGE

DEPARTMENT	NUMBER	COURSE DESCRIPTION	GRADE	COURSE TAKEN	CREDITS EARNED	GRADE POINTS
COMPUTER SCIENCE	153	COBOL	A	4	4	16.0
MATHEMATICS	201	CALCULUS	A	3	3	12.0

CURRENT SEMESTER TOTALS			
CREDITS TAKEN	CREDITS EARNED	GPA	TOTAL POINTS
7	7	4.00	28.0

SEMESTER: WI87

STUDENT NUMBER: 381124188

CUMULATIVE TOTALS			
CREDITS TAKEN	CREDITS EARNED	GPA	TOTAL POINTS
44	44	3.39	149.2

STUDENT NAME & ADDRESS	LOCAL ADDRESS (IF DIFFERENT)
BRIAN CONNORS 686 FRANKLIN HART, MI 48282	

2. *CLASS LIST*

A class list must be produced for each section of each course; a sample class list is shown in Figure B.2. Note that space is provided for the grades. At the end of the term, the instructor will fill in the grades and return a copy of the class list. The grades will then be posted.

FIGURE B.2
Sample class list for Marvel College

CLASS LISTS

DEPARTMENT: CS COMPUTER SCIENCE TERM: FA87
COURSE: 153 COBOL (4 CREDITS)
SECTION: B
SCHEDULE CODE: 2366

TIME: 1:00 - 1:50 M,T,W,F
PLACE: 118 SCR

INSTRUCTOR: 462 DIANE JOHNSTON

STUDENT NUMBER	STUDENT NAME	CLASS STANDING	GRADE
000625321	ARTHUR ADAMS	4	
.	.	.	
.	.	.	
.	.	.	
.	.		

3. GRADE VERIFICATION REPORT

The grade verification report is identical to the class list shown in Figure B.2 except that grades have been filled in. It is sent back to the section instructor after the grades have been processed. The instructor can use the report to verify that the grades were entered accurately.

4. TIME SCHEDULE

The time schedule, which is shown in Figure B.3, lists all sections of all courses to be offered during a given semester. Each section has a unique four-digit schedule code. The time schedule lists the schedule code; the department offering the course; the course number; the section letter; the title of the course; the instructor of the course; the time at which the course meets; the room in which the course meets; the number of credits generated by the course; and the prerequisites for the course. In addition to the information shown in the figure, the time schedule includes the date the semester begins; the date the semester ends; the date finals begin; the date finals end; and the last date at which students may withdraw from a course.

```
COURSE #   CODE #   SECT      TIME                    ROOM      FACULTY

              .         .          .                    .          .
              .         .          .                    .          .
              .         .          .                    .          .


CHEMISTRY (CHM)    OFFICE: 341 NSB

111    CHEMISTRY I                                 4 CREDITS
          1740      A   10:00-10:50 M,T,W,F    102 WRN   JOHNSON
          1745      B   12:00-12:50 M,T,W,F    102 WRN   LAWRENCE
              .         .          .                    .          .
              .         .          .                    .          .
              .         .          .                    .          .

       PREREQUISITE: MATHEMATICS 110

112    CHEMISTRY II                                4 CREDITS
          1790      A   10:00-11:50 M,W         109 WRN   ADAMS
          1795      B   12:00- 1:50 T,R         102 WRN   NELSON
              .         .          .                    .          .
              .         .          .                    .          .
              .         .          .                    .          .

       PREREQUISITE: CHEMISTRY 111

114    . . . .
```

FIGURE B.3
Sample time schedule for Marvel College

5. REGISTRATION REQUEST FORM

A sample registration request form is shown in Figure B.4. This form is used to request classes for the following semester. Students indicate the sections for which they wish to register by entering the sections' schedule codes; for each of these sections, they may also enter a code for an alternate section. Students who cannot be placed in the section they request will be placed in the alternate section, provided there is room.

REGISTRATION REQUEST FORM

STUDENT NUMBER: 000625321   TERM: FA87
         NAME: ARTHUR ADAMS
LOCAL ADDRESS: 571 ALDEN   PERMANENT ADDRESS: 4672 WESTCHESTER
         CITY: GRANDVIEW   CITY: TRENT
        STATE: MICH   STATE: MICH
          ZIP: 49101   ZIP: 48222

                    SCHEDULE CODES
            PRIMARY   ALTERNATE

     1.
     2.
     3.
     4.
     5.
     6.
     7.
     8.
     9.
    10.

FIGURE B.4
Sample registration request form for Marvel College

6. STUDENT SCHEDULE

A sample student schedule form is shown in Figure B.5. This form shows the schedule for an individual student for a given semester.

FIGURE B.5
Sample student schedule for Marvel College

STUDENT SCHEDULE

STUDENT NUMBER: 000625321   TERM: FA87
         NAME: ARTHUR ADAMS
LOCAL ADDRESS: 571 ALDEN   PERMANENT ADDRESS: 4672 WESTCHESTER
         CITY: GRANDVIEW   CITY: TRENT
        STATE: MICH   STATE: MICH
          ZIP: 49101   ZIP: 48222

SCHEDULE CODE	DEPARTMENT	COURSE NUMBER	COURSE DESCRIPTION	SECTION	CREDITS	TIME	ROOM
2366	COMPUTER SCIENCE	153	COBOL	B	4	1:00 – 1:50 M,T,W,F	118 SCR
.	.	.	.	.	.	.	.
.	.	.	.	.	.	.	.
.	.	.	.	.	.	.	.
			TOTAL CREDITS		16		

7. FULL STUDENT INFORMATION REPORT

A sample full student information report is shown in Figure B.6. It gives complete information about a student, including his or her majors and all grades received to date.

FIGURE B.6
Sample full student
information report for
Marvel College

```
                        FULL STUDENT INFORMATION
        STUDENT NUMBER: 000625321          TERM: FA87
                  NAME: ARTHUR ADAMS
         LOCAL ADDRESS: 571 ALDEN     PERMANENT ADDRESS: 4672 WESTCHESTER
                  CITY: GRANDVIEW                  CITY: TRENT
                 STATE: MICH                      STATE: MICH
                   ZIP: 49101                       ZIP: 48222

        MAJOR 1: INFORMATION SYS.    DEPT: COMPUTER SCIENCE   ADVISOR: MARK LAWRENCE
        MAJOR 2: ACCOUNTING          DEPT: BUSINESS           ADVISOR: JILL THOMAS
        MAJOR 3:                     DEPT:                    ADVISOR:
```

TERM	DEPARTMENT	COURSE NUMBER	COURSE DESCRIPTION	CREDITS	GRADE EARNED	GRADE POINTS
FA85	MATHEMATICS	110	CALC. I	4	A	16
	HISTORY	201	WESTERN CIV	3	B	9
	ENGLISH	101	AMER. LIT.	3	A	12
WI86	MATHEMATICS	111	CALC. II	4	B	12
	COMPUTER SCIENCE	151	PASCAL	4	B	12

```
        CREDITS ATTEMPTED: 60
          CREDITS EARNED: 60
             GRADE POINTS: 195
          GRADE POINT AVG: 3.25
           CLASS STANDING: 2
```

8. FACULTY INFORMATION REPORT

This report lists all faculty by department and contains each faculty member's ID number, name, address, office, phone number, current rank, and starting date of employment. It also lists the number, name, and local and permanent address of each of the faculty member's advisees, along with the code number and description of the major in which the faculty member is advising each one and the code number and description of the department in which this major is housed. (You will recall that this department need not be the one to which the faculty member is assigned.)

9. WORK VERSION OF THE TIME SCHEDULE

This report is similar to the original time schedule (see Figure B.3) but is designed for the college's internal use. It shows the current enrollments in each section of each course as well as the maximum enrollment permitted per section. It is more up-to-date than the time schedule itself. (When students register for courses, enrollment figures are updated on the work version of the time schedule;

and when room or faculty assignments are changed, this information is also updated. A new version of this report that reflects the updated figures is then printed.)

10. COURSE REPORT

This report lists, for each course, the code and name of the department offering the course, the course number, the description of the course, and the number of credits awarded. Also listed is the department and course number for each prerequisite course.

UPDATE (TRANSACTION) REQUIREMENTS

In addition to being able to add, change, and delete any of the entities mentioned in the report requirements, the update requirements include the following.

1. ENROLLMENT

When a student attempts to register for a section of a course, determine whether he or she has received credit for all prerequisites to the course. If the student is eligible to enroll in the course and if the number of students currently enrolled in the section is less than the maximum enrollment, enroll the student.

2. POST GRADES

For each section of each course, post the grades indicated on the copy of the class list returned by the instructor, and produce a grade verification report.

3. PURGE

Section information, including grades assigned by the section, is retained for two semesters following the end of the semester, at which time the information is removed from the database. (Grades assigned to students are retained by course, but not by section.)

3   INFORMATION LEVEL DESIGN

Some consideration should be given to overall requirements before the methodology is applied to individual user requirements. Scanning the design, we come up with the following list of possible entities: department, major, faculty member, student, course, and semester.

Your list may be different. You may have included the entity "section", for example, or "grade". On the other hand, you may not have included "semester". In the long run, as long as the list is fairly reasonable, it won't make much difference. In fact, you may remember that this step is really not even necessary. The better we do our job now, however, the simpler the process will be later on.

We now assign a primary key to each of these entities. In general, this will require some type of consultation with the user. We may need to ask the user directly for the required information, or we may be able to obtain it from some type of survey form. Let's assume that having had such a consultation, we have named a relation for each of these entities and have assigned primary keys as follows:

```
DEPARTMENT (DEPARTMENT_CODE,
MAJOR (MAJOR_NUMBER,
FACULTY (FACULTY_NUMBER,
STUDENT (STUDENT_NUMBER,
COURSE (DEPARTMENT_CODE, COURSE_NUMBER,
SEMESTER (SEMESTER_CODE,
```

Note that the primary key for the COURSE relation consists of two attributes, DEPARTMENT_CODE (such as CS) and COURSE_NUMBER (such as 153). Both are required.

At this point, we could also determine initial relationships among these entities and add appropriate foreign keys to implement these relationships. If we wanted to have a graphical representation of the design, we could also create a preliminary E-R diagram corresponding to it.

We now begin to examine the individual user views, create relations for them, represent any keys, and merge them into the design. First of all, we must decide exactly what the user views are. In the list of requirements, the term user view never appeared. Instead, a general description of the system was given, together with a collection of report requirements and another collection of update requirements. How do these requirements relate to user views?

Certainly, each report requirement and each update requirement can be thought of as a user view. What do we do with the general description? Do we think of each paragraph (or perhaps each sentence) in it as representing a user view, or do we use it to furnish additional information about the report and update requirements? Basically, both approaches are acceptable. The second approach is often easier, however, and we shall follow it here. We shall think of the report and update requirements as user views and use the statements in the general description to give additional information about these views wherever needed. We will also consider the general description during the review process to ensure that all the functionality that it describes can be satisfied by our final design.

We now turn to the user views. First let's take one of the simpler user views: report 10, the course report. (Technically, the user views can be examined in any order. Sometimes we take them in the order in which they are listed. In other cases, we may be able to come up with a better order. Often, examining some of the simpler user views first is a reasonable approach.)

Three comments are in order before we proceed with the design. First, with some of the user views, we will take a "good" approach to determining relations; i.e., we will carefully determine the entities and relationships between them and use this information in creating the relations. This means that from the outset the collection of relations created will be in or close to 3NF. With other user views, we will create a single relation that potentially contains some number of repeating groups. In these cases, as we will see, the normalization process will still produce a correct design, but it will also involve more work. In practice, the more experience a designer has had, the more likely he or she is to create 3NF relations immediately. Second, many of the decisions concerning foreign key restrictions will be made arbitrarily. You can assume that appropriate users have been interviewed concerning the relationships and restrictions and that their responses have led to the decisions found in the example. Third, the name of an entity or attribute may vary from one user view to another, and this requires resolution. We will illustrate this process but, in general, will have used names that are exactly the same.

Before treating each individual user view, we will restate the requirements for the view.

USER VIEW 1: COURSE REPORT

> *This report lists, for each course, the code and name of the department offering the course, the course number, the description of the course, and the number of credits awarded. Also listed is the department and course number for each prerequisite course.*

Forgetting for the moment the requirement to list prerequisite courses, the basic relation necessary to support this report would be as follows:

COURSE (DEPARTMENT_CODE, DEPARTMENT_NAME, COURSE_NUMBER,
    COURSE_TITLE, NUMBER_OF_CREDITS)

in which the combination of DEPARTMENT_CODE and COURSE_NUMBER uniquely determine all of the other attributes. In this relation, DEPARTMENT_CODE determines DEPARTMENT_NAME, and thus the relation is not in 2NF (an attribute depends on only a portion of the key). To correct this situation, the relation is split into:

COURSE (DEPARTMENT_CODE, COURSE_NUMBER, COURSE_TITLE,
    NUMBER_OF_CREDITS)
DEPARTMENT (DEPARTMENT_CODE, DEPARTMENT_NAME)

The DEPARTMENT_CODE in the first relation is a foreign key identifying the second.

In order to maintain prerequisite information, we need the relation PREREQ:

PREREQ (DEPARTMENT_CODE, COURSE_NUMBER,
    PREREQ_DEPARTMENT_CODE, PREREQ_COURSE_NUMBER)

(See the discussion of the relation PREREQ in chapter 6, section 6 if you are not clear on the structure of this relation. The only difference between this relation and the PREREQ relation in that section is that there the attribute, COURSE_CODE, uniquely identified a course, whereas here *both* DEPARTMENT_CODE *and* COURSE_NUMBER are required.

   The DBDL version of these relations is shown in Figure B.7, and the result of merging these relations into the cumulative design is shown in Figure B.8. Notice that the DEPARTMENT and COURSE relations have merged with the existing DEPARTMENT and COURSE relations in the cumulative design. In the process, the attribute DEPARTMENT_NAME was added to the DEPARTMENT relation, and the attributes COURSE_TITLE and NUMBER_OF_CREDITS were added to the COURSE relation. In addition, the attribute DEPARTMENT_CODE in the COURSE relation was made a foreign key. Since the PREREQ relation was totally new, it was added to the cumulative collection in its entirety.

```
DEPARTMENT (DEPARTMENT_CODE, DEPARTMENT_NAME)

COURSE (DEPARTMENT_CODE, COURSE_NUMBER, COURSE_TITLE,
          NUMBER_OF_CREDITS)
    FK   DEPARTMENT_CODE → DEPARTMENT

PREREQ (DEPARTMENT_CODE, COURSE_NUMBER, PREREQ_DEPARTMENT_CODE,
          PREREQ_COURSE_NUMBER)
    FK DEPARTMENT_CODE, COURSE_NUMBER → COURSE DLT CSCD
    FK PREREQ_DEPARTMENT_CODE, PREREQ_COURSE_NUMBER →
                                        COURSE DLT CSCD
```

FIGURE B.7
DBDL for user view 1

```
DEPARTMENT (DEPARTMENT_CODE, DEPARTMENT_NAME)

MAJOR (MAJOR_NUMBER)

FACULTY (FACULTY_NUMBER)

STUDENT (STUDENT_NUMBER)

COURSE (DEPARTMENT_CODE, COURSE_NUMBER, COURSE_TITLE,
          NUMBER_OF_CREDITS)
    FK   DEPARTMENT_CODE → DEPARTMENT

PREREQ (DEPARTMENT_CODE, COURSE_NUMBER, PREREQ_DEPARTMENT_CODE,
          PREREQ_COURSE_NUMBER)
    FK DEPARTMENT_CODE, COURSE_NUMBER → COURSE DLT CSCD
    FK PREREQ_DEPARTMENT_CODE, PREREQ_COURSE_NUMBER →
                                        COURSE DLT CSCD

SEMESTER (SEMESTER_CODE)
```

FIGURE B.8
Cumulative collection
after user view 1

USER VIEW 2: FACULTY INFORMATION REPORT

> *This report lists all faculty by department and contains*
> *each faculty member's ID number, name, address,*
> *office, phone number, current rank, and starting date*
> *of employment. It also lists the number, name, and*
> *local and permanent address of each of the faculty*
> *member's advisees, along with the code number and*
> *description of the major in which the faculty member*
> *is advising each one and the code number and descrip-*
> *tion of the department in which this major is housed.*

This user view involves three entities: departments, faculty, and advisees. Applying the tips from chapter 6, we can create three relations:

```
DEPARTMENT  (
FACULTY  (
ADVISEE  (
```

The next step is to assign a primary key to each relation. Before doing so, however, we should briefly examine the relations in the cumulative collection and use the same names for any relations or attributes that are already there. In this case, we would use DEPARTMENT_CODE as the primary key for the DEPARTMENT relation and FACULTY_NUMBER as the primary key for the FACULTY relation. There is no ADVISEE relation in the cumulative relation, but there is a STUDENT relation. Since advisees and students are the same, we choose to rename the ADVISEE relation STUDENT and use STUDENT_NUMBER as the primary key, yielding

```
DEPARTMENT  (DEPARTMENT_CODE,
FACULTY  (FACULTY_NUMBER,
STUDENT  (STUDENT_NUMBER,
```

(Another alternative would be to keep the names ADVISEE and ADVISEE_ NUMBER in this user view and record in the data dictionary the fact that these are synonyms for STUDENT and STUDENT_NUMBER, respectively. Such relations would still be merged as though the names were STUDENT and STUDENT_ NUMBER, but when subschemas were created for this user view, they could be renamed as ADVISEE and ADVISEE_NUMBER, if we so desired. In general, we try to avoid the use of synonyms unless there is a compelling reason to use them, and, in such cases, we make sure that the reason is very carefully documented.)

Next, we add the remaining attributes to these relations.

DEPARTMENT (<u>DEPARTMENT_CODE</u>, DEPARTMENT_NAME)
FACULTY (<u>FACULTY_NUMBER</u>, NAME, ADDRESS, CITY, STATE,
    ZIP, OFFICE_NUMBER, PHONE_NUMBER, CURRENT_RANK,
    START_DATE, DEPARTMENT_CODE)
STUDENT (<u>STUDENT_NUMBER</u>, NAME, LOCAL_ADDRESS, LOCAL_CITY,
    LOCAL_STATE, LOCAL_ZIP, ADDRESS, CITY, STATE, ZIP,
    MAJOR_NUMBER, MAJOR_DESCRIPTION,
    MAJOR_DEPARTMENT_CODE, FACULT_NUMBER, FACULTY_NAME)

The department code is included in the FACULTY relation, since there is a one-to-many relationship between departments and faculty. Since a student can have more than one major, the information concerning majors (numbers, description, department, and the number and name of the faculty member who advises this student in this major) is a repeating group.

Since the key to the repeating group in the student relation is the major number, removing this repeating group yields

STUDENT (<u>STUDENT_NUMBER</u>, NAME, LOCAL_ADDRESS, LOCAL_CITY,
    LOCAL_STATE, LOCAL_ZIP, ADDRESS, CITY, STATE, ZIP,
    <u>MAJOR_NUMBER</u>, MAJOR_DESCRIPTION,
    MAJOR_DEPARTMENT_CODE, FACULTY_NUMBER,
      FACULTY_NAME)

Converting this relation to 2NF produces

STUDENT (<u>STUDENT_NUMBER</u>, NAME, LOCAL_ADDRESS,
    LOCAL_CITY, LOCAL_STATE, LOCAL_ZIP, ADDRESS,
    CITY, STATE, ZIP)
MAJOR (<u>MAJOR_NUMBER</u>, MAJOR_DESCRIPTION,
    MAJOR_DEPARTMENT_CODE, MAJOR_DEPARTMENT_NAME)
ADVISES (<u>STUDENT_NUMBER</u>, <u>MAJOR_NUMBER</u>, FACULTY_NUMBER)

Some dependencies must be removed to create 3NF relations: OFFICE_NUMBER determines PHONE_NUMBER in the FACULTY relation, and MAJOR_DEPARTMENT_CODE determines MAJOR_DEPARTMENT_NAME. Removing these dependencies produces the following collection of relations:

DEPARTMENT (<u>DEPARTMENT_CODE</u>, DEPARTMENT_NAME)
FACULTY (<u>FACULTY_NUMBER</u>, NAME, ADDRESS, CITY, STATE,
    ZIP, OFFICE_NUMBER, CURRENT_RANK, START_DATE,
    DEPARTMENT_CODE)

STUDENT (<u>STUDENT_NUMBER</u>, NAME, LOCAL_ADDRESS, LOCAL_CITY,
      LOCAL_STATE, LOCAL_ZIP, ADDRESS,
      CITY, STATE, ZIP)
ADVISES (<u>STUDENT_NUMBER</u>, <u>MAJOR_NUMBER</u>, FACULTY_NUMBER)
OFFICE (<u>OFFICE_NUMBER</u>, PHONE_NUMBER)
MAJOR (<u>MAJOR_NUMBER</u>, MAJOR_DESCRIPTION, MAJOR_
      DEPARTMENT_CODE)

It may seem that there should be another relation consisting of MAJOR_
DEPARTMENT_CODE (the primary key) and MAJOR_DEPARTMENT_NAME. The
MAJOR_DEPARTMENT_CODE attribute in the MAJOR relation would be a foreign
key matching this other relation. This relation, however, is really the DEPART−
MENT relation already in place, with slightly different names. Thus there is no
need for the this relation. Rather, the MAJOR_DEPARTMENT_CODE in the MAJOR
relation will be a foreign key required to match the existing DEPARTMENT relation. In fact, at this point we might choose to rename MAJOR_DEPARTMENT_
CODE as, simply, DEPARTMENT_CODE. In the final collection of relations, there
is no confusion as to the meaning of this DEPARTMENT_CODE; it is the code of
the department that houses the major.

Let's assume that we have renamed MAJOR_DEPARTMENT_CODE in this
fashion and made the necessary foreign key decisions. The DBDL representation
is shown in Figure B.9, and the result of merging these relations into the cumulative design is shown in Figure B.10. (Note that the local address, city, state, and
zip are allowed to be null.) The tables STUDENT, FACULTY, MAJOR, and
DEPARTMENT merge into existing tables with the same primary keys and with the
same names. Nothing new is added to the DEPARTMENT table in the process, but
the other tables all receive additional columns. In addition, the FACULTY table
also receives two foreign keys, OFFICE_NUMBER and DEPARTMENT_CODE.

FIGURE B.9
DBDL for user view 2

DEPARTMENT (<u>DEPARTMENT_CODE</u>, DEPARTMENT_NAME)

STUDENT (<u>STUDENT_NUMBER</u>, NAME, LOCAL_ADDRESS*, LOCAL_CITY*,
          LOCAL_STATE*, LOCAL_ZIP*, ADDRESS, CITY, STATE, ZIP)

OFFICE (<u>OFFICE_NUMBER</u>, PHONE_NUMBER)

FACULTY (<u>FACULTY_NUMBER</u>, NAME, ADDRESS, CITY, STATE, ZIP,
          OFFICE_NUMBER, CURRENT_RANK, START_DATE,
          DEPARTMENT_CODE)
     FK   OFFICE_NUMBER → OFFICE
     FK   DEPARTMENT_CODE → DEPARTMENT

MAJOR (<u>MAJOR_NUMBER</u>, MAJOR_DESCRIPTION, DEPARTMENT_CODE)
     FK   DEPARTMENT_CODE → DEPARTMENT

ADVISES (<u>STUDENT_NUMBER</u>, FACULTY_NUMBER, <u>MAJOR_NUMBER</u>)
     FK   STUDENT_NUMBER → STUDENT   DLT CSCD
     FK   FACULTY_NUMBER → FACULTY
     FK   MAJOR_NUMBER → MAJOR

The MAJOR table receives one foreign key, DEPARTMENT_CODE. The tables ADVISES and OFFICE are brand new and are thus added directly to the cumulative collection of relations.

FIGURE B.10
Cumulative collection
after user view 2

DEPARTMENT (DEPARTMENT_CODE, DEPARTMENT_NAME)

STUDENT (STUDENT_NUMBER, NAME, LOCAL_ADDRESS*, LOCAL_CITY*,
      LOCAL_STATE*, LOCAL_ZIP*, ADDRESS, CITY, STATE, ZIP)

OFFICE (OFFICE_NUMBER, PHONE_NUMBER)

FACULTY (FACULTY_NUMBER, NAME, ADDRESS, CITY, STATE, ZIP,
      OFFICE_NUMBER, CURRENT_RANK, START_DATE,
      DEPARTMENT_CODE)
    FK OFFICE_NUMBER → OFFICE
    FK DEPARTMENT_CODE → DEPARTMENT

MAJOR (MAJOR_NUMBER, MAJOR_DESCRIPTION, DEPARTMENT_CODE)
    FK DEPARTMENT_CODE → DEPARTMENT

ADVISES (STUDENT_NUMBER, FACULTY_NUMBER, MAJOR_NUMBER)
    FK STUDENT_NUMBER → STUDENT DLT CSCD
    FK FACULTY_NUMBER → FACULTY
    FK MAJOR_NUMBER → MAJOR

COURSE (DEPARTMENT_CODE, COURSE_NUMBER, COURSE_TITLE,
      NUMBER_OF_CREDITS)
    FK DEPARTMENT_CODE → DEPARTMENT

PREREQ (DEPARTMENT_CODE, COURSE_NUMBER, PREREQ_DEPARTMENT_CODE,
      PREREQ_COURSE_NUMBER)
    FK DEPARTMENT_CODE, COURSE_NUMBER → COURSE DLT CSCD
    FK PREREQ_DEPARTMENT_CODE, PREREQ_COURSE_NUMBER →
                            COURSE DLT CSCD

SEMESTER (SEMESTER_CODE)

USER VIEW 3: REPORT CARD

> *At the end of each semester, report cards must be produced. A sample report card is shown in Figure B.1.*

Report cards are fairly complicated documents. The appropriate underlying relations are certainly not immediately apparent. In this view, we will illustrate tips for obtaining information from existing documents.

The first step is to list all of the attributes on the document and give them appropriate names (see Figure B.11). After this has been done, the functional dependencies that exist between these attributes should be listed. The information necessary to determine functional dependencies must ultimately come from the user, although we can often make fairly accurate guesses for most of them. If the functional dependencies are not represented on any documentation we have been given, such as a survey form, we may well have to go directly to the users to obtain the necessary information.

DEPARTMENT_NAME
COURSE_NUMBER
COURSE_TITLE
GRADE
CREDIT_TAKEN_IN_COURSE
CREDITS_EARNED_IN_COURSE
GRADE_POINTS_FROM_COURSE
CREDITS_TAKEN_THIS_SEMESTER
CREDITS_EARNED_THIS_SEMESTER
GPA_THIS_SEMESTER
TOTAL_POINTS_THIS_SEMESTER
POINT_CREDITS_CUMULATIVE
CREDITS_TAKEN_CUMULATIVE
CREDITS_EARNED_CUMULATIVE

GPA_CUMULATIVE
TOTAL_POINTS_CUMULATIVE
SEMESTER_CODE
STUDENT_NUMBER
NAME
ADDRESS
CITY
STATE
ZIP
LOCAL_ADDRESS
LOCAL_CITY
LOCAL_STATE
LOCAL_ZIP

FIGURE B.11
Attributes on report cards for Marvel College

Let's assume that this has been done at Marvel College and that Figure B.12 shows the results. The student number alone determines many of the other attributes. In addition to the student number, the semester must be listed in order to determine credits taken and earned, grade point average (GPA), and total points this semester. The combination of a department description (such as COMPUTER SCIENCE) and a course number (such as 153) determines a course title and the number of credits. Finally, the student number, the semester (season and year), and the course (discipline and course number) are required in order to determine an individual grade in a course, the credits earned from the course, and the grade points in a course. (The semester is required, since students can take the same course in more than one semester at Marvel College. Further, let's assume that upon checking with the users we have learned that they want to allow for the possibility that credits offered by a course may vary from one semester to another and even, possibly, from one student to another.)

STUDENT_NUMBER →
    CREDITS_TAKEN_CUMULATIVE
    CREDITS_EARNED_CUMULATIVE
    GPA_CUMULATIVE
    TOTAL_POINTS_CUMULATIVE
    NAME
    ADDRESS
    CITY
    STATE
    ZIP
    LOCAL_ADDRESS
    LOCAL_CITY
    LOCAL_STATE
    LOCAL_ZIP

STUDENT_NUMBER, SEMESTER_CODE →
    CREDITS_TAKEN_THIS_SEMESTER
    CREDITS_EARNED_THIS_SEMESTER
    GPA_THIS_SEMESTER
    TOTAL_POINTS_THIS_SEMESTER

DEPARTMENT_NAME, COURSE_NUMBER →
    COURSE_TITLE
    CREDITS_TAKEN_IN_COURSE

STUDENT_NUMBER, SEMESTER_CODE, DEPARTMENT_NAME,
        COURSE_NUMBER →
    GRADE
    CREDITS_EARNED_IN_COURSE
    GRADE_POINTS_FROM_COURSE

The next step is to create a collection of relations that will support this user view. A variety of approaches will work. We could combine all of the attributes into a single relation, which would then be converted to 3NF. (In such a relation, the combination of discipline, course number, course title, grade, and so on would

FIGURE B.12
Functional dependencies among attributes on report cards

be a repeating group.) Or we could use the functional dependencies to determine the following collection of relations:

```
STUDENT (STUDENT_NUMBER, NAME, ADDRESS, CITY, STATE, ZIP,
     LOCAL_ADDRESS, LOCAL_CITY, LOCAL_STATE, LOCAL_ZIP,
     CREDITS_TAKEN, CREDITS_EARNED,
     GPA, TOTAL_POINTS)
STUDENT_SEMESTER (STUDENT_NUMBER, SEMESTER_CODE,
     CREDITS_TAKEN, CREDITS_EARNED, GPA, TOTAL_POINTS)
COURSE (DISCIPLINE_DESCRIPTION, COURSE_NUMBER,
     COURSE_TITLE, CREDITS_TAKEN_IN_COURSE)
STUDENT_GRADE (STUDENT_NUMBER, SEMESTER_CODE,
     DEPARTMENT_NAME, COURSE_NUMBER,
     GRADE, CREDITS_EARNED_IN_COURSE,
     GRADE_POINTS_FROM_COURSE)
```

These relations are all in 3NF. The only change we should make concerns the DEPARTMENT_NAME attribute in the STUDENT_GRADE relation. You will recall that when we encounter an attribute for which there exists a determinant not in the relation, the determinant should be added to the relation. In this case, DEPARTMENT_CODE determines DEPARTMENT_NAME, and we add DEPARTMENT_CODE to the relation. In the normalization process, DEPARTMENT_NAME will then be removed and placed in another relation whose key is DEPARTMENT_CODE. This other relation will merge with the DEPART-MENT relation without the addition of any new attributes. The resulting STUDENT_GRADE relation is:

```
STUDENT_GRADE (STUDENT_NUMBER, SEMESTER_CODE,
     DEPARTMENT_CODE, COURSE_NUMBER,
     GRADE, CREDITS_EARNED_IN_COURSE,
     GRADE_POINTS_FROM_COURSE)
```

Before representing this design in DBDL, let's take a close look at STUDENT_SEMESTER. It is true that the attributes within it, CREDITS_TAKEN, CREDITS_EARNED, GPA, and TOTAL_POINTS, which all refer to the current semester, do, in fact, appear on report cards. Let's assume that after checking further we find that they are all easily calculated from other fields on the report card during the actual production of report cards. Then, rather than store them in the database, we will merely make sure that the program that produces report cards performs the necessary calculations. For this reason, we will remove the relation STUDENT_SEMESTER from the collection of relations to be documented and merged. (If these attributes are also required by some other user view in which the same computations are not as practical, they may yet find their way into the database when that user view is analyzed.)

Q&A

Write the DBDL representation of these relations, including foreign key specifications. Note any synonyms between this user view and the cumulative design, and resolve them. Merge the result into the cumulative design.

Answer:

See Figure B.13.

```
DEPARTMENT (DEPARTMENT_CODE, DEPARTMENT_NAME)

STUDENT (STUDENT_NUMBER, NAME, LOCAL_ADDRESS*, LOCAL_CITY*,
         LOCAL_STATE*, LOCAL_ZIP*, ADDRESS, CITY, STATE, ZIP,
         CREDITS_TAKEN, CREDITS_EARNED, GPA, TOTAL_POINTS)

OFFICE (OFFICE_NUMBER, PHONE_NUMBER)

FACULTY (FACULTY_NUMBER, NAME, ADDRESS, CITY, STATE, ZIP,
         OFFICE_NUMBER, CURRENT_RANK, START_DATE,
         DEPARTMENT_CODE)
    FK  OFFICE_NUMBER → OFFICE
    FK  DEPARTMENT_CODE → DEPARTMENT

MAJOR (MAJOR_NUMBER, MAJOR_DESCRIPTION, DEPARTMENT_CODE)
    FK  DEPARTMENT_CODE → DEPARTMENT

ADVISES (STUDENT_NUMBER, FACULTY_NUMBER, MAJOR_NUMBER)
    FK  STUDENT_NUMBER → STUDENT   DLT CSCD
    FK  FACULTY_NUMBER → FACULTY
    FK  MAJOR_NUMBER → MAJOR

COURSE (DEPARTMENT_CODE, COURSE_NUMBER, COURSE_TITLE,
        NUMBER_OF_CREDITS)
    FK  DEPARTMENT_CODE → DEPARTMENT

PREREQ (DEPARTMENT_CODE, COURSE_NUMBER, PREREQ_DEPARTMENT_CODE,
        PREREQ_COURSE_NUMBER)
    FK DEPARTMENT_CODE, COURSE_NUMBER → COURSE DLT CSCD
    FK PREREQ_DEPARTMENT_CODE, PREREQ_COURSE_NUMBER →
                                       COURSE DLT CSCD

SEMESTER (SEMESTER_CODE)

STUDENT_GRADE (STUDENT_NUMBER, SEMESTER_CODE, DEPARTMENT_CODE,
        COURSE_NUMBER, GRADE, CREDITS_EARNED, GRADE_POINTS)
    FK  STUDENT_NUMBER → STUDENT   DLT CSCD
    FK  SEMESTER_CODE → SEMESTER
    FK  DEPARTMENT_CODE, COURSE_NUMBER → COURSE
```

FIGURE B.13
Cumulative design
after user view 3

USER VIEW 4: CLASS LIST

> **A class list must be produced for each section of each course; a sample class list is shown in Figure B.2. Note that space is provided for the grades. At the end of the term, the instructor will fill in the grades and return a copy of the class list. The grades will then be posted.**

Let's assume that after examining the sample class list report, we decide to create a single relation (actually an unnormalized relation) that contains all of the attributes on the class list, with the student information (number, name, class standing, and grade) as a repeating group. (Applying the tips for determining the relations to support a given user view would lead more directly to the result, but, for the sake of giving the example, we'll assume we haven't done that here.) The unnormalized relation created in this fashion would be:

```
CLASS_LIST (DEPARTMENT_CODE, DEPARTMENT_NAME,
      SEMESTER_CODE
    COURSE_NUMBER, COURSE_TITLE, NUMBER_OF_CREDITS,
    SECTION_LETTER, SCHEDULE_CODE, MEETING_TIME,
    MEETING_PLACE, INSTRUCTOR_NUMBER,
    INSTRUCTOR_NAME,

    STUDENT_NUMBER, NAME, CLASS_STANDING, GRADE)
```

Note that we have not as yet indicated the primary key. To identify a given class within a particular semester requires either the combination of department code, course number, and section letter or, more simply, the schedule code. Taking the schedule code as the primary key, however, is not quite adequate. Since the information from more than one semester will be on file at the same time and since the same schedule code could be used in two different semesters to represent totally different courses, the primary key must also contain the semester code. When we remove the repeating group, this primary key expands to contain the key for the repeating group, in this case the student number. Thus, converting to 1NF yields:

```
CLASS_LIST (DEPARTMENT_CODE, DEPARTMENT_NAME,
      SEMESTER_CODE,
    COURSE_NUMBER, COURSE_TITLE, NUMBER_OF_CREDITS,
    SECTION_LETTER, SCHEDULE_CODE, MEETING_TIME,
    MEETING_PLACE, INSTRUCTOR_NUMBER, INSTRUCTOR_NAME,
    STUDENT_NUMBER, NAME, CLASS_STANDING, GRADE*)
```

Converting to 3NF yields the following collection of relations:

```
DEPARTMENT (DEPARTMENT_CODE, DEPARTMENT_NAME)
SECTION (SEMESTER_CODE, SCHEDULE_CODE, DEPARTMENT_CODE,
     COURSE_NUMBER, SECTION_LETTER, MEETING_TIME,
     MEETING_PLACE, INSTRUCTOR_NUMBER)
INSTRUCTOR (INSTRUCTOR_NUMBER, INSTRUCTOR_NAME)
STUDENT_IN_CLASS (SEMESTER_CODE, SCHEDULE_CODE,
     STUDENT_NUMBER, GRADE*)
STUDENT_GENERAL (STUDENT_NUMBER, NAME, CLASS_STANDING)
COURSE (DEPARTMENT_CODE, COURSE_NUMBER, COURSE_TITLE,
     NUMBER_OF_CREDITS)
```

Why was the grade included?

Answer:

Although the grade is not actually printed on the class list, it will be entered on the form by the instructor and later returned for posting. A later report, called the grade verification report differs from the class list only in that the grade is printed. Thus, the grade will ultimately be required and it is legitimate to deal with it here. Since at this point the grade is unknown, the grade field should be allowed to be null.

Write the DBDL representation of these relations, including foreign key specifications. Determine the presence of any synonyms with regard to this user view and the cumulative design. Resolve such synonyms and merge the result into the cumulative design.

Answer:

See Figure B.14.

```
DEPARTMENT (DEPARTMENT_CODE, DEPARTMENT_NAME)

STUDENT (STUDENT_NUMBER, NAME, LOCAL_ADDRESS*, LOCAL_CITY*,
     LOCAL_STATE*, LOCAL_ZIP*, ADDRESS, CITY, STATE, ZIP,
     CREDITS_TAKEN, CREDITS_EARNED, GPA, TOTAL_POINTS,
     CLASS_STANDING)

OFFICE (OFFICE_NUMBER, PHONE_NUMBER)

FACULTY (FACULTY_NUMBER, NAME, ADDRESS, CITY, STATE, ZIP,
     OFFICE_NUMBER, CURRENT_RANK, START_DATE,
     DEPARTMENT_CODE)
     FK  OFFICE_NUMBER → OFFICE
     FK  DEPARTMENT_CODE → DEPARTMENT
```

FIGURE B.14a
Cumulative design after user view 4 (continued on next page)

```
MAJOR (MAJOR_NUMBER, MAJOR_DESCRIPTION, DEPARTMENT_CODE)
      FK   DEPARTMENT_CODE  →  DEPARTMENT

ADVISES (STUDENT_NUMBER, FACULTY_NUMBER, MAJOR_NUMBER)
      FK   STUDENT_NUMBER  →  STUDENT   DLT CSCD
      FK   FACULTY_NUMBER  →  FACULTY
      FK   MAJOR_NUMBER  →  MAJOR

COURSE (DEPARTMENT_CODE, COURSE_NUMBER, COURSE_TITLE,
        NUMBER_OF_CREDITS)
      FK   DEPARTMENT_CODE  -  JEPARTMENT

PREREQ (DEPARTMENT_CODE, COURSE_NUMBER, PREREQ_DEPARTMENT_CODE,
        PREREQ_COURSE_NUMBER)
      FK DEPARTMENT_CODE, COURSE_NUMBER  →  COURSE DLT CSCD
      FK PREREQ_DEPARTMENT_CODE, PREREQ_COURSE_NUMBER  →
                                    COURSE DLT CSCD

SEMESTER (SEMESTER_CODE)

STUDENT_GRADE (STUDENT_NUMBER, SEMESTER_CODE, DEPARTMENT_CODE,
        COURSE_NUMBER, GRADE, CREDITS_EARNED, GRADE_POINTS)
      FK   STUDENT_NUMBER  →  STUDENT   DLT CSCD
      FK   SEMESTER_CODE  →  SEMESTER
      FK   DEPARTMENT_CODE, COURSE_NUMBER  →  COURSE

SECTION (SEMESTER_CODE, SCHEDULE_CODE, DEPARTMENT_CODE,
        COURSE_NUMBER, SECTION_LETTER, MEETING_TIME,
        MEETING_PLACE, FACULTY_NUMBER)
      FK   SEMESTER_CODE  →  SEMESTER
      FK   DEPARTMENT_CODE, COURSE_NUMBER  →  COURSE
      FK   FACULTY_NUMBER  →  FACULTY

STUDENT_IN_CLASS (SEMESTER_CODE, SCHEDULE_CODE,
        STUDENT_NUMBER, GRADE*)
      FK   SEMESTER_CODE, SCHEDULE_CODE  →  SECTION   DLT CSCD
      FK   STUDENT_NUMBER  →  STUDENT   DLT CSCD
```

USER VIEW 5: GRADE VERIFICATION REPORT

The grade verification report is identical to the class list shown in Figure B.2 except that grades have been filled in. It is sent back to the section instructor after the grades have been processed. The instructor can use the report to verify that the grades were entered accurately.

Since the only difference between the class list and the grade verification report is that the grades are printed on the latter, the user views will be quite similar. In fact, since we made provision for the grade when treating the class list, the views are identical, and no further treatment of this view is required.

USER VIEW 6: TIME SCHEDULE

The time schedule, which is shown in Figure B.3, lists all sections of all courses to be offered during a given semester. Each section has a unique four-digit schedule code. The time schedule lists the schedule code; the department offering the course; the course number; the section letter; the title of the course; the instructor of the course; the time at which the course meets; the room in which the course meets; the number of credits generated by the course; and the prerequisites for the course. In addition to the information shown in the figure, the time schedule includes the date the semester begins; the date the semester ends; the date finals begin; the date finals end; and the last date at which students may withdraw from a course.

The attributes on the time schedule are as follows: term (which is a synonym for semester code); department code; department name; location; course number; course title; number of credits; schedule code; section letter; meeting time; meeting place; and name of instructor. The time schedule also contains the starting and ending date of the semester, the starting and ending date of the exam period, and the last withdrawal date.

We could create a single relation containing all of these attributes and then normalize the relation; or we could apply the tips presented in chapter 6 for determining the collection of relations. In either case, we ultimately create the following collection of relations:

```
DEPARTMENT (DEPARTMENT_CODE, DEPARTMENT_NAME, LOCATION)
COURSE (DEPARTMENT_CODE, COURSE_NUMBER, COURSE_TITLE,
       NUMBER_OF_CREDITS)
SECTION (TERM, SCHEDULE_CODE, DEPARTMENT_CODE,
     COURSE_NUMBER, SECTION_LETTER, MEETING_TIME,
     MEETING_PLACE, INSTRUCTOR_NUMBER)
INSTRUCTOR (INSTRUCTOR_NUMBER, INSTRUCTOR_NAME)
SEMESTER (SEMESTER_CODE, START_DATE, END_DATE,
     EXAM_START_DATE, EXAM_END_DATE,
     LAST_WITHDRAWAL_DATE)
```

(Actually, given the attributes in this user view, the SECTION relation would contain the instructor's name. There was no mention of instructor number. In general, as we saw earlier, it's a good idea to include determinants for attributes whenever possible. In this example, during the merge step, we might notice that there is an attribute, INSTRUCTOR_NUMBER, that determines INSTRUCTOR_NAME. This attribute would then be added to the SECTION relation, at which

point the SECTION relation would not be in 3NF. Converting to 3NF will produce
the collection of relations shown above.)

Write the DBDL representation of these relations, including foreign key specifications. Identify any
synonyms with regard to this user view and the cumulative design, and resolve them. Merge the
result into the cumulative design.

Answer:

See Figure B.15.

DEPARTMENT (DEPARTMENT_CODE, DEPARTMENT_NAME, LOCATION)

STUDENT (STUDENT_NUMBER, NAME, LOCAL_ADDRESS*, LOCAL_CITY*,
         LOCAL_STATE*, LOCAL_ZIP*, ADDRESS, CITY, STATE, ZIP,
         CREDITS_TAKEN, CREDITS_EARNED, GPA, TOTAL_POINTS,
         CLASS_STANDING)

OFFICE (OFFICE_NUMBER, PHONE_NUMBER)

FACULTY (FACULTY_NUMBER, NAME, ADDRESS, CITY, STATE, ZIP,
         OFFICE_NUMBER, CURRENT_RANK, START_DATE,
         DEPARTMENT_CODE)
    FK OFFICE_NUMBER → OFFICE
    FK DEPARTMENT_CODE → DEPARTMENT

MAJOR (MAJOR_NUMBER, MAJOR_DESCRIPTION, DEPARTMENT_CODE)
    FK DEPARTMENT_CODE → DEPARTMENT

ADVISES (STUDENT_NUMBER, FACULTY_NUMBER, MAJOR_NUMBER)
    FK STUDENT_NUMBER → STUDENT   DLT CSCD
    FK FACULTY_NUMBER → FACULTY
    FK MAJOR_NUMBER → MAJOR

COURSE (DEPARTMENT_CODE, COURSE_NUMBER, COURSE_TITLE,
         NUMBER_OF_CREDITS)
    FK DEPARTMENT_CODE → DEPARTMENT

PREREQ (DEPARTMENT_CODE, COURSE_NUMBER, PREREQ_DEPARTMENT_CODE,
         PREREQ_COURSE_NUMBER)
    FK DEPARTMENT_CODE, COURSE_NUMBER → COURSE DLT CSCD
    FK PREREQ_DEPARTMENT_CODE, PREREQ_COURSE_NUMBER →
                                      COURSE DLT CSCD

SEMESTER (SEMESTER_CODE, START_DATE, END_DATE,
          EXAM_START_DATE, EXAM_END_DATE, LAST_WITHDRAWAL_DATE)

STUDENT_GRADE (STUDENT_NUMBER, SEMESTER_CODE, DEPARTMENT_CODE,
          COURSE_NUMBER, GRADE, CREDITS_EARNED, GRADE_POINTS)
    FK STUDENT_NUMBER → STUDENT   DLT CSCD
    FK SEMESTER_CODE → SEMESTER
    FK DEPARTMENT_CODE, COURSE_NUMBER → COURSE

FIGURE B.15a
Cumulative design
after user view 6
(continued on
following page)

```
SECTION (SEMESTER_CODE, SCHEDULE_CODE, DEPARTMENT_CODE,
         COURSE_NUMBER, SECTION_LETTER, MEETING_TIME,
         MEETING_PLACE, FACULTY_NUMBER)
    FK  SEMESTER_CODE → SEMESTER
    FK  DEPARTMENT_CODE, COURSE_NUMBER → COURSE
    FK  FACULTY_NUMBER → FACULTY

STUDENT_IN_CLASS (SEMESTER_CODE, SCHEDULE_CODE,
         STUDENT_NUMBER, GRADE*)
    FK  SEMESTER_CODE, SCHEDULE_CODE → SECTION  DLT CSCD
    FK  STUDENT_NUMBER → STUDENT  DLT CSCD
```

USER VIEW 7: REGISTRATION REQUEST FORM

A sample registration request form is shown in Figure B.4. This form is used to request classes for the following semester. Students indicate the sections for which they wish to register by entering the sections' schedule codes; for each of these sections, they may also enter a code for an alternate section. Students who cannot be placed in the section they request will be placed in the alternate section, provided there is room.

The collection of relations to support this user view includes a STUDENT relation that consists of the primary key, STUDENT_NUMBER, and all of the attributes that depend only on STUDENT_NUMBER, such as NAME, LOCAL_ADDRESS, and so on. Since all of the attributes in this relation are already in the STUDENT relation in the cumulative collection, this relation will not add anything new and we will not discuss it further here.

The portion of this user view that is not already present in the cumulative collection concerns the primary and alternate schedule codes that students request. A relation to support this portion of the user view must contain both a primary and an alternate schedule code. It must also contain the number of the student making the request. Finally, to allow the flexibility of retaining this information for more than a single term, the relation must also include the term in which the request is made. This leads to the following relation:

```
REGISTRATION_REQUEST (STUDENT_NUMBER,
       PRIMARY_SCHEDULE_CODE,
     ALTERNATE_SCHEDULE_CODE, TERM)
```

For example, if student 123 were to request the section whose schedule code is 2345, with 2396 as an alternate for the FA87 semester, the row (123, 2345, 2396, "FA87") would be stored. The student number, the primary schedule code, and the term are required in order to uniquely identify a particular row. In

addition, since a student is not required to furnish an alternate schedule code, the
alternate schedule code must accept nulls.

Q&A

Write the DBDL representation of these relations, including foreign key specifications. Identify any
synonyms pertaining to this user view and the cumulative design, and resolve them. Merge the result
into the cumulative design.

Answer:

    See Figure B.16.

DEPARTMENT (<u>DEPARTMENT_CODE</u>, DEPARTMENT_NAME, LOCATION)

STUDENT (<u>STUDENT_NUMBER</u>, NAME, LOCAL_ADDRESS*, LOCAL_CITY*,
        LOCAL_STATE*, LOCAL_ZIP*, ADDRESS, CITY, STATE, ZIP,
        CREDITS_TAKEN, CREDITS_EARNED, GPA, TOTAL_POINTS,
        CLASS_STANDING)

OFFICE (<u>OFFICE_NUMBER</u>, PHONE_NUMBER)

FACULTY (<u>FACULTY_NUMBER</u>, NAME, ADDRESS, CITY, STATE, ZIP,
        OFFICE_NUMBER, CURRENT_RANK, START_DATE,
        DEPARTMENT_CODE)
    FK OFFICE_NUMBER → OFFICE
    FK DEPARTMENT_CODE → DEPARTMENT

MAJOR (<u>MAJOR_NUMBER</u>, MAJOR_DESCRIPTION, DEPARTMENT_CODE)
    FK DEPARTMENT_CODE → DEPARTMENT

ADVISES (<u>STUDENT_NUMBER</u>, FACULTY_NUMBER, <u>MAJOR_NUMBER</u>)
    FK STUDENT_NUMBER → STUDENT DLT CSCD
    FK FACULTY_NUMBER → FACULTY
    FK MAJOR_NUMBER → MAJOR

COURSE (<u>DEPARTMENT_CODE</u>, <u>COURSE_NUMBER</u>, COURSE_TITLE,
        NUMBER_OF_CREDITS)
    FK DEPARTMENT_CODE → DEPARTMENT

PREREQ (<u>DEPARTMENT_CODE</u>, <u>COURSE_NUMBER</u>,
<u>PREREQ_DEPARTMENT_CODE</u>, PREREQ_COURSE_NUMBER)
    FK DEPARTMENT_CODE, COURSE_NUMBER → COURSE DLT CSCD
    FK PREREQ_DEPARTMENT_CODE, PREREQ_COURSE_NUMBER →
                         COURSE DLT CSCD

SEMESTER (<u>SEMESTER_CODE</u>, START_DATE, END_DATE,
        EXAM_START_DATE, EXAM_END_DATE, LAST_WITHDRAWAL_DATE)

FIGURE B.16a
REGISTRATION—REQUEST
(STUDENT—NUMBER)

FIGURE B.16a
(continued)

```
STUDENT_GRADE (STUDENT_NUMBER, SEMESTER_CODE, DEPARTMENT_CODE,

          COURSE_NUMBER, GRADE, CREDITS_EARNED, GRADE_POINTS)
     FK   STUDENT_NUMBER → STUDENT  DLT CSCD
     FK   SEMESTER_CODE → SEMESTER
     FK   DEPARTMENT_CODE, COURSE_NUMBER → COURSE


SECTION (SEMESTER_CODE, SCHEDULE_CODE, DEPARTMENT_CODE,
          COURSE_NUMBER, SECTION_LETTER, MEETING_TIME,
          MEETING_PLACE, FACULTY_NUMBER)
     FK   SEMESTER_CODE → SEMESTER
     FK   DEPARTMENT_CODE, COURSE_NUMBER → COURSE
     FK   FACULTY_NUMBER → FACULTY


STUDENT_IN_CLASS (SEMESTER_CODE, SCHEDULE_CODE,

          STUDENT_NUMBER, GRADE*)
     FK   SEMESTER_CODE, SCHEDULE_CODE → SECTION  DLT CSCD
     FK   STUDENT_NUMBER → STUDENT  DLT CSCD
```

FIGURE B.16b
Cumulative design
after user view 7

```
REGISTRATION_REQUEST (STUDENT_NUMBER,
PRIMARY_SCHEDULE_CODE,
          ALTERNATE_SCHEDULE_CODE*,
SEMESTER_CODE)
     FK   STUDENT_NUMBER → STUDENT  DLT CSCD
     FK   SEMESTER_CODE, PRIMARY_SCHEDULE_CODE → SECTION DLT CSCD
     FK   SEMESTER_CODE, ALTERNATE_SCHEDULE_CODE* → SECTION
                                                  DLT CSCD
```

USER VIEW 8: STUDENT SCHEDULE

> *A sample student schedule form is shown in Figure*
> *B.5. This form shows the schedule for an individual*
> *student for a given semester.*

Suppose that we had created a single unnormalized relation to support the student schedule. This unnormalized relation would contain a repeating group representing the lines in the body of the schedule. The relation would thus be:

```
STUDENT_SCHEDULE (STUDENT_NUMBER, TERM, NAME,
     LOCAL_ADDRESS,
     LOCAL_CITY, LOCAL_STATE, LOCAL_ZIP, ADDRESS,
     CITY, STATE, ZIP,
```

SCHEDULE_CODE, DEPARTMENT_NAME, COURSE_NUMBER

COURSE_TITLE, SECTION_LETTER,

NUMBER_OF_CREDITS, MEETING_TIME, ROOM)

At this point, we remove the repeating group to convert to 1NF, yielding the following:

STUDENT_SCHEDULE (STUDENT_NUMBER, TERM, NAME,
    LOCAL_ADDRESS,
    LOCAL_CITY, LOCAL_STATE, LOCAL_ZIP, ADDRESS,
    CITY, STATE, ZIP, SCHEDULE_CODE, DEPARTMENT_CODE,
    COURSE_NUMBER, COURSE_TITLE, SECTION_LETTER,
    NUMBER_OF_CREDITS, MEETING_TIME, ROOM)

Note that the key expands to include SCHEDULE_CODE, which is the key to the repeating group. Converting to 2NF produces:

STUDENT (STUDENT_NUMBER, NAME, LOCAL_ADDRESS, LOCAL_CITY,
    LOCAL_STATE, LOCAL_ZIP, ADDRESS, CITY,
    STATE, ZIP)
STUDENT_SCHEDULE (STUDENT_NUMBER, TERM, SCHEDULE_CODE)
SECTION (TERM, SCHEDULE_CODE, DEPARTMENT_CODE,
    COURSE_NUMBER, COURSE_TITLE, SECTION_LETTER,
    CREDITS, MEETING_TIME, ROOM)
COURSE (DEPARTMENT_CODE, COURSE_NUMBER, COURSE_TITLE,
    NUMBER_OF_CREDITS)

Removing the attributes that depend on the determinant of DEPARTMENT_CODE, COURSE_NUMBER from SECTION to convert to 3NF produces:

STUDENT (STUDENT_NUMBER, NAME, LOCAL_ADDRESS, LOCAL_CITY,
    LOCAL_STATE, LOCAL_ZIP, ADDRESS, CITY,
    STATE, ZIP)
STUDENT_SCHEDULE (STUDENT_NUMBER, TERM, SCHEDULE_CODE)
SECTION (TERM, SCHEDULE_CODE, DEPARTMENT_CODE,
    COURSE_NUMBER, SECTION_LETTER, MEETING_TIME,
    ROOM)
COURSE (DEPARTMENT_CODE, COURSE_NUMBER, COURSE_TITLE,
    NUMBER_OF_CREDITS)

USER VIEW 9: FULL STUDENT INFORMATION REPORT

> **A sample full student information report is shown in
> Figure B.6. It gives complete information about a student, including his or her majors and all grades received
> to date.**

Suppose we attempted to place all of the attributes on the student information report in a single unnormalized relation. The relation has two separate repeating groups, one for the different majors a student may have and the other for all the courses the student has taken. The full relation would be:

STUDENT_INFO (STUDENT_NUMBER,

  MAJOR, DEPARTMENT_CODE, ADVISOR_NAME,

  TERM_TAKEN, COURSE_DEPARTMET COURSE_NUMBER,

  COURSE_TITLE, NUMBER_OF_CREDITS, GRADE_EARNED,

  GRADE_POINTS, TOTAL_CREDITS_ATTEMPTED,
  TOTAL_CREDITS_EARNED, TOTAL_GRADE_POINTS,
  GRADE_POINT_AVERAGE, CLASS_STANDING)

In converting to 1NF, if there are more than two repeating groups they are separated, producing:

STUDENT_BASIC (STUDENT_NUMBER, TOTAL_CREDITS_ATTEMPTED,
  TOTAL_CREDITS_EARNED, TOTAL_GRADE_POINTS,
  GRADE_POINT_AVERAGE, CLASS_STANDING)
STUDENT_MAJOR (STUDENT_NUMBER,

  MAJOR, DEPARTMENT_CODE, ADVISOR_NAME)
STUDENT_COURSE (STUDENT_NUMBER,

  TERM_TAKEN, COURSE_DEPARTMENT, COURSE_NUMBER,

  COURSE_TITLE, NUMBER_OF_CREDITS, GRADE_EARNED

  GRADE_POINTS)

Converting these to 1NF and including ADVISOR_NUMER, which is a determinant for ADVISOR_NAME, produces:

STUDENT_BASIC (STUDENT_NUMBER, TOTAL_CREDITS_ATTEMPTED,
     TOTAL_CREDITS_EARNED, TOTAL_GRADE_POINTS,
     GRADE_POINT_AVERAGE, CLASS_STANDING)
STUDENT_MAJOR (STUDENT_NUMBER, MAJOR, DEPARTMENT_CODE,
     ADVISOR_NUMBER, ADVISOR_NAME)
STUDENT_COURSE (STUDENT_NUMBER, TERM_TAKEN,
     COURSE_DEPARTMENT, COURSE_NUMBER,
     COURSE_TITLE, NUMBER_OF_CREDITS,
     GRADE_EARNED, GRADE_POINTS)

STUDENT_COURSE is not in 2NF, since COURSE_TITLE and NUMBER_OF_
CREDITS depend only on the COURSE_DEPARTMENT, COURSE_NUMBER com-
bination. STUDENT_MAJOR is not in 2NF, since DEPARTMENT depends on
MAJOR. Removing these dependencies produces:

STUDENT_BASIC (STUDENT_NUMBER, TOTAL_CREDITS_ATTEMPTED,
     TOTAL_CREDITS_EARNED, TOTAL_GRADE_POINTS,
     GRADE_POINT_AVERAGE, CLASS_STANDING)
STUDENT_MAJOR (STUDENT_NUMBER, MAJOR, ADVISOR_NUMBER,
     ADVISOR_NAME)
MAJOR_INFO (MAJOR, DEPARTMENT_CODE)
STUDENT_COURSE (STUDENT_NUMBER, TERM_TAKEN,
     COURSE_DEPARTMENT, COURSE_NUMBER,
     GRADE_EARNED, GRADE_POINTS)
COURSE (COURSE_DEPARTMENT, COURSE_NUMBER,
     COURSE_TITLE, NUMBER_OF_CREDITS)

Other than STUDENT_MAJOR, all of these relations are in 3NF. Converting
STUDENT_MAJOR to 3NF produces the following:

STUDENT_MAJOR (STUDENT_NUMBER, MAJOR, ADVISOR_NUMBER)
ADVISOR (ADVISOR_NUMBER, ADVISOR_NAME)

USER VIEW 10: WORK VERSION OF THE TIME SCHEDULE

This report is similar to the original time schedule (see Figure B.3) but is designed for the college's internal use. It shows the current enrollments in each section of each course as well as the maximum enrollment permitted per section. It is more up-to-date than the time schedule itself. (When students register for courses, enrollment figures are updated on the work version of the time schedule; and when room or faculty assign-

ments are changed, this information is also updated.
A new version of this report that reflects the updated
figures is then printed.)

The only difference between the work version of the time schedule and the
time schedule itself (see user view 6) is the addition of two attributes for each
section: current enrollment and maximum enrollment. Since these two attributes
depend only on the combination of the term and the schedule code, they would be
placed in the SECTION relation of user view 6 and, after the merge, would be in
the SECTION relation in the cumulative design.

The cumulative design thus far is shown in Figure B.17.

FIGURE B.17a
Cumulative design
after user view 10
(continued on
following page)

```
DEPARTMENT (DEPARTMENT_CODE, DEPARTMENT_NAME, LOCATION)

STUDENT (STUDENT_NUMBER, NAME, LOCAL_ADDRESS*, LOCAL_CITY*,
         LOCAL_STATE*, LOCAL_ZIP*, ADDRESS, CITY, STATE, ZIP,
         CREDITS_TAKEN, CREDITS_EARNED, GPA, TOTAL_POINTS,
         CLASS_STANDING)

OFFICE (OFFICE_NUMBER, PHONE_NUMBER)

FACULTY (FACULTY_NUMBER, NAME, ADDRESS, CITY, STATE, ZIP,
         OFFICE_NUMBER, CURRENT_RANK, START_DATE,
         DEPARTMENT_CODE)
    FK  OFFICE_NUMBER → OFFICE
    FK  DEPARTMENT_CODE → DEPARTMENT

MAJOR (MAJOR_NUMBER, MAJOR_DESCRIPTION, DEPARTMENT_CODE)
    FK  DEPARTMENT_CODE → DEPARTMENT

ADVISES (STUDENT_NUMBER, FACULTY_NUMBER, MAJOR_NUMBER)
    FK  STUDENT_NUMBER → STUDENT   DLT CSCD
    FK  FACULTY_NUMBER → FACULTY
    FK  MAJOR_NUMBER → MAJOR

COURSE (DEPARTMENT_CODE, COURSE_NUMBER, COURSE_TITLE,
        NUMBER_OF_CREDITS)
    FK  DEPARTMENT_CODE → DEPARTMENT

PREREQ (DEPARTMENT_CODE, COURSE_NUMBER,
        PREREQ_DEPARTMENT_CODE PREREQ_COURSE_NUMBER)
    FK DEPARTMENT_CODE, COURSE_NUMBER → COURSE DLT CSCD
    FK PREREQ_DEPARTMENT_CODE, PREREQ_COURSE_NUMBER →
                                    COURSE DLT CSCD

SEMESTER (SEMESTER_CODE, START_DATE, END_DATE,
          EXAM_START_DATE, EXAM_END_DATE, LAST_WITHDRAWAL_DATE)
```

```
STUDENT_GRADE (STUDENT_NUMBER, SEMESTER_CODE, DEPARTMENT_CODE,
        COURSE_NUMBER, GRADE, CREDITS_EARNED, GRADE_POINTS)
    FK   STUDENT_NUMBER → STUDENT   DLT CSCD
    FK   SEMESTER_CODE → SEMESTER
    FK   DEPARTMENT_CODE, COURSE_NUMBER → COURSE

SECTION (SEMESTER_CODE, SCHEDULE_CODE, DEPARTMENT_CODE,
        COURSE_NUMBER, SECTION_LETTER, MEETING_TIME,
        MEETING_PLACE, FACULTY_NUMBER, CURRENT_ENROLLMENT,
        MAXIMUM_ENROLLMENT)
    FK   SEMESTER_CODE → SEMESTER
    FK   DEPARTMENT_CODE, COURSE_NUMBER → COURSE
    FK   FACULTY_NUMBER → FACULTY

STUDENT_IN_CLASS (SEMESTER_CODE, SCHEDULE_CODE,

        STUDENT_NUMBER, GRADE*)
    FK   SEMESTER_CODE, SCHEDULE_CODE → SECTION   DLT CSCD
    FK   STUDENT_NUMBER → STUDENT   DLT CSCD

REGISTRATION_REQUEST (STUDENT_NUMBER, PRIMARY_SCHEDULE_CODE,
        ALTERNATE_SCHEDULE_CODE*, SEMESTER_CODE)
    FK   STUDENT_NUMBER → STUDENT   DLT CSCD
    FK   SEMESTER_CODE, PRIMARY_SCHEDULE_CODE → SECTION DLT CSCD
    FK   SEMESTER_CODE, ALTERNATE_SCHEDULE_CODE* → SECTION
                                               DLT CSCD
```

Since the process of determining whether a student has had the prerequisites for a given course involves examining the grades (if any) received in these prior courses, it makes sense to analyze the user view that involves grades (post grades) before treating the user view that involves enrollment.

USER VIEW 11: POST GRADES

> **For each section of each course, post the grades indicated on the copy of the class list returned by the instructor, and produce a grade verification report.**

There is a slight problem with posting grades. Grades must somehow be posted by section (e.g., we must record the fact that student 000625321 received an A in the section of CS 153 whose schedule code was 2366 during the fall 1987 semester) in order to produce the grade verification report. On the other hand, for the full student information report, there is no need to have any of the grades related to an *actual section* of a course. Further, since section information, including these grades, is only to be kept for two semesters (see the description of PURGE in the user requirements), grades would be lost after two semesters if they were kept by section only, since section information would be purged at that time.

A viable alternative is to post two copies of the grade; one copy would be associated with the student, the term, and the section, and the other copy would be associated only with the student and the term. The first copy would be used for the grade verification report and the second for the full student information report. Report cards would probably utilize the second copy, although not necessarily.

Thus, we would have two grade relations:

GRADE_BY_SECTION (<u>STUDENT_NUMBER</u>, DEPARTMENT_CODE, COURSE_NUMBER, <u>SCHEDULE_CODE</u>, <u>SEMESTER_CODE</u>, GRADE)

and

GRADE_BY_STUDENT (<u>STUDENT_NUMBER</u>, DEPARTMENT_CODE, <u>COURSE_NUMBER</u>, <u>SEMESTER_CODE</u>, GRADE)

Since the DEPARTMENT_CODE and COURSE_NUMBER in GRADE_BY_SECTION depend only on the concatenation of SCHEDULE_CODE and SEMESTER_CODE, they will be removed from GRADE_BY_SECTION during the normalization process and will be placed in a relation whose primary key is the concatenation of SCHEDULE_CODE and SEMESTER_CODE. This relation will be combined with the relation SECTION in the cumulative design without adding new fields. The GRADE_BY_SECTION relation that is left will be merged with STUDENT_IN_CLASS without adding new fields. Finally, the GRADE_BY_STUDENT relation will be combined with the STUDENT_GRADE relation in the cumulative design without adding any new fields. Thus, treatment of this user view does not change the cumulative design.

USER VIEW 12: ENROLLMENT

> **When a student attempts to register for a section of a course, determine whether he or she has received credit for all prerequisites to the course. If the student is eligible to enroll in the course and if the number of students currently enrolled in the section is less than the maximum enrollment, enroll the student.**

With the data already in place in the overall design, we can determine what courses a student has taken. We can also determine the prerequisites for a given course. The only remaining issue is the ability to enroll a student in a course. This is similar to the problem encountered in the design exercise in section 6 of chapter 6, where we saw that what is required is another relation, ENROLL. In this case, since information must be retained for more than one semester, we must include the semester code in the relation. (We must have the information that student 123 enrolled in section 2345 in SU87 rather than in FA87, for example.) The additional relation is as follows:

ENROLL (<u>STUDENT_NUMBER</u>, <u>SEMESTER_CODE</u>, <u>SCHEDULE_CODE</u>)

The primary key of this relation matches the primary key of the relation STUDENT_IN_CLASS in the cumulative design. The fields occur in a different order here, but that makes no difference. Thus, this relation will merge with STUDENT_IN_CLASS. There are no new fields to be added, so the cumulative design remains unchanged.

USER VIEW 13: PURGE

Section information, including grades assigned by the section, is retained for two semesters following the end of the semester, at which time the information is removed from the database. (Grades assigned to students are retained by course, but not by section.)

Periodically, certain information that is more than two terms old is to be removed from the database. This includes all information concerning sections of courses, such as the time, the room, and the instructor, as well as information about the students in the section and their grades. The grade each student received will remain in the database by course but not by section. For example, we will always retain the fact that student 123 received an A in CS 153 during the fall semester of 1987, but, once the data for that term is purged, we will no longer know the precise section of CS 153 that awarded this grade.

If we examine the current collection of relations, we see that all of the data to be purged is already included in the cumulative design and, so nothing new needs to be added at this point.

FINAL INFORMATION-LEVEL DESIGN

The design that has been produced is now reviewed to ensure that the user views can be met. You should conduct this review on your own to make certain you understand how the requirements of each user can indeed be satisfied. We will assume that this review has taken place and that no changes have been made. Thus, Figure B.17 shows the final information-level design.

Two other types of documentation could have been produced during the preceding steps. The first is a list of the do-

FIGURE B.18a
Domain definitions for final design

```
•••••••••••••••••• DOMAIN DEFINITIONS ••••••••••••••••••••••••
```

DOMAIN	TYPE	DESCRIPTION	RESTRICTIONS
ADDRESS	C(25)	STREET ADDRESSES	
CITY	C(25)	CITIES	
CLASS_STANDING	D(1)	CLASS STANDINGS	MUST BE 1 FOR FRESHMAN, 2 FOR SOPHOMORE, 3 FOR JUNIOR OR 4 FOR SENIOR
COURSE_ DESCRIPTION	C(25)	COURSE DESCRIPTIONS	
COURSE_NUMBER	D(3)	COURSE NUMBERS	
CREDITS	D(3)	NUMBER OF CREDITS	
DATE	D(6)	DATES	HAS FORM YYMMDD
DEPARTMENT_CODE	C(3)	DEPARTMENT CODES	
DEPARTMENT_NAME	C(25)	DEPARTMENT NAMES	
ENROLLMENT	D(3)	COURSE ENROLLMENTS	
FACULTY_NUMBER	D(4)	FACULTY NUMBERS	
GPA	D(3,2)	GRADE POINT AVERAGES	MUST BE BETWEEN 0.00 AND 4.00
GRADE	C(1)	GRADES	MUST BE "A", "B", "C", "D", "F", OR "I" (INCOMPLETE)
GRADE_POINTS	D(3)	GRADE POINTS	OBTAINED BY MULTIPLYING THE NUMBER OF CREDITS OF "A" BY 4, THE NUMBER OF CREDITS OF "B" BY 3, OF "C" BY 2, OF "D" BY 1 AND ADDING THE RESULT
MAJOR_NUMBER	D(3)	MAJOR NUMBERS	
MEETING_TIME	C(20)	MEETING TIMES	IDENTIFIES START AND ENDING TIMES AND DAYS OF THE WEEK
NAME	C(25)	PERSON NAMES	
NUMBER_OF_ CREDITS	D(1)	NUMBER OF CREDITS GRANTED BY A COURSE	MUST BE BETWEEN 1 AND 5
PHONE_NUMBER	D(4)	OFFICE PHONE NUMBERS	MUST BEGIN WITH A 3
RANK	C(9)	FACULTY RANKS	MUST BE "INSTRUCTOR", "ASST PROF", "ASSO PROF", or "PROFESSOR"
ROOM	C(7)	ROOM NUMBERS	CONSIST OF 3 DIGIT NUMBER AND 3 CHARACTER BUILDING ABBREVIATION, ("110 NSB")
SCHEDULE_CODE	D(4)	SCHEDULE CODES (CODES THAT UNIQUELY IDENTIFY SECTIONS OF COURSES IN A GIVEN SEMESTER	
SECTION_LETTER	C(1)	SECTION LETTERS	
SEMESTER_CODE	C(4)	SEMESTER CODES	HAS FORM SSYY WHERE SS IS EITHER FA FOR FALL, WI FOR WINTER, OR SU FOR SUMMER AND YY IS THE YEAR
STATE	C(2)	STATES	
STUDENT_NUMBER	D(9)	STUDENT NUMBERS	
ZIP	D(9)	ZIP CODES	

mains that were used together with the relationship between the tables and columns that were defined and these domains. This documentation for the completed design is shown in Figure B.18 on the opposite page, right and below. The second is a pictorial representation, typically an E-R diagram or something equivalent to it. This could be used whenever the designer thought it would be helpful. A pictorial representation of the final design is shown in Figure B.19 on page 706.

The diagram shown in the figure is similar to an E-R diagram that follows the newer version of the E-R model as discussed in chapter 8. Some slight changes have been made which simplify the drawing. Rather than represent one-to-many relationships by labeling one end of the relationship with "1" and the other with "N", an arrow is drawn from the "1" to the

```
************* TABLE AND COLUMN DEFINITIONS ********************
```

TABLE	COLUMN	DOMAIN	COMMENTS
ADVISES	STUDENT_NUMBER	STUDENT_NUMBER	
	FACULTY_NUMBER	FACULTY_NUMBER	
	MAJOR_NUMBER	MAJOR_NUMBER	
COURSE	DEPARTMENT_CODE	DEPARTMENT_CODE	
	COURSE_NUMBER	COURSE_NUMBER	
	COURSE_TITLE	COURSE_TITLE	
	NUMBER_OF_CREDITS	NUMBER_OF_CREDITS	
DEPARTMENT	DEPARTMENT_CODE	DEPARTMENT_CODE	
	DEPARTMENT_NAME	DEPARTMENT_NAME	
	LOCATION	ROOM	
FACULTY	FACULTY_NUMBER	FACULTY_NUMBER	
	NAME	NAME	
	ADDRESS	ADDRESS	
	CITY	CITY	
	STATE	STATE	
	ZIP	ZIP	
	OFFICE_NUMBER	ROOM	
	CURRENT_RANK	RANK	
	START_DATE	DATE	
	DEPARTMENT_CODE	DEPARTMENT_CODE	
MAJOR	MAJOR_NUMBER	MAJOR_NUMBER	
	MAJOR_DESCRIPTION	MAJOR_DESCRIPTION	
	DEPARTMENT_CODE	DEPARTMENT_CODE	
OFFICE	OFFICE_NUMBER	ROOM	
	PHONE_NUMBER	PHONE_NUMBER	
PREREQ	DEPARTMENT_CODE	DEPARTMENT_CODE	
	COURSE_NUMBER	COURSE_NUMBER	
	PREREQ_DEPARTMENT_CODE	DEPARTMENT_CODE	
	PREREQ_COURSE_NUMBER	COURSE_NUMBER	
REGISTRATION_REQUEST	STUDENT_NUMBER	STUDENT_NUMBER	
	PRIMARY_SCHEDULE_CODE	SCHEDULE_CODE	
	ALTERNATE_SCHEDULE_CODE	SCHEDULE_CODE	
	SEMESTER_CODE	SEMESTER_CODE	

TABLE	COLUMN	DOMAIN	COMMENTS
SECTION	SEMESTER_CODE	SEMESTER_CODE	
	SCHEDULE_CODE	SCHEDULE_CODE	
	DEPARTMENT_CODE	DEPARTMENT_CODE	
	COURSE_NUMBER	COURSE_NUMBER	
	SECTION_LETTER	SECTION_LETTER	
	MEETING_TIME	MEETING_TIME	
	MEETING_PLACE	ROOM	
	FACULTY_NUMBER	FACULTY_NUMBER	
	CURRENT_ENROLLMENT	ENROLLMENT	
	MAXIMUM_ENROLLMENT	ENROLLMENT	
SEMESTER	SEMESTER_CODE	SEMESTER_CODE	
	START_DATE	DATE	
	END_DATE	DATE	
	EXAM_START_DATE	DATE	
	EXAM_END_DATE	DATE	
	LAST_WITHDRAWAL_DATE	DATE	
STUDENT	STUDENT_NUMBER	STUDENT_NUMBER	
	NAME	NAME	
	LOCAL_ADDRESS	ADDRESS	
	LOCAL_CITY	CITY	
	LOCAL_STATE	STATE	
	LOCAL_ZIP	ZIP	
	ADDRESS	ADDRESS	
	CITY	CITY	
	STATE	STATE	
	ZIP	ZIP	
	CREDITS_TAKEN	CREDITS	
	CREDITS_EARNED	CREDITS	
	GPA	GPA	
	TOTAL_POINTS	GRADE_POINTS	
	CLASS_STANDING	CLASS_STANDING	
STUDENT_GRADE	STUDENT_NUMBER	STUDENT_NUMBER	
	SEMESTER_CODE	SEMESTER_CODE	
	DEPARTMENT_CODE	DEPARTMENT_CODE	
	COURSE_NUMBER	COURSE_NUMBER	
	GRADE	GRADE	
	CREDITS_EARNED	CREDITS	
	GRADE_POINTS	GRADE_POINTS	
STUDENT_IN_CLASS	SEMESTER_CODE	SEMESTER_CODE	
	SCHEDULE_CODE	SCHEDULE_CODE	
	STUDENT_NUMBER	STUDENT_NUMBER	
	GRADE	GRADE	

"N". Thus, the arrowhead always represents the "many" part of the relationship. Also, we have not put the diamond inside the rectangles for composite entity types (types used to implement many-to-many relationships). Any rectangle with more than one arrow entering it represents such an

FIGURE B.18b
Table and column definitions for final design specifying underlying domains

entity. Thus, we can easily distinguish such entities without cluttering the diagram any further. (With these slight changes, the diagram is, for practical purposes, a data structure diagram, as discussed in chapter 8.) Finally, the only relationships that are given a name are those for which there may be a question concerning the meaning of the relationship. In this figure, the relationships that are in that category are "has prereq", "is prereq", "primary", and "alternate".

In general, on such a diagram, we would still represent the collection of fields that constituted each entity. We would also indicate which relationships were existence dependencies and which were ID dependencies. However, if the diagram is used only to give a pictorial representation of a DBDL design, such information is unnecessary since it is all contained within the DBDL documentation. (You will recall that existence dependencies and ID dependencies are not terms within DBDL but that they correspond to certain key restrictions that are easily recognized.)

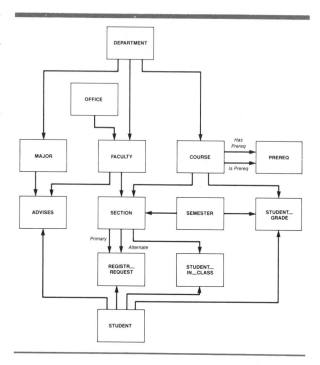

FIGURE B.19
Pictorial representation of the final information level design

SUBSCHEMAS

At this point, subschemas may be created for each user. They will be represented as a collection of relations and/or views. If we use only relations, the subschema for a given user will typically be the final version of 3NF relations to support the user view that was merged into the design, together with any required foreign key restrictions. The subschema for the first user view treated in the Marvel College design could thus be as follows:

```
DEPARTMENT (DEPARTMENT_CODE, DEPARTMENT_NAME)
COURSE (DEPARTMENT_CODE, COURSE_NUMBER, COURSE_TITLE,
        NUMBER_OF_CREDITS)
    FK   DEPARTMENT_CODE → DEPARTMENT
PREREQ (DEPARTMENT_CODE, COURSE_NUMBER,
        PREREQ_DEPARTMENT_CODE, PREREQ_COURSE_NUMBER)
    FK   DEPARTMENT_CODE, COURSE_NUMBER → COURSE
    FK   PREREQ_DEPARTMENT_CODE, PREREQ_COURSE_NUMBER →
        COURSE
```

This subschema represents a projection of the DEPARTMENT relation, a projection of the COURSE relation, and the complete PREREQ relation.

.4 MAPPING TO THE RELATIONAL MODEL

We will assume that the relational model system to be used supports primary keys but not foreign keys. The collection of relations will be precisely the collection of relations in the final information-level design. Further, since the system supports primary keys, these will not require any special treatment. The collection of relations is shown in Figure B.20.

FIGURE B.20
Collection of relations
in design for a
relational model
DBMS

```
DEPARTMENT (DEPARTMENT_CODE, DEPARTMENT_NAME, LOCATION)

STUDENT (STUDENT_NUMBER, NAME, LOCAL_ADDRESS*, LOCAL_CITY*,
         LOCAL_STATE*, LOCAL_ZIP*, ADDRESS, CITY, STATE, ZIP,
         CREDITS_TAKEN, CREDITS_EARNED, GPA, TOTAL_POINTS,
         CLASS_STANDING)

OFFICE (OFFICE_NUMBER, PHONE_NUMBER)

FACULTY (FACULTY_NUMBER, NAME, ADDRESS, CITY, STATE, ZIP,
         OFFICE_NUMBER, CURRENT_RANK, START_DATE,
         DEPARTMENT_CODE)

MAJOR (MAJOR_NUMBER, MAJOR_DESCRIPTION, DEPARTMENT_CODE)

ADVISES (STUDENT_NUMBER, FACULTY_NUMBER, MAJOR_NUMBER)

COURSE (DEPARTMENT_CODE, COURSE_NUMBER, COURSE_TITLE,
        NUMBER_OF_CREDITS)

PREREQ (DEPARTMENT_CODE, COURSE_NUMBER, PREREQ_DEPARTMENT_CODE,
        PREREQ_COURSE_NUMBER)

SEMESTER (SEMESTER_CODE, START_DATE, END_DATE,
          EXAM_START_DATE, EXAM_END_DATE, LAST_WITHDRAWAL_DATE)

STUDENT_GRADE (STUDENT_NUMBER, SEMESTER_CODE, DEPARTMENT_CODE,
               COURSE_NUMBER, GRADE, CREDITS_EARNED, GRADE_POINTS)

SECTION (SEMESTER_CODE, SCHEDULE_CODE, DEPARTMENT_CODE,
         COURSE_NUMBER, SECTION_LETTER, MEETING_TIME,
         MEETING_PLACE, FACULTY_NUMBER, CURRENT_ENROLLMENT,
         MAXIMUM_ENROLLMENT)

STUDENT_IN_CLASS (SEMESTER_CODE, SCHEDULE_CODE,
                  STUDENT_NUMBER, GRADE*)

REGISTRATION_REQUEST (STUDENT_NUMBER, PRIMARY_SCHEDULE_CODE,
                      ALTERNATE_SCHEDULE_CODE*, SEMESTER_CODE)
```

The foreign key restrictions must be enforced by programmers. These restrictions are shown in Figure B.21 on the following page. For sake of efficiency, an index (nonunique) will be created on each of these foreign keys.

The fields that must allow nulls are the local address fields, the GRADE field in the STUDENT_IN_CLASS relation, and the ALTERNATE_SCHEDULE_CODE field in the REGISTRATION_REQUEST relation. In each of the character fields in

───

```
FACULTY
      FK   OFFICE_NUMBER  →  OFFICE
      FK   DEPARTMENT_CODE  →  DEPARTMENT

MAJOR
      FK   DEPARTMENT_CODE  →  DEPARTMENT

ADVISES
      FK   STUDENT_NUMBER  →  STUDENT   DLT CSCD
      FK   FACULTY_NUMBER  →  FACULTY
      FK   MAJOR_NUMBER  →  MAJOR

COURSE
      FK   DEPARTMENT_CODE  →  DEPARTMENT

PREREQ
      FK DEPARTMENT_CODE, COURSE_NUMBER  →  COURSE DLT CSCD
      FK PREREQ_DEPARTMENT_CODE, PREREQ_COURSE_NUMBER  →
                                      COURSE DLT CSCD

STUDENT_GRADE
      FK   STUDENT_NUMBER  →  STUDENT   DLT CSCD
      FK   SEMESTER_CODE  →  SEMESTER
      FK   DEPARTMENT_CODE, COURSE_NUMBER  →  COURSE

SECTION
      FK   SEMESTER_CODE  →  SEMESTER
      FK   DEPARTMENT_CODE, COURSE_NUMBER  →  COURSE
      FK   FACULTY_NUMBER  →  FACULTY

STUDENT_IN_CLASS
      FK   SEMESTER_CODE, SCHEDULE_CODE  →  SECTION   DLT CSCD
      FK   STUDENT_NUMBER  →  STUDENT   DLT CSCD

REGISTRATION_REQUEST
      FK   STUDENT_NUMBER  →  STUDENT   DLT CSCD
      FK   SEMESTER_CODE, PRIMARY_SCHEDULE_CODE  →  SECTION DLT CSCD
      FK   SEMESTER_CODE, ALTERNATE_SCHEDULE_CODE*  →  SECTION
                                              DLT CSCD
```

FIGURE B.21
Foreign key restricitons in design for a relational model DBMS (each foreign key requires a non-unique index)

this group, blank can be used to represent null without causing any problem. In the single numeric field, LOCAL_ZIP, we can use zero to represent null.

There are no secondary or candidate keys in this design.

B.5   MAPPING TO THE CODASYL MODEL

To create a design for a CODASYL system, we create a record type for each relation in the final information-level design. Initially, the attributes of each relation are the fields in the corresponding record. Foreign keys are removed, and sets are created to fulfill the same role. (If relation B contains a foreign key identifying relation A, the foreign key is removed and a set is created in which A is the owner and B is the member.) Finally, any record with its primary key intact at the end of this process is assigned a location mode of CALC on this primary key. All others are assigned a location mode of VIA SET. (If there is more than one choice for the set, one is chosen arbitrarily at this point.)

The results obtained by applying this procedure to the final information-level design for Marvel College are shown in Figures B.22 and B.23. The records and the corresponding fields are shown in Figure B.22. Any record with a field (or combination of fields) underlined as the key will be CALC on this key. All others will be VIA SET, using the indicated set. Note that some of the record types contain no fields, a perfectly acceptable situation. The sets are shown in

FIGURE B.22
CODASYL records
(CALC keys
underlined)

```
DEPARTMENT (DEPARTMENT_CODE, DEPARTMENT_NAME, LOCATION)

STUDENT (STUDENT_NUMBER, NAME, LOCAL_ADDRESS*, LOCAL_CITY*,
         LOCAL_STATE*, LOCAL_ZIP*, ADDRESS, CITY, STATE, ZIP,
         CREDITS_TAKEN, CREDITS_EARNED, GPA, TOTAL_POINTS,
         CLASS_STANDING)

OFFICE (OFFICE_NUMBER, PHONE_NUMBER)

FACULTY (FACULTY_NUMBER, NAME, ADDRESS, CITY, STATE, ZIP,
         CURRENT_RANK, START_DATE)

MAJOR (MAJOR_NUMBER, MAJOR_DESCRIPTION)

ADVISES ()
    VIA S_STUDENT_ADVISES

COURSE (COURSE_NUMBER, COURSE_TITLE, NUMBER_OF_CREDITS)
    VIA S_DEPARTMENT_COURSE

PREREQ ()
    VIA S_HAS_PREREQ

SEMESTER (SEMESTER_CODE, START_DATE, END_DATE,
          EXAM_START_DATE, EXAM_END_DATE, LAST_WITHDRAWAL_DATE)

STUDENT_GRADE (GRADE, CREDITS_EARNED, GRADE_POINTS)
    VIA S_STUDENT_STUDENT_GRADE

SECTION (SCHEDULE_CODE, SECTION_LETTER, MEETING_TIME,
         MEETING_PLACE, CURRENT_ENROLLMENT,
         MAXIMUM_ENROLLMENT)
    VIA S_SEMESTER_SECTION

STUDENT_IN_CLASS (GRADE*)
    VIA S_SECTION_STUDENT_IN_CLASS

REGISTRATION_REQUEST ()
    VIA S_STUDENT_REGISTRATION_REQUEST
```

Figure B.23 on the following page. The name of the set, the owner record type, and the member record type are listed for each set. Each set is assumed to be AUTOMATIC and MANDATORY unless otherwise noted. In this design, the only exception is S_ALTERNATE, which is MANUAL, since the corresponding foreign key is allowed to be null. Each set will include both owner and prior pointers. Set insertion modes may be assigned arbitrarily at this time.

FIGURE B.23
CODASYL sets

SET	OWNER	MEMBER	COMMENT
S_OFFICE_FACULTY	OFFICE	FACULTY	
S_DEPARTMENT_FACULTY	DEPARTMENT	FACULTY	
S_DEPARTMENT_MAJOR	DEPARTMENT	MAJOR	
S_STUDENT_ADVISES	STUDENT	ADVISES	
S_FACULTY_ADVISES	FACULTY	ADVISES	
S_MAJOR_ADVISES	MAJOR	ADVISES	
S_DEPARTMENT_COURSE	DEPARTMENT	COURSE	
S_HAS_PREREQ	COURSE	PREREQ	
S_IS_PREREQ	COURSE	PREREQ	
S_STUDENT_STUDENT_GRADE	STUDENT	STUDENT_GRADE	
S_SEMESTER_STUDENT_GRADE	SEMESTER	STUDENT_GRADE	
S_COURSE_STUDENT_GRADE	COURSE	STUDENT_GRADE	
S_SEMESTER_SECTION	SEMESTER	SECTION	
S_COURSE_SECTION	COURSE	SECTION	
S_FACULTY_SECTION	FACULTY	SECTION	
S_SECTION_STUDENT_ IN_CLASS	SECTION	STUDENT_IN_CLASS	
S_STUDENT_STUDENT_ IN_CLASS	STUDENT	STUDENT_IN_CLASS	
S_STUDENT_REGISTRATION_ REQUEST	STUDENT	REGISTRATION_REQUEST	
S_PRIMARY	SECTION	REGISTRATION_REQUEST	
S_ALTERNATE	SECTION	REGISTRATION_REQUEST	MANUAL

It should now be a simple matter to create the schema DDL for the chosen CODASYL system, using the information given in Figures B.22 and B.23. Specific details concerning the format of the individual fields can be obtained from the information provided by the domain list and by the list in Figure B.18 that shows corresponding fields and domains.

Any special restrictions, such as the foreign key restrictions shown in Figure B.21, together with any other restrictions that programmers must enforce should now be recorded in the manner discussed in chapter 12.

As we saw earlier, Figure B.19 is effectively a data structure diagram for this design.

B.6 CALCULATING SPACE REQUIREMENTS

Using the initial CODASYL design for Marvel College, we will illustrate the calculation of space requirements. We are going to assume that the CODASYL system we are using has the characteristics discussed in chapter 12 in the material on calculating space requirements. We will also assume that PRIOR and OWNER pointers have been requested for all sets.

Let's suppose that the following physical requirements have been obtained for the system at Marvel College: There are 25 departments offering 750 different courses; 300 faculty members housed in 250 different offices; 35 different majors available; and 6,000 students. On the average, half the students have a double major. A perusal of the catalog produces an estimate of 300 prerequisites that must be stored in the database. General grades must be kept in the database for 20 semesters (it is estimated that this will mean storing up to 150,000 grades). Since registration requests are retained for one semester beyond the one in which the request was made, 12,000 registration requests could be in the database at any time. Also, at any time, the database must be able to hold information concerning 1,600 sections of courses. Total enrollment in all of these sections would be approximately 30,000 students. (In calculating this figure, we count students once for each section in which they are enrolled. Thus, a student enrolled in 5 courses will be counted 5 times.)

A translation of the above information into numbers of occurrences for each of the record types in the design gives:

DEPARTMENT — 25
COURSE — 750
FACULTY — 300
OFFICE — 250
MAJOR — 35
STUDENT — 6000
ADVISES — 9000 (half of the students have two majors)
PREREQ — 300
SEMESTER — 20
STUDENT—GRADE — 150,000
REGISTRATION—REQUEST — 12,000
SECTION — 1,600
STUDENT—IN—CLASS — 30,000

The calculation for the required size of the database, given these requirements, is shown in Figures B.24 and B.25. In Figure B.24, the number of pointers for each record type is calculated. The first column gives the number of calc chain pointers in each occurrence. Each CALC record has a calc chain pointer; other records do not. Thus, this number is either 1 or zero. The next column indicates the number of sets in which the record participates as the owner. For each of these sets the record will contain two pointers, and the next column gives the result of

RECORD TYPE	CALC PTR	OWNS SETS	# OF PTRS	MEMBER SETS	# OF PTRS	TOTAL PTRS
ADVISES	0	0	0	3	9	9
COURSE	0	4	8	1	3	11
DEPARTMENT	1	3	6	0	0	7
FACULTY	1	2	4	2	6	11
MAJOR	1	1	2	1	3	6
OFFICE	1	1	2	0	0	3
PREREQ	0	0	0	2	6	6
REGISTR._REQUEST	0	0	0	3	9	9
SECTION	0	3	6	3	9	15
SEMESTER	1	2	4	0	0	5
STUDENT	1	4	8	0	0	9
STUDENT_GRADE	0	0	0	3	9	9
STUDENT_IN_CLASS	0	0	0	2	6	6

FIGURE B.24
Calculations giving the number of pointers for each record type

multiplying by 2 the number of sets in which the record is the owner. (Remember that prior and owner pointers will be picked for all sets. Since owner records do not contain owner pointers, each owner record will contain two pointers, a next pointer and a prior pointer. Each member record, in contrast, will contain three, a next pointer, a prior pointer, and an owner pointer.) The next column gives the number of sets in which the record participates as a member, and the following column gives the result of multiplying this number by 3. The final column gives the total number of pointers for the record type.

Figure B.25 shows the actual calculations. The first column gives the number of bytes of system data for each record type. In each case, this number is four. The second column gives the number of bytes of data in records of each type. The third column gives the number of pointers and is taken directly from Figure B.24. Assuming that each pointer is three bytes long, these numbers are each multiplied by 3, giving the number of space occupied by these pointers. The results are stored in the fourth column. Adding system data, user data, and space for pointers together yields the total space (in bytes) required for a single record of each type. These numbers are stored in the fifth column. The sixth column represents the number of occurrences of records of each type that must be stored in the database (see the preceding list). Multiplying the figures in the fifth and sixth columns yields the total space required by all occurrences of records of each type. These figures are stored in the final column.

RECORD TYPE	SYSTEM DATA	USER DATA	# OF PTRS	PTRS SPACE	TOTAL SPACE	# OF OCCUR.	SPACE REQUIRED
ADVISES	4	0	9	27	31	9,000	279,000
COURSE	4	31	11	33	68	750	51,000
DEPARTMENT	4	35	7	21	60	25	1,500
FACULTY	4	105	11	33	142	300	42,600
MAJOR	4	28	6	18	50	35	1,750
OFFICE	4	11	3	9	24	250	6,000
PREREQ	4	0	6	18	22	300	6,600
REGISTR._ REQUEST	4	0	9	27	31	12,000	372,000
SECTION	4	38	15	45	87	1,600	139,200
SEMESTER	4	34	5	15	53	20	1,060
STUDENT	4	144	9	27	175	6,000	1,050,000
STUDENT_ GRADE	4	7	9	27	38	150,000	5,700,000
STUDENT_ IN_CLASS	4	1	6	18	23	30,000	690,000
							8,340,710

Effective page length
= 4096 - 12 (used by system) - 174
    (1 less than the length of the
    longest record)
= 3910

Number of pages in 100% full database
= 8,340,710 / 3910
= 2134

Number of pages in 80% full database
= 2134 * 1.25
= 2668
= 2700 (rounded)

Required database size is **2700** pages.

The total of figures in the final column (8,340,710) represents the total amount of space that will be required to store all occurrences of all records. To convert this into a number of pages for the database, three additional steps are required. First, the effective page length is calculated. From the total space on a page (4,096 bytes), we subtract the amount of space that is required on each page for general system data (12 bytes). Next, we subtract a number that is one less than

FIGURE B.25
Space calculations

the length of the longest record. (See the discussion of these calculations in chapter 12 if the reason for doing this is not clear to you.) In this example, the result is 3,910. Dividing this figure into the total number of bytes required produces the number of pages required for a database that is *totally full*, in this case 2,134 pages. Finally, assuming that we desire the database to be about 80 percent full, we multiply this figure by 1.25, obtaining a size of about 2,700 pages.

7 CALCULATING LRAs

To illustrate the process of calculating LRAs, we will perform the particular calculation for the number of LRAs that is required to produce the time schedule.

The first step in the production of the time schedule is to locate the appropriate semester. Since the SEMESTER record is calc, this requires 1 LRA of the SEMES-TER record.

At this point, each section owned by that semester must be accessed. Since the 1,600 sections mentioned in the requirements are for two semesters, we would expect the semester that we just found to own approximately 800 sections. Thus, 800 LRAs of the SECTION record are required.

For each of these 800 sections accessed, we must find the faculty member that owns the section. Since owner pointers are included in all sets in this design, finding the faculty member that owns a section requires only a single LRA. Thus, 800 LRAs of the FACULTY record are required to find the faculty members that own each of the 800 sections.

For each of these 800 sections that are accessed, we must also find the course that owns the section. Again, since owner pointers are included in all sets in this design, finding the course that owns a section requires only a single LRA. Once a course has been found, the department that owns the course must also be located. As before, this requires only a single LRA. Therefore, finding the courses that own each of the 800 sections and the departments that own each of these courses requires 800 LRAs of the COURSE record and 800 LRAs of the DEPARTMENT record.

In total, 1 LRA of the SEMESTER record, followed by 800 LRAs each of the SECTION, FACULTY, COURSE, and DEPARTMENT records, is required, for a grand total of 3,201 LRAs.

To calculate associated transport volume, we multiply the number of LRAs of each record type by the associated record length. In this case, the computation would be

```
TRANSPORT VOLUME =      1 *   53           (SEMESTER)
                   + 800 *   87           (SECTION)
                   + 800 *  142           (FACULTY)
                   + 800 *   68           (COURSE
                   + 800 *   60           (DEPARTMENT)
                 = 53 + 69,600 + 113,600 + 54,400 + 48,000
                 = 285,653 (bytes)
```

Once all the LRAs and corresponding transport volumes have been calculated for a given design alternative, they are multiplied by the appropriate weights and then the weighted figures are added together. Regarding the time schedule, the weight will probably be quite low, since the report is run very infrequently (once per semester).

The final figures obtained in this process for each design alternative are compared, as are the figures concerning the amount of space required for the database by each of the design alternatives.

To illustrate the effect of a change to the design on LRAs and transport volume, let's assume that we have decided to include the name of the faculty member who teaches a given section as part of the section record. This will add an extra 25 bytes to the data portion of each occurrence of the section record, thus adding 40,000 bytes (25 times 1600) to the space required for the database. It means that once an occurrence of SECTION is accessed, there is no longer a need to access the FACULTY record. Removing the 800 LRAs of the FACULTY record from the computations results in 2,401 LRAs being required to produce the time schedule. The new calculations for transport volume would be

```
TRANSPORT VOLUME =      1 *   53           (SEMESTER)
                    + 800 *  112           (SECTION)
                    + 800 *   68           (COURSE)
                    + 800 *   60           (DEPARTMENT)
                  = 53 + 89,600 + 54,400 + 48,000
                  = 192,653 (bytes)
```

These calculations reflect the new record length of each occurrence of SECTION as well as the fact that occurrences of FACULTY no longer need to be accessed in the production of the report. Thus, fewer LRAs are required and transport volume is decreased. The disadvantages of such a change include the increase in the size of the database and the problems associated with the fact that names of faculty members would be stored redundantly.

EXERCISES

Discuss the effect of the following changes on the design for the Marvel College requirements.

1. A given section of a course may have more than one instructor, and each instructor is to be listed on the time schedule.
2. Each department offers only a single major.
3. Each department offers only a single major, and each faculty member may only advise students in the major that is offered by the department to which the faculty member is assigned.
4. Each department offers only a single major, and each faculty member may only advise students in the major that is offered by the department to which the faculty member is assigned. In addition, a student may only have a single major.

5. There is an additional transaction requirement: Given a student's name, find the student's number.

6. More than one faculty member may be assigned to one office.

7. The number of credits earned in a particular course may not vary from student to student or from semester to semester.

8. Instead of a course number, course codes are used to uniquely identify courses; i.e., department numbers are no longer required for this purpose. However, it is still important to know which courses are offered by which departments.

9. On the registration request, a student may designate a number of alternates along with his or her primary choice. These alternates are listed in a priority order, with the first one being the most desired and the last one being the least desired.

10. **** *SPECIAL PROJECT* ****

Complete the information-level design for the following set of requirements. After you have done this, create an initial design for a relational system as well as an initial design for a CODASYL system that is similar to the one discussed in the text.

PREMIERE PRODUCTS REQUIREMENTS

Premiere Products has decided to expand its operation and has determined that a database should be designed to handle the new requirements. A database is needed that will satisfy the following requirements.

GENERAL DESCRIPTION

Premiere Products is a distributor. It buys products from its vendors and sells these products to its customers. The Premiere Products operation is divided into territories. Each customer is represented by a single sales rep, who must be assigned to the territory in which the customer resides. Although each sales rep is assigned to a single territory, more than one may be assigned to the same territory.

When a customer places an order, the order is assigned a number. The customer number, the order number, the customer purchase order (PO) number, and date are entered. (Customers can place orders by sending in a purchase order. For orders that are placed in this fashion, the PO number is recorded.) For each part that is ordered, the part number, quantity, and quoted price are entered. (When it is time for the user to enter the quoted price, the price from the master price list for parts is displayed on the screen. If the quoted price is the same as the actual price, no special action is required. If not, the user enters the quoted price.) The order may also contain special charges, for which a description of the charge and the amount of the charge is entered. Finally, an order may include comments, in which case the comment is entered. Following this, a form is printed that is a combination order acknowledgement/picking list. This form, which is shown in Figure B.26 on the following page, is sent to the customer as a record of the order he or she has placed. A copy of the form is also used when the time comes to "pick" the merchandise that was ordered in the warehouse.

Until the order is filled, it is considered to be an *open* order. When the order is filled (which may be some time later), it is said to be *released*. At this point, an invoice (bill) is printed and sent to the customer, and the customer's balance is increased by the amount of the invoice. The order may have been filled completely or it may have been partially filled (for less than the full amount originally requested). In either case, since the goods have been shipped, the order is considered to have been filled and is no longer considered an open order. (Another possibility is to allow back orders when the order cannot be completely filled. In this case, the order would remain open but only for the back-ordered portion. Premiere Products does not allow back orders, however.) When an invoice (see Figure B.27 opposite) is generated, the order is removed from the file of open orders. Summary information is stored concerning the invoice (number, date, customer, invoice total, and freight) until the end of the month.

ORDER ACKNOWLEDGEMENT/PICKING LIST

DATE: 10/15/87   ORDER 12424

PREMIER PRODUCTS
146 NELSON PLACE
ALLENDALE, MI 49401

SOLD TO: SMITH RENTALS
153 MAIN ST.
SUITE 102
GRANDVILLE, MI 49494

SHIP TO: A & B SUPPLIES
2180 HALTON PL.
ARENDVILLE, MI 49232

CUSTOMER	P.O. NO.	ORDER DATE	SLS REP
1354	P0335	10/02/87	10 - SAM BROWN

QUANTITY ORDER	QUANTITY SHIP	ITEM NUMBER	DESCRIPTION	PRICE	AMOUNT
6		AT414	LOUNGE CHAIR	42.00	252.00
4		BT222	ARM CHAIR	51.00	204.00

	ORDER TOTAL
	456.00

FIGURE B.26
Order acknowledgement/ picking list for Premiere Products

Companies like Premiere Products employ basically two methods for accepting payments from customers: open items and balance forward. In the open-item approach, customers make payments on specific invoices. An invoice remains on file until it is completely paid. In the balance-forward approach, customers simply have balances. When an invoice is generated, the customer's balance is increased by the amount of the invoice. When a payment is made, the customer's balance is decreased by the amount of the invoice. Premiere Products uses the balance-forward approach.

At the end of each month, customers' accounts are updated and aged. (The description of month-end processing in the requirements that follow contains details of the update and aging process.) Statements, an aged trial balance (defined under report requirements), a monthly cash receipts journal, a monthly invoice register, and a sales rep commission report are printed. Cash receipts and invoice summary records are then removed from the database. Month-to-date fields are set to zero. If it is also the end of the year, year-to-date fields are set to zero.

TRANSACTION REQUIREMENTS

1. Enter/edit territories (territory number and name).
2. Enter/edit sales reps (sales rep number, name, address, city, state, zip, MTD

sales, YTD sales, MTD commission, YTD commission, and commission rate). Each sales rep represents a single territory. (MTD stands for month-to-date and YTD stands for year-to-date.)

3. Enter/edit customers (customer number, name, first line of address, second line of address, city, state, zip, MTD sales, YTD sales, current balance, and credit limit). A customer may have a different name and address to which goods will be shipped, called the "ship-to" address.) Each customer has a single sales rep and resides in a single territory. The sales rep must represent the territory in which the customer resides.

4. Enter/edit parts (part number, description, price, MTD and YTD sales, units on hand, units allocated, and reorder point). Units allocated are the number of units that are currently "spoken for", i.e., the number of units of this part that are currently present on some open orders. The reorder point is the lowest value that is acceptable for units on hand without reordering the product. On the stock status report, which will be described later, any part for which the number of units on hand is less than the reorder point will be indicated by an asterisk.

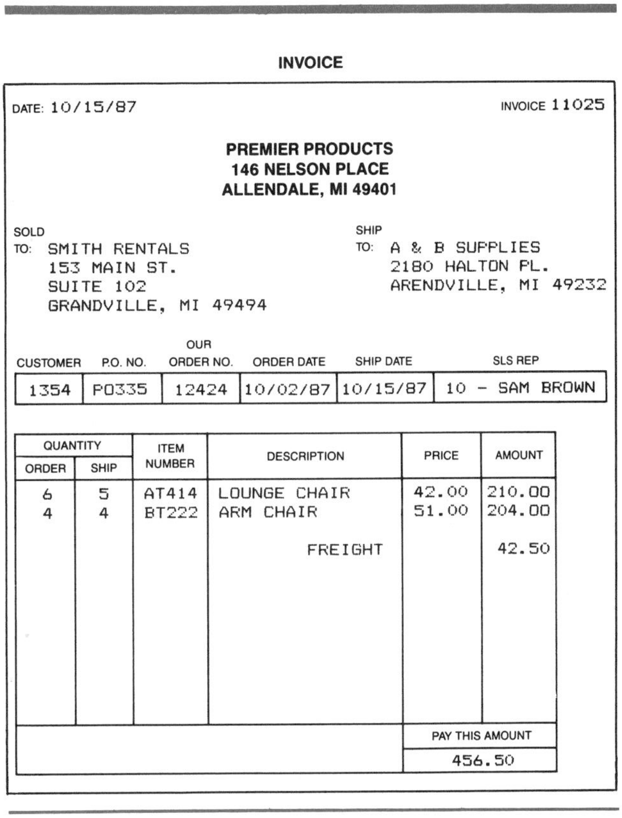

5. Enter/edit vendors (vendor number, name, address, city, state, zip). In addition, for each part supplied by the vendor, enter/edit the part number, the price the vendor charges for the part, the minimum order quantity that the vendor will accept for this part, and the expected lead time for delivery of this part from this vendor.

6. Order entry (order number, date, customer, customer PO number, and the order detail lines). An order detail line consists of a part number, description, number ordered, and quoted price. Each order detail line includes a sequence number that is entered by the user. Detail lines on an order must print in order of this sequence number. The system should calculate and display the order total. After all orders for the day have been entered, order acknowledgements (see Figure B.26) are printed. In addition, for each part ordered, the units allocated for the part must be increased by the number of units that were ordered.

FIGURE B.27
Invoice for Premiere Products

7. Invoicing cycle:
   a. Enter the numbers of the orders to be released. For each order, enter the ship date for invoicing and the amount of the freight. Indicate whether the order is to be shipped in full or partially shipped. If it is to be partially shipped, enter the number shipped for each order detail line. The system will generate a unique invoice number for this invoice.
   b. Print invoices for each of the released orders. A sample invoice is shown in Figure B.27.
   c. Update files with information from the invoices just printed. For each invoice, the invoice total is added to the current invoice total, the current balance, and MTD and YTD sales for the customer who placed the order. The total is also added to MTD and YTD sales for the sales rep who represents the customer, and the total, multiplied by the sales rep's commission rate, is added to MTD commission earned and YTD commission earned. For each part shipped, units on hand and units allocated are decremented by the number of units of the part that were shipped. MTD and YTD sales of the part are increased by the product of the number of units shipped and the quoted price.
   d. Create invoice summary record for each invoice printed. These records contain the invoice number, date, customer, sales rep, invoice total, and freight.
   e. Delete all of the released orders.
8. Receive payments on account (customer number, date, amount). Each payment is assigned a number. The amount of the payment is added to the total of current payments for the customer and is subtracted from the current balance of the customer.

REPORT REQUIREMENTS

1. Territory list.
   For each territory, list the number and name of the territory, the number, name, and address of each of the sales reps in the territory, and the number, name, and address of each of the customers represented by these sales reps.
2. Customer master list.
   For each customer, list the number and both the address and the ship-to address. Also list the number, name, address, city, state, and zip of the sales rep who represents the customer and the number and name of the territory in which the customer resides.
3. Open orders by customer.
   This report lists open orders organized by customer and is shown in Figure B.28 on the opposite page.
4. Open orders by item.
   This report lists open orders organized by item and is shown in Figure B.29 on the opposite page.
5. Daily invoice register.
   For each invoice produced on a given day, list the invoice number, the invoice date, the customer number, the customer name, the freight, and the invoice total. A sample of this report is shown in Figure B.30 on the opposite page.

```
10/08/87              PREMIERE PRODUCTS              PAGE 1
                  CUSTOMER OPEN ORDER REPORT

ORDER    ITEM      ITEM         ORDER    ORDER     QUOTED
NUMBER   NUMBER    DESCRIPTION  DATE     QTY       PRICE

CUSTOMER 1354 - SMITH RENTALS

 12424   AT414    LOUNGE CHAIR  10/02/87    6       42.00
 12424   BT222    ARM CHAIR     10/02/87    4       51.00

CUSTOMER 1358 - ...........

   .        .          .           .        .         .
   .        .          .           .        .         .
   .        .          .           .        .         .
   .        .          .           .        .         .
```

FIGURE B.28
Open orders report
(by customer)

FIGURE B.29
Open orders report
(by item)

```
10/08/87                    PREMIERE PRODUCTS                       PAGE 1
                          ITEM OPEN ORDER REPORT

 ITEM     ITEM          CUSTOMER    CUSTOMER         ORDER   ORDER    ORDER   QUOTED
NUMBER  DESCRIPTION     NUMBER      NAME             NUMBER  DATE     QTY     PRICE

AT414 LOUNGECHAIR       1354    SMITHRENTALS       12424  10/02/87    6      42.00
                          54    KAYLAND ENTERPRISES12489  10/03/87    8      42.00
                                                    TOTAL ON ORDER -  14

BT222 ARM CHAIR         1354    SMITHRENTALS       12424  10/02/87    4      51.00
                          .          .                .       .       .
                          .          .                .       .       .
                          .          .                .       .       .
                          .          .                .       .       .
```

```
10/16/87                    PREMIERE PRODUCTS                       PAGE 1
                  DAILY INVOICE REGISTER FOR 10/15/87

INVOICE   INVOICE    CUSTOMER    CUSTOMER       SALES              INVOICE
NUMBER    DATE       NUMBER      NAME           AMOUNT   FREIGHT   AMOUNT

 11025    10/15/87     1354    SMITH RENTALS    414.00    42.50    456.50
   .         .           .          .             .         .        .
   .         .           .          .             .         .        .
   .         .           .          .             .         .        .
   .         .           .          .             .         .        .
   .         .           .          .             .         .        .

                                              2,840.50   238.20   3,078.70
```

6. Monthly invoice register.

   The monthly invoice register has the same format as the daily invoice register but includes all invoices for the month.

FIGURE B.30
Daily invoice register

7. Stock status report.

For each part, list the part number, description, price, MTD and YTD sales, units on hand, units allocated, and reorder point. For each part for which the number of units on hand is less than the reorder point, an asterisk should appear at the far right of the report.

8. Reorder point list.

This report has the same format as the stock status report. Other than the title, the only difference is that parts for which the number of units on hand is greater than or equal to the re-order point will not appear on this report.

9. Vendor report.

For each vendor, list the vendor number, name, address, city, state, and zip. In addition, for each part supplied by the vendor, list the part number, description, the price the vendor charges for the part, the minimum order quantity that the vendor will accept for this part, and the expected lead time for delivery of this part from this vendor.

10. Daily cash receipts journal.

For each payment received on a given day, list the number and name of the customer who made the payment, together with the amount of the payment. A sample of the report is shown in Figure B.31.

```
10/05/87            PREMIERE PRODUCTS                PAGE  1
                DAILY CASH RECEIPTS JOURNAL

PAYMENT         CUSTOMER        CUSTOMER                PAYMENT
NUMBER          NUMBER          NAME                    AMOUNT

  .                .               .                       .
  .                .               .                       .
  .                .               .                       .
5807             1354          SMITH RENTALS           1,000.00
  .                .               .                       .
  .                .               .                       .
  .                .               .                       .

                                                      12,235.50
```

FIGURE B.31
Daily cash receipts journal

11. Monthly cash receipts journal.

The monthly cash receipts journal has the same format as the daily cash receipts journal but includes all cash receipts for the month.

12. Customer mailing labels.

A sample of the three-accross mailing labels the system is to print is shown in Figure B.32 on the following page.

```
SMITH RENTALS           KAYLAND ENTERPRISES          JOHN & SONS, INC.
153 MAIN ST.            267 29TH ST                  5563 CRESTVIEW
SUITE 102               WYOMING, MI 48222            ADA, MI 49292
GRANDVILLE, MI 49494

  .                        .                            .
  .                        .                            .
  .                        .                            .
```

FIGURE B.32
Customer mailing labels

13. Statements.

    Monthly statements are to be produced; a sample is shown in Figure B.33.

14. Monthly sales rep commission report.

    For each sales rep, list his or her number, name, address, MTD sales, YTD sales, MTD commission earned, YTD commission earned, and the commission rate.

15. Aged trial balance.

    The aged trial balance is a report containing the same information that is printed on the statements.

MONTH-END PROCESSING

Month-end processing consists of taking the following actions at the end of each month:

1. Update customer account information. In addition to the customer's actual balance, the system must maintain a record stating how much of what the customer owes is current debt, incurred within the last 30 days, how much is owed for more than 30 but less than 60, more than 60 but less than 90, and more than 90. While the actual balance, current invoice total, and current payment total are updated whenever an invoice is produced or a payment is received, these aging figures are updated only at month end. The actual update process is as follows:

   a. The payments within the last month are credited to the over 90 figure. Any excess is credited first to the over 60 figure, then to the over 30 figure, and then to the current figure. If there is still an excess, it is credited to the current month's invoices.

   b. The figures are then rolled. The over 60 amount is added to the over 90 amount. The over 30 amount becomes the new over 60 amount. The current amount becomes the new over 30 amount. Finally, the current month's invoice total becomes the new current amount.

   c. Statements and the aged trial balance are printed.

   d. The current invoice total is set to zero, the current payment total is set to zero, and the previous balance is set to the current balance in preparation for the coming month.

      To illustrate, let's assume that before the update begins, the figures for customer 1354 are as follows:

DATE 11/01/87

PREMIERE PRODUCTS
146 NELSON PLACE
ALLENDALE, MI 49401

SMITH RENTALS   CUSTOMER NUMBER: 1354
153 MAIN ST.   SLSREP: 10 - SAM BROWN
SUITE 102
GRANDVILLE, MI 49494   LIMIT 5,000.00

INVOICE NUMBER	DATE	DESCRIPTION	TOTAL AMOUNT
10945	10/02/87	INVOICE	1,230.00
	10/05/87	PAYMENT	1,000.00CR
11025	10/15/87	INVOICE	456.50
	10/22/87	PAYMENT	500.00CR

OVER 90	OVER 60	
.00	198.50	TOTAL DUE >>>>>> 2,325.20

OVER 30	CURRENT	
490.20	1,686.50	

PREVIOUS BALANCE	CURRENT INVOICES	CURRENT PAYMENTS
2,138.70	1,686.50	1,500.00

FIGURE B.33
Statements

```
CURRENT  BALANCE:    2,325.20      PREVIOUS  BALANCE:  2,138.70
CURRENT  INVOICES:   1,686.50            CURRENT:     490.20
CURRENT  PAYMENTS:   1,500.00            OVER  30:    298.50
                                         OVER  60:    710.00
                                         OVER  90:    690.00
```

The current payments (1,500.00) are subtracted from the OVER 90 figure (690.00), reducing the OVER 90 figure to zero and leaving an excess of 810.00. This excess is subtracted from the OVER 60 figure (710.00), reducing the OVER 60 figure to zero and leaving an excess of 100.00. This excess is subtracted from the OVER 30 figure (298.50), reducing this figure to 198.50. At this point, all the figures are rolled and the CURRENT figure is set to the current invoice total. This produces the following:

```
CURRENT  BALANCE:    2,325.20      PREVIOUS  BALANCE:  2,138.70
CURRENT  INVOICES:   1,686.50            CURRENT:   1,686.50
CURRENT  PAYMENTS:   1,500.00            OVER  30:    490.20
                                         OVER  60:    198.50
                                         OVER  90:      0.00
```

Statements and the aged trial balance are now produced, after which the PREVIOUS BALANCE, CURRENT INVOICES, and CURRENT PAYMENTS figures are updated, yielding:

```
CURRENT  BALANCE:    2,325.20      PREVIOUS  BALANCE:  2,325.20
CURRENT  INVOICES:       0.00            CURRENT:   1,686.50
CURRENT  PAYMENTS:       0.00            OVER  30:    490.20
                                         OVER  60:    198.50
                                         OVER  90:      0.00
```

2. Print the monthly invoice register and the monthly cash receipts journal.
3. Print a monthly sales rep commission report.
4. Zero out all MTD fields. If it also happens to be year end, zero out all YTD fields.
5. Remove all cash receipts and invoice summary records. (In practice, such records would be moved to a historical type of database in order to allow for the possibility of future reference. For the purposes of this illustration, we have disregarded this fact.)

CHAPTER 1 – INTRODUCTION TO DATABASE MANAGEMENT

1. Redundancy occurs when the same data item is stored in more than one place. For instance, several pieces of faculty data, such as a faculty member's name and address, may be stored in more than one file. This is wasteful of space and creates potentially severe update problems.

3. Bill's initial concern was that all of the programs would have to deal with the mechanics of manipulating the underlying database structure and as a result would be more complicated. He was also worried that a problem that affected a single program could damage the whole database structure. Bill's concern would be justified with programs that had to perform such manipulation. The use of a DBMS, however, relieves programs of this responsibility.

5. Entities are represented by files, attributes by fields, and relationships by common fields in separate files.

7. A database contains within its structure a description of itself that makes the database a logically complete structure.

9. More than one user has access to the data. Otherwise, the database would be inaccessible to the majority of users at any point in time.

11. A data model is a classification of approaches to database management. It has two components: structure and operations. The three main data models are the hierarchical model, the network model, and the relational model.

13. CODASYL proposed standards for database management systems. A number of systems have been developed following the CODASYL standards.

15. In general, economy of scale refers to the fact that the collective cost of several combined operations may be less than the sum of the cost of the individual operations. Database processing makes this type of combination possible.

17. DBA is database administration, i.e., the person or group that has charge of the database. The DBA balances conflicting user requirements, enforces general standards, and establishes security standards.

19. A database has integrity if data in the database satisfies any integrity constraints (i.e., rules concerning which data values are considered valid) which have been established.

21. Since in the database approach the data is in a single database rather than in a collection of separate files, it is easier to obtain data from multiple areas than it would be in a file-oriented approach. Even within a single area, the possibility of accessing data in a number of different ways is advantageous in the development of new programs to satisfy requests. Further, the advent of high-level languages associated with database management systems allows users to write some of their own programs, with the result that they can rapidly obtain access to data in the database.

23. Data independence occurs when the structure of the database can change without requiring the programs that access the database to change. It is achieved in the database environment through the use of external views or subschemas. Each program accesses data through an external view. The underlying structure of the database can change, without requiring a change in the external view; thus, the program would not have to change. (There is an obvious stipulation. If the change to the database structure were to invalidate this user view, then the user view and consequently the program would have to change. An example of such a change would be the deletion of a field required by the program from the database structure.)

25. Since a DBMS is such a large software product, it occupies a substantial amount of both disk space and internal memory.
27. Since all users now depend on the database, if the database is unavailable, all users are affected. With a file-oriented approach, if a given file was unavailable, only the users of that file were affected; other users could proceed with their processing.

CHAPTER 2 - FUNCTIONS OF A DATABASE MANAGEMENT SYSTEM

1. The DBMS should handle all of the details of manipulating the database when users attempt to store, retrieve, or update data.
3. The DBMS must be aware of at least some of the information in the catalog in order to function. Therefore, if the information is not maintained by the DBMS or a related product, some of it must be kept in two different places, which creates redundancy problems.
5. A logical transaction is a sequence of steps that will accomplish what is perceived by the user as a single task. Changing the address of customer 124 is an example of a logical transaction requiring the update of only a single record. Adding an order and all associated order lines is an example of a logical transaction requiring multiple updates.
7. When a transaction is committed, all of its updates are made permanent and available to other users. When a transaction is aborted, any updates already completed are undone.
9. A transaction might be aborted because a deadlock has occurred or because the data is faulty (e.g., after some of the updates have been completed, it is discovered that the next update cannot occur because there is nonnumeric data in a field that is supposed to be numeric). A transaction might be aborted because of a computer crash that occurs while the transaction is being processed.
11. Locking is the process of assigning locks to users on portions of the database in order to prevent other users from updating these portions for the period during which the user holds the lock.
13. Two-phase locking occurs when there are two distinct phases of locking: a growing phase, in which locks are acquired but no locks are released, and a shrinking phase, during which all locks are released and no further locks are acquired. Suppose user A releases a lock before successfully completing a transaction, at which time user B updates the record on which user A held the lock. If user A's transaction is later aborted, user A's updates will be undone. In the process, however, user B's update to the record on which A held and later released a lock will also be undone.
15. If a user holds a shared lock on a portion of the database, other users may read but not update this portion. If a user holds an exclusive lock on a portion of the database, no other user may access this portion in any way. If only exclusive locks are used, then the action of a user reading data, which by itself does not cause a problem, will prevent all other users from accessing this portion of the database. This can create severe contention problems.
17. Recovery is the process of returning the database from an incorrect state to one that is known to be correct.
19. A backup copy of the database is made before the update is run. If the database is later damaged, then the backup copy is copied over the live copy and the update is rerun.

21. The journal is the record of updates to the database. For each update, a before image and an after image of the portion of the database affected by the update are typically stored in the journal. In addition, when a transaction is committed, a record of this fact is stored in the journal.

23. Forward recovery is the process of starting with a backup copy of the database that is no longer current and bringing it forward by effectively repeating the updates that have taken place. It is accomplished by first copying the backup copy of the database over the live copy and then applying the after images of committed transactions that are stored in the journal to the database. It is appropriate when damage has made the live copy of the database unusable.

25. If the transaction has just occurred, it can potentially be rolled back. If a period of time has intervened, rollback may not be practical, in which case the data is corrected by entering an offsetting transaction.

27. Security is the protection of the database from unauthorized access.

29. Since any user can access only the data present in his or her subschema, omitting records and/or fields from that user's subschema prevents him or her from having access to them.

31. A given user can take a given action on a given object. These actions are usually supported through the combination of subschemas and passwords.

33. Privacy is the right of an individual to have certain information concerning him or her kept confidential. It is through appropriate security measures that privacy can be ensured.

35. Integrity occurs when data in the database satisfies any constraints that have been placed on it. An integrity constraint is a condition that data in the database must satisfy or a condition under which certain types of processing must take place or must not take place.

37. Logical data independence occurs when changes to the logical structure of the database do not affect programs that access the database. This permits the database structure to be altered in order to keep pace with changing requirements without requiring massive changes to programs.

39. The DBMS should furnish services to assist in making changes to the database structure, to gather and report statistics concerning database usage, and so on.

CHAPTER 3 - RELATIONAL MODEL I

1. A relation is a two-dimensional table in which
   a. The entries are single-valued.
   b. Each column has a distinct name, called the attribute name.
   c. All of the values in a given column are values of the same attribute.
   d. The order of columns is immaterial.
   e. Each row is distinct.
   f. The order of rows is immaterial.

3. The primary key is the attribute or collection of attributes that uniquely identifies a given row. A foreign key is an attribute in one relation that is required to match the primary key of another relation. Foreign keys provide a mechanism for explicitly specifying relationships between different relations.

5. If there is a one-to-one relationship between two entities, the two can be represented in a single relation that contains all attributes of both entities. Alternatively, a relation can be created for each entity, with each relation containing the primary key of the other.

7. Suppose entity A is represented by relation A and entity B is represented by relation B. A many-to-many relationship between entity A and entity B is implemented by creating a third relation whose key is the concatenation of the keys of relation A and relation B.

9. In the natural join, the column used for the join operation appears only once. In the equijoin it appears twice (once from each table). In the theta-join, a condition other than equality is used. Finally, in the outer join, rows from one table that do not match any rows in the other table still appear, with the corresponding values for the other table set to null.

CHAPTER 4 – RELATIONAL MODEL II

1. An attribute, B, is functionally dependent on another attribute, A, (which may be a collection of attributes) if a value for A determines a single value for B at any time.

3. An attribute A (or collection of attributes) is a candidate key for relation R if all attributes in R are functionally dependent on A and no subcollection of the attributes in A also has this property.

5. A relation is in first normal form if it does not contain repeating groups. This is precisely the same as the "normalized" relation of chapter 3.

7. A relation is in third normal form if it is in second normal form and the only determinants it contains are candidate keys. If a relation is not in third normal form, there is a determinant, B, that is not a candidate key. Since B is a determinant, there is at least an attribute, C, in the relation that depends on B. Since B is not a candidate key, a given value of B can occur in many rows in the table. Since C depends on B, the value of C in each of these rows must be the same, which creates redundancy and a variety of update problems concerning attribute C.

9. A relation is in fourth normal form if it is in third normal form and contains no multivalued dependencies.

CHAPTER 5 – RELATIONAL MODEL III

1. Entity integrity: No attribute that participates in the primary key may accept null values. This property guarantees that entities have an identity, i.e., that there is a way to distinguish one from another, namely, through the primary key.
   Referential integrity: If a relation, A, contains a foreign key that matches the primary key of a relation, B, values of this foreign key must either match the value of the primary key for some row in relation B or be null. This ensures that the database has integrity as far as the relationship specified by the foreign key is concerned (in other words, there will be no row in A that is associated with a nonexistent row in B).

3. They furnish logical data independence. They allow different users to view the same data in different ways. By including only the columns a given user needs in his or her view, the database seems much simpler to the user, and the portion of the database not included in the view is not available to him or her, which furnishes a measure of security.

5. A view, although it may be defined as a join of several tables, is still perceived as a single table by the user of the view. For some users, this is sufficient. Others require more than a single table in their subschema (or external schema). Thus, a view is best characterized as a subset of a subschema. Some subschemas will be single views; others may consist of a collection of views.

7. Indexes speed up retrieval. The disadvantages of using indexes are that they must be updated

when data in the database changes, which adds overhead, and that they occupy space that is technically not necessary.

9. a. A system in which data is perceived by the user as tables is called *tabular*.

b. A system that also supports the SELECT, PROJECT, and JOIN operations independently of any predefined access paths is called *minimally relational*.

c. A system that supports the full relational algebra is called *relationally complete*.

d. A system that supports the full relational algebra and the two integrity rules is called *fully relational*.

11. The structure of a table can be changed in SQL by using the ALTER command. In general, new columns may be added, old columns may be deleted, and the name and/or physical characteristics of old columns may be changed. (Not all systems that support SQL allow all of these changes.)

13. Embedded SQL commands in COBOL programs are identified to the precompiler by being preceded by EXEC SQL and followed by END-EXEC. Host variables are the normal COBOL variables (i.e., the nondatabase variables). They are distinguished from the database column names in embedded SQL commands by being preceded by a colon.

15. Like many other languages, COBOL is designed to process a single record at a time. There are no facilities in the language to handle a situation like the one that is created when a SELECT statement returns multiple records (rows). Cursors allow the result of such a SELECT statement to be presented to COBOL one row at a time.

17. The COMMIT command marks the end of a successful transaction; all updates can be made permanent. ROLLBACK indicates an abort; all updates since the last COMMIT are undone. The COMMIT thus marks the end of a logical transaction (and also the beginning of the next). A program can use the ROLLBACK to trigger a transaction abort. (The system might also abort a transaction.)

19. A user-defined procedure could be written to check that certain integrity constraints have been met before data is permitted to be added or modified. There are two significant limitations to user-defined procedures in DB2: they must be written in assembly language, and they cannot perform any database accesses.

21. EQUEL is the embedded version of QUEL. In EQUEL a block of code contained between two lines of code which are both "## [" is treated as a loop that will be executed repeatedly, one time for each row that has been retrieved.

23. Integrity constraints are specified in INGRES with the DEFINE INTEGRITY command. When an update occurs that would affect a column for which an integrity constraint has been specified, the update command is modified so that the constraint cannot be violated.

CHAPTER 6 - DATABASE DESIGN I

1. The inputs to the design process that are useful during the information-level design are the reports that must be produced; the inquiries that must be supported; the output that must be sent to other systems; update transactions that must be processed; calculations that must be performed; restrictions that must be enforced; and synonyms used within the organization. The inputs that are useful during the physical-level design are the number of occurrences of the various entity types; the frequency with which reports will be printed; report lengths; response time requirements; and any special security conditions that must be enforced.

3. The goal of the information-level design is a design that satisfies the user requirements as cleanly as possible. The goal of the physical-level design is twofold: acceptable performance and retaining as much of the cleanness of the information-level design as possible.

5. The process of designing a database to support a complex set of requirements is too complex to be achieved in a single step. Separation of the overall problem into a consideration of user views is a method of breaking down the process into smaller, more manageable pieces.

7. a. REPRESENT EACH USER VIEW AS A COLLECTION OF RELATIONS. A collection of relations that will support the user view is created.

   b. NORMALIZE THESE RELATIONS. The relations created in step 1 are converted to 4NF.

   c. REPRESENT ALL KEYS. Primary, candidate, secondary, and foreign keys are documented at this point.

   d. REPRESENT ANY OTHER RESTRICTION. Any restrictions not covered in the previous steps are represented at this point.

   e. MERGE THE RESULT OF THE PREVIOUS STEPS INTO THE DESIGN. The relations and restrictions for the user view are added to the cumulative design. Relations with identical primary keys are combined.

   The above steps are repeated for each user view.

CHAPTER 7 – DATABASE DESIGN II

1. Existing documents tell us nothing about any additional requirements that are included in the new system for which the design is being completed. Further, the underlying assumptions and requirements are not always clear from the document itself. We need additional input from the users.

3. Processing information is used in the physical design process. Rather than interview the users in two separate steps, we try to obtain and document the information that is required for both steps in the design process.

5. For a column to allow nulls means that the special value "NULL" is a legal value for this column; i.e., effectively the column does not need to have a value. An entity, B, is an entity subtype of an entity, A, if every occurrence of B is also an occurrence of A. If an attribute of an entity, A, can be null, there is effectively an entity subtype, B, consisting of all the occurrences of A for which the attribute is not null. In DBDL, if B is an entity subtype of A, the entire primary key of B will be a foreign key matching A.

7. Encoded data is data in which codes have been substituted for the regular values. Since the codes will, in general, be much shorter than the data that has been encoded, a significant savings in space may result from encoding. On the other hand, unless it is acceptable to the user to be presented with only the codes, the original data must be substituted for the codes when the data is presented to the user. This creates additional overhead that would not be required if the data had not been encoded.

9. Each user should review the information that has been assembled concerning his or her view of data before the actual design process begins in order to ensure that the information is correct. As each view is merged, the cumulative design should be reviewed to ensure that the user view can indeed be supported. This is done to make sure the merge was accomplished properly. Finally, after all user views have been treated and merged, the cumulative design is reviewed to ensure not only that each user view can be satisfied but in the best possible way.

11. A computerized tool to assist in the database design process should accept as input functional or multivalued dependencies, or alternatively 3NF or 4NF relations. It should produce as output various reports and/or graphical representations of possible database designs. It should allow for user override of any decisions that it might make. It should be iterative, allowing user interaction along the way to refine the design. In the physical-design part of the process, it should accept processing requirements and suggest alternative physical designs for specific systems that are optimal with respect to the given requirements.

13. A "bottom-up" methodology starts with a collection of specific user requirements and ultimately synthesizes a design from these requirements. A "top-down" methodology starts with a general overall database design representing the basic corporate entities and relationships and continually refines the design until a design that will satisfy the individual requirements is produced. A top-down methodology gives a global feel to the project; there is always an idea of where the project is headed, which is not true with a strict bottom-up approach. On the other hand, a bottom-up approach provides a rigorous way of handling each user requirement. With the top-down approach, a bad start in determining an initial design can cause real problems at some later point in the process, but with a bottom-up approach, it is not necessary to have an initial overall design from which to proceed.

    DBDL, in its basic form, is an example of a bottom-up methodology. A simple modification can allow DBDL to provide the benefits of both types of methodologies. Before beginning the specific treatment of individual user views, the views are reviewed for the purpose of determining the basic entities and relationships that are present. At this point, each entity is represented by a relation. The primary key is the only attribute that needs to be listed for the relation. Additionally, foreign keys may be included for each of the one-to-many relationships, although this is not absolutely essential, since these foreign keys will emerge as the individual user views are treated later.

15. In a later article, Chen proposed a change to the E-R model. In the new version, only entities can have attributes. Further, entities that are introduced to implement many-to-many relationships have a special name; they are called composite entities and are represented as a diamond inside a rectangle.

CHAPTER 8 – CODASYL MODEL I

1. CODASYL (the COnference on DAta SYstems Languages) set up a task group, the DBTG (DataBase Task Group) to develop standards for database management systems. The DBTG, which published an initial report in 1971, became a permanent part of CODASYL in 1972. At that time, its name was changed to the DDLC (Data Description Language Committee).

3. A set type is a one-to-many association between record types. This is the construction that is used to implement relationships in the CODASYL model. A set type is the general structure. A set occurrence is a specific example of a set type. This would consist of a single occurrence of the record type that constitutes the "one" part of the association and all the occurrences of the "many" record type that are associated with it.

5. The schema is the overall logical view of a database.

7. The DDL (data definition language) is used to describe the logical characteristics of the database and of individual users' views of the database. The DML (data manipulation language) is used to manipulate the database. The DMCL (device media control language) is used to

describe the physical characteristics of the database.

9. Including the SET IS PRIOR PROCESSABLE clause requests that prior pointers be maintained for this set. This in turn will make any process that involves finding a prior occurrence within a set occurrence more efficient. This includes not only attempting to find the prior occurrence in a program but also the process of deleting record occurrences or disconnecting record occurrences from a set occurrence. In such an operation, the record immediately prior to the record that is to be removed must point to the record immediately after. Finding the record that is immediately after is easy, since the NEXT pointer points directly to it. The process of finding the record that is immediately prior can be very difficult and inefficient unless prior pointers are used. Thus, the inclusion of prior pointers makes this operation much more efficient. On the other hand, prior pointers require space, and update operations must now also update prior pointers. Since prior pointers are technically not necessary (the same operations would be possible without them, just less efficient), both of these represent unnecessary overhead.

11. The storage class of a record within a set indicates whether or not the record is to be inserted into an occurrence of the set automatically during a STORE command. If the storage class is AUTOMATIC, the record will be inserted. If the storage class is MANUAL, it will not.

13. Including the LINKED TO OWNER clause in a set description requests that owner pointers be maintained within the member record occurrences in this set. This makes the process of finding the owner occurrence for any member occurrence much more efficient (there is no need to follow around the rest of the chain to locate the owner if owner pointers exist). On the other hand, owner pointers occupy space and must be maintained by the system. Since they are technically not required, this represents unnecessary overhead.

15. The special register DB-STATUS is used by the DBMS to notify the program of any problems that occurred when accessing the database. If anything abnormal occurred during the execution of any DML command, DB-STATUS will be set to a value that indicates the type of problem. Programs can then test DB-STATUS and take appropriate action.

17. The current of run unit is the last record of any type that was found or stored. It is the object of the GET, MODIFY, ERASE, CONNECT, DISCONNECT, and RECONNECT commands. The current of run unit is updated by the FIND and STORE commands.

CHAPTER 9 - CODASYL MODEL II

1. There are two advantages to such a use of declaratives. First, we can set our own flag and thus use our own condition names to improve readability in the remainder of the PROCEDURE DIVISION. Second, we can indicate the action that we wish taken in the event something unforeseen occurs when the database is being accessed in the DECLARATIVES. Once this has been done, we don't have to worry about it in the rest of the PROCEDURE DIVISION. If it were not for this use of DECLARATIVES, we would have to have a special test after every DML command.

3. A system-owned set is a set in which the owner is the reserved word SYSTEM. A system-owned set has only one occurrence. This occurrence is thus a chain containing all the occurrences of the member record type. Any processing that requires accessing all occurrences of a given record type could thus use a system-owned set in which the desired record type is the member. Without a system-owned set, we would have to examine the entire area, searching for records of the given type (using FIND NEXT ... WITHIN AREA). There are two advantages to using a

system-owned set. First, the entire area does not have to be searched and second, the set can be sorted in an appropriate fashion so that when the records are retrieved, they are already in some appropriate order. There are two disadvantages. First, since the set is technically not necessary, the space occupied by the set pointers together with the maintenance of these pointers causes unnecessary overhead. Second, in some situations it is actually better to search the entire area. If we are looking for one thousand records in a 100-page database, accessing all one thousand records by sequentially scanning the entire database requires only 100 disk accesses. On the other hand, if the records are CALC and thus are randomly distributed throughout the database, accessing all one thousand records, using a system-owned set, could require close to one thousand disk accesses. (If a record to be accessed is on a page already in memory, no further disk access is required. If the records are randomly distributed, the chance of the next record to be accessed being already in memory is not good. There is some change, however, and that is why it might not take all one thousand disk accesses.)

5. Normally, the execution of most DML commands will update some currency indicator or indicators in a prescribed way. If we wish to do so, it is possible to prevent the system from updating one or more of these indicators by using the RETAINING CURRENCY clause. The actual clause is RETAINING CURRENCY FOR . . . . The FOR is followed by REALM, SETS, RECORD, or a specific list of sets. Any currency that indicator mentioned in such a clause will not be updated as a result of the execution of the command.

7. The two new conditions for the IF statement are the tenancy condition and the member condition. The tenancy condition (IF set-name MEMBER . . .) is used to determine whether or not the current of run unit is actually a member of the named set. The member condition (IF set-name IS EMPTY . . .) is used to determine whether or not the current set occurrence of the named set has any members.

9. If we were to remove the line index for a deleted record, the line index for all the records on the page that followed the deleted record would change. This is unacceptable, since records throughout the database point to these records on the basis of the previous value.

11. Using logical records promotes data independence. This means that a change to the database structure might only require a change in the manner in which a logical record was constructed by the DBMS. Programs that used this logical record would not need to change. Further, the use of logical records may result in increased productivity, since programmers don't have to worry about the details of database navigation when using them.

13. After a user has described the database to the ASF, the system will "automatically" create a small application system that supports simple updating of and reporting on the data in the database.

15. Like a derived stored table, a view also has a defining query. Unlike a derived stored table, a view is not actually stored. Instead, it is created dynamically as it is needed.

17. Data is perceived by users as tables in both systems. Both support the SELECT, PROJECT, and JOIN operations, although DB2 supports them in a much more dynamic fashion. They are only supported as part of view definitions in IDMS/R, not as part of a true interactive query, as they are in DB2. IDMS/R does not support the full relational algebra, as does DB2. Neither system currently provides full support for the integrity rules.

19. When a COMMIT is executed all locks are released. When a user is the victim in a deadlock situation, an automatic ROLLBACK occurs.

21. The tabular structure of the relational model is simpler. There is only one construction, the table (or relation). In the CODASYL model there are two constructions: records and sets. In the

relational model, relationships are implicit. In the CODASYL model, they are explicit.

23. In general, the simplicity of the structure and operations of the relational model make relational systems easier to use than CODASYL systems. Most CODASYL systems offer query languages whose ease of use approaches that of the relational model. These languages suffer from two drawbacks, however. There is no standardization among such languages (as there is for SQL). Second, in complex queries, users have to deal with database navigation.

CHAPTER 10 – THE HIERARCHICAL MODEL

1. A node is a record type or record occurrence.
   A branch is a one-to-many relationship between two nodes.
   The root is the top-most node in the hierarchy.
   A descendant is any node connected by branches beneath a given node.
   A parent is a node directly above another node, located where both nodes are connected by a branch (the "one" node in a one-to-many relationship).
   A child is a node directly below another node, located where both nodes are connected by a branch (the "many" node in a one-to-many relationship).
   Twins are two or more child node occurrences of the same node type, and they have the same parent occurrence.

3. A hierarchical path is the top-to-bottom route taken in accessing (reaching) a given node occurrence. Access begins at the root node and proceeds from parent to child occurrence until the required node occurrence is reached. Using preorder traversal, node occurrences are retrieved from top to bottom (following the hierarchical path) and from left to right.

5. DL/I logical relationships allow a segment to have two parents. The segment has both a physical parent and a logical parent. The unidirectional logical relationship is a one-way relationship going from the logical child segment to the logical parent segment. The bidirectional logical relationship retains the pointers from logical child to logical parent and additionally has a pointer connecting the logical parent to the first logical child occurrence, which then points to the next logical child, and so forth.

7. HDAM permits random access through hashing to root segment occurrences and access to dependent segment occurrences through pointers stored in each segment. Sequential access to root segments is not possible unless a secondary index is also used. HIDAM permits sequential and random access through an index to root segment occurrences and access to dependent segment occurrences through pointers stored in each segment.

9. In a logical relationship, a virtual segment is a segment that does not physically exist but appears to the user as if it did exist. (Contrast Figures 10.14 and 10.16.)

11. A PCB is a program communication block and is one of the components of a PSB. The PCB identifies, among other things, which database (by name) will be used; this database must have been previously defined through a DBD.

13. GU, GN, GNP, GHU, GHN, and GHNP are the six DL/I function codes used for retrieval. DLET, REPL, and ISRT are the three DL/I function codes used for updating.

15. The current position is the segment occurrence accessed by the most recently executed GU, GN, GNP, GHU, GHN, GHNP, or ISRT DL/I function code.

17. Use any of the hold versions of the retrieval function codes when you need to replace (REPL) or delete (DLET) the retrieved segment occurrence.

19. Various answers are possible. Use Figure 10.20 as a guideline for the relative advantages and disadvantages of each data model.

CHAPTER 11 – INVERTED FILE MODEL

1. The inverted file model is not one of the three generally accepted data models, but DBMS's that follow it do not fit any of the three models. Also, some DBMS products that do follow one of the three data models use an inverted file structure for physically storing secondary keys behind the scenes.

3. An inverted file is a file that is associated with a normal data file and has as its key a nonkey field from the data file. The inverted file allows access to the data file on the basis of values of the inverted file key field. A secondary key is a field other than the primary key that is used for random access to records in the file. A partially inverted file is a file in which only some, not all, of the fields in the file are secondary keys. A fully inverted file is a file in which all nonprimary key fields are established as secondary keys.

5. The data records themselves and the ISN are stored in data storage. Stored in the associator are database, file and field definitions, the address converter, and inverted lists (files) for each descriptor.

7. A descriptor is a field that serves as either a primary or secondary key and that has an inverted list maintained for it. In the inverted list, a given value of a descriptor has a list of ISNs having that descriptor value. The address converter positionally relates the ISN to the block number in data storage that contains the record with that ISN value.

9. An elementary field is a field that permits a single value per record. A multiple-value field is a field that can have multiple values per record, up to a maximum of 191 values. In other words, it is a repeating data item. A group is a combination of consecutive fields, both elementary and multiple-value. A periodic group is a group that repeats within a record.

11. The ADABAS F I ND command does not retrieve data storage records. Rather, the F I ND command retrieves a list of ISNs that satisfy the search criteria specified as part of the F I ND command. The READ command retrieves either an entire data storage record or selected fields within the record.

13. ADABAS does not handle full data verification and does not automatically provide for referential integrity.

    DL/I does not handle full data verification and will delete all descendant segment occurrences when a parent segment occurrence is deleted.

CHAPTER 12 – DATABASE DESIGN III

1. Create a relation for each relation in the final information-level design. The attributes of each relation will be precisely the same as those in the information-level design. Implement the various keys, primary, candidate, secondary, and foreign, using features of the DBMS if such

features exist. If not, document the fact that programs must enforce such features. Finally, document any other restrictions that programs must enforce.

3. The general process of mapping to a hierarchical system is similar to that of mapping to a CODASYL system. In fact, the same rules can be applied to produce an initial network. The sets in this network become the parent-child relationships. If the network created is not a hierarchy, it must be converted to a hierarchy or collection of hierarchies. In IMS, this would most likely be accomplished through the use of logical child relationships.

5. The factors to consider are the space occupied by the data itself; the space occupied by pointers; the space occupied by any indexes; the space occupied by any special data maintained by the DBMS; any space inherently wasted by the DBMS; and space intentionally wasted by users. The last category includes any space left for future growth and space left vacant to achieve satisfactory performance from hashing routines.

7. A logical access map is a diagram that shows the sequence in which records are accessed to satisfy a given application.

CHAPTER 13 – THE FOURTH-GENERATION ENVIRONMENT

1. Machine language during the first; assembly language during the second.

3. Programmer shortage, increased demand for programs, and problems inherent with traditional methods of system development.

5. Uploading is the transfer of data from the personal computer environment to the mainframe computer environment. Downloading is the transfer of data from the mainframe computer environment to the personal computer environment. Figure 13.3 shows how data flows during downloading; just reverse the arrows for the uploading process.

Figure 13.3 shows how data flows during downloading; just reverse the arrows for the uploading process.

7. A data dictionary system is a system that stores, maintains, and reports on the contents of the firm's data dictionary.

9. Select from the following: name, aliases, description and definition, type, representation, length, output format, default value, validation rules, derivation formula, number of occurrences, responsible users, security, key information, database location, frequency of use and update, and where-used information.

11. Entry and maintenance, control and management, reporting, and software environment interaction.

13. Using a procedural language, the programmer must specify in detail how to accomplish the solution to the given problem. With a nonprocedural language, the programmer specifies what is to be accomplished but not how to accomplish it.

15. A query language is a nonprocedural language for retrieving information from a database.

17. A precompiler combines its own language features with those of a typical programming language such as COBOL; the combined source code is compiled by the precompiler and then compiled by the programming language's compiler. A skeletal program is the skeleton of a high-level language program; a programmer adds language statements for the specific problem to be solved.

19. Prototyping is the process of rapidly creating a working version of the complete system.

21. Icons are special screen symbols that serve as representations of the functions they perform.

CHAPTER 14 – DATABASE ADMINISTRATION

1. Money, materials, machines, personnel, data, and information.

3. Based on Figure 14.1, internal sources of data should be selected from purchasing, receiving, inventory, production, sales, distribution, billing, collection, and paying. External destinations of information should be selected from federal government, state government, local government, stockholders, vendors, advertising, lenders, customers, unions, competitors, and community. Other answers are possible.

5. Each company determined the exact position of DBA on the basis of its management philosophy, its then existing organizational structure, its degree of experience in the use of computers, its size, and the specific responsibilities and authority placed in the hands of DBA.

7. Top-level management commitment and involvement is the most critical, since without it the success of the DBMS environment will be limited.

9. This is not normally a realistic goal, since it represents a very complex undertaking and may not be in the best interests of the firm to pursue.

11. Typical skills (see figure 14.5) include interpersonal skills, mature judgment, communication skills, technical skills, and an understanding of the business and its data needs.

13. Top-level education and commitment, enterprise planning, hardware/software requirements planning, and policy formulation.

15. Seven of the recurring costs of a DBMS environment are software maintenance; hardware maintenance and depreciation; ongoing training; DBA personnel; TP and communications maintenance; various supplies; and computer system overhead.

17. Business Systems Planning is a widely-used planning methodology created by IBM that provides a step-by-step process to develop a comprehensive plan for an organization's information requirements.

19. Knowledge of the overall goals and objectives of an enterprise helps the DA understand the direction of the enterprise and helps identify business functions that may be necessary in the future. It also gives an indication of planned future growth.

21. Quick-payback applications of a manageable size whose benefits far exceed their costs are always wise choices.

23. The distribution of responsibilities among several people with checks and balances on their work so that the potential for security problems can be minimized.

25. A security officer has primary responsibility for security in the firm.

27. Amount of permanent disk used; amount of temporary disk used; terminal connect time; CPU time; number of tape mounts; main memory used; and number of lines of print.

29. Five DBA application functions are standards and procedures, data dictionary management, training, overall coordination, and database loading.

31. Five DBA technical functions are DBMS support; test/production environments; database design; DBMS performance; and keeping abreast of technological changes.

33. DBA is responsible for the conceptual and internal data-level designs and serves in an advisory capacity to the systems analysts and designers for the external data-level design.

35. Among the many types of performance statistics are the following: number of terminal users; number of transactions per transaction type; program execution time; number of database accesses per transaction, per database record type and per disk pack; database pages with high access rates; transactional response time; user terminal connect time; ad hoc queries processed,

and their characteristics; batch program execution time; and the number of database accesses per batch program.

CHAPTER 15 – ALTERNATIVES

1. Databases on computer networks may be split over several sites in the network, which requires a special type of database management system, called a distributed database management system to manage the data.
3. A distributed database management system (DDBMS) is a DBMS that is capable of supporting and manipulating distributed databases. It contrast, a DBMS does not have the capability of dealing with databases that are not completely contained on one machine.
5. The local site is the site at which the user is currently operating. A remote site is any other site in the network.
7. Replication is the storing of the same data item at more than one site in the network. It is done to speed access to data (data accessed at the local site does not require additional communication time). The benefit is that users at each of the sites where the replicated data is stored can access that data more efficiently than they could if the data were stored only at a remote site. The main problem concerns update: when replicated data is updated, all copies of the data around the network must be updated.
9. Data fragmentation is the dividing of a logical object, like the collection of all records of a given type, among the various locations in a network. Its main purpose is to place data at the site where it is most often accessed.
11. a. Since each location can keep its own data, greater local control can be exercised over it.
    b. In a well-designed distributed system, capacity can often be increased at only one site rather than for the whole database. Capacity can be further increased through the addition of new sites to the network.
    c. Other users can continue their processing even though a site on the network is unavailable. In a centralized system, no users can continue processing if the database is unavailable.
    d. Data available locally can be retrieved much more efficiently than data stored on a remote, centralized system.
13. All the same issues are encountered when concurrency is treated in a centralized system, but two other issues are encountered as well: local deadlock, which means that two users at the same site are in deadlock, and global deadlock, which means that two users at different sites are in deadlock.
15. The complete data dictionary may be stored at a single site. A complete copy of the data dictionary may be stored at every site. The entries in the dictionary may be distributed among the sites in the network (possibly with replication).
17. In the physical-level design process, in addition to all the usual factors, communication time must be considered in the choice of an optimum design.
19. a. Since the mainframe is free to perform other functions while the database computer is accessing the database, parallel processing is possible and improvements in performance can be achieved. On the other hand, if a database request only retrieves a single record, there is actually more overhead than before, since the mainframe sends a request to the database computer, which then accesses the database to retrieve the record and finally sends the

retrieved record back to the mainframe. Without a database computer, the mainframe would simply have retrieved this record directly from the database on disk.

b. If a host computer is managing a database, there exists the possibility for someone to bypass the DBMS and access the database directly. When a database computer is used, users must go through it to access the database; it is impossible to bypass it. On the other hand, the potential exists for users to fool the database computer into believing that they are legitimate users even though they are not. If they do so, these users will be able to access the database.

c. The possibility exists of hooking several host computers to the same database computer. Another possibility is to hook several database computers to a single host computer. These options allow great flexibility in configuring systems to specific needs, but their implementation causes the system to become effectively a distributed system, which means it is susceptible to the problems associated with such systems.

d. A database computer is a specialized machine built to serve a single purpose; consequently it is much simpler than a typical mainframe. On the other hand, the entire system, including both the host and the database computer, is more complex than a system in which a database computer is not used.

e. Since database computers are much simpler than a typical mainframe, they are potentially more reliable; fewer things can go wrong. This reliability may be offset, however, by the presence of additional hardware and software, which can cause other things to go wrong.

21. a. Users can define new tables to the system in an easy and flexible way.

b. Users can modify the structure of existing tables in an easy and flexible way.

c. Users can enter data through a form on the screen without having to write any programs to support this activity.

d. Users can create custom forms in some easy fashion.

e. Users can create reports that include related data from several tables in an easy way.

f. Users can write programs in some full procedural programming language that can access the database.

APPENDIX A – FILE AND DATA STRUCTURES

1. A logical transaction is a user request to accomplish a single task. A logical record is an individual user's view of a data record in the database. A physical record is one unit of data transferred between memory and disk. A logical transaction may require the processing of multiple logical records, and a logical record may require the access of multiple physical records.

3. Intrafile clustering involves records from one file, while interfile clustering involves records from two or more files.

5. A primary key is a field(s) that has a unique value for each record in the file. Random access is permitted for a field that is a secondary key; this field does not have to be unique. A sequence key is a field that determines the order of records within the file. There may be more than one field in each case.

7. The formula applied with a key-addressing technique results in a unique disk address, while a hashing formula does not guarantee a unique address.

9. When collision occurs on a given page, a pointer field within the page indicates which page received the relocated record. If multiple collisions occur, the pointer field chains together the relocated records.

11. When an indexed file is initially created by means of the block-splitting technique and when full pages are split into two or more pages by means of this technique, each page is only partially filled which leaves free space distributed throughout the file to allow for future additions to the file.

13. Both the inverted file and the multilist structures have an index, with one record for each unique key field value. For the inverted file, this index has a pointer to a lower-level index that contains the addresses of all records with that key field value. For the multilist, this index has a pointer to a logical record with that key field value. Each logical record has a pointer field that chains together all other fields with that particular key field value.

15. There can be seven children per node at a maximum. For a two-level B-tree, forty-eight keys can be stored at a maximum (the root can have six keys; each of the root's seven children can have six keys, or forty-two total level 1 keys; adding six and forty-two gives forty-eight keys).

GLOSSARY

Abort a transaction To undo all of the updates already completed for the *transaction*.

Access method A file organization, together with the set of possible access techniques.

Active data dictionary A data dictionary that documents the firm's data and that interacts with other software components.

ADABAS The Adaptable DAta BAse System, an inverted model DBMS from Software AG of North America, Inc.

After image A record of a portion of a database after a change has been made.

Alias An alternative name for a given table (used in SQL).

ANSI The American National Standards Institute.

ANSI/SPARC The American National Standards Institute/Standards Planning and Requirements Subcommittee.

ANSI/SPARC model A model of data proposed by *ANSI/SPARC* that includes external, conceptual, and internal schemas.

Application generation The process of developing an application system.

Application generator Software tool that allows rapid development of an application system.

Applied When a database is changed to match either before or after images stored in a log or journal, we say these images have been applied.

Artificial intelligence A computer-based system that performs functions normally associated with intelligent human behavior.

Attribute A property of an entity.

Authorization rule A rule indicating the conditions (constraints) under which a given person or group (the subject) can take a certain type of action on a set of database entities (the object).

B-tree A widely used multilevel index structure in which multiple keys and pointers are stored in each tree node.

Bachman diagram A diagram of the records and sets in a network database. Also called a *data structure diagram*.

Back-end computer See *database computer*.

Back-end machine See *database computer*.

Backup A copy of a database. Used to recover the database when the database has been damaged or destroyed.

Base table An existing, permanent table in a relational database.

Before image A record of a portion of a database before a change was made.

Bidirectional relationship A two-way logical relationship in a DL/I database which uses pointers in the logical parent and child segments.

Bill-of-materials relationship In manufacturing, the relationship between a parent part and its component parts. The classic example of a many-to-many relationship between an entity and itself.

Block See *page*.

Blocking factor The number of logical records in a block or page.

Boyce-Codd normal form (BCNF) A relation is in Boyce-Codd normal form if it is in second normal form and the only determinants it contains are candidate keys. Also called third normal form in this text.

Branch The connection between two nodes in a tree structure.

Bridge facility A data dictionary software interface occurring prior to the execution of the DBMS. Also called a *static interface*.

Buffer A memory area holding one or more blocks of data.

Candidate key A minimal collection of attributes (columns) in a relation on which all attributes are functionally dependent but which was not necessarily chosen as the primary key, the main direct access vehicle to individual tuples (rows).

Catalog A source of information on the types of entities, attributes, and relationships in a database.

Checkpoint A time at which updates to the database which are in progress are made permanent. In some cases, systemwide checkpoints are used; in others, checkpoints pertain only to individual transactions.

Children Nodes that are direct descendants of other nodes in a tree structure.

Ciphering See *encryption*.

Clustering The grouping of logical records in a database on the basis of usage patterns.

CODASYL COnference on DAta SYstems Languages. The group that developed COBOL and that proposed the CODASYL model for database management.

CODASYL model The model for database management systems proposed by CODASYL. Falls within the general network model of data. Not a standard, although it has been used in the development of many systems.

Collision The result of two or more records ending up with the same hash function value in direct organization.

Commit The process of completing all updates for a logical transaction, making them permanent, and making the results available to other users.

Communications network A number of computers configured in such a way that data can be sent from any one computer in the network to any other.

Composite In the entity-relationship model, an entity used to implement a many-to-many relationship.

Compression The packing of data on disk by, for example, removing trailing spaces and leading zeros.

Concatenation Combination of attributes. To say a key is a concatenation of two attributes, for example, means that a combination of values of both attributes is required to uniquely identify a given tuple.

Conceptual schema The global organizational view of data.

Concurrent update Multiple updates taking place to the same file or database at almost the same time. Also called *shared update*.

Coordinator In a distributed network, the site that directs the *two-phase commit* process. Often, it is the site that initiates the transaction.

Coupling A relationship between two ADABAS files that have a descriptor field in common.

Cross-reference A record used to implement a many-to-many relationship. Also called a *link record*.

Currency A concept used to indicate position within a CODASYL database.

Currency indicator A conceptual pointer maintained by a CODASYL DBMS to establish a current record of a run unit, record type, set type, or realm.

Cursor In embedded SQL, a pointer to a collection of rows returned by the query that defines the cursor. Used to allow the processing of the multiple rows returned by SQL in a record-at-a-time oriented language.

Data Base Task Group The group originally appointed by CODASYL to develop specifications for database management systems.

Data definition language A language used to communicate the structure of a database to the database management system.

Data dictionary A central storehouse of data about the firm's data.

Data entry database A DL/I Fast Path database restricted to a root segment and up to seven child segment types.

Data fragmentation The process of dividing a logical object, such as the collection of records of a certain type, among various locations in a *distributed database*.

Data independence The property that allows the structure of the database to change without requiring changes to application programs.

Data Language/I See *DL/I*.

Data manipulation language A language used to manipulate the data in the database.

Data model A classification scheme for database management systems. A data model addresses two aspects of database management: *structure* and *operations*.

Data structure diagram A diagram of the records and sets in a network database.

Database A structure that can house information about multiple types of entities and about relationships among the entities.

Database action diagram (DAD) A diagram showing the actions that must be taken by an application program.

Database administrator The individual responsible for the database. The head of database administration.

Database computer A computer whose sole purpose is to perform database activities on behalf of another computer. Also called *back-end computer*, *back-end machine*, or *database machine*.

Database description See *DBD*.

Database design The process of determining the content and arrangement of data in the database in order to support some activity on behalf of a user or group of users.

Database Design Language (DBDL) A relational-like language used to represent the result of the database design process.

Database machine See *database computer*.

Database management system A software package designed to manipulate data in a database on behalf of a user.

Database navigation The process of finding a path through the relationships in a database to satisfy a given request.

Data communication The process of sending data from one computer to another.

DB2 A relational DBMS offered by IBM.

DBA Database administration. The individual or group responsible for the database. (Sometimes the acronym stands for database administrator.)

DBD A DL/I database description defining the physical database. DBD is an acronym for database description.

DBDL See *Database Design Language*.

DBMS Database management system.

DBTG The Data Base Task Group, the group originally appointed by CODASYL to develop specifications for database management systems.

DDL Data definition language.

Deadlock A state in which two or more users are each waiting for resources held by the other(s).

Deadly embrace Another name for deadlock.

Defining query The query used to define the structure of a view.

Dependency diagram A diagram indicating the dependencies among the attributes in a relation.

Descendant A node beneath another node in a tree structure.

Descriptor An ADABAS primary or secondary key.

Determinant An attribute that determines at least one other attribute.

Differential file A file of changes to be made to data in a database. This file is consulted first when users access a database to determine whether the records to be retrieved have been changed in any way.

Direct access Another name for *random access*.

Direct organization A physical file structure by which records are accessed at a disk address on the basis of a formula applied to the value of a field in the record.

Distributed database A database that is stored on computers at several sites of a computer network and in which users can access data at any site in the network.

Distributed database management system A database management system that is capable of manipulating distributed databases.

Distributed free space Unfilled record slots in a file reserved for future additions.

Division-remainder method A direct-organization hashing technique whose formula uses the remainder as the disk address.

DL/I Data Language/I, the database definition and manipulation component of IBM's hierarchical model DBMS, IMS.

DML Data manipulation language.

Domain A pool from which the values for an attribute must be chosen.

Domain-key normal form A relation is in domain-key normal form if every constraint on the relation is a logical consequence of the definitions of keys and domains.

Downloading Data transfer from mainframe to personal computer.

Dynamic interface A data dictionary software interface that takes place during the execution of the DBMS. Also called a *runtime interface*.

Encryption The transformation of data into another form before it is stored in the database. The data will be returned to its original form for any legitimate user accessing the database. Also called *encyphering* or *ciphering*.

Encyphering see *Encryption*.

Entity An object (person, place, or thing) of interest.

Entity integrity The rule that no attribute that participates in the primary key may accept *null* values.

Entity subtype Entity A is an entity subtype of entity B if every occurrence of A is also an occurrence of B.

Entity-relationship (E-R) model A graphic model for database design in which entities are represented as rectangles and relationships are represented as diamonds connected by arrows to the entities they relate.

Equijoin A type of *join* in which both columns used in the join appear in the result.

Essential set A set that cannot be removed from a CODASYL database structure without incurring the loss of a relationship.

Exclusive lock A type of lock on a resource which prohibits other users from accessing the resource in any way.

Existence dependency In the *entity-relationship model*, a dependency in which one of the entities depends on the other for its existence.

Expert system A knowledge-based system dedicated to a specific field of expertise.

Extension The data in a relation at a given point in time. It can be visualized as a "filled-in" table.

External schema In the *ANSI/SPARC model*, the application program's view of the database.

External view The application program's view of the database.

Fast Path DL/I's high-speed capability.

Fifth-generation software Emerging software exhibiting functions of artificial intelligence.

Fifth normal form (5NF) A relation is in fifth normal form if every join dependency is implied by the candidate keys.

File organization Physical structure of a file.

First normal form (1NF) A relation is in first normal form if it does not contain repeating groups. (Technically this is part of the definition of a relation.)

Flat file structure A two-dimensional table.

Folding method A direct-organization hashing technique whose formula uses the sum of groups of the key's digits as the disk address.

Foreign key An attribute (or collection of attributes) in a relation whose value is required either to match the value of a primary key in another relation or to be null.

Fourth-generation environment Current software environments with a DBMS and data dictionary at their core and other software components integrated with these core components.

Fourth-generation language (4GL) A programming language with both procedural and nonprocedural features.

Fourth normal form (4NF) A relation is in fourth normal form if it is in third normal form with no multivalued dependencies.

Fragmentation transparency The property that means users do not need to be aware of any *data fragmentation* (splitting of data) that has taken place in a *distributed database*.

Free-standing data dictionary A data dictionary system that executes independently of a specific DBMS. Also called an *independent* or *stand-alone* data dictionary.

Fully inverted file A file in which inversion takes place on all fields.

Fully relational The expression used to refer to a DBMS in which users perceive data as tables, which supports all the operations of the *relational algebra*, and which supports *entity* and *referential integrity*.

Functionally dependent An attribute, B, is functionally dependent on another attribute, A (or possibly a collection of attributes), if a value for A determines a single value for B at any one time.

Functionally determine Attribute A functionally determines attribute B if B is *functionally dependent* on A.

Global deadlock *Deadlock* in a distributed system that cannot be detected solely at any individual site.

Growing phase A phase during an update in which new *locks* are acquired but no locks are released.

Hash function A formula used in direct organization to transform the primary key into a disk address. Also called a *hashing algorithm*, a *hashing routine*, or a *randomizing routine*.

Hashing A direct-organization technique for transforming a primary key to a disk address that does not guarantee a unique address.

Heterogeneous DDBMS A *distributed DBMS* in which at least two of the local DBMS's are different from each other.

Hierarchical model Tree-structured DBMS.

Hierarchical path The path followed in the process of accessing nodes in a tree structure.

Homogeneous DDBMS A *distributed DBMS* in which all of the local DBMS's are the same.

Host language A language such as COBOL in which database commands may be embedded.

Hybrid system A DBMS that combines features of two or more data models.

ID dependency In the *entity-relationship model*, a relationship in which one entity depends on the other for identification.

IDMS A CODASYL DBMS that is offered by Cullinet.

IDMS/R A DBMS with both CODASYL and relational features that is offered by Cullinet.

IMS A hierarchical DBMS offered by IBM.

Index A file relating key values and logical records with those key values. Also called an *index file*.

Indexed organization A physical file structure consisting of the data file and a separate index file.

Indexed random organization Indexed organization in which data records are not stored physically in primary key sequence.

Indexed sequential organization Indexed organization in which data records are physically stored in primary key sequence.

Inessential set A set that can be removed from a CODASYL database structure without incurring the loss of a relationship.

Information center The department in an enterprise which makes software tools available to users and trains them in their use.

Information level of database design The step during *database design* in which the goal is to create a clean DBMS-independent design that will support user requirements.

INGRES A relational DBMS that is offered by Relational Technology.

Integrated data dictionary A data dictionary system executing with one or more specific DBMS's. Also called a *dependent* data dictionary.

Integrity A database has integrity if all integrity constraints that have been established for it are currently met.

Integrity constraint A condition that data within a database must satisfy. Also, a condition that indicates types of processing that may or may not take place.

Intension The permanent part or structure of a relation. It can be viewed as the listing of attributes or columns in a relation.

Internal schema The view of the database as seen by the computer.

Internal sequence number See *ISN*.

Interrelation constraint A condition that involves two or more relations.

Intersection data The data in a link record.

Inverted file A data structure for which an index has been created for a secondary key field. Also called an *inverted list*.

Inverted file model A DBMS that is based on an inverted file structure.

Inverted list See *inverted file*.

ISAM IBM's indexed sequential access method.

ISN ADABAS's internal sequence number, a unique number automatically assigned to each record in a file.

Join In the *relational algebra*, the operation in which two tables are connected on the basis of common data.

Journal A record of all changes to the database. Used to recover a database that has been damaged or destroyed. Also called a *log*.

Journaling The process of maintaining a *journal* or *log*.

Key-addressing A direct-organization technique for transforming a primary key to a unique disk address.

Knowledge-based system Fifth-generation software consisting of a database of data (knowledge) and rules that can draw inferences from the stored knowledge.

Linear search A collision-management technique that locates records in a nearby page.

Link record A record used to implement a many-to-many relationship. Also called a *cross-reference*.

Linked list A data structure that uses pointers to connect records in a logical sequence. Also called a *pointer chain*.

Local deadlock Deadlock that can be detected totally at one site in a distributed system.

Local site From a user's perspective, the site in a distributed system at which the user is working.

Location mode A two-part strategy consisting of one strategy for placing records in a database and a companion strategy for finding those records at some later time. Also called an *access method*.

Location transparency The property that means users do not need to be aware of the location of data in a *distributed database*.

Lock granularity The amount of the database that is locked when locks are acquired. Can be a field, record, page, or the entire database.

Locking The process of placing a lock on a portion of a database, which prevents other users from accessing that portion.

Log A record of all changes to the database. Used to recover a database that has been damaged or destroyed. Also called a *journal*.

Logical access map (LAM) A diagram that shows the sequence of accesses to data in a database by an application program.

Logical data independence The property that allows the logical structure of the database to change without requiring changes to application programs.

Logical database An individual user's view of the database.

Logical record access (LRA) The process of accessing any record in a database. A logical record access occurs whether or not the record happens already to be in memory. Used in estimating performance.

Logical transaction A sequence of steps or updates that will accomplish what is perceived by the user as a single task.

Lower conceptual domain The portion of an *entity-relationship* diagram in which *domains* are defined.

Main storage database A DL/I Fast Path memory-resident database restricted to root-only segments.

Manual set A set in a CODASYL database for which retention is manual. Member occurrences in such a set will automatically not be connected to a set occurrence by virtue of the STORE command.

Many-to-many relationship A relationship between two entities in which each occurrence of each entity type is related to many occurrences of the other entity type.

Mapping The process of creating an initial design for the DBMS that will be used in an application from the final information-level design.

Member record type In a CODASYL set, the record type that is the "many" part of the one-to-many relationship.

Message Data sent from one computer to another.

Microcomputer DBMS A DBMS that can be used on a microcomputer.

Minimally relational A DBMS in which users perceive data as tables and which supports at least the SELECT, PROJECT, and JOIN operations of the *relational algebra* without requiring any predefined access paths.

Multidependent If there is a *multivalued dependency* of attribute B on attribute A, B is multidependent on A.

Multi-determine If there is a *multivalued dependency* of attribute B on attribute A, A multi-determines B.

Multimember set A CODASYL set with more than one *member record type*.

Multivalued dependency In a relation with attributes A, B, and C, there is a multivalued dependency of attribute B on attribute A if a value for A is associated with a specific collection of values for B independently of any values for C.

Natural join A type of *join* in which only one of the columns used in the join appears in the result.

Natural language A language in which users communicate with the computer through the use of normal English questions and commands.

Navigation See *database navigation*.

Network A structure containing record types and explicit one-to-many relationships between these record types.

Network model A *data model* in which the structure is a network and the operations involve navigating the network (following the arrows in a data structure diagram).

Node A record in a tree or hierarchical structure. An index page in a B-tree data structure.

Nonprocedural language A language in which the user specifies the task to be accomplished rather than the steps necessary to accomplish the task.

Nonkey attribute An attribute that is not part of the primary key.

Nonloss decomposition A decomposition of a relation through projections which allows the original data to be reconstructed.

Normal form See *first normal form*, *second normal form*, *third normal form*, *Boyce-Codd normal form*, and *fourth normal form*.

Normalization Technically, the process of removing repeating groups to produce a *first normal form* relation. Sometimes used to indicate the process of producing a *third normal form* relation, which is the goal of part of the database design process.

Null A special value meaning "unknown" or "not applicable."

Occurrence A specific example of a structure, such as the record for student Lee Adams. Distinguished from *type*, which means the structure itself (for example, the general student record).

One-to-many relationship A relationship between two entities in which each occurrence of the first entity type is related to many occurrences of the second entity type but each occurrence of the second entity type is related to only one occurrence of the first entity type.

One-to-one relationship A relationship between two entities in which each occurrence of the first entity type is related to one occurrence of the second entity type and each occurrence of the second entity type is related to one occurrence of the first entity type.

Operation One of the two components of a *data model*. The facilities given users of the DBMS to manipulate data within the database.

Optimizer The component of a DBMS that will select the best way to satisfy a query.

Order In a tree structure, the maximum number of children a node can have.

Outer join A type of *join* in which rows in one table that do not match rows in the other table are still included in the result.

Overflow area A separate area used in indexed organization and in collision management for direct organization. Records are placed and accessed in this area if they cannot be added at their optimal disk address.

Owner record type In a CODASYL set, the record type that is the "one" part of the one-to-many relationship.

Page The unit of data that is transferred between memory and disk. Also called *block* or *physical record*.

Parent A node that is located directly above another node in a tree structure is said to be the parent of the other node.

Partial dependency A dependency of an attribute on only a portion of the primary key.

Partially inverted file A file in which inversion takes place on only some of the fields.

Passive data dictionary A data dictionary providing documentation of the firm's data only.

Password A word that must be entered before a user can access certain computer resources.

Physical data independence The property that allows the underlying physical structure of the database to change without requiring changes to application programs.

Physical level of database design The step during *database design* in which a design for a given DBMS is produced from the final information level design.

Physical record See *page*.

Physical record access (PRA) The process of transferring a record from the database to the disk. Unlike a *logical record access*, a physical record access does not occur if the record happens already to be in memory.

Pointer array An alternative method for implementing *sets* in a CODASYL database. Permits more efficient implementation of sorted sets than the normal chain implementation.

Pointer chain See *linked list*.

Preorder traversal Top-to-bottom and left-to-right *hierarchical path* followed through a tree structure.

Primary copy In a distributed database with replicated data, the copy that must be updated in order for the update to be deemed complete.

Primary index For indexed organization, the index file based on the primary key.

Primary key A minimal collection of attributes (columns) in a relation on which all attributes are functionally dependent and which is chosen as the main direct access vehicle to individual tuples (rows). See also *candidate key*.

Privacy The right of an individual to have certain information concerning him or her kept confidential.

Procedural language A language in which the user must specify the steps necessary to accomplish a task instead of merely specifying the task itself.

Program generator A language facility that generates a second- or third-generation language program.

Program specification block See *PSB*.

Promote a lock To change the status of a lock from shared to exclusive.

Prototype A working version or model of an application system.

Prototyping The use of fourth-generation software that permits us to rapidly create an application system prototype.

PSB A DL/I program specification block used to define a logical database.

QBE Query-by-example. A *data manipulation language* for relational databases in which users indicate the action to be taken by filling in portions of blank tables on the screen.

Qualify To indicate the relation (table) of which a given attribute (column) is a part by preceding the attribute name with the relation name. For example, CUSTOMER.ADDRESS indicates the attribute named ADDRESS within the relation named CUSTOMER.

QUEL A data manipulation language used by the INGRES DBMS.

Query facility A facility that enables users to easily obtain information from the database.

Query language A language that is designed to permit users to easily obtain information from the database.

Query-by-Example (QBE) See *QBE*.

Random access A type of access in which records are accessed directly without the need to access other records in the file. Also called *direct access*.

Recovery The process of restoring to a correct state a database that has been damaged or destroyed.

Recursive set A CODASYL set in which the owner and member records are of the same type.

Redundancy Duplication of data.

Referential integrity The rule that if a relation, A, contains a *foreign key* matching the primary key of another relation, B, then the values of this foreign key must either match the value of the primary key for some row in relation B or be null.

Relation A two-dimensional table in which all entries are single-valued.

Relational algebra A relational *data manipulation language* in which relations are created from existing relations through the use of a set of operations.

Relational calculus A relational *data manipulation language* which is based on the predicate calculus of mathematical logic.

Relational database A collection of relations.

Relational model A *data model* in which the structure is the *table* or *relation* and the operations strictly involve the data in these tables.

Relationally complete A term applied to any relational *data manipulation language* that can accomplish anything that can be accomplished through the use of the relational calculus. Also applied to a DBMS that supplies such a data manipulation language.

Relationship An association between entities.

Relative record number The number of a record relative to the start of a file.

Remote site From a user's perspective, any site other than the one at which the user is working.

Replicated Data that is duplicated at more than one site in a distributed database.

Replication transparency The property that means users do not need to be aware of any *replication* that has occurred in a *distributed database*.

Report generator See *report writer*.

Report writer A nonprocedural language for producing formatted reports from data in a database. Also called a *report generator*.

Resource utilization billing A technique for billing users of the computer environment on the basis of computer resources they use.

Rollback The process of undoing changes that have been made to a database.

Root The topmost node in a tree structure.

Runtime interface See *dynamic interface*.

Save A backup copy.

Schema A description of the overall structure of the database.

Screen generator An interactive facility for creating and maintaining display and data entry formats for screen forms.

Second normal form (2NF) A relation is in second normal form if it is in first normal form and no nonkey attribute is dependent on only a portion of the primary key.

Secondary index For indexed organization, an index file that is based on a secondary key.

Secondary key An attribute or collection of attributes that is of interest for retrieval purposes (and that is not already designated as some other type of key).

Security The protection of the database against unauthorized access.

Segment A node or record in a DL/I hierarchical structure.

Self-describing A term applied to a structure that contains a description of itself. To say a database is self-describing means that no external source need be consulted to determine the structure of the database.

Sequence field A DL/I *sequence key*.

Sequence key A field or group of fields within a record that determines the order of records within the file.

Sequential access A type of access in which records are stored and retrieved in a file in a predetermined order.

Sequential organization A physical file structure consisting of records that are stored in the physical sequence in which they occur during processing.

Set The CODASYL implementation of a one-to-many relationship.

Shared lock A type of lock that permits other users to access the resource for retrieval only.

Shared update Multiple updates taking place to the same file or database at almost the same time. Also called *concurrent update*.

Shrinking phase A phase during an update in which all locks are released and no new locks are acquired.

Singular set A CODASYL set with only one occurrence. Also called a *system-owned set*.

Sizing Determining the required levels of computer resources.

Sorted set A CODASYL set in which insertion is SORTED BY DEFINED KEYS.

Special register Special item available to users of CODASYL systems in application programs. The most important of the special registers is DB-STATUS, which is used by the DBMS to convey any error that occurred during processing.

SQL Structured Query Language. A very popular relational *data manipulation language* that is used in DB2 and many other DBMS's.

Static interface See *bridge facility*.

Statistical database A database intended to supply only statistical information.

Structure One of the two components of a *data model*. The manner in which the system structures data or, at least, the manner in which the users perceive that the data is structured.

Structured Query Language (SQL) See *SQL*.

Subschema An application program's view of the database.

Synonyms Two or more records having the same hash function value.

System-owned set A CODASYL set with only one occurrence. Also called a *singular set*.

Table Another name for a relation.

Tabular A DBMS in which users perceive data as tables but which does not furnish any of the other characterstics of a relational DBMS.

Teleprocessing (TP) monitor A system software product that controls a host computer's terminal communications and the application programs executed by the terminal users.

Theta-join A type of *join* in which the join condition is something other than equality.

Third normal form (3NF) A relation is in third normal form if it is in second normal form and if the only determinants it contains are candidate keys. (Technically this is the definition of Boyce-Codd normal form, but in this text the two are used synonymously.)

Three-way logic A type of logic in which, in addition to "true" and "false", there is a third possibility: "maybe."

Transaction See *logical transaction*.

Transaction processing Processing that is controlled by a TP monitor.

Transport volume The volume of data that is transported from disk to memory (and memory to disk) during processing.

Tree A data structure that resembles a tree, with a single root at the top and its branches leading toward the bottom.

Tuning The process of changing aspects of a database design in order to improve performance.

Tuple The formal name for a row in a table.

Twin A node in a tree structure that has the same parent as another node is said to be the twin of the other node.

Two-phase commit An approach to the commit process in distributed systems in which there are two phases. In the first phase, each site is instructed to prepare to commit and must indicate whether the commit will be possible. After each site has responded, the second phase begins: If every site has replied in the affirmative, all sites must commit. If any site has replied in the negative, all sites must abort the transaction.

Two-phase locking An approach to *locking* in which there are two phases: a *growing phase*, in which new locks are acquired but no locks are released, and a *shrinking phase*, in which all locks are released and no new locks are acquired.

Type A structure itself (for example, a student record). Distinguished from *occurrence*, which means a specific example of a structure, such as the record for student Lee Adams.

Unnormalized relation A structure that satisfies the properties required to be a relation with one exception: repeating groups are allowed.

Union-compatible Two relations that have the same number of columns and in which corresponding columns have the same domain. Such relations can be combined with the UNION, INTERSECTION, and DIFFERENCE operations of the *relational algebra*.

Update anomaly An update problem that can occur in a database owing to a faulty design.

Uploading Data transfer from personal computer to mainframe.

Upper conceptual domain The portion of an *entity-relationship* diagram in which the entities and relationships are defined.

User view The view of data that is necessary to support the operations of a particular user.

User-defined procedure A procedure defined by users that will automatically be invoked at the appropriate time by the DBMS.

Victim In a deadlock situation, the deadlocked user whose transaction will be aborted to break the deadlock.

View An application program's or individual user's view of the database.

Weak entity type In the E-R model, an entity type that depends on another entity type for its existence.

INDEX

boldfaced page numbers indicate the major discussion for that topic